Antitrust and Regulation

The International Library of Critical Writings in Business History

Series Editor: Geoffrey Jones
                       Professor of Business History,
                       University of Reading

Antitrust and Regulation

Edited by

Giles H. Burgess, Jr.

Professor of Economics,
Portland State University

An Elgar Reference Collection

Published by
Edward Elgar Publishing Limited
Gower House
Croft Road
Aldershot
Hants GU11 3HR
England

Edward Elgar Publishing Limited
Distributed in the United States by
Ashgate Publishing Company
Old Post Road
Brookfield
Vermont 05036
USA

CIP catalogue records for this book are available from the British Library and the US Library of Congress

ISBN 1 85278 451 2

Printed in Great Britain at the University Press, Cambridge

Contents

Acknowledgements

The editor and publishers wish to thank the following who have kindly given permission for the use of copyright material.

Academic Press, Inc. for article: Yoshi Tsurumi (1978), 'The Case of Japan: Price Bargaining and Controls on Oil Products', *Journal of Comparative Economics*, **2**, 126–43.

American Economic Association for articles: Willard E. Hotchkiss (1914), 'Recent Trust Decisions and Business', *American Economic Association Papers and Proceedings*, **IV** (1), 158–72; Thomas S. Ulen (1980), 'The Market for Regulation: the ICC from 1887 to 1920', *American Economic Association Papers and Proceedings*, **70** (2), 306–10; John C. Panzar (1980), 'Regulation, Deregulation and Economic Efficiency: The Case of the CAB', *American Economic Association Papers and Proceedings*, **70** (2), 311–15; Robert W. Harbeson (1958), 'The Clayton Act: Sleeping Giant of Antitrust?', *American Economic Review*, **XLVIII**, 92–104; Richard Schmalensee (1987), 'Horizontal Merger Policy: Problems and Changes', *Journal of Economic Perspectives*, **1** (2), 41–54; Thomas M. Jorde and David J. Teece (1990), 'Innovation and Cooperation: Implications for Competition and Antitrust', *Journal of Economic Perspectives*, **4** (3), 75–96.

American Marketing Association, Chicago, Illinois for article: Corwin D. Edwards (1950), 'Trends in Enforcement of the Antimonopoly Laws', *Journal of Marketing*, **XIV** (5), 657–65.

Antitrust Bulletin for articles: Ernest Gellhorn (1986), 'Climbing the Antitrust Staircase', *Antitrust Bulletin*, **XXXI**, 341–57; Toshiaki Nakazawa and Leonard W. Weiss (1989), 'The Legal Cartels of Japan', *Antitrust Bulletin*, **XXXIV** (3), 641–53.

Basil Blackwell Ltd. for article: Frederic C. Benham (1931), 'The Economic Significance of Public Utilities', *Economica*, **XI** (31–34), 26–36.

Leslie Hannah for his own article: (1979), 'Mergers, Cartels and Concentration: Legal Factors in the U.S. and European Experience', in Horn and Kocka (eds.), *Law and the Formation of the Big Enterprises in the 19th and Early 20th Centuries*, 306–16.

Harvard University Press for excerpt: Morton Keller (1980), 'Regulation of Large Enterprise: The United States Experience in Comparative Perspective', in Chandler and Daems (eds.), *Managerial Hierarchies*, 161–81.

Kluwer Academic Publishers for excerpt: O.E. Williamson (1983), 'Antitrust Enforcement: Where it has Been; Where it is Going', in John Craven (ed.), *Industrial Organization, Antitrust and Public Policy*, 41–65.

Oxford University Press for article: Thomas Sharpe (1985), 'British Competition Policy in Perspective', *Oxford Review of Economic Policy*, **1** (3), 80–94.

President and Fellows of Harvard College, Harvard Business School for articles: Benjamin J. Klebaner (1964), 'Potential Competition and the American Antitrust Legislation of 1914', *Business History Review*, **38** (2), 163–85; Thomas K. McCraw (1975), 'Regulation in America: A Review Article', *Business History Review*, **XLIX** (2), 159–83; Clyde O. Ruggles (1945), 'Government Control of Business', *Harvard Business Review*, **XXIV** (1), 32–50.

The RAND Corporation for article: George J. Stigler (1971), 'The Theory of Economic Regulation', *Bell Journal of Economics and Management Science*, **2** (1), 3–21.

University of Chicago Press for articles: Thomas E. Sunderland (1951), 'Changing Legal Concepts', *Journal of Business*, **XXIV** (4), 235–52; John Jewkes (1958), 'British Monopoly Policy 1944–56', *Journal of Law and Economics*, **I**, 1–19; Richard C. Bernhard (1960), 'English Law and American Law on Monopolies and Restraints of Trade', *Journal of Law and Economics*, **III**, 136–45; Eugene Rotwein (1964), 'Economic Concentration and Monopoly in Japan', *Journal of Political Economy*, **LXXII**, 262–77.

University of Pennsylvania Law Review for article: Richard A. Posner (1979), 'The Chicago School of Antitrust Analysis', *University of Pennsylvania Law Review*, **127** (4), 925–48.

Yale Journal on Regulation for articles: Elizabeth E. Bailey and William J. Baumol (1984), 'Deregulation and the Theory of Contestable Markets', *Yale Journal on Regulation*, **1** (2), 111–37; Harry G. Broadman and Joseph P. Kalt (1989), 'How Natural is Monopoly? The Case of Bypass in Natural Gas Distribution Markets', *Yale Journal on Regulation*, **6** (2), 181–208; Alfred E. Kahn (1990), 'Deregulation: Looking Backward and Looking Foward', *Yale Journal on Regulation*, **7** (2), 325–54.

Every effort has been made to trace all the copyright holders but if any have been inadvertently overlooked the publishers will be pleased to make the necessary arrangement at the first opportunity.

In addition the publishers wish to thank the library of The London School of Economics and Political Science and The Alfred Marshall Library, Cambridge University, for their assistance in obtaining these articles.

Introduction

The collection of articles in this volume has been chosen to reflect a century of changes in regulation: changes in the way regulations are used to alter the organization and conduct of business, changes in the laws themselves, and changes in the attitudes of scholars towards regulation. In the US, the laws governing the conduct of business – that is, public-utility and antitrust regulations – are more closely connected than is commonly understood. The political pressure for control over monopoly, which culminated in the Sherman Antitrust Act in 1890, had previously led to the passage of the Interstate Commerce Commission Act in 1887 to regulate the railroads, as well as to other state public utility regulation laws adopted before that.

Government Regulation and its Effect on Business

Antitrust and public-utility laws to regulate business were thus first established in the last quarter of the 19th century in the US. While innovative, these specific regulations were based upon much older and rather widely held principles, as indicated by Morton Keller in Chapter 2. It may be impossible to establish conclusively the reasons for their adoption at this particular time and place, but it is tempting to offer at least a tentative explanation. First, both antitrust and public-utility regulations are designed to limit the acquisition and/or exercise of power by business enterprise. Second, the laws and customs of the United States were strongly opposed to the accumulation of power to control the lives of others – either by government or by individuals. Third, the rapid restructuring of the economy brought on by the 'industrial revolution' challenged the more traditional checks on the size and power of business which had been provided, in the US, by state laws governing corporations. In a number of states in the 19th century, state corporate charters prohibited interstate and inter-corporate dealings, but the growth in markets and increased open violations of the law overwhelmed and effectively crippled the ability of state governments to exercise control over business power. The Standard Oil 'Trust', a device designed to circumvent the laws of the State of Ohio, came to represent to a broad segment of the American public the evil embodiment of corporate giantism which the Sherman Antitrust Act of 1890 was intended to control. Thus, while economic changes taking place in the late 19th century in the US may have been roughly parallel to those in Britain and elsewhere at the time, their political impact in the US may well have been unique.

Comparing the late 19th and early 20th century political/economic attitudes towards business combinations in the US, Britain and Germany, Keller finds significant differences. The US was least tolerant. Britain, by contrast, accepted the right of business to associate freely, while Germany encouraged cartels to advance the public interest. In Chapter 1, Leslie Hannah also compares regulations, but to a different end. Hannah is concerned with how US attitudes on antitrust – its intolerance of cartels combined with its *de facto* acceptance of mergers –

encouraged the development of large-scale enterprise. He suggests that certain differences among nations in their industrial organization may be attributed to differences in regulation.

Expansion of Antitrust Regulation in the US

In Chapter 3, C.F. Taeusch reflects upon the process which brought the Sherman Act into existence, ascribing its adoption to uniquely American attitudes towards business and government. In particular Taeusch contrasts the general treatment of restraint of trade in the US – both in common law and in the Sherman Antitrust Act – with decisions taken about the same time in England regarding the Mogul Steamship case.

In the first 20 or so years, US antitrust law was subjected to a period of definition. Through a series of trials and extensive judicial review, precise content was given to the vague language proscribing various acts of 'combination in restraint of trade' and 'monopolization'. The results surprised many who doubted that the Sherman Antitrust Act could or would deal with the growth of giant enterprise since, even to those of vastly divergent views (from advocates of laissez-faire capitalism at one extreme to proponents of large-scale government intervention at the other) such growth seemed to be inherent in industrialization. Thus, the government's success in cases against American Tobacco Company and Standard Oil of New Jersey, leading to court-ordered divestitures which diminished the size and market power of the dominant firms in tobacco and oil, came as a most welcome victory for those in the middle who sought measured reform. Willard Hotchkiss provides us with one contemporary view of these events in Chapter 4. He deals with the then current intellectual controversy in economics over the efficiency of the 'trusts'; he doubts that scale economies could account for the sweeping consolidations which had occurred in such industries as oil and tobacco, and favours the remedies taken in those cases. He also expresses satisfaction with the status of the law which implied that, by the 'Rule of Reason', firms would carry the burden of proof to show that their behaviour (or size) was justified.

Thus began the period of expansion of antitrust law in the US. The early victories of 1911 – *U.S. v Standard Oil of N.J.* and *U.S. v American Tobacco Company* – were celebrated by supporters of antitrust regulation who called for new legislation to provide even stronger weapons in their arsenal. The Clayton Act and the Federal Trade Commission (FTC) Act of 1914 were the product of these pressures. (In later years, the Robinson-Patman Act (1936) and the Kefauver-Celler Act (1950) would be added as well.) While popular sentiment weighed heavily in favour of antitrust in the years preceding 1920, there were continued disagreements among reformers about how best to proceed; the passage of the two new laws in 1914 reflects this fact rather than being simply a matter of legislative overkill.

The FTC Act established an administrative body with broad discretion to deal with 'unfair methods of competition'; it was favoured by that group which had long believed that corporate giants could be effectively controlled only by direct regulation, somewhat akin to the regulation of public-utility enterprise.

The Clayton Act patched together legislative solutions to what at the time were perceived to be serious shortcomings of the Sherman Act. One dimension of reform dealt with the threshold issue: how big or how powerful did a firm have to become before it exceeded the tolerance of the law? The Clayton Act declared that a single merger (as one example of proscribed actions) was illegal if the effect was 'to tend to create a monopoly or to substantially lessen competition'. The other dimension of reform dealt with the emerging discretion of the trial court (presumed by many to be presided over by pro-business judges): how serious would a violation of law have to be before it exceeded the limits permitted by the 'Rule of Reason'? As the Clayton Act contained no criminal provisions, it eliminated tests of unlawful intent – a potentially elusive factual issue – which the 'Rule of Reason' had attached to the Sherman Act. Under the Clayton Act, it was only necessary for the government (or private plaintiff) to show that the merger it opposed, or any of the other proscribed acts it sought to enjoin, had an unlawful effect.

In Chapter 5, B.J. Klebaner surveys the legislation of 1914 and offers some interesting observations regarding it. He suggests that the influence of professional economists was far greater in shaping the 1914 laws than it had been in the case of the Sherman Act. Specifically, Klebaner asserts there was growing resistance among economists to the notion that potential competition could act as an effective constraint on the 'trusts', and growing fear that unfair competition and destructive tactics could serve to deflect entry. Klebaner insists that many professionals seemed ready to assign to the state responsibility for safeguarding the ability of the market to function properly.

In the years that immediately followed, however, reformers almost certainly lost both heart and patience. With the war and the armistice, the recovery and prosperity of the 1920s, other matters eclipsed antitrust reform in the popular mind. And more to the point, antitrust seemed to lose ground. The 'steel trust' survived a challenge in the US Steel case when the Supreme Court, rejecting the government's position, declared that 'mere size is no offence'. At the same time, 'big business' seemed to be growing more powerful; in the rapidly expanding market for automobiles in the 1920s, for example, Ford and General Motors emerged to dominate the largest of all industries. However, dramatic changes in antitrust were still to come.

With the Great Depression and the New Deal, broad economic reforms began to unfold, including those affecting antitrust. In the legislative arena, the Robinson-Patman Act (1936) amended the price discrimination provisions of the Clayton Act by making it unlawful to discriminate in price where the effect might result in 'injury to competition', a phrase which would eventually come to mean that *ad hoc* price-cutting was unlawful. The desires of earlier reformers for the government to protect small, independent firms began to be realized. In the judicial arena, there were aggressive prosecutions of existing law, while the appointment of more sympathetic judges and justices created new law. The scope of the 'Rule of Reason' was limited (in some cases the Rule was simply eliminated completely) by the establishment of *Per Se* rules; the Sherman Act began to be applied by the courts (much like the Clayton Act) to declare whole categories of actions to be illegal *per se* – that is, whether or not criminal purpose and restrictive effects were involved. Symbolic of the 'new Sherman Act' was the Appeal Court's decision in *U.S. v Alcoa* (1945): Alcoa's monopoly in aluminium was unlawful because it had been built and preserved by actions 'to embrace each new opportunity' in the market. Alcoa was held responsible for having eliminated, via preemption, the opportunity for potential competitors to emerge. Regulation of the market by antitrust had thus progressed a great deal.

The reactions to the changes were by no means universally favourable. While many welcomed the more muscular involvement of government, others were critical. In Chapter 6, Thomas Sunderland conveys the types of objections raised by those disturbed by the direction in which US antitrust was moving at mid-century. Sunderland complains that, while the Sherman and Clayton Acts had been designed to keep competition vigorous, the newer legislation (Robinson-Patman) and interpretations (*Alcoa*) softened competition and made life easier for the individual competitor. His criticisms are directed at both the new rules of antitrust (condemning certain types of competitive behaviour *per se*), and at its new objectives (protecting individual firms and the principle of their 'rights to compete' rather than the competitive process and the principle of the market).

On the other hand, those favouring tough antitrust standards were not totally satisfied either. In Chapter 7, C.D. Edwards reflects the position of many who felt that even more stringent regulation of business was needed. Edwards expresses the belief that the problem of size had not been directly addressed by the law. He argues that 'bigness' has two major implications. First, large firms lead to high market concentration; concentration in turn lends itself to a form of understanding, similar in effect to unlawful conspiracy but beyond the reach of law. Second, big firms have a latent power to coerce which, though similar in effect to unfair business practices, is not illegal in itself. To thwart bigness, Edwards favours the legislation then pending to amend and strengthen the antimerger provisions of the Clayton Act (the Kefauver-Celler Act of 1950).

The antimerger amendment to the Clayton Act was successful in passage; it empowered the government (or a private plaintiff) to oppose mergers of assets, a loophole in the original Clayton Act; it also permitted application of the law to vertical and conglomerate mergers, another oversight in the original. The new legislation was accompanied by further expansion of the law in the courts. Important case precedents established new principles for antimerger law: (1) it could be used to prevent minor increases in market concentration (*U.S. v Brown Shoe* (1960)), as distinguished from changes which definitively 'lessen competition or tend to create a monopoly'; and (2) it could be used to prevent mergers which strengthen and perhaps increase the efficiency of larger firms if the result is to place smaller, less efficient firms at a disadvantage (*U.S. v Von's Grocery* (1967)). The mood of this era, in which antitrust came to be used as a force to promote competition in the sense of eliminating the advantages of the large, well-positioned firm, is captured in R.W. Harbeson in Chapter 8 who reports on the DuPont case: the large block of stock ownership of the du Pont family and its associated business interests in General Motors was found to be unlawful due to the presumed 'insider' advantages which it gave Dupont over competitors for sales of paints and fabrics to auto makers. In the late 1960s, American antitrust had become a very powerful force in shaping the organization of industry. But a change would soon become apparent.

Retrenchment in Antitrust Regulation

The 1970s and 1980s brought about a relaxation of particular antitrust rules: certain business practices and market structures which earlier had been targeted by law enforcement agencies were now condoned. At the same time that some were seeking to make antitrust even stronger – through the proposed adoption of the Industrial Reorganization Act to forcibly break up industries with existing high levels of concentration – the general mood swung in the opposite direction. Academics and practitioners alike displayed more concern for the economic consequences of antitrust enforcement in terms of efficiency than they had done just a short time before. Why was this so? On the practical level, economic stagnation, the oil embargo and increased competition from Europe and Japan all conspired to suggest that US business needed help in the form of an antitrust law more tolerant towards 'big business', a law which sought to encourage efficiency rather than handicap large firms by supporting many competitors. And on the intellectual level, newer ideas began to replace the old in terms of the theory of industrial organization.

Still, it is easy to exaggerate what has happened. Changes which have taken place relate more to the temper than the letter of the law. The most important changes are to be found in two areas: (1) reversals by the Supreme Court of certain *per se* rules which had earlier established as illegal entire categories of business practices; and (2) modifications in the enforcement agencies' standards for selecting merger cases. In terms of the former, the plaintiff or prosecution must once again show anticompetitive effect in order to establish unlawful conduct. For example, the new rulings have made it possible, barring proof of restraint of trade effects, for manufacturers to assign exclusive territories to their dealers (*Continental TV v Sylvania* (1977)) and to establish resale price maintenance contracts with dealers (*Business Electronics v Sharp* (1988)). In terms of the latter, it is no longer presumed that horizontal and/or vertical mergers by larger firms will necessarily lessen competition; the FTC and the Antitrust Division have adopted guidelines which permit them to consider whether or not benefits to efficiency might result from a merger.

The papers by O.E. Williamson and R.A. Posner (Chapters 9 and 10) express the reaction of some who generally approve of the direction of change. Posner argues that price-cutting and vertical contracting practices of larger firms, for example, should never have been condemned *per se*. He also rejects the 'leverage' theory – the notion that a large firm has inherent advantages in competing with a small one – which in the heyday of antitrust had been used to justify increased government power to control the organization of industry. Williamson asserts, however, that strategic behaviour by the large established firm might create a form of leverage, summarizing recent analyses of preemptive behaviour. Such behaviour, he feels, is dangerous to the preservation of competition and should therefore be targeted by the law. Thus there continue to be differences in opinion, even though these have narrowed in the current era of antitrust.

Ernest Gellhorn follows the twists and turns of US antitrust history in his article entitled 'Climbing the Antitrust Staircase' (Chapter 11). Gellhorn describes a four-stage evolution of antitrust: (1) a contractual phase in which the courts applied – with great hesitation – a literal interpretation of the Sherman Act; (2) an analytical phase in which the 'Rule of Reason' was developed; (3) a structural phase in which *per se* rules and structural tests of illegality were applied; and (4) the current economics phase encompassing new analyses and new rules. According to Gellhorn, each phase reflects changes in the understanding of the workings of the market. He indicates that antitrust still needs to improve its ability to differentiate between competitive and monopolistic behaviour, but expresses the belief that in the end external factors – that is, the state of the economy – are likely to override rational analysis.

R. Schmalensee describes the new era in Chapter 12 in terms of the law on mergers, claiming that the attitudes of professional economists towards mergers have changed. Schmalensee also details the parallel changes in antitrust law enforcement which have occurred. Compared to the past, academics and lawyers both see competition as a more robust process and are willing to tolerate increases in firm size and market concentration provided that entry is relatively free. Schmalensee reflects these contemporary attitudes and is concerned primarily with fine-tuning the new rules.

The article by T.M. Jorde and D.J. Teece (Chapter 13) contains a different twist. Until recently, the US has been the primary laboratory in the development of antitrust. But Jorde and Teece call for reform in the law dealing with joint ventures – reform allowing greater cooperation among competitors – with major emphasis given to the fact that US law on restraint of trade places domestic firms at a great disadvantage *vis-à-vis* foreign competition. They cite Japanese law in particular as being more permissive in allowing competitors to develop and commercialize new technology. Historically, judicial interpretations of US law on restraint of trade prohibit *per se* all agreements between competitors. And while the National Cooperative Research Act of 1984 has allowed an exception for joint ventures to the general rule on restraint of trade, Jorde and Teece argue that it is too narrow, permitting R&D activity only. They seek changes on two related fronts: (1) relaxing the *per se* rules which ban cooperation, and (2) modifying American law to conform to standards set by other nations.

Antitrust Regulation in Great Britain and Japan

Historically, treating competition as a matter of serious public concern has been the exclusive province of the US, with notable exceptions in other New World nations such as Canada, Australia and New Zealand. Elsewhere, monopoly and combinations in restraint of trade were taken to be the norm. However, the end of World War II seemed to signal a change. For reasons of its own, Britain adopted the Monopoly and Restrictive Practices Act in 1948, thus initiating a series of changes in British law regarding the treatment of antitrust and the concept of competition. In contrast, antitrust law was adopted in Japan under coercion. The US Occupation Government imposed an antitrust law upon Japan which carried forward even after the period of occupation ended. This too began a tradition, but one in which Japanese antitrust law gradually devolved from its beginnings as a foreign transplant.

Antitrust history has become richer in diversity. In this broader perspective, antitrust law has now been individually embraced by a number of nations; it has also been incorporated as part of the political and economic system of the EEC. What began as US policy has become international but (as we have also seen in Chapter 13) the process of transplantation and adaptation has rebounded and ultimately led to change or calls for change to relax the US position.

The traditional British policy of laissez-faire may have been fundamentally pro-competitive, but it also tolerated the development of monopolies and cartels. John Jewkes states in Chapter 14 that even the cautious beginnings represented by the Monopolies and Restrictive Practices Act of 1948 were therefore a dramatic move for the nation to make. The law established a Monopolies Commission to study the effects of market conditions which might be contrary to the public interest and to recommend action in the event that serious problems were discovered. However, in contrast to US antitrust law, there was no presumption that monopoly was destructive of the public interest. Jewkes offers his explanation of why Britain opted to place greater reliance upon competition at this time and how this decision led to the subsequent adoption of the Restrictive Trade Practices Act of 1956.

R.C. Bernhard describes the Restrictive Practices Act of 1956 and contrasts it with comparable US law in Chapter 15. Bernhard argues that British law was narrower in scope than the Sherman Act's broad prohibition of 'any contract, combination or conspiracy' in restraint of trade. In Britain, the law requires registration of restrictive agreements which are presumed to be contrary to the public interest; these are investigated by a Restrictive Practices Court finally to determine whether the public interest may be aided by the agreement (in contrast to the *per se* illegality of restraints in the US). Bernhard makes the further contrast that, in the event of a restrictive agreement being determined contrary to the public interest, it is voided by the court rather than being declared illegal, and the parties involved are not subject to punishment.

The subsequent evolution of British law has been captured by Thomas Sharpe in Chapter 16. Sharpe points out how a number of changes have led to expanding the coverage of the law – mergers, statutory monopolies (i.e., single firms with 25 per cent of the market), 'complex monopolies' – resulting in a wider range of conditions now being subject to investigation as restrictive practices. Sharpe argues that the most important change in the structure of British law was provided by the Competition Act of 1980, which permits selective investigation by the Office of Fair Trading of business practices which distort competition. In his comprehensive survey, Sharpe finds that significant changes have reshaped British law but suggests, nevertheless, that it remains an *ad hoc* system for the investigation and remedy of some market defects; he argues that it does not comprise a fully-fledged antitrust policy in the sense of the US model.

Since the Meiji Restoration of 1878, the government of Japan has acted to cultivate economic growth and development. In so doing, Japan has relied upon a mixture of private initiative and public intervention. This combination was believed to have fuelled the militarism of the Japanese prior to World War II. Thus, when the post-war Occupation Government of Japan acted to establish a vigorous antitrust policy, it was motivated by a desire to alter the structure of the Japanese economy: to deconcentrate industry and to sever the ties between government and the *zaibatsu* – family-dominated holding companies. But in Chapter 17, Eugene Rotwein describes the conflict between the transplanted policy and the structure of the Japanese economy; he explains that the pre-war *zaibatsu* came to be replaced by modern *zaibatsu* which were organized in the form of financial holding companies around giant banks. Because the Fair Trade Commission had so much discretion and the law was so flexible, the post-occupation government was free to pursue a traditional policy of partnership with business, thus bypassing the US-inspired plan for massive deconcentration. Rotwein argues that the Japanese tolerance for restrictiveness and its pursuit of other national priorities were incompatible with the antitrust policy designed by the Occupation Government. The JFTC had to compete with MITI, the Ministry of International Trade and Industry, for example, and was willing to sanction the establishment of 'depression' and 'rationalization' cartels and to permit restrictions designed to strengthen the export-import position of Japan.

Yoshi Tsurumi argues in Chapter 18 that the Japanese economy is organized along the lines of indicative planning, with antitrust policy playing a subordinate role; he describes it as a system in which administered market competition is the controlling force. But he suggests that the degree of governmental control ebbed in the 1950s and 1960s with expansive economic growth. However, Tsurumi identifies the oil crisis of 1973 as a turning point, the resulting rapid inflation causing public sentiment to favour tighter controls over big business. Because of political pressure, the JFTC received greater support to regulate monopoly, and MITI, whose interests had previously almost exclusively reflected its business clients, became more sensitive to the public interest. Tsurumi explains these changes in the context of the oil crisis and Japanese policies designed to give monopsonistic power to its oil-using industries to resist price increases.

T. Nakazawa and L.W. Weiss then address another issue in which antitrust has been subordinated to broader economic policy. Dealing with conditions that might in other nations be treated as the proper subject of an incomes policy – temporary or permanent excess capacity in specific industries – the Japanese have sanctioned depression and/or rationalization cartels to control supply. In an implied comparison with the US, Nakazawa and Weiss assess the actions of the JFTC in this policy area and offer the judgement that antitrust – and competition – have suffered as a result.

Expansion of Public Utility Regulation in the US

The regulation of 'natural monopoly' and of business franchised by the State has a long history which predates the settlement of the Thirteen colonies. But the development of public utility regulation as we now know it began in the late 19th century in the US, propelled by the same popular demand for government control of monopoly as that which led to the establishment of antitrust laws. The so-called Granger laws established state-by-state regulation of the railroads which (unique to the US) were operated as private enterprises and which were viewed by the farmer-Populist as the most rapacious of modern monopolists. As state legislatures extended control over price to other related industries – the business of storing grain, for example – the affected business firms tested the constitutionality of the regulations. In *Munn v Illinois* (1877), the Supreme Court determined that business 'affected with the public interest' could lawfully be regulated without violating constitutional protection of private property. The American concept of the public utility – at least in legal terms – was born.

Congress passed the Act to Regulate Commerce, known as the Interstate Commerce Commission Act, in 1887. This was a landmark in two respects: (1) it established federal governmental control over interstate rail operations, and (2) it created an agency, the ICC, for the express purpose of administering regulations. Some years later, in the 1930s to be precise, federal regulatory agencies began to mushroom. But in the meantime, public utility regulation continued to be concentrated at the state and local level as the public utility sector gradually expanded to include suppliers of water, gas and electricity, operators of streetcars and taxicabs, etc.

F.C. Benham captures the essence of the early period of regulation in the US, examining in Chapter 20 the economic rationale of regulation: that certain industries possess 'natural monopoly' characteristics, and that regulation of them permits the state to use the natural monopolies' low-cost advantages for the 'public good' by holding the monopolists' power in check (including their power to discriminate in price). Benham also provides a concise history of legal institutions, explaining why the process of public utility regulation developed as it did in the United States, as opposed to Great Britain, for example.

The fact that regulations were often adopted in response to calls to protect the public interest does not necessarily mean, however, that the public interest was always effectively served by them. T.S. Ulen surveys the conditions which existed both before and after the passage of the ICC Act in Chapter 21. Others have suggested that the railroads had an interest in securing regulation as a means to enforce cartel pricing in their industry, which had occasionally experienced price wars following rapid expansion of capacity. Ulen finds that, contrary to any simple theory of regulation, there is no clear pattern of serving the interests either of the public or of industry. He suggests that, between 1887 and 1920, the only clear winner may have been the ICC itself, in view of the greatly expanded powers it enjoyed.

In Chapter 22, C.O. Ruggles traces the expansion of regulation from its beginnings through the turbulent period of the 1930s. He shows that for nearly 50 years following *Munn v Illinois* (1877), the courts generally resisted any government action to extend its authority to regulate industry in the 'public interest'. After *Nebbia v New York* (1934) opened the floodgates, however, government could regulate any line of business it chose. Given the opportunity to act, together with a New Deal confidence in 'social engineering' (that is, reliance upon the government instead of the market for the management of economic affairs), Congress and the Administration acted to extend federal regulation to a number of 'competitive' industries. The change was such that the logical justification for a new regulation often turned the traditional one on its head – the problem was not monopoly, but too much competition! In a relatively short period of time, federal regulations were drawn up to include telecommunications (1934), motor carriers (1935), air carriers (1938), natural gas transport by pipeline (1938), and extended to include natural gas production by the Supreme Court (1954). The regulations often relied upon minimum pricing floors and entry control to limit competition; even agriculture (1938) was covered, with acreage allotments and price supports for some selected commodities. Within this context, Ruggles examines the difficulties with and wisdom of price and entry regulation as it existed after a period of broad expansion.

Retrospective assessments of public utility regulation began to appear at this time; one of the most well-developed was that offered by George Stigler (Chapter 23). Stigler systematically rejects the 'public interest' theory of regulation, offering instead a 'private interest' theory which asserts that regulations (to be read as protection) are demanded by certain economic groups and duly supplied by government. Thus public utility regulation is not considered as the traditional means of government seeking to offset or eliminate market failures, but as implied in political economic analyses, with government in the market for selling favours.

Thomas McCraw offers a comprehensive survey of the original explanations and the later reinterpretations of regulation in Chapter 24. He finds that the 'public interest' did lose much of its original meaning during the New Deal era, and that the legislative process seems to have been 'captured' by successful economic interests claiming their well-being to be equivalent to the public good. Instead of seeking one consistent theory to explain the process, however, McCraw develops the theme that government has over time pursued different aims in adopting regulation; these have included containing monopoly, limiting competition, promoting industry, protecting consumers, etc. The salient fact, in McCraw's view, is that, with such an assortment of purposes, regulation is not of a piece; it has not been nor cannot be logically consistent.

The Era of Deregulation

The 1970s brought a change in direction once again which increased market control and reduced government control. In a decade which was as remarkable as that of the 1930s, federal economic regulation (i.e., control of price and entry) was lifted or significantly reduced from airlines (1978), trucking (1980), railroads (1980), long-distance telecommunications (1982) and the production of natural gas (1985). It can certainly be argued that underlying the changes was a renewed commitment to the 'public interest': protections of existing operators in the affected industries were stripped away over loud objections. It can also be argued that underlying the changes was a new understanding of both 'natural monopoly' and competition; the concept of 'contestability' introduced a new dimension into the discussion of the appropriateness of public utility regulation. Finally, deregulation in public utilities to some extent parallels the contemporary change in antitrust, with more emphasis placed upon efficiency and competition and less emphasis upon (and faith in) protection of competitors.

John Panzar provides an interesting comparison in Chapter 25 of the 1938 decision to regulate airlines and the 1978 decision to deregulate them, arguing that each might have been appropriate – in the 'public interest' – in its time. Discussing the latter, Panzar deftly cuts through the popular oversimplifications of the issues and helps to clarify the search for an optimal policy by highlighting certain significant differences between total and partial deregulation.

In Chapter 26, Elizabeth Bailey and William Baumol develop the broader theme of the move towards deregulation during the 1970s and 1980s and the role played by 'contestability' – the use of a credible threat of entry to discipline an incumbent seller (even a monopolist) in the same manner as 'old-fashioned' competition. Using illustrations from several industries, Bailey and Baumol show how the contestability theory can be applied to the task of defining the optimal scope of regulation and the increased reliance upon the market, the result being a coherent reorganization of both the structure of regulation and of the industry itself.

Harry Broadman and Joseph Kalt explore another dimension of the change in regulation in Chapter 27: the increased reliance upon competition, even in the very process of regulating the natural monopolist. Traditionally, the market tended to be regarded either as a natural monopoly or competitive in toto. But more recent analyses seek to define the boundaries of 'natural monopoly' more carefully. Broadman and Kalt deal with this issue in the context of price regulation in natural gas distribution. Traditionally, local gas distributors bought and resold natural gas to their customers, serving as exclusive agents for the dual purposes of supplying transport and the commodity itself. Large customers now have the option of buying gas directly from the wholesale source at a competitive price and buying transportation services from the distribution company at a regulated price. This 'bypass' option eliminates the longstanding practice, under regulation, of setting prices for industrial customers high enough above cost to subsidize low prices for households. Broadman and Kalt survey bypass, concluding that on the whole it represents a triumph of economics over politics: state and local public utility commissions may be prevented by the Federal Energy Regulatory Commission (which mandates bypass) from currying favour of the many at the expense of the few.

Finally, Alfred Kahn offers a review of and prospectus for deregulation in Chapter 28. Having served as CAB Chairman at the time when federal airline regulation was abandoned (and having acted as a leading advocate for deregulation), Kahn's personal views have always proved interesting. Here he discusses the shortcomings of competition – such as those seen in the reduction in quality of service and the increase in price discrimination in airlines. However, he asserts that the process of regulation is even more prone to institutional failure than is the market. Nevertheless, Kahn suggests that regulation will continue to be important as a means of serving the 'public interest' in the core of the public utility sector: changes are likely to be limited to a greater willingness to rely more heavily upon competition (as in the case of bypass) to assist in regulating price. As for the deregulated sector, such as transportation and communications for example, Kahn suggests that a better level of success will be achieved in reaching the goals set under deregulation if government performs its competition-supporting tasks well, such as antitrust enforcement.

And so we see, once again, the interconnections between the two forms of regulation in the US. The recent trend to deregulate industry, which was subjected for a time to direct price and entry controls, is a recommitment to competition. But regulatory reform also implies that government should continue to bear a responsibility – now through antitrust – to serve the public interest.

Part I
Government Regulation and its Effect on Business

[1]

LESLIE HANNAH

Mergers, Cartels and Concentration: Legal Factors in the U.S. and European Experience

I

The growth of the modern corporation has been an ubiquitous phenomenon in the modern world. The supplementation of market transactions by the "visible hand" of corporate bureaucrats, the divorce of capital ownership from managerial control, the economies of large-scale operation, and (though the evidence for this is more ulusive) the increase in market power (by dominant firms and/or cartels) have been recognised as common to the development of capitalism in the United States, France, Germany, Britain and a wide range of other countries with advanced living standards, and also, through the international corporation, in many smaller and less developed economies. In most countries the roots of modern, large-scale organisation can be traced at least as far back as the three or four decades before the First World War, though there are differences in the rate of adoption of the new legal and managerial structures of the modern corporate economy. In the period before 1914, for example, it seems that the United States and Germany led the industrial world in introducing large-scale corporate organisation, whereas Britain retained a stronger inherited structure of family enterprise and market-based industrial organisation for a longer period, in harness with her less dominant fledgling large corporations[1].

In all countries it has been recognised that a necessary precondition for the widespread adoption of modern industrial organisation is the enactment of legislation facilitating what in English law is known as the joint-stock, limited liability company. The availability of general incorporation cheapens and popularises a process of corporate establishment and growth which previously was only available through relatively expensive parliamentary (or other state-initiated) enactment. There are two aspects of modern corporate development to which this facility is crucial: in the expansion in size of operations (both in larger-scale plants and through multi-plant operation, integration and diversification); and in the divorce of ownership and control. Strictly, general incorporation is not a necessary condition for the first of these characteristics

---

1 See e.g. J. *Kocka* u. H. *Siegrist*, this volume, pp. 79 ff.; A. D. *Chandler* Jr. and H. *Daems* (eds.), Managerial Hierarchies: New Views on the Growth of Big Business in the Western World, Harvard 1980.

of modern industrial organisation. In new, fast-growing industries, especially, a family firm can achieve very large size by reaping the entrepreneurial rents of the innovator and ploughing-back profits, without seeking capital from a wider range of shareholders, or even adopting corporate form or quoted company status. Thus family firms (some of them incorporated – some not) could build up substantial capital assets and large-scale, multi-plant operations without losing control of the firm. As early as 1795, the Peel family owned 23 mills in Britain, and later in the nineteenth century the Wills family built up a very large international business in cigarettes without alienating control to outside capital holders. Even in the twentieth century, though a firm like Morris Motors in the British car industry was compelled to incorporate and seek outside capital, William Morris did so for many years without letting the *ordinary* capital – and hence voting control – out of his own hands. Much the same is true of the controlling families in many European business concerns, though, despite exceptions such as the Fords, it was becoming increasingly rare in the United States by 1914 for family ownership to persist in large organisations[2].

Large-scale enterprises were, then, possible before general limited liability legislation, and family firms persisted many years after such legislation. In many other cases, however, it was a necessary precondition of the successful raising of capital that the shareholders should not be held individually liable for the debts of the company in which they were only "sleeping" partners. Where capital requirements were large and ploughback of profits was an inadequate means of raising it – as in the overseas trading companies of the seventeenth century or the canal undertakings of the late eighteenth and nineteenth centuries – national legislatures had usually been willing to enact special legislation conferring limited liability on the shareholders of specific companies. The general joint stock legislation of 1844–56 in Britain thus merely made general a facility which had already been widely adopted in chartered trading companies, canal and railway undertakings, etc[3]. Much the same was true in the legislation enacted in most European countries and in North America to create limited liability; special charters or alternate forms like the Kommanditgesellschaft auf Aktien had pre-dated the general law. General enabling legislation for the modern corporate form had come earlier in Belgium and Holland, and was adopted by the American states at various dates in the mid-to-late – nineteenth century, by France in 1863/68, and in Germany in 1870 – 72. Further developments in the national laws made them especially conducive to the development of large-scale enterprise. The holding company, for example, made the joint stock company a more flexible form of control and in some countries, e. g. Britain, was judged to be legitimate if the business of the controlled subsidiaries

---

2 L. *Hannah*, The Rise of the Corporate Economy, London 1976, chapters 2 and 5; A. D. *Chandler*, Jr., The Visible Hand, Cambridge/Mass. 1977.

3 H. A. *Shannon*, The coming of general limited liability, in: Economic History, vol. 2, 1931/32, pp. 267–91; id., The First 5000 limited liability companies and their duration, in: Economic History, vol. 2, 1931/32, pp. 396–419, *id.*, The limited companies of 1866–1883, in: EHR, vol. 4, 1932–34, pp. 290–316; G. *Todd*, Some Aspects of joint stock companies 1844–1900, in: EHR, vol. 4, 1932–34, pp. 466–71; J. B. *Jefferys*, The denomination and character of shares 1855–1885, in: EHR, vol. 16, 1946, pp. 45–55.

accorded with the aims of the parent company as laid down in the corporate charter: the articles of association. Elsewhere legislative change was necessary to facilitate this development: for example, the exceptionally liberal law of New Jersey in 1888 conferred a general right upon corporations to purchase stock in another corporation, and many of the major U.S. holding companies were registered under that law[4]. Holding companies also made merger very much simpler, and merger became a major source of growth for large companies around the turn of the century in the United States and elsewhere.

II

If developments of limited liability companies were a necessary condition for the *widespread* adoption of modern corporate forms and large scale operation, they were not a sufficient condition. Indeed, in the early years the new companies, as many contemporaries predicted, were not particularly successful. In Britain, for example, a high proportion of the joint stock companies registered under the new legislation of 1844–56 ended in bankruptcy, and, precisely because of their limited liability, the directors of limited companies were distrusted by those with whom they traded. Shareholders, also, were given ample cause to distrust the men who dealt in (but often did not themselves own) the shares of their companies and there was a considerable amount of fraudulent promotion. Markets in shares in industrial companies developed only slowly, and many of the early limited liability shares with a widely-spread ownership were risky and were traded in thin markets, often informally rather than trough a stock exchange[5]. By the end of the nineteenth century, however, some of the glaring loopholes in the company law had been tightened up, and stock market or other institutions had developed which provided effective supervision and helped prevent the most glaring frauds. In Germany, the supervisory board (Aufsichtsrat) provided a means by which major shareholding groups could establish some controls over the managers. In Britain and the United States informal selfregulation by the stock exchanges provided the best protection for the stockholders; but it was not until the 1930s in the USA and the 1940s in Britain that really effective state legislation offered better guaranteees against inadequate information for the investor[6].

I have suggested elsewhere that, in Britain at least, the absence of effective company laws requiring the disclosure of information to investors prevented the development of takeover bids by *outsider* groups which have been a major force making for indus-

---

4 E. g. R. L. *Nelson*, Merger Movements in American Industry 1895–1956, Princeton 1959, pp. 64–70.

5 See the sources listed in note 3 above.

6 E. g. N. *Horn* in this volume, pp. 123–81 above; E. V. *Morgan* and W. A. *Thomas*, The Stock Exchange, London 1962. For a more sceptical view of the efficiency of regulation see e. g. G. J. *Benston*, "The Effectiveness and Effects of the SEC's Accounting Disclosure Requirements, in: H. G. *Manne* (ed.), Economic Policy and the Regulation of Corporate Securities, Washington 1969, pp 23–79

trial concentration in many industrial countries, especially in the United States and Britain since the Second World War[7]. It is clear, however, that by the end of the nineteenth century the adoption and elaboration of the new corporate forms by *insider* groups promoting large-scale, merged enterprises was widespread. The largest merger wave occurred in the United States where, between 1896 und 1905, the largest 100 corporations increased their size on average by a factor of four (mainly by merger), gaining control of 40% of the nation's industrial capital[8]. Mergers and close associations in cartels also prospered in Germany at the same time, and Germany developed a range of large-scale corporations comparable in some respects to those in America. In Britain, by contrast, though joint stock organisation was widely adopted, the pre-1914 merger movement was limited to fewer industries and created smaller-scale enterprises. It was not until the 1920s that developments in holding companies and mergers comparable in intensity and significance for the corporate economy occurred there[9].

If there were differences in the rate of adoption of the new forms, in time and space, then, there were also distinct uniformities which arose essentially from economic rather than legal factors. The industries in which large-scale corporations appeared were much the same in all countries. Large-scale plants were required in the modern sectors of chemicals and automobiles, coordinated research and development programmes were required in the electrotechnical and chemical industries; vertical integration was economic in a range of industries in which management proved better able to control and monitor vertical production flows. Thus the large corporation appeared in the relevant industries at much the same time in advanced industrial countries, though particular market situations in individual countries led to some deviations from the general pattern in particular periods[10].

The timing of movements toward increased concentration (and especially of those which depended on merger activity) also derived from similar factors in each country. Short-term fluctuations in merger activity in the United States and the United Kingdom have been found to be closely related to the trade cycle, and especially to stock exchange prices in those countries[11]. When share prices were rising, the number of mergers increased; when share prices fell, merger activity also declined. This suggests that the dynamics of the financial market are a possible causal influence. There have been a number of attempts to analyse the relationship more closely, none of them en-

---

7 L. *Hannah*, Takeover Bids in Britain before 1950, in: Business History, vol 16, 1974, pp. 65–77.

8 D. *Bunting* and J. *Barbour*, Interlocking Directorates in Large American Corporations 1896–1964, in: BHR, vol. 45, 1971, p. 317, n. 1.

9 L. *Hannah*, Mergers in British Manufacturing Industry 1880–1918, in: *Oxford Economic Papers*, vol. 26, 1974 pp. 1–29; L. *Hannah* and J. A. *Kay*, Concentration in Modern Industry: Theory Measurement and the U. K. Experience, London 1977, chapter 5.

10 See e. g. the forthcoming conference volume edited by A. D. *Chandler* and H. *Daems*, Managerial Hierarchies.

11 *Nelson*, Merger Movements; *Hannah*, Mergers.

tirely satisfactory[12]. It is difficult to agree, for example, that when share prices are high, capital is cheap and thus firms will find it cheap to buy another firm, for the *cost* of that other firm will also reflect high share prices. However if the acquired firms are not quoted on the stock exchange but are privately held this objection does not hold. In this case, the family holders of the shares are likely to have more stable expectations about their prospects than stock market investors during an upswing in share prices. In a share boom, then, promoters are able to boost the value of share in quoted companies and offer shares (or, via a new issue, cash) which seem especially attractive. They are thus better able in a stock market upswing to entice controlling families to sell their shares and hence control. The transfer of shares (with the acquired company becoming a subsidiary of a quoted holding company) was a major source of growth in the early years of large corporations (though it was less common in later decades as unquoted companies decreased in importance), and explains much of the correlation between share prices and merger activity in these years. The correlation did, however, remain in later periods (when most acquired firms were quoted ones) and it may be that more recent explanations of the phenomenon – for example, that share prices act as a proxy for optimistic entrepreneurial expectations[13] – also played a part in earlier periods. While the data is less good it appears that a similar, though less strong, correlation can be observed in France and Germany between financial and economic conditions and merger activity, suggesting that even in countries with rather different financial and corporate structures, comparable factors were at work[14].

III

Despite the characteristics of the rise of the corporate economy which are common to all countries, there remains the problem of explaining major differences in the pace and direction of these changes in the various countries, in particular in explaining why the United States and Germany led in introducing large scale enterprise, while Britain and other countries generally appear to have lagged. Kocka and Siegrist have adopted a modified version of the Gerschenkron thesis and suggest that large corporations (often coordinated by banks) were a means of economising on rare entrepreneurial talent and overcoming market imperfections in Germany[15]. In the United States, market

---

12 E. g. R. L. *Nelson*, Business Cycle Factors in the Choice between Internal and External Growth, in: W. W. *Alberts* and J. E. *Segall* (eds.), The Corporate Merger, Chicago 1966 pp. 52–66; M. *Gort*, An Economic Disturbance Theory of Mergers, in: Quarterly Journal of Economics, vol. 83, 1969, pp. 624–42.

13 C. P. *Mayer*, Share Prices, Growth and Mergers, unpublished B. Phil. thesis, Oxford 1976.

14 *Kocka*, The Rise of the modern business enterprise in Germany, in: *Chandler/Daems*, Managerial Hierarchies. M. *Levy-Leboyer*, Le patronat francais, a-t il été Malthusien?", in: Le Mouvement Social, 1974, pp. 3–49.

15 See their contribution to this volume.

imperfections have also been allocated a role. Davis has argued that high levels of U.S. concentration can be accounted for by imperfections in the capital market (compared with the more highly developed British market) and by the more complex financial flows required by the rapidly changing U.S. economy[16]. No doubt social factors like the German bureaucratic tradition and the French and British attachment to the family firm must also play their part in any comprehensive explanation of international differences. The contributions to a recent conference at Harvard to discuss Chandler's propositions on the „visible hand" of management made it clear that, despite clear convergence in the course of industrialisation, market conditions varied considerably from country to country; and that to equate a lag in merger activity and large-scale organisation to a lag in economic progress is to oversimplify the varying requirements of disparate economies[17].

In the context of this conference, however, the most relevant hypotheses are those which relate to the impact of antitrust laws (or their absence) on the differential rates of adoption of modern corporate forms. The thesis, still occasionally advanced by U.S. economists, that their antitrust laws account for historically lower levels of merger activity and of concentration in the U.S. have now been largely discredited: partly because the purported *explicanda* (fewer mergers, lower concentration) are not true, and partly because the loopholes in the Sherman and Clayton acts prior to the Celler – Kefauver amendment of 1950 were so great as to render the legislation effective in only a limited number of cases[18]. More recently both Chandler and the present author have argued the case for the opposite thesis: that the U.S. antitrust laws actually encouraged merger because they tolerated that path to monopoly power while they more effectively outlawed the alternative pathway via cartels and restrictive practices[19].

The evidence for this view is derived principally from a comparison of Britain with the United States. The timing and relative intensity of the merger waves in the United States has been explained in part by the existence of antitrust laws outlawing cartels in the U.S; while U.S. firms operating in Britain found that they could achieve monopolistic ends by joining cartels (which remained legal in Britain, and in Europe generally until after the Second World War). Yet to view mergers and cartels purely as alternatives is to oversimplify. It is clear that mergers can in some circumstances – where there are economies of scale or integration, for example, – achieve ends to which

16 L. *Davis*, The Capital Markets and Industrial Concentration: The U.S. and U.K., a Comporative Study, in: EHR, vol. 19, 1966, pp. 255–72. The article presents an interesting thesis, which, however, falls down on empirical investigation. Cf. Hannah, Mergers, p. 15, n. 3; *Chandler*, Visible Hand, p. 373.

17 *Chandler/Daems*, Managerial Hierarchies.

18 E. g. G. *Stigler*, The Economic Effects of the Antitrust Laws, in: *id*, Organisation of Industry, Homewood/III. 1968, pp. 259–95; and cf. e. g. C. *Eis*, The 1919–1930 Merger Movement in American Industry, unpublished Ph. D. thesis, CUNY 1968 (University Microfilms 68–11, 221); L. *Hannah*, The Political Economy of Mergers in Manufacturing Industry in Britain between the Wars, unpublished D. Phil. thesis, Oxford 1972, pp. 60–66.

19 *Chandler*, Visible Hand, chapter 10; *Hannah*, Rise pp. 157–58.

a looser cartel is not normally able to aspire. More seriously for the hypothesis, it is evident that cartels are not only *alternatives* to mergers, but are also in an important sense *complements*. Indeed, in Britain cartels had their heyday between the 1930s and the 1950s: that is *after* the great wave of the 1920s had already increased the market power of corporations: as a supplement (and not merely an alternative) to mergers.

The symbiotic relationship between mergers and cartels is not surprising. Cartels, especially in countries like the U.S.A. (where they were illegal) or in Britain (where their agreements were often not legally enforceable), are fragile. The temptation of the "chiseller" to cut prices or to increase production above quotas or to offer secret rebates is great, and the chance of detection by cartel partners low. As the number of firms in an industry declines, however, the effect of any one firm on the market is greater: detection of chiselling and policing of cartel agreements by the members becomes more feasible. An oligopoly has thus been widely recognised to be more conducive to the successful operation of cartels than a disaggregated market structure with many small firms. The potential gains (for both the firms and the public) from cartel regulation may also be greater in the conditions of imperfect competition which may follow from the concentrated market structure created by a prior merger wave[20]. Where competition is imperfect, for example, there may be advantages to regulating competitive advertising costs, or to rationalising production facilities by inter-firm agreement[21].

The complexity of this dual alternative/symbiotic relationship of mergers and cartels goes some way to explaining why Germany at first sight seems to fit uneasily in the simple model of the two as alternatives which is implied in the comparison of Britain and the United States[22]. In 1897 the highest German court ruled that cartel agreements were legal, and Germany was widely recognised as the spiritual homeland of cartels. By 1905, it has been estimated, 25% of output was controlled by cartels and the proportion subsequently rose to 50%. Yet the predominance of large-scale enterprise was, we have seen, more noticeable prior to the 1920s in Germany than in Britain. The conclusion that contrasts in antitrust laws explain *the major part* of the contrast between industrial concentration in the various exonomies can, then, rightly be rejected. In Germany, as elsewhere, cartels were not only potential alternatives to merger but were in important senses complements to them. German cartels have been treated by some writers[23] as a form of forward vertical integration, which are not just alternatives to the U.S. style of vertical integration through formal expansion of the firm, but are also complements to horizontal mergers of businesses (mergers which were sometimes a

---

20 *Hannah* and *Kay*, Concentration pp. 10–18.

21 The regulation of competitive advertising coasts has been an important function of eartels in e.g. the soap industry, and cartels establishing common conditions of sale existed both in Britain and Germany.

22 As remarked by *Kocka* and *Siegrist*, p. 95, on which the following paragraph draws; for comparable estimates of cartel penetration in Britain see J. D. *Gribbin*, (ed.), Survey of International Cartels and Internal Cartels 1944, 1946, London, (micrographed, available from Central Library, Department of Industry, 1 Victoria Street, London S. W. I.).

23 E. g. *Kocka* and *Siegrist* in this volume, pp. 62 f., 82, for the most explicit treatment in this fashion.

precondition of successful forward integration in both America and Germany). Cases were also noted in which the establishment of a cartel encouraged vertical integration by merger because it enabled firms legally to circumvent their established cartel quotas by internalising what had formerly been production for the market. In Germany, then, economic upswings like that of the later 1890s produced not only more merger activity but also more cartels, and cartels occurred in industries where high levels of concentration had already been established by merger activity[24].

To recognise the complexity of the relationship is not, however, to deny that entrepreneurs sometimes face mergers and cartels as alternatives as well as complementary options. To the extent that this is true in particular industries and at particular times, the presence of an antitrust law outlawing cartels may legitimately be said to be a factor explaining why mergers are more common in some economies than in others. The impact of the law is shown most clearly in the United States where legal developments shifted the balance of advantage in monopolisation away from cartels and toward mergers. The Knight decision on section 2 of the 1890 Sherman Act in 1895 eased the path of monopolisation by merger, while the Addyston Pipe decisions of 1898–9 made it clear that pools and cartels would receive much harsher treatment. Though there were many other factors contributing to it, the unprecedented merger wave in the U.S.A. which followed received some impetus from these legal decisions[25]. In Britain there were neither antimerger nor anticartel statutes, but a leading common law decision in the Mogul case in 1891 established the legitimacy of cartels or "conspiracies" in restraint of trade. Members of cartels were sometimes unable to enforce their agreements on members in the British courts, but otherwise the cartel option was an attractive one to British firms. Thus American entrepreneurs when they entered the British market were advised by their bankers that the American method of monopolisation – by merger – was not necessary and that much the same end could be achieved in Britain by a cartel. Significantly the enactment of an effective anti-cartel law – the Restrictive Trade Practices Act in 1956 – contributed, as the Sherman Act had in America many years earlier, to a wave of merger activity of very large proportions[26]. In the case of Germany, also, entrepreneurs were aware that mergers and cartels could be alternatives as well as complements: this is clear for example, in the discussions about the development of the Ruhr Coal Syndicate before the First World War. Industrialists in Germany, especially after the Supreme Court decision of 1897 that cartel obligations were binding in law, had freedom to choose between the alternatives without significant legal intervention. The gradations between the two forms of monopolisation were, it seems, more of a continuum in Germany: the sales syndicate, for example, could become a strong organisation in its own right and it was sometimes a short step from that to a full merger of interests. In Germany, perhaps more than in

---

24 E. *Maschke*, Outline of the History of German Cartels from 1873 to 1914, in: F. *Crouzet* W. H. *Chaloner* and W. M. *Stern* (eds.), Essays in European Economic History 1709–1914, London 1969 [translation of article originally appearing in *Vortragsreihe der Gesellschaft für Westfälische Wirtschaftsgeschichte*, Heft 10, 1964], pp. 226–58.

25 *Nelson*, Merger movements.

26 *Hannah*, Mergers.

any other country, the interaction of the alternative and complementary aspects of the various routes to monopolisation is most evident.

It is evident, then, that a single variable equation in which the independent variable (antitrust law) is held to explain the dependant variable (level of merger activity or industrial concentration) will not contribute much to an understanding of the problem. The discussion of the impact of law – or indeed of any other variable – cannot in a complex economy be treated in these simplistic terms. Rather we must consider the whole range of interacting variables together in a more subtle model of the determinants of international differences in the corporate economy. While such a model would certainly have economic and financial variables (over time and between different national economies) at its centre, it is unlikely that it would completely rule out antitrust factors of the kind we have identified in cross-country comparisons.

Fusionen, Kartelle und Konzentration. Rechtliche Faktoren in der amerikanischen und europäischen Entwicklung 1880–1914

Zusammenfassung

Die Einführung von Gesellschaftsformen mit beschränkter Haftung durch die Gesetzgebung war sowohl in den USA wie auch in Europa ein Faktor, der die Entwicklung von Großunternehmen erst ermöglichte. Die Entwicklung der Gesellschaftsform der holding company erleichterte ebenfalls die Herausbildung größerer Unternehmenskomplexe. Um aber internationale Ähnlichkeiten und Unterschiede im Grad der Anwendung der neuen Gesellschaftsformen und der damit verbundenen Herausbildung von Großunternehmen zu verstehen, muß man sich den ökonomischen und technologischen Faktoren zuwenden: den Techniken, mit denen integriert und Großbetriebe geschaffen wurden, den überlieferten Marktinstitutionen und der Entwicklung der Aktienmärkte. Zum Beispiel hat man eine deutliche positive Korrelation beobachtet zwischen der Fusionsaktivität (die marktbeherrschende Unternehmen hervorbringt) und dem Niveau der Aktienkurse: Dies legt die Vermutung nahe, daß selbst in Ländern mit unterschiedlichen finanziellen Institutionen und differierendem Gesellschaftsrecht ähnliche finanzielle Faktoren diesen Fusionsbewegungen zugrundeliegen.

In übermäßig vereinfachten Vergleichen zwischen Großbritannien und den Vereinigten Staaten ist die Antitrust-Gesetzgebung als ein Grund für den höheren Konzentrationsgrad der Wirtschaft in den USA angeführt worden: indem sie Fusionen zuließ, Kartelle aber gesetzlich ausschloß, so wird argumentiert, habe die US-Antitrust-Gesetzgebung einen Anreiz zur Konzentration geschaffen. Bezieht man jedoch Deutschland in den Vergleich mit ein, dann ist es schwierig, diese These in ihrer einfachen Form aufrecht zu erhalten: Deutschland war gegenüber Kartellen sogar noch toleranter als Großbritannien, erreichte aber nichtsdestoweniger einen hohen Konzentrationsgrad. Es steht zu vermuten, daß die Beziehung zwischen Fusionen und Kartellen komplexer ist, als das einfache Modell es impliziert: Fusionen und Kartelle (und die Auswirkungen von Antitrust-Gesetzen herauf) sollten als potentiell *komplementäre* ebenso wie potentiell *alternative* Unternehmensstrategien verstanden werden. Brauchbare Vergleiche zwischen Ländern hinsichtlich der Wirkung von Antitrust-Gesetzen erfordern somit eine komplexere, multivariable, Wechselwirkungen berücksichtigende Analyse des Konzentrationsproblems.

Titles quoted

Benston, G. J., The Effectiveness and Effects of the SEC's Accounting Disclosure Requirements, in: H. G. *Manne* (ed.), Economic Policy and the Regulation of Corporate Securities, Washington 1969.

Bunting, D. and *Barbour*, J., Interlocking Directorates in Large American Corporations 1896–1964, in: BHR, vol. 45, 1971, pp. 317–35.

Chandler, A. D., Jr., The Visible Hand: The Managerial Revolution in American Business, Cambridge/Mass. 1977.

– and H. *Daems* (eds.), Managerial Hierarchies: New Views on the Growth of Big Business in the Western World, Harvard 1980.

Davis, L., The Capital Markets and Industrial Concentration: The U. S. and U. K., a Comparative Study, in: EHR, vol. 19, 1966, pp. 255–72.

Eis, C., The 1919–1930 Merger Movement in American Industry, unpublished Ph.D. thesis, CUNY 1968.

Gribbin, J. D., (ed.), Survey of International Cartels and Internal Cartels 1944, 1946, London (micrographed).

Gort, M., An Economic Disturbance Theory of Mergers, in: Quarterly Journal of Economics, vol. 83, 1969, pp. 624–42.

Hannah, L., The Rise of the Corporate Economy, London 1976.

–, Mergers in British Manufacturing Industry 1880–1918, in: Oxford Economic Papers, vol. 26, 1974, pp. 1–20.

–, Takeover Bids in Britain before 1950, in: Business History, vol. 16, 1974, pp. 65–77.

–, The Political Economy of Mergers in Manufacturing Industry in Britain between the Wars, unpublished D. Phil. Thesis, Oxford 1972.

–, and *Kay*, J. A., Concentration in Modern Industry: Theory Measurement and the U. K. Experience, London 1977.

Jefferys, J. B., The denomination and character of shares 1855–1885, in: EHR, vol. 16, 1946, pp. 45–55.

Kocka, J., The Rise of the Modern Business Enterprise in Germany, in: *Chandler/Daems*, Managerial Hierarchies.

Levy-Leboyer, M., Le patronat francais, a-t il été Malthusien? in: Le Mouvement Social, 1974, pp. 3–49.

Maschke, E., Outline of the History of German Cartels from 1873 to 1914, in: F. *Crouzet*, W. H. *Chaloner* and W. M. *Stern* (eds.), Essays in European Economic History 1789–1914, London 1969, pp. 226–58.

Mayer, C. P., Share Prices, Growth and Mergers, unpublished B. Phil. thesis, Oxford 1976.

Morgan, E. V. and *Thomas*, W. A., The Stock Exchange, London 1962.

Nelson, R. L., Business Cycle Factors in the Choice between Internal and External Growth, in: W. W. *Alberts* and J. E. *Segall* (eds.), The Corporate Merger, Chicago 1966, pp. 52–66.

–, Merger Movements in American Industry, 1895–1956, Princeton U. P. 1959.

Shannon, H. A., The coming of general limited liability, in: Economic History, vol. 2, 1931/32, pp. 267–91.

–, The First 5000 limited liability companies and their duration, in: Economic History, vol. 2, 1931/32, pp. 396–419.

–, The limited companies of 1866–1883, in: EHR, vol. 4, 1932–34, pp. 290–316.

Stigler, G., The Economic Effects of the Antitrust Laws, in: idem, Organisation of Industry, Homewood/Ill. 1968, pp. 259–95.

Todd, G., Some Aspects of joint stock companies 1844–1900, in: EHR, vol. 4, 1932–34, pp. 46–71.

[2]

Excerpt from Alfred Chandler and Herman Daems (eds), *Managerial Hierarchies*, 161–81

5/ Regulation of Large Enterprise: The United States Experience in Comparative Perspective

Morton Keller

REGULATION OF THE MARKET is as old as the market itself. For as long as society has enjoyed the benefits of enterprise, it has sought to check its excesses. Medieval authorities sought to enforce a just price and forbade usury; early modern times saw extensive mercantilist efforts to bend economic activity to the interests of the state. English common law gradually developed constraints on monopolies and contracts in restraint of trade and on objectionable trade practices such as forestalling, engrossing, and regrating. Regulation has been as much a part of the history of Western capitalism as trade, investment, entrepreneurship, and technology.

During the late nineteenth and early twentieth centuries, that history took a new turn. The large business enterprise emerged as the primary instrument of production and distribution. The merger of firms into large-scale combinations, the integration of production and distribution within firms, and the steady accretion of company control in the hands of salaried managers were widespread and consequential developments. In recent years emergence of big business has been the subject of a rich and revealing historical literature.

The regulatory response to this development, however, has not been the beneficiary of comparable historical analysis. Substantial work has been done, of course, on the judicial and administrative regulation of the large enterprise, particularly in the United States, but this literature tends to dwell on the impact (or lack of impact) of regulation on the enterprises it is regulating. It has less to say about the development of public policy toward big business as a historical phenomenon with its own form and character. Nor has there been comparative analysis of the strategy and structure of regulation to match the recent literature on the managerial revolution in a number of Western countries.

What follows is a tentative attempt at such an overview. This essay examines the regulatory response to the rise of big business as a distinctive historical development, passing through discernible phases of evolution through the nineteenth and early twentieth centuries. In it I try to see that process in comparative perspective (though with special attention to the United States). My underlying assumption is that both the growth of large enterprise and the regulatory response were parts of a more general theme: the effort of the private and public institutions of the West to come to terms with the awesome new economic power unleashed by industrial development and technological change.[1]

THE NINETEENTH CENTURY

The large enterprises that appeared in a number of Western countries during the nineteenth century had a number of things in common. The needs of investment capital, production, management, and marketing transcended national boundaries, and everywhere public policy was called on to respond to the rise of industrial capitalism. It did so, however, in ways that were profoundly affected by the character of each country's history and culture.

Statutory and legal frameworks of business regulation differed among Western nations in timing and character. The French structure of business regulation arose in response not to the coming of large enterprise but to the French Revolution. The law of March 2, 1791, proclaimed the freedom of industry and commerce from state restrictions; the Civil Code of 1804 stripped fraudulent or unlawful contracts of their legal force and defined commercial illegality as acts "contrary to good

morals or to public order"; the Commercial Code of 1807 regulated a variety of business practices; and the Penal Code of 1810
imposed penalties on those who "effect or attempt to effect an
artificial increase or reduction in the price of a product." These
acts were designed to underpin the Revolution's break with
the restrictive, merchantilist economic policies of the *ancien
régime*.[2]

Nineteenth-century French commercial law and legislation
—typified by the Companies Act of 1867, which minimized government restraints on the creation of firms—reflected the primacy of small, often family-sized units in the nation's economic
life. Trade associations came under legal restraint when they
threatened local market relations (as in an influential 1851 case
involving Calais lumber merchants). Businessmen's agreements
restricting competition for a specific period of time were upheld
by the courts, but not when they imposed an unlimited prohibition on competition in a particular locale as well.[3] Toward
the end of the nineteenth century, the competitive threat
of German cartels loomed larger, and domestic pressure to allow
business combines grew. Prerevolutionary mercantilist and guild
traditions reappeared in a new guise. An 1884 law legitimated
professional societies, labor unions, and trade associations. But
what one legal expert has called "the ghost" haunting French
regulatory law continued to be "the suppression of freedom"
in commercial affairs. In this area, as elsewhere in French life
during the nineteenth and early twentieth centuries, individualism and corporatism engaged in never-ending conflict
with one another. Big business in France made its way in a
society with strong commitments both to laissez-faire and family-
sized enterprises and to state-supported, large-unit consolidation.[4]

German commercial law closely resembled the French
model. The Prussian Trade Regulation Act of September 7,
1811, which restricted the powers of guilds and abolished the
price-fixing authority of the police, echoed the French statute of
1791. The German Civil Code of 1896 followed the French Civil
Code of 1804 in declaring that "a transaction in violation of
good morals is void" and that someone "who designedly injures
another in a manner violating good morals" is liable to indem-

nification. The 1896 Statute against Unfair Competition was based on several articles of the French Code.[5]

The language of French economic liberalism thus entered into German law, but there was no equivalent of the French Revolution to foster a liberal alternative to Germany's corporative past. In the 1870s United States ambassador Andrew White called the ever more numerous German cartels "some new form of guilds." German courts readily legitimated cartels and their practices. The Bavarian Landgericht held in 1888 that "it was not *contra bonos mores* for business men belonging to a branch of industry which is suffering from a depression to get together and enter into agreements regulating the ways and means of operating their industry with a view to promoting recovery. On the contrary such course of action would seem incumbent upon prudent business men." The Reichsgericht in the Saxon Wood Pulp Cartel case of 1897 affirmed that cartels were often in the interest of the public as well as of their members, for if prices fell too far then society itself would suffer.[6] These decisions displayed the strong German inclination to accept tightly organized forms of economic activity, without the French disposition to support a market system dominated by freely competing family-sized firms. For all the similarity of language in the two nations' laws, *pro bono publico* had a very different meaning for each of them.

The British regulatory response was no less idiosyncratic. As in the case of France, economic liberalism secured a strong foothold in nineteenth-century English public policy. The Companies Act of 1862 was as much a bulwark of entrepreneurial freedom as the French law of 1867, and the Board of Trade did little to impede an orgy of railroad incorporation in the 1840s. Cartels at first met with opposition from courts steeped in the antimonopoly attitudes of nineteenth-century English common law. *Hilton* v. *Eckersley* (1856) held a mill-owners' cartel to be against the public interest: "They agree to carry on their trade not freely as they ought to do, but in conformity with the will of others; and this not being for a good consideration is contrary to public policy."[7]

By the end of the century, however, the British tradition of economic liberalism and free trade had to come to terms with the fact that cartels were an important part of the nation's economic life. In two major cases, *Mogul* v. *McGregor* (1889) and *Maxim* v. *Nordenfelt* (1894), modern British cartel policy emerged. The court in the *Mogul* case upheld a rebate granted by a cartel of steamship lines to its exclusive customers. *Maxim* enforced the ancillary covenant of an armaments cartel in which the defendant had agreed not to sell munitions anywhere for twenty-five years. Major elements of modern British regulatory policy are evident in these decisions. In sharp contrast to the United States experience, judges were inclined to exercise self-restraint in economic controversies: "To draw a line between fair and unfair competition, between what is reasonable and unreasonable, passes the power of the Courts" (*Mogul*); "In England, at least, it is beyond the jurisdiction of her tribunals to mould and stereo-type national policy" (*Maxim*). A relatively cohesive and homogeneous business community made arbitration rather than litigation the preferred mode of conflict resolution. (A major British arbitration act was passed in 1889; no significant arbitration law was passed in the Uinted States until the 1920s.)[8]

While it may seem that the British acceptance of cartel practices was similar to that of the Germans, its underlying rationale was very different. British policy rested on a belief in enterpreneurial freedom and the sanctity of contracts that overrode any distinction between the cartel and the individual businessman, or even between fair and unfair competition, which, as one of the *Mogul* judges said, "would impose a novel fetter upon trade." Another spoke of "the injustice of not allowing an association of traders to do those things which could be done by an amalgamation of the same persons."[9] German cartel policy, in contrast, assumed that the public good was best served by restraints on competition. These are quite dissimilar conceptions of the public good, and the difference in part explains why German public policy was so much more positively helpful to cartelization than was its British counterpart.[10]

The United States regulatory response to the rise of large enterprise differed sharply from the European experience. On the face of things, it was a policy suffused with paradox. The nation with the strongest traditions of individualism, voluntarism, localism, and hostility to the active state nevertheless developed the most elaborate, extensive system of legal and statutory regulation. The seedbed of integrated big business produced a regulatory system that more than any other was committed to fostering small-unit competition; the land of the trust became the land of antitrust.

For much of the nineteenth century, United States economic policy was not unlike that of France and England. It, too, was dedicated to the precepts of liberalism and laissez-faire. General-incorporation laws made chartering little more than an administrative formality; few constraints were placed on corporations' internal affairs. Indeed, the states heartily competed to see which could be most attractive to chartered companies. The already permissive New Jersey corporation law was further liberalized in 1899, so that "the conduct and conditions of [a corporation's] . . . business are treated as private and not public affairs." The external impact of corporations—on customers, competitors, and society at large—was another matter, however. Conflicting economic interests, public opinion, and party politics fostered a steady growth of legislative and judicial supervision, based on the states' chartering authority and on their police power to protect the public health, safety, and welfare.[11]

The conflict between the internal pressure on corporations to pursue autonomy and the external pressure on them for accountability attained a scale and intensity in the United States that had no European analogue. Why was this so? Surely in part because of the rapidity with which big business came to the country and the scale it attained. The sense of a sudden change in economic life, and thus in the life of the society at large, was far more intense in the United States than in Europe. What was more, this corporate-managerial revolution occurred in a society with no older tradition of feudalism, corporatism, or social and political hierarchy. Nowhere were nineteenth-century individualism and laissez-faire less challenged by opposing social values; nowhere did big business develop faster or further. The result was a politics of regulation—and a regulatory system—unique in character.

The railroads were the United States' first big business, and railroad supervision was the first great regulatory battleground.

From the 1820s to the 1870s, states, counties, and towns oscillated between providing freedom and subsidies for railroads to expand and seeking to mitigate or regulate the effects of that expansion. As consolidation in the late nineteenth century made the railroads truly national enterprises, regulation became a national issue as well. E. L. Godkin of the *Nation* presciently warned in 1873: "The locomotive is coming in contact with the framework of our institutions. In this country of simple government, the most powerful centralizing force which civilization has yet produced must, within the next score years, assume its relations to that political machinery which is to control and regulate it."[12]

In 1887 Congress responded to more than a decade of agitation for federal railroad regulation by enacting the Interstate Commerce Act. This law defined and laid down the penalties for rate discrimination and created an Interstate Commerce Commission (ICC) with the power to investigate and prosecute violators. In the years that followed, railroads continued to expand and consolidate, and new regulatory laws were added. These included the Elkins Act of 1903, designed to end rebates to favored customers; the Hepburn Act of 1906, granting rate-making power to the ICC; the Mann-Elkins Act of 1910, which set up a Commerce Court to review rate and other disputes; the Adamson Act of 1916, prescribing an eight-hour day for railroad workers; and the Esch-Cummins Act of 1920, which returned the railroads to private ownership after a wartime hiatus of government operation.

This record cannot be characterized either as one of subservience to the railroads or as a coherent national railroad policy. The interests involved were too varied, conflicting, and effervescent for either tendency to prevail. Some larger railroads wanted federal regulation to serve as a substitute for rate pooling, which consistently failed because the courts refused to enforce it. Other lines favored state supervision; still others opposed all regulation, state or federal. The interests of small railroads often conflicted with those of the larger lines. Commercial, agricultural, and industrial shippers were no less varied; their attitudes toward regulation differed according to their size and location and the extent of the rail service currently available to them. Railroad labor unions and public opinion in general were also factors to be reckoned with. So too were the regulators themselves: state railroad commissions, state legislators, Congress and the President, the ICC, and, not least, the state and federal courts. It is not surprising that the United States system of railroad regulation was conspicuous for its scale and extent—and for its inability to promote the development of a stable, rationalized, and efficient national railroad system.[13]

The performance of the ICC reveals how difficult it was to have a viable form of national administrative supervision in a federalist, pluralistic polity. During the first ten years of its existence, the commission handed down rulings on more than 800 rate controversies, but the size, complexity, and intensely competitive character of the railroad business and the limits on the ICC's power (its decisions could be reviewed by the courts) severely limited its impact. The commission adopted a judicial rather than an administrative model from the first. Its initial chairman, the former judge and legal treatise writer Thomas M. Cooley, announced, "The Commissioners realize that they are a new court, . . . and that they are to lay the foundations of a new body of American law." The major achievements of the ICC by 1900 were to bring about greater uniformity in railroad accounting and the classification of operating costs and greater publicity about the conduct of the railroad business. Closer control was not possible; nor, thought Chairman Cooley, was it desirable: "The perpetuity of free institutions in this country requires that the political machine called the United States Government be kept from being overloaded beyond its strength. The more cumbrous it is the greater power and intrigue and corruption under it."[14]

Similar conditions attended the creation and early application of the Sherman Antitrust Act. The use of the trust and later the holding company to evade state laws forbidding one corporation from holding the stock of another unloosed strong public fears of corporate power. The corporate trust—"a perfectly new device in the law"—had a disturbing ambiguity about it. One commentator wrote in 1887, "The Standard Oil has grown to be a more powerful—corporation, shall we call it? or what? for this is one of the questions—than any other below the national government itself."[15] The trust in the generic sense of a "huge, irresponsible, indeterminate" corporation became the object of widespread public, legislative, and judicial concern. By 1890 ten states had passed antitrust laws, and six state supreme courts had found trust agreements to be illegal as monopolies, conspiracies in restraint of trade, or against public policy. The Sherman Act, adopted by a virtually unanimous congressional vote in 1890, outlawed "every contract, combination in the form of trust or otherwise, or conspiracy, in restraint of trade or commerce." The sweep and vagueness of this formulation, and the law's reliance on the courts rather than on an administrative agency to determine when it had been violated, avoided the risk that the Supreme Court would declare it unconstitutional. Beyond that, the language of the Sherman Act reflected the prevailing uncertainty as to just what form regulation should take—and just what should be regulated.[16]

Not surprisingly, the Sherman Act at first proved to be no more effective as a regulatory device than the ICC. In the 1890s the Department of Justice lacked the personnel, the money, and the inclination to prosecute offenders vigorously. The courts, too, severely limited the utility of the act. They held that a firm might well dominate its sector of the economy without doing anything illegal, and they developed a distinction between legitimate business practices and "illegal commercial piracy." In its *E. C. Knight* decision of 1895, the Supreme Court held that even though the American Sugar Refining Company controlled over 90 percent of the nation's sugar-refining capacity, it did not violate the Sherman Act because it was engaged in manufacturing, not in interstate commerce. In a series of decisions from 1897 to 1899, however, the Court made it clear that the Sherman Act would be applied—and applied vigorously —against trading and pricing cartels.[17]

By the end of the nineteenth century a distinctive public policy toward the large enterprise had emerged in the United States. In contrast with the European situation, pools, trusts, and cartels had little or no legal standing, but holding companies (particularly of manufacturing firms) were acceptable combinations. Furthermore, despite the creation of the ICC, regulation was being handled primarily through litigation and court decisions, not through administrative decrees. The *form* of regulation—a mass of state laws, the Interstate Commerce and Sherman Acts, and constant and heavy litigation—indicated the widespread popular distrust of big business; the regulatory *function* reflected the diversity of interests at play, the political power of large enterprise, and the weakness of the administrative state.

The Early Twentieth Century

In the years after 1900, large enterprises throughout the West tended more and more to resemble one another. By 1930 the 100 largest firms in the United States and in Great Britain each accounted for about 25 percent of the net manufactured output of their countries. They were no less alike in their managerial, marketing, and financial structures. In 1901 the English observer Henry Macrosty commented that "after a century of competition we find that a new motive is gripping the industrial world, the desire to put an end to competition, while maintaining the private ownership and direction of industry."[18]

Might the same be said of public policy? Did regulatory structures, particularly those of Germany, Great Britain, and the United States, respond in similar ways to the emergence of mature systems of big business? Certainly there are grounds for arguing that such a convergence of policy did in fact take place. The administrative state—regulatory agencies, administrative law, and the like—grew in all countries. The goals of rationalization and efficiency appealed to political as well as corporate leaders. One study of British political thought from 1890 to 1914 is aptly titled *The Quest for National Efficiency;* an interpretation of American politics and society during this period is called *The Search for Order.*[19]

The regulatory policies of leading industrial nations appeared to converge during the course of the early twentieth century, in pace with the increasing uniformity of large enterprises. "By the time the [First World] War came," said A. H. Feller, "corporation law throughout Europe had reached a certain level of stability." By the 1920s courts in the United States had come closer to the European willingness to accept cartel practices. At the same time, Germany, which established its Cartel Court in 1923; Great Britain, which conducted its first trust investigation in 1919; and France, which passed a law penalizing excessive company profits in 1926, began to echo the American policy of paying heed to the dangers as well as celebrating the advantages of bigness and combination. In the late nineteenth century, regulatory policy everywhere established the ground rules that accompanied the emergence of big business; in the early twentieth century the emphasis shifted to accommodating regulation to mature systems of large enterprise.[20]

Nevertheless, a closer look at the record suggests that underlying national differences continued to leave their mark on regulatory policy. Each country had its own mode of supervision, its own politics of regulation, its own way of dealing with specific issues such as boycotts, tying contracts, price cutting, and resale-price maintenance. Public policy continued to reflect the fact that large enterprise functioned in distinct and distinctive national milieus.[21]

Big business in Germany had a much closer relationship to the policies of the state than was the case in Great Britain or the United States. The atavistic character of the Kaiser and his court had a heavy and often oppressive weight on the career of a leading businessman like Albert Ballin of the Hamburg-Amerika Line. At the same time, the freedom of firms to form cartels remained secure and uncontested. It was, said one commentator, "a right somewhat akin to the right to make use of a highway, and only subject to correction of abuses of power." As Ballin observed, the United States government could require the dissolution of a syndicate, while under German law its dissolution could be a punishable offense.[22] German courts repeatedly ruled that cartels protected the interests of the nation against the selfishness of individuals. A Reichstag committee investigating cartels in the early 1900s was critical of numerous practices—particularly those of the steel cartel—but recommended no restrictive legislation; nor was any enacted. The courts treated cartel cases in terms of the law of industrial property rights, patents, trade regulations, copyrights, and the like. In contrast to the United States' emphasis on antitrust law, there was no cartel law as such in Germany until after World War I.[23]

The German Cartel Law of 1923, the first statute to refer specifically to cartels, created a Cartel Court with the power to adjudicate charges of abuses by these associations. On the face of things this was a regulatory device comparable to the American Federation Trade Commission. The Cartel Court heard

more than 2,000 complaints during the 1920s, but the relief
that it granted rarely went beyond allowing the aggrieved party
to withdraw from the cartel. For the most part, the court sustained cartel boycotts (*Sperre*) of nonmembers and "loyalty rebates" to exclusive customers. It exercised little or no restraint
on the pace of cartelization; one estimate is that there were 1,500
cartels in 1923 and 2,500 in 1925. Although the Company Act of
1930 (which copied the British Companies Act of 1928) brought
German company law into closer accord with that of other
countries, only organized labor and the Socialists challenged the
structure of cartelization that had become so prevalent in German enterprise. No organized counterforce of competing business interests, no countertradition of free-market competition
left its mark on early twentieth-century German public policy
toward the large enterprise.[24]

Though there were many similarities between the reform
politics of Edwardian British Liberalism and early twentieth-
century progressivism in the United States, antitrust was not
one of them. The major British concern in the years after 1900
was not the power of big business but its efficiency—that is, its
capacity to compete with its German and American rivals.

The consolidation and integration of British firms, always
slower than that of their overseas counterparts, quickened during World War I and after. A number of businessmen, politicians, and publicists in the 1920s called for the "rationalization" of industry. Some hoped that the Board of Trade might
play a role in this regard comparable to that of Herbert Hoover's
Department of Commerce. Moreover, British regulatory policy
increasingly concerned itself with the internal management of
firms. The Companies Department of the Board of Trade won
independent status in 1904, a year after the creation of the
Bureau of Corporations in the United States Department of
Commerce and Labor. Successive Companies Acts—those of
1900, 1908, and especially 1928—tightened government supervision of the formation and management of firms and the issuance of securities, in much the same way as the United States'
Federal Trade Commission Act of 1914 and Securities Exchange
Act of 1934.[25]

Yet the major thrust of British public policy toward large

enterprises—in dramatic contrast with the German pattern—
was to keep state involvement at a minimum. Arbitration rather
than litigation remained the preferred mode of resolving conflicts among firms; "arrangements and understandings and gen-
tlemen's agreements" more extensive "than the average man
ever dreamed of" continued to be the norm.[26] Far less big-
business litigation came before the British than before the
United States courts. Eleven of the 50 largest industrial corporations in the United States faced government-initiated law-
suits in the appellate courts during the early twentieth century;
none of the 50 leading British firms were so involved. The major
United States firms were parties to about 300 appellate cases
through 1906, and about 350 from 1907 to 1916. The comparable British firms figured in only 22 reported cases between
1895 and 1935.[27]

Nor was there a pronounced and vigorous judicial response
to combination as such. One observer concluded in 1925 that
"speaking broadly, and as a practical matter, the law does not
forbid monopoly at all." He found, however, that only 11 cases
involving the power of cartels came before the courts between
1829 and 1925 (8 of these from 1898 on). Six involved challenges
to contractual arrangements between cartels and outside parties;
given the courts' respect for sanctity of contract, it is not surprising that all were decided in favor of the cartels. When the
cartel sought to enforce its provisions against its own members
in 4 other cases, however, the decision in 3 went against the
combine.[28] A 1937 review of British legal obstacles to industrial
integration concluded that "the progress of industrial integration by means of contractual association proceeds without assistance from the legislature and in face of considerable opposition from the common law; but this opposition varies in its
intensity and success."[29] Perhaps the fairest judgment is that public policy both reflected and sustained the halting, uncertain
progress of British business consolidation during the early twentieth century.

The ostensible goal of regulation in the United States after
1900 was clear enough. "The policy of the law looks to competition," observed a federal court in 1900; "the fundamental purpose of the Sherman Act was to secure equality of opportunity

and to protect the public against the evils commonly incident to the destruction of competition," the Supreme Court concluded in 1923.[30] Yet this was the period during which big business in the United States took its modern form. How, in fact, did regulatory law and legislation cope with the growing disparity between public-policy theory and economic reality?

During the years before World War I, concern over the size, structure, practices, and power of the large enterprise had a central place in American public life. James Bryce observed in 1905 that the dominant issue in American politics "was the one least discussed in Europe: I mean the propriety of restricting industrial or mercantile combinations of capitalists."[31] This was a direct response to the rapidity and scale of corporate consolidation in the United States. It was also part of a broader, pervasive fear of social change that expressed itself in a variety of forms: prohibition, restriction of immigration, legalized racial segregation, the conservation movement. This larger context helps explain why the regulatory goals of antitrust were so much stronger in the early twentieth-century United States than in any other Western society.

The vast literature on the trusts, that appeared in the years after 1900 was divided between two schools of thought. The first saw corporate consolidation as a sinister social development and called for policies designed to maintain a system of free competition among roughly comparable business units. The other saw large enterprise as a progressive force that held out the promise of greater efficiency, lower costs, and labor peace. These attitudes stemmed not from traditional class divisions but rather from particular individual or group interests. Samuel Gompers of the American Federation of Labor welcomed the rise of big business; small businessmen were among the most ardent supporters of antitrust policies.[32] Given this range of views, it is not surprising that American regulatory policy, in sum, was neither sharply adverse toward nor warmly protective of large enterprise. Rather, it may best be seen as a complex, varied response to an equally complex and varied economic system.

Early twentieth-century national regulation developed in a kind of counterpoint to state corporation law. Wiley B. Rutledge, Jr., concluded in 1937, "During the half-century in which the Federal Government has been extending its control over corporate enterprise, the states have been engaged simultaneously in abrogating their control." During the decade from 1915 to 1925, a deluge of state laws legitimated no-par stock offerings. In the late 1920s a number of commonwealths—among them California, Illinois, Michigan, Ohio, and Pennsylvania—made their corporation laws still more liberal than they had been before. As Rutledge observed, "In general, they are designed to give the maximum freedom to the incorporators, and to adjust statutory provisions to the requirements of the large scale mass production enterprise."[33]

Federal policies followed a more tortuous path. By the end of the nineteenth century it seemed clear that, while the courts would not uphold trusts or cartels, they were ready to allow manufacturing firms to combine into holding companies. This trend was a helpful prelude to the great burst of industrial mergers around 1900. Alfred D. Chandler, Jr., has noted that "after 1899 lawyers were advising their corporate clients to abandon all agreements or alliances carried out through cartels or trade associations and to consolidate into single, legally defined enterprises."[34]

If judicial policy helped set the stage for the turn-of-the-century merger movement, it also contributed to its end. The slowdown of mergers after 1902 coincided not only with the satiation of the market for industrial securities but also with the Supreme Court's 1904 *Northern Securities* decision, the first to suggest that a holding company might be vulnerable to the Sherman Act. Thereafter (with an occasional spectacular exception, such as the public utilities combines of the 1920s) corporate growth occurred more often through managerial investment in production, marketing, research, and other facilities than through consolidations fostered by promoters and investment bankers. Meanwhile, Sherman Act antitrust actions multiplied. The new Bureau of Corporations provided the government with better fact-gathering facilities; the Expediting Act of 1903 gave priority in the federal courts to Sherman Act and ICC cases; and the Department of Justice was strengthened by larger appropriations and the creation of an Antitrust Division.

During Theodore Roosevelt's presidency (1901–1909), 44 Sherman Act suits were filed; under William Howard Taft (1909–1913) the number rose to 90.[35]

The Supreme Court's *Standard Oil* and *American Tobacco* decisions were the most important in pre–World War I antitrust law. They forced two of the largest corporate holding companies to break up into separate (and theoretically competing) firms. More significantly, the Court's adoption of the "rule of reason" in applying the Sherman Act meant that the character and practices of large enterprises, not their size or the percentage of the industry that they controlled, would determine their liability. Flexible (and highly complex and technical) considerations would henceforward characterize United States antitrust law.[36]

The *American Tobacco* case nicely demonstrates how the character of regulation had changed in accord with the new technology, managerial structure, and marketing conditions of big business. The complexity of the American Tobacco Company's corporate structure (there were several layers of holding companies) and the intermixture of production and marketing functions made its dissolution very difficult. Each of the numerous component companies of the American Tobacco combine had to be dealt with as an individual conspirator in restraint of trade: "Every concern made brands owned by some other concern, or had made for it by some one of the other companies a brand or brands which it owned." The several kinds of American Tobacco equities also had to be treated separately; the interests of bondholders, preferred stockholders, and common stockholders often conflicted with one another. The complex dissolution plan that followed on the Court's decision was worked out in a series of conferences by American Tobacco officials, company lawyers, federal circuit-court judges, and the Attorney General and his staff. The settlement created new, supposedly independent firms—Liggett and Myers, P. Lorillard, and others–out of the original American Tobacco combine. Efforts were made to assure these new companies the brand names, factories, distribution facilities, and earning power necessary to compete on reasonable terms with the mother firm. At the same time, it was recognized that "the business itself offers insuperable obstacles to the creation of perfect competitive conditions under any method of distribution." In fact, the tobacco industry retained an essentially oligopolistic character. Here was regulation far more complex in its character and ambiguous in its results than simple antitrust.[37]

The Clayton and Federal Reserve Acts of 1914 were passed at the end of the formative period of big business in the United States, just as the Interstate Commerce and Sherman Acts marked its beginning. As might be expected, the later laws had much in common with the complex and articulated mode of legal regulation that had emerged in step with large enterprise. The Clayton Act exempted labor unions and agricultural marketing associations from the Sherman Act and forbade specific business practices such as price discrimination, tying contracts, and interlocking directorates that "substantially lessen competition or tend to create a monopoly." In sum, it adapted the Sherman Act to new economic conditions by specifying what sorts of associations were permissible and what sorts of behavior were not.

The Federal Trade Commission Act made "unfair methods of competition in commerce" as illegal as conspiracies in restraint of trade. More important, it was the charter of administrative (as distinct from judicial) oversight of the modern business enterprise. For the first time, a government agency—the Federal Trade Commission–was given a broad grant of power (in the words of the act) to investigate corporations' "organization, business, conduct, practices, and management . . . and relation to other corporations and to individuals" and to issue legally enforceable cease and desist orders. As with the Clayton Act, the emphasis now was more on the practices than on the structure of big business.[38]

By 1914 the framework of regulation, like the structure of big business that it regulated, was largely in place. Public policy had not necessarily become more straightforward, however. It is true that trade associations were fostered by the Republican administrations of the 1920s and that a series of Supreme Court decisions stretching from *United States* v. *United States Steel* (1920) to *Appalachian Coals* v. *United States* (1933) upheld combinations and cartel practices. Other decisions, however, such as *American Column and Lumber* v. *United States* (1921), held otherwise. And although tying contracts and resale-price

178 / Morton Keller

maintenance won wide support in British and German law, American courts in the 1920s dealt severely with these anti-competitive devices. The legal historian James Willard Hurst has concluded after a review of three generations of United States antitrust law, "What stands out as most basic in the record is the lack of well-defined, comprehensive, sustained planning of public action affecting concentration of private economic control."[39]

This indeterminacy was due not only to the political and economic power of big business but also to the variety and range of the interests at play. As Hurst observes, "Growing diversity of the economy produced growing diversity of competing special interests." Thus the American Newspaper Publishers' Association, anxious to lower the price of newsprint, was a prime mover in the antitrust suit against the International Paper Company. Similarly, Kansas oil producers, reacting to a price cut imposed on them by Standard Oil, put pressure on Congress to order the investigation that led to antitrust actions against that firm.[40] Technological change brought its own, new forms of business competition and regulatory pressure: between railroads and trucks, between coal and oil producers, among the producers of new products competing for the same consumer dollars. The result, in Hurst's words, was that "the regulatory situation might well be too cloudy on the merits to make possible dogmatic judgments of where the public interest lay."[41]

Similar conflicts of interest doubtless existed in other nations, but the size and scale of the United States economy and the decentralized character of the political and legal process made this pluralistic war of all against all a uniquely important part of the American regulatory system.

Notes

1. See Alfred D. Chandler, Jr., *The Visible Hand: The Managerial Revolution in American Business* (Cambridge, Mass., 1977); Leslie Hannah, ed., *Management Strategy and Business Development: An Historical and Comparative Study* (London, 1976); Herman Daems and Herman van der Wee, eds., *The Rise of Managerial Capitalism* (The Hague, 1974); David S. Landes, *The Unbound Prometheus: Technological Change and Industrial Development in Western Europe from 1750 to the Present* (Cambridge, 1969).

2. Francis Déak, "Contracts and Combinations in Restraint of Trade

in French Law: A Comparative Study," *Iowa Law Review* 21 (1935–1936): 397–454, especially pp. 417–419.

3. See Theodore Zeldin, *France 1848–1945: Ambition, Love and Politics* (Oxford, 1973), pt. 1, secs. 5–7; Déak, "Contracts and Combinations," p. 402.

4. John Wolff, "Business Monopolies: Three European Systems in their Bearing on American Law," *Tulane Law Review* 9 (1935):325–377, especially pp. 333–334; see also Francis Walker, "The Law Concerning Monopolistic Combinations in Continental Europe," *Political Science Quarterly* 20 (1905):27–36; V. G. Venturini, *Monopolies and Restrictive Trade Practices in France* (Leyden, 1971), chap. 1.

5. Reinhold Wolff, "Social Control through the Device of Defining Unfair Trade Practices: The German Experience," *Iowa Law Review* 21 (1935–1936):355–396, especially p. 357.

6. White is quoted in Heinrich Kronstein, "The Dynamics of German Cartels and Patents. I," *University of Chicago Law Review* 9 (1941–1942): 646; for these cases, see J. Wolff, "Business Monopolies," pp. 328–333; see also Walker, "Monopolistic Combinations," pp. 14–21.

7. Hilton v. Eckersley, 119 Eng. Rep. 781, 793 (6 El. & Bl. 47 (1856)). See also Richard Brown, "The Genesis of Company Law in England and Scotland," *Juridical Review* 13 (1901):185–204; Henry Parris, *Government and the Railways in Nineteenth Century Britain* (Toronto, 1965).

8. Mogul v. McGregor, L.R. 23 Q.B.D. 598, 617 (1889), [1892] A.C. 25; Maxim v. Nordenfelt [1894] A.C. 535, 553–554.

9. Mogul v. McGregor, L.R. 23 Q.B.D. at 617.

10. See J. Robertson Christie, "Contracts in Restraint of Trade," *Juridical Review* 12 (1900):283–303; Felix H. Levy, "The Sherman Law and the English Doctrine," *Cornell Law Quarterly* 6 (1920–1921):45ff.

11. Edward Q. Keasbey, "New Jersey and the Great Corporations," *Harvard Law Review* 13 (1899):210–211; Morton Keller, *Affairs of State: Public Life in Late Nineteenth Century America* (Cambridge, Mass., 1977), pp. 409–422.

12. Quoted in James A. Garfield, *The Future of the Republic: Its Dangers and Its Hopes* (Cleveland, 1873), p. 20.

13. Ari and Olive Hoogenboom, *A History of the ICC: From Panacea to Palliative* (New York, 1976), is a good survey of the subject and its literature.

14. Quoted in Keller, *Affairs of State*, pp. 429–430; see also Henry C. Adams, "A Decade of Federal Railway Regulation," *Atlantic Monthly* 81 (1898):433–443.

15. Charles B. Elliott, "The Consolidation of Corporations Existing under the Laws of Different States," *Central Law Journal* 17 (1883):383; F. J. Stimson, "Trusts," *Harvard Law Review* 1 (1887):133–134.

16. Stimson, "Trusts," p. 143; Keller, *Affairs of State*, pp. 434–438.

17. See Hans B. Thorelli, *The Federal Antitrust Policy: Origination of an American Tradition* (Baltimore, 1955), chaps. 7–8; United States v. E. C. Knight Co., 156 U.S. 1 (1895); United States v. Trans-Missouri Freight

180 / MORTON KELLER

Ass'n, 166 U.S. 290 (1897); United States v. Joint Traffic Ass'n, 171 U.S. 505 (1898); Addystone Pipe and Steel Co. v. United States, 175 U.S. 211 (1899).

18. Leslie Hannah, *The Rise of the Corporate Economy: The British Experience* (Baltimore, 1976), pp. *ix–x;* Henry Macrosty, *Trusts and the State* (London, 1901), p. 12.

19. G. R. Searle, *The Quest for National Efficiency: A Study in British Politics and British Political Thought, 1899–1914* (Berkeley, 1971); Robert H. Wiebe, *The Search for Order, 1877–1920* (New York, 1967).

20. A. H. Feller, "The Movement for Corporate Reform: A World-Wide Phenomenon," *American Bar Association Journal* 20 (1934):347–348; see also Robert Liefmann, *Cartels, Concerns and Trusts* (New York, 1932), pp. 175ff.

21. See Fritz E. Koch, "Methods of Regulating Unfair Competition in Germany, England, and the United States," *University of Pennsylvania Law Review* 78 (1930):693–712, 854–878.

22. See U.S. Congress, Senate, Committee on Interstate Commerce, *Trusts in Foreign Countries* (Washington, D.C., 1912), pp. 115–116. See also Lamar Cecil, *Business and Politics in Imperial Germany, 1888–1918* (Princeton, 1967), especially pp. 114ff.

23. See William Notz, "Recent Developments in Foreign Anti-Trust Legislation," *Yale Law Journal* 34 (1924–1925):163; R. Wolff, "Social Control," pp. 358–359.

24. Liefmann, *Cartels*, pp. 168–170; R. Wolff, "Social Control," pp. 376–381; National Industrial Conference Board, *Rationalization of German Industry* (New York, 1931), pp. 39, 45. See also William C. Kessler, "German Cartel Regulation under the Decree of 1923," *Quarterly Journal of Economics* 50 (1935–1936):680–693.

25. Hannah, *Rise of the Corporate Economy*, pp. 29ff.; Conservative Party, *Industry and the State: A Conservative View* (London, 1927), p. 24; Bishop C. Hunt, "Recent English Company Law Reform," *Harvard Business Review* 8 (1930):183.

26. P. L. Payne, "The Emergence of the Large-Scale Company in Great Britain, 1870–1914," *Economic History Review*, 2nd ser. 20 (1967):526.

27. Case figures from *American Digest, 1658–1896* (Saint Paul, 1897–1904); *Decennial Edition of the American Digest, 1897–1906* (Saint Paul, 1908–1912); *All England Law Reports Annotated Index and Table of Cases, 1895–1935* (London, 1936). Company lists from Payne, "Emergence," pp. 539–541.

28. F. D. Simpson, "How Far Does the Law of England Forbid Monopoly?" *Law Quarterly Review* 41 (1925):393–394ff.

29. Geoffrey Vickers, "Legal Obstacles to Industrial Integration," *Law Journal* 84 (1937):237.

30. United States v. Chesapeake & Ohio R.R., 105 F. 93 (C.C.S.D. Ohio, 1900); Ramsey Co. v. Bill Posters' Ass'n, 260 U.S. 501, 512 (1923).

31. James Bryce, "America Revisited: The Changes of a Quarter-Century," *Outlook* 79 (1905):847.

32. See Thorelli, *Antitrust Policy,* chap. 6; Paul T. Homan, "Industrial Combination as Surveyed in Recent Literature," *Quarterly Journal of Economics* 44 (1929–1930):345–375.

33. Wiley B. Rutledge, Jr., "Significant Trends in Modern Incorporation Statutes," *Washington University Law Quarterly* 22 (1937):309, 337.

34. Chandler, *Visible Hand,* pp. 333–334.

35. Thorelli, *Antirust Policy,* pp. 534–537; Oswald W. Knauth, *The Policy of the United States toward Industrial Monopoly* (New York, 1914), pp. 86, 92.

36. Standard Oil Co. of New Jersey v. United States, 221 U.S. 1 (1911); United States v. American Tobacco Co., 221 U.S. 106 (1911). See also Henry Seager and Charles A. Gulick, Jr., *Trust and Corporation Problems* (New York, 1929), chaps. 8, 11, 19.

37. Albert C. Muhse, "The Disintegration of the Tobacco Combination," *Political Science Quarterly* 28 (1913):249–278, especially pp. 254, 276. See also William Z. Ripley, ed., *Trusts, Pools and Corporations,* rev. ed. (Boston, 1916), chap. 8; Revis Cox, *Competition in the American Tobacco Industry, 1911–1932* (New York, 1933).

38. James W. Hurst, *Law and Social Order in the United* (Ithaca, 1977), pp. 246–247; Gregory Hankin, "Functions of the Federal Trade Commission," *Illinois Law Quarterly* 6 (1923–1924):188.

39. Hurst, *Law and Social Order,* p. 266. See also Ellis W. Hawley, "Herbert Hoover: The Commerce Secretariat and the Vision of an 'Associative State,' 1921–1928," *Journal of American History* 62 (1974):116–140; United States v. United States Steel, 251 U.S. 407 (1920); Appalachian Coals, Inc., v. United States, 288 U.S. 377 (1921); on tying contracts, see United Shoe Machinery Co. v. United States, 258 U.S. 433 (1922); Edwin R. A. Seligman and Robert A. Love, *Price Cutting and Price Maintenance: A Study in Economics* (New York, 1932).

40. Hurst, *Law and Social Order,* p. 217. On the paper trust suit, see Morton Keller, *In Defense of Yesterday: James M. Beck and the Politics of Conservatism* (New York, 1958), pp. 68–69; on the Kansas oil producers, see Francis Walker, "The Oil Trust and the Government," *Political Science Quarterly* 23 (1908):18–46.

41. Hurst, *Law and Social Order,* p. 218.

Part II
Expansion of Antitrust Regulation in the US

[3]

BUSINESS AND THE SHERMAN LAW

C. F. TAEUSCH

Perhaps much of the criticism of anti-trust legislation, especially of the Sherman Act, has been due to a misconception of the laws and of the conditions which produced them. The Sherman Act was intended by its framers to extend the principles of English common law to the new business situation which was developing in America, and to regulate this business in socially desirable ways (pp. 447–451, 461–462).

In England, in contrast to the developing American policy of control of combinations, the legal and legislative tendency has been to leave the business man free to organize in order to cope with new situations (pp. 451–456). The policy of regulation by court, statute, and even by business itself is much more highly developed in the United States than in England (pp. 457–460).

CRITICISMS of the Sherman law and other anti-trust legislation, such as the Clayton Act and the Federal Trade Commission Act, have been as persistent as they have been ineffective in removing such laws from the statute books. True, subsequent legislation—such, for example, as the Shipping Board Act of 1916, the Transportation Act of 1920, and the Webb-Pomerene Act—has considerably modified the incidence of anti-trust legislation, while judicial interpretation has restored certain common-law principles that appeared for a while to have been superseded. But the chief restrictive principle of the three major anti-trust acts still remains, indicating that forty years of protest by business men has had only a peripheral effect. This is a phenomenon which invites explanation.

It will be the purpose of this paper to subject our anti-trust legislation to such an analysis as will disclose its historic import. This will entail examining both the nature of the protest against such legislation and the object against which this protest has been directed. Have the criticisms of business men been leveled against an object that can really be modified? It may be that our anti-trust legislation is not what its critics think that it is, in which case much of the energy expended in the objections or attempted modifications could be conserved or better directed.

THE SHERMAN LAW   447

Has the Sherman law been the causal agent it was intended and has been supposed to be, controlling business benignantly or malevolently as points of view differ? Or may it paradoxically have been merely the effect or the symptom of the conditions it was intended to control? If the latter possibility is the real situation, then business men have been fighting a shadow and may be likened to medical practitioners who superficially treat a rash which is symptomatic of a deeper-seated organic ailment.

The Origin of the Sherman Act

The first obvious step in the analysis of the situation would be to discover what the author of the Sherman Act himself had in mind. This may be difficult to discover, and even when discovered it may be found to be beside the point. But at least it is a fact that Senator Sherman said that he intended to extend the anti-monopoly common-law rules, which then were available in the several State jurisdictions, to interstate and foreign commerce, which were subject only to federal jurisdiction.[1] The statement that there was no common law in the United States, although it prevailed in most of the several States of the Union, appeared in the speech of Senator Vest[2] and also in Senator Hoar's reply to Senator Kenna's question: "Is monopoly prohibited at common law? If so, why does this bill denounce monopoly?" Senator Hoar went on to say: "The great thing which this bill does, except affording a remedy, is to extend the common-law principles, which protected fair competition in trade in old times in England, to international and interstate commerce in the United States."[3] In view of the fact that Senator Hoar was a member of the Judiciary Committee, to which the Sherman bill had been referred[4] and which reported back the substitute bill which was finally accepted, Senator Hoar practically writ-

---

[1] *Congressional Record*, 51st Congress, p. 2456; the argument was amplified on pp. 2457 and 2459, and also in Sherman's autobiography, *Recollections of Forty Years*, pp. 832–836.
[2] *Congressional Record*, 51st Congress, p. 2603.
[3] *Ibid.*, p. 3152.
[4] Sherman was a member of the Finance Committee, which reported the bill.

C. F. TAEUSCH

ing the whole of the substitute bill, the idea back of this piece of legislation is clear.

It is unnecessary to develop in detail the practical means and fallacious reasoning employed by Sherman to effect a continuity between the common law and the new Act.[5] It remained for Senator Platt to discover the untenability of such a position,[6] a position, however, which unquestionably represented the attempt to meet the new dynamic forces of business, and its extension beyond State confines, and at the same time to conserve the political-legal metaphysics of our federal system, a metaphysics which was to dominate the reasoning of the courts for ten years subsequent to the enactment of the law. In this sense, Senator Morgan's frontal attack was more nearly to the point than was Senator Platt's observation. Morgan said: "It is very true that we use common-law terms here and common-law definitions in order to define an offense which is itself comparatively new [*sic*], but it is not a common-law jurisdiction that we are conferring upon the circuit courts of the United States. It is Federal jurisdiction, arising under the Constitution of the United States. If it did not arise there we could not confer it."[7]

Anyone acquainted with our doctrine of judicial review might have known that the judicial interpretation of the statute would not be determined by the intentions or remarks of the framers of the law. In an early case[8] arising under the Sherman Act, the Circuit Court did examine the debates in Congress, "in order to determine the history of the evil which

[5] Sherman thought that the federal courts could be empowered to employ common-law rules by having the wording of the Sherman Act stress the *parties* to the conspiracy rather than the *nature of the cause*. The first draft of the Act was absolute and plenary, stressing the *substance* of the Act; the next four were based on the commerce clause of the constitution; the second and particularly the sixth drafts stressed the *parties* involved. *Ibid.*, pp. 2463 and 2600. Equally interesting is the fallacy whereby Chief Justice White later did effect the continuity of the common law and the Sherman Act. This fallacy consisted in an ambiguous use of the term "rule of reason;" the phrase "of reason" could be interpreted as either an objective or a subjective genitive. The fallacy persisted in the use of the adjective "reasonable," which was sometimes used to modify "construction of the common law rule" and sometimes to qualify "restraint of trade." Standard Oil Company *v.* U. S., 221 U. S. 1, 66 (1911).

[6] *Congressional Record*, 51st Congress, p. 2607.

[7] *Ibid.*, p. 3149.

[8] U. S. *v.* Debs, 64 Fed. 724 (1894).

the legislation was intended to remedy," but the Court pointed
out that it could not take the views or purposes expressed in
debates in Congress for determining the construction of statutes. The Court further pointed out that the chairman of
the Judiciary Committee himself had stated: "Now just what
contracts, what combinations in the form of trusts, or what
conspiracies will be in restraint of trade or commerce, mentioned in this bill, will not be known until the courts have
construed and interpreted this provision."[9]

Justice Peckham still further minimized the importance of
congressional debates in affecting judicial decisions.[1] It was
not until 1911, when Justice White bound the Sherman Act
to the common law,[2] that the intentions of the 51st Congress
were re-examined. Justice Holmes had refused even to consider the title of the enacted bill: "I stick to the exact words
used" [in the body of the Act],[3] although Justice Lacombe
had held that "although the title to an act cannot control its
words, it may furnish some aid in showing what was in the
mind of the legislator."[4] Although the District Court in the
Trans-Missouri case[5] had considered the business conditions
described in the 51st Congress as necessitating the Sherman
law, this decision was later reversed in the Supreme Court.
In line with this situation, it is also highly significant that
practically none of the trusts or combinations mentioned in
the Senate debates as particularly flagrant offenders were
sued or prosecuted during the decade following the enactment of the Sherman law. A statute might have a history;
but, once it was enacted, the law was to be interpreted as
worded. Judicially considered, the Sherman Act was a Topsy
or a Minerva, conceived too soon after the publication of

---

[9] *Congressional Record*, 51st Congress, p. 4089.
[1] U. S. *v.* Trans-Missouri Freight Association, 166 U. S. 290, 318, 327 (1897).
[2] Standard Oil Company of New Jersey *et al. v.* U. S., 221 U. S. 1, 50.
[3] U. S. *v.* Northern Securities Company, 193 U. S. 197, 403 (1904).
[4] Dueber *v.* Howard, 66 Fed. 637, 643 (1895). The title of Sherman's original bill was: "An Act to declare unlawful, trusts and combinations in restraint of trade and production." Later, the title of the enacted bill became: "An Act to protect trade and commerce against unlawful restraints and monopolies."
[5] 53 Fed. 440, 455 (1892).

C. F. TAEUSCH

Darwin's *Origin of Species* for anyone to think that it had a previous growth or development.

The Common-Law Doctrine of Monopoly

In his dissenting opinion in the Sugar Trust case,[6] Justice Harlan argued that a federal court could have denied relief, on common-law principles, to a party bringing suit to enforce an agreement to acquire the possession of all the sugar refineries in the United States. The interesting point about this supposititious case is that no specific cases were cited— probably because no such cases existed! Even up to the beginning of Roosevelt's administration, only four cases were so defended. One of three possibilities is implied: the absence of a federal common law, or the newness of trusts and combinations so that no federal cases could yet have arisen, or the indisposition of business men to have recourse to the courts in order to enforce their agreements.

This last-named alternative must be given due consideration. American business men were effecting agreements which were sanctioned by the anticipation of economic rather than of legal consequences. This was recognized by Justice Peckham in his statements that "a company desirous of deviating from the rates agreed upon would face a disastrous rate war" and that "under these circumstances the agreement prevents competition."[7] Business had discovered a sanction for its agreements, more powerful even than the provision, e.g., in the Trans-Missouri Association, for a fine in case of breach: the sanction of continued participation in group business profits. And it was the discovery and recent use of this business sanction which had practically negated the old common-law control over such agreements.

The common-law control over monopolies or conspiracies in restraint of trade was not in the main a positive control; it consisted rather in the refusal of the courts to entertain suits for breach of contract on the part of those who had made an

---

[6] U. S. *v.* E. C. Knight Company *et al.*, 156 U. S. 1, 38 (1895).
[7] U. S. *v.* Joint Traffic Association, 171 U. S. 505, 564 (1898).

THE SHERMAN LAW   451

agreement in the furtherance of monopoly or in restraint of trade and who wished to enforce the contract by law against any member of the agreement who later breached it. The theory underlying the common law in this respect was that such agreements could be expected to break up of their own accord. For the materialization of the intent to raise or maintain prices, aside from inducing more competitors to invade the field, would tempt some members of the agreement to secure an advantage by selling at less than the agreed price. The experiences of the European cartels indicate the essential and practical soundness of the common-law theory. But the psychology of the American business man had, even by 1890, deviated sufficiently from that of the individualistic Englishman, especially by developing a group consciousness in connection with more highly integrated business associations, to make the common law less effective than it was in the land of its origin.

Therefore, the whole argument regarding the enactment of the common-law rule into federal legislation, prominent in the debates in Congress at the time the Sherman law was enacted, and revived in the functional interpretations of the Supreme Court twenty years later, is not so important in explaining the significance of the law as is the other prominent feature of the Sherman Act, the provision for a positive indictment for offences which the common law simply refused to enforce. This distinction still further supports the view, developed in this paper, that the Sherman law has become historically significant, not only as an instrument of social-economic control, but also as a symptom of developing American business conditions, the full import of which is just now becoming apparent.

The Mogul Steamship Case

Without continuing the above line of reasoning any further, a totally different approach to the situation may be made. At the very time that the Sherman law was being discussed and enacted in the United States Congress, a leading case involving the same situation was pending in the English courts. Although this fact is well known to students of the subject and is constantly referred to in that connection, a description of the situation is not available in general literature and may therefore be of interest here.

The Mogul Steamship Company, an English firm incorporated in 1883, was engaged in the ocean carrying trade, a part of which included the transporting of tea from China to England. In 1884 the Company had joined a "conference" of steamship owners trading in and out of Hankow, for the purpose of maintaining freight rates by preventing a large number of ships from appearing for tea cargoes at the peak of the tea season and thereby taking the "cream" of the business away from those companies that operated all the year around.

The Mogul Steamship Company, for whatever reason, was not included in the conference in 1885, but sent steamers up the river to Hankow. Additional conference steamers were sent up the river, with the result that rates became unremunerative. The Mogul Steamship Company met the competitive rates rather than allow their vessels to sail away empty, but brought suit against the members of the conference, charging them with a conspiracy in restraint of trade.[8] In the meantime the conference had come to an end in August, 1885, and in the summer of 1886 the rate of freight was determined by free competition in an open market. The case, which was twice appealed, presents a fairly complete description of the status of the common-law rules in England, at that time, regarding monopoly and restraint of trade. In each of the three decisions, the conference was held not to have done anything wrongful or malicious, nor to have committed a misdemeanor, and the acts of the members of the conference were held not to have been unlawful. In the first appeal,[9] Lord Esher, Master of the Rolls, found in favor of the plaintiff, thus placing on the records the complete argument of the Mogul Steamship Company; but he was outvoted by the other two judges of the court.

---

[8] Mogul Steamship Company *v.* McGregor, Gow and Company *et al.*, Law Reports 21 Queen's Bench Division 544 (1888).

[9] *Ibid.*, L.R. 23 Q.B.D. 598 (1889).

THE SHERMAN LAW

The economic realism exhibited by the English justices is indicated by Lord Coleridge's remark, in the original judgment, that "certain Sir Philip Sydney's of the day were urging counsels of perfection which it would be silly indeed to make the measure of the rough business of the world as pursued by ordinary men of business."[1] This attitude was continued by Lord Justice Bowen, in the first appellate decision, dissenting from Lord Esher:

> If the English law distinguishes between acts done jointly by a combination of capitalists and similar acts done by a single man of capital . . . , one rich capitalist may innocently carry competition to a length which would become unlawful in the case of a syndicate with a joint capital no larger than his own, and one individual merchant may lawfully do that which a firm or partnership may not. What limits, on such a theory, would be imposed by law on a joint-stock company limited, is a problem which might well puzzle a casuist. The truth is that the combination of capital for purposes of trade and competition is a very different thing from such a combination of several persons against one, with a view to harm him, as falls under the head of an indictable conspiracy.[2]

Lord Morris, in the House of Lords, repeating Lord Justice Bowen's argument, said:

> I am not aware of any stage of competition called 'fair' intermediate between lawful and unlawful. The question of 'fairness' would be relegated to the idiosyncrasies of individual judges.[3]

And Lord Bowen had significantly said:

> It is not the province of judges to mould and stretch the law of conspiracy in order to keep pace with the calculations of political economy. If peaceable and honest combinations of capital for purposes of trade competition are to be struck at, it must, I think, be by legislation, for I do not see that they are under the ban of the common law.[4]

This statement was made on July 13, 1889. The Sherman Law was enacted July 2, 1890. The English decisions and the American enactment strikingly illustrate the contrast between the regulative attitude underlying our political-economic activities and the laissez-faire policy prevailing in the English courts. The situation confronting the two governmental bodies was almost identical. As Lord Halsbury, L.C., stated the case in the House of Lords, to which final appeal had been taken:

---

[1] *Ibid.*, L.R. 21 Q.B.D. 544, 552.
[2] *Ibid.*, L.R. 23 Q.B.D. 598, 617.
[3] *Ibid.*, 1892 Appeal Cases 25, 51.
[4] *Ibid.*, L.R. 23 Q.B.D. 598, 620.

C. F. TAEUSCH

An associated body of traders endeavor to get the whole of a limited trade into their own hands by offering exceptional and very favorable terms to customers who will deal exclusively with them; so favorable that but for the object of keeping the trade to themselves they would not give such terms; and if their trade were confined to one particular period they would be trading at a loss; but in the belief that by such competition they would prevent rival traders competing with them, and so receive the whole profits of the trade to themselves.[5]

That the problem is still of current interest in America, and has not been settled by the Sherman law, is indicated by the recent protest of the United States Lines against the Ward Line's invasion of the lucrative holiday trade between New York and Havana. The United States Lines maintain a year-round schedule between New York and Havana and have naturally resented the sporadic attempts of outsiders to "skim off the cream" of the traffic at peak periods. The Shipping Act of 1916, Sec. 15, provides that "conferences" of American lines shall be exempt from the provisions of the Sherman law if the Shipping Board approves their arrangements. But such exemptions from the Sherman law are few and they are strictly defined.

The Status of the Common Law in England

In agreeing with Lord Justice Bowen against Lord Esher, Lord Justice Frye traced the movements in the common law and statutes of England during the preceding several centuries. The general tenor of statutory development in England, he said, had been in the direction of freeing business men from prohibitions against combination. The older penal statutes against regrating (cornering the market) and similar acts of combination had been repealed early in the reign of George III,[6] leaving the common law to its unaided operation. Furthermore, the statutes of 1871 and 1875,[7] enlarging the power of combination among workmen as well as among masters, positively signified the tendency of English law to take cognizance of the fact that industry and business required organization as a method of coping with new situations.[8] In

---

[5] *Ibid.*, A.C. 25, 35 (1892).

[6] 12 Geo. 3, c. 71. Practically made complete in 1844 (7 and 8 Vict., c. 24).

[7] 34 and 35 Vict., c. 31; and 39 and 40 Vict., c. 22.

[8] L.R. 23 Q.B.D. 598, 629. See also Lord Bramwell's statement in the House of Lords, A.C. 25, 27 (1892).

brief, the repeal of English statutes against monopoly, during a period of a little over a century, had resulted in a situation in which the control over monopoly consisted largely in the refusal of the courts to enforce monopoly agreements. "[Such] contracts are not illegal in any sense except that the law will not enforce them. It does not prohibit the making of such contracts; it merely declines, after they have been made, to recognize their validity. The law considers the disadvantage so imposed upon the contract a sufficient shelter to the public."[9]

This did not mean that agreements in restraint of trade were not subject to positive action. As Lord Coleridge had pointed out,[1] an indictment could be brought by the state if a public wrong, as defined in the statutes, could be proved; the public had a right to interfere whether damages to individuals could actually be proved or not. He referred to two cases[2] in which nothing was done in fact but in which conviction followed the mere entering of the agreement: no one was harmed, though the public offence was complete. But the situation regarding civil actions was, of course, otherwise: "If a combination is lawful; or, being unlawful there is no damage, an action will not lie."[3]

Lord Esher had relied largely on the decision of Justice Crompton in Hilton *v.* Eckersley[4] for his position. Eckersley, one of a number of masters who had signed an agreement not to sell except under certain circumstances, was sued for the penalty for failing to observe the agreement. Justice Crompton had held that the bond was void and therefore not actionable, but that it was indictable. Lord Campbell, an associate justice, agreed that the bond was void and therefore not actionable, but asserted that it was also not indictable. Lord Esher, in the Mogul case, agreed with Justice Crompton; but Lord Justice Bowen denied the validity of this view

---

[9] Bowen, L. J., L.R. 23 Q.B.D. 598, 619.

[1] L.R. 21 Q.B.D. 544, 548 ff.

[2] The Bridgewater case (unreported) and Rex *v.* de Berenger, 3 M. and S. 67, 76, Bayley, J.

[3] L.R. 21 Q.B.D. 544, 549.

[4] 6 E. and B. 47.

C. F. TAEUSCH

and reverted to the common-law view of Lord Campbell. He cited Wickens *v.* Evans,[5] in which a regional distribution of sales territory was held to be not against the public interest, because it was expected to fail of its own accord owing to the fact that legal enforcement would be denied the combination.

A broader and yet succint account of the development of common-law policy in England is to be found in a recent publication,[6] which shows how the policy of the common law in England "came to reflect the growing flexibility of English society and English industry." The case against monopolies, the seventeenth century "germ seed of the modern legal doctrine condemning private monopoly for its tendency to injure the public interests," was directed, not against a man's conduct of his own business, but "solely against the pretended right to stop others from making and selling what [he himself] was making." This was the exact point at issue in the Mogul case and involves a distinction which the American business man so often fails to perceive. It is this distinction which has enabled the English courts to avoid the paradox of maintaining the business liberty implied in "competition" by legal enforcement. As George Unwin has shown,[7] the English courts managed to circumscribe the existing gild control, not to the end of enlarging state regulation, but in the interests of individual self-determination. Where state control became necessary in the case of obvious abuses of an individualistic system of economics, the concepts of "restraint of trade" and "conspiracy" were evolved to differentiate interferences with others from the reasonable implications of business activity and growth. In the nineteenth century, even "restraint of trade" was largely abandoned because of the prevailing laissez-faire doctrine; while there also occurred a "remarkable relaxation" in applying the concept of "conspiracy" to restraints of trade, both in judicial decisions and

---

[5] 3 Y. and J. 318.

[6] *Mergers and the Law*, prepared by Myron W. Watkins, National Industrial Conference Board (New York, 1929), chap. 1.

[7] *Industrial Organization in the Sixteenth and Seventeenth Centuries* (London, 1904), cited by Watkins, *op. cit.*, p. 8.

in statutory modifications of the comon law. "For this faith [in the efficacy of free contract], English industrial experience may be responsible," an experience which was almost wholly absent in the United States until comparatively recently.

Developments in the United States

Aside from the factual contrast between the English judicial views expressed in the Mogul case and the American legislative views expressed in the Sherman law, broader differences had developed in the two countries due to their geographic isolation and the legal-political separation effected by the American Revolution. It was well and good for John Marshall to assert the continuity of the common law in spite of the political divorce from England, and for Chief Justice White in 1911 to reconcile the Sherman law with common-law doctrine and to integrate them in the Standard Oil and American Tobacco cases. But such views could not brush aside the historic differences that were inevitable in the separate development of the two countries. The United States had experienced nothing to compare with the nineteenth-century Manchester school of liberalism and its new emphasis on the doctrine of laissez faire; not only had we not developed sufficiently industrially, but we were much more orthodox in clinging to the views of monopoly that arose at the time of the Tudors and Stuarts, views which were brought to this country by the earlier English immigrants but which England had outgrown by the nineteenth century. Just as the colonists and the writers of the federal Constitution resorted to a system of "checks and balances" to curb both executive and legislature, because of the traditional fears that had been generated by an earlier English experience with absolute monarchy and colonial experiences with parliamentary tyranny, so the growth of American business units in the latter part of the nineteenth century conjured up visions of statutory monopolies and royal trade prerogatives that had ceased to exist in England for over a century and which had never existed in the United States.

C. F. TAEUSCH

England, on the other hand, had experienced no such development of religious sects as characterized nineteenth-century America; such as, for example, the "community spirit" of Puritanism, exercised more frequently in the direction of "reform" movements and attempts to effect "uniformity" of behavior, but also providing a basis for business associations and agreements that deviated widely from traditional English individualism subsequent to the Commonwealth. True, our pioneering experience had materially developed an agrarian individualism that was comparable to the individualistic note of the Puritan as well as of other religious faiths, conspicuously that of the Quaker, the Scotch Presbyterian and the German Pietist. But both of these factors—physical and religious—must be distinguished from the business and industrial individualism of the Englishman, and both together were obviously but a paradoxical part of the complex which constituted American behavior; a complex which included as early as 1890 a degree of business co-operation which made the traditional common-law rules, still operative in individualistic England, of little effect in controlling American economic relations.

Trade-association activities in the United States are far more extensive in scope than they are in England; their relatively recent appearance as overt accomplishments is no indication of the antiquity of their underlying psychological backgrounds. The organization of American industry is not only on a larger scale than it is in England; it is much more highly integrated. Our business leaders who complain of the attempted regulative activities of Church and state should have their attention directed to the autocratic control which is exercised within American industry itself. In the recent merger movement, autonomy of the constituent companies is the exception, not the rule, at least in contrast with the decentralization of management observed in English amalgamation; and we have not by any means been free in America from the attempt on the part of business men to use the lash on Churches, the Y.M.C.A., newspapers, or colleges and uni-

THE SHERMAN LAW

versities, in order to make these supposedly independent social agencies conform to the business view. The phenomenon of external control is widespread and is not peculiar to the enactment of the Sherman law. A basic condition of the appearance of this phenomenon is the fact that the principle of controlling and regulating the conduct of others, introduced into America by the Calvinistic sects, is as dominant in the United States as it is in Scotland, Switzerland, and parts of Germany; Calvinism was seldom more than a minority force in England.[8] The pooling and exchange of trade information among rival businesses is but another, and happier, manifestation of the psychological attitude previously developed in a religious sense in the Puritan "community."

Another very definite difference in the conditions underlying English and American business is presented by our protective tariff.[9] In the Senate debate on the Sherman bill, much was made of this point by Southern senators, who contended that a lowering of the tariff wall would effect the results aimed at by the bill.[1] One can very definitely gather the impression, from the replies of the Northern Republican members, that the shot told, and it is not difficult to infer that their almost unanimous support of the Sherman bill resulted, at least partly, from the fear that the alternative would be an attack upon the sacred tariff. Viewed from this angle, the Sherman law was a legal appendage that had to go with the tariff hide; and if in the course of succeeding decades the tail began to wag the dog, it must be remembered that such frequently is the broader result of legislative endeavors to correct particular social or economic situations.

[8] Tawney, G. A., *Religion and the Rise of Capitalism* (New York, 1926). True, the medieval Church had earlier exercised such controls, but the direct effect of Catholic doctrine has not been felt in the United States, at least prior to the recent influx of immigration from southern Europe; it certainly was not an important factor when the Sherman law was enacted.

[9] The absence of a protective tariff in England was referred to by Justice Bowen, in the Mogul case, as a factor in the efficacy of the common law in preventing monopolies. L.R. 23 Q.B.D. 598, 620.

[1] No less than eight bills were introduced in the House of Representatives, 51st Congress, to declare trusts and combinations unlawful. Six of these bills were introduced by Southern representatives; four provided for importation, free of duty, of articles handled by trusts or combinations.

C. F. TAEUSCH

That the Senate was not aware of certain forces in American business life, now quite certainly present and then probably in their incipient stages, is indicated indirectly by its attitude regarding the persons who were to be protected by the Sherman law. All through the debate in the Senate, the individual *consumer* or the *seller of farm products* is regarded as the aggrieved party, the person to be protected against the power and greed of the business monopoly. Indeed, this point was stressed by one of the most vigorous opponents of the bill, Senator George, of Mississippi, who held as a practical objection to the bill the fact that the consumer or farmer would be impotent, because of his limited means, to bring suit against a wealthy corporation.[2] Nowhere in the debate was much attention paid to the purchaser of "producers' goods" or to the competitor of "big" business; in this sense, Justice Holmes was right in disregarding the final title of the Act. It was assumed by the Senate that most business men, especially the large competitors, could and would look out for themselves; such protection as was accorded them was incidental to the rights of the consumer to purchase commodities at "fair" prices.

The history of the Federal Trade Commission indirectly shows how this traditional ecclesiastical view has persisted. For a number of years the Commission proceeded against individual businesses largely on the ground that the purchaser-consumer had been harmed by the particular practice. Until a very few years ago, the Commission had not yet discovered that the incidence of "unfair trade practices" could also be on business itself; and once it did adopt this point of view, by establishing the "trade practice submittal," it was criticized by the courts for extending its jurisdiction to matters "not affecting the public interest." In short, a governmental device, originated by Herbert Hoover in the Department of Commerce on the basis of the principle of business self-government and restated by him again and again as president as a necessary development in meeting modern business condi-

[2] *Congressional Record,* 51st Congress, p. 1767.

tions, has been blocked by the Supreme Court with exactly
the same democratic political philosophy that actuated Congress originally in passing the Sherman Act, a philosophy
which the Church has held throughout its history.

Conclusion

It is not to be wondered at that the state, viewing with
alarm the development of business power, should have had
recourse to such an instrument as the Sherman law. The
fact that Congress did not anticipate certain other implications of the newer positive business philosophy—such as,
e.g., the justification of high wages on the ground of their
great purchasing value, the ruthless junking of obsolete equipment and methods, the relatively greater importance of mer-
chandising and marketing than production, and the relatively
free exchange of business information among competitors[3]—
may explain why the Sherman law was not made either more
or less stringent than it was. The Sherman law can be sufficiently explained on the ground that the state recognized with
fear a new power on the social horizon: Business. The aggregate power had been present in society from earliest times,
but it had been scattered among many individuals. Now
these forces were converging into organizations which constituted a new kind of social energy, comparable in size and
strength and value with state and Church. The presence of
this rival, with tremendous autonomous possibilities, although
but vaguely estimated, was not to be tolerated by the ever-
jealous state; the Church had always been perfectly clear in
its attitude toward Mammon and lucre.

The possibility of a benign or generous business policy, especially on the part of an achieved monopoly, did not occur
to the framers of the Sherman Act—any more than it has occurred to some business men! And not until 1925 did the
Supreme Court of the United States assert[4] that it would no
longer assume as a major premise that business men normally

---

[3] It has recognized the principle in the tariff and in the laws restricting immigration.
[4] "Trade Association Cases," 268 U. S. 563 and 588, 45 Sup. Ct. 578 and 586.

C. F. TAEUSCH

were prompted by greed and cupidity. The autonomous regulation of business—early manifesting itself in associations which did not disintegrate of their own accord when the common-law sanctions were denied their agreements, and which could be curbed only by the positive statutory provisions of the Sherman Act—has in the meantime become nation-wide, and even world-wide in its scope; and is now occupied with the development of policies, ethical as well as economic, which are not only intended to keep business clear of governmental or legal entanglements, but which also are rapidly and intensively developing a doctrine as well as a technique of self-regulatory business functions.

The most significant feature of the Sherman law was, therefore, not its purposes or its subsequent achievements, but its symptomatic indication of the fact that Business was a growing social power and that the law was viewing this with apprehension. There is no denying the remedial activities of the law: business itself was not sufficiently aware of the obligations attaching to the development of its social power and needed an external corrective. And the Sherman law may still be regarded as a necessary potential curb even though its actual employment be considerably lessened or even misapplied. The repeal of the Sherman law has been advocated again and again, but its retention could be defended solely on the ground that it is a perpetual reminder to business that freedom from the law can best be achieved by proper self-government.

The enactment of the Sherman law exhibited an attempt to conserve the political and legal values against the encroachments of the economic on the pattern of social values. It need not be regarded either as a cure-all or a kill-joy; the cure and the joy are to be discovered rather in autonomous business health, a condition which is amenable to direct and self-attention without the assistance of either Church or state.

[4]

RECENT TRUST DECISIONS AND BUSINESS

By Willard E. Hotchkiss
Northwestern University

Dissolution of several giant combinations by court decree, though perhaps the most dramatic circumstance in recent trust history, is by no means the only important one. Court decisions during the past two or three years have raised many other questions than the question of dissolution, and the record in pending litigation is still adding to the number. Besides this, important reports of the Bureau of Corporations and other branches of the government have collected and disseminated material facts previously unavailable. Finally, discussion of the question is gradually being focused around specific legislative proposals, based for the most part on assumptions concerning trust efficiency quite different from the views current at an earlier date. From all this a new stage in the evolution of the trust question is easily recognized.

Neither the time available for the preparation of this paper, nor the author's previous study of the subject justify an attempt to present significant new material. The paper, therefore, will be directed primarily toward an effort to set forth, as the author sees them, some of the current phases of the question, and if possible to suggest profitable lines of further inquiry.

Considered from the standpoint of immediate effects, the topic of the session has to do, among other things, with the possible connection between government trust activity and the present situation in business. Accepting the current belief that there is at present a depression in business of whatever degree of seriousness, how much of the situation may fairly be credited to the attitude of the government, and of this in turn what part is attributable to the activity of the Department of Justice and the courts? Unquestionably, during the past year, the prospect of tariff and currency legislation, added to the uncertainty of developments concerning trusts, have tended to postpone the inauguration of extensive new enterprises. However wholesome the ultimate effects of new legislation or decisions of the courts, it is quite obvious that, as a psychological influence, changes in the governmental situation may have a large part in bringing on a depression for which conditions are ripe. Even if we should accept the "Wall Street push-button theory" of panics, the psychological element would be none the less present, though operating along other than the traditionally accepted lines.

To the extent that a composite view of the business mind can be secured, it seems to reveal hopefulness with respect to the currency and readiness to make adjustments to the new tariff. Indications are not lacking, however, that this attitude is based in part on an assumption that the activity of the Department of Justice with respect to trusts is to be considerably diminished.

A feeling that the Attorney General has it in his power to hale into court representatives of business enterprises covering a wide range of activity is clearly a circumstance which affects many interests other than those directly subject to attack. It is not difficult, moreover, to hear it asserted with reference to particular cases that the activity of the department of justice is or has been largely a matter of individual caprice or political hazard. In view of such inferences, the discretion exercised by the Attorney General and the manner of its exercise becomes an important factor in the discussion.

The Sherman anti-trust law, in contrast to many of the state anti-trust laws, is expressed in general terms. It declares illegal the contracting, combining, or conspiring to restrain trade or commerce among the states or with foreign nations, and the monopolizing or attempting, combining, or conspiring to monopolize any part of such trade or commerce. In deciding whether these offenses have been committed, the courts, and before them the Department of Justice, have to face essentially two questions: (1) Do the facts as they appear in the particular case show a combination which by its very existence constitutes monopoly or restraint of trade? (2) Do the facts point to conduct on the part of individuals or corporate bodies which indicates a purpose to do the things which the act enjoins?

The second sort of consideration involves not primarily the question of illegal combination, but rather the question of what constitutes unfair and illegal competition. Beginning with the Standard Oil and Tobacco cases, decisions up to the present have hinged largely on specific acts of restraint and particular methods of exercising economic power. Practices resorted to by a large industrial unit in competition with smaller units or in averting potential competition have contained the crucial points. The following are some of the specific questions, several of which are

160   *American Economic Association*

likely to be presented to the Attorney General in a single prima facie case.

Is it permissible for manufacturers or distributors to pool their interests, and by means of lists or trade letters essentially to boycott dealers who handle outside competitive products or who violate restrictions concerning retail price? Is it legal to maintain a system of espionage on competitors? Are there any restrictions on the right of a concern to employ competitors' servants when circumstances indicate a well-defined policy of using this method to obtain competive trade secrets and to drive the competitor out of business? What are the limits of control to be exercised by the holder of a patent over the patented article and its accessories? To what extent and under what forms may the makers of brands and trade-mark goods coerce the distributors of their products? May the manufacturers of a group of commodities, some competitive and some non-competitive, compel dealers to handle exclusively their competitive products as a condition of securing the monopoly product? Is it legitimate for a large corporation to fix an unremunerative price in the territory of a local competitor when circumstances point to a purpose of eliminating the competitor from the field? May the integration of an industry be accomplished or attempted by using monopoly returns in one branch of the industry to support rate wars with the purpose of destroying competition in another branch? May controlled companies be run as independents?

It is quite clear that some one of these questions, usually several of them, have been involved in most of the recent cases passed upon by federal courts, and they clearly contain the gravamen of charges in several other cases now pending. Competitive methods are notably in the foreground in the Cash Register case, the Bathtub case, the United Shoe Machinery case, and in the Oil and Tobacco cases.

Chief Justice White, speaking for the Supreme Court, has set forth in forcible language in the Tobacco case the influence of specific acts in bringing the Court to the decision reached in that case. Using the language of the Court:

The history of the combinations is so replete with the doing of acts which it was the obvious purpose of the statute to forbid, so demonstrative of the existence from the beginning of a purpose to acquire dominion and control of the tobacco trade, not by the mere exertion of the ordinary right to contract and to trade, but by methods devised in order to monopolize the trade by driving competitors out of business, which were ruthlessly carried out upon

Recent Trust Decisions and Business 161

the assumption that to work upon the fears or play upon the cupidity of competitors would make success possible. We say these conclusions are inevitable, not because of the vast amount of property aggregated by the combination, not because alone of the many corporations which the proof shows were united by resort to one devise or another. Again, not alone because of the dominion and control over the tobacco trade which actually exists, but because we think the conclusion of wrongful purpose and illegal combination is overwhelmingly established by the following considerations: [The opinion then proceeded to specify among other things several acts of the sort above enumerated.]

Conceding the wide discretion of the Attorney General, it may fairly be questioned whether, with due regard to his oath of office, he can in the future safely omit to take cognizance of specific acts of prima facie violation when the courts already have established the illegality of similar practices. Whenever the fact of combination is complicated by evidence of unfair and coercive methods, then at least the burden of responsibility for securing business peace must rest squarely on defendants.

Admitting the Attorney General's power in many cases to prosecute or not to prosecute, as well as the possibility that political considerations may enter into particular cases, it is doubtless still true that the enforcement of the Sherman law, in the main, has had, and still has, a patriotic and beneficial purpose.

If a diminution of activity by the Department of Justice should mean delay in clarifying the legal standards governing competition, this, from the business standpoint, could scarcely be regarded as a beneficent result. Without reference to the merits of the Administration view concerning the efficacy of competition, the serious need of a definition for fair competition is clear, —a definition which will promote rivalry based on the relative efficiency of different economic units, and eliminate rivalry based on brute force.

There is some analogy between the law of fair and unfair competition and the law of fraud. Notwithstanding border-line cases with reference to which it is impossible to say categorically that a certain procedure does or does not constitute fraud, an attorney is able to advise his client with a fair degree of assurance what constitutes a fraudulent precedure,—with reference to fraud there is a comprehensive body of law. This, though highly in the interest of business stability, is not yet the case with reference to unfair competition.

Whatever the disturbing influence of agitation the question of unfair competition ought to be settled with as little delay as practicable. Whether it is dealt with by the legislature or by the courts, it is quite clear that it never can be settled as long as practices which the public conscience condemns are tolerated.

Dissolution of trusts presents an essentially different problem from those just considered. In the Oil and Tobacco cases the improbability of otherwise being able to terminate unfair methods explains why dissolution was ordered. Dissolution *per se* raises at once, among other things, the question of the relative efficiency of trusts considered from the long-time view and with respect to every aspect of the particular line of business concerned.

In approaching this phase of the topic it should be made clear at the outset that the discussion has to do with efficiency in the productive rather than the acquisitive sense. Productive efficiency, moreover, needs to be defined in terms broad enough to include, not only the making and distributing of goods to satisfy existing wants, but also considerations of permanent national productivity and well-being.

At the time the great industrial trusts were being formed, it was widely assumed that, whatever the dangers they might entail, they surely would be able to make and distribute goods more economically than smaller units of production. It should be noted, however, that this view met with no uniform acceptance by economists. Professor Bullock, in his article entitled "Trust Literature: Survey and Criticism,"[1] published in 1901, submitted, in a masterly analysis, reasons for skepticism concerning trust efficiency which require surprisingly little revision today.

Considering the history of trusts during the last decade, it is still worth while to introduce a discussion of their efficiency by the question, "Why were the trusts organized?" There is no doubt that the kind of competition which had obtained in many industries during the late eighties and nineties had been exceedingly wasteful and destructive. On the other hand, court records, government reports, and a mass of other public data make it hardly necessary to point out that producing and distributing efficiency was largely an afterthought in connection with trust formation. It appears quite obvious that the two impelling forces—one or both of which really explain the launching of the great industrial trusts—were *market control* and the *profits of organization.*

[1] *Quart. Jour. Econ.*, vol. XV, Feb. 1901. Reprinted in Ripley, W. Z., *Trusts, Pools and Corporations.*

Recent Trust Decisions and Business   **163**

The security market at the beginning of the present century, the corporation law of New Jersey, and knowledge in the use of cut-throat competition were circumstances peculiarly favorable to the pursuit of these objects. Returns in the form of promoters' and syndicate managers' profits to be secured from the creation and flotation of new securities were an all-sufficient incentive for bringing enterprises together and organizing them into a trust. Inasmuch as securities based on hopes which in turn were based on prospective market control could easily be marketed, it was possible to pay prices for good plants which no former earning power would have justified and to bring other plants into subjection. Immediate incentive in some cases, compulsion in other cases, was sufficient to bring about a sale, the terms of which bore but secondary relation to past or future earnings from operation.

Admitting that the situation just described gave most of the trusts at the start a handicap of heavy obligations and expensive and inefficient plants, the real question today is, "Have they made good since that time?" What criteria are available by which their efficiency can be ascertained?

For the steel trust the Bureau of Corporations has made an approach to the question of efficiency through an analysis of costs. The significance of these figures is disputed, but so far as I am aware no specific criticism of them has been put forth in such a way as to contain affirmative evidence of superior efficiency.

The Bureau report shows also what is well known, that the steel trust during the period of its existence has been able to put market value under a large part of the water in its original capitalization. Obviously, other factors than the economical production of steel influence this showing. There are no figures which would justify an attempt to evaluate these other factors, but control of ore and market control have figured largely.

With reference to ore, some of the control has now been relinquished, but for the period as a whole the ore position has been a strong asset. If it were possible to conceive a government policy which regarded ore deposits as public property to be utilized and developed exclusively for the general welfare, would the corporation have been able to occupy such a favorable position? The difficulty of a categorical answer to such a question does not make it the less a fair one.

With reference to market control, there are conditions under which this might enhance productive efficiency in the national sense, notably if it prevented reckless overproduction or cut-throat competition,—what is called demoralization of trade. One of the acts of the Steel Corporation concerning which there is a large weight of favorable opinion is its policy of maintaining prices just after the panic of 1907. If comparison were made with an earlier period of recurring pools followed by reckless competition, when steel was spoken of as intermittently "prince" or "pauper," it might be argued that market stability in iron and steel could be accomplished only through the trust.

Business men in and out of trusts unquestionably are coming to feel that price maintenance with reference to certain aspects of trade is a highly desirable policy. While, from the public stand-point, there clearly are indications that this form of coöperation, even in the absence of a formal pool, frequently goes far beyond legitimate market needs, it probably will be found desirable in working out future policy with respect to competition to permit open—not secret—price maintenance under proper restrictions when situations so demand. The very fact, however, that men are coming more and more to this view, raises serious question whether, even in iron and steel, either a trust or a pool will be necessary in the future to accomplish the needed result.

The action with respect to steel prices after 1907 represents, of course, merely a "standing pat" on permanent policy. The serious questions surrounding this policy when regarded as per-manent and the disquieting rumor that the policy narrowly es-caped abandonment at the very time the public occasion for its maintenance arose create grave doubt whether in general, or in emergencies like 1907, a trust in the long run will prove the safest conservator of business stability.

Admitting, without prejudice to opposite contention, some merit in a policy of price maintenance, its success in the case of steel would seem to rest on factors which have little to do with corporation efficiency. The tariff has continued, up to the present year, to protect from foreign competition; overlapping ownership with railroads, the largest purchasers of steel, has created in some measure community of interest between buyers and sellers scarcely favorable to price depression; most important of all, the period during which the steel trust has been in operation has been one peculiarly of unprecedented demand for steel products,—a demand

Recent Trust Decisions and Business **165**

which only roughly could have been anticipated at the time the United States Steel Corporation was organized.

Concluding this line of argument, if we accept that the advance in steel securities is due to the control of ore and control of market, and if it can be shown that the success of these policies, whatever their merit or demerit on public grounds, is not necessarily related to any economies in making and distributing steel, it becomes quite clear that advance in securities shows nothing concerning the relative efficiency of the trust.

There are other figures and other ways in which they might be connected with the general subject of efficiency, but it may seriously be questioned whether there are any figures available from which affirmative mathematical evidence of the steel trust's superior efficiency could be shown.

The factors to be considered in other industries obviously would not be exactly the same as for steel. In a so-called horizontal combination made up merely of similar plants the situation would be less complex. It is perhaps clear that the study of each sort of business presents its own difficulties and that conclusions concerning efficiency must be, in every case, specific rather than general. This, however, merely emphasizes the complicated nature of the general problem and the necessity of further specification before any assumptions of superior efficiency can be accepted.

Among the chief economies of combination which are set forth in general terms are the better utilization of men, machines, and materials, saving from by-products, comparison of methods and results in different plants, eliminating sales costs, facilities in pushing foreign trade. Some of these items are perhaps not capable of representation in comparative cost sheets, but some of them which are such, for example sales costs of farm machinery, do not appear as economies in those combinations where they would naturally be expected.

All of the above items are so obviously conditioned by the nature of the particular business, that, except as discussion is based on a cost showing of individual concerns, very little progress can be made by discussing them in general terms. In connection with all of them, however, it is plain that the protagonists of combination still fail to distinguish between combination and large-scale business as much as they did a dozen years ago when

Professor Bullock, in the article above cited, criticized them on this ground. It has scarcely been shown that the theoretical advantages of trusts, except those which raise negative presumptions on grounds of public policy, might not have been secured by much smaller units.

Quite obviously, business in this country is likely to be carried on in the future, to a great extent, in large units; but this is by no means equivalent to asserting that the trust form of organization will be a dominant factor. Both economic theory and practical experience in production have established the law of diminishing returns with respect to plant size. When, however, the point of maximum plant productivity has been reached, it may be possible to combine ten plants into a single organization and still achieve notable economies with respect to the distribution of product. Economies of a legitimate sort in the business or financial organization of a concern may also be realized by such combination.

Accepting, however, the distinction between plant efficiency and corporation efficiency, is it reasonable to suppose that combination of plants can go on indefinitely without experiencing disadvantages similar to those which appear with increase in the size of plant; or, if this is true, does it necessarily indicate that there would still be a balance of advantage from the integration of a whole industry by bringing together allied and subsidiary enterprises in a consolidated concern?

The testimony of persons whose familiarity with industrial organization merits respect indicates that when combination is carried too far there are dangers, at least, of an administrative nature which might be grouped under the two heads of *cumbersomeness* and *stagnation*. One line of theoretical argument against monopoly combinations which, so far as I am aware, has never been adequately answered, is the contention that an assured monopoly control in an industry will inevitably discourage enterprise.

In the tobacco industry there is now evidence of active competition along certain lines. The testimony of a person who perhaps more than any other is familiar with details of organization in that industry indicates that the younger men in the different organizations regard dissolution distinctly with favor. They find they are nearer the center of things and that therefore their enterprise and individual efficiency meets with greater re-

Recent Trust Decisions and Business   **167**

sponse.[2] Is this perhaps a side light on the argument that trusts
engender stagnation?

A detailed history of inventions, with a parallel record of those
to be credited respectively to trusts and to independents in the
same line of trade, would be of interest in this connection; or,
again, a comparison with foreign countries where the same industries have not been directly affected by trusts. While it is
easy to point to significant contributions of particular trusts along
the line of invention, there is a widespread belief that the trusts
tend to stifle the utilization of new inventions and processes.
Obviously the showing in this regard for the short period under
consideration would prove nothing with reference to the permanent influence of combinations.

As to the charge of cumbersomeness, there are here and there
indications that, even in the absence of government activity, some
of the trusts are trying to readjust their business in such a way
as to break up organization and operating control into smaller
units. One of the reasons given on creditable testimony for the
lack of disturbance in the oil and tobacco industries as result of
dissolution, was that disintegration proceeded along lines already
contemplated by those organizations in the interest of greater
efficiency.[3]

Uniformity in corporation law; a greater responsibility to
stockholders on the part of corporation officers and directors;
regulation of transactions in which men as promoters and syndicate managers do business with themselves as the officers of corporations; elimination of unfair competition;—these are reforms

[2] On the other side, it is to be noted that one effect of dissolution has been to
necessitate enormous expenditure for building up a demand for paying brands,
—this due to the fact that by the dissolution proceedings some of the companies were left without such brands.

[3] Some writers have emphasized, as does Professor Bullock (*loc. cit.*, p. 199),
the extraordinary legal and organization expenses which combinations incur.
He speaks of the "cost of employing the most skilled legal talent to steer the
combination just close enough to the law;" also of the "expenses necessary for
'legislative' and 'educational' purposes and the outlays for stifling competition
or the continual 'buying out' of would-be rivals." If coercive methods and
unfair competition are separately considered as above, it is scarcely permissible, in considering relative productivity, to feature too strongly handicaps of
this sort. When we contend for the elimination of all combination advantages
to which negative presumptions attach on grounds of public policy, we must
also be ready to eliminate possible disadvantages which would disappear were
the practices of combinations made to conform to the public good.

admittedly long overdue. Without necessarily agreeing with those who contend that the timely enactment of these measures would have prevented the trust movement, it is still reasonable to maintain that in the absence of other causes than efficiency trusts could not have reached anything like their present strength.

Conceding that the superior efficiency of combinations has not been established, what are the prospects that our present knowledge could, within a reasonable period of time, be so supplemented by further investigation as substantially to increase the assurance with which the subject could be handled?

Existing reports of the Bureau of Corporations have given us an enormous mass of information concerning trusts. Their great contribution in outlining and forecasting methods of investigation is universally recognized. It is still clear, however, that the inquiries of the Bureau have one great drawback. If the same ability and training which have gone into these reports could have been organized in such a way as to command an authority like that of the Interstate Commerce Commission, the influence of the reports on the trust situation would have been tremendously enhanced.

The actual carrying out of inquiries, as well as the later phases of their organization, has usually been under the supervision of some one person. This is a normal procedure, and while apparently it has not discouraged the coöperation of the whole Bureau force in developing scientific methods of approach, it has, however, tended to identify each of the reports with an individual. Rightly or wrongly, interested persons have felt that they could safely question specific findings, provided they were able to give. plausible reasons for their objections. The complexity of subject matter is well calculated to confuse persons whose interest does not bring them in direct contact with the facts. All of these circumstances makes it desirable that the government body which carries on investigation of this sort should, by its formal organization and the dignity of its position, command the greatest possible authority not only with students but with the general public.

The Commissioner of Corporations has proposed a further inquiry into trust efficiency. Is this practicable on general principles? and if so, has the Commissioner at his disposal, or is he likely to have, the instrumentalities by which a comprehensive study of efficiency could be undertaken? It is not within the province of this paper to outline the scope and method of such an investigation. Obviously, there would be much greater difficulty in providing for the inquiry a basis of uniform, or at least standard, accounts than has confronted the Interstate Commerce Commission in prescribing uniform accounting for the railroads. However, if some board or trade commission, occupying a position in the public esteem like that of the Interstate Commerce Commission, were to lay down the lines which an inquiry should take and prescribe its methods, the results, as far as they went, would command general acceptance.

Even a temporary commission *ad hoc*, if the training and personality of its members carried weight, might obtain a similar result. Under such conditions, it seems reasonable to suppose that an investigation might be carried on which would supplement existing reports, cover industries not yet investigated, and add materially to our knowledge of trust efficiency. The value of a comprehensive study undertaken now would be enhanced by the fact that some of the dissolved trusts could figure in any comparison made. Considering the magnitude of such a study there is ground for skepticism whether Congress would readily appropriate sufficient funds. It is also doubtful whether the work could be completed within the limits of a single Presidential term.

Less comprehensive inquiries by the Bureau unaided, if the reports were individually well managed, would be valuable, as past reports have been, but it is not to be expected that they would result in any epoch-making addition to our knowledge of trust efficiency.

If the whole truth could be revealed it probably would show for each industry investigated some items in which the advantage would be on the side of trusts, while in others combination would mean loss. The extent to which such items could be shown in balanced parallel columns would vary both with the industry and the specific items. Obviously, no inquiry would lead to uniformity of net results for different industries.

We already have come to accept monopoly as the normal and economical condition in the so-called public service enterprises. None of the arguments against trust efficiency have tended seriously to undermine this assumption. If it is true that some industries can advantageously be carried on as complete monopolies, others in very large units, and still others in smaller units, investigation, if it has the effect of moderating the policy of dissolution pending further knowledge, may possibly serve to prevent the breaking up of combinations which are economically and politically justified. Obviously, it is no inconsistency to look with favor on an effort to dissolve a combination like the tobacco trust and at the same time to be extremely skeptical about the result of dissolving the so-called telephone and telegraph trust.

In introducing the discussion of efficiency, emphasis was laid on the necessity of considering efficiency in the productive, rather than the acquisitive, sense; also upon the necessity of defining productive efficiency with reference to permanent national productivity and well-being. The most cursory consideration of a highly integrated industry like iron and steel, in which trust influence is carried through every intermediate process from raw material to a great variety of finished products, reveals such stupendous problems affecting both resources and men that the efficiency of the trust at every turn is interwoven with questions of public policy. Other trusts, perhaps in less measure, present a similar situation.

Relative efficiency, then, can only partially be revealed by any sort of formal investigation; if it were revealed there would still remain questions of law and policy upon which, in the last analysis, the perpetuation or dissolution of particular trusts must ultimately hinge. While the distinctions between questions of trust methods and the question of combination *per se* is necessary for clear thinking, trust practices, historically and potentially, are so interwoven with the fact of bigness that the trust problem from the government policy standpoint is and will remain one problem.

From this it results that the benefits to accrue from further inquiry into trust efficiency would come primarily in the way of a more illuminating publicity and in laying the foundation for the permanent work of an industrial or trade commission rather than in any service they might render in forming the basis for dissolution proceedings.

Up to this point the possibility of dissolving combinations has been assumed. Before the Oil and the Tobacco decisions, this possibility was by no means admitted, and in one of these cases, at least, it seems apparent that control has not been successfully dissipated. Without attempting to argue the physical possibility of dissolution, knowledge of the procedure in the Tobacco case and in subsequent cases leaves little doubt that dissolution *per se* is entirely practicable. There is still doubt whether dis-

Recent Trust Decisions and Business 171

sipation of financial control can immediately be accomplished by court action. Precautions against coercive control similar to those taken in the Tobacco case can be devised, however, in such a way that with the lapse of time the tendency will be in the direction of competition.[4] From this standpoint the present active competition in the tobacco industry is encouraging. No thoughtful person will expect that the exact condition which preceded combination will be restored.

As this paper has tried to proceed from the standpoint of business welfare, one further question should perhaps be raised. Granted that the breaking up of trusts is intrinsically desirable, may not the disturbance to business from repeated dissolutions be so great as to over-balance possible advantages? The extreme care shown by the courts up to this time, and the action of some of the trusts in hastening to dissolve themselves, are calculated to allay fear of this sort. Such developments as those in the oil and tobacco industries prior to dissolution, and those which appear to be under way in some other industries at the present time, indicate perhaps that dissolution is along the line of present economic development. If the actual execution of the work can be placed in the hands of an efficient trade commission, it does not seem probable that the danger of disturbance to business need figure largely in the policy to be pursued.

To summarize a discussion which deals so largely with unanswered questions is exceedingly difficult. Concerning the efficiency of trusts, the meagerness of specific proof of economies claimed, the entire absence for any trust of anything like a balance of advantages against disadvantages, the continued reliance on hypothetical benefits,—these have made the trusts peculiarly vulnerable to the persistent and well organized challenge of their economic justification by the administration now in power. It may safely be assumed that from the efficiency standpoint the burden of proof has shifted to the trusts. There are no facts which would justify a careful student in regarding the efforts to dissolve trusts as an economic calamity. The Sherman law, which so often in the past has been hailed as a monument of political folly, is clearly attaining a more respectable place in public esteem.

[4] For a description of these precautionary measures, see Muhse, A. C., "The Disintegration of the Tobacco Trust," *Political Science Quarterly*, June 1913; also Stevens, W. M., *Industrial Combinations and Trusts*, New York, 1913, pp. 440-461.

Leaving the question of efficiency out of account, it is possible to set forth certain definite favorable results of government trust activity. In the first place, the trust movement has been subjected to a large amount of publicity, the net result of which has been to break the spell of the trusts in the public mind. This publicity has made us realize for one thing that the bureaucracy of capital may be as dangerous to national productivity and progress as a bureaucracy of public officials. It has also created a demand for still more illuminating publicity which, in the long run, is bound to have a wholesome effect.

The carrying through of the Tobacco and Oil cases, whatever we may think of the ultimate disposition of those cases, has created a reasonable ground for assurance that the Government may proceed with any trust policy which is finally considered wise, without being embarrassed by a feeling of impotence.

Perhaps the greatest of all the specific services to business which the Sherman anti-trust law and the decisions under it have rendered is found in the progress toward a definition of legitimate competition. This has given an effectual impetus to efforts directed toward raising the moral level upon which competition and all the business of the nation in the future will be carried on.

The present situation is one in which the government is unquestionably in the possession of tremendous power, for the use of which there are comparatively few effective legal checks. The intimate and growing connection between government and business seems destined, moreover, to give any administration greater and greater power to influence by its policy the course of business affairs. In such a situation business welfare is bound to depend, in many instances, upon political responsibility and the character of officers rather than upon concrete legal restraints.

Whatever the momentary disturbance accompanying the trust activity of government during recent years, the signs of growing recognition of public responsibility on the part of great business enterprises more than compensates for any drawbacks which the details of the situation may have brought. Without falling prey to over-sentimental optimism one can still maintain that the co-operation for public ends which such a recognition implies will, in the long run, make for the continued development and prosperity of wholesome business.

[5]

By Benjamin J. Klebaner
ASSOCIATE PROFESSOR OF ECONOMICS
THE CITY COLLEGE OF THE CITY UNIVERSITY OF NEW YORK

Potential Competition and the American Antitrust Legislation of 1914

❧ *The concepts of actual and potential competition as natural checks on trusts are examined through the literature which accompanied the framing and passage of the Clayton and Federal Trade Commission acts. The contributions of professional economists to these discussions are especially significant in the evolution of the public policies ultimately adopted.*

Public concern over the trust problem in the United States between 1890 and 1914 was mirrored in the considerable contemporary literature on the subject.[1] Of particular importance to these discussions was the participation of many professional economists. Their thinking directly and indirectly influenced the antitrust legislation of 1914 in a way that cannot be said of the Sherman Act of 1890.[2] A survey of the more important of these professional writings should improve our comprehension of the implications of the vague phraseology of the Clayton and Federal Trade Commission acts. Especially relevant is the discussion generated over the concepts of actual and potential competition as natural checks on large-scale enterprise, popularly called "trusts."

POTENTIAL COMPETITION: A NATURAL CHECK ON TRUSTS

Clear-cut refinement of market categories of the type Edward Chamberlin has made familiar in our own day, is not to be found in most pre-1914 analyses of competition and monopoly. A rigorous and systematic definition of perfect competition was first attempted by Francis Y. Edgeworth in 1881, but it was not until forty years later that Frank Knight presented a complete formulation.[3] In the

---

[1] Appleton P. C. Griffin, *List of Books (with references to periodicals) Relating to Trusts* (3rd ed., Washington, 1907); Library of Congress, *List of References on Trusts 1907–1913* (Washington, 1913).

[2] Hans B. Thorelli, *The Federal Antitrust Policy* (Baltimore, 1955), p. 567. Allyn A. Young, "The Sherman Act and the New Antitrust Legislation," *Journal of Political Economy*, vol. XXIII (May, 1915), p. 204.

[3] George J. Stigler, "Perfect Competition, Historically Contemplated," *Journal of*

meantime, successive editions of Alfred Marshall's *Principles* (1890–1920) defined free competition simply as a situation where "buyers generally compete with buyers and sellers compete freely with sellers." He stated explicitly that his analysis did not assume competition was perfect.[4] Marshall's most distinguished American contemporary, John Bates Clark, did not specify anything more definite for competition than "the healthful rivalry in serving the public."[5]

Trusts, however defined, could not oppress the public, it was often argued. "Potential competition," defined by Clark as "competition of the mill that is not yet built but will be built if the trust becomes too extortionate," acted as an effective natural restraint on the trusts.[6] In the absence of legal barriers "the active influence of the potential competitor" was ever present, according to George Gunton. This friend of Standard Oil stated in 1888 that the "economic effect is substantially the same as if the new competitor were already there." As the community accumulates "surplus capital," Gunton reasoned, the probability of new competition is heightened.[7] Two decades later William Howard Taft similarly pointed to the "enormous floating capital awaiting investment" in good times; rarely, he thought, would it take more than a year for potential competition to become effective. The Republican presidential candidate of 1908 drew the usual conclusion: "Existence of actual plant is not . . . . necessary to potential competition."[8]

Political Economy, vol. LXV (February, 1957), pp. 6, 11. On the relationship between Chamberlinian market categories, earlier economic theorizing, and antitrust, see: Shorey Peterson, "Antitrust and the Classic Model," *American Economic Review*, vol. XLVII (March, 1957), pp. 60–78.

[4] Alfred Marshall, *Principles of Economics* (8th ed., New York, 1946), p. 341. The first edition has identical wording. A similarly vague definition appears in his *Industry and Trade* (London, 1919), p. 653. P. W. S. Andrews remarks, in Thomas Wilson and P. W. S. Andrews (eds.), *Oxford Studies in the Price Mechanism* (Oxford, 1951), p. 142, that as long as entry is possible, Marshall considers the industry competitive. Beginning with the second (1891) edition, Marshall included the sentence about perfect competition. *Principles* (9th ed., 2 vols., New York, 1961), vol. II, p. 569.

[5] John Bates Clark, *Essentials of Economic Theory* (New York, 1907), p. 374. See also Benjamin J. Klebaner, "Trusts and Competition; John Bates Clark and John Maurice Clark," *Social Research*, vol. XXIX (Winter, 1962), pp. 475–80.

[6] John Bates Clark, "The Real Dangers of the Trusts," *Century Magazine*, vol. LXVIII (October, 1904), p. 955; Charles J. Bullock, "Trusts and Public Policy," *Atlantic Monthly*, vol. LXXXVII (June, 1901), p. 741; William M. Coleman, "Trusts from an Economic Standpoint," *Journal of Political Economy*, vol. VIII (December, 1899), pp. 29–30; George A. Rich, "Trusts Their Own Corrective," *Popular Science Monthly*, vol. XLIV (April, 1894), p. 741.

[7] George Gunton, "The Economic and Social Aspects of Trusts," *Political Science Quarterly*, vol. III (September, 1888), p. 403; H. Hayes Robbins, "Powers and Perils of the New Trusts," *Gunton's Magazine*, vol. XVI (June, 1899), pp. 198–99; similarly, Gunton, *Principles of Social Economics* (New York, 1891), pp. 404, 406, 407. See also: Charles F. Beach, Jr., "Facts About Trusts," *Forum*, vol. VIII (September, 1889), p. 69; Beach, Jr., *The Trust: An Economic Evolution* (Chicago, 1894), p. 12; George E. Roberts, "Why the Trusts Cannot Control Prices," *American Monthly Review of Reviews*, vol. XX (September, 1899), p. 307. Roberts was director of the Mint.

[8] William H. Taft, *Presidential Addresses and State Papers* (New York, 1910), p. 15; see also p. 526. In our day, Joseph A. Schumpeter felt "creative destruction" was important even when "merely an ever-present threat." *Capitalism, Socialism, and Democracy* (3rd ed., New York, 1950), p. 85.

Andrew Carnegie had emphasized in 1889 that only freedom to compete was needed to make exceptional profits temporary. By 1900 he could point to the "ghosts of numerous departed trusts which aimed at monopolies." The final report of the United States Industrial Commission affirmed in 1902 that under modern conditions "a monopoly cannot abuse its power to any great extent without rivals springing up to dispute its supremacy." Perhaps the most important facts brought out by the Commission, in the opinion of an Illinois economist, were those revealing "the development of new competition side by side with the great consolidations." [9]

Economists agreed that in the absence of legal or natural monopoly or control of a basic material, a trust could not permanently exact excessive profits, thanks to the operation of potential competition.[10] In much the same vein as Gunton and Taft, the argument of surplus capital appeared in writings of Professors Franklin H. Giddings (1887) and Charles J. Bullock (1898). There was "always a large amount of uninvested capital seeking profitable employment." This would curb the price-raising tendencies of businessmen, the American Philosophical Society was told in 1903.[11] Economists pointed out that not only newcomers, but also existing (albeit small) firms already in the industry threatened the would-be perfect monopolist.[12]

LIMITATIONS OF POTENTIAL COMPETITION

Unlike the spokesmen for the trusts, however, some economists called attention to the limitations of potential competition. Its working was stayed by the existence of excess capacity in an in-

[9] Andrew Carnegie, "The Bugaboo of Trusts," *North American Review*, vol. CXLVIII (February, 1889), p. 150; "Popular Illusions about Trusts," *Century Magazine*, vol. LX (May, 1900), p. 149. See also: Henry Wood, *Political Economy of Natural Law* (Boston, 1894), pp. 66, 71; William R. Peters, "Benefits of Trusts," John P. Peters (ed.), *Labor and Capital* (New York, 1902), p. 53; U. S. Industrial Commission, *Report* (19 vols., Washington, 1900–1902), vol. XIX, p. 614; Maurice H. Robinson, "The Report of the Industrial Commission: V – Trusts," *Yale Review*, vol. XI (November, 1902), pp. 293–94.

[10] Jeremiah W. Jenks, "Trusts in America," *Economic Journal*, vol. II (January, 1892), pp. 92–93, 99; Richard T. Ely, *Monopolies and Trusts* (New York, 1900), p. 252; Theodore Marburg, "Trusts in America," *Economic Review*, vol. XI (January, 1901), p. 67; Irving Fisher, *Elementary Principles of Economics* (3rd ed., New York, 1912), p. 330.

[11] Franklin H. Giddings, "The Persistence of Competition," *Political Science Quarterly*, vol. II (March, 1887), p. 67; Charles J. Bullock, *Introduction to the Study of Economics* (Boston, 1897), p. 325; also in 3rd ed. (New York, 1908), p. 339; Bullock, in A. B. Nettleton (ed.), *Trusts or Competition?* (Chicago, 1900), p. 121; C. Stuart Patterson, *The Problem of Trusts* (Philadelphia, 1903), p. 9. The idle capital argument was also used by the De Pauw University economist James R. Weaver, in Chicago Conference on Trusts, *Speeches* (Chicago, 1900), p. 297, and in Lyman Horace Weeks, *The Other Side* (New York, 1900), p. 74. Marshall referred to potential competition in an 1890 presidential address, "Some Aspects of Competition," without using the phrase. A. C. Pigou, *Memorials of Alfred Marshall* (London, 1925), p. 288.

[12] Frank W. Blackmar, *Economics* (Topeka, 1900), p. 437; same in (New York, 1907) edition, p. 457; Gilbert H. Montague, *Trusts of To-day* (New York, 1904), p. 78.

dustry.[13] The slow response of potential competitors was one explanation offered for very large profits earned year after year without attracting rivals.[14] Considerable time might be required to gain a foothold in an industry, Harvard's Silas Macvane noted in 1890. To construct a large plant took time.[15] The sheer magnitude of the necessary outlay might deter entry.[16] President E. Benjamin Andrews of Brown University, one of the few economists who was very dubious of the effectiveness of potential competition, found no economic laws which could "prevent the permanent existence of monopolies" exacting excessive prices. Even if the minimum capital needed in many industries was forthcoming, he told the American Social Science Association in 1889, months or years might elapse before the new firm could produce.[17] There was always a chance that a new rival might join forces with an existing trust. An even stronger trust might arise "out of the ruins of the first," Edward W. Bemis warned. "Trusts have more frequently driven competition from the field, than has competition the trusts," John Bascom of Williams College insisted in 1895.[18]

Many supporters of the combination movement claimed that actual competition was hopeless. Bullock of Harvard pointed out that if this claim was indeed true, the remedial power of potential competition was put in doubt. Moreover, monopoly "fairly and honestly" achieved could undersell rivals, thereby deterring new

[13] Harry E. Montgomery, *Vital American Problems* (New York, 1908), pp. 10–11; Jeremiah W. Jenks, *The Trust Problem* (Rev. ed., New York, 1903), p. 69; William M. Collier, *The Trusts* (New York, 1900), pp. 126–27; O. M. W. Sprague, in "Governmental Price Regulation — Discussion," *American Economic Review*, suppl. III (March, 1913), p. 137.

[14] Henry C. Adams, "Trusts," American Economic Association, *Publications*, 3rd ser., vol. V (May, 1904), pp. 96–97; Jenks, *Trust Problem*, p. 70; Montgomery, *Vital American Problems*, p. 13; Charles Van Hise, *Concentration and Control* (New York, 1912), p. 84; Edwin R. A. Seligman, *Principles of Economics* (New York, 1914), p. 369; in the 1st ed. (New York, 1905), on p. 368.

[15] Silas Macvane, *Working Principles of Political Economy* (New York, 1890), p. 117; Collier, *Trusts*, p. 116; James E. Le Rossignol, *Monopolies Past and Present* (New York, 1901), p. 241; Editorial, "The Real Danger in Trusts," *Century Magazine*, vol. LX (May, 1900), p. 153; Montgomery, *Vital American Problems*, p. 10.

[16] Macvane, *Working Principles*, p. 117; Victor S. Yarros, "The Trust Problem Restudied," *American Journal of Sociology*, vol. VIII (July, 1902), p. 73; Charles W. Baker, *Monopolies and the People* (3rd ed., New York, 1899), p. 159; Nettleton (ed.), *Trusts*, p. 79; Jenks, in *Amendment of the Sherman Antitrust Law* (Hearings, Senate Judiciary Committee, Washington, 1908), p. 109; Eliot Jones, *The Trust Problem in the United States* (New York, 1921), p. 277.

[17] E. Benjamin Andrews, "The Economic Law of Monopoly," *Journal of Social Science*, vol. XXVI (February, 1890), pp. 6, 11, 12. In 1894 he saw "the competitive system . . . fast giving way to . . . combination. It could benefit society greatly if men improved morally." "The Combination of Capital," *International Journal of Ethics*, vol. IV (April, 1894), p. 334.

[18] Alsen F. Thomas, *The Slavery of Progress* (New York, 1910), pp. 21–22; Edward S. Meade, "The Limitations of Monopoly," *Forum*, vol. XXXI (April, 1901), p. 217; Edward W. Bemis, "The Trust Problem — Its Real Nature," *Forum*, vol. XXVIII (December, 1899), p. 420; Edward D. Durand, "The Trust Problem," *Quarterly Journal of Economics*, vol. XXVIII (May, 1914), pp. 398–99. Durand's Harvard lectures also appeared in book form (Cambridge, 1915); John Bascom, *Social Theory* (New York, 1895), p. 410. See also 56 Cong., 1 Sess., *House Reports*, No. 1501, p. 5.

firms from appearing in the industry despite high profits.[19] Economists thus cited a variety of practical reasons why potential competition could not always be counted on to eliminate monopolistic pricing.

UNFAIR COMPETITION OBSTRUCTS POTENTIAL COMPETITION

Destructive tactics employed by existing firms were widely held to be a major (when not the main) obstacle to entry into their markets.[20] Combinations seeking complete control, Taft explained in 1914, used various devices of an "unfair character. . . . in order to keep out or destroy new competition." Professor Thomas N. Carver pointed out that "the more effectively the organization can terrorize the trade, and the greater the artificial risks it can create, the less competition it will have and the larger profits it can make." This Harvard economist saw the danger of competition "lapsing into the brutal struggle for existence, where self-interest leads to uneconomic as well as to economic, to destructive as well as to productive activity."[21]

Unfair competition took a variety of forms. William H. S. Stevens, the leading authority (and subsequently assistant chief economist of the FTC) analyzed in detail no fewer than eleven methods: local price cutting, bogus independents, fighting ships [22] and brands, tie-ins, exclusive dealings, rebates and preferential contracts, acquisitions of exclusive or dominant control of machinery or goods used in manufacturing, "manipulation,"[23] boycotts, espionage, and coercive threats and intimidation. These tactics prevented potential competitors from becoming actual rivals of existing firms.[24] Stevens therefore advocated the prohibition of "any method except produc-

---

[19] Bullock, "Trusts and Public Policy," pp. 741–42; Walter E. Clark, "Control of Industrial Monopoly," *Rollins Magazine*, vol. II (July, 1912), p. 7; Jenks, in *Amendment of the Sherman Antitrust Law*, p. 108.

[20] Nettleton (ed.), *Trusts*, p. 80; Baker, *Monopolies*, pp. 85, 253; Herbert J. Davenport, *Outlines of Economic Theory* (New York, 1896), p. 205; Davenport, *Economics of Enterprise* (New York, 1913), p. 485. On the other hand, Charles J. Bullock, "Trust Literature: A Survey and a Criticism," *Quarterly Journal of Economics*, vol. XV (February, 1901), p. 204, argued that capitalists would not be permanently intimidated by destructive competition.

[21] William H. Taft, *The Anti-Trust Act and the Supreme Court* (New York, 1914), pp. 128–29; Thomas N. Carver, *The Distribution of Wealth* (New York, 1904), p. 267; Carver, *Essays in Social Justice* (Cambridge, 1915), p. 108.

[22] A fighting ship is used by a shipping conference to prevent a new line from getting business by the former's quoting unprofitable rates.

[23] Stevens uses the term for "certain practices and methods which have occasionally appeared."

[24] William H. S. Stevens, "Unfair Competition: I," *Political Science Quarterly*, vol. XXIX (June, 1914), pp. 283; *ibid*.: II (September, 1914), 489; Stevens, *Unfair Competition* (Chicago, 1917), p. 221. Earlier Stevens had written . . . "if the Sherman Act can eliminate certain piratical and predatory methods of competition, a larger proportion of the 'natural' tendency toward combination would dissolve into the thin air." "A Group of Trusts and Combinations," *Quarterly Journal of Economics*, vol. XXVI (August, 1912), p. 642.

tion and selling efficiency which prevents potential competition from becoming actual competition."[25] Ban unfair competition, it was often said, and only deserving trusts would survive.[26]

As a major (if not the basic) means of dealing with the trust problem, leading economists — among them John Bates Clark, J. Laurence Laughlin (Chicago), Herbert J. Davenport (Cornell), Henry R. Seager (Columbia), Frank A. Fetter (Princeton) and Frank W. Taussig (Harvard) — came to favor legislation forbidding all forms of unfair competition.[27] Attorney General Philander C. Knox expressed the conviction (1903) that monopoly would be impossible in the United States "if competition were assured of a fair and open field and protected against unfair, artificial and discriminating practices."[28]

Among these forms of unfair competition, many observers especially singled out price discrimination as a deterrent to potential competition. Already in 1889 Charles W. Baker, associate editor of *Engineering News* and author of the first comprehensive American study of the monopoly problem, demanded a law providing for nondiscrimination.[29] William M. Collier, Special Assistant Attorney General to enforce the antitrust laws in 1903–1904, had urged in 1900 that corporations be compelled to sell to all on equal terms.[30] John Bates Clark's authoritative voice spoke out in favor of a policy of uniform f.o.b. mill prices with some exceptions. Such a policy, Theodore Marburg told the National Conference on Trusts and Combinations (Chicago, 1907), "would re-establish the industrial 'open door' through which the potential competitor may enter."[31] Economists of the standing of Taussig, Bullock, Fetter,

[25] Stevens, "Unfair Competition: I," p. 490.

[26] Bruce Wyman, "Constructive Trust Control," *World To-Day*, vol. XXI (January, 1912), p. 1585; Clark, "Control of Industrial Monopoly," p. 8; Henry R. Seager, *Introduction to Economics* (3rd ed., New York, 1905), p. 508.

[27] John Bates Clark, "How to Deal with the Trusts," *Independent*, vol. LIII (May 2, 1901), p. 1003; J. Laurence Laughlin, *The Elements of Political Economy* (Rev. ed., New York, 1896), p. 71; Laughlin, in *Changes in Interstate Commerce Laws* (Hearings, Senate Interstate Commerce Committee, Washington, 1911–1912), p. 1004; Davenport, *Outlines*, p. 314; Henry R. Seager, "Government Regulations of Big Business in the Future," *Annals of the American Academy of Political and Social Science: Industrial Competition and Combination*, vol. XLII (July, 1912), p. 244, hereafter cited as *Annals*, XLII; Seager, *Principles of Economics* (New York, 1913), p. 469; Frank A. Fetter, *Principles of Economics* (New York, 1904), p. 332 (original in italics); again in 1913 ed., p. 332; Frank W. Taussig, in "Governmental Price Regulation — Discussion," *American Economic Review*, suppl. III (March, 1913), p. 132.

[28] *Senate Documents*, 57 Cong., 2 Sess., No. 73, p. 16.

[29] Baker, *Monopolies*, pp. 247, 249, 253. Baker was prepared to legalize contracts in restraint of trade and permit the establishment of monopolies.

[30] Collier, *Trusts*, p. 310.

[31] John Bates Clark, *The Control of Trusts* (New York, 1901), pp. 64–66; John Bates and John Maurice Clark, *Control of Trusts* (New York, 1912), p. 192; Theodore Marburg, in National Civic Federation, *Proceedings of the National Conference on Trusts and Combinations* (New York, 1908), p. 105. See also Ernest G. Stevens, *Civilized Commercialism* (New York, 1917), p. 170.

and Laughlin, as well as President Charles Van Hise of the University of Wisconsin all wanted to forbid price discrimination.[32] In 1902, the conservative United States Industrial Commission came out for stringent legislation making price discrimination for the purpose of destroying competition a crime.[33]

Among prominent scholars, Jeremiah W. Jenks of Cornell was almost alone on the other side. He emphasized the usefulness of discrimination when rivals wished to make headway against a great combination. Similarly, Gilbert H. Montague, though opposed to fraud, disparagement, and coercion, felt that both law and ethics sanctioned "free competition by underselling." [34]

One particular form of price discrimination, railway rebates, was sometimes stressed. To Henry Carter Adams, then chief ICC statistician, the railway problem was "at the bottom of the trust problem." A few months later the Democratic platform described rebates and discriminations by transportation companies as "the most potent agency" promoting and strengthening unlawful trusts. Other economists, Clark, Bemis, Bullock, Laughlin, and Edwin R. A. Seligman among them, although not necessarily going this far, agreed as to the need for strong laws against favoritism to large shippers.[35]

As economists analyzed the actual operation of competition in the rough-and-tumble of the market place, they were generally led to assign to the state the function of "jealously safeguarding the privileges of the potential competitor," to use the words of Theodore Marburg, vice-president of the American Economic Association in 1901. John Bates Clark also warned that "potential competition will be weak if the government shall do nothing to strengthen it." A theorist who wrote more extensively on the trust problem than any other American economist, Clark called on government to preserve "the right of every potential competitor of a trust to enter a field of business and to call on the law for protection whenever he is in danger of being unfairly clubbed out of it." Professor Fetter like-

[32] Van Hise, *Concentration*, p. 226. Van Hise was a geologist by profession. In his address before the National Convention of the Progressive Party, Theodore Roosevelt pronounced Van Hise's main thesis "unquestionably right." *Progressive Principles* (New York, 1913), p. 144; Frank W. Taussig, *Principles of Economics* (2 vols., New York, 1911), vol. II, p. 429; Bullock, *Elements*, p. 195; Fetter, *Principles*, p. 332, found also in 3rd ed. (New York, 1913), p. 332.

[33] U.S. Industrial Commission, *Report*, vol. XIX, p. 650.

[34] Jenks, *Trust Problem*, presents a hypothetical example of how a small firm might be harmed (pp. 325–26); Gilbert H. Montague, "The Ethics of Trust Competition," *Atlantic Monthly*, vol. XCV (March, 1905), p. 421. Montague had recently left Harvard's Department of Economics to embark on a distinguished career as an antitrust lawyer.

[35] Adams, "Trusts," p. 105; see also Bemis, "The Trust Problem — Its Real Nature," p. 120; Kirk H. Porter (comp.), *National Party Platforms* (New York, 1924), p. 248; Bullock, *Elements*, p. 193; John Bates Clark, in Chicago Conference on Trusts, *Speeches*, p. 408; J. Laurence Laughlin, *Industrial America* (New York, 1906), p. 136; Edwin R. A. Seligman in Frank Fayant (ed.), "What Is To Be Done with the Trusts?" *New York Times Magazine Section* (December 5, 1909), p. 2.

wise thought (1905) that the proper direction of trust control lay in "maintaining potential competition through fair and free conditions of industry." Even George Gunton would "stringently . . . prohibit all arbitrary barriers to the easy mobility and the safe concentration of capital and productive enterprise." Thomas N. Carver spoke for most American economists when he insisted that Adam Smith's "invisible hand" could produce beneficent results only in the presence of "proper government interference and control." Unchecked by appropriate legislation, a trust could enjoy "no small measure of monopolistic power," Clark declared.[36]

Some economists believed in the sufficiency of a policy of preventing unfair competition. They reasoned like Bruce Wyman of Harvard Law School that fair competition would always be possible if unfair competition were forbidden.[37] Other writers, however, stressed the need for measures going beyond a ban on unfair competition. Laughlin considered the abolition of tariffs on trust-made goods "the one powerful means" to secure effective competition.[38] At the same time he supported legislation to ban unfair competition.

On this last point, agreement among impartial students was well-nigh universal. After all, even a believer in the inevitability of monopoly or the economic advantages of large-scale production should be prepared to test his theory under proper (i.e., fair) conditions of competition. The Clarks pointed out that "survival in predatory competition is likely to mean something else than fitness for good and efficient production." As a 1910 editorial in the Nation urged: "Let monopolies arise where, in the ordinary course of things, and without resort to unfair means, competition dies away; but do not let competition be killed with a club." Only in this way could the "natural monopoly of superior efficiency" be distinguished from "artificial monopoly," to use Laughlin's description of good and bad trusts.[39]

[36] Marburg, in National Civic Association, Proceedings, p. 332 (original in italics); Clark, Essentials, pp. 384, 385; Fetter, Principles, p. 332 (original in italics found in 1st and 3rd eds.); George Gunton, "Trusts and How to Deal with Them," Chautauquan, vol. X (March, 1890), p. 703; Carver, Essays, p. 109; Clark, "The Real Dangers of the Trusts," p. 955. In the 4th ed. of his popular Trust Problem, Jenks for the first time stated: "in the fair field, kept deliberately open let the honest cost-cheapening monopoly be welcomed, if it come" (New York, 1917), p. 276.

[37] Bruce Wyman, "Unfair Competition by Monopolistic Corporations," Annals, XLII p. 73; a similar statement is in his Control of the Market (New York, 1911), pp. 264-65.

[38] Laughlin, Industrial America, p. 133. A more moderate recommendation was made by John Bates Clark, "Monopoly and Tariff Reduction," Political Science Quarterly, vol. XIX (September, 1904), p. 389. Cf. George H. Walker, "What Shall be Done about the Trusts?" Washington State Bar Association, Proceedings Eleventh Annual Session (Olympia, 1899), p. 97. A critique of the popular theory is Frank L. McVey, "Trusts and the Tariff," Journal of Political Economy, vol. VII (June, 1899), pp. 382-84. Baker (Monopolies, 1899 ed., p. 257) had little faith in potential competition but urged removing the tariff where a trust earned enormous profits.

[39] John D. Clark, The Federal Trust Policy (Baltimore, 1931), p. 104; Clark and Clark, Control, p. 200; Robert L. Raymond, "Industrial Combinations: Existing Law and Suggested

COMBINATION AND LIMITS ON SIZE

Combination as such — distinguished from the unfair tactics which merged firms might use — was no special concern to most students of the trust problem. Crusading Henry D. Lloyd wrote in 1896 that combination neither could nor should be prevented, but when it acquired the power to "crush competition and manipulate prices . . . something must be done!" As Professor William Folwell of Minnesota told the National Civic Federation in 1912, "Take from corporations the power to exploit, to overcapitalize and monopolize, and 'scale' may be left to the operation of economic forces." [40] By the 1890's economists generally viewed the combination movement as a normal evolution of the competitive system. Dissolution was "hopeless as a permanent policy. The fact of combination and of monopoly tendency must be faced," Taussig told the Chicago Conference on Trusts (1907). [41]

Protesting that trusts were not a "natural growth," Edward Meade of the University of Pennsylvania was in the minority when he forecast increased efficiency and lower costs of production following the break-up of the larger combinations. On the other side, Jenks criticized the Supreme Court's *Tobacco* and *Oil* decisions of 1911 for insufficiently appreciating the efficiency of the great combinations, even though they might be monopolies. [42]

Men with legal training shared Jenks' viewpoint. To William M. Coleman trusts were "absolutely indispensable to the attainment of the ideal state in which men of the highest possible development produce the greatest possible amount of the most advantageous commodities." Impressed with the inherent soundness of the combination principle, a legal scholar like Wyman argued for regulation rather than destruction of the trusts. "If it is true that not all competition is beneficent," stated the *Independent* in 1914, "it is no less true that not all combination is harmful." [43]

Legislation," *Journal of Political Economy*, vol. XX (April, 1912), pp. 313, 319; "Monopolies and the Law," *Nation*, vol. XC (January 6, 1910), p. 4; J. Laurence Laughlin, "Good and Bad Trusts," *World To-Day*, vol. XXI (January, 1912), p. 1588.

[40] Caroline A. Lloyd, *Henry Demarest Lloyd* (2 vols., New York, 1912), vol. I, pp. 289–90. Similarly, John Bascom wrote in 1895 that "Combination, an inevitable incident of progress, must be accepted and brought into submission to our common life." *Social Theory*, p. 413. Folwell, in National Civic Federation, *The Trust Problem* (New York, 1912), p. 369. *Cf.* the comments of Seager and Baker in *ibid.*, pp. 362, 391.

[41] Jeremiah W. Jenks, "Trusts in the United States," *Economic Journal*, vol. II (March, 1892), p. 71; Thorelli, *Federal Antitrust*, p. 376; Taussig, in National Civic Federation, *Proceedings*, p. 376.

[42] Edward S. Meade, "The Fallacy of 'Big Business,'" *Annals*, XLII, p. 88; contrast Donald Dewey, *Monopoly in Economics and Law* (Chicago, 1959), p. 8; Jeremiah W. Jenks, "Economic Aspect of the Recent Decisions of the United States Supreme Court on Trusts," *Journal of Political Economy*, vol. XX (April, 1912), p. 357. Jenks would protect "the public interest from direct harm" by legislation or court action, but would keep "the benefits of combination," *ibid.*

[43] Coleman, "Trusts from an Economic Standpoint," p. 33; Wyman, *Control of the*

Economists differed, however, on the significance of market share. Even an 85 per cent market share did not confer monopoly power on a firm in an industry where competitors were freely in existence and entry was not obstructed, according to Jenks, author of the *Trust Problem*, a standard work which went through more editions than any other in the field. Professor E. Dana Durand, on the other hand, reasoned that the mere combining of the greater part of an industry, quite apart from cut-throat practices, would give the firm "an appreciable degree of monopoly power." The Minnesota economist argued cogently that banning unfair competition could only serve as an adjunct to a policy forbidding combination. In the congressional debate on the 1890 legislation Senator John Sherman, quoting the New York Supreme Court, asked where was there room for another firm once an all- or nearly all-embracing combination had been formed. As William M. Collier pointed out, combining all the plants capable of supplying the entire market leads to at least a temporary monopoly; this restraint on competition justified laws against "such all-absorbing combination." Another lawyer, Charles P. Howland, saw monopoly deriving from the size of corporations. He wanted limits set on capitalization depending on the size of the national market; if no firm were allowed to grow so large as to fill the market, at least some competition would be restored.[44]

For a long time John Bates Clark was leader of the school which thought that banning unfair competition was all that was needed to make potential competition effective. By 1912, even he was prepared to place some restriction on the size of corporations. Clark, who had once described "the rigorous individualists" who advocated strict laws against consolidation as "bulls against the comets, one and all," now included in his list of remedies for the trust problem preventing combinations from growing to such a size that competition with them would be impossible. He favored breaking them up when they had grown that large. A firm controlling half the market might be required to prove that enough competition remained "to safeguard the interests of the public." Before a Senate

---

Market, pp. 263, 276; See also Robert L. Raymond, "The Federal Antitrust Act," *Harvard Law Review*, vol. XXIII (March, 1910), p. 378, and Ernest G. Stevens, "Civilized Commercialism," *American Law Review*, vol. XLVIII (May–June, 1914), pp. 433, 438; *Independent*, vol. LXXVII (1914), p. 80.

[44] Jeremiah W. Jenks, in Herbert Friedman, "The Trust Problem," *Yale Law Journal*, vol. XXIV (April, 1915), pp. 502–503; Hadley, however, thought that the larger the percentage controlled, "the larger the chance that a monopoly may in fact exist," *ibid.*, p. 502; Durand, "The Trust Problem," pp. 389, 401; Sherman, in *Congressional Record*, 51 Cong., 2 Sess., 2460 (March 21, 1890); Collier, *Trusts*, p. 130; Howland, "Monopolies: The Cause and the Remedy," *Columbia Law Review*, vol. X (February, 1910), pp. 102, 106; Robert R. Reed proposed a $200,000,000 capital limit, except by special act of Congress. "American Democracy and Corporate Reform," *Atlantic Monthly*, vol. CXIII (February, 1914), p. 267.

committee he conceded in 1914 that there were difficulties in setting a precise limit on size. The rule of reason might be applied by court or commission in this connection, based on whether or not the market was monopolistic. Dissolution prospects would, he hopefully maintained, strengthen "other measures for checking the development of further monopolies." [45]

Also in 1912, Van Hise, who was convinced that potential competition was not a sufficient regulator in more than 90 per cent of the cases, proposed that a firm with over half of any line be considered an unreasonable restraint of trade, i.e., one which did not permit free competition. Somewhat inconsistently he informed the House Committee on Interstate Trade in 1914 that whether one, two, or even five firms comprised an industry made little difference, because they could "cooperate perfectly to control the market;" hence the need for government regulation. [46]

An economist then at Van Hise's university, Thomas S. Adams, told the National Civic Federation that a firm controlling over 40 per cent of an industry should be regarded *ipso facto* as a combination in restraint of trade. In the event the firm had acquired this share without engaging in unfair competition he wanted a commission to regulate its prices. [47]

In practice, the closest Congress came to considering a limit on size was the recommendation of the Stanley Committee in 1912, found also in the La Follette bill of 1913, which would have established a rebuttable presumption of unreasonable restraint of trade when a firm had more than 30 per cent of the relevant market. One committee member, Representative John A. Sterling (Illinois), urged the dissolution of the great combinations. Even if monopolistic power had been achieved by natural growth, he advocated a limit on the amount of capital that a firm could have. Another committee member, Representative Augustus P. Gardner (Massachusetts), doubted that elimination of unfair competition would suffice to restore competition: "Mere bigness . . . may result in a more or less perfect monopoly." Representative Dick T. Morgan of Oklahoma saw the alternatives for the giant corporation as size limits or government supervision. [48]

[45] Clark, in *Annals*, XLII, p. 66; Clark, "The Real Dangers of the Trusts," p. 958; Clark and Clark, *Control*, pp. 194–95; John Bates Clark, in *Interstate Trade* (Hearings, Senate Interstate Commerce Committee, Washington, 1914), p. 364. A similar proposal is in Lewis H. Haney, *Business Organization and Combination* (Rev. ed., New York, 1914), p. 409.

[46] Van Hise, in *Interstate Trade*, p. 98; and in *Interstate Trade Commission* (Hearings, House Interstate and Foreign Commerce Committee, Washington, 1914), pp. 348–49; Van Hise, *Concentration*, pp. 227, 252.

[47] National Civic Federation, *Proceedings*, pp. 492–93.

[48] Stanley Bill, H.R. 26130 (1912), in U.S. Congress, *Bills and Debates in Congress*

In 1907, William Jennings Bryan reactivated the old proposal for federal licensing of interstate corporations, with maximum limits on the share which one firm could control, based on experience. The Democratic platform of 1908 proposed the licensing of interstate corporations before they could control 25 per cent of an industry, and prohibiting control of more than 50 per cent. As its share increased from 25 to 50 per cent, Bryan suggested (during the 1908 campaign), the licensed firm should stop expanding.[49]

Theodore Roosevelt considered the Bryan proposal even "more foolish" than the antitrust law. In his seventh annual presidential message (December, 1907) he had specifically opposed corporations whose formation or operations involved monopoly. Roosevelt wanted a giant whose position had been attained "by sheer baseness and wrong doing" to be broken up. However, there was no point in dissolving firms whose sole offense was their size, he explained in the *Outlook* (1912). Large size he identified with efficiency. Since his early days as President he had argued publicly for federal regulation and supervision of big business. He did not visualize that it would be any more difficult to regulate Standard Oil or United States Steel than to regulate a large railroad.[50]

In his attitude toward bigness President William H. Taft was in essential agreement with his predecessor. His inaugural address (two years before the Supreme Court announced the Rule of Reason) proposed an amendment to the antitrust law which included the right to combine for the sake of efficiency, while distinguishing combination "formed with the intent of creating monopolies." In this context, combinations which continued to grow beyond the point of economy of management characteristic of

Relating to Trusts (3 vols., Washington, 1914), vol. III, p. 2542; La Follette Bill, S. 2552 (1913), *ibid.*, vol. III, pp. 3118–19. Cummins' bill would have had the trade commission judge whether the capital of a firm was so extensive as to "destroy or prevent substantially competitive conditions in the general field of industry in which such corporation is engaged," *ibid.*, vol. III, pp. 2430–31; elsewhere he argued for a 25 per cent limit, *Congressional Record*, 63 Cong., 1 Sess., 4283 (August 29, 1913). See also: Sterling, in *House Reports*, 62 Cong., 2 Sess., No. 1127, p. 345, and *Congressional Record*, 62 Cong., 2 Sess., 10529–30 (August 8, 1912); Gardner, in *ibid.*, 10627 (August 9, 1912); Morgan, in *Interstate Trade Commission*, p. 170.

[49] William J. Bryan, "Dissolution and Prevention," *The Reader*, vol. IX (May, 1907), p. 578; Porter (comp.), *Platforms*, p. 277; Bryan, *Speeches* (2 vols., New York, 1913), vol. II, pp. 136–37.

[50] Elting E. Morison, *et al.* (eds.), *Letters of Theodore Roosevelt* (8 vols., Cambridge, 1951–1954), vol. VI, p. 1129; *Compilation of the Messages and Papers of the Presidents* (20 vols., New York, n. d.), vol. XV, p. 7078 (Seventh Annual Message); Theodore Roosevelt, "The Trusts, the People, and the Square Deal," *Outlook*, vol. XCIX (November 18, 1911), p. 655; "The Taft-Wilson Trust Programme," *Outlook*, vol. CII (September 21, 1912), p. 105; *Messages and Papers of the Presidents*, vol. XIV, p. 6648; George E. Mowry, *The Era of Theodore Roosevelt, 1900–1912* (New York, 1958), pp. 132–33. In a 1903 speech before Milwaukee businessmen, Roosevelt described big corporations as "the result of an inevitable process of economic evolution," quoted in Walter F. Meier, "What Attitude Should Government Assume toward Trusts?" *American Journal of Sociology*, vol. IX (September, 1903), p. 213.

efficient, large-scale firms demonstrated monopolistic intent. The law was violated only where the purpose or necessary effect of the combination was to stifle actual and potential competition and establish a monopoly.[51]

Woodrow Wilson too was not opposed to size *per se*. "I am for big business and I am against the trusts," he flatly stated during the campaign of 1912. His party's platform, though less explicitly than in 1908, wanted to forbid by law "the control by any one corporation of so large a proportion of any industry as to make it a menace to competitive conditions." [52] This idea was forgotten in the antitrust legislation of 1914.

Publicity As a Remedy

Publicity was often proposed to help make potential competition effective. The theory here was that knowledge of high profits would lure competitors into the field, while public opinion would moderate the trust's exactions. Henry C. Adams considered publicity "the first step" in the solution of the trust problem. Jenks saw publicity as the "most effective means" to force the passing on to the public of the savings of combination. Many businessmen shared Waddill Catchings' faith that little if any further trust legislation would be needed beyond a publicity statute.[53]

In 1900 and again in 1902 the United States Industrial Commission recommended that large corporations be required to submit "properly audited" annual reports. The Bureau of Corporations (1903–1914) operated on the theory of publicity which, in the words of Commissioner Luther Conant, Jr., had the "broader motive of maintaining an open field for fair competition." [54] Publicity, then,

[51] *Messages and Papers of the Presidents*, vol. XVI, p. 7369. See also vol. XVII, pp. 7651, 7655, and Taft, *Presidential Addresses*, p. 527.
[52] Woodrow Wilson, *The New Freedom* (New York, 1913), pp. 180, 191; Ray Stannard Baker, *Woodrow Wilson* (6 vols., Garden City, 1927–1937), vol. IV, p. 357. Porter (comp.), *Platforms*, p. 322.
[53] Frank N. Judson, *The Rightful Relation of the State to Private Business Associations* (St. Louis, 1890), p. 16; Baker, *Monopolies* (1889 ed.), pp. 254–55; *ibid.* (1899 ed.), p. 357; Gunton, "Trusts and How to Deal with Them," p. 703; Robert L. Raymond, "A Statement of the Trust Problem," *Harvard Law Review*, vol. XVI (December, 1902), p. 90; Seligman, *Principles* (1914 ed.), p. 640; Taussig, *Principles*, vol. II, p. 433; Seager, in *Annals*, XLII, p. 244; Henry C. Adams, "What is Publicity?" *North American Review*, vol. CLXXV (December, 1902), p. 904; Jeremiah W. Jenks, in *Amendments to Sherman Antitrust Law* (Hearings, Senate Judiciary Committee, Washington, 1914), p. 307; Jenks, *Trust Problem* (1900 and 1914 eds.), pp. 223–24; Jenks, in *Amendment of the Sherman Antitrust Law*, p. 109; Catchings, head of Central Foundry Co., in *Interstate Trade Commission*, pp. 54–55.
[54] U.S. Industrial Commission, *Report*, vol. I, p. 6; U.S. Commissioner of Corporations, *Annual Report*, 1912 (Washington, 1913), p. 3. By 1902 it was said that the inadequacy of publicity as a remedy had been "widely recognized." Yarros, "The Trust Problem Restudied," p. 68.

shared with a ban on unfair competition the distinction of being the least controversial and most widely proposed trust remedies.

CONGRESS AND POTENTIAL COMPETITION: THE 1890's

In the debate on the antitrust measure of 1890, congressmen had expressed concern for what was soon to become widely known as "potential competition." Senator Sherman explained that one of the purposes of his original bill was "to prevent and control combinations made with a view to prevent competition." Trusts, he thought, had "a uniform design to prevent competition." One of the six unlawful purposes of a trust enumerated in Senator John H. Reagan's bill of 1890 was "to prevent competition." The section in the law of 1890 making unlawful every contract in restraint of trade was held to render superfluous a proposed amendment denouncing every agreement "for the purpose of preventing competition." [55] By passing the Sherman Act, Congress aimed to outlaw "artificial obstacles to entry;" private restrictions on competition were to be eliminated and prevented. As Myron Watkins later pointed out, "we were committed to the principle of offering full protection to . . . potential producers." [56]

Senator George Hoar, one of the sponsors of the bill which eventually became the Sherman Act, explained that the 1890 measure was intended to protect "fair competition" in interstate commerce. After the Supreme Court in 1895 defeated the government's efforts to break up the Sugar Trust, many friends of an antitrust policy proposed a constitutional amendment. If such action were taken, Congress would have "power to maintain an open field for honest competition," according to the House Judiciary Committee. Chairman George W. Ray specifically saw the need for laws which would maintain "fair and open opportunity to enter and engage in every honest pursuit." [57] With the Northern Securities (1904) and subsequent decisions, it became clear that constitutional amendment was not necessary in order to deal with the trust problem.

[55] Sherman, in *Congressional Record*, 51 Cong., 1 Sess., 2457, 2459, 2569 (March 21, 24, 1890); Reagan, in *ibid.*, 51 Cong., 1 Sess., 2469 (March 21, 1890); Culberson, in *ibid.*, 51 Cong., 1 Sess., 5951 (June 11, 1890); Young, "The Sherman Act and the New Antitrust Legislation," p. 213. Justice Holmes went so far as to argue that "there is no combination in restraint of trade, until something is done with the intent to exclude strangers to the combination from competing with it in some part of the business which it carries on." *Northern Securities Co. v. U.S.*, 193 U.S. 197, p. 409 (1905) (dissent).

[56] John M. Lishan, "The Sherman Act" (Ph.D. Dissertation, Harvard University, 1958), p. 38. Thorelli, *Federal Antitrust*, p. 571. See also John Perry Miller, *Unfair Competition* (Cambridge, 1941), p. 25. Myron W. Watkins, "The Sherman Act: Its Design and Its Effects," *Quarterly Journal of Economics*, vol. XLIII (November, 1928), p. 42.

[57] Hoar, in *Congressional Record*, 51 Cong., 1 Sess., 3152 (April 8, 1890); *House Reports*, 56 Cong., 1 Sess., No. 1501, p. 33; Ray, in *Congressional Record*, 56 Cong., 1 Sess., 6306 (May 31, 1900).

The Rule of Reason: Attack on the Sherman Act

Certain quarters were dissatisfied with Supreme Court decisions from 1897 on, which appeared to forbid all contracts restraining trade. Montague estimated that two-thirds of the country's business was thereby being conducted "in defiance of law." Strict enforcement of the Sherman Act would prohibit "the normal growth of large commercial enterprise," he complained. The law appeared not to confine itself to forbidding unreasonable restraints of trade.[58]

The "rule of reason," enunciated in May, 1911 in the historic Standard Oil and Tobacco decisions, was hailed by economist Seager: the Supreme Court's interpretation condemning only unreasonable restraints had turned the law into "a constructive and regulative measure of reform." Law-Professor Wyman saw reasonableness as the common law standard by which "good" trusts would be separated from the "bad." New York corporation lawyer Felix Levy took issue with the 1912 Democratic platform allegation that the rule weakened the Sherman Act.[59]

While some denounced the rule of reason for weakening the Sherman Act, others thought the rule did not go far enough in that direction. Professor Laughlin claimed business was slowing up because the antitrust law was uncertain in its meaning. The Sherman Act was attacked before the American Mining Congress in October, 1911, as "a wet blanket upon industry." The law of 1890 was "an anachronism," according to James M. Beck, and "little more than a delusion:" men could not be compelled to compete if they did not want to. The law was "destructive in purpose and application," according to Arthur Eddy, the lawyer who wrote a famous plea for open price associations in 1912.[60]

---

[58] Gilbert H. Montague, "Defects of the Sherman Antitrust Law," *Yale Law Journal*, vol. XIX (December, 1909), pp. 88, 107, 109, reprinted almost verbatim as "Trust Regulation Today," *Atlantic Monthly*, vol. CV (January, 1910), pp. 1–8. The President of the National Association of Clothiers, Marcus M. Marks, also urged that reasonable agreements be made lawful in "Effects of Anti-Trust Legislation on Business," *Annals of the American Academy of Political and Social Science*, vol. XXXII (July–December, 1908), p. 48.

[59] Henry R. Seager, "The Recent Trust Decisions," *Political Science Quarterly*, vol. XXVI (December, 1911), pp. 610–11; Wyman, *Control of the Market*, p. 234; Levy, in *Trust Legislation* (Hearings, House Judiciary Committee, Washington, 1914), pp. 241, 247–48.

[60] Laughlin, "Good and Bad Trusts," p. 1586; D. W. Kuhn, *Sherman Anti-Trust Law* (Address before American Mining Congress, October, 1911), p. 5; James M. Beck, "The Supreme Court Decisions: The Quandary," *North American Review*, vol. CXCIV (July, 1911), p. 70. Beck was U.S. Solicitor-General, 1921–1925; he favored a government tribunal to hear complaints, *Annals*, XLII, p. 300. Arthur J. Eddy, *The New Competition* (New York, 1912), p. 333. The President of the Virginia Bar Association urged the repeal of the Sherman Act on the grounds that competition should not be the life of trade, and the "absolutely uncertain and vague" law did not distinguish between good and bad trusts. J. F. Bullitt, "The Present Status of the Trust Question," Virginia State Bar Association, *Report of the Twenty-fourth Annual Meeting* (n.p., 1912), pp. 170, 182.

ANTITRUST LEGISLATION OF 1914   177

In the 1890's it had been urged that industries be given the right to combine "under proper supervision" and to agree on reasonable prices and avoidance of competitive excesses. In the years just preceding the enactment of the antitrust legislation of 1914, Van Hise was perhaps the outstanding non-business proponent of an amendment to the Sherman Act which would permit combinations in restraint of trade involving division of territories and agreements on output and even prices provided they were not detrimental to the public welfare.[61]

Other critics argued the Sherman Act had failed to solve the monopoly problem, or to prevent the maturation of monopoly. Indeed, according to Jenks, it had "tended to breed monopoly" by forbidding certain other restraints.[62]

Despite such attacks, there was widespread support for the Sherman Act as a measure to ensure fair competition and to prevent exclusion.[63] Almost unanimous support for the principle of the Sherman Act, and a determination that big business should be regulated appeared in the replies to a questionnaire sent to 16,000 representative Americans by the National Civic Federation. Advocates of repeal or liberalizing amendments were people who had been violating the law, attorney Samuel Untermyer pointedly observed. Among popular authors, support for the Sherman Act policy was even more common than among scholars.[64]

Certainly the Taft administration made vigorous use of the 1890 law. More prosecutions of business combinations were instituted from 1909 to 1913 than during Theodore Roosevelt's two terms. Taft considered the law "the expression of the effort of a freedom-loving people to preserve equality of opportunity." He told Congress in December, 1912 that the trust question was "gradually solving itself" by enforcement of the Sherman Act.[65]

[61] Aldace F. Walker, "Unregulated Competition Self-Destructive," *Forum*, vol. XII (December, 1891), p. 515; Walker, "Anti-Trust Legislation," *Forum*, vol. XXVII (May, 1899), p. 262. Walker was a member of the original ICC, 1887–1889; from 1889–1892 he was connected with the Trunk Line and Central Traffic Associations; after 1894 he headed the Santa Fe. Van Hise, in *Interstate Trade*, pp. 95, 96; Van Hise, in *Trust Legislation*, p. 557; see also F. P. Fish (Boston attorney) in *ibid.*, p. 1511 and L. C. Boyle (Kansas City attorney for the Yellow Pine Manufacturers Association), *Interstate Trade Commission*, p. 442.

[62] Rep. Dick Morgan, in *Trust Legislation*, p. 4; Dean William D. Lewis, University of Pennsylvania Law School, in *ibid.*, p. 399; J. Newton Baker (D.C. attorney), "Regulation of Corporations," *Yale Law Journal*, vol. XXII (February, 1913), p. 329; Jenks, in *Amendments to Sherman Antitrust Law*, p. 302.

[63] Bennett, attorney for manufacturers of printing presses, in *Trust Legislation*, p. 301; Dushkind, attorney for Independent Tobacconists Association of N.Y.C., in *ibid.*, p. 702; Charles A. Boston, "The Spirit behind the Sherman Anti-Trust Law," *Yale Law Journal*, vol. XXI (March, 1912), pp. 358, 371.

[64] National Civic Federation, *Proceedings*, p. 8; Samuel Untermyer, "The Supreme Court Decisions: The Remedy," *North American Review*, vol. CXCIV (July, 1911), p. 77; Thorelli, *Federal Antitrust*, p. 576.

[65] *Messages and Papers of the Presidents*, vol. XVII, p. 7655 (1911 Annual Message);

OPEN DOOR FOR BUSINESS: THE POLICY OF THE 1914 LAWS

During the presidential campaign of 1912 Woodrow Wilson spoke of his desire to create a situation "where every man knows that the business community is open for him to enter and that he will be welcome." The New Freedom was concerned with "men who are on the make rather than the men who are already made." Wilson therefore wanted to "check those who use big business to crush little business, who use power to prevent anybody coming into competition with their power by a power and intelligence of his own." His first annual message proposed that the 1890 law be left unaltered, but urged supplementary legislation to "clarify it." The aim — much sought after by businessmen and endorsed by the three major party platforms in 1912 — was to "practically eliminate uncertainty." [66]

Maintenance of competition remained the dominant philosophy and, though seldom mentioned explicitly in congressional discussions of the antitrust measures of 1914, potential competition was probably in the mind of legislators.[67] The Senate Committee on Interstate Commerce, reporting on its 1913 hearings, stressed the importance of creating and preserving competitive conditions so that actual competition would be most likely to take place. In the unusual case where there was no actual competition, there would at least be "a potential competition tending to prevent undue prices and unfair practices." The aim of the 1914 laws, Senator Thomas J. Walsh succinctly stated, was "to preserve competition where it exists, to restore it where it is destroyed, and to permit it to spring up in new fields." Senator William E. Chilton stressed the purpose "to create competition, to fix it so that there is an incentive for the little man to come in and take the field or a part of the field which is now occupied absolutely by these gigantic corporations," not to destroy or stop big business. President Wilson similarly described the 1914 legislation as aiming to make "men in a small way of

---

Congressional Record, 62 Cong., 3 Sess., 897 (December 19, 1912). See also Attorney-General George W. Wickersham, *The Administration's Anti-Trust Record* (Washington, 1912), p. 26.

[66] Woodrow Wilson, *Public Papers* (ed. by R. S. Baker and W. E. Dodd, 6 vols., Garden City, 1925–1927), vol. I., p. 29; Wilson, *New Freedom*, pp. 17, 191, 221; John W. Davidson (ed.), *A Crossroads of Freedom* (New Haven, 1956), p. 516; see also *ibid.*, pp. 78, 269, 464. For a similar stress on a free field see W. R. Hammond (Atlanta Judge), "Evil and Cure of Monopolistic Business Tendency," Georgia Bar Association, *Report of the Twenty-ninth Annual Session* (Macon, 1912), pp. 129, 131; Albert Shaw (ed.), *Messages and Papers of Woodrow Wilson* (2 vols., New York, 1924), vol. I, p. 42 (1913 Annual Message); *ibid.*, vol. I, p. 52 (1914 Special Message on Trusts).

[67] E. Dana Durand, "The Trust Legislation of 1914," *Quarterly Journal of Economics*, vol. XXIX (November, 1914), p. 73. *Cf.* Jones, *Trust Problem*, p. 335; Clark, *Federal Trust Policy*, p. 168.

business as free to succeed as men in a big way and to kill monopoly in the seed." [68]

CLAYTON ACT APPROACH

Compared to the aspirations of some antitrust advocates, the Clayton Act was "so weak that you cannot tell it from water," as Wilson wrote to Colonel Edward House. Senator James A. Reed (Missouri) exaggerated, however, when he described the measure as proclaiming "Peace on earth, good will toward the trusts." After all, the 1914 measure left the Sherman Act intact. The intention of Congress was to supplement the 1890 act, making certain practices — such as tying clauses and price discrimination — illegal which in themselves were not covered by the earlier law, and thus "to arrest the creation of trusts, conspiracies, and monopolies in their incipiency and before consummation." Some of these practices, such as price discrimination, had been singled out for condemnation prior to 1914. Tying clauses involving a patented product, however, had been upheld by the courts.

Prevention of monopoly rather than prosecution of trusts after they had been in operation was at the heart of the Clayton Act's approach. Congress forbade certain tactics "where the effect . . . *may* be to substantially lessen competition or tend to create a monopoly" and not merely where competition had already been damaged or eliminated. This was in harmony with the theory that it was preferable to keep "the field open for the beneficent effect of competition rather than wait until those channels of competition have been blocked up and then try to open them with a knife," as Henry L. Stimson phrased it in 1911.[69]

FTC AND POTENTIAL COMPETITION

A similar philosophy motivated the Federal Trade Commission Act. Senator Francis G. Newlands, the author, argued that making unfair competition unlawful would "protect the pygmies against the giants of the business and open the lines of competition." Senator Henry F. Hollis envisioned the FTC as "policing competition, so

[68] *Senate Reports*, 62 Cong., 3 Sess., No. 1326, pp. 3–4; Walsh, in *Congressional Record*, 63 Cong., 2 Sess., 16145 (October 5, 1914); Chilton, in *ibid.*, 14326 (August 27, 1914); Wilson, *Public Papers*, vol. I, p. 189; see also, *ibid.*, vol. II, p. 318.

[69] Arthur S. Link, *Woodrow Wilson and the Progressive Era, 1910–1917* (New York, 1954), p. 73; Reed, "The New Way with the Trusts," quoted in *Literary Digest*, vol. XLIX (October 24, 1914), p. 778; *Senate Reports*, 63 Cong., 2 Sess., No. 698, p. 1; Henry L. Stimson (Secretary of War in Taft's Cabinet), *Address at the Republican Club New York City on December 15, 1911*, p. 6.

as to protect small businessmen, keep an open field for new enterprise, and prevent the development of trusts." The last, of course was related to the widespread view that unfair competition was (in the words of a House group endorsing the bill) the one effective means of "establishing and maintaining a monopoly" in the absence of control of raw materials or transportation discrimination. To prevent unfair competition was therefore "the most certain way to stop monopoly at the threshold." As Representative Rufus Hardy told the House in 1911, "By . . . ruinous competition combination builds itself into monopoly." [70]

The idea of a trade commission was in the air in the first decade of the twentieth century. Americans felt that regulation had to accompany combination. President Roosevelt envisioned it in 1907 as functioning to ratify "reasonable agreements between, or combinations of corporations." Wyman had suggested using the Sherman Act to dissolve combinations restraining trade, while a commission regulated firms with "substantial control over their market." Senator Newlands, the staunchest congressional advocate of the trade commission idea, explained in 1911 that the proposed agency would preserve "the good arising from commercial combination," while "curing the pernicious practices connected therewith." [71]

Commissioner of Corporations Herbert K. Smith argued for administrative regulation because application of the Sherman Act through the courts was haphazard. The Republican platform of 1912 viewed the commission as an agency for the prompt administration of the law. The Senate report on the FTC bill agreed that a commission would help to enforce the 1890 law. Moreover, the experts could aid the courts in fashioning effective dissolution decrees. [72] Advocates also envisioned the commission in the role of adviser to businessmen on the legality of their plans. [73]

[70] Newlands in *Congressional Record*, 63 Cong., 2 Sess., 12939 (July 29, 1914); Hollis, in *ibid.*, 12146 (July 15, 1914); 63 Cong., 2 Sess., *House Reports*, No. 1142, pp. 18–19; George Rublee, "The Original Plan and Early History of the Federal Trade Commission," *Academy of Political Science Proceedings*, vol. XI (January, 1926), pp. 117–18; Hardy, in *Congressional Record*, 62 Cong., 1 Sess., 1232 (May 16, 1911). The notion that monopoly was built on unfair practices was challenged by Progressive Donald Richberg in *Trust Legislation*, p. 419.

[71] Talcott Williams, "No Combination Without Regulation," *Annals of the American Academy of Political and Social Science*, vol. XXXII (July–December, 1908), p. 258; *Messages and Papers of the Presidents*, vol. XIV, p. 7079; Bruce Wyman, in *Annals*, XLII, p. 71; *Congressional Record*, 62 Cong., 1 Sess., 1212 (May 15, 1911).

[72] Herbert K. Smith, in *Amendments to Sherman Antitrust Law*, p. 333; see also, William Draper Lewis, in *Trust Legislation*, p. 398; Porter (comp.), *Platforms*, pp. 341, 354; *Senate Reports*, 63 Cong., 2 Sess., No. 597, pp. 9, 10, 12.

[73] James R. Garfield (ex-Secretary of the Interior), *Annals*, XLII, pp. 144–45; Henry R. Towne (of Yale and Towne), in *Trust Legislation*, p. 524.

Two groups, otherwise at odds, supported the commission idea. One — which included the Progressives — wanted to regulate what appeared to be inevitable monopolies. The other, which embraced the congressional sponsors of the 1914 measures, wanted to destroy monopoly and employ the commission as an instrument to preserve competition. Senator Newlands cleverly argued (1911) that a commission would not commit the country permanently to either school's approach.[74] Some opponents of the mild measure which became law in 1914 feared that it was the first step to the adoption of the policy of regulating rather than destroying private monopoly. To allay such misgivings, the House report on the bill pointed out that the commission had no power "to make terms with monopoly or in any way to assume control of business." [75]

By mid-1914 Wilson, originally critical of the Progressives' proposal for a strong trade commission came to advocate the Brandeis-Rublee plan for an effective regulatory agency for business. In the process he scrapped his original concept of an antitrust statute which would define trade restraints in precise terms.[76] The Commission, hailed by Professor Durand as "a great forward step," turned out to be "the most important feature of the new trust legislation," as he remarked shortly after the event.[77]

By the time Wilson submitted his special message on trusts and monopolies (January 20, 1914), Congress had already enacted two major measures which were intended in part to have an impact on this problem: tariff reduction and creation of a central banking system. For decades elimination of protectionism had been the main antitrust proposal of the Democratic Party. The Underwood Tariff of 1913 made a start in this direction. Creation of the Federal Reserve System followed a warning by the Pujo Committee that the "inner group" of leading banks had been "more destructive of competition than anything accomplished by the trusts, for they strike at the very vitals of potential competition in every industry that is under their protection." [78] The Federal Reserve System was established on a decentralized basis so as to make it impossible for

[74] *Senate Reports*, 63 Cong., 2 Sess., No. 597, p. 10; Gerard C. Henderson, *The Federal Trade Commission* (New Haven, 1925), pp. 21, 22; Henry R. Seager and Charles A. Gulick, Jr., *Trust and Corporation Problems* (New York, 1929), p. 415; Newlands, in *Senate Reports*, 63 Cong., 2 Sess., No. 597, p. 27.

[75] Dushkind, in *Trust Legislation*, pp. 711–712; *House Reports*, 63 Cong., 2 Sess., No. 533, p. 7.

[76] Link, *Wilson and the Progressive Era*, pp. 72–73. In his Special Message on Trusts, January 20, 1914 (*loc. cit.*, note 66), pp. 85–86, Wilson advocated a trade commission. Durand, "The Trust Legislation of 1914," pp. 78, 90, 97; Porter (comp.), *Platforms*, p. 341 (Progressive plank).

[77] Wilson, Special Message on Trusts, January 20, 1914, pp. 81–88 (*loc. cit.*, note 66).

[78] House Banking and Currency Committee, *Report of the Committee . . . to Investigate the Concentration of Control of Money and Credit* (Washington, 1913), p. 161.

the New York financial leaders to control the central bank. Yet another weapon intended to deal with banker control was forged in Section 8 of the Clayton Act.

HOLDING COMPANIES AND CORPORATE REFORM

In his January, 1914 statement Wilson observed that agreement was general that the holding company should be prohibited. Four years earlier Taft had made a similar recommendation for inclusion in a proposed federal incorporation law, reasoning that the device "has been such an effective agency in the creation of the great trusts and monopolies." The holding company facilitated the elimination of competition because a controlling interest in a firm could be purchased at small cost, Senator Theodore E. Burton pointed out.[79] Another important count against the holding company was that it was used to exploit minority shareholders.[80] The House Judiciary Committee considered a corporation whose primary purpose was to hold the stock of other companies "an abomination;" Section 7 of the Clayton Act was to eliminate the evil as far as possible.[81] Contrary to Wilson's original (impractical) notion, not all holding companies would be banned under this provision.

Effective antitrust action was linked, in the opinion of many, with restrictions on corporate powers and conduct, to be achieved (as a rule) by federal incorporation.[82] Some went so far as to claim that monopoly would be destroyed if corporate privileges — illustrated by the right of firms to hold the stock of other companies — were confined.[83] It remained for Chester Wright of the University of Chicago to point out that reform of corporation law would help only in a small way to solve the monopoly problem — insofar as

[79] Wilson, *Special Message on Trusts*, January 20, 1914, p. 87 (*loc. cit.*, note 66); Taft, *Special Message*, January 7, 1910, *Messages and Papers of the Presidents*, vol. XVII, p. 7455; Theodore E. Burton, *Corporations and the State* (New York, 1911), p. 122. For a lawyer's arguments against holding companies see J. Newton Baker, "Regulation of Corporations," p. 330. For a lawyer's favorable attitude see Albert H. Walker, in *Trust Legislation*, p. 1396.

[80] Clark and Clark, *Control*, p. 191; Untermyer, in *Trust Legislation*, p. 858.

[81] *House Reports*, 63 Cong., 2 Sess., No. 627, p. 17. John Bates Clark also used the term "abomination" in "After the Trusts, What?" *World To-day*, vol. XXI (November, 1911), p. 1296. E. Dana Durand commented that Section 7 of the Clayton Act added "nothing of real value to the Sherman Act." "The Trust Legislation of 1914," p. 83. For the legislative history of Section 7, see David D. Martin, *Mergers and the Clayton Act* (Berkeley, 1959), chap. 2.

[82] Burton, *Corporations*, p. 174; Frederick H. Allen (corporation attorney), in *Trust Legislation*, p. 1168; R. M. Benjamin, "The Evolution and Prevention of Trusts and Monopolies," *Albany Law Journal*, vol. LXVIII (August, 1906), p. 246. A comprehensive discussion of remedies for corporate abuses is found in Haney, *Business Organization*, pp. 383–402.

[83] Robert R. Reed, "American Democracy and Corporate Reform," *Atlantic Monthly*, vol. CXIII (February, 1914), p. 259; Reed, in *Interstate Trade Commission*, pp. 332–33, 344; Reed, in *Trust Legislation*, pp. 591, 625.

promoters' profits stimulated the formation of trusts. He correctly observed: [84]

> . . . totally abolish all the evils of the corporation, stock-watering, manipulation, defrauding creditors, injuring minority stockholders, excessive promoters' profits, and all the rest, and you will still have the problem of trusts on your hands. Conversely, if you were so successful as to abolish all the trusts in creation, you would still have to face these evils which are due to our lax corporation laws.

Thoroughgoing corporate reform, however, was not on the program of action for the New Freedom.

THE LEGACY OF 1914

Spokesmen for laissez-faire — among them the eminent corporation lawyer John Dos Passos — looked to "the natural laws of trade" to "prevent or break up most commercial monopolies." [85] Between 1890–1914 the view became widespread that markets could function satisfactorily only if potential competition were an ever-present threat. Economists (and some others) pointed out that unregulated cut-throat competition often destroyed the possibilities of potential competition. They insisted that government assume the responsibility of forbidding activities which impeded the working of potential competition.

Price discrimination, exclusive dealing, holding-company acquisitions — business devices enumerated in the original Clayton Act as unlawful when they might "substantially lessen competition or tend to create a monopoly" — all menace potential competition. The "unfair methods of competition" declared unlawful in the FTC Act of 1914 can also reasonably be interpreted to include the variety of devices endangering potential competition.

The half-century which has elapsed since the passage of the two measures cannot be said to have seen the realization of the aspirations of some of the more enthusiastic supporters of the idea that a specialized independent agency aided by statutes forbidding various forms of unfair business conduct were adequate to preserve competition in the American economy.[86] Moreover, uncertainty was not eliminated in the 1914 laws, which left intact the rule of reason

---

[84] Chester W. Wright, "The Trust Problem: Prevention versus Alleviation," *Journal of Political Economy*, vol. XX (June, 1912), p. 582.
[85] John R. Dos Passos, *Commercial Trusts* (New York, 1901), p. 63.
[86] John Perry Miller, "Woodrow Wilson's Contribution to Antitrust Policy," in Earl Latham (ed.), *The Philosophy and Policies of Woodrow Wilson* (Chicago, 1958), pp. 134, 143.

interpretation of the Sherman Act. Indeed, the courts extended the principle to the Clayton Act as well.

Nevertheless, the antitrust heritage of 1914 remains of value even in today's world. Pure and perfect competition were repudiated as "direct goals of antitrust policy" by the eminent lawyers and economists who reported on the antitrust laws in 1955 to the Attorney General; but these men emphasized the fundamental importance of "relative freedom of opportunity for entry of new rivals . . . for effective competition in the long run." In effect, they restated the main point of the message of serious students of the trust problem between 1890 and 1914. A recent study of big business concludes that "the threat of competitive innovation and entry is continuous and omnipresent." [87] To the extent that this is true, the 1914 laws have contributed to the result. Antitrust decisions which focus on potential competition [88] are in the spirit of the thinking which lay behind the 1914 Clayton and Federal Trade Commission acts.

[87] Attorney-General's National Committee to Study the Antitrust Laws, *Report* (Washington, 1955), pp. 326, 334; A. D. H. Kaplan and Alfred Kahn, "Big Business in a Competitive Society," *Fortune,* vol. XLVII (February, 1953), sec. 2, p. 4.

[88] American Bar Association Section on Antitrust Law, *Proceedings,* vol. XII (Chicago, 1958), pp. 105–202, esp. pp. 177, 186, 202.

[6]

THE JOURNAL of BUSINESS

of the University of Chicago

| Volume XXIV | OCTOBER 1951 | Number 4 |

CHANGING LEGAL CONCEPTS[1]

THOMAS E. SUNDERLAND[2]

THIS is the first of four lectures on the general subject "Big Business and Public Policy." As a part of that larger field, I have been asked to develop the subject "Changing Legal Concepts." Accordingly, I shall address myself to the Sherman Act and to related antitrust laws. I will endeavor to explore the attitude of the courts and outline the trend of recent judicial decisions.

The phenomenon of change is not a peculiar characteristic of the law. Even in the field of science, what is regarded as immutable one day is later found to be quite untenable. Economists, also, constantly revise their premises.

What makes the lawyer's path a thorny one, especially in the antitrust field, is the fact that changes frequently are quite unscientific in origin. The evolution of legal doctrine unfortunately does not stem mainly from the application of logical processes to the analysis of factual data. Rather, developments in the law are all too often dictated by the ebb and flow of political viewpoints and social objectives, more often than not deriving their impetus from the activities of minority pressure groups.

The business lawyer's predicament is aggravated by the very general provisions and vague content of the antitrust laws. It does not help, obviously, that the different statutes seem to conflict with one another. Thus the Sherman and the Clayton Acts were designed to keep competition vigorous, while the Robinson-Patman and Miller-Tydings Acts, for example, were designed to lessen or soften competition by making business life easier for the individual competitor. Numerous writers have commented on the conflicting theories behind our antitrust legislation,[3] and even the Supreme Court has referred to it within the last month.[4]

---

[1] An address delivered February 7, 1951, under the auspices of the Executive Program Club in association with the University of Chicago.

[2] General counsel, Standard Oil Company (Indiana).

[3] The best treatment of this subject and summary of the literature on this conflict in our laws is found in *Geographic Pricing Practices—Basing Point Selling* by William Simon (Chicago: Callaghan & Company, 1950), particularly Chapter IV, "Protecting Competition vs. Protecting Competitors."

[4] The apparent divergence between the Sherman Act and the Robinson-Patman Act received recent comment from the Supreme Court in Standard Oil Company (Indiana) v. Federal Trade Commission, decided January 8, 1951.

Before attempting to discuss the new and significant cases, let me describe briefly the principal antitrust laws. Thereafter I shall review the recent decisions in order to bring out what, to my mind, are two dominant trends in the law:

First, is the disposition to attack big business blindly. The tendency is to protect the individual small competitor, without regard for his efficiency, against the hazards of competition, rather than to preserve and to protect competition and the competitive system as such.

Second, but not mutually exclusive, is the tendency to condemn various types of competitive conduct automatically as a matter of law. This process involves the elimination of any investigation into the facts to determine whether the broad prohibitions of the law have in fact been offended and whether competition has actually been hindered.

THE STATUTES

THE SHERMAN ACT

In taking up the statutes, first and foremost is the Sherman Act. Section 1 declares unlawful "Every contract, combination in the form of trust or otherwise, or conspiracy in restraint of trade or commerce." Section 2 condemns "every person who shall monopolize, or attempt to monopolize, or combine or conspire with any other person to monopolize any part of interstate commerce."

There has been no single moment from the day that the Sherman Act became law back in 1890, that its precise meaning and scope, even contemporaneously, could be stated with any degree of assurance. Apparently this basic antitrust law was written in general terms so that its broad principles might be applied by the courts to fit a great variety of situations

which might arise.[5] The language of the Act, as a matter of fact, falls so far short of conveying any readily comprehensible meaning that it is usually ignored by the courts.[6]

It was not until the Sherman Act had been on the books for twenty years that there was finally resolved the controversy as to whether Section 1 was to be read literally, so as to condemn *every* agreement or understanding among competitors, or whether the so-called "rule of reason" was to be applied. In 1911, in the famous cases in which the Supreme Court ordered the dissolution of the old Standard Oil trust[7] and the Tobacco trust,[8] the view finally prevailed that only "unreasonable" restraints upon competition fell within the ban of the statute—i.e., that the "rule of reason" is implicit in the Sherman Act.

The critical questions the courts must answer in applying the rule of reason are: What is the real nature of the transaction complained of? What effect has the

[5] As Chief Justice Hughes said, the broad terms of the Sherman Act have "... a generality and adaptability comparable to that found to be desirable in constitutional provisions." Appalachian Coals Inc. v. United States, 288 U.S. 344, 360 (1933); Sugar Institute v. United States, 297 U.S. 553, 600 (1936).

[6] As Mr. Justice Stone observed: "In consequence of the vagueness of its language, perhaps not uncalculated, the courts have been left to give content to the statute. . . ." Apex Hosiery Co. v. Leader, 310 U.S. 469, 489 (1940).

More recently Mr. Justice Reed expressed the same thought when he said: ". . . the courts have been given by Congress wide powers in monopoly regulation. The very broadness of terms such as restraint of trade, substantial competition and purpose to monopolize have placed upon courts the responsibility to apply the Sherman Act so as to avoid the evils at which Congress aimed." United States v. Columbia Steel Co., 334 U.S. 495, 526 (1948).

[7] Standard Oil Company of New Jersey v. United States, 221 U.S. 1, 60 (1911).

[8] United States v. American Tobacco Company, 221 U.S. 106 (1911).

challenged activity upon competitive conditions? Careful analysis of the probable or actual economic consequences is called for. Only by looking at the end result of the particular practice is it possible to determine whether competition was unreasonably restrained.[9]

THE CLAYTON AND FEDERAL TRADE COMMISSION ACTS

The Clayton Act became law in 1914 under President Wilson.[10] It was aimed at specific competitive practices so as to bar, in their incipiency, those activities which were deemed to have been utilized to eliminate competition and aid monopoly.[11]

Thus the Clayton Act forbade price discrimination (Section 2), tying clauses, full line forcing and exclusive dealing (Section 3), the acquisition of the capital stock of a competitor (Section 7), and interlocking directorates among compet-

ing firms (Section 8). If some of these statutory phrases are not fully understood at the moment, I am sure they will become clear as we discuss the cases. However, these practices were barred only where it could be shown that "the effect may be to substantially lessen competition or tend to create a monopoly."

This qualifying language was originally regarded as importing the "rule of reason" into the Clayton Act, leaving the courts to judge, in the individual case, whether under all of the circumstances the practice complained of probably[12] would have the evil effects at which the law was aimed.[13]

The Federal Trade Commission Act, passed simultaneously with the Clayton Act, contained a broad prohibition against "unfair methods of competition."[14]

THE ROBINSON-PATMAN ACT

The Robinson-Patman Act, although treated often as a separate statute, is in fact an amendment to Section 2 of the Clayton Act. It is designed to deal more comprehensively than the original law with price discriminations that injure competition.

---

[9] The substance of the "rule of reason" was probably best set forth in Mr. Justice Brandeis' well-known dictum in the Chicago Board of Trade case, where he stated:

". . . But the legality of an agreement or regulation cannot be determined by so simple a test, as whether it restrains competition. Every agreement concerning trade, every regulation of trade, restrains. To bind, to restrain, is of their very essence. The true test of legality is whether the restraint imposed is such as merely regulates and perhaps thereby promotes competition or whether it is such as may suppress or even destroy competition. To determine that question the court must ordinarily consider the facts peculiar to the business to which the restraint is applied; its condition before and after the restraint was imposed; the nature of the restraint and its effect, actual or probable. The history of the restraint, the evil believed to exist, the reason for adopting the particular remedy, the purpose or end sought to be attained, are all relevant facts." Chicago Board of Trade v. United States, 246 U.S. 231, 238 (1918).

[10] The exoneration of United Shoe Machinery Company, under the Sherman Act, furnished some of the inducement for the passage of the Clayton Act. United States v. United Shoe Machinery Co., 247 U.S. 32 (1918).

[11] United Shoe Machinery Corporation v. United States, 258 U.S. 451 (1922).

[12] In the Morton Salt case the court indicated that the "possibility" of injury to competition is the test under the Robinson-Patman Act. It is obvious that the change of one word (from "probable" to "possible") can have far-reaching significance. Federal Trade Commission v. Morton Salt Co., 334 U.S. 37 (1948).

[13] See case(s) cited *infra*, note 19.

[14] By employing the phrase "unfair methods of competition" in place of the narrower term "unfair competition," Congress advisedly adopted a phrase that does not "admit of precise definition, but the meaning and application of which must be arrived at by . . . 'the gradual process of judicial inclusion and exclusion.' " Federal Trade Commission v. R. F. Keppel & Bro., Inc., 291 U.S. 304, 312 (1934). The Wheeler-Lea Amendment of 1938 extended the jurisdiction of the Trade Commission under the Trade Commission Act to include unfair or deceptive acts or practices, as well as unfair methods of competition.

Those are the principal statutes. In discussing recent developments in the interpretation of these laws, it will facilitate matters if the discussion is divided under four general headings: (1) the abandonment of the rule of reason and the substitution in its place of the doctrine of illegality *per se* (that is to say, automatic illegality); (2) the development of the doctrine of implied conspiracy; (3) the development of the doctrine that a corporation may conspire with its own subsidiary company (or affiliated company), and possibly may conspire with itself (i.e., with its own officers); and (4) brief reference to a variety of strange developments under the Robinson-Patman Act.

Adequate consideration of any one of these topics could require more time than is allotted to me altogether, as I am sure you will appreciate. Of necessity, I shall paint in broad strokes and endeavor to depict the broad legal trends.

I. ILLEGALITY PER SE

After 1911 the "rule of reason" was an integral part of our Antitrust Laws, and only those activities which unreasonably restrained competition or tended toward a monopoly were condemned by the courts. The recent trend in the law has been dominated by the tendency to restrict the scope of the rule of reason under both the Sherman and the Clayton Acts, and to hold competitive practices illegal in and of themselves, without permitting any investigation to determine whether real harm has been done to the competitive system. Many practices are now held to be "illegal *per se*," which means that they are held to be illegal automatically, regardless of whether it could be shown, by the evidence, that the purposes of the law were in no way thwarted.

The illegality *per se* doctrine is directly opposed to the rule of reason. Under the rule of reason, as stated earlier, there must be careful inquiry and analysis as to all of the facts and circumstances to determine whether the challenged practice actually involves the evils at which the law is aimed. Under the *per se* doctrine, a conclusive presumption prevails that the practice in question has consequences prohibited by the statute, and evidence to the contrary will not be accepted.

The type of practice first held to be illegal *per se* was price fixing.[15] No defense by way of justification can be offered to a charge that competitors have agreed among themselves on prices.[16]

Boycotting is another practice which is held to be illegal *per se*. Thus, an agreement among competitors not to deal with a particular buyer or seller is automatically condemned.[17] It may well be argued that no combination of sellers or buyers should under any circumstances be permitted to sit in judgment on the practices of anyone. On the other hand, as long as the justification for their conduct would always be open to full judi-

---

[15] United States v. Trenton Potteries Co., 273 U.S. 392, 398 (1927).

[16] This ruling has been extended to include any "tampering" with the price structure by two or more competitors acting together. "Any combination which tampers with price structures is engaged in an unlawful activity." United States v. Socony-Vacuum Oil Co., 310 U.S. 150, 221 (1940). See also Kiefer-Stewart Co. v. Seagram & Sons, Inc., United States Supreme Court, decided Jan. 2, 1951 (fixing maximum resale prices held illegal *per se*).

[17] ". . . Under these circumstances it was not in error to refuse to hear the evidence offered, for the reasonableness of the methods pursued by the combination to accomplish its unlawful object is no more material than would be the reasonableness of the prices fixed by unlawful combination." Fashion Originators' Guild v. Federal Trade Commission, 312 U.S. 457, 468 (1941). See also Eastern States Retail Lumber Dealers' Association v. United States, 234 U.S. 600 (1914).

cial scrutiny under the rule of reason, it can certainly be argued that some activity coming under the heading of —>"boycotting" is not only justified, but even affirmatively in the public interest. For example, suppose that some automobile dealers pursued the practice of substituting inferior parts in new automobiles in order to remove and resell the original parts at a substantial profit. If the automobile companies formed an organization to police this type of activity in order to protect the public, I for one could see no harm in such an organization. Under the *per se* doctrine, however, such activity would be held to be automatically illegal.

Recently the *per se* doctrine has been extended into more controversial fields. The International Salt Company sold an automatic dispenser of salt tablets and required its customers to buy their supplies of salt tablets for use in this dispenser from the company. This "tying" together of the sale of a dispensing machine with the sale of salt tablets is, of course, a "tie-in" sale within the meaning of the Clayton Act. Section 3 of that Act makes tie-in sales illegal but—and this is important—*only* "where the effect . . . may be to substantially lessen competition or tend to create a monopoly. . . ." The Salt Company was held guilty by the Supreme Court of violating Section 3, although its total sales of salt through this device were so small that it is difficult to believe that there was any substantial effect on competition.[18] Previously, the effects of such a "tying clause" would have been studied carefully by the court, and, in the absence of affirmative proof of any unreasonable lessening of competition, no violation of the law would have been found.[19] In the

Salt case, however, the tie-in sale of the dispenser and the salt was held to be illegal regardless of any proof that competition in the salt industry was affected in any substantial way.[20] The principle was enunciated that it was unreasonable *per se* to foreclose competitors from any market of significant size.

So-called "exclusive dealing" arrangements are very common in the business world. Retail stores of all kinds often carry one brand or one line exclusively. We can all think of examples, whether it be shirts, suits, electrical devices, etc. Other competing retailers will carry another line of merchandise made by a competing manufacturer. The same is usually true in the gasoline business—the retail dealers find it a good business practice to carry only one brand of gasoline and usually the same line of oils, greases, etc. On the West Coast some "exclusive dealing" arrangements in petroleum supplies were made a matter of contract between the supplier and the retail gasoline dealer. However, in June 1949, such "exclusive dealing" contracts were held to be illegal *per se*, in a case involving the Standard Oil Company of California.[21]

[18] International Salt Company v. United States, 332 U.S. 392 (1947).

[19] Standard Fashion Company v. Magrane-Houston Company, 258 U.S. 346 (1922); International Business Machines Corp. v. United States, 298 U.S. 131, 136 (1936); Federal Trade Commission v. Sinclair Refining Company, 261 U.S. 463 (1923); Pick Manufacturing Company v. General Motors Corporation, 299 U.S. 3 (1936); Federal Trade Commission v. Curtis Publishing Company, 260 U.S. 568 (1923). Compare: Federal Trade Commission v. Gratz, 253 U.S. 421 (1920); Compare also: International Shoe Co. v. The Federal Trade Commission, 280 U.S. 291 (1930).

[20] "It was not established that equivalent machines were unobtainable, it was not indicated what proportion of the business of supplying such machines was controlled by [the] defendant, and it was deemed irrelevant that there was no evidence as to the actual effect of the tying clauses upon competition." Standard Oil Company v. United States, 337 U.S. 293, 305 (1949).

[21] Standard Oil Company v. United States, 337 U.S. 293 (1949).

That company's sales to independent dealers under these exclusive dealing contracts comprised less than 7 per cent of the gasoline sales on the West Coast, so that it could hardly be claimed that the practice tended to create a monopoly. But what is important here is that the company wanted to show that its exclusive dealing contracts did not in fact restrict competition. However, such evidence was rejected by the court as immaterial.

The Supreme Court decided in this case that exclusive dealing contracts are automatically illegal, without making any inquiry into the economic consequences of the practice. In so doing, the court stated as a principal reason that courts are ill-suited for determining the economic consequences of practices such as exclusive dealing. If mere difficulty in passing upon the economic consequences of competitive practices is justification for holding them automatically illegal, we have a situation that suggests the story of a judge in a frontier community who insisted that the accused prisoner receive a "fair trial." However, this judge saw no reason for delaying the execution of the death sentence until the end of the trial. The difference in our exclusive dealing case is this: A fair trial is dispensed with altogether, and the defendant is held guilty as a matter of law.[22]

Interestingly enough Mr. Justice Douglas, in his dissent in this Standard of California case, predicted that the outlawing of exclusive dealing con-

tracts would encourage the oil companies to take over the retail operations themselves, and thus eliminate many small businessmen. Douglas was firmly convinced that the court's decision outlawing these contracts would lead to monopoly. Mr. Justice Frankfurter, writing for the majority, was equally firmly convinced that exclusive dealing is harmful per se. In view of the sharp divergence of opinion between members of the Supreme Court as to what the actual consequences of the challenged activity might be, it is all the more startling for the court to refuse to permit any inquiry whatever into the real consequences of exclusive dealing.[23]

If proof of economic consequences is unnecessary under the Clayton Act, why should not the doctrine of illegality per se be further extended under the Sherman Act? Needless to say, the Department of Justice has not overlooked this possibility. In the recent motion picture dissolution case, which has resulted in the divorcement of motion picture produc-

[22] In a recent District Court case, where the trial judge permitted testimony on the effect of exclusive dealing contracts in the tin can industry, he refused to ban exclusive dealing contracts of no greater duration than one year. United States v. American Can Co., 87 F. Supp. 18, 32 (N.D. Calif. 1949); cf. Federal Trade Commission Order re Motion Picture Advertising Service Co., Inc., CCH Trade Regulation Service, Vol. 3, para. 14.503.

[23] The full impact of the court's decision is demonstrated by the dissenting opinion of Mr. Justice Jackson, stating, in part (337 U.S. 293, 321, 322 (1949)): ". . . the only possible way for the courts to arrive at a fair determination is to hear all relevant evidence from both parties and weigh not only its inherent probabilities of verity but also compare the experience, disinterestedness and credibility of opposing witnesses. This is a tedious process and not too enlightening, but without it a judicial decree is but a guess in the dark. That is all we have here and I do not think it is an adequate basis on which to upset long-standing and widely practiced business arrangements."

See also, M. A. Adelman, Address before National Petroleum Association, April 13, 1950: "Economists' interest in requirements contracts is: How do they affect competition? Do they make it stronger or weaker—on prices or service or anything else? Do they make for greater or lesser efficiency in gasoline distribution? For them, accordingly, by far the most important thing about the Standard of California case was that these issues were clearly seen and consciously thrust aside."

tion from theatre ownership, the Justice Department strongly urged that the vertical integration of the defendants should be held to be illegal *per se*.[24] The court, while it did not rule out the possibility for future cases, found it unnecessary to apply this doctrine in that particular case in order to decide for the Government.

In the *Columbia Steel* case,[25] which involved the acquisition by a subsidiary of the United States Steel Corporation of the assets of the Consolidated Steel Company on the West Coast, only one vote on the Supreme Court prevented a holding that, due to the size of the U.S. Steel Corporation, the acquisition in question was illegal *per se*. A bare majority of the Supreme Court, applying the rule of reason, held that this acquisition of Consolidated "seems to reflect a normal business purpose rather than a scheme to circumvent the law." 334 U.S. 495, 533.

That size, in and of itself, did not violate the law was first decided in the original *Steel* case in 1920.[26] Later this rule was somewhat qualified by Mr. Justice Cardozo in the *Swift* case,[27] when he held that "size carries with it an opportunity for abuse that is not to be ignored when the opportunity is proved to have been utilized in the past." In the more recent

Tobacco case[28] Mr. Justice Burton, instead of referring to "mere size," used the term "power to exclude competition," and held that possession of this power is itself a violation of Section 2 of the Sherman Act, "provided that it is coupled with the purpose or intent to exercise that power."[29] And in the *Aluminum* case, although the possession by Alcoa of 90 per cent of the aluminum ingot production was held by Judge Learned Hand not to prove a violation of Section 2 of the Sherman Act by itself, the extra element required to prove an offense, over and above mere size, was provided by the fact that Alcoa had progressively embraced each new opportunity that it found to fortify its dominant position. In other words, Alcoa was not content to sit tight and stagnate—it continued to grow, taking every normal opportunity to expand its business, but in the process did not resort to unlawful practices at any time.[30] Nevertheless,

---

[24] United States v. Paramount Pictures, Inc., 334 U.S. 131 (1948). Referring to this case, Mr. Justice Douglas subsequently remarked that "a majority of the court could not be obtained for holding illegal *per se* the vertical integration in the motion picture industry." Standard Oil Company v. United States, 337 U.S. 293, 315 (1949), Mr. Justice Douglas, dissenting, footnote, p. 318.

[25] United States v. Columbia Steel Company, 334 U.S. 495 (1948).

[26] United States v. United States Steel Corporation, 251 U.S. 417, 451 (1920); United States v. International Harvester Company, 274 U.S. 693, 708 (1927).

[27] United States v. Swift & Company, 286 U.S. 106, 116 (1932).

[28] American Tobacco Company v. United States, 328 U.S. 781 (1946). In United States v. Griffith, 334 U.S. 100, 107 (1948), Mr. Justice Douglas reiterated his view that monopoly power, however acquired, may stand condemned under Section 2 of the Sherman Act even though it remains unexercised. See, also, United States v. Paramount Pictures, Inc., 334 U.S. 131, 174 (1948), where size is referred to as "... an earmark of monopoly power. For size carries with it an opportunity for abuse."

[29] See Rostow, *Monopoly under the Sherman Act: Power or Purpose?* 43 Ill. L. Rev. 745, 770–776 (1949).

[30] "... It insists that it never excluded competitors; but we can think of no more effective exclusion than progressively to embrace each new opportunity as it opened, and to face every newcomer with new capacity already geared into a great organization, having the advantage of experience, trade connections and the elite of personnel. Only if we interpret 'exclusion' as limited to maneuvers not honestly industrial, actuated solely by a desire to prevent competition, can such a course indefatigably pursued, be deemed not 'exclusionary.'" United States v. Aluminum Co. of America, 148 F. 2d 416, 431 (2nd Cir. 1945).

Alcoa was found to have violated the law.

So the situation as of today is that mere size is not yet illegal *per se*.[31] However, less and less is required, in addition to proof of mere size, to constitute a violation of the Sherman Act.

Recently the President has signed a bill[32] extending Section 7 of the Clayton Act to cover acquisitions of assets as well as acquisitions of capital stock. With the legislative history indicating a Congressional purpose to overrule the *Columbia Steel* case, there now exists a new vehicle for gaining majority support in the Supreme Court for the doctrine that any acquisition of a competitor is illegal *per se*. The significance of the amendment to Section 7 is demonstrated by the experience of the Minnesota Mining and Manufacturing Company just a few weeks ago. That company felt compelled to abandon its plans for the acquisition of the assets of another company, solely on account of the passage of the bill referred to, although the proposed acquisition had been considered entirely lawful under the pre-existing law because it had no actual adverse effect on competition.[33]

We can certainly conclude that, as far as the Clayton Act is concerned, it is abundantly clear that the rule of reason is being displaced by the doctrine of illegality *per se*. Under the Sherman Act, the pressure further to restrict the application of the rule of reason is unremitting. For the moment, a bare majority of the court has declined to apply the illegality *per se* doctrine to corporate integration, merger cases, or cases involving charges of undue economic concentration. But we must not forget that if the minority on the Supreme Court had been able to muster one additional vote—then the corporate integration in the motion picture cases and the acquisition involved in the *Columbia Steel* case might have been held to be illegal *per se* under the Sherman Act.

2. IMPLIED CONSPIRACY

You will recall that the Sherman Act makes unlawful a *conspiracy* in restraint of trade. Accordingly, the term "conspiracy" is an important one in the antitrust field. Originally and until recently it meant just what the word implies: i.e., actual agreement or understanding among competitors to accomplish what the law forbade. Uniform conduct of competitors was not unlawful unless it could be proved that the uniformity resulted from actual agreement, and not simply from action based upon the enlightened self-interest of the individual participants. Thus the practice of competitors in following the prices of a so-called "price leader" in an industry was held to be entirely innocent, and formerly met with the Supreme Court's express approval.[34] That all competitors followed the same system of pricing—even the following of a basing-point system— was formerly not considered, in and of itself, to prove conspiracy where there was no evidence that the various competitors did so by actual agreement.[35]

[31] Address of Assistant Attorney General Bergson, *Bigness in Business*, before the New York State Bar Association, January 25, 1950. See: A New Look at Antitrust Enforcement Trends, Antitrust Law Symposium—1950 Edition, CCH, March 20, 1950, p. 85.

See also United States v. National Lead Company, 332 U.S. 319 (1947).

[32] Public Law 899, 81st Cong., 2nd Sess. (1950).

[33] 96 Cong. Rec. 16667–8 (Dec. 13, 1950); N.Y. Times, Dec. 30, 1950.

[34] United States v. United States Steel Corporation, 251 U.S. 417, 448 (1920); United States v. International Harvester Co., 274 U.S. 693, 708 (1927).

[35] Cement Mfrs. Protective Assn. v. United States, 268 U.S. 588 (1925); Maple Flooring Mfgrs. Assn. v. United States, 268 U.S. 563 (1925).

CHANGING LEGAL CONCEPTS   243

Currently, however, conspiracy is inferred, or presumed, simply on the ground that all the circumstances are consistent with its existence.[36] As stated by an eminent economist,[37]

"... The courts have certainly gone a long way in accepting various kinds of market behavior as evidence of a conspiracy among firms; so far, indeed, that it seems appropriate to inquire whether market behavior rather than conspiracy has not become the test of illegality."

The time was when a lawyer could safely advise his client that if the client had not consulted or agreed with his competitors he could not be charged with having conspired to restrain trade. Today a seller may be held guilty of conspiracy to fix prices even though he had no communication or understanding whatsoever with any of his competitors.[38]

Out of the whole cloth, the courts fabricate this theory: The conduct of one seller may, under some circumstances, be construed as an "invitation" to its competitors to follow its practice. If competitors in fact do follow similar practices—for example, have the same pricing policy announced by one of their number—then that fact can be construed to be an "acceptance" of the original "invitation" and the consummation of a conspiracy for which all can be convicted. As stated by the Supreme Court, "Acceptance by competitors, without previous agreement, of an invitation to participate in a plan the necessary con-

sequences of which, if carried out, is restraint of interstate commerce, is sufficient to establish an unlawful conspiracy under the Sherman Act."[39]

When "implied conspiracy" means actual conspiracy proved by circumstantial evidence, there can be no objection, because circumstantial proof has universal acceptance in the law. When, however, conspiracy is judicially inferred, in the absence of any evidence of agreement or understanding, merely on the ground that the state of competition is said to be substantially such as might prevail under a conspiracy, then something other than conspiracy has been made the offense. For example, consider this paradox: Any businessman knows that competition, itself, often drives competing concerns to identical prices in the same area, particularly for a homogeneous product. However, these competitors, whose actions might be only those which a prudent man would adopt, run the risk of being charged with conspiracy to violate the law. The first seller, depending upon the method employed to announce the new price, may be held, by the mere announcement, to have invited others to charge the same price. And when they do charge a similar price, they may be guilty of implied conspiracy.

There is another development along the same line. The Federal Trade Commission has coined the phrase "conscious parallelism of action," which is cleverly designed to make non-conspiratorial conduct take on an air of willful concert of action. On the theory that most people are in favor of virtue and are against sin, the battle is half won if a practice being attacked can be tagged with a label which makes it sound sinful. In the

[36] See Interstate Circuit, Inc. v. United States, 306 U.S. 208 (1939); United States v. Masonite Corp., 316 U.S. 265 (1942); American Tobacco Co. v. United States, 328 U.S. 781 (1946).

[37] Mason, *The Current Status of the Monopoly Problem in the United States*, 62 Harv. L. Rev. 1265, 1277 (1949).

[38] United States v. Masonite Corporation, 316 U.S. 265 (1942).

[39] Interstate Circuit v. United States, 306 U.S. 208, 227 (1939).

Rigid Conduit case,[40] there were four-teen corporate defendants before the Federal Trade Commission. Two of the fourteen were acquitted under the first count of a complaint which charged a conspiracy to maintain uniform prices; but, on the same evidence, these same two were held guilty under the second count, which rested on mere "conscious parallelism": i.e., the individual use of a pricing system, with knowledge that other sellers also used it. The Court of Appeals held, in effect, that these two defendants were guilty of conspiracy when, admittedly, they had not in fact conspired or attempted to do so. Star-tling as the proposition may seem, on the appeal of this case the Supreme Court was evenly divided (4 to 4), thus affirm-ing the lower court but preventing an authoritative determination.[41] No opin-ions are written under such circum-stances, so that we have no clue to the thinking of any members of the Supreme Court.[42]

It must be clear, even from this brief review, that businessmen and lawyers must revise their concept of a "con-spiracy" under the Sherman Act. When the business practice under consideration is a type that might be considered offen-sive under the antitrust laws *if* accom-plished by conspiracy, it is increasingly likely that conspiracy will be inferred, or

will be held to exist legally if not actually —or the need for proving conspiracy will be dispensed with altogether.[43] While we have not reached the point where mere uniformity, without more, is deemed to be conspiracy, certainly proof of conspiracy in the old-fashioned sense has been largely done away with.[44]

3. CONSPIRACY WITHIN A CORPORATE ORGANIZATION

Closely related to the tendency to dis-pense with proof of conspiracy, even under a law making conspiracy the es-sence of the charge, is the increasing trend toward elimination of any need to show conspiracy—by holding, as a mat-ter of law, that corporate activity is con-spiratorial in its nature. Corporate action necessarily involves the joint action of the corporate personality and at least one officer; from these elements a con-spiracy may be found to exist.

Let me hasten to say that no case has

[40] Triangle Conduit & Cable Co. v. Federal Trade Commission, 168 F. 2d 175 (7th Cir. 1948), *affirmed* (by an equally divided court), *sub nomine* Clayton Mark & Co. v. Federal Trade Commission, 336 U.S. 956 (1949).

[41] The doctrine of "conscious parallelism," once established, can be pushed to absurd length. Com-pare Milgram v. Loew's, Inc., CCH Trade Reg. Serv., para. 62,733 (E.D. Pa. 1950), where the court held that there was similarity of business practices (individual distributors refused to license first run films to a drive-in theatre) such as to con-stitute an actionable "conspiracy," notwithstand-ing that the proof was that each distributor indi-vidually thought his course of action would be the more profitable to him and acted accordingly.

[42] Furthermore, no matter how this question may be finally resolved under the Clayton and Sher-man Acts, the Federal Trade Commission is free to resort to Section 5 of the Federal Trade Com-mission Act when it decides to condemn competitive activity, although actual agreement or understand-ing cannot be proved. A dictum of Mr. Justice Black in the *Cement* case is that "existence of a 'combina-tion' is not an indispensable ingredient of an 'un-fair method of competition.'" Federal Trade Com-mission v. Cement Institute, 333 U.S. 683 (1948), footnote at page 721, citing Federal Trade Com-mission v. Beech-Nut Packing Co., 257 U.S. 441, 455 (1922). Apparently, the Commission need only conclude that the conduct of the parties has an aroma of conspiracy, in order to issue a cease and desist order.

[43] Note the startling comment in the Preliminary Report of Select Committee on Small Business on Antitrust Law Enforcement, H.R. Rep. No. 3236; 81st Cong., 2nd Sess. 35 (1951):
"... the growing difficulty of getting data on conspiracy, may well force the [Federal Trade] Commission to make illegality turn on the existence of trade-restraining effects, without the allegation of conspiracy."

[44] Compare Mr. Justice Jackson, concurring in Krulewitch v. United States, 336 U.S. 440, 445, 451–452 (1949).

yet held that every corporate act amounts to a conspiracy. But, as recently as January 2nd of this year, a unanimous Supreme Court found a corporation and its wholly-owned subsidiary guilty of conspiring with each other, because they simultaneously refused to sell to a customer which failed to maintain suggested resale prices. The court stated, expressly, that the two companies (parent and subsidiary), acting individually, might lawfully have refused to deal with the customer.[45]

In the *General Motors* case,[46] the automobile company had a wholly-owned subsidiary engaged in the automobile finance business. General Motors was held guilty of conspiring with this wholly-owned subsidiary to require its dealers to do their financing through this subsidiary. In the *Yellow Cab* case,[47] where a group of companies under common control were alleged to have conspired to restrain trade, the court sustained the charge with the statement that "The test of illegality under the Act is the presence or absence of an unreasonable restraint on interstate commerce. . . . The corporate interrelationships of the conspirators . . . are not determinative of the applicability of the Sherman Act." 332 U.S. 218, 227.

In other words, even though the Sherman Act makes the existence of a conspiracy the essence of the wrong, it is not important to consider first whether there is or is not a combination or conspiracy.

The important question is this: Would the transaction be abhorrent to the law *if* accomplished by conspiracy? When the answer to that question is in the affirmative, then the court by-passes the statute and holds that the affiliated companies and their officers are "deemed" to have conspired, although there is no actual conspiracy.[48] Without doubt, even a single corporation can be guilty of conspiring with its own officers on this theory.[49] Senator Sherman, if he were alive today, would be amazed at the current interpretation of the statute which bears his name.

We have discussed the tendency, under the Sherman and Clayton Acts, to hold various practices and transactions to be automatically illegal and to bar proof of actual economic consequences. Thereafter we examined the tendency to forego proof of conspiracy, even in cases where conspiracy is the essence of the charge, and to condemn certain types of conduct as amounting to a conspiracy despite the absence of any proof of actual conspiracy.

I turn next to the consideration of a few of the many remarkable developments under the Robinson-Patman Act.

4. TRENDS UNDER THE ROBINSON-PATMAN ACT

The sale of a commodity at two different prices to two different purchasers constitutes a "price discrimination" under the Robinson-Patman Act.[50] Sales to different customers at different prices are very familiar in the business world.

[45] Kiefer-Stewart Co. v. Seagram & Sons, Inc., CCH Trade Reg. Serv., para. 62,737 (U.S. Jan. 2, 1951). The court stated that the rule that affiliated companies can be guilty of conspiracy to violate the antitrust laws was especially applicable in this case because the companies involved had held themselves out as competitors.

[46] United States v. General Motors Corp., 121 F. 2d 376 (7th Cir. 1941), *cert. denied*, 314 U.S. 618 (1941).

[47] United States v. Yellow Cab Co., 332 U.S. 218 (1947).

[48] In addition to the cases mentioned, see also Schine Chain Theatres v. United States, 334 U.S. 110 (1948).

[49] See Note, "Are Two or More Persons Necessary to Have a Conspiracy under Section 1 of the Sherman Act?" 43 Ill. L. Rev. 551 (1948).

[50] Sec. 2 Clayton Act, 38 Stat. 730; 15 U.S.C. 12 ff.; Public, No. 212, 63d Cong. (1914) as amended by Robinson-Patman Act, 49 Stat. 1526; 15 U.S.C. 13; Public, No. 692, 74th Cong. (1936).

There are a variety of reasons for this, including traditional quantity discount schedules, long-term supply contracts which keep prices from fluctuating with day-to-day quotations, etc. The Robinson-Patman Act prohibits price discriminations however, *only* "where the effect . . . may be substantially to lessen competition or tend to create a monopoly. . . ." It therefore becomes important to know under what circumstances the courts will decide that a price discrimination has caused the statutory injury to competition.

In the recent *Morton Salt* case,[51] involving a charge of price discrimination, the essential "injury to competition" was found to exist although no effort was made to prove actual injury to competition and where the evidence simply showed that one of two competing customers was charged a slightly higher price than the other. The Salt Company charged $1.60 per case if the purchase was less than a carload quantity. For carload purchases the price per case was $1.50—a quantity discount of 10 cents per case. Of all of Morton's customers, $99\frac{9}{10}$ per cent were able to buy in carload quantities, and only one-tenth of 1 per cent had to buy in less than the carload quantities. With the discount so small in proportion to the price of the product, and with salt itself such a small item in most wholesale and retail businesses, and with only one-tenth of 1 per cent of Morton's business not receiving the benefit of the carload discount, the dissenting opinion points out that it was ". . . farfetched even to find it reasonably *possible* that competition would be *substantially* affected." 334 U.S. 37, 60–61. Nevertheless, the majority of the court held that the carload discount was

a violation of the Robinson-Patman Act.

The *Morton Salt* case is significant for two reasons. First, because another type of illegality *per se* is suggested. Once again a rule-of-thumb is adopted which eliminates the need for proof of actual harmful consequences. No real injury need be shown, in the sense of injury which will lessen competition generally, or even the ability of a particular seller to compete. Congress purported to outlaw only *certain* price differences—i.e., those which may be injurious to competition—nevertheless, the court holds that any difference in price automatically creates the required statutory injury[52] and, therefore, that *all* such price differences are outlawed. The court has certainly amended the statute in this respect! Under such a test it would not matter that the customer paying the higher price prospered and expanded his business, while the one receiving the lower price went bankrupt. Theoretically, the prosperous buyer could sue the bankrupt one for treble damages!

Of equally great significance is the obvious confusion in the *Morton Salt* case between "injury to competition" and "injury to a competitor." The fact that an individual competitor is adversely affected by some transaction does not indicate that competition or the competitive system has been endangered. A recent report of a Congressional Committee,[53] adopted by both Houses, makes this point very clear in the following language:

"Competition is a contest between sellers for the business of a buyer. In such a contest one seller gets the order while other sellers lose the

---

[51] Federal Trade Commission v. Morton Salt Co., 334 U.S. 37 (1948).

[52] See also Elizabeth Arden Sales Corp. v. Gus Blass, 150 F. 2d 988 (8th Cir. 1945), *cert. denied*, 326 U.S. 773 (1945).

[53] Conf. Rep. on Sen. Bill 1008, H.R. Rep. No. 1422, 81st Cong., pp. 5, 6; Simon, *Geographic Pricing Practices—Basing-Point Selling, infra*, p. 94.

order. That is competition. The seller who did not get the order may feel injured, but that does not mean that competition has been injured. In any competitive economy we cannot avoid injury to some of the competitors. The law does not, and under the free enterprise system it cannot, guarantee businessmen against loss. That businessmen lose money or even go bankrupt does not necessarily mean that competition has been injured. 'Competition,' Mr. Justice Holmes observed, 'is worth what it costs.'

We must always distinguish between injury to competition and injury to a competitor. To promote and protect competition is the primary function of the antitrust laws. However, we cannot guarantee competitors against all injury. This can only be accomplished by prohibiting competition."

Yet in the *Morton Salt* case, the court seemed to concern itself exclusively with whether an individual customer of Morton Salt might have been injured. Whether competition in the Salt business was actually affected, was not considered. The contrary would seem to be evident from the few facts that I have stated.

The confusion between "injury to a competitor" and "injury to competition" is further exemplified in a Robinson-Patman case involving my own company which was recently decided by the Supreme Court. In *Standard Oil Company* v. *Federal Trade Commission*,[54] the Supreme Court, by a narrow margin, reversed a Court of Appeals decision which would have made injury to a competitor the test of whether it was a de-

fense to a charge of "price discrimination" to prove that the lower price was quoted in good faith to meet a competitor's lower price.

Involved in the case were these facts: Standard sold gasoline to both jobbers and retail service station dealers in Detroit. The service station operators objected to the jobbers selling to other retail dealers at prices below Standard's price to its dealers—and also objected that these jobbers were, in some cases, making retail sales at cut prices in competition with them. Standard proved, as its defense, that these jobbers had been solicited by other suppliers, that they could have bought comparable gasoline at the same or lower prices from these other suppliers if Standard refused to meet the lower prices quoted by them. Standard relied on the express words in the statute, making the good-faith meeting of a competitor's lower price a complete defense to a charge of price discrimination. The Trade Commission rejected this defense, however, solely on the basis of its finding that some of Standard's retail dealer customers were injured.[55]

Completely overlooked by the Commission and by the Court of Appeals, which sustained its ruling, was the relationship of the matter at issue to the maintenance of a competitive system. If, because his customers may be adversely affected in their competition with others, a seller is to be prevented from competing by meeting the lower prices of his competitors, the functioning of the competitive system is thwarted. Fortu-

---

[54] Decided January 8, 1951, not yet officially reported, rev. 173 F. 2d 210 (1949). Because of space limitations, it is not possible to discuss the statutory interpretation and legislative history problems to which so much attention is given in the Court's opinion. For discussions of this case, see Adelman, *Integration and Antitrust Policy*, 63 Harv. L. Rev. 27 (1949); Berger and Goldstein, *Meeting Competition under the Robinson-Patman Act*, 44 Ill. L. Rev. 315 (1949); Austern, *Required Competitive Injury and Permitted Meeting of Competition*, Robinson-Patman Act Symposium, 1947, Commerce Clearing House, p. 63.

[55] The Commission's own summary of the testimony of the allegedly injured service-station operators was that "they lost many customers." See Adelman, *Integration and the Antitrust Laws*, 63 Harv. L. Rev. 27, 71; also Adelman, *Antitrust Upside-Down Cake and Eat It Too*, Fortune Magazine, March, 1950.

nately, however, the Supreme Court recognized the significance of this problem and held in favor of recognizing the good-faith meeting of competition. "It is enough to say," the Court stated, "that Congress did not seek by the Robinson-Patman Act either to abolish competition or so radically to curtail it that a seller would have no substantial right of self-defense against a price raid by a competitor" (p. 17).

Collateral aspects of the case just mentioned involved the legality under the Robinson-Patman Act of functional discounts and of integration. Standard was simply selling to its jobbers at a normal jobber price level. The circumstance which gave rise to the case was that the jobber-customers in question had integrated their activities by combining jobbing and retail functions. The effect of the Supreme Court's decision is that a supplier may give the usual functional discount to a jobber who engages in both jobbing and retailing, where the supplier is meeting in good faith an equally low price offered to the jobber by a competing seller. In the absence of good-faith meeting of competition, the granting of even the usual functional discount to a jobber, particularly if he has integrated operations involving both jobbing and retailing, remains of doubtful legality.

In the pending *Spark Plug* cases,[56] the staff of the Federal Trade Commission is strenuously opposing any difference in the price at which spark plugs are sold as original equipment to automobile manufacturers, on the one hand, and to wholesale suppliers of replacement plugs, on the other, unless the price difference can be justified on the basis of differences in costs of manufacturing or distributing. Despite the difference in function between the wholesaler and the consumer (car manufacturer), the Trade Commission staff is insisting that such price differences are illegal. This is a direct attack on the so-called functional discount, which has been a familiar feature of American business for many years.

SUMMARY AND GENERAL DISCUSSION

Some of these developments in the application of our Antitrust Laws seem to me to have serious implications. Some of you may have the same feeling in whole or in part. However, all is not lost as yet. By a single vote in the merger and integration cases, and virtually the same narrow margin[57] in the *Standard Oil* Robinson-Patman Act case, complete approval of the tendencies in the law to which I have adverted has thus far been avoided. But the pressure in the directions mentioned continues to be strong. A change of a single Justice on the Supreme Court could eliminate the last barriers to the fulfilment of the dreams of the antitrust prosecutors.

As I have watched these trends develop in the law, it has seemed to me that underneath the surface is a rather deep-seated suspicion of big business, which has been taken advantage of by those who want to redesign the business and industrial setup in this country. For them, and the politician as well, the attack on big business is as safe politically as a crusade against sin. As a consequence, it has not always been necessary to be entirely objective.

Also—and this is more distressing—

[56] In the matter of Champion Spark Plug Company (Docket No. 3977); In the matter of General Motors Corp., A.C. Spark Plug Company (Docket No. 3886); In the matter of Electric Auto-Lite Company (Docket No. 5624).

[57] The decision in the case was by a vote of 5 to 3, Justice Minton not participating. However, as Judge of the Court of Appeals, he wrote the opinion for that Court which the Supreme Court reversed.

there are sincere and capable economists who believe in and support many of the legal trends which I have mentioned. Outstanding among these is Mr. Corwin Edwards, who will follow me in this lecture series.

I do not pretend to be qualified to challenge Mr. Edwards in the economic field which he has made his life's work. But in reading his recent book,[58] I was especially concerned over his treatment of bigness, or what he calls "the concentration of economic power."

His analysis is replete with the manifold ways in which this power "may" or "can" be abused,[59] and he sums up with the statement that, "By use of the types of power that have been described above, a giant enterprise *can* sap the vigor and attenuate the usefulness of competition." He adds, "The power of the great concern *may* create difficulties for new competitors who wish to enter its field of activity" (p. 105).[60] There are altogether many pages of such inductive analysis of the ways in which large companies are capable of abusing their economic power.

It is not shown that large enterprises are in actuality a menace to the public or to the small businessman. On the contrary, Mr. Edwards suggests (p. 109) that "the pros and cons of big business" are "inadequately known." If so, should we not endeavor to ascertain all the facts? That would seem fair enough. However, I surmise that Mr. Edwards would be a little impatient with this question. He indicates that there is no time for further study, because, he says, "Our large enterprises are growing by accretion, and their power appears to show an increasing momentum. There is a substantial risk that, before the diagnosis of big business is completed, the independence of small enterprises will have been destroyed . . ." (*id.*).

Mr. Justice Douglas, in his dissent in the *Standard of California* case, takes up the cry: "Monopoly has flourished. Cartels have increased their hold on the nation. The trusts wax strong. There is less and less place for the independent. . . ."[61] Again, however, no documentation is offered.

I prefer Professor Adelman's approach, when he states: "But heated assertions are not proof in economics any more than they are in law. We need to learn the actual facts in each case. . . ."[62]

While Mr. Edwards reaches out to gather in all possible abuses that can or might arise from large size, I failed to

---

[58] *Maintaining Competition* (New York: McGraw-Hill Book Co., 1949).

[59] *Viz.*, "This bargaining power *can* be used to raise prices without significant reduction in volume of sales. The *inducement* to use it, etc." (p. 93); ". . . the large enterprise *may* adopt monopolistic policies . . ." (p. 94); "Strength in one market *may* be used to increase strength in another . . ." (p. 95); ". . . it *may* adopt a policy of high prices for materials and relatively low markups above these prices in its own sales of products . . ." (p. 98); ". . . the giant concern *can* deprive [small enterprises] of independent initiative and force them into a tacit vassalage" (p. 101).

[60] Cf. ". . . our consideration should be not what the corporation had power to do or did, but what it has now power to do and is doing. . . ." United States v. United States Steel Corp., 251 U.S. 417, 444 (1920).

[61] Standard Oil Co. of California v. United States, 337 U.S. 293, 318 (1949).

[62] Address before National Petroleum Association, April 13, 1950. Judge Jerome Frank admonishes that: "Those who, oversimplifying economic problems, thoughtlessly urge the elimination of virtually all monopolies, not only disregard the unavoidable existence of monopolistic elements in almost all kinds of competition but dangerously invite a program which, by neglecting socially valuable aspects of some industrial integrations ('oligopolies') in some mass production industries, might tragically reduce our living standards. Monopoly-phobia, like most phobias, is both a symptom and a cause of a neurotic tendency which, in refusing bravely to face facts, cannot yield intelligent guidance." Concurring opinion, Standard Brands v. Smidler, 151 F. 2d 34, 42 (2nd Cir. 1945).

note any substantial effort on his part to illuminate the opposite side of the coin.

No less an authority than the Secretary of Commerce assured us recently that, "The development of big business has been accompanied by growth in the size of the market and by increased competition, with the result that the relative productive share of the larger corporations is substantially less today than it was half a century ago." The facts he gives in support of this conclusion are illuminating.[63]

About a year ago Professors Lintner and Butters of the Harvard Business School faculty analyzed a report of the Federal Trade Commission on the subject of the effect of mergers on industrial concentration.[64] The Commission's report had led a member of Congress to say: "If the trend of mergers and acquisitions continues, small business will ultimately disappear as an important factor in American industry." The members of the Harvard Business School faculty indicate that their analysis of the same materials relied upon by the

Trade Commission causes them to reach "essentially the opposite conclusion." It would certainly appear that the case against big business had not been proved very conclusively.

I think we should all deprecate the practice of depicting big business as a monster and using that false image to frighten the public. There is too much at stake to permit our laws to develop on the basis of emotion or witch-hunting. If, as Mr. Edwards states, the facts are not yet known, then we should concentrate our energies upon developing them. I am hopeful that the succeeding speakers in this lecture series will find time to discuss the basic factual question of whether big business is destroying small enterprises, and whether the so-called concentration of economic power is the threat that it is sometimes claimed to be.

My own feeling is that bigness in business is quite inevitable, and is here to stay, even apart from the need for large enterprises to make available in great quantities the machines of war.[65] If we can look forward to conditions of peace, it seems to me that the preservation and continued improvement of our high standard of living is dependent to an important extent upon the mass production methods which only large enterprises make possible. As the Secretary of Commerce has said: "Much of the research, production and distribution which have made us great industrially

---

[63] Address before Minneapolis Chamber of Commerce, April 13, 1950. Mr. Sawyer stated in part (pp. 5–6):

"It is currently stated, and believed by many, that the big companies have gobbled up practically all of the little companies. The fact is that between 1940 and 1947 all corporations in the country with assets over $100,000,000 added only 2.1 percent by the acquisition of other businesses. Their share of total assets acquired during this period amounted to 0.8 percent of all industrial assets. Many of the big companies have grown, to be sure, but the large part of this growth has come from retained earnings and new financing.

"Furthermore, whereas in 1900 there were approximately 21 business firms for each one thousand persons, in 1949—after all the gobbling up of the little firms was supposed to have taken place—there were 26 business firms per thousand people."

[64] Lintner and Butters, *Effect of Mergers on Industrial Concentration, 1940–1947.* "The Review of Economics and Statistics," February, 1950.

[65] See the recent advertisement of N. W. Ayer, Inc., Saturday Evening Post, November 11, 1950: "Who, other than Stalin, believes American business is too big—now?"

"Not only is bigness here to stay, but bigness—including big business, big unions and big government—is both essential and inevitable in a modern industrial system. Even the small band to whom the fight against it is a religious cause—a very small band but a devoted, noisy, and well entrenched one —have largely accepted these facts; they fight on only to sell their lives dearly." Drucker, *How Big Is Too Big?* Harper's Magazine, July 1950, p. 24.

can only come from the concentration of financial strength and contacts which are the privilege of big business, so-called."[66]

Far from stifling smaller firms, big business is probably the principal source of opportunities for those individuals possessing the initiative and ambition to start a new business on their own. I doubt if there are many large industries that do not count upon many thousands of small suppliers, and do not require as many small businessmen to act as distributors, fabricators, and service agencies for their products. Take du Pont as an example. It relies upon 30,000 business firms as suppliers and has 80,000 business firms as customers. Over 350 independent firms have built up prosperous businesses of their own based on Cellophane—only one of du Pont's products. As the president of that company has testified, "Du Pont is essential to small business, small business is essential to du Pont."[67]

If a great number of individuals have preferred to seek careers within the large corporations, I submit that it is not because the predatory practices of the large companies have limited the opportunities in the field of small business.

The whole attack on big business re-flects a defeatist economic-stagnation approach to the monopoly problem. It is an offshoot of the pessimistic economic philosophy of the depression years, which prophesied that the loss of our frontier and the growing maturity of our industrial system spelled stagnation.[68] It presupposes that dramatic new inventions, new techniques, and technological changes will not be forthcoming in the future. It thus reflects a lack of faith in the continuance of the dynamic character of our system, which has brought so many benefits in the past. An appraisal of the monopoly problem cannot possibly start from such an unfounded premise.

Are the large industries of the country secure from competitive challenge today? Can they risk taking the complacent view that their positions cannot be undermined? Only the myopic and unaware, and those who would ignore our entire economic history, would answer in the affirmative.

New and different methods of doing business and new products have repeatedly overturned pre-existing businesses and brought new ones to the fore.

Even the most vocal advocates of the doctrine that bigness is bad, *per se*, recognize this phenomenon. Thus Professor Rostow concedes that in our system there is still a good deal of scope for innovation and enterprise. "New men and new ideas," he states, "keep bursting through the neat fences of existing interests, either with new firms or new techniques."[69]

---

[66] Sawyer, *supra*, at p. 12.

[67] Testimony before Monopoly Power Subcommittee of House Judiciary Committee, pp. 8, 11, Nov. 15, 1949.

In addition, Mr. Fairless testified for U.S. Steel that: "The startling fact is that nearly 40 per cent of all the money that we took in from all of our customers last year went to 54,000 suppliers from whom we had to purchase goods and services; and at least 50,000 of these suppliers were small businesses. The same is true every year. Moreover we sold our finished products and materials to approximately 110,000 customers; some of whom were individuals, some of whom were large enterprises, but about 90,000 of whom we classify as small customers." *Statement before the House Judiciary Subcommittee on the Study of Monopoly Power*, p. 4 (April 26, 1950).

[68] Hansen, *Full Recovery or Stagnation* (New York: Norton & Co., 1938), pp. 313, 315.

[69] Rostow, "*Monopoly under the Sherman Act: Power or Purpose?*" 43 Ill. L. Rev., 745 (1949).

"This constant change to the new, the more efficient, is the very heart of the process of effective competition. Unless read and applied in the light of its broad purposes, therefore, the 'New Sherman Act' may develop a serious contradiction." *Trouble Begins in the "New" Sherman Act: The Perplexing*

Competition pressures develop not only from within an industry but also from the outside from new inventions and new products. Many new names have found important places in the radio industry, especially since the inception of television. We are all aware of what airplanes and trucks are doing to the railroads. Those who have had to meet the competition of plastics and synthetics will tell you that the status quo offers no haven. And it is not too soon to speculate on what wide-scale use of atomic energy will do to existing fuel and power industries. A striking example of a competitive pressure developing from within an industry is the introduction of the supermarket in the grocery industry—a development that originated with the smaller elements in the business and which the large chains had to meet.

I would urge the courts to revert to

Story of the A & P Case. Yale L. J., Vol. 58, No. 6, May 1949, p. 969.

the rule of reason; to avoid scare words, rules-of-thumb, and assumptions; and to employ doctrines of automatic illegality only with the utmost caution. The decision in each case that is brought should depend upon whether under all the facts and circumstances it is shown that competition has in fact been unduly restrained. Through a realistic, as distinguished from a doctrinaire, application of the Antitrust Laws, business transactions and practices which further competition will be given a free rein, and only those which in actuality stifle or restrict competition will be condemned.

I also urge a re-examination of those laws and statutory interpretations which, in the guise of protecting the competitive system, are in reality aimed at shielding the individual competitor from the hazards of competition. If we truly believe that competition provides the most efficient mechanism to bring about a balanced distribution of goods and services at fair prices, we should avoid throwing road blocks into its path.

[7]

TRENDS IN ENFORCEMENT OF THE ANTIMONOPOLY LAWS

CORWIN D. EDWARDS
Federal Trade Commission

EDITOR'S NOTE: *This paper was presented before the American Business Law Institute on December 28, 1949. Where such terms as "this year" and "last month" appear in it, they refer to the calendar year 1949. In presenting the paper, Mr. Edwards said that it is an expression of his personal views—not a statement of the official views of the Federal Trade Commission.*

THE enforcement of the laws against monopoly appears to be entering a transition stage. A few years ago, at the outbreak of the war, most of the important antimonopoly cases were concerned with abuse of patent rights or participation in international cartels. In the patent field there was a no-man's land of uncertain law at the boundary between the patent laws and the antitrust laws. In the international cartel field many conspiracies to allocate world markets in ways that had political as well as economic significance had been too long neglected.

Today the patent cases and the international cartel cases have become almost as commonplace as cases of price fixing among members of a trade association. Many of the uncertainties about the bearing of the antitrust laws upon patents have been removed by judicial decision. Successful proceedings against international cartels have proved to be substantially similar to proceedings against domestic conspiracies to fix prices, allocate markets, and coerce or destroy competitors. Patent cases and cartel cases continue to be frequent and important, like cases involving the older forms of domestic price fixing. But their nature and their contribution to the maintenance of competition has become clear.

THE PROBLEM OF SIZE OF FIRM

Today a new set of issues is coming to the fore. It springs from a growing awareness of the significance of the size and power of great corporations which are not monopolies in the old-fashioned sense, and from concern over the effectiveness and subtlety of the means by which such corporations can coerce their competitors and control their markets. There is a ferment of interest in problems associated with bigness, not only in the law enforcement agencies but in the Congress and in the courts. A sub-committee of the House Judiciary Committee, which has been exploring means of strengthening the American competitive policy, has focussed much of its time and attention upon the concentration of economic power. Testifying before this committee, the Assistant Attorney General in charge of the Antitrust Division of the Department of Justice urged investigation of various factors that cause excessive concentration, including mergers, consolidations and acquisitions, huge amounts of capital available for investment in the hands of big corporations, and control over natural resources and raw materials. In a 1948 report on the merger movement, the FTC renewed its long standing recommendation that the Clayton Act be amended to prevent corporations from acquiring the assets of their competitors where the effect may be to substantially lessen competition. A bill for this purpose has passed the House of Representatives and will be pending before the Senate when Congress reconvenes. In an emphatic dissent in the

California Standard Oil case, Mr. Justice Douglas said last summer that the trend of judicial opinion has deflected the antitrust laws in a way that favors monopoly. He said that the laws had been made sharply effective against loose price fixing arrangements, illegal extensions of the power of a patent, and overt monopolistic tactics, but that "when it comes to monopolies built in gentlemanly ways— by mergers, purchases of assets and control and the like—the teeth have been largely drawn from the Act."

My purpose in this paper is not to review expressions of discontent with the present laws, nor to analyze the various problems associated with bigness and the extent to which existing law does or does not provide a satisfactory means to cope with them. I shall confine myself to a more limited subject—the way in which the problem of bigness has affected, and is affecting, the cases brought by the law enforcement agencies.

In spite of a good deal of public clamor which asserts the contrary, cases under the present antimonopoly laws are not based upon a charge that bigness is unlawful per se. The Court of Appeals for the Seventh Circuit recently declared that this is not the law, in an opinion, delivered this year, which sustained the conviction of New York Great Atlantic & Pacific Tea Company for violating the Sherman Act. The Assistant Attorney General in charge of the Antitrust Division has repeatedly said that he starts antitrust proceedings not because a company is big but because it uses its size for unlawful practices or purposes. Nevertheless, the peculiar status of the large corporate enterprise has a substantial effect upon most of the proceedings in which large enterprises are involved. As the court said in the A & P decision already mentioned, size becomes an

earmark of monopoly power because it carries with it opportunity for abuse. The step from bigness to control of the market is a short one, and there are many ways in which lawful bigness develops into unlawful conspiracy or monopoly.

PRICE CONSPIRACY

In an industry dominated by a few large concerns, the problem of price fixing conspiracy changes its character. So long as enterprises are small and numerous, there can be no conspiracy that does not leave a broad and unmistakable trail. If prices are to be fixed, small and numerous concerns must get together, must take and record formal decisions, and must set up machinery to determine whether or not decisions are being carried out. Collective activities like these are clearly different from the ordinary exercise of managerial discretion in running a competitive business. But when enterprises become few and large the picture changes. Executives of all important concerns in an industry can come together around a lunch table or on a golf course. Continuous close association can provide the basis for informal understanding with a miniumm of written record and a minimum of subsequent policing. The mechanics of reaching an agreement, in other words, are no longer obvious. Furthermore, an agreement among large companies can often be made to look like the ordinary conduct of business, so that a casual observer does not see or understand it and the expert investigator has difficulty ascertaining its character. It is no accident that in recent proceedings in which conspiracy to fix prices has been charged, those who were accused have protested loudly that they were merely engaged in competition and have accused the law enforcement agencies of trying to prevent them from acting independently in their own business interest.

In a highly concentrated industry the typical price fixing arrangement develops simply and subtly. As concerns become larger and fewer, each large enterprise becomes aware that competition with its large rivals may be a costly and risky business because of the power of those rivals and their ability to stand great losses. There is a persistent incentive for each large enterprise to seek out customers or market areas or types of product that are relatively unimportant to the other big producers; for it is easier to expand where opposition is absent or weak than where it is strong. Thus, so far as possible, the big enterprises bypass, supplement, or complement each other instead of competing with each other. As the business in which they are directly competitive decreases in amount and importance, they have a decreasing incentive to take risks and sacrifice profits in a struggle over that business. It is much simpler for each of them to recognize the primacy of the others as to parts of the market in which those others have some sort of tactical advantage or historical claim, hoping that in return its own primacy will be recognized where it has or claims advantage. Such a live-and-let-live policy is likely to mitigate and moderate competition in any field that is occupied by a few large enterprises. Yet it takes only a modest increase in the precision and tightness of this kind of mutual acquiescence in leadership to bring about a price fixing conspiracy as effective as any old-fashioned document signed in blood. A hardening of the intent to defer to each leader's decisions within the area of his leadership; some device to identify the portion of the market in which each large concern is to take the lead; some device to inform the followers about the

decision of the leader so that they can follow readily—add only these elements, and the marketing policies of the large enterprises can march together with unerring precision. In some industries the purpose to avoid competition and the necessary devices to make such a conspiracy effective were worked out crudely in meetings and formal agreements decades ago when enterprises were smaller and more numerous, so that now, when concerns are fewer and larger, the purpose is taken for granted and the means have become well understood trade practices that require no further tinkering. In some industries, if there ever were such formal agreements there is no evidence of them. So far as the record shows, an accretion of trade practices has gone along with a slowly developing mutual understanding, which now has the legal significance and the economic effect of complete agreement. In some industries the NRA period set the pattern with Government sanction, and trade practices established under the code have been continued by general tacit assent. Whatever the historical peculiarities of the particular industry, the pattern of this kind of conspiracy allocates among the principal concerns in the industry the authority to take the lead in making price decisions applicable to particular parts of the industry's business, and assigns to all concerns in the industry the obligation to follow the established leader except where they are themselves leaders.

The difficulties in coping with this kind of conspiracy lie in obtaining evidence and devising effective remedies rather than in developing legal concepts. When minds meet in an arrangement to fix prices, an illegal conspiracy has been established regardless of the subtlety of the process by which the result is brought about. The problem that confronts a law-enforcement agency is to determine when the minds have met and to bring together proof of the fact. In this kind of conspiracy prices are likely to be identical because all the followers accept and duplicate the leader's prices. But under conditions of intense competition prices may be identical too. The investigator's problem is to examine the trade practices through which leaders are selected and knowledge of their decisions is disseminated, in a search for overt agreements on some of the supporting details; and if such overt agreements are lacking, as they may be, to examine the marketing practices of the industry in great detail in order to see whether there are circumstances that cannot be explained by competition but can be explained only by the existence of conspiracy. Proof in such a conspiracy case is likely to depend largely upon circumstantial evidence, much of which is economic evidence about the behavior of prices, the flow of commodities, the relation of prices to costs, and similar matters. In the FTC's price fixing cases attention has often centered upon minutiae which were important, not for themselves, but because identical behavior in such matters is hard to achieve without careful and concerted planning. The courts have been hospitable to economic evidence and to circumstantial evidence, and consequently the laws against monopoly have been effective tools for use against subtle conspiracies. But the cost of investigating and trying a conspiracy case has gone up, so that the complexity of the problem of proof limits the speed and scope of enforcement activity.

The greatest difficulty confronting a law enforcement agency about this kind of conspiracy is provision of a satisfactory remedy after the case is won. Merely to punish the offenders and rely in the future upon deterrent effects of anticipated punishment is likely not to be enough; for, once this kind of conspiracy has become well established, it is so built into the institutions of the market that mere observance of the same trade practices, the same methods of price quotation, and the like, may be sufficient so keep the conspiracy going. What is needed is a break between the past and the future. Yet the nature of the break is not easy to devise. Parties to the conspiracy may be required to change their methods of quoting prices or to cease using their old means of exchanging price information. An effort may be made to introduce uncertainties that prevent one seller from knowing in advance what another seller will do. Sellers may be enjoined from continuing to respond to the old signals in the old way. Buyers may be given new opportunities to protect themselves. But however ingenious such remedies may be, they all involve two dangers: first, that the Government may prescribe ways of doing business that are not suited to economic conditions in the industry and that unduly hamper private initiative; and second, that the parties to the conspiracy may be able, by slight changes in their methods of doing business, to develop new ways of determining who shall be leader in each part of the market and of disseminating information about what each leader has decided to do.

Thus where companies have become big and few, their bigness jeopardizes effective enforcement of the law against price fixing.

UNFAIR COMPETITIVE PRACTICES

Bigness has a similar effect on the enforcement of the law against coercive practices and against practices that exclude competitors from the market. When enterprises are numerous and small, the means available for one which wishes to coerce its fellows are relatively crude and easy to detect. Indeed, joint action by a number of small enterprises is likely to be necessary if they are to coerce anyone effectively. It is easy to prevent boycotts and similar forms of intimidation and exclusion.

By contrast, the coercive influence which a large concern can exert upon a smaller one may leave no clear trail. The resources of the great enterprise may be so large, and its capacity to use them for the destruction of any selected small rival may be so obvious, as to make the mere existence of the large concern a standing threat that to incur its displeasure is to risk a business death sentence. In such instances docility is induced in the small enterprise through its own imagination, and the large enterprise enjoys the benefits thereof without threatening or engaging in any overt act. The classic example of this kind of docility is found in the testimony of the president of the Riverside Metal Company before the Temporary National Economic Committee. When asked why he had not reduced the price of his product when the price of his raw material fell, he replied, "Well, of course, I would not make a reduction in the base price of beryllium copper unless the American Brass made a price reduction in beryllium copper." When asked if this meant that he exercised no individual judgment as to the price he charged for his product, he replied, "Well, I think that is about what it amounts to; yes, sir," and added, "The industry is one of price leadership and a small company like ours, making less than 1½ per cent of the total, we have to follow. . . . " He said no one had told him that he must follow. He was then asked, "Did you have a feeling that something might happen if you didn't?" He replied, "I don't know what would happen." To the question, "You don't want to find out, do you?" he made no answer.

Unless power to coerce is to be regarded as unlawful even when not overtly exercised, situations like this present nothing for the law enforcement agency to proceed against. The independence and initiative of small business are eaten away and competition stops while the large enterprise basks in the sun without flexing its muscles.

When the large enterprise acts to coerce or exclude its small competitors, however, the law enforcement agencies take action in their turn. Recent cases contain a variety of examples of practices with a coercive or exclusive effect which big concerns are charged with using. In some of these cases the courts have sustained the charges, whereas in others the truth or falsity of the allegations has not yet been adjudicated.

In the case against the New York Great Atlantic and Pacific Tea Company, the circuit court of appeals emphasized the company's refusal to make further purchases from suppliers who would not give it a differential price advantage and treated this refusal as the equivalent of an unlawful boycott because of the size and power which A & P enjoyed. The court also treated the company's sale of food below cost at retail in some areas as a monopolistic practice because of the company's ability to subsidize these sales from the proceeds of its business in other areas in a way that small independent competitors could not do. In the case against American Can Co., decided last November, the district court held that the systematic refusal of the company to lease its can-closing machines to canners who do not contract to buy from the company all the cans they will require over a five-year period violates Section 3 of the Clayton Act, in view of the position which American

Can occupies in the industry. In the National Lead case, the Supreme Court held in 1948 that patent exchanges of the kind engaged in by the defendants were not inherently unlawful but were instruments of unlawful restraint when they were established between two companies which together controlled the market. The fact that there had been no challenge of the validity of any of the patents was treated by the court as persuasive evidence of the power and restructive intent of the combination. In the Schine Chain Theatre case, terminated by consent decree last June, the decree forbids the company to bid on more than 60 per cent of the first-run films offered for exhibition in towns where there are bidders that are not members of the Schine Chain. Each theatre that is a member of the chain is also required to bid independently for its own requirements. In the Northern Pacific Railway Co. case, instituted last May, the Government charges that, in granting leases for land, the company has required that supplies shipped to the lessees and products produced by the lessees shall be carried exclusively over the Northern Pacific Railway and that the products shall be sold to vendees who will also ship exclusively over that railway.

Most significant of all in indicating the close connection between coercive and exclusive activity, on the one hand, and size, on the other, are the cases involving the vertical integration of a large company or the alliance of two or more large companies that are vertically related in the market. In the Paramount Pictures case, the courts have found the Sherman Act violated by the fact that a large film producer and distributor owns large numbers of strategically placed moving picture theatres. The opinion in the case holds that vertical integration is not illegal per se, but that it becomes so

when it becomes part of a scheme to control an appreciable segment of the market, or where there is the power and purpose to exclude competitors. After considerable litigation over remedies, a consent decree was entered under which a considerable number of theatres will be sold by Paramount, in order to create an opportunity for the appearance of independent first-run competitors, and the rest of the theatres will be owned by a separate company, subject to a voting trust designed to prevent control of policy by Paramount.

In the Western Electric case, the Government charges that Western has acquired an unlawful monopoly of the manufacture of telephone equipment through the fact that American Telephone and Telegraph Co., which controls Western, makes substantially all of its purchases from Western and requires the operating companies controlled by A.T.&T. to buy from Western also. The Government asks that A.T.&T.'s control of Western be terminated, that Western be divided into three companies, that patents be thrown open for general license, and that A.T.&T. and its subsidiaries be required to buy their telephone equipment through competitive bidding.

The duPont case, filed last June, is the most ambitious and significant expression of the general principle that underlies this group of cases. The duPont Co. is said to own, directly or indirectly, about 23 per cent of the stock of General Motors and about 19 per cent of the stock of U. S. Rubber, and through this stock ownership, supplemented by interlocking directors and officers, to control both of these large companies. As a result of this relationship, it is charged, the three companies reciprocally provide markets for each other on preferential terms; duPont grants secret discriminatory rebates to General Motors; U. S. Rubber gives preferential prices to General Motors; there is an exchange of technological information sometimes on an exclusive and sometimes on a preferential basis; fields of manufacture are so divided that none of the three companies competes inconveniently with the other two; and concerns which supply goods to any one of the three are induced to buy their own requirements from the three companies rather than from the competitors of these companies.

Whether or not particular charges in the foregoing cases are well founded, the broad principle of the cases is, in my opinion, correct and of outstanding significance. It is that acts which have no coercive or exclusive effect when performed by small competitors may acquire such effects when they are performed by large companies. Conditions attached to sales or leases may enable the large seller to preempt the market. Aggressive use of buying and selling power may entail discriminations that necessarily destroy small rivals. Preference for particular customers or sources of supply may cease to be a mere harmless exercise of the freedom to select customers and become instead a sufficient means to enable the preferred concern to dominate or monopolize its own market. Thus, as the courts have recognized in recent cases, special limits upon the activity of great enterprises may become necessary to prevent these giants from attaining or perpetuating a coercive control over their rivals and from depriving their rivals of the opportunity to do business.

Monopoly Power

Closely related to these problems of coercion and exclusion is the problem of monopoly power. In the old concept of monopoly, a single giant concern was able both to exploit its customers and to coerce, intimidate, or exclude its small competitors. In an increasing number of industries, this concept is obsolete. Most of the market is shared among two, three, four, or five large enterprises, which may be of comparable size. Any one of them may have power to coerce or intimidate the remaining small enterprises, but they cannot coerce or intimidate each other. Where these large concerns act in concert, they are likely to give rise to the problem of conspiracy that I have already discussed. But where each has staked out a sphere of influence sufficiently separate from the others to avoid competition and to make conspiracy unnecessary, there is a new type of monopoly problem. In such instances each large enterprise controls a part of the market, and collectively the large enterprises control all of it. Yet no one of them has the position and unmatched power of the old-fashioned monopoly.

The law enforcement agencies are in process of facing this problem squarely, and there is some indication that the courts will entertain proceedings directed against this kind of monopoly power. Ever since 1890, the Sherman Act has forbidden monopolization of "any part" of commerce. In recent cases this provision has been so interpreted that the law can be applied against such group monopolization. In the chain store cases, the Department of Justice concurrently made charges of monopoly against Great Atlantic & Pacific Tea Company, Kroger Grocery and Baking Company, and Safeway Stores, in spite of the fact that these great food distributing enterprises jointly occupy the field of retail food distribution and, in some parts of the country, occupy it alongside each other. A & P was convicted, and the conviction was sustained on appeal. The other two cases were settled by pleas and fines. In the meat packing case, instituted last summer, the Department of Justice is requesting that each of the great meat packers be dissolved on the ground that collectively they enjoy a monopoly of the packing business.

Moreover, the law is being so interpreted that if a seller is the sole or principal supplier of a single customer the relationship may be called monopoly provided that customer constitutes a significantly large part of the total available market. This principle, clearly enunciated by the court in the Yellow Cab case, is being invoked by the Department of Justice in the current proceeding against duPont, General Motors, and U. S. Rubber, already referred to. Purchases by General Motors, in particular, are regarded as so large a part of the total market available to suppliers of materials for automobile manufacture that preemption of the General Motors part of the market is thought to constitute monopolization of a part of commerce.

Until the meat case and the duPont case, and perhaps other similar cases, have been finally decided, it will not be possible to say whether or not the present law covers the entire problem of divided monopoly. It is clear, however, that bigness can, and frequently does, raise the problem. Because of the development of groups of large concerns, proceedings against monopoly become necessary in more industries and under more complicated circumstances than would otherwise be the case. At the same time, the distinction between unlawful monopoly and the lawful operation of a relatively large enterprise becomes smaller and less sharp.

Conclusion

Thus, whether one is concerned with conspiracy, with unfair competitive practices, or with monopoly, the growth of large business enterprises has tended to complicate the problem, to enhance the difficulties of the law enforcement agencies, and to make it necessary for law enforcement activities to challenge types of behavior and of business structure that would have remained unchallenged in a world of small business. Speaking in 1939 on the subject, "Can the Antitrust Laws Preserve Competition?" I pointed out that large business units raise problems of leadership and of group monopoly, and remarked that, when large concerns do not overtly conspire as to their terms of sale, successful proceedings in group monopoly cases "would require either that the Government prove that a tacit conspiracy existed among those involved or that the Government establish a new principle, as yet untested in the courts, that there may be monopoly as the joint effect of the separate action of members of a group as well as monopoly in a single enterprise." I pointed out, too, that the alternative remedies available to the Government in such proceedings were to insist that in making prices the companies should individually "give different weight to various strategic considerations than they now individually give" or else to seek dissolution of the large concerns. Since that speech, proceedings against the subtler forms of conspiracy have become more ambitious and have been, on the whole, successful, and different forms of challenge to what I then called group monopoly have developed. The law enforcement agencies have not yet solved to their own satisfaction the problem of how to limit or influence the business decisions of individual large enterprises in such a way as to avoid tacit conspiracy and the exercise of monopolistic control. The Department of Justice has given increased attention to various types of proceeding for dissolution and divestiture. The FTC has emphasized its need for stronger legal weapons to prevent objectionable types of bigness from developing through mergers.

It may be that at some future date the Congress will decide that some degree of bigness is so dangerous to the public interest as to be inherently objectionable and will amend our substantive law in accord with this decision. I am not concerned here with the question whether or not that is likely to happen, nor with the question whether or not it should happen. Even if the purposes and standards of the law remain what they are today, the logic of events is likely to force the law enforcement agencies in the future, as it has forced them in the recent past, to pay increased attention to the size of business enterprises. For great size creates manifold opportunities to conspire and to exercise monopoly power, and in curbing conspiracies and monopolies there is frequent need to curb the behavior of large enterprises in a way that the behavior of small enterprises need not be curbed, and there is also frequent need to reduce the size and alter the structure of large enterprises where their size and structure are such as to have monopolistic consequences. Though bigness is not unlawful in itself, unlawful conditions that grow out of bigness can be dealt with successfully only by a policy that takes full account of the size and power that produced these unlawful conditions.

[8]

THE CLAYTON ACT: SLEEPING GIANT OF ANTITRUST?

By Robert W. Harbeson*

Thus, over 40 years after the enactment of the Clayton Act, it now becomes apparent for the first time that Section 7 has been a sleeping giant all along. Every corporation which has acquired a stock interest in another corporation after the enactment of the Clayton Act in 1914, and which has had business dealings with that corporation is exposed, retroactively, to the bite of the newly discovered teeth of Section 7.[1]

The foregoing passage from the minority opinion of the United States Supreme Court in *United States v. E. I. du Pont de Nemours and Company et al.*, handed down June 3, 1957, suggests the great legal and economic significance which at least some members of the Court attach to this decision. A similar view has been widely echoed in the business and financial press. For example, *Fortune* comments editorially that the decision is "potentially the most important antitrust development since Justice Edward Douglass White enunciated the 'rule of reason' in the Standard Oil Case in 1911."[2] The important word in this statement is "potentially"; without minimizing the importance of the increased scope which this decision gives to the antitrust laws it seems likely that the unanswered questions which it raises and the uncertainties which it creates may be of equal if not greater significance.

In the *du Pont* decision the Supreme Court held, 4 to 2, that the purchase by du Pont in 1917-19 of a 23 per cent stock interest in General Motors violated Section 7 of the Clayton Act, in that through this purchase "du Pont intended to obtain, and did obtain, an illegal preference over its competitors in the sale to General Motors of its products, and a further illegal preference in the development of chemical discoveries made by General Motors."[3] The proceeding began in June 1949 as a civil action in the United States District Court for the Northern District of Illinois, the government charging that du Pont's stock ownership in General Motors violated both Sections 1 and 2 of the Sherman Act and Section 7 of the Clayton Act. The government's complaint named, in addition to du Pont and General Motors, two holding companies owning large blocks of du Pont and General Motors stock—

---

* The author is professor of economics at the University of Illinois.

[1] *U. S. v. E. I. du Pont de Nemours and Co. et al.*, 353 U.S. 586 (1957), at p. 611; hereafter cited as *U.S. v. du Pont.*

[2] "Brennan on Bigness," *Fortune*, July 1957, LVI, 91.

[3] *U.S. v. du Pont*, p. 608.

Christiana Securities Company and Delaware Realty and Investment Corporation—and also the Wilmington Trust Company, United States Rubber Company, and members of the du Pont family.

Judge La Buy dismissed the government's complaint, holding that du Pont did not control General Motors, that there had been no limitation or restraint upon General Motors' freedom to deal with competitors of du Pont or to develop its chemical discoveries, and that there was no basis for a finding that there was or had been any reasonable probability of an illegal restraint within the meaning of the Clayton Act.[4] The government appealed despite the fact that, reportedly, government attorneys felt that the District Court's decision was "airtight."[5] However, in appealing, the government limited the complaint to du Pont, General Motors, and the two holding companies mentioned above. The appeal, like the original complaint, charged violations both of Sections 1 and 2 of the Sherman Act and Section 7 of the Clayton Act, but the latter apparently was included only as an afterthought or make-weight; according to Justice Burton the government referred to it only in the closing pages of its brief and for a few minutes in its oral argument. Nevertheless the majority of the Supreme Court rested its decision solely on the ground that a violation of Section 7 of the Clayton Act was involved.[6] The decision of the District Court was reversed and the case remanded to it for determination, after further hearing, of the equitable relief necessary and appropriate to eliminate the effects of the unlawful stock acquisition involved.

In reaching the foregoing conclusion the majority of the Supreme Court extended the scope of the Clayton Act in three ways. First, it was held that Section 7, even prior to the Celler amendments of 1950, covered vertical as well as horizontal acquisitions of stock; that is, acquisitions of stock of customer or supplier companies as well as stock of competitors. In the Court's words, "any acquisition by one corporation of all or any part of the stock of another corporation, competitor or not, is within the reach of the section whenever the reasonable likelihood appears that the acquisition will result in a restraint of commerce or in the creation of a monopoly of any line of commerce."[7] Prior to the present decision Section 7 in its original form had, except in one

[4] *U.S. v. E. I. du Pont de Nemours and Co. et al.*, 126 F. Supp. 235 (1954).

[5] "The Bite of the G. M. Decision," *Business Week*, June 8, 1957, p. 42.

[6] The relevant portion of Section 7 in its original form reads as follows: "That no corporation engaged in commerce shall acquire, directly or indirectly, the whole or any part of the stock or other share capital of another corporation engaged also in commerce where the effect of such acquisition may be to substantially lessen competition between the corporation whose stock is so acquired and the corporation making the acquisition or to restrain such commerce in any section or community or tend to create a monopoly of any line of commerce."

[7] *U.S. v. du Pont*, p. 592.

instance, been applied only to horizontal acquisitions;[8] the 1950 amendments made it clear that all kinds of acquisitions and mergers, vertical and conglomerate as well as horizontal, were covered; but the present case was governed by the Clayton Act in its pre-1950 form.

Second, it was held that, although prior cases under Section 7 were brought at or near the time of the stock acquisition involved, this fact does not mean that the government is foreclosed from bringing an action at any time when a threat of substantial lessening of competition or restraint or monopoly of any line of commerce is evident. The Court pointed out that the purpose of the Clayton Act was to arrest the foregoing tendencies in their incipiency and that: " 'Incipiency' in this context denotes not the time the stock was acquired, but any time when the acquisition threatens to ripen into a prohibited effect. . . . To accomplish the congressional aim, the Government may proceed at any time that an acquisition may be said with reasonable probability to contain a threat that it may lead to a restraint of commerce or tend to create a monopoly of a line of commerce."[9] In the present case the suit was brought 30 years after the stock acquisition involved took place.

Third, the relevant market for purposes of determining whether there had been a substantial lessening of competition as a result of the stock acquisition in question was held to be the market for automobile finishes and fabrics and not the entire industrial market for finishes and fabrics of all sorts. The Court held that "automotive finishes and fabrics have sufficient peculiar characteristics and uses to constitute them products sufficiently distinct from all other finishes and fabrics to make them a 'line of commerce' within the meaning of the Clayton Act."[10] It was noted that General Motors accounted for upwards of two-fifths of the total sales of automotive vehicles in the United States and that in 1946 and 1947 du Pont supplied approximately two-thirds of General Motors' requirements for finishes and 40 to 50 per cent of its requirements for fabrics. Hence the requirements for establishing a violation of Section 7, namely, that the market involved be "substantial" and that the firm involved supply a "substantial" part of that market, were satisfied.

This holding stands in sharp contrast to that in the *Cellophane*[11] case a year earlier, in which du Pont was held not to have violated the Sher-

[8] Prior to 1950 there was one lower-court decision arising out of a private treble-damage suit which held that Section 7 covered vertical stock acquisitions. *Ronald Fabrics Co. v. Verney Brunswick Mills, Inc.,* C C H Trade Cases 57514 (D.C. S.D. N.Y., 1946).

[9] *U.S. v. du Pont,* p. 597.

[10] *Ibid.,* pp. 593-94.

[11] *U.S. v. E. I. du Pont de Nemours and Co.,* 351 U.S. 377 (1956). See also G. W. Stocking and W. F. Mueller, "The Cellophane Case and the New Competition," *Am. Econ. Rev.,* March 1955, XLV, 29-63.

man Act despite the fact that it was one of only two producers of cellophane and accounted for 75 per cent of the output of that commodity.
It was held that the relevant market was not that for cellophane but for
all flexible wrapping materials and that cellophane's 17.9 per cent share
of the latter market was too small to sustain a finding that du Pont was
guilty of monopolizing within the meaning of Section 2 of the Sherman
Act.

In addition to the foregoing specific findings the Court by implication made two further points. First, the percentage of stock ownership
necessary to establish control may be substantially less than a majority. Under the circumstances of the present case du Pont's 23 per cent
ownership in General Motors was found to be sufficient to establish
control. Second, while it must be shown that a vertical stock acquisition results in excluding competitors from a "substantial" share of the
relevant market in order to establish a violation of Section 7 it is not
necessary that they be completely excluded. In the present case competitors of du Pont supplied a substantial share of General Motor's requirements for finishes and fabrics and the bulk of its requirements for
a number of other products which could have been secured from du
Pont. As with the definition of the relevant market, the significance of
the foregoing features of the present decision will depend upon future
interpretations.

The Court also found it necessary to demonstrate that du Pont's
commanding position as supplier of finishes and fabrics to General
Motors was not achieved on competitive merit alone but resulted from
the elimination of competitive suppliers consequent upon du Pont's
stock acquisition. In support of its conclusion the Court reviewed the
circumstances antecedent to the acquisition and documents purporting
to show du Pont's purpose in making the acquisition. Some years prior to
the acquisition of the General Motors stock the du Pont Company, long
dominant in the manufacture of military and commercial explosives,
had decided to expand its business into other fields. The desirability of
this step was emphasized by the decision in 1908 of the United States
to construct and operate plants to supply explosives for the armed
forces. A search for other uses of nitrocellulose, the principal raw material used in the manufacture of smokeless powder, revealed outlets in
the manufacture of lacquers, celluloid, artificial leather, and artificial
silk. Expansion into these fields by du Pont was begun by the purchase
in 1910 of the Fabrikoid Company, then the largest manufacturer of
artificial leather. The expansion program was barely started, however,
when the first world war intervened and made it necessary for du Pont
greatly to enlarge its facilities for producing explosives. The need to
find post-war uses for these enlarged facilities stimulated du Pont to

continue its expansion program into other fields during the war years, $90 million being set aside for this purpose.

The trial court found evidence that at or near the time of du Pont's purchase of General Motors stock officials of du Pont were well aware that the latter was a large consumer of some of the commodities which their organization was producing in increasing quantities. John J. Raskob, then treasurer of du Pont, apparently was the principal promotor of the idea that his company should make an investment in General Motors in order to insure that it would supply a predominant share of the latter's requirements for finishes, fabrics, and other products. He was supported in this view by Pierre S. du Pont, then president of the du Pont Company, who had acquired personal holdings of General Motors stock in 1914, and by William C. Durant, founder and, for some time, president of General Motors. Two circumstances facilitated the eventual purchase of General Motors stock by du Pont. First, when Durant and the banking interests controlling General Motors deadlocked on the choice of a Board of Directors in 1915 they resolved the deadlock by agreeing to name Pierre S. du Pont chairman of the General Motors Board, and to make Pierre du Pont, Raskob, and two nominees of Pierre du Pont neutral directors. Second, $50 million of du Pont's $90 million expansion fund was still in hand. The first block of General Motors stock was purchased by du Pont in 1917. In recommending this purchase to the du Pont Finance Committee Raskob said that "Our interest in the General Motors Company will undoubtedly secure for us the entire Fabrikoid, Pyralin [celluloid], paint and varnish business of those companies, which is a substantial factor."[12] Du Pont's annual reports to its stockholders in 1917 and 1918 likewise emphasized that the purchase would result in the company obtaining a new and substantial market for its products. In view of the foregoing evidence the majority of the Supreme Court felt that there was no basis for concluding that the acquisition could qualify for Section 7's exemption of purchases made "solely for investment."

Immediately after the stock acquisition J. A. Haskell, du Pont's sales manager and vice president, became General Motors' vice president in charge of the operations committee, and documentary evidence revealed his intention to pave the way for more general adoption of du Pont products. In the Court's words:

> Haskell set up lines of communication within General Motors to be in a position to know at all times what du Pont products and what products of du Pont competitors were being used. It is not pure imagination to suppose that such surveillance from that source made an impressive im-

---

[12] Quoted in *U.S. v. du Pont*, p. 602.

pact upon purchasing officials. It would be understandably difficult for them not to interpret it as meaning that a preference was to be given to du Pont products. Haskell also actively pushed the program to substitute Fabrikoid artificial leathers for genuine leather and sponsored use of du Pont Pyralin sheeting through a liaison arrangement set up between himself and the du Pont sales organization.[13]

The Court concluded that whereas prior to the stock acquisition du Pont's sales to General Motors were relatively insignificant, as a result of the foregoing activities "du Pont quickly swept into a commanding lead over its competitors, who were never afterwards in serious contention."[14] By 1921, 4 of General Motors' 8 operating divisions bought from du Pont their entire requirements of paints and varnishes; 5, their entire requirements of Fabrikoid; 4, their entire requirements of rubber cloth; and 7, their entire requirements of Pyralin. The Fisher Body division for many years refused to use du Pont products. The explanation probably is that when General Motors acquired the Fisher Body Company a voting trust was established which gave the Fisher brothers more autonomy in the management of the business than was enjoyed by the other operating divisions and enabled them to withstand efforts of high-ranking du Pont and General Motors executives to induce them to switch to du Pont from their accustomed sources of supply.

The Court conceded that "Competitors did obtain higher percentages of the General Motors business in later years although never high enough at any time substantially to affect the dollar amount of du Pont's sales."[15] It also conceded that "considerations of price, quality and service (of the products concerned) were not overlooked by either du Pont or General Motors" but held that the wisdom of this business judgment could not obscure the fact "plainly revealed by the record, that du Pont purposely employed its stock to entrench itself as a primary supplier of General Motors' requirements for automotive finishes and fabrics."[16] Finally, the fact that the executives of both companies acted fairly and on the basis of honest conviction concerning the best interests of their respective companies, without any attempt to overreach du Pont's competitors or anyone else, was dismissed as irrelevant on the ground that it was not necessary to show intent to restrain competition or to create a monopoly in order to prove a violation of Section 7.

Justice Burton, joined by Justice Frankfurter, in a long minority

[13] *Ibid.*, p. 603.
[14] *Loc. cit.*
[15] *Ibid.*, p. 605.
[16] *Ibid.*, p. 606.

opinion attacked the reasoning and conclusions of the majority. The minority's reading of the legislative history of the Clayton Act convinced them that vertical acquisitions of stock were to be reached, if at all, only by provisions of the Clayton Act other than Section 7. They pointed out that for 40 years this interpretation of Congressional intent had been followed administratively by the Department of Justice and Federal Trade Commission and contended that this should be regarded as persuasive evidence of the proper scope of Section 7. They objected to the majority's ruling that lawfulness at the time of the suit rather than at the time of the stock acquisition was controlling, on the ground that "The result is to subject a good-faith stock acquisition, lawful when made, to the hazard that the continued holding of the stock may make the acquisition illegal through unforeseen developments," and that "such a view is not supported by the statutory language and violates elementary principles of fairness."[17]

The majority were accused of being guilty of a logical fallacy in concluding that "because du Pont over a long period supplied a substantial portion of General Motors' requirements of paints and fabrics, its position must have been obtained by misuse of its stock interest rather than competitive considerations."[18] In support of the contrary interpretation the minority pointed out that each of the General Motors operating divisions bought independently and that the volume of purchases from du Pont varied greatly from one division to another; that although du Pont is General Motors' principal paint supplier the latter in recent years had bought as much as 30 per cent of its paint from competitors; that du Pont has had much less success than its competitors in selling to General Motors products other than finishes and fabrics; and that the fact that du Pont supplies a larger proportion of General Motors' requirements of finishes and fabrics than of other automobile manufacturers can be explained on grounds other than its stock interest in General Motors. For example, Ford follows the policy of making most of its own finishes and fabrics, with du Pont supplying most of these materials which the company itself does not manufacture. Chrysler follows the policy of selecting for each product a single supplier to whom it can be the most important customer, choosing Pittsburgh Plate Glass for paint and Texileather for fabrics.

The minority dismissed the documentary evidence relied upon by the majority to prove du Pont's intent to secure noncompetitive preferences—the letters and reports of Raskob, Haskell, and others—as being in each case "a matter of disputed significance which cannot be evalu-

[17] *Ibid.*, p. 622.
[18] *Ibid.*, p. 643.

ated without passing on the motivation and intent of the author."[19] It was said that, read in the context of the situations to which they were addressed, they were consistent with the District Court's conclusion that no restriction was placed on General Motors' freedom to buy as it chose and that General Motors' buyers did not regard themselves as being in any way restricted. The minority also contended that the Supreme Court should have accepted the lower court's interpretation of the facts in the case, since its findings were supported both by contemporaneous documents and by oral testimony and since the question of the credibility of the witnesses was of great importance and the trial judge was in a position to evaluate their credibility at first hand.[20]

Finally, economists may be interested in the minority's criticism of the Court's concept of the relevant market. They held that the record did not support the majority's decision that the relevant market was that for automotive finishes and fabrics; on the other hand, the record did show that other finishes and fabrics were competitive with those in question, and that therefore the relevant market was that for all industrial finishes and fabrics. The majority were criticized for including sales of du Pont's "Dulux," which is not used on automobiles, in computing du Pont's share of the market for automotive finishes and for excluding the sales of its "Duco" automotive finishes which are made for nonautomotive uses.[21] The comment was made, à la Schumpeter,[22] that "If Duco is to be treated as a separate market solely because of its initial superiority, du Pont is being penalized rather than rewarded for contributing to technological advance."[23] On the basis of the minority's definition, du Pont's share of the relevant market in 1947 was less than

---

[19] *Loc. cit.*

[20] Two principal criticisms of the *du Pont* decision from a legal standpoint are suggested by the above discussion of the minority opinion. One concerns the proper scope of judicial review; it is said that the lower court's findings of fact should have been sustained since they were not clearly erroneous and were supported both by oral testimony and contemporaneous documents. The other criticism is that in holding that the original Section 7 applied to vertical as well as horizontal acquisitions and that lawfulness at the time of bringing suit rather than at the time of acquisition was controlling, the Court disregarded 40 years of administrative interpretation and all the precedents except one lower-court decision. Underlying this criticism is the contention that regard for precedent gives predictability to law and guards against capricious or illogical changes in rulings, and that if precedents become outmoded as a result of changing conditions or changing social policies the proper remedy is legislative action.

[21] If the relevant market were taken to be that for all du Pont finishes for both automotive and nonautomotive uses General Motors' share in recent years, according to the minority, would range from 14 to 25 per cent. While this is considerably smaller than the share as computed by the majority's method it would still seem to be "substantial."

[22] J. A. Schumpeter, *Capitalism, Socialism and Democracy*, 3rd ed. (New York, 1950), Ch. 7, 8.

[23] *U.S. v. du Pont*, p. 651.

3.5 per cent for finishes and about 1.6 per cent for fabrics. From this it was concluded that the Clayton Act was not violated by du Pont's stock acquisition because it did not foreclose competitors from a substantial share of the relevant market or significantly limit the competitive opportunities of others trading in that market.

Economists would disagree with the minority's contention that automotive finishes are indistinguishable from other industrial finishes or that Duco is indistinguishable from other finishes. The mere fact that the latter was a patented product is at least presumptive evidence that it is significantly differentiated from other finishes. Moreover each such differentiated product has a distinct market; whether the "relevant market" for antitrust purposes is to be considered the market for a single product in the narrowest sense or as comprising a group of markets of closely related products is necessarily a policy question depending upon what degree of monopoly power is regarded as permissible.

While the present decision extends the scope of the antitrust laws in ways described above this conclusion is subject to certain qualifications. First, the holding which extends the Clayton Act in its pre-1950 form to vertical stock acquisitions is not likely to be of great importance. It was early discovered that the original Clayton Act covered acquisitions of stock but not of assets;[24] in view of this loophole it is unlikely that there were many vulnerable stock acquisitions in the pre-1950 period. For the period since 1950 the holding is superfluous in view of the Celler amendments which extend the coverage of the Clayton Act to all types of mergers and acquisitions, vertical, horizontal, and conglomerate, whether achieved by the purchase of stock or the purchase of assets. Second, there are definite limitations on the retroactive aspect of the holding which permits suit to be brought at any time, following a stock acquisition, when a probable violation of the Clayton Act can be established. This is both because of the probable fewness of vulnerable stock acquisitions in the pre-1950 period and because of the need on the part of the antitrust enforcement agencies to conserve their time and resources for dealing with important current cases. Where acquisition of assets is involved there is the additional limitation that suit must be brought before the assets become scrambled to such an extent as to make divestiture impracticable. However, the holding in the present case is important in that it will enable the enforcement agencies to deal retroactively with some recent, post-1950, acquisitions, and by removing the time factor, especially in the case of stock acquisitions, should materially strengthen enforcement in the future.

[24] See *F.T.C. v. Western Meat Co., Thatcher Mfg. Co. v. F.T.C., Swift and Co. v. F.T.C.,* 272 U.S. 554 (1926); *Arrow-Hart and Hegeman Electric Co. v. F.T.C.,* 291 U.S. 587 (1934).

The significance of the present case, as indicated at the outset, perhaps depends less upon what it decided, important though these points
are, than upon the answers which will ultimately be given to the numerous important questions which it poses. For the case raises more questions than it answers. Since the decision rests to a large extent upon
facts peculiar to the du Pont-General Motors relationship much uncertainty has been created concerning the extent to which a similar
conclusion will be reached in future cases under Section 7 of the Clayton Act which involve different fact situations.[25] One area of uncertainty concerns the definition of the relevant market which will be
adopted in future acquisition cases. Will a narrow concept of the relevant market comparable to that adopted in the present decision be retained in future Clayton Act cases? Will a narrow concept of the relevant market be adopted in Clayton Act cases while a broader definition
is retained (following the precedent of the *Cellophane* decision) in
Sherman Act cases?

A second area of uncertainty concerns the percentage of ownership
by one corporation in another which will be vulnerable under Section 7.
Under the circumstances of the present case du Pont's 23 per cent ownership of General Motors stock was held to be sufficient to establish the
fact of control. However, it cannot be assumed that this is necessarily
a firm figure; the percentage of ownership which will be held to establish the fact of control may be higher or lower in future cases under
Section 7 depending upon the degree of interference by the acquiring
corporation in the affairs of the corporation a stock interest in which
has been acquired, the absolute size and market shares of the acquiring
and acquired corporations, and other factors.

A related question concerns the extent to which the rulings in the du
Pont case with regard to the relevant market and percentage of ownership necessary to establish the fact of control will serve as precedents
in future cases involving joint stockholdings by two or more corporations in a third corporation. Another related question concerns the
possible bearing of the present case upon vertical integration involving
the acquisition of the entire capital stock or assets of a customer or
supplier corporation. In view of the fact that since 1950 the Clayton
Act has applied to acquisitions of assets as well as of stock the question
arises whether a corporation will be more or less vulnerable if it acquires, or has acquired, a customer or supplier corporation outright
than if it acquires merely partial stock ownership. More specifically,
will a concept of the relevant market comparable to that adopted in the

[25] See also Betty Bock, "Antitrust Polarity: The Two du Pont Decisions," *Conference
Board Bus. Record,* July 1957, XIV, 325-31.

present case be adopted in cases involving complete vertical integration? In this connection much importance attaches to the outcome of the pending Federal Trade Commission complaint against the acquisition by the Union Carbide and Carbon Corporation of the assets of the Visking Corporation, one of its principal customers. This is the Commission's first action against a so-called "forward-vertical" merger.

A third area of uncertainty concerns the bearing of the absolute size and market shares of the acquiring and acquired firms upon the vulnerability of acquisitions under Section 7. Would the present decision have been different if one or both of the industries represented by du Pont and General Motors were less concentrated, or if the market share of either or both of these firms had been smaller? What is the minimum market share which could qualify as "substantial" within the meaning of the Clayton Act? Would the decision have been different if the absolute size, as distinct from the market share, of du Pont and/or General Motors had been materially smaller?

A final question concerns the remedies which will be invoked to give effect to the Supreme Court's decision in the du Pont case. The Supreme Court in remanding the present case to the District Court noted that the latter had "wide discretion" in adapting remedies to the requirements of the individual case. The question of remedies in the present proceeding is particularly difficult because of the magnitude of the divestiture involved. The sale of du Pont's holdings of some 63 million shares of General Motors, currently worth about $2.4 billion, would represent the largest government-ordered disposal of property ever made. Sale of the stock in the open market over any short period would drastically depress the price of the shares and might have other undesirable repercussions. Even assuming that it were possible to dispose of the stock on the open market without appreciable depression of its price this solution would be undesirable from du Pont's standpoint because of tax considerations. The Company would be subject to a huge capital gains tax—estimated at between $500 and $600 million—while the du Pont stockholders would pay income taxes at the regular rates on such part of the proceeds as might be distributed in dividends.

The government has filed a divestiture plan intended to accomplish the eventual disposal of the General Motors stock while minimizing the foregoing difficulties. The plan calls for depositing all of the General Motors stock with a court-appointed trustee who, in turn, would parcel it out over a ten-year period to du Pont stockholders other than Christiana Securities Company, Delaware Realty and Investment Corporation, and stockholders of the latter. The distribution would be made in proportion to each shareholder's interest in the du Pont Company.

Christiana, Delaware, and the stockholders of Delaware, together accounting for about 40 per cent of the du Pont stock, would be excluded from the distribution by reason of their representing the interest of the du Pont family. The government proposes that these parties' share of the General Motors stock be disposed of at public or private sale over a ten-year period, with the other du Pont stockholders being given the first opportunity to purchase the stock. During the ten-year divestiture period voting rights to the General Motors stock would be lodged with du Pont stockholders other than Christiana, Delaware, and the stockholders of Delaware. The voting rights attached to the latter parties' share of the General Motors stock would be prorated among the other du Pont stockholders until the stock is sold. The purpose of these arrangements is to prevent an important residue of common control of du Pont and General Motors from remaining in the hands of the du Pont family.

The government's plan prohibits du Pont, Christiana, and Delaware from acquiring or holding, directly or indirectly, any General Motors stock or from exercising any kind of influence or control over General Motors. Du Pont and General Motors are prohibited from having interlocking directorates and common officers; from entering into any agreement, understanding, or arrangement for joint ownership or operation of any commercial or manufacturing enterprise; and from granting exclusive patent rights to each other. In addition, du Pont and General Motors are prohibited from entering into any contract, agreement, or understanding which requires that General Motors purchase any specific percentage of its requirements of any product from du Pont, or which grants to du Pont the first or a preferential right to manufacture or sell any chemical discovery made by General Motors.

Du Pont's plan for divestiture has not yet (January 1958) been filed, but it is reported unofficially that the Company favors placing its holdings of General Motors stock in a nonvoting trust without any requirement that the stock be sold. Unless an agreement can be reached between the parties it is highly probable that the District Court's decision with regard to remedies will be appealed to the Supreme Court.

The foregoing analysis, in the opinion of the writer, demonstrates that the *du Pont* decision materially increases the ability of the enforcement agencies to maintain if not enhance the strength of competitive forces in the economy, and that potentially its influence in this direction could be much greater. The decision will, therefore, be applauded by those who favor a strong antimonopoly policy, but even those who oppose such a policy and the larger number who are defeatists concerning its possibilities would find it difficult to deny that stockholdings of the type here involved make little or no economic contribution from the social viewpoint and that, potentially at least, they may be socially disadvantageous. The Celler amendments and the *du Pont* decision have materially increased the stature of Section 7 of the Clayton Act, but whether the decision deserves the appellation of "sleeping giant" will depend upon future judicial rulings concerning the numerous important questions which the decision poses.

Part III
Retrenchment in Antitrust Regulation

[9]

Excerpt from *Antitrust Economics*, 320–43

13

Antitrust Enforcement: Where it has Been; Where it is Going

Antitrust, which once enjoyed widespread support, has come under withering attack from a variety of quarters recently. Many of the critics regard antitrust as an anachronism, and openly counsel that it be abolished. But some hold the opposite view. They urge that antitrust enforcement be strengthened, and recall the Warren Court years with nostalgia.

Critics of the first kind appear to be dismayed over the difficulties experienced by US auto, steel, and other industries as compared with the robust successes of the Japanese. A reshaping of the relations among firms and between business and government along the lines of the Japanese model is widely held to be attractive. The details of the Japanese model remain somewhat obscure, however, and its transferability to the US scene is problematic. Until the model is more fully worked out, its net benefits assessed, and its transferability demonstrated, it would appear to be judicious to regard reforms along these lines as speculative. For the purposes of this chapter therefore, my examination of antitrust will remain within the framework of US experience.

A decade is a useful interval over which to observe and report on antitrust developments. The 1960s, 1970s, and 1980s can each, I think, be usefully characterized as an antitrust era. Specifically, concentration and entry barrier analysis flourished in the 1960s. Efficiency analysis gained ascendancy in the 1970s, and I expect the 1980s to be the period when the analysis of strategic behavior comes of age. Arguments that antitrust should be abolished would be easier to understand had there been no substantial progress during the 1970s or if the problems of the 1980s were inconsequential. Inasmuch, however, as antitrust made remarkable progress during the 1970s and since difficult problems of

Research on this chapter was facilitated by a grant from the National Science Foundation. Reprinted from *Industrial Organization, Antitrust and Public Policy*. ed. John Craven, Klurver–Nihjoff Publishing, Boston (1983), pp. 41–68, with permission.

strategic behavior remain unresolved, calls for the abolition of antitrust are premature if not uninformed.

Antitrust enforcement in the 1960s is briefly examined in the first section of this chapter. The reforms of the 1970s are reviewed next. Some of the concerns and recent developments relating to strategic behavior are then treated and unresolved enforcement dilemmas for the 1980s are addressed. Concluding remarks follow. I argue that, whereas reliance on entry barrier arguments was excessive in the 1960s, much of this was redressed by a shift of attention to efficiency, in all of its forms, in the 1970s. Difficult strategic behavior issues have, nevertheless, surfaced and this area is presently in great flux.[1] Considerable research resources have recently been directed at these issues – as a result of which there is a prospect for better resolution in the latter part of this decade.

I.   The 1960s

The 1960s was the era when market-power analysis flourished. This was partly due to earlier theoretical, empirical, and policy studies in which entry barriers were prominent, but it was also because antitrust economics was sorely lacking in two other respects. First, there was a general undervaluation of the social benefits of efficiency. Second, there was a widespread tendency to regard efficiency very narrowly – mainly in technological terms. An awareness of transactions costs, much less a sensitivity to the importance of economizing thereon, had scarcely surfaced. Instead, the firm was held to be a production function to which a profit maximization objective had been assigned. Subject to rudimentary economy-of-scale considerations, the efficient boundaries of firms were taken as given. Accordingly, efforts to reconfigure firm and market structures that went beyond these natural boundaries were assessed almost exclusively in market-power terms.

The intellectual basis for market-power analysis was provided by Joe Bain in the 1950s, especially in his book *Barriers to New Competition* (1956). Many of the antitrust ramifications of this approach to industrial organization were set out by Carl Kaysen and Donald Turner very shortly thereafter in their book *Antitrust Policy: An Economic and Legal Analysis* (1959). The decade of the 1960s witnessed further applications of this line of reasoning and widespread adoption of entry barrier arguments by the courts.

Illustrations of the success of entry barrier reasoning are the *Procter & Gamble* and *Schwinn* cases, both of which were decided by the Supreme

---

[1] A shift of the traditional entry barrier approach in the direction of strategic behavior was signaled by the influential paper of Richard Caves and Michael Porter (1977).

Court in 1967.[2] The first of these cases was anticipated by the Federal
Trade Commission's opinion in *Foremost Dairies*, where the Commission
ventured the view that the necessary proof of violation of section 7
'consists of types of evidence showing that the acquiring firm possesses
significant power in some markets *or* that its overall organization gives it
a decisive advantage in efficiency over its small rivals.'[3] Although Donald
Turner, among others, was quick to label this as bad law and bad
economics (1975, p. 1324) in that it protects competitors rather than
promotes the welfare benefits of competition, the Commission carried
this reasoning forward in *Procter & Gamble* and linked it with barriers
to entry in the following way:[4]

In stressing as we have the importance of advantages of scale as a factor
heightening the barriers to new entry into the liquid bleach industry, we reject,
as specious in law and unfounded in fact, the argument that the Commission
ought not, for the sake of protecting the 'inefficient' small firms in the industry,
proscribe a merger so productive of 'efficiencies.' The short answer to this
argument is that, in a proceeding under section 7, economic efficiency or any
other social benefit resulting from a merger is pertinent only insofar as it may
tend to promote or retard the vigor of competition.

This emphasis on entry barriers and the low regard accorded to economies
also appears in the Supreme Court's opinion. Thus the Court observed
that Procter's acquisition of Clorox may[5]

... have the tendency of raising the barriers to new entry. The major competitive
weapon in the successful marketing of bleach is advertising. Clorox was limited
in this area by its relatively small budget and its inability to obtain substantial
discounts. By contrasts, Procter's budget was much larger; and, although it would
not devote its entire budget to advertising Clorox, it could divert a large portion
to meet the short-term threat of a new entrant. Procter would be able to use its
volume discounts to advantage in advertising Clorox. Thus, a new entrant would
be much more reluctant to face the giant Procter than it would have been to face
the smaller Clorox.
  Possible economies cannot be used as a defense to illegality.[6]

The aforementioned insensitivity to transaction cost economizing was

---

[2] *Federal Trade Commission* v. *Procter & Gamble Co.*, 386 US 568 (1967); *United States*
v. *Arnold Schwinn & Co.* 388 US 365 (1967).
  [3] *Foremost Dairies, Inc.*, 60 FTC 944, 1084 (1962), emphasis added.
  [4] Quoted from Bork (1978, p. 254).
  [5] *Federal Trade Commission* v. *Procter & Gamble Co.*, 386 US 568, 574 (1967).
  [6] Although perverse applications of economies reasoning are much less common today,
occasional aberrations nevertheless appear. See footnote 28, for an example.

coupled with a preoccupation with entry barriers in reaching the *Schwinn* decision. Donald Turner, who was then the head of the Antitrust Division, succinctly expressed the prevailing attitude toward nonstandard or unfamiliar business practices as follows: 'I approach territorial and customer restrictions not hospitably in the common law tradition, but inhospitably in the tradition of antitrust law.'[7] This view, which I shall refer to as the inhospitality tradition, was widely held among antitrust specialists during the 1960s. Rather than presume – or at least investigate the possibility – that vertical restrictions served affirmative economic purposes, it was assumed instead that they were designed to enhance market power. Specifically, the Government argued that 'Schwinn's strenuous efforts to exclude unauthorized retailers from selling its bicycles suggest that, absent these restraints, there would be a broader retail distribution of these goods with the resulting public benefits (including lower price) of retail competition.'[8] Since the Government believed that it was 'unnecessary to create quality images' because products that are objectively superior would be self-evident, and since product differentiation can adversely affect the condition of entry, Schwinn's efforts to effect differentiation were held by the Government to be contrary to the public interest.

Accordingly, antitrust enforcement in the 1960s can be described as a period during which market-power concerns were virtually determinative. The benefits of economies were wilfully disregarded, and the evidence of economies was narrowly restricted to those with technological origins. A series of reactions, many of which were needed correctives, was set in motion by the excesses to which this type of reasoning was given.

II.   The 1970s

The reconceptualizing of antitrust issues that occurred during the late 1960s and early 1970s is sketched below. This mainly entailed a shift away from entry barriers to address economic organization from the standpoint of what economic purposes are being served. Two of the cases that were decided during the 1970s in which this shift is reflected will be briefly described.

A.   EFFICIENCY ANALYSIS

The reforms of antitrust enforcement in the 1970s had their origins in critiques of the 1960s. These include (a) the insistence of the Chicago

---

[7] The quotation is attributed to Turner by Stanley Robinson 1968 NY State Bar Association, Antitrust Symposium, p. 29.

[8] Jurisdictional Statement for the United States at 14, *United States* v. *Arnold Schwinn & Co.* 388 US 365 (1967). For a discussion, see Williamson (1979a, pp. 980–5).

School that antitrust issues be studied through the lens of price theory; (b) related critiques of the entry barrier approach; (c) application of the partial-equilibrium welfare-economics model to an assessment of the trade-offs between market power and efficiency; and (d) a reformulation of the theory of the modern corporation whereby transaction-cost-economizing considerations were brought to the fore. An additional contributing factor was the reorganization of the economics staff of the Antitrust Division. Whereas previously the staff economists were used almost exclusively to support the legal staff in the preparation and litigation of cases, they were now asked to assess the economic merits of cases before filing.

The Chicago School approach has been set out by Richard Posner (1979) elsewhere. Although it is possible to quibble with Posner's rendition of Harvard versus Chicago (as these were viewed in the 1960s), it is nevertheless clear that the efficiency orientation favored by Aaron Director (and his students and colleagues) has stood the test of time rather well. Thus whereas Director's views on tie-ins, resale-price maintenance, and the like were widely regarded as suspect – 'In some quarters the Chicago School was regarded as little better than a lunatic fringe' (Posner, 1979, p. 931) – this approach enjoys wider respect today.[9] But Chicago, or at least the diehard branch, has, in the process of applying price theory to antitrust, insisted on an uncommonly narrow formulation. (Specifically, as discussed below, the diehard-Chicago approach to the study of strategic behavior is myopic and simplistic. This has a bearing, however, more on the enforcement issues of the 1980s than to those of the 1970s.)

Given Chicago's price theory orientation, many of the criticisms of the entry barrier approach understandably originated there as well. Objections of two kinds were registered. The first of these held that the basic entry barrier model, as set out by Bain (1956) and elaborated by Franco Modigliani (1958), purported to be but did not qualify as an oligopoly model. As George Stigler put it, the entry barrier model solved the oligopoly problem by murder: 'The ability of the oligopolists to agree upon and police the limit price is apparently independent of the sizes and numbers of oligopolists' (1968, p. 21). Put differently, the model did not address itself to the mechanics by which collective action was realized. Instead, it simply assumed that the requisite coordination to effect a limit-price result would appear. As discussed below, recent models in the entry barrier traditon have avoided this problem by explicitly casting the analysis in a sitting monopolist–duopoly framework. Addressing the issues of entry in this more limited context has analytical advantages, but applications outside of the dominant-firm context are appropriate only upon a showing

---

[9] The recent Areeda and Turner antitrust treatise is an example. See Posner (1979, pp. 933–8) for a discussion of the earlier Kaysen and Turner book as compared with the Areeda and Turner treatise.

that the necessary preconditions to effect oligopolistic coordination are satisfied.

The other objection to entry barrier analysis relates to public policy misuses of entry barrier reasoning. That the condition of entry is impeded is neither here nor there if no superior structural configuration – expressed in welfare terms – can be described. However obvious this may be on reflection, this was not always the case. Rather, there was a widespread tendency to regard barriers of all kinds as contrary to the social interest. But as Robert Bork has put it, 'The question for antitrust is whether there exist artificial entry barriers. These must be barriers that are not forms of superior efficiency and which yet prevent the forces of the market ... from operating to erode market positions not based on efficiency' (1978, p. 311, emphasis added).

The distinction between remediable and irremediable entry impediments thus becomes the focus of attention. Little useful public policy purpose is served, and considerable risk of public policy mischief results, when conditions of an irremediable kind are brought under fire. Mistaken treatment of economies of scale illustrates what is at stake. Thus, suppose that economies of scale exist and that the market is of sufficient size to support the larger of two technologies. Since superior outcomes will be attributable to the less efficient technology only under very unusual conditions, net social benefits ought presumably to be attributed to these scale-economy conditions. To describe such economies as barriers to entry, however, does not invite this conclusion; to the contrary, mistaken welfare judgments are encouraged. Many of the enthusiasts of entry barrier analysis have been reluctant to concede such hazards.

That efficiency benefits were held in such low regard in the 1960s is partly explained by the widespread opinion that, as between two structural alternatives – one of which simultaneously presents greater market power and greater efficiency than the other – the more competitive structure is invariably to be preferred. This view was supported by the implicit assumption that even small anticompetitive effects would surely swamp efficiency benefits in arriving at a net valuation. The FTC opinion that 'economic efficiency or any other social benefit ... [is] pertinent only insofar as it may tend to promote or retard the vigor of competition'[10] – where competition is defined in structural terms – is a clear indication of such thinking.

Application of the basic partial-equilibrium welfare-economics model to an assessment of market power versus economies trade-offs disclosed that to sacrifice economies for reduced market power came at a high cost (Williamson, 1968). Although the merits of this framework remain open to dispute (Posner, 1975, p. 821), the general approach, if not the

---

[10] See footnote 4 *supra*.

framework itself, has since been employed by others. Bain was among the first to acknowledge the merits of an economies defense in assessing mergers (1968, p. 658). Wesley Liebeler (1978), Robert Bork (1978), and Timothy Muris (1979) have all made extensive use of the partial-equilibrium trade-off model in their insistence that antitrust enforcement that proceeds heedless of trade-offs is uninformed and contrary to the social interest.

A common argument against trade-off analysis is that the courts are poorly suited to assess economic evidence and arguments of this kind (Bok, 1960). In fact, a simple sensitivity to the merits of economies is sufficient to avoid the inverted reasoning of *Foremost Dairies*; and although errors of the *Schwinn* kind are avoided only upon recognizing that economies can take transaction cost as well as technological forms, the mistakes of the inhospitality tradition also become less likely once this step has been taken.

Whereas technological innovations were easily accommodated within a production function framework (and economists have devoted considerable attention to these matters) organizational innovation is alien to this framework (and, as of the early 1960s, had been generally neglected). The publication of Alfred Chandler's book *Strategy and Structure* (1962) represented the opening wedge in an effort to develop a deeper understanding of the importance of organizational innovation and its relation to the study of the modern corporation. Chandler focused on the shift from the traditional hierarchical structure (or unitary form) to the multidivisional (or M-form) structure. This innovation first appeared in the 1920s and was imitated and widely adopted thereafter. Chandler argued that the new structure had deep rationality properties that permitted the firm to realize superior results in both strategic and operating respects. It was uninformed and untenable to argue that internal organization was a matter of indifference after the appearance of Chandler's book.

Independently, Armen Alchian (1969) and Richard Heflebower (1960) also recognized that organization form had an important bearing on economic performance. They advanced the proposition that corporations were discharging functions ordinarily associated with the capital market. The internal-resource allocation, incentive, and control attributes of the modern corporation were subsequently discussed and developed by others (Williamson, 1970, 1975). This in turn led to a more general study of firm and market structures whereby the issue of mediating transactions was addressed not as a datum but as an economizing issue. Although this insight owes its origins to Ronald Coase's classic 1937 paper, it was not until the 1970s that the issues were operationalized.

Whereas both the production function approach and inhospitality tradition regarded markets as the natural, hence efficient, way by which to mediate transactions between technologically separable entities, this presumption was unacceptable once firms were described not as production functions but as governance structures. Whether transactions should be mediated by markets, hierarchies, or mixed modes was thus an issue to be investigated by assessing the transaction-cost ramifications of each. Such a comparative institutional undertaking involved (a) dimensionalizing transactions, (b) describing alternative governance structures, and (c) recognizing that transaction costs would be economized by matching governance structure with transactions in a discriminating way (Williamson, 1971, 1975, 1979b).

This approach to the study of economic organization disclosed that many nonstandard or unfamiliar business practices that were, at best, puzzling, when assessed in technological terms, were in fact the outcome of rational transaction-cost-economizing efforts. Vertical integration, vertical market restrictions, and aspects of conglomerate and multinational organization were all re-examined to advantage. Organizational innovations that had hitherto been regarded as presumptively unlawful, under the inhospitality tradition, were thus accorded greater sympathy. Indeed, subject to the condition that certain structural thresholds (mainly high concentration coupled with barriers to entry) are not exceeded, a presumption that organizational innovations have the purpose and effect of economizing on transaction costs is warranted.[11] This is a rather drastic departure from the mistaken views of the 1960s.

B. TWO CASES

It is a credit to the growing sophistication of antitrust that the 1970s witnessed a shift away from asserted, but often only imagined, entry barrier effects to consider the affirmative purposes served by new business configurations. This occurred both with respect to mergers-for-economies as well as vertical market restrictions (and other nonstandard business practices). The 1975 decision of the Federal Trade Commission to vacate the administrative law judge's order and dismiss the complaint in the *Budd Company* case illustrates the shift in mergers-for-economies

---

[11] Developing this takes us beyond the scope of the current chapter, but it has been addressed elsewhere (Williamson, 1981). Among the leading organizational innovations during the past 150 years that have important transaction cost economizing attributes are (a) the appearance of managerial hierarchies in the railroads in the 1860s; (b) selective forward integration out of manufacturing into distribution that occurred at the end of the nineteenth century; (c) the invention of the multidivisional structure in the 1920s and its subsequent diffusion following the Second World War; (d) the extension of multidivisionalization to manage diversified lines of commerce (the conglomerate); and (e) the further application of this to promote technology transfer in the multinational enterprise.

thinking.[12] The complaint had stressed Budd's importance as a potential entrant into narrowly defined lines of commerce and held that the benefits conferred by Budd on the acquired firm (Gindy) disadvantaged small rivals. The Commission rejected the complaint counsel's narrow definition of the market and regarded the acquisition as procompetitive – in that the acquisition relieved Gindy of financial and other handicaps that it had experienced previously. The upside-down valuation of economies in *Foremost Dairies* and *Procter* was thus recognized as a perversion of sound antitrust economics.

The Supreme Court's decision in 1977 in the *GTE–Sylvania* case also corrected mistaken reasoning of the 1960s, specifically that of *Schwinn*. Contrary to *Schwinn*, the Court held that[13]

[vertical] restrictions, in varying forms, are widely used in our free market economy. As indicated above, there is substantial scholarly opinion and judicial authority supporting their economic utility. There is relatively little authority to the contrary. Certainly there has been no showing in this case, either generally or with respect to Sylvania's agreement, that vertical restrictions have or are likely to have a 'pernicious effect on competition' or that they 'lack ... any redeeming virtue'. ... Accordingly, we conclude that the per se rule in *Schwinn* must be overruled.

The 1960s preoccupation with competition, often amounting to no more than a concern over competitors coupled with a naive view of the modern corporation, was thus substantially redressed.

III. Strategic Behavior: A Progress Report

The main issue on the research agenda for industrial organization during the next decade is the study of strategic behavior – by which I mean efforts by established firms to take up advance positions or respond contingently to rivalry in ways that discipline actual and discourage potential competition. Whether such behavior exists, what forms it takes, how widespread each type is, and what antitrust ramifications attach thereto, are all open to dispute.

Although a great deal of research talent has been directed to these issues in the past few years and real progress has been made, we still have a long way to go before the main issues can be thought to be settled. Unlike efficiency analysis, where industrial organization could draw upon

---

[12] Budd Co. [1973–1976 Transfer Binder] Trade Regulation Reporter CCTT, para. 20, 998 (FTC No. 8848 18 Sept. 1975).

[13] *Continental TV Inc. et al.* v. *GTE–Sylvania Inc.* 433 US 36, 45 (1977).

applied welfare economics for assistance, the study of strategic behavior poses puzzles that are quite novel. The need for new theory has not gone unnoticed and a number of applied theorists have been developing new models designed to answer these requirements.

Although this work is progressing rapidly, it is still in early stages of development. As matters stand presently, established firms have considerable latitude in responding defensively to new rivalry. Unlike the entry barrier era of the 1960s, where courts were quick to find anticompetitive purpose lurking behind innocent and efficient practices, the courts in the 1970s have been very cautious in evaluating claims of predation and strategic abuse by dominant firms.[14] This is partly because agreement is lacking on criteria for discerning admissible from excessive competitive replies to new rivalry. Additionally, there are problems in translating proposed criteria to operational measures that the courts can apply with confidence. Related to both of these is the hazard, to which the courts have been alert, that firms that complain they are subject to predatory pricing (and other unlawful practices) may, in fact, be seeking protectionist relief from legitimate, albeit complex, rivalrous behavior. Also, the enforcement ramifications of some of the new models have yet to be worked out.

A. DIEHARD CHICAGO

The distinguishing characteristic of what Posner has referred to as 'diehard Chicagoans' (1979, p. 932) is a reluctance to confront strategic behavior in any but a very narrow context. The favored approach, as illustrated most recently by the commentary of John McGee (1980), has been to insist upon studying strategic behavior issues in myopic terms.[15]

Predatory Pricing

McGee's survey of the recent predatory pricing literature is mainly negative with one conspicuous exception. McGee advises readers that 'Robert Bork's formulation of the problem commands attention' (1980, p. 293) and concludes that, 'In his masterful analysis of the US antitrust laws, Robert H. Bork shows why predatory price cutting would be rare or nonexistent even if there were no legal rules against it' (1980, pp. 316–17). Although I agree that Bork has made important contributions to the study of antitrust,[16] McGee and I differ on our assessment of

---

[14] For references to the relevant cases, see Ordover and Willig (1981, p. 70, n. 2).

[15] Although McGee was not among those identified by Posner as being a member of the diehard school, McGee has since volunteered that he qualifies for membership (1980, p. 292, n. 15).

[16] See my review of Bork's book in Williamson (1970a).

Bork's treatment of strategic behavior in general and predatory pricing in particular.

Thus Bork poses the problem of predatory pricing by considering a firm with an 80 per cent market share that 'wishes to kill a rival with 20 per cent in order to achieve the comforts and prerogatives of monopoly status' (1978, p. 149). He concludes, upon examining the rationality of such an undertaking, that predatory pricing of this kind is 'most unlikely to exist' (1978, p. 155). But the case that Bork considers is a very special and relatively uninteresting kind. As discussed below, the full ramifications of predatory pricing are not disclosed by focusing on a dominant firm's efforts to destroy a rival that has already committed itself by investing in specialized human and physical capital (and hence needs only to recover its variable costs to remain viable during the predatory siege).

McGee is nevertheless attracted to this formulation and therefore regards predatory pricing as insignificant. Indeed, his preferred legal rule on predatory pricing is to ignore it altogether (McGee, 1980, p. 317). Upon recognition, however, that some rule must be adopted, McGee understandably endorses the most permissive predatory pricing rule that has yet to be proposed: the Areeda–Turner marginal-cost-pricing rule.[17] In fact, this rule has found favor in many courts. But as Paul Joskow has explained, this has occurred because of a pressing need to fill a void and 'not because of the triumph of economic efficiency considerations in the interpretation of antitrust statutes' (1980, p. 202).

Voids can be filled, of course, in many ways. One of the reasons the courts were attracted to a marginal-cost-pricing rule, I conjecture, is that they perceived the dangers that more stringent rules would encourage protectionist abuses and accordingly favored a very permissive standard. In the process, however, of reducing the risk of what Joskow and Alvin Klevorick (1979, p. 223) refer to as 'false-positive' error – that is, incorrectly declaring something predatory that in fact is efficient – the courts have accepted a huge risk of 'false-negative' error – that is, allowing behavior that is, in fact, predatory to continue.

Although a consensus on this issue has not yet developed, there is widespread concern that a marginal-cost-pricing standard is defective.[18] A basic problem with this criterion is that it appeals to static-welfare-economics arguments for support while predatory pricing is unavoidably

---

[17] This rule is mainly associated with the 1975 paper of Phillip Areeda and Donald Turner. McGee, however, observes that he originated the rule ten years earlier (McGee, 1980, p. 290).

[18] Janusz Ordover and Robert Willig, in a recent paper, develop cost-based criteria that they contend are in the spirit of Areeda and Turner (Ordover and Willig, 1981, pp. 9, 16). In fact, however, their double test – the price exceeds both average and marginal cost – is much more stringent, and they nowhere propose average variable cost as a suitable surrogate, the operational result at which Areeda and Turner arrive.

an intertemporal issue. As William Baumol succinctly puts it, static analysis of the kind in which Areeda and Turner rely is 'inadequate ... because it draws our attention from the most pressing issues that are involved' (1979, p. 2). The 'nub of the problem ... [is] the intertemporal aspect of the situation' (1979, p. 3).

The Condition of Entry

As a result of persistent criticism, much of it originating with Chicago, it is now widely recognized that the entry barrier arguments of the 1960s were much too sweeping. But such a demonstration does not establish that this entire tradition should be rejected. The possibilities that remediable impediments to entry might arise, and that such circumstances are identifiable, ought to be considered. Consistent with his neglect of strategic factors, Bork seems unwilling to entertain such possibilities. This unwillingness is due chiefly to his implicit assumption that labor and capital markets operate frictionlessly, so that every market outcome is presumptively a merit outcome and further discussion is pointless. Once transaction costs are admitted, however, the assumption of frictionlessness no longer applies, the possibility of introducing strategic impediments to entry arises, and the main argument needs to be qualified. To be sure, the exceptions may not be numerous and the difficulties of informed or efficacious intervention may be great. Such defects might better be tolerated, therefore, rather than made subject to public policy review and attempted rectification. But this is a separate argument. Neither Bork nor others of the antientry barrier belief have addressed the entry barrier issues on these grounds. Since the frictionlessness assumptions on which Bork implicitly relies are unacceptable to many students of antitrust, continuing dispute over the nature and importance of entry barriers is to be expected.

Recent Headway

Objections that have been or could be leveled at early entry barrier models and related applications to predatory pricing include: (a) the structural preconditions are not carefully stated; (b) whether it is more attractive to bar rather than accept entry is assumed but not demonstrated; (c) attention is focused on total costs, but the composition of costs and the characteristics of assets matter crucially and have been neglected; (d) the incentives to engage in predation are weak; and (e) cost asymmetries between established firms and potential entrants are asserted but rarely addressed. Recent work has made headway with each of these issues.

Structural Preconditions. As discussed above, the early entry barrier models purported to be oligopoly models. But the question of how oligopolists managed to achieve effective concurrence of market action –

with respect to price, output, investment, and so forth – was not addressed. The relevance of those models outside of the dominant firm context was thus questionable.

Recent models in the entry barrier tradition have essentially abandoned the oligopoly claim. The issues are posed instead in a duopoly context between a sitting monopolist and a potential entrant. Those who would apply these models to oligopoly presumably have the heavy burden of demonstrating their applicability.

Similar care has been taken in assessing claims of predation. The hazard here is that the legal process will be misused to discourage legitimate rivalry. There is growing agreement that the structural preconditions that must be satisfied before claims of predation are seriously entertained are very high concentration coupled with barriers to entry (Williamson, 1977, pp. 292–3). Joskow and Klevorick (1979, pp. 225–31) and Ordover and Willig (1981) concur and propose a two-tier test for predatory pricing. The subset of industries for which strategic behavior warrants public policy scrutiny would thus appear to be the following: (a) the sitting monopolist–duopolist situation; (b) regulated monopolies; (c) dominant-firm industries; and (d) what William Fellner has referred to as 'Case 3 oligopoly' (1949, pp. 47–9) – which is an industry where an outside agency (for instance, a union) enforces collective action.[19]

Rationality of Pre-entry Deterrence. In principle, entry can be deterred in any of three ways: (a) by expanding output and investment in the pre-entry period, thereby discouraging the incentive to enter; (b) by threatening aggressive post-entry responses; and (c) by imposing cost disadvantages on rivals. The second of these is addressed below. The first is in the spirit of Bain and Modigliani and has been dealt with more recently by Avinash Dixit, who models the entry problem in a duopoly context (1979, 1980). This permits him simultaneously to display and assess the profitability and feasibility of having the sitting monopolist adopt any of three postures: (a) behave in an unconstrained-monopoly fashion; (b) expand output and investment so as to deter entry; and (c) accept entry by taking up a Stackelburg-leadership position in relation to the entrant. Dixit demonstrates that entry deterrence is optimal when fixed costs are of intermediate degree; the complaint that entry deterrence is an imposed, rather than derived, result can be dismissed if the requisite conditions are satisfied.

Costs, Assets, and Credibility. The standard entry barrier model assumes that potential entrants have access to the same long-run average total cost curve as do estabished firms. But the composition of costs between fixed

---

[19] It has been argued that the United Mine Workers performed this function in the bituminous coal industry (Williamson, 1968).

and variable is ignored. This poses the following anomaly: extant firms and potential entrants are indistinguishable if all costs are variable. The only effective entry-deterring policy in circumstances where all costs are variable is setting price equal to total cost, which is to say that entry deterrence is without purpose. The crucial role of fixed costs in early deterrence is evident from an examination of Dixit's (1979) formulation of the entry problem.

Even granting that entry deterrence sometimes is optimal, another question arises as to how large a monopoly distortion can develop by reason of temporal asymmetry (the sitting monopolist has assets in place at the outset) and fixed-cost conditions. Schmalensee has recently addressed this issue and shows that the pre-entry present value of excess profits that can be realized by established firms 'cannot exceed the capital (start-up) cost of a firm of minimum efficient scale,' and that scale economies are therefore of little quantitative importance from a welfare standpoint (1980, pp. 3, 8). This result is questionable, however, because it ignores the reputation-effect incentives discussed below.

A related issue that has come under scrutiny is the matter of credible threats. This goes to the issue of what post-entry behavior is appropriately imputed to the sitting monopolist. As Curtis Eaton and Richard Lipsey observe (1980, p. 721), both credible and posturing threats take the same form – 'If you take action X, I shall take action Y, which will make you regret X.' But credible and noncredible threats are distinguishable in that the party issuing the threat will rationally take action Y only if credibility conditions are satisfied. If the Nash response to X is indeed to take action Y, the threat is credible. But if, despite the threat, X occurs and the net benefits accruing to the party issuing the threat are greater if he accommodates (by taking action Z rather than Y), then the threat will be perceived as posturing rather than credible. Since such threats will be empty, Eaton and Lipsey have urged that analysis of strategic behavior focus entirely on threats for which credibility is satisfied. The translation of this argument into investment terms discloses that the sitting monopolist must invest in durable, *transaction-specific assets* if he is to successfully pre-empt a market and deter entry.[20]

Reputation Effects. Bork's original assessment of the benefits of predation, McGee's commentary thereon, the Areeda–Turner criterion for assessing predation, Schmalensee's measures of welfare distortion, and the Eaton and Lipsey treatment of credible threats all address the issue of entry and predation in a very narrow context. A large, established firm is confronted

---

[20] Asset specificity can take three forms: site specificity, physical asset specificity, and human asset specificity. For a discussion of these issues in transaction cost terms and an assessment of their organizational ramifications, see Williamson (1979b).

with a clearly defined threat of entry and its response is assessed entirely in that bilateral context. The rationality of killing a rival (Bork, 1978) or of deterring an equally efficient firm (which has not yet made irreversible commitments) becomes the focus of attention (Eaton and Lipsey, 1980, 1981). If, however, punitive behavior carries signals to this and other firms – in future periods, in other geographic areas, and, possibly, in other lines of commerce – such analyses may understate the full set of effects on which the would-be predator relies in his decision to discipline a rival. Assessing this requires that the issue of predation be addressed in a teaching and learning context – which, since teaching and learning models are not well developed, is not easy, and is somewhat speculative.

Recognition that reputation effects can be important has nevertheless been growing and there has been some headway in dealing with the issues. The general point has been made by Christian von Weizsacker in the context of what he refers to as the extrapolation principle (1981, pp. 72–3):

One of the most effective mechanisms available to society for the reduction of information production cost is the principle of extrapolation. By this I mean the phenomenon that people extrapolate the behavior of others from past observations and that this extrapolation is self-stabilizing, because it provides an incentive for others to live up to these expectations. ... By observing others' behavior in the past, one can fairly confidently predict their behavior in the future without incurring further costs ...

[This] extrapolation principle is deeply rooted in the structure of human behavior. Indeed it is also available in animal societies. ... The fight between two chickens does not only produce information about the relative strengths in the present, but also about relative strength in the future.

Whereas Eaton and Lipsey and others have emphasized that only credible threats will effectively deter rivals and that credibility is realized by making pre-emptive investments, reference to reputation opens up the possibility that behavior matters. If, however, all of the objective factors pertinent to rivalry are fully disclosed, what is it that a firm can credibly do to alter preceptions?

The answer to this puzzle, as to many others in economics, is that the fiction of complete knowledge facilitates analysis, but sometimes obscures the core issues. Obscuration is a special hazard where competition of a small-numbers kind with repeat play is involved.

David Kreps and Robert Wilson have addressed the issues by observing that the general problem with so-called noncredible threats is that 'the competitor realizes that if faced with a *fait accompli* of entry, the monopolist will find it optimal to accept this entry. Thus the believability of the threat is tenuous; perhaps the competitors will simply call the monopolist's bluff and enter' (Kreps and Wilson, 1980, p. 2). But while others terminate the analysis here, Kreps and Wilson go on to pose the following dilemma: 'if the monopolist carries out the [noncredible] threat, then he will become known for being tough, and this will deter subsequent challenges and therefore be to his long-run advantage. Today's entrant, realizing that the monopolist will meet today's challenge in order to deter challenges in the future, believes that the threat is credible and thus does not enter' (1980, p. 2).

Kreps and Wilson evaluate the behavioral aspects of credibility by considering a series of examples of noncooperative games. The two crucial features are (a) there must be uncertainty regarding the sitting monopolist's payoffs, and (b) the game involves repeated play. While the specific source of uncertainty is not important, they nevertheless offer several possibilities: 'There may be uncertainty concerning the monopolist's production function. The monopolist may derive nonpecuniary benefits from fighting, or he may gain pecuniary benefits indirectly in another of his activities. He may simply be irrational . . . [or there may be] uncertainty about the monopolist's discount rate' (p. 24).

With respect to repeated play, they observe that 'the play of early rounds may be overwhelmingly influenced not by immediate payoffs but by considerations of what information is being transmitted' (p. 58). This incentive to develop a reputation for toughness is especially great where the sitting monopolist 'plays against a sequence of different opponents, none of whom [has] the ability to foster a reputation' (p. 58). Accordingly, whereas credible-threat conditions must be fully satisfied in a full-information game, quasi-credibility may do if there is payoff uncertainty and repeat play.[21]

Applications pose the question of whether the circumstances where reputation-effect incentives are strong can be recognized. An important consideration is whether local entry is being attempted into a small sector of the total market in which the established firm enjoys dominance. Exploratory entry into a local geographic market, or into one or a few products in a much broader line of related products, would presumably enhance the appeal of a teaching response. The likelihood that the observed behavior is strategic is increased in the degree to which (a) the response is intensively focused on the local disturbance (is carefully crafted to apply only to the market where entry is attempted) and (b) goes beyond

---

[21] Assessing investment behavior is made more complex as a consequence. Thus even if a firm is 'unable to use excess capacity or a highly developed sales network profitably . . . *if* its opponents think that the firm might be able to use that capacity/sales network to engage in profitable predation, then the firm may wish to develop that capacity/sales network' so as to confirm the fear (Kreps and Wilson, 1980, p. 61).

a simple defensive response (for example, holding output unchanged in the face of entry) to include a punitive aspect (for example, increasing output as the reply to entry).

Cost Asymmetries. Areeda and Turner (1975) and, more recently, Ordover and Willig (1981, pp. 13–14) take the position that the predatory impact of a price reduction by a dominant firm can be judged by whether such a reduction will exclude an equally efficient rival. As I have argued elsewhere, this is a peculiar criterion for assessing the welfare benefits of contingent increases in output– 'now it's here, now it isn't, depending on whether an entrant has appeared or perished' (Williamson, 1977, p. 339). I did not, however, comment on the costs incurred by the entrant except in passing (1977, pp. 296, 303–4). This is a regrettable oversight, since Ordover and Willig, like Areeda and Turner before them, argue that whenever an incumbent's costs are lower than the entrant's, 'a price just below the rival's cost does earn the incumbent some profit ... and therefore induces exit without violation of our standard of predation' (1980, p. 14). Inasmuch as they make no reference to the contrary, Ordover and Willig appear to have reference to the full pecuniary costs experienced by the rival. In consideration of the series of strategic-cost disadvantages that an entrant experiences or may be made to bear in relation to an established firm, this is surely a dubious criterion.

There are two points here, the first of which is that history matters in assessing costs. Temporal cost differences can arise in operating cost, cost of capital, and learning-curve respects. The second point is that the established firm may, by its own actions, be responsible for cost differences of the first two kinds and may contribute to the third.

Operating-cost Asymmetries. The possibility that a potential entrant experiences cost disadvantages by reason of strategic forward integration into distribution has been addressed by Bork (1978, pp. 156–8). Thus suppose that the dominant firm experiences identical costs whether its product is distributed by integrated or independent dealers. Forward integration may nevertheless be attractive because this has the effect of raising the costs to potential rivals. If potential entrants that would otherwise enjoy cost parity (say in terms of manufacturing costs) must, because of foreclosure, simultaneously create a distribution capability to effect entry, and if *additional* costs are incurred in creating a side-by-side distribution network that would be avoided by utilizing (or expanding) existing, but nonintegrated, distribution capacity, forward integration may be presumed to have been undertaken for the purpose of creating strategic operating-cost asymmetries.

Capital Cost Differentials. Assume, for the purposes of the argument here, that the potential entrant would experience identical distribution costs to those of the established firm if it were to enter both manufacturing and distribution stages rather than manufacturing alone. Suppose also, however, that the would-be entrant has demonstrated competence only at the manufacturing stage. Two-stage entry thus requires it to raise funds for an unfamiliar second stage to which the capital market can be expected to attach a risk premium (Williamson, 1975, pp. 110–12; 1979b, pp. 962–4). Accordingly, cost parity between established firm and potential rival can be upset by capital cost differentials.

The capital costs of would-be entrants can further be increased if established firms can quasi-credibly threaten to engage in post-entry predation. If the 'suppliers of capital to [potential] entrants perceive that the risks in the particular markets are greater than they had previously thought them to be, the cost of capital to new entrants will rise' (Joskow and Klevorick, 1979, p. 231).

Learning Effects. The proposition that costs are a function not merely of the scale and scope of a firm's activity but also of the cumulative output was set out by Armen Alchian in 1959. Only recently, however, have the strategic ramifications been addressed. One of the complications that is introduced by learning effects is that the test of remunerative pricing by dominant firms in early-stage growth industries is much more difficult (Williamson, 1977, p. 323). Current costs need to be reduced by the discounted effect on future costs in making the assessment. As Michael Spence puts it, 'When there is a learning curve, the short-run output decision is a type of investment decision. It affects the accumulated output, a stock, and through it, future costs and market position' (1981, p. 1).

But there is more to it. First and foremost, the established firm, which enjoys the benefits of lower costs by reason of accumulated output, will never be confronted with an equally efficient rival if costs comparisons are made in the immediate post-entry period and learning curves are important. Second, out of recognition of the intertemporal cost effects, the established firm may have an incentive to engage in aggressive pricing designed to 'reduce the return to competitors investing in expanded market shares' (Spence, 1981, p. 41). Additionally, the established firm may upset efforts to achieve cost parity by threatening (perhaps with good cause) to bring law suits should the entrant attempt to shorten the learning period by hiring away key employees.

The upshot is that the *equally efficient rival criterion is primarily suited to static circumstances where historical differences and contrived cost asymmetries may be presumed to be absent*. This scenario is evidently favored by those who take a narrow view of predation and advocate a marginal cost pricing standard. To the extent, however, that actual circumstances are not accurately described in this way, allowance for cost differences may be necessary if an informed assessment of predation is to be realized.[22]

IV. Unresolved Dilemmas

The study of strategic behavior has made remarkable progress since the late 1970s. A number of troublesome problems nevertheless remain. These include: (a) whether efforts to curb predation should focus primarily on price and output, or if other aspects of rivalry should be included; (b) inasmuch as rules governing predation set up incentives for established firms to preposition, should allowance be made for prepositioning in assessing the merits of alternative rules; and (c) whether victims of mistaken predation should be accorded protection.

A. DIMENSIONS

Although they are not independent, the study of strategic behavior is usefully split into *ex ante* and *ex post* parts. *Ex ante* behavior takes the form of pre-entry investment (in capacity, research and development, promotion, the offer of multiple brands, and so on) while *ex post* behavior involves specific adaptations by dominant firms contingent upon entry. As between the two, aggressive strategic behavior in *ex post* respects is widely believed to be the more reprehensible, but there are complicating factors here as well.

Christian von Weizsacker's work on innovation is instructive in this regard. He distinguishes between progressive and mature industries and observes that the positive externalities of innovation are especially strong in a progressive industry due to the 'possibility of generating the next innovation' (1981, p. 150). A welfare assessment of the intertemporal incentives to engage in innovation in a progressive industry leads von Weizsacker to conclude that 'a pricing action by an incumbent, which by reasonable standards is not considered a predatory action in a nonprogressive industry, [*a fortiori*] cannot be called a predatory action in a progressive industry' (1981, p. 210).

A somewhat different aspect is emphasized by Ordover and Willig, who, in an important paper, contend that *ex post* 'manipulation of the

---

[22] F. M. Scherer observes that 'Entry at or near the minimum optimal scale into significant oligopolistic markets is [rare] ... Indeed, it is sufficiently rare that it usually receives considerable attention in the relevant trade press' (1980, p. 248). Many models of predatory pricing ignore this and argue that only output that is produced by an equally efficient rival is socially valued.

product set can frequently be more effective than price cutting as an anticompetitive tactic' (1981, p. 18). Two types of tactics are examined. The first entails 'the introduction of a new product that is a substitute for the products of the rival firm and that endangers its viability by diverting its sales. The second tactic is employed in the context of systems rivalry. It consists of the constriction in the supply of components that are vital to consumers' use of the rival's product, coupled with the introduction of systems components that enable consumers to bypass their use of the rival's products' (p. 19). Although both their criterion for assessing predation as well as the practicability of implementing their rules for assessing strategic R&D and the upward repricing or withdrawal of pre-existing components complementary to a rival may be disputed, the issues have nevertheless been structured in a useful way. Follow-on studies will surely make use of this framework.

But what should be done in the meantime when the law is confronted with problems that run well ahead of the theory? SCM Corporation asked for compulsory licensing relief in its complaint that Xerox had excluded SCM from the plain-copier market,[23] and Berkey Photo argued that unannounced product innovations by Kodak placed it at an unfair disadvantage.[24] The FTC has also brought some rather ambitious strategic behavior suits. A collusive strategy of brand proliferation formed the basis of its complaint against the principal producers of ready-to-eat cereals (Kellogg, General Mills, General Foods, and Quaker Oats),[25] and the FTC subsequently charged duPont with making pre-emptive investments in the titanium-dioxide market.[26]

Except for cases that are patently protectionist (and some of these have a protectionist flavor), there are no happy choices. Put differently, trade-offs proliferate and our capacity to evaluate them is very primitive. Thus, although some reject these suits with the observation that 'Plaintiffs arguments in the high-technology cases of the 1970s rests implicitly on an atomistic theory of competition which posits an organized economy with no changes in technology, no shifts in consumer tastes, no change in population – and no future that is essentially different from the past' (Conference Board, 1980, p. 18), this is really a red herring. Strategic behavior is an interesting economic issue *only* in an intertemporal context where uncertainty is featured. The high-technology cases are plainly of this kind, and arguably involve strategic calculations in which private and

[23] *SCM Corp.* v. *Xerox Corp.* (DC Conn 1978) 1978–2 Trade Cases, Para. 62, 392.

[24] *Berkey Photo, Inc.* v. *Eastman Kodak Co.* (DC NY 1978) 1978–1 Trade Cases, par. 62, 392.

[25] *FTC* v. *Kellogg et al.*, Docket No. 8883.

[26] *FTC* v. *E. I. du Pont de Nemours & Co.*, Complaint, Docket No. 9108, 5 Aprill 1978 CCH Trade Regulation Reporter, transfer binder, Federal Trade Commission Complaints and Orders, 1976–1979, Par. 21, 407.

social valuations differ. The courts have understandably been cautious in moving ahead in this area. Assuming that these are matters that can be re-examined as a deeper understanding of the issues and a capacity to make informed trade-offs develops, this would appear to be the responsible result.

B. PREPOSITIONING

A primary focus on *ex post* price and output behavior does not, however, mean that *ex ante* investments should be ignored entirely. Indeed, if comprehensive comparisons of the welfare ramifications of alternative predatory pricing rules are to be attempted, differential *ex ante* consequences, if they exist, should presumably be included.

The ways by which firms will preposition in relation to different rules have been addressed by Spence (1977), Salop (1979), Dixit (1979, 1980), and Eaton and Lipsey (1980, 1981) in relation to entry deterrence in general and by Williamson (1977) as entry deterrence applies to predation. The general argument here is that an 'established firm can alter the *outcome* to its advantage by changing the initial conditions. In particular, an irrevocable choice of investment allows it to alter its post-entry marginal cost curve, and thereby the post-entry equilibrium' (Dixit, 1980, p.96). This line of reasoning has been applied to the study of predation with the following result: each predatory pricing rule predictably gives rise to 'pre-entry price, output, and investment adjustments on the part of dominant firms whose markets are subject to encroachment. To neglect the incentives of rules whereby dominant firms made *pre-entry adaptive responses of a strategic kind* necessarily misses an important part of the problem' (Williamson, 1977, p. 293).

There is less than unanimity, however, over whether these prepositioning effects should be taken into account. Recent supporters of the marginal cost/equally efficient rival pricing rule (McGee, 1980; Ordover and Willig, 1981) ignore the prepositioning ramifications of alternative rules. Whether this is because they believe them to be unimportant or beyond the purview of responsible analysis is unclear. For the moment, the matter of prepositioning incentives and their relevance for rule assessment is under dispute.

C. MISTAKEN PREDATION

A troublesome question arises where predatory pricing is attempted in circumstances where the structural preconditions described previously are not satisfied. I will refer to this class of events as 'mistaken predation,' in that even if the predator is successful in driving a rival from the market it will fail to realize anything but very transient market power benefits.

A significant excess of price over cost cannot be supported for any but a short period of time where rivals are many and entry is easy. Where this obtains, an attempt at predation is mistaken because a correct assessment of the net benefits will disclose that they are negative.

The fact that attempted predation is mistaken does not, however, guarantee that it will never occur. Where it does, should the victims be entitled to relief by bringing suit and recovering damages? The application of the type of reasoning employed by Joskow and Klevorick would suggest a negative answer. The hazard is that many of the suits brought by firms in competitive industries would have the purpose of relieving these firms from legitimate rivalry rather than attempted predation. Since mistaken predation will presumably be rare or, at least, not repeated, the 'false positive errors – that is ... errors that involve labeling truly competitive price cuts as predatory' (Joskow and Klevorick, 1979, p. 223) would appear to be high and augur against allowing suits of this kind. Some firms would be victimized as a result, however, and other students of predation may assess the hazards differently.

V. Conclusion

The 1960s was a decade when antitrust was preoccupied with measures of concentration and entry barriers. Such a narrow formulation facilitated easy enforcement – to the extent that Justice Stewart was moved to observe that 'the sole consistency that I can find under section 7 is that the government always wins'[27] – but sometimes at the expense of an informed welfare assessment of the issues. Three factors contributed to this condition. First, it was widely believed that oligopolistic collusion was easy to effectuate. Second, wherever entry barriers were discovered they were held to be anticompetitive and antisocial, there being a great reluctance to acknowledge trade-offs. And third, the business firm was thought to be adequately described as a production function to which a profit maximization objective had been assigned.

These views had two unfortunate consequences. For one thing, anything that contributed to market power – offsetting benefits notwithstanding – was held to be unlawful. Second, nonstandard or unfamiliar business practices that departed from autonomous market contracting were also held to be presumptively unlawful. If the natural way by which to mediate transactions between technologically separable entities is through markets, surely any effort by the firm to extend control beyond its natural (technological) boundaries must be motivated by strategic purpose.

Matters changed in the 1970s, as a greater appreciation for efficiency

---

[27] Dissenting opinion in *US* v. *Von's Grocery Inc.* 384 US 270 (1966).

benefits developed, and as the conception of the firm as a governance
structure took hold. The perverse hostility with which efficiency differentials were once regarded gave way to an affirmative valuation of efficiency
benefits,[28] and business practices that were previously suspect, because
they did not fit comfortably with the view of the firm as a production
function, were reinterpreted in a larger context in which – implicitly, if
not explicitly – transaction cost economizing was introduced. As a
consequence, antitrust errors and enforcement excesses of the 1960s were
removed or reversed in the 1970s.

Despite progress with these matters, antitrust cannot settle back to a
quiet life. Other difficult antitrust issues relating to strategic behavior
have recently surfaced, and existing criteria for assessing the lawfulness
of strategic practices are actively under dispute. Significant headway with
a number of strategic behavior issues has nevertheless been made and
more is in prospect. The study of strategic behavior has been clarified in
the following significant respects: (a) severe structural preconditions in
both concentration and entry barrier respects need to be satisfied before
an incentive to behave strategically can be claimed to exist; (b) attention
to investment and asset characteristics is needed in assessing the condition
of entry – specifically, nontrivial irreversible investments, of a transaction-
specific kind have especially strong deterrent effects; (c) history matters
in assessing rivalry – both with respect to the leadership advantage enjoyed
by a sitting monopolist as well as in the incidence and evaluation of
comparative costs; and (d) reputation effects are important in assessng
the rationality of predatory behavior.

This last has a bearing on two crucial aspects of the strategic behavior
issue. For one thing, those who argue that strategic behavior can be
disregarded unless credible threat conditions are fulfilled have overstated
the case. This is not to suggest that the study of credible threats cannot
usefully inform the analysis of strategic behavior. But if knowledge is
imperfect then dominant firms can alter expectations by posturing (as
well as by objectively fulfilling credibility conditions), in which event
precommitments need not be as extensive as the credible threat literature
would indicate. Second, myopic assessments of strategic behavior understate the incentives to engage in predation. Those who focus on the
incentive to kill a specific rival are ignoring what may often be the stronger
incentive – that is, to develop a reputation that will subsequently help to
deter this and other firms in later periods, in other geographic markets,

---

[28] Vigilance is, nevertheless, necessary lest retrogression occur. Thus the Government's
lead attorney advised the court in *US* v. *Occidental Petroleum* (Civil Action No. C-3-78-
288) that the acquisition of Mead by Occidental was objectionable because it would permit
Mead to construct a large 'Greenfield plant, which was the most efficient and cost-effective
treatment,' and that this would disadvantage Mead's rivals.

and in other lines of commerce.

Among the issues actively under dispute in the study of strategic behavior are the following: (a) whether the equally efficient rival criterion is a useful one;[29] (b) whether the assessment of predatory pricing rules should make allowance for prepositioning incentives;[30] (c) whether strategic behavior should focus primarily on *ex post* contingent responses or can also be responsibly extended to include *ex ante* investments;[31] and (d) what remedies should be sought.[32] Clarification on these as well as sharpening of the issues enumerated in the preceding paragraph can be expected as the 1980s progress. I expect that antitrust enforcement regarding strategic behavior will be in much better shape at the end of the decade as a result of intervening scholarship. I furthermore anticipate that the continued need for antitrust will be demonstrated – and, alarmist cries for the abolition of antitrust will be discredited – in the process.

[29] Lest there by any doubt, I regard this as a seriously flawed criterion.

[30] I believe that they should, though this complicates the analysis.

[31] My own view is that antitrust is best advised to focus – at least for the present – on *ex post* contingent behavior. Behavior that goes beyond being merely defensive to include a punitive aspect is especially reprehensible and, arguably, is also the easiest to assess. Accordingly, contingent behavior that is directed not merely at the immediate rival but has a teaching-and-learning aspect is properly made the principal focus of antitrust enforcement against predation – at least until the state of the art for modeling and assessing strategic behavior is significantly advanced from where it stands presently.

[32] Not only are welfare assessments of *ex ante* entry-deterring behavior very subtle (von Weizsacker, 1980, 1981), but meaningful relief for *ex ante* investments may be difficult to fashion. Unless, therefore, a clear showing of welfare losses is made and efficacious relief can be devised, caution would appear to be warranted before pressing antitrust to hold that *ex ante* investments are unlawful.

[10]

THE CHICAGO SCHOOL OF
ANTITRUST ANALYSIS

RICHARD A. POSNER †

The use of the term "Chicago" to describe a body of antitrust views to which I, among others, am thought to subscribe is very common. I shall argue in this paper that although there was a time when the "Chicago" school stood for a distinctive approach to antitrust policy, especially in regard to economic questions, and when other schools, particularly a "Harvard" school, could be discerned and contrasted with it, the distinctions between these schools have greatly diminished. This has occurred largely as a result of the maturing of economics as a social science, and, as a corollary thereto, the waning of the sort of industrial organization that provided the intellectual foundations of the Harvard school. More generally, this change can be attributed to the fact that the diversity in fundamental premises among economists studying antitrust questions has substantially diminished. No longer is it such a simple thing to identify a Harvard or a Chicago position on issues of antitrust policy. Partly this is a matter of growing consensus; partly of a shift from disagreement over basic premises, methodology, and ideology toward technical disagreements of the sort that would be found even in a totally nonideological field.

Part I of this paper recounts the development of the Chicago school of antitrust analysis, and, more briefly, of the Harvard school. The sharpest differences between them are assignable to the 1950's and early 1960's. Part II discusses a number of areas in which the positions of the two school have since overlapped, converged, or crossed over, with special reference to predatory pricing. Part III considers the issue in which traces of the traditional Chicago-Harvard confrontation are most conspicuous—the issue whether to break up leading firms in highly concentrated industries. The general conclusion of the paper is that it is no longer worth talking about different schools of academic antitrust analysis.

I. THE CHICAGO AND HARVARD SCHOOLS: THE FOUNDATIONS

The basic features of the Chicago school of antitrust analysis are attributable to the work of Aaron Director in the 1950's. Di-

† Lee and Brena Freeman Professor of Law, University of Chicago. The helpful comments of Robert Bork, Kenneth Dam, William Landes, George Stigler, and Donald Turner on a previous draft are gratefully acknowledged.

926 *UNIVERSITY OF PENNSYLVANIA LAW REVIEW* [Vol. 127:925

rector formulated the key ideas of the school,[1] which were then elaborated on by students and colleagues such as Bowman, Bork, McGee, and Telser.[2] These ideas did not, I believe, emerge from a full-blown philosophy of antitrust. Rather, they were the product of pondering specific questions raised by antitrust cases, and only in retrospect did it become clear that they constituted the basis of a general theory of the proper scope of antitrust policy. In summary form the key ideas may be stated as follows:

1. A tie-in (*i.e.*, requiring a buyer to buy a second product as the condition of buying the first) is not a rational method of obtaining a second source of monopoly profits, because an increase in the price charged for the tied product will, as a first approximation, reduce the price that the purchaser is willing to pay for the tying product. A tie-in makes sense only as a method of price discrimination, based on the fact that the amount of the tied product bought can be used to separate purchasers into more or less elastic demanders of the tying product. There is no need to worry about price discrimination, however, because it does not aggravate the monopoly problem. On the contrary, price discrimination is a device by which the monopolist in effect seeks to serve additional consumers, *i.e.*, those having the more elastic demands, who might be deterred by the single monopoly price that would be charged in the absence of discrimination. Thus, price discrimination brings the monopolist's output closer to that of a competitive market and reduces the misallocative effects of monopoly.

2. From the standpoint of the manufacturer imposing it, resale price maintenance is not a rational method of distribution if its effect is to give dealers monopoly profits. Yet manufacturers, if permitted, often will impose it. The explanation is that, by preventing price competition among dealers, resale price maintenance encourages dealers to offer consumers presale services (such as point

---

[1] Director formulated his ideas mainly orally. *But see* Director & Levi, *Law and the Future: Trade Regulation*, 51 Nw. U.L. Rev. 281 (1956).

[2] *See, e.g.*, Bork, *Vertical Integration and the Sherman Act: The Legal History of an Economic Misconception*, 22 U. Chi. L. Rev. 157 (1954); Bowman, *Tying Arrangements and the Leverage Problem*, 67 Yale L.J. 19 (1957); McGee, *Predatory Price Cutting: The Standard Oil (N.J.) Case*, 1 J.L. & Econ. 137 (1958); Telser, *Why Should Manufacturers Want Fair Trade?*, 3 J.L. & Econ. 86 (1960). For the most complete and most orthodox statement of the Chicago position see R. Bork, The Antitrust Paradox (1978); for an anthology in which Chicago writings are heavily represented see The Competitive Economy: Selected Readings (Y. Brozen ed. 1974). My own views, which closely resemble but are not identical to the more orthodox Chicago position espoused by Bork, are expressed in R. Posner, Antitrust Law (1976).

of sale advertising, inventory, showroom display, and knowledge-able sales personnel) up to the point at which the cost of these services at the margin just equals the price fixed by the manufac-turer. Such services, which enhance the value of the manufacturer's product to consumers and hence the price he can charge the dealers, might—because of "free-rider" [3] problems—not be provided if price competition among dealers were permitted.

3. Selling below cost in order to drive out a competitor is un-profitable even in the long run, except in the unlikely case in which the intended victim lacks equal access to capital to finance a price war. The predator loses money during the period of predation and, if he tries to recoup it later by raising his price, new entrants will be attracted, the price will be bid down to the competitive level, and the attempt at recoupment will fail.[4] Most alleged instances of below-cost pricing must, therefore, be attributable to factors other than a desire to eliminate competition.

These ideas generated others. The tie-in analysis, for instance, was extended to vertical integration in general. To illustrate, it makes no sense for a monopoly producer to take over distribution in order to earn monopoly profits at the distribution as well as the manufacturing level. The product and its distribution are com-plements, and an increase in the price of distribution will reduce the demand for the product.[5] Assuming that the product and its distribution are sold in fixed proportions, and thus that the price discrimination analysis is inapplicable, the conclusion is reached that vertical integration must be motivated by a desire for efficiency rather than for monopoly.

The analysis of resale price maintenance generalized readily to other restrictions on distribution, such as exclusive territories and exclusive outlets. The predatory-pricing analysis generalized to other methods by which firms were thought to hurt others by hurt-ing themselves—for example, by demanding that purchasers sign longer-term contracts than they desire, in order to deny a market to competing sellers: a rational purchaser would demand compensa-tion for accepting such a disadvantageous term.

---

[3] A "free rider" in this context would be a dealer who undersold competing dealers by selling the product itself at a lower price while relying on them to provide the necessary presale services to the customer.

[4] Rather than suffer financial loss as a result of a price war, the rational would-be monopolist would buy out the competing company.

[5] This is the same reason why manufacturers would not want their dealers to cartelize distribution and why, therefore, Director sought an alternative explanation for resale price maintenance.

From these various analyses, a conclusion of great significance for antitrust policy emerges: firms cannot in general obtain or enhance monopoly power by unilateral action [6]—unless, of course, they are irrationally willing to trade profits for position. Consequently, the focus of the antitrust laws should not be on unilateral action; it should instead be on: (1) cartels and (2) horizontal mergers large enough either to create monopoly directly, as in the classic trust cases,[7] or to facilitate cartelization by drastically reducing the number of significant sellers in the market. Since unilateral action, as I have defined the term, had been the cutting edge of antitrust policy for a great many years, to place it beyond the reach of antitrust law, as Director and his followers seemed to want to do, implied a breathtaking contraction in the scope of antitrust policy.

What was the source of Director's heterodox thinking? Because of Director's close personal and professional associations with Milton Friedman, it is common to think that Director's antitrust analysis was the product of conservative (which is to say, "liberal" in the nineteenth-century sense of the term) antipathy to government intervention in the economy. I question this view. I believe Director's conclusions resulted simply from viewing antitrust policy through the lens of price theory. Each of his ideas was deducible from the assumption that businessmen are rational profit-maximizers, the deduction proceeding in accordance with the tenets of simple price theory, *i.e.*, that demand curves slope downward, that an increase in the price of a product will reduce the demand for its complement, that resources gravitate to the areas where they will earn the highest return, etc. "Simple" and "easy" are not the same thing, however. Although the analytic tools used by Director were simple, the insights they yielded were extremely subtle. Certainly they were resisted for many years.

Yet it is still fair to ask why the application of price theory to antitrust should have been a novelty. The answer, I believe, is that in the 1950's and early 1960's, industrial organization, the field of economics that studies monopoly questions, tended to be untheoretical, descriptive, "institutional," and even metaphorical.[8]

---

[6] By this I mean action that does not involve agreement with a competitor. It may, of course, involve agreement with a customer or supplier, and generally does: even a sale below cost involves at least an implicit contract between seller and purchaser.

[7] *See, e.g.*, United States v. American Tobacco Co., 221 U.S. 106 (1911); Standard Oil Co. v. United States, 221 U.S. 1 (1911).

[8] Its flavor is well conveyed in the writings of Edward S. Mason. *See, e.g.*, E. MASON, ECONOMIC CONCENTRATION AND THE MONOPOLY PROBLEM (1957). For a representative application of 1950's-style industrial organization to antitrust prob-

Casual observation of business behavior, colorful characterizations (such as the term "barrier to entry"), eclectic forays into sociology and psychology, descriptive statistics, and verification by plausibility took the place of the careful definitions and parsimonious logical structure of economic theory. The result was that industrial organization regularly advanced propositions that contradicted economic theory.

An example is the "leverage" theory of tie-ins that Donald Turner, a Harvard economist in the Edward Mason and Joe Bain tradition, espoused shortly after Director had developed his price-discrimination theory of tie-ins.[9] The leverage theory held that if a seller had a monopoly of one product, he could and would monopolize its indispensable complements as well, so as to get additional monopoly profits. Thus, if he had a patented mimeograph machine, he would lease the machine at a monopoly price and also require his lessees to buy the ink used in the machine from him and charge them a monopoly price for the ink. This procedure, however, makes no sense as a matter of economic theory. The purchaser is buying a service, mimeographing. The pricing of its components is a mere detail; it is, rather, the total price of the service that he cares about. If the seller raises the price of one component, the ink, the purchaser will treat this as an increase in the price of the service. If the machine is already being priced at the optimal monopoly level, an increase in the price of the ink above the competitive level will raise the total price of the service to the consumer above the optimal monopoly level and will thereby reduce the monopolist's profits.

There was a similar confusion in the concept of a "barrier to entry," a concept that played—and still plays—a large role in thinking about competition. Suppose that it costs $10,000,000 to build the smallest efficient plant to serve some market; then, it was argued, there is a $10,000,000 "barrier to entry," a hurdle a new entrant would have to overcome to serve the market at no disadvantage vis-à-vis existing firms.[10] But is there really a hurdle? If the $10,000,000 plant has a useful life of, for example, ten years, the annual cost to the new entrant is only $1,000,000. Existing firms bear the same annual cost, assuming that they plan to replace their

---

lems see C. KAYSEN, *United States v. United Shoe Machinery Corporation: An Economic Analysis of an Anti-trust Case* (1956).

[9] *See* Turner, *The Validity of Tying Arrangements Under the Antitrust Laws,* 72 HARV. L. REV. 50, 60-62, 63 n.42 (1958).

[10] *See* C. KAYSEN & D. TURNER, ANTITRUST POLICY 73 & n.33 (1959).

plants. The new entrant, therefore, is not at any cost disadvantage after all.

Advertising presents a similar situation. A new entrant, to get his product accepted in the market, may have to launch it with an expensive advertising campaign. Again, this is a capital expenditure, because the effect of the campaign will not be fully used up in the first year. There is no reason to expect the annual cost of this capital expenditure to be any higher than that of firms in the market. They too must spend money on advertising to keep the consumer interested in their products. Most advertising, in fact, depreciates more rapidly than most plants; [11] therefore, it is a lesser "barrier to entry" than having to build a plant (although in the traditional analysis it was considered a greater one). Neither the plant nor the advertising is a barrier in any useful sense.

The Chicago school's view of advertising is especially noteworthy because of the importance that advertising had assumed in the Harvard thinking on antitrust.[12] Advertising played a dual role in that thinking. First, it was one of the most important barriers to entry. Second, it was used as the riposte to the free-rider argument about why manufacturers imposed resale price maintenance. The Harvard position was that overcoming the free-rider problem and thereby increasing the provision of presale services by the retailer was not a social benefit, because those services were forms of advertising, and advertising enables the manufacturer more effectively to differentiate his brand from competitors' brands, thereby creating or enhancing barriers to entry. The underlying assumption is that consumers are irrational and manipulable, and the Chicago theorist rejects this assumption as inconsistent with the premises of price theory. The rational consumer will pay for advertising (in the form of a higher price for the advertised brand) only to the extent that advertising reduces his costs of search. The

---

[11] The depreciation rate of advertising has been found to be very high in industries that advertise heavily—such as the cosmetics (13% a year) and cereals (37%) industries. *See* Ayanian, *Advertising and Rate of Return*, 18 J.L. & ECON. 479, 499 (1975).

[12] Unlike other tenets of the old industrial organization, the hostility to advertising, though largely abandoned in the new Areeda and Turner treatise, P. AREEDA & D. TURNER, ANTITRUST LAW (1978); *see* note 41 *infra*, continues to command considerable, though diminished, academic support. *See, e.g.,* W. COMANOR & T. WILSON, ADVERTISING AND MARKET POWER (1974). For the Chicago position, see Brozen, *Entry Barriers: Advertising and Product Differentiation,* in INDUSTRIAL CONCENTRATION: THE NEW LEARNING 115 (1974); Telser, *Advertising and Competition,* 72 J. POLITICAL ECON. 537 (1964). For recent discussions see D. WORCESTER, WELFARE GAINS FROM ADVERTISING: THE PROBLEM OF REGULATION (1978); Butters, *A Survey of Advertising and Market Structure,* 66 AM. ECON. REV. PAPERS & PROC. 392 (1976).

services provided by advertising are therefore real services. In fact, they are indistinguishable from those yielded by a better product—and it is never suggested that making one's product genuinely better than those of competitors or potential competitors creates a "barrier to entry."

A clue to the nature of the Harvard school of industrial organization is that its practitioners were so fond of doing studies of competition in particular industries—airlines, tin cans, aluminum, rayon, Douglas firs, etc. These studies exemplified the particularistic and non-theoretical character of the field. The powerful simplifications of economic theory—rationality, profit maximization, the downward-sloping demand curve—were discarded, or at least downplayed, in favor of microscopic examination of the idiosyncrasies of particular markets.

The "kinked demand curve," "workable competition," "cut-throat competition," "leverage," "administered prices," and the other characteristic concepts of the industrial organization of this period had this in common: they were not derived from and were often inconsistent with economic theory, and in particular with the premises of rational profit maximization. They were derived from observation, unsystematic and often superficial, of business behavior. Director's approach was the opposite. He explained tie-ins, resale price maintenance, and other business behavior described in antitrust cases not by studying the practices but by looking for an explanation for them that squared with basic economic theory.[13] When they first began to emerge in the articles written by his colleagues, students, and disciples, Director's ideas made little impact either on scholarly opinion or on policy. In some quarters the Chicago school was regarded as little better than a lunatic fringe. Kaysen and Turner's *Antitrust Policy,* the classic statement of the Harvard school, published in 1959, contains virtually no trace of any influence of the Chicago school.[14]

Twenty years later, the position is dramatically changed. Partly as a result of George Stigler's attacks on the intellectual foundations of traditional industrial organization [15] and partly as a

[13] It is a curiosity, and a source of regret, that to this day very few of Director's ideas have been subjected to systematic empirical examination.

[14] They do offer a brief discussion of the price discrimination theory of tie-ins. *See* C. KAYSEN & D. TURNER, *supra* note 10, at 157. Elsewhere, however, the authors seem to be espousing the leverage theory. *Id.* 154, 157. But the discussion is unclear, as is Turner's brief reference to the price discrimination theory in his early article on tie-ins. *See* Turner, *supra* note 9, at 63 n.42.

[15] *See* G. STIGLER, THE ORGANIZATION OF INDUSTRY (1968) [hereinafter cited as ORGANIZATION OF INDUSTRY], collecting his major articles on industrial organiza-

result of the growing sophistication of economic analysis, the traditional industrial organization is becoming discredited in academic circles. The Chicago school has largely prevailed with respect to its basic point: that the proper lens for viewing antitrust problems is price theory. At the same time, some of the specific ideas first advanced by Aaron Director have been questioned, modified, and refined, resulting in the emergence of a new animal: the "diehard Chicagoan" (such as Bork and Bowman) who has not accepted any of the suggested refinements of or modifications in Director's original ideas.

The work of Director and his followers focused on the question when, if ever, a firm can unilaterally obtain or maintain monopoly power. The question when a firm can obtain such power by collaboration with its competitors received less attention. Partly, perhaps, for tactical reasons (not to seem to reject antitrust policy in its entirety), the members of the Chicago school would sometimes denounce price fixing. But it is unlikely that they regarded even price fixing, let alone oligopoly, as a serious problem. In the classical economic tradition running from Smith to Marshall, the tradition in which the Chicago school operates, a clear recognition of the propensity of sellers to attempt collusion was conjoined with a general indifference to, and sometimes an explicit rejection of, the desirability of imposing legal sanctions on collusion. This complacency (if one can call it that) rested on the belief that cartels were, first, highly unstable because of the propensity of members to cheat (so long as the cartel was not legally enforceable), and, second, in the long run futile in the absence of substantial barriers to entry. Collusion might still be attempted frequently if attempting it was cheap, but it would rarely succeed and its overall misallocative effects would be too slight to warrant inevitably costly public proceedings.

Given this tradition, given the Chicago school's rejection of the expansive notion of "barriers to entry," given the lack of any clear theoretical basis for oligopoly theory (and its accouterments such as the kinked demand curve), given Harberger's tiny estimate of the welfare costs of monopoly,[16] given the atheoretical, ad hoc, and unsupported character of the efforts to avoid the implications of Harberger's analysis by ascribing to oligopolists failures of innovation or cost control, it was not to be expected that the Chicago

tion. *See also* G. STIGLER & J. KINDAHL, THE BEHAVIOR OF INDUSTRIAL PRICES (1970).

[16] *See* Harberger, *Monopoly and Resource Allocation*, 44 AM. ECON. REV. PAPERS & PROC. 77 (1954).

school would attach great importance to vigorous prosecution of colluders. But such enforcement activity, in contrast to that directed against unilateral monopolizing acts, was not deplored.

George Stigler's work in the late 1950's and early 1960's, however, did focus on collusion and thus served to complete the edifice of Chicago antitrust thought. A series of articles [17] chipped away at the apparatus that the traditional industrial organization had constructed to analyze collusion. In its place Stigler proposed a general theory of collusion that embraced oligopoly, *i.e.,* collusion not involving explicit communication, as a special case.[18] He approached the question of collusion by asking, in the manner of a price theorist rather than an industrial-organization man, when the benefits of collusion, in higher profits, exceed the costs (of preventing cheating) to the individual seller. The rate of entry, the elasticity of demand, the concentration of buyers, and other factors were identified. Many of these factors had been noted by the oligopoly theorists; Stigler's contribution was to show that every facet of the collusion question, including tacit collusion or oligopoly behavior, could be analyzed using the tools of price theory.

Stigler's analysis did not deny the possibility of collusion, even of the tacit variety. But it did suggest that tacit collusion would be a problem only at very high levels of concentration,[19] and in so doing cast grave doubt on the necessity for draconian measures, whether under section 7 of the Clayton Act or section 2 of the Sherman Act, for preventing tacit collusion by arresting or destroying concentration.[20]

By 1969, then, an orthodox Chicago position (well represented in the writings of Robert Bork) had crystallized: only explicit price fixing and very large horizontal mergers (mergers to monopoly) were worthy of serious concern.

II. The Growing Convergence of the Two Schools

The basic tenet of the Chicago school, that problems of competition and monopoly should be analyzed using the tools of general

---

[17] *See* articles collected in Organization of Industry, *supra* note 15.

[18] G. Stigler, A *Theory of Oligopoly,* in Organization of Industry, *supra* note 15, at 39.

[19] *Id.* 57, 59. *See also* Kessel, *A Study of the Effect of Competition in the Tax-Exempt Bond Market,* 79 J. Political Econ. 706, 727 (1971).

[20] *See* President's Task Force Report on Productivity and Competition (1969), *reprinted in* 1 *Small Business and the Robinson-Patman Act: Hearings on H. Res. 66 Before the Special Subcomm. on Small Business and the Robinson-Patman Act of the House Select Comm. on Small Business,* 91st Cong., 1st Sess. 271 (1969).

934   *UNIVERSITY OF PENNSYLVANIA LAW REVIEW*   [Vol. 127:925

economic theory rather than those of traditional industrial organization, has triumphed. The concepts and methods of traditional industrial organization are increasingly discredited in economics as practiced in the leading universities and this change is beginning to be reflected in the application of economics to antitrust law. The new Areeda and Turner treatise [21] is a notable example of this point, although the treatise, perhaps because it is addressed primarily to practitioners rather than scholars, does not explicitly acknowledge the modification or abandonment of many of Professor Turner's earlier views. At the same time, the application of price theory to antitrust law has not left the pioneering work of Director and his followers untouched.

Let us consider now how the passage of years has affected some of the specific controversies between the Chicago and Harvard schools.

1. *Tie-ins.* The leverage theory of tie-ins early gave way in Harvard thinking to a barriers-to-entry theory.[22] A tie-in was said to complicate entry because the new entrant would have to produce the tied as well as the tying product. When the motive for tying is price discrimination, however, the producer of the tying product need not assume control over any part of the production of the tied product, let alone produce it all. Instead, all that is required is that he act as an intermediary between the producer and the ultimate consumer so that he can reprice it in accordance with his discriminatory scheme.[23] A new entrant will be able to obtain the tied product from the same source that the existing firm obtains it from.

One element (and an important one) of the Chicago analysis is, however, subject to criticism: the assumption that price discrimination is on the whole socially beneficial because it moves the monopolist's output closer to the competitive level and hence reduces the misallocative effects of monopoly. As Joan Robinson pointed out long ago, if price discrimination is not perfect (and it

---

[21] P. AREEDA & D. TURNER, *supra* note 12. Another important example, less dramatic only because the author is too young to have had earlier published views to recant, is Ernest Gellhorn's *Antitrust Law and Economics.* E. GELLHORN, ANTITRUST LAW AND ECONOMICS 257-60, 283-85 (1976).

[22] The barrier-to-entry theory of tie-ins appears in Kaysen and Turner's treatise. C. KAYSEN & D. TURNER, *supra* note 10, at 157. As pointed out above, it is not clear whether Kaysen and Turner also espoused the leverage theory. *See* note 14 *supra.*

[23] It is hardly credible, for example, that the A.B. Dick Company was trying to take over the production of ink in the United States. *See* Henry v. A.B. Dick Co., 224 U.S. 1, 11 (1911).

never is), it may lead to a smaller, rather than a larger, output than single-price monopoly.[24] For example, many of the heavy users of mimeograph machines might be deterred by an ink tie-in that had the effect of raising the price of the machine and the loss of output might not be offset by greater business from small users, even though on balance the monopolist's profits were higher (higher profits, rather than greater output, being the purpose of price discrimination). Even a larger output may not result in a smaller misallocation. The price-discriminating monopolist breaks up his demand curve into a series of separate demand curves for different groups of customers. Within each of these submarkets he sells the output that equates his marginal revenue to his marginal cost. The total misallocation brought about by the price-discriminating monopolist is the sum of the misallocations in each submarket, and may easily exceed the misallocation caused by a monopolist charging a single price and producing a smaller output.[25]

Other criticisms of the Chicago position have also been made. Professor Williamson, for instance, has noted that price discrimination involves extra transaction costs—specifically, the costs of preventing the low-price purchasers from reselling to the high-price purchasers (arbitrage)—which reduce the welfare gains from a higher output—if output is in fact higher.[26] It has also been argued that, by increasing the expected gains from monopolizing, price discrimination increases the investment in monopolizing—which may not be socially desirable. Indeed, the costs of creating and maintaining monopolies may exceed the misallocative costs resulting from the smaller output of monopolized compared to competitive markets.[27]

In the light of such criticism, the original Chicago analysis of the effects of tie-ins now seems a little oversimple. Nevertheless,

---

[24] J. ROBINSON, THE ECONOMICS OF IMPERFECT COMPETITION 190-94 (1933). *See also* P. SAMUELSON, FOUNDATIONS OF ECONOMIC ANALYSIS 42-45 (1947). Bork thinks it likely that price discrimination, even if imperfect, will generally result in a larger output than a single-price monopoly. R. BORK, *supra* note 2, at 397. He relies for this conclusion primarily on Joan Robinson's analysis, but I cannot find anything in her analysis that supports any general conclusion regarding the output effects of discriminatory versus nondiscriminatory monopoly.

[25] I am indebted to Dennis Carlton for having pointed this out to me.

[26] O. WILLIAMSON, MARKETS AND HIERARCHIES: ANALYSIS AND ANTITRUST IMPLICATIONS 11-13 (1975).

[27] *See* Posner, *Exclusionary Practices and the Antitrust Laws*, 41 U. CHI. L. REV. 506, 510-13 (1974). Bork criticizes the argument on the ground that some monopolies are a byproduct of socially desirable activity, *e.g.*, innovation, and in those cases the effect of price discrimination in making monopoly more profitable, and hence inducing greater resources to be expended on obtaining it, need not occasion concern. R. BORK, *supra* note 2, at 396. The point is correct. *See* Posner, *supra*, at 513-14. But it is different from the point that price discrimination is socially desirable because it leads to a larger output of the monopolized product.

the conclusion that tie-ins should not be forbidden seems both correct [28] and increasingly influential on academic opinion.

2. *Vertical integration.* Here too the leverage theory was eventually replaced by a barriers-to-entry theory (the economic analysis of vertical integration being, as I have indicated, symmetrical with that of tie-ins).[29]   The thinking was that if, for example, supplier *A* acquires all of his retail outlets, *B*, in order to compete, will have to open his own chain of outlets. This, in turn, will make *B*'s entry more costly. The steps in this analysis are illogical, however, and evidence of monopolization by such means scant or nonexistent.[30] *A* will find it very costly to buy more outlets than he needs. *B*, on the other hand, will not have to open his own outlets to enter; if his entry is anticipated, the outlets will be there to greet him. Moreover, even if *B* did have to open his own retail outlets, the higher capital cost of his entry would still be no greater than the (also higher) capital cost to *A* of being a retailer as well as a manufacturer. The analysis does not depend on whether retail outlets are cheap or expensive to build or acquire or on whether the integration in question is forward into distribution or backward into raw-material, or other, supply. The essential point is that the cost to the monopolist of integrating is prima facie the same as the cost to the new entrant of having to integrate.[31] The validity of this analysis is not affected even if the result of integration is completely to deny the new entrant access to some essential input except by dealing with the existing firms in the market. The cost to the existing firms is still the same as to the new entrant, although now it is in the form of an opportunity cost. Suppose, for example, that kryptonite is an indispensable input in the manufacture of widgets. *A* owns all the kryptonite in the universe and also manufactures widgets. He could, of course, refuse to sell kryptonite to *B*, a prospective entrant into widget production. The cost to *A* of this refusal is the price *B* would have been willing to pay. Stated differently, by his control of kryptonite *A* can extract any monopoly

---

[28] *See* R. POSNER, *supra* note 2, at 178-83.

[29] *See* C. KAYSEN & D. TURNER, *supra* note 10, at 120-21. Kaysen and Turner also espoused a leverage theory of vertical integration. *Id.* 121-22.

[30] *See* Peltzman, *Issues in Vertical Integration Policy*, in PUBLIC POLICY TOWARD MERGERS 167 (1969).

[31] This assumes equal access to capital markets and equal cost of obtaining capital. These assumptions have been criticized by Professor Williamson, Williamson, Book Review, 83 YALE L.J. 647, 656-57 (1974), among others. In only one respect, however, and that a minor one, can this position be sustained, at least in the absence of evidence that has so far not been forthcoming. *See* text accompanying note 61 *infra*.

rents available in the widget industry without denying a place in widget manufacture to others firms. If there is a proper antitrust objection, it is to the kryptonite monopoly rather than to vertical integration.

Yet, despite the force of these arguments, it is incorrect to dismiss entirely the possibility of monopolistic consequences from vertical arrangements. The above arguments assume that, as in the case of the manufacturer-retailer, the relevant inputs, *e.g.*, the manufactured product and its distribution, are combined in fixed proportions to produce the final output (the sale at retail). Suppose, however, that some input is used in variable proportions with other inputs to produce the final output, *e.g.*, uranium and enrichment services in the production of nuclear fuel. If one of the inputs is monopolized, causing its price to rise in relation to those of other inputs, the output manufacturer will seek to reduce the proportion in which he uses this input and, instead, use more of the other inputs. The possibility of such substitution acts as a partial check on the monopoly power of the input monopolist. Assume, however, that the input producer buys the input user. This will eliminate the threat of substitution and so reduce the elasticity of demand for the input in question.[32] Even so, it does not follow that the merger should be prohibited, for one of its effects is that the inputs will now be used in the proportions that minimize the true social costs of manufacturing the output. But it cannot be said that such a merger, merely because it is vertical, cannot possibly increase monopoly. So saying, I do not mean to suggest that such an equivocal and perhaps remote[33] danger warrants reversing the growing support, at least in academic circles, for a permissive policy toward vertical mergers and vertical integration generally.

The change in thinking that has been brought about by the Chicago school is nowhere more evident than in the area of vertical integration. Kaysen and Turner, writing in 1959, advocated forbidding any vertical merger in which the acquiring firm had twenty

---

[32] *See* Vernon & Graham, *Profitability of Monopolization by Vertical Integration*, 79 J. POLITICAL ECON. 924 (1971), *discussed in* McGee & Bassett, *Vertical Integration Revisited*, 19 J.L. & ECON. 17 (1976). *See also* Blair & Kaserman, *Vertical Integration, Tying, and Antitrust Policy*, 68 AM. ECON. REV. 397 (1978), and references cited therein. Blair and Kaserman note that the same result can be obtained by the input monopolist's tying potentially substitutable inputs to the sale of the input he controls. They offer no example showing that this has ever been done.

[33] A very recent paper suggests, on theoretical grounds, that monopoly power is unlikely to be increased substantially. *See* Mallela & Nahata, *Theory of Vertical Control With Variable Proportions* (forthcoming in *Journal of Political Economy*). A similar conclusion is reached by Bork. *See* R. BORK, *supra* note 2, at 229-31.

percent or more of its market.[34] Areeda and Turner, writing in
1978, express very little concern with anticompetitive effects from
vertical integration. In fact, as between a rule of per se illegality
for vertical integration by monopolists and a rule of per se legality,
their preference is for the latter.[35]

   3. Restricted distribution. As noted above, the Harvard reply
to the Chicago analysis of resale price maintenance was that the
benefit that the manufacturer sought to obtain by restricting competition among his distributors, *i.e.*, presale services, was actually a
social evil, because these services resulted in "product differentiation," a barrier to entry.[36] Facing no close substitutes for his brand
because it was differentiated in the consumer's eyes from competing
brands,[37] the producer could charge a monopoly price. If the case
of fraudulent advertising is put to one side, the conclusion that
advertising and related promotional methods create monopoly
power, at least in any sense relevant to antitrust policy, cannot be
derived from the premises of economic theory. Consumers will not
pay more for one brand than for another unless the first is cheaper
or better.[38] Advertising can make an advertised brand cheaper by
reducing the consumer's search costs by an amount greater than
the difference in nominal price between that brand and nonad-
vertised brands of the same product. The same point can be made
with respect to the other presale services, *e.g.*, display, that are
encouraged by restricted distribution.

   The new industrial organization, which relates advertising to
the costs of search, has transformed advertising from a social evil
into a social benefit,[39] and in so doing has fatally undermined the
Comanor riposte to the Director-Telser theory of resale price main-
tence. Although inter-school differences relating to the welfare
effects of advertising remain,[40] the position of the Chicago school

---

[34] C. KAYSEN & D. TURNER, *supra* note 10, at 133.

[35] 3 P. AREEDA & D. TURNER, *supra* note 12, ¶ 726b. Areeda and Turner are
discussing vertical integration by internal expansion rather than by merger, but their
analysis implies a tolerant attitude toward either form.

[36] *See* text accompanying note 12 *supra*.

[37] *See* Comanor, *Vertical Territorial and Customer Restrictions: White Motor
and Its Aftermath*, 81 HARV. L. REV. 1419, 1425-33 (1968).

[38] This assumes, of course, that the consumer is rational. That is one of the
standard assumptions of economic theory. It is not equivalent to assuming that the
consumer is omniscient. Indeed, the existence of consumer search costs is an
important reason why there is advertising. *See* Nelson, *Advertising as Information*,
82 J. POLITICAL ECON. 729 (1974).

[39] *See* references in D. WORCESTER, *supra* note 12, at 209.

[40] This is indicated by Professor Richard Nelson's comments on this paper which
follow.

on restricted distribution has become the orthodox academic position.[41]   The decision in *Continental T.V., Inc. v. GTE Sylvania Inc.*[42] suggests that it is well on its way to becoming the legal position as well.

4. *Predatory pricing.*   McGee's famous article on the Standard Oil Trust [43] combined the startling empirical finding that the trust, contrary to popular and academic belief, had not engaged in predatory pricing, with theoretical arguments for doubting the rationality of the practice.   One of McGee's major arguments—that the trust would not have used predatory pricing because it is cheaper to buy a competitor than to sell below cost—was vulnerable to the criticism of being irrelevant to present-day circumstances, since acquiring a major competitor is clearly and unconcealably unlawful whereas predatory pricing may be difficult to detect.   There is, however, a deeper problem with the McGee argument: it neglects strategic considerations.   Assume that it is lawful to buy a rival. It does not follow that a firm will never resort to predatory pricing. After all, it wants to minimize the price at which it buys its rivals, and that price will be lower if it can convince them of its willingness to drive them out of business unless they sell out on its terms.   One way to convince them of this is to engage in predatory pricing from time to time.

Since classical (or, one might add, modern) economics contains no generally accepted theory of strategic behavior, it is not surprising that the Chicago school should not have been particularly concerned with predatory pricing.   Eliminate strategic considerations, and it becomes impossible to construct a rational motivation for predatory pricing without assuming (very uncongenially to a Chicagoan) asymmetric access to the capital markets for financing a period of below-cost selling.   But to ignore strategic considerations is not satisfactory.   Even without having a well-developed theory of strategic behavior, one can easily imagine circumstances in which predatory pricing, at least in the absence of legal prohibition, would be a plausible policy for a profit-maximizing seller to

---

[41] The new Areeda and Turner treatise essentially adopts the Chicago position on advertising, in the course of discounting the significance of advertising as a barrier to entry.   See 2 P. AREEDA & D. TURNER, *supra* note 12, ¶ 409d.   For Turner's earlier contrary views see Turner, *Advertising and Competition*, 26 FED. B.J. 93 (1966).

[42] 433 U.S. 36 (1977), *discussed in* Posner, *The Rule of Reason and the Economic Approach: Reflections on the Sylvania Decision*, 45 U. CHI. L. REV. 1 (1977).

[43] McGee, *supra* note 2.

follow. Suppose that he sells in many markets, and his rivals sell in only one or a few markets each. If he sells below cost in one market, his losses there are an investment that will be recouped with interest in his other markets in the form of more timid competition from the rivals in those markets. Knowing that the multi-market seller can obtain substantial gains from a demonstrated willingness to sell below cost for an extended period of time in one market, the local victim may not think it worthwhile to try to outlast him.

To be sure, the administrative and error costs of trying to prevent this sort of thing may outweigh its dangers to the competitive process. That, however, is a different point. My point is that predatory pricing is not irrational. It is not in the same category with, for example, attempting to get a second monopoly through tying. Bork is able to place predatory pricing in the irrational category only by failing to mention the possibility of strategic behavior.[44]

Additional evidence for the decline of "schools" of antitrust economics is the position that Areeda and Turner (both of the Harvard Law School) have taken on predatory pricing. Their influential article on the subject (and the amplification of the article in their new treatise) is an essay in price theory.[45] Strategic considerations, the sort of thing the traditional industrial organization embraced eagerly, *e.g.*, in oligopoly theory, are not mentioned, and skepticism of the likelihood of predatory pricing is registered.[46] Using the basic premises of classical price theory, Areeda and Turner argue that the only price that should be condemned as predatory is one below short-run marginal cost. Any higher price implies an opportunity to utilize scarce resources more fully by lowering price and expanding output. This is pure textbook price theory unadorned by any of the concepts of traditional industrial organization.

It is not surprising that Professor Scherer, a leading adherent of traditional industrial organization thinking, launched a sweeping attack on the Areeda-Turner article,[47] or that Professor Williamson

---

[44] R. BORK, *supra* note 2, at 144-55.

[45] Areeda & Turner, *Predatory Pricing and Related Practices Under Section 2 of the Sherman Act*, 88 HARV. L. REV. 697 (1975); 3 P. AREEDA & D. TURNER, *supra* note 12, ¶ 711.

[46] A curiosity of the Areeda and Turner treatment is that no theory of why predatory pricing would ever occur is suggested.

[47] Scherer, *Predatory Pricing and the Sherman Act: A Comment*, 89 HARV. L. REV. 869 (1976); *see* Areeda & Turner, *Scherer on Predatory Pricing: A Reply*, 89 HARV. L. REV. 891 (1976); Scherer, *Some Last Words on Predatory Pricing*, 89 HARV. L. REV. 901 (1976).

criticized Areeda and Turner for ignoring strategic considerations in designing a rule against predatory pricing.[48] What is, perhaps, surprising is that I attacked Areeda and Turner as unduly permissive.[49] Unfortunately, my attack bogged down in a terminological dispute. I said that the proper criterion of predatory pricing was selling below long-run rather than short-run marginal cost with intent to destroy an equally or more efficient rival *and* that short-run marginal cost is lower than long-run marginal cost even when the firm is operating at its full (optimal) capacity, because some of elements of long-run marginal cost are fixed in the short run. Areeda and Turner pounced on the assertion that short-run marginal cost is below long-run marginal cost at full capacity. They pointed out that it would be costlier for a firm already operating at full capacity to expand in the short run than in the long run, for only in the long run could the firm make the adjustments in plant scale, etc., necessary to optimize production at a higher level.[50] I accept this criticism. Although I continue to be troubled by cases, potentially significant in the predatory-pricing context, in which long-run marginal cost might be *thought* to exceed short-run marginal cost even without excess capacity,[51] these cases can be dealt with by careful definition of the relevant terms.

---

[48] *See* Williamson, *Predatory Pricing: A Strategic and Welfare Analysis*, 87 Yale L.J. 284 (1977).

[49] *See* R. Posner, *supra* note 2, at 191-93.

[50] 3 P. Areeda & D. Turner, *supra* note 12, ¶ 715a, at 168 n.7.

[51] To illustrate very simply the kind of problem that led me to my original formulation, imagine a firm that at its current level of production makes 100 units at a total cost of $1,000.00, this cost consisting of (1) a rental of $500.00 for the factory premises and (2) labor and materials (short-run variable) costs of $5.00 per unit. The firm decides to cut price and expand output for the sole purpose of driving a more efficient rival out of the market. The firm's new production level is 101 units. At this level of production, which is greater than optimal, the labor and materials cost of the last unit is, say, $5.50; but rent, a fixed debit, is unchanged. The firm's short-run marginal cost is then $5.50. What is its long-run marginal cost? We must ask what the landlord would charge when the lease comes up for renewal if the output of the firm has risen. Presumably, the rental will be higher— suppose it is $5.00 higher. (The figure is not particularly important, so long as it is large enough to make the long-run marginal cost curve of the firm higher than at the current level; if it is lower, the present output of the firm cannot be optimal.) Assume further that in the long run the labor and materials cost of expanding output by one unit would be $5.10. Then the long-run marginal cost, that is, the cost in the long run of expanding output from 100 to 101 units, is $10.10. But the short-run marginal cost is only $5.50 despite the fact that the expansion is from the level of production that is optimal given the firm's existing plant, work force, etc.

As another example, suppose there are some workers who divide their time between production and maintenance. To expand output, the firm shifts these workers entirely into production. In the short run, the increased labor cost of production may be completely offset by the reduction in maintenance expense; in the long run, the maintenance expense is, if anything, higher.

But this is a side issue that only obscures the serious problems of the short-run marginal cost standard. The lesser problem is that the standard gives the would-be predator an incentive to maintain excess capacity and thereby reduce his short-run marginal costs, an incentive the predator might have anyway in order to make his threat to sell below cost more credible.[52] The greater problem is that the administrative difficulties of basing the legal rule on the concept of short-run marginal cost are so acute as to have led Areeda and Turner themselves to reject short-run marginal cost as the operational standard and instead substitute average variable cost. *Yet they continue to defend that standard by reference to the arguments, such as they are, for allowing firms to cut price to short-run marginal cost.* Average variable cost could be much below short-run marginal cost.[53] A standard of average variable cost should be defended on its own merits, rather than by reference to a different standard for which it is the crudest possible proxy. But Areeda and Turner do not attempt to defend an average variable cost standard, save as a proxy for short-run marginal cost.

What is the point of having such a low price floor? It would be unusual for a firm that wanted to engage in predatory pricing to set a price equal to or only slightly above zero. It would set a price designed to make its competitors' business unprofitable at minimum cost to itself. Any firm that sells at a price equal to its average variable costs, a price that doesn't cover any of its fixed costs (let alone generate any return on investment), will be unprofitable. Therefore, even if the competitor is somewhat more efficient than the predator, a price equal to the predator's variable costs, and hence close to the competitor's variable costs, should be an effective predatory price. Areeda and Turner allude to this possibility in a cryptic footnote. They write:

> One can posit a case in which (1) one rival has lower variable costs but higher total costs than the other, (2) their

---

The second example suggests the way to reconcile my analysis with the conventional textbook formulation. We can say that the added future maintenance cost resulting from the shift of workers from maintenance to production is actually one of the short-run marginal costs of stepping up production and that the higher rental that will be negotiated for the future period is actually a short-run marginal cost of the present increase in production.

[52] *See* Spence, *Entry, Capacity, and Oligopolistic Pricing*, 8 Bell J. Econ. 534 (1977).

[53] In my example, *see* note 51 *supra*, Areeda and Turner would, I take it, regard short-run marginal cost as somewhere above $10.10 (since that is the long-run marginal cost at the higher level of output). But the average variable cost is only a shade over $5.00.

joint capacity exceeds the demand at a price that would be profitable to both, and hence (3) marginal-cost pricing by the first rival would drive out the second, which is the more efficient producer in the long run when capital facilities have to be replaced. But even in such a case, the appropriate short-run solution is production by the rival with the lowest variable costs. Obviously, one would not want that firm to replace its facilities, but a rational firm would not do so if the cheaper technique were available to it, or if others could freely enter using that technique.[54]

The last sentence in effect denies the possibility of predatory pricing by asserting that a rational firm would not replace its facilities if the cheaper technique were available to it or if others could "freely enter" with that technique. The first alternative, the availability of the cheaper technique, simply retracts the premise of the discussion—that there is a competitor who is "the more efficient producer in the long run when capital facilities have to be replaced." If a predator is always as efficient in the long run as his competitors, there is little reason to forbid predatory pricing. A more efficient competitor can exclude a less efficient one without pricing below cost and thereby losing money in the short run. To have a rational basis, a rule against predation must assume that firms sometimes want to cling to their markets although they are less efficient than their rivals, *i.e.,* the "cheaper technique" is *not* available to them.

The second alternative suggested is free entry by firms as efficient as the excluded competitor. There are two ways in which to interpret the meaning of free entry here. One is that there is no need to worry about predatory pricing if there are many potential entrants waiting in the wings: the predator cannot possibly deter them all. If so, there is little reason to have any rule against predatory pricing. Alternatively, Areeda and Turner may be suggesting that predatory pricing is possible only where there are barriers to entry. This, however, neglects strategic considerations, which do not depend on the existence of barriers to entry.[55]

The quoted passage fails to take the problem of predatory pricing seriously. It implies that no rational firm would engage in predatory pricing if its long-run marginal costs were higher than those of its victims. If this is so (which I question on the basis of

54 3 P. Areeda & D. Turner, *supra* note 12, ¶ 715a, at 168 n.7.

55 *See* O. Williamson, Markets and Hierarchies: Analysis and Antitrust Implications 145-48 (1075).

944   *UNIVERSITY OF PENNSYLVANIA LAW REVIEW*   [Vol. 127:925

the strategic considerations suggested earlier), why is it necessary to forbid predatory pricing? Predatory pricing against less efficient firms is not a serious danger since they can be excluded by pricing at or above cost. Areeda and Turner may think that business irrationality is sufficiently common to warrant a rule against predatory pricing.[56] In any event, if there is sufficient danger of predatory pricing to warrant having a legal rule, as Areeda and Turner for whatever reason believe, that danger is triggered when a firm that is less efficient than its rivals cuts its price to its variable costs in order to make it unprofitable for those rivals to enter or remain in the market. Indeed, to repeat an earlier point, it is hard to see why a predator would ever have to price below that level in order to discourage rivals.

Whoever is correct in the debate over predatory pricing, one thing is clear: the debate is no longer one between schools that employ consistently different and ideologically tinged premises to reach predictably opposite results.

III. Remaining Differences

There is one very important area in which traces of the traditional differences between Chicago price theorists and Harvard industrial organizationists persist: the two schools continue to disagree over the significance of concentration and the wisdom of a policy of deconcentration. Williamson and many other lawyers and economists continue to believe that persistently high concentration in an industry warrants breaking up the leading firms. Brozen, Demsetz, Stigler, Baxter, and others disagree (the last two named, it should be noted, are defectors from the ranks of the deconcentrators).[57] Areeda and Turner, as will be seen, appear to take an intermediate position.

The heart of the difference is not over the strength of the positive correlation, found in many studies, between concentration and profitability but over the explanation for it. The Harvard school, still identifiable as such on this issue, contends that the correlation is explained by the fact that the leading firms in highly concentrated industries employ "conscious parallelism" to avoid price competition and thereby earn abnormal profits. The Chicago school does

---

[56] It is difficult to determine their precise position because they do not explain under what circumstances they would expect predatory pricing to occur.

[57] *Industrial Concentration: The New Learning* contains a very full version of this debate. Industrial Concentration: The New Learning (H. Goldschmid, H. Mann & J. Weston eds. 1974).

not deny that concentration is a factor that facilitates collusion of a sort difficult to detect, although it attaches less significance to concentration per se than do the oligopoly theorists. It asks, rather, how it is that excessive profitability can persist without attracting new entry that will cause prices to fall to the competitive level. The Harvard school, after all, wants to restructure only the persistently concentrated industries. If the leading firms in such industries are able, by virtue of concentration, to obtain supra-competitive profits, these profits should act as a magnet to other firms in the economy and their entry will deconcentrate the industry. That is what happened to the steel industry in the years following the formation of U.S. Steel Corporation in 1901.[58] Persistent concentration implies either that the market in question simply does not have room for many firms (economies of scale) or that some firms are able persistently to obtain abnormal profits by cost reductions or product improvements that competitors and new entrants are unable to duplicate.[59] Neither case is an attractive one for public intervention designed to change the market structure.

The Harvard reply is that there is an alternative explanation for persistent concentration in particular industries: barriers to entry. Because Stigler's definition of a barrier to entry, as a cost that differentially affects new entrants compared to firms already in the market,[60] is now generally accepted, the search is for costs having this characteristic. The most sophisticated quester, Oliver Williamson, has found one: the uncertainty of the new entrant's prospects may force him to pay a higher risk premium to obtain capital than existing firms must pay.[61] This is a legitimate point. But it is difficult to believe that such a difference in the cost of capital would be enough to prevent entry if the firms in a market were charging prices substantially above their costs. The risk premium is unlikely to be a large fraction of the new entrant's costs. Interest and profit are rarely more than ten percent of a manufacturing firm's sales price and often they are a much smaller percentage. Thus, even if a new entrant had to pay a ten percent higher interest rate and (expected) return to shareholders to attract the necessary capital, its total costs would be only about one percent higher than those of the firms already in the market. There is no doubt that the differential risk premium is smaller if the new en-

---

[58] *See* ORGANIZATION OF INDUSTRY, *supra* note 15, at 108.

[59] *See, e.g.,* Peltzman, *The Gains and Losses from Industrial Concentration,* 20 J.L. & ECON. 229 (1977).

[60] *See* ORGANIZATION OF INDUSTRY, *supra* note 15, at 67-70.

[61] *See* Williamson, *supra* note 31, at 656-59.

trant is a well-established firm in other markets, as will typically be the case, and, to the extent that the risk is diversifiable, the risk premium will be still smaller or even disappear entirely. Another important source of new entry, viewing the term functionally rather than lexicographically, is the expansion of the existing small firms in the market. In response to supracompetitive pricing, a fringe of small firms in a market may be able to expand output moderately without incurring significantly higher capital costs than those borne by the larger firms in the market. All in all, it seems far-fetched to base a policy of deconcentration on the allegedly higher borrowing costs of new entrants in concentrated markets.

Williamson has also argued that if a firm once grows big, for whatever reason, there is no reason to expect it to decline as a result of the random shocks to which it and other market participants will be subjected over time.[62] But he neglects a crucial factor. The firm is by hypothesis charging a supracompetitive price as a result of the interdependence or collusion fostered by the concentrated market structure in which it finds itself. That price will attract new firms (or, what amounts to the same thing, expansion by the smaller firms in the market) and the oligopolist will either have to cut price or surrender market share. In the former case, profits will fall and in the latter, concentration will decrease. The persistence of high concentration *together with* excess profitability remains to be accounted for.

Deconcentration policy, then, is critically dependent upon belief in the existence of substantial barriers to entry in many industries. Once "barrier to entry" was redefined as a differentially higher cost borne by the new entrant, the plausibility of supposing that barriers to entry are common, or commonly substantial, diminished sharply. The deconcentrators are thus arguing from an abandoned premise. This can be seen most clearly by comparing the discussion of barriers to entry in Kaysen and Turner's *Antitrust Policy* and in Areeda and Turner's *Antitrust Law*. Both books are concerned over the anti-competitive consequences of deconcentration, although the latter much more qualifiedly so, and only at much higher levels of concentration.[63] The view of barriers to entry, however, is very different in the two books.[64] To Kaysen and

---

[62] *See* Williamson, *Dominant Firms and the Monopoly Problem: Market Failure Considerations*, 85 Harv. L. Rev. 1512, 1518-19 (1972).

[63] *Compare* C. Kaysen & D. Turner, *supra* note 10, at 27, 72, 104 n.6 *with* 2 P. Areeda & D. Turner, *supra* note 12, ¶¶ 406b, 407d & 408c.

[64] *Compare* C. Kaysen & D. Turner, *supra* note 10, at 73-74 *with* 2 P. Areeda & D. Turner, *supra* note 12, ¶ 409.

Turner they are numerous and include economies of scale, capital requirements, scarce know-how and inputs, and product differentiation. No rigorous definition of barrier to entry is offered; nor do the authors deduce the concept of barriers to entry from the assumption that business firms act as rational profit maximizers. The important point, however, is that, believing barriers to entry to be numerous and prevalent, the authors have a rational basis for wanting to deconcentrate concentrated markets. Areeda and Turner greatly pare down the list of barriers to entry. Because they utilize Stigler's definition of a barrier to entry, they are led to exclude economies of scale entirely. The related size-of-capital barrier is discarded also and product differentiation is discounted on the basis of a view of advertising that is close to the Chicago view. The only barriers that remain are: (1) the Williamson risk-premium version of the capital barrier and (2) control of scarce input.[65] Thus, Areeda and Turner largely discard the concept of barrier to entry, finding some of the barriers theoretically invalid and others empirically unimportant; such "pure" barriers as remain surely cannot explain much concentration. And although Areeda and Turner do not expressly discuss the dependence of deconcentration theory on the belief in the existence of high and pervasive barriers to entry, they do draw quite different policy implications concerning persistent high concentration from Kaysen and Turner. Whereas the earlier book recommended a policy of deconcentration, the later book recommends remedial action, whether under existing antitrust provisions or new legislation, only where there is proof of noncompetitive performance.[66] There is more than a nuance of difference between these two views. Here, then, is further evidence that even in the most important area where distinctive "Harvard"

---

[65] Legal barriers to entry such as patents are quite properly ignored as beyond the reach of antitrust policy. As a detail, I think Areeda and Turner are wrong to treat control of a scarce input as a barrier to entry into the output market. *See* 2 P. AREEDA & D. TURNER, *supra* note 12, ¶ 409b. To treat it so is a version of the leverage fallacy. If a seller of widgets controls an indispensable input into widget production, call it manganium, he will have little incentive to restrict entry into the widget market. His control of manganium will enable him to extract all of the economic rents obtainable in the widget market without selling any widgets, let alone trying to control the widget market. (To be sure, I am ignoring considerations of input substitution in the variable-proportions case and of price discrimination, but these are second-order considerations and are in any event not the basis on which Areeda and Turner deem control of a key input a barrier to entry.) Alternatively, if the scarce input is not a good but, say, the services of an extraordinarily skilled manager, he will presumably extract all (or more realistically most) of the benefits that his services confer on the firm, in the form of a rent; consequently, the firm's costs may be little lower than those of other firms in the market, or of prospective entrants.

[66] *See, e.g.,* 3 P. AREEDA & D. TURNER, *supra* note 12, ¶ 840.

and "Chicago" approaches remain discernible, the process of convergence is well under way.[67]

CONCLUSION

Although this paper has not attempted an exhaustive canvass of rival theories of antitrust analysis,[68] it has, I hope, said enough to persuade the reader that the oldest and most persistent stereotype in antitrust economics, that of the Chicago school, bears little relationship to the current state of academic thinking. Changes of mind within both the Chicago school and its principal rival, which I have called the Harvard school, have produced a steady trend toward convergence. Differences remain, but increasingly they are technical rather than ideological.[69]

---

[67] A further aspect of the Chicago-Harvard difference on deconcentration arises from the difference between the deep distrust of government intervention that is associated with the Chicago School of Economics (in the broader, Milton Friedman sense) and the (rapidly diminishing) complacency toward such intervention associated with traditional Harvard-M.I.T. economic thinking. Deconcentration is a more ambitious form of public control than is usually involved in antitrust enforcement, so one's attitudes toward the capabilities of regulatory-type governmental interventions naturally come into play. That is why adherents of the Chicago school believe it unsound to base a policy of deconcentration on the assumption that a deconcentration proceeding is a swifter method than entry itself of deconcentrating markets in which there are no barriers to entry in the technical sense but in which entry at minimum cost requires substantial time.

[68] I have not, for instance, discussed the "transactional cost" analysis associated with Oliver Williamson. That analysis combines elements of Harvard thinking with elements of the thought of Ronald Coase and elements of the Carnegie-Mellon school. I have also not mentioned Richard Markovits, who has revived Chamberlain's brand of old-fashioned industrial organization, the populist school associated with Willard Mueller and others, or the diehard industrial organizationists such as Michael Mann.

[69] Professor Richard Nelson, whose comments on this paper follow, evidently disagrees. But he is a careful reader neither of my work nor of the recent journal literature that he purports to summarize. He suggests, for example, that the recent Chicago writing denies the possibility of adjustment lags or costs in new entry into a concentrated industry. But a recognition of that possibility is in fact an important aspect of the work of Stigler, *see* ORGANIZATION OF INDUSTRY, *supra* note 15, at 108, and of me, *see, e.g.*, Posner, *supra* note 2, at 29; note 66 *supra*. He implies that the Chicago school has ignored uncertainty, information, and search costs: on the contrary, the current interest in these subjects stems from George Stigler's pioneering article on the economics of information. *See* G. Stigler, *The Economics of Information*, in ORGANIZATION OF INDUSTRY, *supra* note 15, at 171. And the Chicago school's analysis of advertising differs from the traditional Harvard view precisely in bringing consumer search costs into the analysis. *See, e.g.*, Nelson, *supra* note 38. The role of transaction costs in explaining vertical integration, although latterly associated with Oliver Williamson, stems from the early article by Coase. Coase, *The Nature of the Firm*, 4 ECONOMICA 506 (1937).

More important, while Professor Nelson argues that some of the very recent literature modifies or refines the economic theory underlying the Chicago school's analysis, nowhere does he state that the literature supports a more active antitrust policy than the Chicago analysis recommends, or for that matter a different antitrust policy. His analysis appears to have no policy implications.

[11]

The Antitrust Bulletin/Summer 1986   341

Climbing the antitrust staircase

BY ERNEST GELLHORN*

Introduction

In the space of about 15 years, antitrust has moved from a time when the guiding principle seemed to be that the government always wins[1] to a situation where critics frequently charge that the government never sues.[2] While both comments are obviously overstatements, there is more than a kernel of truth in each. The question arises, therefore, whether recent differences in the direction of antitrust policy are solely ones of philosophy and political power. Are the antitrust policies and judgments under President Reagan, as compared with antitrust rulings while Jimmy Carter or Gerald Ford was president, explained simply by the fact that we now have a conservative, business-oriented regime in power unwilling to enforce antitrust with the same vigor as prior administrations? Or is something more significant taking place?

I believe that a careful examination of antitrust trends and current practices reveals substantial shifts in the center of antitrust analysis and economic understanding. And this redirection is likely to continue regardless of which party controls the

---

* Attorney, Jones, Day, Reavis & Pogue; formerly, Dean and Galen J. Roush Professor of Law, Case Western Reserve University.

1 United States v. Von's Grocery Co., 384 U.S. 270, 301 (1966) (Stewart, J.) ("The sole consistency that I can find is that in litigation under Section 7, the Government always wins").

2 *See* Seiberling, *Congress Makes the Laws: The Executive Should Enforce Them*, 53 ANTITRUST L.J. 175 (1984).

executive branch. This conclusion is supported by the fact that many recent changes have been confirmed by courts even though only about one-third of all federal judges have been appointed by Mr. Reagan, including only one member of the Supreme Court. It seems, in other words, that something more than naked power is operating to refocus antitrust enforcement.

In determining what other, perhaps more rational factors are deciding the course of antitrust, I propose first to examine earlier shifts in antitrust doctrine and then to explore some of the forces that have forged these changes. They are, I believe, instructive in seeking an understanding of the likely future direction of anti-trust. This is not to suggest, however, that politics and normative values should be discounted. Rather, the thesis of this article is that the future of antitrust is profoundly affected by developing insights into market operations as well as by the state of the economy and the political process. Each has a place and each plays a role in the shaping of antitrust policy.

Four phases of antitrust

The primary operative terms of the major antitrust statutes are extraordinarily brief yet equally vague. The Sherman Act simply prohibits "every contract . . . in restraint of trade" and makes "every person who shall monopolize" subject to liability.[3] The Clayton Act completes this picture by condemning mergers whose effect "may be substantially to lessen competition."[4] These broad, Constitution-like delegations of interpretative authority to the courts have led to a kaleidoscope of reactions over the years, including confusion, hostility, expansive application, and skepti-cism.

Contractual (1890–1910)

The formative years of antitrust, from the adoption of the Sherman Act in 1890 until the establishment of the "Rule of

---

[3]   15 U.S.C. §§ 1-2.

[4]   15 U.S.C. § 17.

Reason" at the time of the statute's majority,[5] were an important if confusing period. When first confronted with this broad responsibility to regulate trade, the courts lacked a sense of direction and often retreated to literalist interpretations of the statutory language. For example, the first antitrust case to reach the Supreme Court held that the manufacture of sugar was not "commerce," and the Court's initial substantive rulings held that agreements to fix prices for all shipments by rail carriers were illegal because the statutory language barred "every contract" in restraint of trade.[6] Similarly, a merger of competing railroads was condemned because it (necessarily) eliminated all competition between the merged lines.[7]

While the results in these cases were often more reasonable than their rationales, the operative tests they created were troublesome. Read as literally as the tests themselves read the Sherman Act, they appeared to mean that almost every contract which supported trade—contracts to sell goods or services, contracts to create a partnership or corporation, or contracts that otherwise intensified competition—could be readily condemned. This obviously went beyond the Court's intentions, so exceptions were quickly created and limiting rules were developed. Nonetheless, the law seemed unduly oppressive, confusing, and rigid. There was no connecting thread for identifying the line between dangerous, undue exercises of private market power and competitive activities that should be promoted or allowed to go unchecked. As one would expect, there was strong pressure for change.

Analytical (1911–1940)

Responding to some of these criticisms, the Court shifted its approach and began to analyze more carefully the practical effects of the challenged business activity. The Congress, it said in

---

5   *See* Standard Oil of N.J. v. United States, 221 U.S. 1 (1911).

6   United States v. Trans-Missouri Freight Ass'n, 166 U.S. 290 (1897).

7   Northern Securities Co. v. United States, 193 U.S. 197 (1904).

344 : *The antitrust bulletin*

Standard Oil of N.J., had meant only to condemn unreasonable restraints of trade.[8] Thus, before finding a practice illegal under the "Rule of Reason," the purpose and likely effect of the practice were to be examined; this could include a close examination of market operations, an industry's history, the scope of competition, and related factors.

This analytical approach to antitrust proved easier to state than apply. Trials became lengthy affairs filled with speculation about the effect of particular practices, as courts were asked to base their conclusions on unknown future market trends. Business success is often as intuitive as it is rigorous; close market analysis may be only the first step. In any case, judges were trained to read legal doctrines rather than make successful business decisions. Recognizing this limitation, they tended to defer to business judgments and the rule of reason became synonymous with antitrust immunity. The principal exception was the Court's prohibition of price-fixing, although even this exception was abandoned temporarily during the Depression of the 1930s.[9] This period was marked by antitrust's continuing search for a unifying theory.

Structural (1940–1970)

Antitrust was restored as a policy tool when the New Deal abandoned its cartel approach to business revival in the late 1930s. Concerned with the time, cost, and results of rule of reason trials, antitrust doctrine increasingly relied on per se rules and structural tests to challenge boycotts, market allocations, vertical restraints, mergers, and monopolies.[10] Oligopoly theory

---

8   221 U.S. at 1.

9   *See* Appalachian Coals, Inc. v. United States, 288 U.S. 344 (1983).

10   *See* Fashion Originators' Guild of America, Inc. v. FTC, 312 U.S. 457 (1941) (boycott); United States v. Topco Associates, Inc., 405 U.S. 596 (1972) (market allocation); United States v. Arnold, Schwinn & Co., 388 U.S. 365 (1967) (vertical restraint); United States v. Von's Grocery Co., 384 U.S. 270 (1966) (merger); United States v. Aluminum Co. of America, 148 F.2d 416 (2d Cir. 1945) (monopolization).

captured the imagination of policy makers and courts. It supplied a seemingly coherent, market-based framework for testing the potential dangers of various arrangements that expanded private economic power.[11]

During this period, the focus of antitrust theory and its rules was on possible misuses of business arrangements. The advantages of monopoly/oligopoly power to producers (and dangers to consumers) were so great—of increased prices and profits from controlled output and entry—that it seemed likely that most restraints served some malign purpose. The difficulties of detecting cartels and oligopolies as well as the inherent problems associated with unwinding complex transactions also favored immediate challenges to practices posing only incipient dangers.

These expansive applications of antitrust were not without their difficulties. Many case results seemed unreasonable and inconsistent with the underlying theory.[12] Trials took as long as ever, since litigants felt compelled to introduce rule of reason-type evidence to answer questions of characterization, *i.e.*, whether a practice fit within a per se category. The process proved awkward since these covert methods misdirected the decision maker's attention and sacrificed the likely accuracy of the outcome.

Economic (1970–   )

The structuralist view of antitrust began to fade even as it was reaching widespread acceptance.[13] The major challenge came from those associated with the "Chicago school," who viewed

---

[11]   *See* J. Bain, Barriers to New Competition (1956); C. Kaysen & D. Turner, Antitrust Policy: An Economic and Legal Analysis (1959).

[12]   *See, e.g.*, FTC v. Brown Shoe Co., 384 U.S. 316 (1966); United States v. Aluminum Co. of America, 377 U.S. 271 (1966) (Alcoa-Rome merger). *See generally*, R. Bork, The Antitrust Paradox (1978).

[13]   *See* Industrial Concentration: The New Learning (H. Goldschmid, H. Mann & J. Weston eds. 1974).

346 : *The antitrust bulletin*

antitrust primarily through the lens of price theory.[14] In addition to questioning the empirical and theoretical foundations of oligopoly theory, they outlined numerous possible benefits from various restraints. These ideas spread from the law reviews to the enforcement agencies and the courts, and there has been a steady retreat in recent years from the once dominant per se approach.[15] Even when the per se rule has not been abandoned, its application has been constrained.[16]

This increasing reliance on economic theory, which began (albeit with a different understanding) under the structuralists, but was now based on the concept of efficiency, has often been controversial. The scope and meaning of various rules—including, for example, the tests for monopolization—are far from clear, as often only part of the "new learning" has been understood or accepted.[17] Moreover, the jury's continuing role in private antitrust litigation has furthered this uncertainty as recent cases have frequently involved nongovernment suits.[18]

Within these limitations, however, it now seems clear that antitrust is generally limited to considering arrangements involv-

---

[14]   *See* Posner, *The Chicago School of Antitrust Analysis*, 127 U. Pa. L. Rev. 925 (1979); R. Bork, *supra* note 12.

[15]   *See, e.g.*, Continental T.V., Inc. v. GTE Sylvania Inc., 433 U.S. 36 (1977); Broadcast Music, Inc. v. CBS, 441 U.S. 1 (1979). *See also* National Soc'y of Professional Engineers v. United States, 435 U.S. 679 (1978); NCAA v. Board of Regents of the Univ. of Okla., 104 S. Ct. 2984 (1984).

[16]   *See* Jefferson Parish Hospital Dist. No. 2 v. Hyde, 104 S. Ct. 1551 (1984); Northwest Wholesale Stationers, Inc. v. Pacific Stationery & Printing Co., 105 S. Ct. 2613 (1985).

[17]   A particularly apt illustration is Justice Stevens' recent opinion in Aspen Skiing Co. v. Aspen Highlands Skiing Corp., 105 S. Ct. 2847 (1985), which emphasized the Sherman Act's focus on efficiency while nonetheless holding that a firm with monopoly power could not alter its joint venture arrangement with a competitor without first giving a business reason for the change.

[18]   *See* Monsanto Co. v. Spray-Rite Service Corp., 104 S. Ct. 1464 (1984); *Aspen Skiing*, 105 S. Ct. at 2847.

ing firms with substantial market power. In most situations an examination of the likely adverse effects must demonstrate substantial impairment of competition before an antitrust court will intervene.

Climbing the antitrust staircase

These shifts in antitrust policy and doctrine may be seen as nothing more than mindless oscillations reflecting political or personal agendas of those currently in power. Indeed, political scientists have often viewed antitrust as a reflection of the continuous struggle between capitalism and populism, with the outcome determined principally by the fortunes of the economy. There is obvious force to this contention as both history and logic suggest that when the economy is strong there is a greater tendency to worry about the misuse of economic power, whereas pressures are often overwhelming to abandon competition theory and accept (and even encourage) cartels during periods of economic dislocation.[19]

If this health-of-the-economy/political-power picture were a complete analysis, antitrust enforcement would simply reflect the swings of a pendulum between various polar and intermediate positions. During periods of economic prosperity antitrust would be expansive and widely used, and vice versa. That has not been the case, however. The prosperity of the 1920s and the recovery of the 1980s were not accompanied by a similar growth in antitrust enforcement. Consider also the reaction to the abandonment of the per se rule for vertical restraints in the *Sylvania* decision.[20] A major shift in antitrust enforcement, it reflected intensive economically based criticism of the prior per se rule. While aspects of *Sylvania* remain controversial, there is widespread agreement that the rule of reason standard adopted by the Court is the appropriate measure for evaluating territorial and

---

19   *See generally*, E. HAWLEY, THE NEW DEAL AND THE PROBLEM OF MONOPOLY 12-34 (1966).

20   *Sylvania*, 433 U.S. at 36.

similar restrictions. This decision has caused a reexamination of numerous doctrines, as its approach of examining the likely justifications and effects of a restraint has now been applied to tie-ins, boycotts, and even price-fixing.[21]

It is particularly significant that the four phases of antitrust have cut across partisan lines and differing economic trends. Antitrust has only generally paralleled the state of the economy. The development of antitrust has been more like the climb of a zigzagging staircase than the swings of a pendulum, with numerous landings at odd intervals and varying degrees of steepness in the steps. The one constant over time has been the incremental development of doctrine and the increasing sophistication of policy. Reflecting its common-law origins, new insights have been added to old ones. The specific lines drawn in the 1982 and 1984 Merger Guidelines might change under a more liberal administration, but the likelihood is that the changes would be modest and the basic framework would be left intact.[22] The general dismissal of the leverage theory that once dominated antitrust is another illustration of the intellectual growth of antitrust.[23]

This is not to deny the political nature of antitrust or its role as a catalyst in the ongoing debate over distribution of society's resources. Similarly, not all cases can be fit into this analysis, and many decisions reflect conflicting views. But the dominant development over the past two phases of antitrust has been the central

---

21   *See* cases cited *supra* noted 16; *Broadcast Music*, 441 U.S. at 1.

22   *See* Alpert & Kitt, *Is Structure All?*, 53 ANTITRUST L.J. 255 (1984) ("As a practical matter, remarkably little has changed: . . . . the primary emphasis continues to be upon structural considerations and, in particular, upon individual firm market shares and industry concentration measures"); Gellhorn, *Government Merger Policy and Practice— 1983*, 52 ANTITRUST L.J. 419 (1983). *See also* John H. Shenefield, Address to New England Antitrust Conference, Cambridge, Mass. (Nov. 14, 1981).

23   *See* H. HOVENKAMP, ECONOMICS AND FEDERAL ANTITRUST LAW 222-24 (1985); Posner, *supra* note 14, at 926, 929, 934-38. *But see* Kaplow, *Extension of Monopoly Power Through Leverage*, 85 COLUM. L. REV. 515 (1985).

role that economic analysis has played and the increasing understanding of policy makers and courts in the operation of markets
and business incentives. This understanding has led to a greater
skepticism of the benefits of antitrust intervention and a new
caution in applying antitrust to disrupt potentially beneficial
market practices. In lawyer's terms, the burden of persuasion has
shifted to those who would prohibit a vertical restraint or stop a
merger, except where the transaction demonstrably increases the
market power of firms with a large share of a concentrated
market.[24]

In large measure, this new antitrust doctrine is more favorable
to business and competitive experimentation. The predisposition
of antitrust enforcers and advisers is to identify permissible
methods for a business to achieve specific ends. To some degree,
of course, this has always been the rule. What has changed in the
past decade is that fewer devices are foreclosed from consideration. For example, a manufacturer who wants to encourage
dealer promotion and servicing can rely on exclusive territories,
customer allocations, and tie-ins more readily than in the past;
less desired methods such a areas of primary responsibility,
reserved accounts, profit pass-overs, etc. are no longer avenues of
first resort. Whether a practice will be approved will depend on
the market power of the participants and the likelihood that it
could enhance competition by increasing efficiency.

On the other hand, increased reliance on the rule of reason
standard has also introduced greater uncertainty and, in some
situations, raised business costs for complying with antitrust
requirements. It is no longer true that a trial under the rule of
reason standard will result in approval of the challenged business
practice. The process of transition from the per se standard to the
rule of reason measure is also far from complete—indeed, it is
unclear whether the courts will ever completely abandon the per
se rule for price-fixing, boycotts, tie-ins, or resale price main-

---

[24]   *See* U.S. Department of Justice Merger Guidelines (1982; rev'd
1984); U.S. Department of Justice Vertical Restraints Guidelines (1985).
See generally, Easterbrook, *The Limits of Antitrust*, 63 Tex. L. Rev. 1
(1984).

tenance—and this heightens the costs of uncertainty. The Department of Justice guidelines and advice on mergers, vertical restraints, joint ventures, patents, etc. may prove helpful in reducing these costs. But the Antitrust Division's use of guidelines to press for change as well as to provide guidance means that they are less important as precedent.

Antitrust is, in other words, in a state of ferment. We are still in the midst of the economic phase and considerable doctrinal development has yet to occur.

Future directions

Analyzing past movements in antitrust is difficult enough without hazarding a guess as to its future direction. I have no reason to suppose that my crystal ball is clearer than anyone else's. Rather than attempting to divine the meanings of a necessarily clouded crystal ball, I thought it would be more helpful to identify some of the factors likely to influence the direction that antitrust may take and to discuss some of the major issues that will determine the slope and direction of the antitrust staircase.

First and perhaps foremost is that fact that the primary ingredients determining the direction of antitrust policy are probably unrelated to antitrust itself. The state of the economy—at least at the extremes—will probably decide the major questions. If the imbalance of trade continues or worsens, efforts to narrow antitrust enforcement in the merger and export areas will not only continue but possibly succeed. Similarly, if the economic downturn often predicted for the late 1980s occurs, and especially if it is steeper than currently envisioned, political pressures to curtail antitrust will intensify. As this suggests, the most favorable climate for the development of an independent, rational antitrust policy seems to be a period of modest economic growth when there is widespread recognition of the need to compete.[25]

[25] Paradoxically, the "need to compete" is probably the greatest when the economy is not performing well and the pressures are the greatest to avoid the rigors of competition.

Similarly, politics and ideology count for something. Two recent leaders of the Antitrust Division, Sanford Litvak and William Baxter, held very different antitrust philosophies. And I cannot conceive of either serving under the other's president. While there were undoubtedly many decisions made by each that the other would also have made, their decisions at the critical margin were very different. Indeed, their differences were often basic and fundamental—as illustrated by their positions on the virtues of resale price-fixing—and undoubtedly had much to do with the changing atmosphere of antitrust since 1980. The point should not be overplayed, however. Messrs. Baxter and Litvak are somewhat unusual cases, at least in their rhetoric, and they probably are not representative of most appointees to lead antitrust.

Of greater significance to the future of antitrust is the accident of Supreme Court appointments. Only one appointment has been made in the past decade, a record unlikely to be matched in the next 10 years. While not a basis for selecting justices, the philosophy of the new appointees and their knowledge of antitrust economics will undoubtedly have much to do with controlling the future direction of antitrust.[26]

It is important for antitrust followers to recall that the economy and politics probably have a greater effect on determining the direction of antitrust enforcement than anything else. To a substantial degree, antitrust is not in control of its own destiny. Nonetheless, there are substantial areas of agreement among most participants in antitrust policy development and this agreement is likely to be reflected in future actions regardless of who wins elections or is appointed to the Supreme Court. These areas of policy agreement tend to set the framework for political maneuver and probably to limit political choices.[27]

---

[26] However, the current list of frequently mentioned possible Supreme Court appointees—Bork, Easterbrook, and Posner—includes an unusually large number of antitrust experts.

[27] This is not always the case, however. General agreement among antitrust observers that the Robinson–Patman Act's prohibition of price discrimination as written is counterproductive has not seemed to have had much impact on Congress.

352 : *The antitrust bulletin*

One such area is the acknowledged relevance of economic analysis to determining antitrust outcomes. The parsing of case precedent or applying simplistic notions of the leveraging of monopoly power is no longer an acceptable basis for developing policy. The focus of antitrust is on consumer welfare and more specifically on whether the challenged activity was aimed at increasing output. The classical perfect-competition paradigm is now firmly established in the antitrust hierarchy; it is the measure against which particular policies and actions are first tested. Increasingly, this also requires sophisticated determinations of the relevant market, the time frame during which a practice or action is to be viewed, and the market power and concentration of those competing in the market. With the development of theories of strategic and opportunistic behavior, contestable markets, etc., it is also clear that the economic data set will not necessarily point policy in only one direction. There will continue to be large areas of judgment where the predisposition of the decider is the single most important element determining the outcome.

The primary effect of this agreement on basic economic analysis will continue to be the identification of a wide branch of cases not suitable for antitrust intervention—even though they were formerly the staple of government as well as private activity. These will include non-price vertical restraints, most conglomerate and many horizontal mergers, and most price discrimination matters (even those that may be technical violations of the Robinson–Patman Act). Antitrust economics will continue to be used most widely to create filters and to identify safe harbors free from antitrust challenge.[28] The reason is not that antitrust is being unduly cut back or made ineffective. Rather, economic analysis demonstrates that the challenged practice cannot impair competition—because of limited market power—and that it serves a likely useful purpose.

Similarly, once prevalent populist notions are unlikely to make a comeback, having been purged from serious antitrust review. These include proposals to establish "no-fault" or indus-

---

[28]   *See* sources cited, *supra* note 24.

trial deconcentration laws for attacking persistent monopolies or concentrated markets, conglomerate merger bills usually aimed at particular industries, and so forth. They have been replaced in recent years by equally implausible (at least from a political standpoint) proposals to eliminate juries from private antitrust cases, to limit treble damages, to modify the merger law, and to repeal the price discrimination law. At this point there is no economic or political consensus on either set of proposals and, unless underlying economic and political forces change radically, it seems unlikely that we will witness major substantive change in the antitrust laws in this century.

Much harder, of course, is to identify future issues in antitrust and how they will be resolved. Despite the absence of any persuasive case justifying the treble-damage jury system for private antitrust actions, I see little likelihood of serious reform. The system has been in place for so long that the burden of persuasion seems to have shifted to those proposing any changes. As the Georgetown Private Damage Project illustrates, the evidence is so difficult to collect and evaluate that one must despair of ever establishing a persuasive case. More easily challenged, although seemingly still impregnable against change, is the current multilayered antitrust enforcement scheme involving three government agencies—state attorney generals, the Federal Trade Commission, and the Antitrust Division. Here the case for consolidation, at least of the FTC and Division's enforcement authority, is particularly powerful.[29]

On a substantive note, there remains considerable room for movement regarding the rules applicable to price-fixing, boycotts, horizontal mergers, and vertical restraints. In particular, numerous Supreme Court decisions are simply irreconcilable or irrational. Both tie-ins and boycotts are subject to per se condemnation "in some cases," but when is unclear.[30] The test for measuring permissible activities of a monopolist was further

[29] *See* Gellhorn, *Regulatory Reform and the Federal Trade Commission's Antitrust Jurisdiction*, 49 TENN. L. REV. 471 (1982).

[30] *See* cases cited *supra* note 16.

confused by the Court's recent *Aspen Skiing* decision, which seems to be a sport in law as well as fact.[31] And the current rules allowing manufacturers to establish exclusive territories but not fix resale prices—yet enforce other non-price restraints with their dealers—cry out for clarification.[32]

However, if the recent past is any indication of the future, observers 10 and 20 years from now will repeat this lament. The genius of the common-law system of antitrust is that a court decides only the case before it and avoids the errors of broad rules encompassing unknown situations. The cost is that inconsistent and sometimes incoherent rules result, intensifying the law's uncertainty. This leads me to suggest (rather than predict) that substantive antitrust doctrine focus on three central issues in the years ahead. One issue is whether we should abandon the per se test in antitrust. The concept began with price-fixing and spread over the years to include both horizontal (boycotts, market allocations) and vertical (tie-ins, exclusive territories) restraints. But as recent cases have shown, even the "hard-core" areas such as price-fixing (*ASCAP*) and boycotts (*Northwest Wholesale*) may involve practices deserving rule of reason analysis.[33] The result is that the per se rule no longer eases antitrust administration or provides business with sound guidance.[34] Its primary effect is to distract antitrust trials into arguments over character-

---

[31]   *See Aspen Skiing*, 105 S. Ct. at 2847; Malina, *Supreme Court Update—1985*, 54 ANTITRUST L.J. 289, 293-95 (1985).

[32]   *See, e.g.*, Easterbrook, *Vertical Arrangements and the Rule of Reason*, 53 ANTITRUST L.J. 135 (1984); Liebler, *1983 Economic Review of Antitrust Developments: The Distinction Between Price and Non-price Distribution Restrictions*, 31 UCLA L. REV. 384 (1983) (vertical restraints, price or non-price, have similar effects and cannot be distinguished on economic or other analytical grounds).

[33]   *See Broadcast Music*, 441 U.S. at 1; *Northwest Wholesale*, 105 S. Ct. at 2613. *See also NCAA*, 104 S. Ct. at 2984.

[34]   *See* Note, *Fixing the Price Fixing Confusion: A Rule of Reason Approach*, 92 YALE L.J. 706 (1983). *See also* Haddock, *Basing-Point Pricing: Competitive vs. Collusive Theories*, 72 AM. ECON. REV. 289 (1982); Liebler, *supra* note 32.

ization that confuse judges and juries and waste substantial societal resources. Courts should instead focus on the likely effects of the questioned activity to determine if it will impair or improve consumer welfare—as is the case under the rule of reason.

A second and related recommendation is that antitrust should focus its attention on fleshing out the meaning of the rule of reason.[35] The much maligned soft drink and beer bills—that provide that a producer's exclusive territorial licenses for wholesalers in these industries cannot be challenged if "substantial and effective competition" exists in the distribution market—may prove to be important steps in this direction.[36] The Vertical Restraints Guidelines reflect a different and, I think, less persuasive approach.[37] Whatever the approach, however, my point is

---

[35]   *See, e.g.*, Easterbrook, *supra* note 32, at 153 ("The Emptiness of the Rule of Reason"); H. HOVENKAMP, *supra*, note 23, at 271 ("Courts are simply incapable of dealing with the kind of nondescript, open-ended 'rule of reason' articulated in *Sylvania*").

For a personal effort, *see* Gellhorn & Tatham, *Making Sense Out of the Rule of Reason*, 35 CASE WES. RES. L. REV. 155 (1984–85).

---

[36]   *See* Soft Drink Interbrand Competition Act, 15 U.S.C. §§ 3501–03; S. 412, Malt Beverage Interbrand Competition Act, 99th Cong., 1st Sess. (1985). I should note that I have contributed to the drafting of these legislative items and testified on their behalf.

These statutes adopt the filter design of the Merger and Vertical Restraints Guidelines also urged in a somewhat different way by Judge Easterbrook (see sources cited *supra* note 24). However, rather than rely initially on market shares and market structures to distinguish between benign and possibly dangerous restraints—increasingly questionable measures in light of the theory of contestable markets (see Baumol, *Contestable Markets: An Uprising in the Theory of Industry Structure*, 72 AM. ECON. REV. 1 (1982)—the soft drink act and beer bill rely on evidence of intense competition to limit antitrust coverage to those practices that might injure consumer welfare. That is, where there is substantial and effective competition, the non-price vertical restraint poses no threat and should be immune from antitrust challenge.

---

[37]   As already noted (see *supra* note 36), the problem of the guidelines is that they automatically equate market structure with the benefits or absence of competition. Increasingly, however, the economic evidence is to the contrary. *See, e.g.*, Alpert & Kitt, *supra* note 22.

356 : *The antitrust bulletin*

that further attention needs to be given to clarifying the application of the reasonableness standard. If it is to play an important role on the center stage of antitrust—as seems to be the direction of Supreme Court cases—its content and approach must be defined.

On the other hand, if the per se rule is to retain validity a third recommendation is that the Court (or, alternatively, the Division) spell out with greater clarity the distinction between suspect horizontal activity and benign vertical arrangements. The problem is particularly acute when a manufacturer of a branded article presses his dealers to promote his product or otherwise seeks to market his product aggressively, particularly against discounters. The current case law is unpredictable and inconsistent. Cases such as *Klor's*,[38] *General Motors*,[39] *Monsanto*,[40] *Sealy*,[41] and *Topco*[42] demonstrate the depth of the current confusion. All involve essentially similar free-rider fact situations, yet their results turn on whether the practice is characterized as horizontal or vertical. Of course, as long as different standards (per se or rule of reason) apply to similar conduct, the horizontal/vertical distinction will not be dispositive. But at least an understandable method for distinguishing horizontal from vertical arrangements would lead to similar cases being decided in the same way.[43]

*   *   *   *

---

[38]   Klor's Inc. v. Broadway-Hale Stores, Inc., 359 U.S. 207 (1959).

[39]   United States v. General Motors Corp., 384 U.S. 127 (1966); *see* Baker, *Interconnected Problems of Doctrine and Economics in the Section One Labyrinth: Is Sylvania a Way Out?*, 67 VA. L. REV. 1457 (1981).

[40]   *Monsanto*, 104 S. Ct. at 1464.

[41]   United States v. Sealy, Inc., 388 U.S. 350 (1967).

[42]   *Topco*, 405 U.S. at 596.

[43]   See, for example, the thoughtful analysis by Professor Liebler suggesting a focus on whether the restraint could directly restrict output as a method for distinguishing horizontal from vertical arrangements. Liebler, *Intrabrand "Cartels" Under GTE-Sylvania*, 30 UCLA L. REV. 1 (1982). *See also* Liebler, Book Review, 66 CALIF. L. REV. 1317, 1334-39 (1978).

Antitrust staircase : 357

The agenda for antitrust has not been shortened by the emphasis on economic analysis in recent years or the introduction of courts and policy makers to price theory. Indeed, it seems likely that only the easiest questions have been answered where there is general agreement among economists. Concepts such as contestable markets or opportunistic behavior may be relatively simple to grasp; yet their application in particular markets to guide antitrust policy makers seems another matter. Even if more sophisticated economic analysis is within the general antitrust lawyer's grasp, it is far from certain that these insights will provide clear answers to basic policies or particular cases.

Antitrust at its core involves values and normative judgments. After close to 100 years of antitrust it is still unclear whether antitrust enforcement significantly contributes to consumer welfare. To some this suggests that those who would intervene in the market must bear a heavy burden, or at least that intervention should be limited to those markets where the likelihood of collusion and injury to consumer welfare is relatively high. Where competitive and monopolistic behavior are basically indistinguishable, the costs of intervention—including the cost to consumer welfare when antitrust is used to restrain competition—must be calculated carefully.

Perhaps the principal lesson from antitrust history for the future is to realize how little we really understand about markets and how they operate.

[12]

Economic Perspectives — Volume 1, Number 2 — Fall 1987 — Pages 41–54

Horizontal Merger Policy: Problems and Changes

Richard Schmalensee

Most knowledgeable economists seem now to agree that the Department of Justice, the Federal Trade Commission, and the courts were excessively hostile to horizontal mergers in the 1960s. Merger policy in the 1960s reflected in part a presumption that mergers rarely lower costs and in part a desire to preserve and protect small business for noneconomic reasons.[1] There also seems to be widespread agreement that the 1984 Merger Guidelines provide a useful general framework for evaluating the economic effects of proposed mergers. However, there is less agreement on the merits of the specific standards set forth in the Guidelines or of those employed in practice, which tend to be more permissive. There is even less agreement on the desirability of proposed changes in the underlying law, Section 7 of the Clayton Act.

In what follows I argue that, while it might be desirable to make small changes in the core language of Section 7, the Reagan administration's proposals for major changes should not be adopted. In particular, it would not be desirable to require courts to consider the efficiency effects of proposed mergers, nor should they be given a long list of other factors that must be considered in merger cases. I also argue that

---

[1] Read, for instance, the Supreme Court's treatment of efficiencies and the virtues of small business in *Brown Shoe*, 370 U.S. 294 (1962) and *Von's Grocery*, 384 U.S. 270 (1966).

■ *Richard Schmalensee is Professor of Economics and Management, Massachusetts Institute of Technology, Cambridge, Massachusetts.*

some changes in the current merger Guidelines and in enforcement policy would be desirable, but I do not think radical reform is called for here either.

Feasible Goals of Merger Policy

The efficiency-minded czar of economic theory, if serving as both enforcement agency and judge, would approve proposed mergers if and only if they would increase consumers' plus producers' surplus. To make this determination, the czar would calculate and evaluate the short-run and long-run effects of each proposed merger on prices, costs, product varieties, information, and the rate and direction of technical change, among other things. If either the market involved or any other affected market were imperfectly competitive, the czar would take account of the associated differences between private and social costs. The calculations would be adjusted to reflect imperfections in information that might distort the actions of buyers or sellers.

Real merger policy must inevitably fall well short of this ideal for three important reasons. First, industrial organization economics is hardly an exact science. Economists cannot testify with the confidence of experts on ballistics or fingerprints—or at least they should not. They cannot now predict the precise quantitative effects of any particular merger on costs or prices, and the net impact on buyers, sellers, and society as a whole is even harder to quantify. A perfect merger czar would need tools and techniques for the analysis of proposed changes in market structure that are not yet available to real economists.

Second, courts cope badly with complexity and tradeoffs. One economist may be able to convince another that the cost-reducing effects of a particular proposed merger will, on balance, probably outweigh its collusion-enhancing effects. However, it is quite another thing to *prove* the case to a jury of high school dropouts or to a judge who spends most of his time trying drug cases or deciding if advertising campaigns are deceptive. A rule of law that permits only mergers that can be *proven* to increase welfare will permit no mergers, while a rule that bars only mergers that can be proven to decrease welfare will stop no mergers. Legislation that would require anything approaching a full-blown cost-benefit analysis would produce both long trials and unpredictable decisions.

Third, while the enforcement agencies rely on professional economists to deal with complexities and tradeoffs in a sophisticated manner, and private enforcement of Section 7 is relatively unimportant,[2] the agencies necessarily operate with very limited information in the pre-merger screening period. Their decisions are often based only on information provided voluntarily by firms seeking to merge. Some balance is provided when rivals or managers seeking to avoid a hostile takeover make submis-

---

[2] That is, even though individuals and corporations can directly file cases under Section 7 without government involvement to attempt to block or undo mergers, private cases under Section 7 are relatively unimportant. Private cases are relatively more important in some other areas of antitrust.

sions, but their evidence is likely to reflect their private interests. Moreover, business decisions are often necessarily based on rough estimates of possible efficiencies that would not come close to satisfying legal standards of proof or even the standards of the seminar room. Thus the enforcement agencies do not have the information or the tools to simulate the behavior of the ideal merger czar.[3] Even if they did, private parties would continue to challenge some mergers the government approved and thus force the courts to decide their fate.

In the face of these difficulties, the best one can hope for in practice is a merger policy that makes few major blunders and operates with enough speed and predictability so as not to become a major source of cost and uncertainty. Such a policy must necessarily rely on presumptions and shortcuts that reflect the current state of economic knowledge and belief.[4]

If one believed, for instance, as many economists did in the 1960s, that horizontal mergers rarely yield non-trivial efficiencies but that non-trivial increases in concentration generally facilitate the exercise of market power, one would argue that all mergers that would increase concentration more than trivially should be stopped. Coupled with clear standards for market definition, such a rule would be relatively simple and predictable. It would, of course, block mergers that would produce efficiencies that more than outweighed any adverse effects on competition. But if such mergers were known or believed to be rare, the expected costs of these errors would be small relative to the costs of protracted and inevitably error-prone evaluation of every challenged merger.

The Role of Efficiency Arguments

Most economists now believe that the link between concentration and collusion is relatively weak. In part this reflects a good deal of cross-section empirical work during the 1970s that casts considerable doubt on the strength—and even the existence—of a positive relation between concentration and profitability.[5] Theory suggests that high levels of concentration may be necessary for effective collusion, but the empirical literature suggests that high concentration is certainly not sufficient. Both theory and empirical analysis indicate that small increases in concentration and increases that leave a market still fragmented are almost certainly harmless. From this perspective,

[3] Despite these difficulties, I feel strongly that the Hart-Scott-Rodino requirement that all large mergers be screened by the government before consummation improves enforcement at relatively low cost and should accordingly be retained. Before this requirement was imposed in 1976, enforcement decisions were based on even less information than at present, and the agencies were often in the position of asking the courts to impose substantial costs by separating merged firms that had already integrated their operations.

[4] For general discussions of the limits of antitrust, see Easterbrook (1984) and Schmalensee (1987). I differ here from the other authors in the symposium only in placing more stress on the inherent limitations of the enforcement agencies and the courts.

[5] For a survey of the relevant literature, see, for instance, Schmalensee (forthcoming). The survey notes that intra-industry cross-section studies of the relation between concentration and price have generally supported the hypothesis that concentration facilitates collusion.

the vast majority of horizontal mergers pose no market power problems and should simply be approved rapidly.

Most economists now also give greater weight to the argument that mergers and other transactions in the market for corporate control often enhance efficiency by displacing inefficient management or exploiting economies of scope or scale. My impression is that this change in attitude cannot be adequately described as a response to new evidence.[6] At any rate, as Williamson (1968) has argued, a small efficiency gain will generally outweigh a large increase in market power.

But this argument does not imply that the *courts* should be given the task of deciding whether efficiencies outweigh the increased risk of collusion in individual cases. Courts cannot perform that task accurately, predictably, or quickly, and case-specific assessments are likely to reflect presumptions and precedents as much as the realities of the case. Greater predictability and speed would be obtained, at little cost in accuracy, if greater confidence that mergers on average produce cost savings would instead increase the burden that must be met by those who seek to prove that any particular merger will facilitate collusion. Thus I would not support legislation requiring the courts to consider the efficiencies likely to arise from particular mergers.

On the other hand, the enforcement agencies should continue to consider possible efficiencies. The agencies can handle collusion-efficiency tradeoffs in a more sophisticated and flexible fashion than the courts; they can use the best available economic techniques and are not constrained by precedent. Moreover, the agencies need not limit their attention to factors the courts would consider. In no area of the law are enforcement decisions always dictated by the letter of the controlling statute. If the enforcement agencies decide not to take action against a particular merger because they feel it would produce substantial efficiencies, private parties can still challenge it on market power grounds.

The pre-merger information that agencies possess is, however, generally inadequate to permit anything approaching a full-blown cost-benefit analysis, even if the available tools of economics permitted such an analysis in principle. I would thus argue that the enforcement agencies should use efficiency arguments only as tiebreakers; strong arguments should tip the scales in close cases. Lack of persuasive efficiency evidence should not result in a merger with little likely collusive impact being challenged, nor should a thick stack of management consultants' reports save a merger that is highly objectionable on market power grounds. And efficiencies that could practically be obtained without the merger should be ignored. Thus I am on balance more comfortable with the treatment of efficiency in the 1982 Guidelines than with that in the 1984 Guidelines.[7]

---

[6] That is, I think the empirical evidence for this proposition is rather thin (but see Jarrell, Gregg A., James A. Brickley, and Jeffrey M. Netter in the next issue of the *Journal of Economic Perspectives*) though there is even less evidence against it. It does seem clear that the affected shareholders generally gain from mergers (Jensen and Ruback, 1983), but this statement does not establish that society as a whole gains.

[7] On a related point, I agree with Fisher's statement elsewhere in this symposium that the Federal Trade Commission seems to have been too ready to believe superficial efficiency arguments in the GM-Toyota case.

Amending Section 7

Let me now turn to the administration's proposals to amend Section 7. I have already dealt with one of these: I do not think the courts should be required to consider efficiencies that might result from proposed mergers. The administration also proposes changing the core language of the law and adding a list of factors—essentially those specified in the Guidelines—that must be "duly considered" in merger cases.

Section 7 now requires the plaintiff to demonstrate that the effect of a proposed merger "may be substantially to lessen competition, or to tend to create a monopoly." The problem is that the word "may" seems to require only that a non-zero probability of harm be demonstrated. This language is perfectly consistent with the unduly restrictive policy of the 1960s, as the courts then found. Since I hold the consensus view that most horizontal mergers have only a tiny probability of raising prices and that many have positive efficiencies, and since I doubt (perhaps naively) that this consensus is likely to be radically revised in the forseeable future, I think the law should require more of those who oppose mergers.

I am thus comfortable with the core language in the administration's proposal, which would require a showing that there be a "significant probability that the merger will substantially increase the ability to exercise market power," where "market power" is then correctly defined as "the ability of one or more firms profitably to maintain prices above competitive levels for a significant period of time."[8] It is worth noting that if this language were written into law, a merger that would permit price to be raised above cost (that is, the competitive price) would be illegal, no matter how much the merger lowered costs. Thus, even if the courts were always required to consider "efficiencies deriving from the acquisition," as the administration proposes, they would be logically compelled ultimately to ignore them subsequently in evaluating the legality of most mergers.

Even if the courts should not be required to balance claimed efficiencies against increases in the likelihood of effective collusion, shouldn't the law specify how the latter should be assessed? Or in terms of the current legislative debate, shouldn't the courts be required to consider all the economically relevant factors (excluding efficiency) spelled out in the Guidelines? I think not.

Section 7, as it stands or with its core language changed as above, requires the courts to judge the likelihood that a merger will have harmful effects but does not specify how that judgement is to be reached. The courts can thus consider any evidence that economists and others persuade them is relevant and ignore everything else. If the courts were given a long list of factors that *must* be considered, as the administration proposes, with no indication as to how they should be measured or

---

[8] More continuity in terminology would be provided if the plaintiff were instead required to show "a substantial probability that the merger will substantially lessen competition or tend to create a monopoly." But this very continuity may create some danger that future courts would confuse "lessening competition" and "removing competitors", as in the decisions cited in footnote 1, above.

weighed in the final decision, merger cases would generally be lengthened. Moreover, since the state of industrial organization economics is such that the longer the list of factors that must be weighed, the more the ultimate outcome reflects judgment, decisions would probably become the less predictable. Such a procedure gives no guarantee of reaching better decisions on average.

A somewhat more attractive approach would be to legislate a "structured rule of reason;" that is, to prescribe the algorithm to be followed in evaluating merger cases. In principle, this approach could prevent the courts from, say, deciding after "due consideration" that conditions of entry are irrelevant to the likelihood of effective collusion. While legislation along these lines might improve merger policy, it would have to be drafted carefully to reflect only the most fundamental economic principles. It would be unwise to write the current Guidelines into law, despite their many virtues.

The main reason is that industrial organization economics does not stand still, but antitrust statutes do.[9] New theory, evidence, and analytical techniques are continually being developed, and professional opinion can shift rapidly. By 1980, the 1968 Guidelines had come to be widely viewed as fundamentally flawed; the 1982 Guidelines simply ignored them. I do not believe that anyone can now describe in detail what analytical approach to horizontal merger evaluation will be considered optimal 20 or even 10 years hence. Since antitrust laws are difficult to amend, legislating the details of today's best practice will almost guarantee years of bad decisions based on outmoded doctrines and methods.

A second reason for not legislating the Guidelines turns on the difference between the enforcement agencies and the courts. While both should make predictable decisions, they necessarily proceed in different ways. Within the agencies, the current Guidelines (whatever they may be at any time) can serve as a flexible framework for structuring analysis. Cases that do not quite fit that framework—for instance, those in which the definition of the relevant market is fundamentally uncertain or in which strategic groups and mobility barriers play a central role in determining industry conduct—can be handled in an ad hoc fashion with the best available tools.[10] The agencies screen enough mergers so that relatively consistent behavior, even if it departs from the published Guidelines, comes to be relatively predictable.

For a judge, however, the law is the law. If the statute and relevant precedents assume there always exists a single clearly correct market definition, for instance, or fail to mention mobility barriers, courts will require that market boundaries be sharply defined and will disregard evidence that mobility barriers are important. The Guidelines as law would necessarily be applied less flexibly and in a less economically sophisticated manner by the courts than they are now applied by the enforcement agencies.

---

[9] The Clayton Act, passed in 1914, has only had two major substantive amendments: the Robinson-Patman Act of 1936, which tightened restrictions on price discrimination, and the Celler-Kefauver Act of 1950, which closed a gaping loophole in Section 7. The substantive cores of Sections 1 and 2 of the Sherman Act have remained untouched since their passage in 1890.

[10] On mobility barriers and strategic groups, see Caves and Porter (1977).

That point made, however, I do not think that the courts should ignore the then-current Guidelines any more than they should ignore any other aspect of the relevant economics literature. Nor, as a practical matter, do they proceed in this fashion. Judicial attitudes toward mergers have changed in ways that reflect the changes in economic thinking embodied in the Guidelines, even though not a word of Section 7 has been altered since 1950. New legislation is clearly desirable only when the weight of precedent makes it impossible for the courts to base decisions on economic realities.[11] And horizontal merger law does not currently face that problem.

I next turn to the Guidelines themselves, considering them both as an outline of enforcement policy and as a message to the courts.

Market Definition and the Concentration Test

Under the current (1984) Guidelines, the enforcement agencies examine market concentration first. If a proposed horizontal merger would increase concentration only slightly or would leave concentration low, it is approved without examination of the other factors discussed in the next section. In this section I consider the Guidelines' approach to market definition and then discuss the use of concentration standards as a threshold test.

The Guidelines define a market as "a product or group of products and a geographic area in which it is sold such that a hypothetical, profit-maximizing firm, not subject to rate regulation, that was the only present and future seller of those products in that area would impose a "small but significant and nontransitory" increase in price above prevailing or likely future levels." Note that market definition under the Guidelines necessarily involves a counterfactual exercise, not a description of observed behavior, an important distinction explored by Scheffman and Spiller (1985) and Spiller and Huang (1986). The Guidelines note that a price increase of 5 percent lasting one year will generally be used in this analysis.

This definition has the great merit of shifting attention away from time-worn issues of substitutability and cross-elasticity and toward the real economic question: the extent to which demand would fall (for whatever reason) if price were increased. Such a shift of attention is appropriate across all of antitrust policy, as Landes and Posner (1981), Schmalensee (1982) and others have argued.

The main weakness of the Guidelines' market definition standard, which is also noted by Fisher in this symposium, is that the price baseline should be "competitive levels" rather than "present and likely future levels." After all, market power is the ability to increase price above the competitive level profitably, not above the current level. It thus makes sense in evaluating mergers to define a market as something that could profitably be monopolized, not as something for which price could be profitably increased over current (possibly monopolistic) levels.

[11] New legislation might be necessary to expunge the vague concept of "submarkets" from the law. I, for one, am tired of explaining to lawyers that I don't know what a "submarket" is because the term is not used in economics and has never been defined clearly by judges.

If only two firms produced salt, for instance, and managed through tacit collusion to charge the monopoly price, a careful analysis would show that price could not be profitably increased above present or likely future levels. Under the Guidelines, "salt" would thus be found not to be a relevant market. If the relevant market were instead found to be "seasonings," a merger between the two salt producers might be allowed because it would not much increase concentration in the "seasonings market." This approach to market definition is not only logically flawed, it is biased in favor of permitting mergers in highly concentrated markets where collusion is already a problem.

In defense of the current definition, White argues in this symposium that the purpose of merger policy is only to prevent a worsening of current performance, which is by assumption impossible in the salt case. But merger policy, like the rest of antitrust policy, should seek to enhance competition where possible. More importantly, while tacit collusion and even explicit collusion often break down, a salt monopolist is unlikely ever to revert spontaneously to competitive behavior. Thus, this salt merger is in fact likely to worsen future market performance.[12]

One could also argue that a "competitive levels" standard would require a finding as to the extent to which current price, which is readily observed, is above marginal cost, which is not easy to measure. This position is strengthened by the recent literature on the limitations of accounting data, which indicates that the reported accounting profitability of individual firms is an unreliable guide to the extent to which they are exercising market power. (See Fisher's paper in this symposium for references.) But this position ultimately amounts to arguing that a clearly biased standard should be elevated to the status of a principle because the correct standard is difficult to implement. It is possible to correct at least roughly for some biases (such as the effect of inflation), and it is surely better to attempt this than to pretend accounting data are unbiased.[13]

The "5 percent for a year" standard for "small but significant and nontransitory" price changes has acquired considerable importance, despite its obvious arbitrariness (which is recognized by the agencies) and the equally obvious impossibility of applying it rigorously with the information available in most merger screening proceedings. The standard is perhaps best understood as mandating a conservative, local, first derivative test, which can be justified by the usual lack of any nonlocal information about cost and demand condition. That is, if a 5 percent price increase would clearly be profitable, an increase large enough to worry about is also likely to be profitable. On the other hand, if a 5 percent increase above competitive levels would not be profitable, even a monopoly over the collection of products and areas

---

[12] Note also that a finding that the market is "salt" would not, under the Guidelines, bar a merger between two small salt producers that would not increase concentration noticeably.

[13] White's example of a proposed merger between a cellophane monopolist and a producer of aluminum foil mainly illustrates that no single method of assessing market power is universally useful. An intelligent enforcement agency that focuses on the basic question—will the merger facilitate the exercise of market power?—rather than on market definition would attack the hypothetical merger if it would make possible an increase in the price of either product.

being considered would not likely cause much social harm. Thus the 5 percent test seems basically sensible, though, in light of the generally small losses associated with a 5 percent increase in price above competitive levels (and the imprecision that inevitably attends the application of any test of this sort), I would be not be much less comfortable with a 10 percent test.

Once the boundaries of the relevant market have been fixed, the level of post-merger concentration and the increase in concentration that the merger would produce are used to select potentially undesirable mergers for further study. Is it sensible to assign such a strategic role to concentration? After all, the link between concentration and the exercise of market power, which once seemed the bedrock of industrial organization, is now widely recognized to be weak. About all that remains of the "old learning" that supported the strict 1968 Guidelines is the belief that high concentration is a necessary condition for the effective exercise of market power.[14]

But this remnant is enough to justify the use of a concentration-based threshold test. The Guidelines should begin with the necessary condition that is easiest to test. This approach permits approval of a large number of harmless mergers quickly and at a relatively low cost. Using any of the other factors discussed below in the threshold test would increase cost and reduce predictability with at best modest improvements in the quality of the selection procedure.

Let me now turn to the standards used for evaluating levels of and changes in concentration under the Guidelines. It is important to note that the HHI has not been proven superior to, say, the four-firm concentration ratio used in the 1968 Guidelines as a predictor of noncompetitive behavior. Nor does much evidence exist that the Guidelines' critical concentration levels—post-merger HHIs of 1000 and 1800—have real economic significance. Essentially no evidence attaches significance to the threshold levels of changes in HHI specified in the Guidelines: 50 if post-merger HHI is above 1800 and 100 if the post-merger HHI is above 1000.[15] It is thus difficult to have defensibly strong feelings one way or another about the Guidelines' concentration tests.

For the sake of completeness, though, I will note that my sense is that the critical concentration levels in the current Guidelines are at least not radically wrong. The available evidence on concentration levels in the U.S. indicates that relatively few markets will be classed as "highly concentrated" by the Guideline standards. This finding is consistent with the fundamental premises that underlie modern antitrust policy: the economy is generally at least workably competitive, and market power is only infrequently a serious social problem.

Indeed, the "high concentration" line is currently drawn about where it was in 1968. As White notes, an HHI of 1800 corresponds roughly to a four-form concentration ratio of 70 percent, which is close to the 1968 Guidelines standard of 75 percent for "high concentration." Moreover, a bit of arithmetic reveals that the "shares of

---

[14] Even this statement is a bit strong, since trade associations have occasionally served to sustain collusive agreements in unconcentrated markets. But merger policy can do little to affect such conduct, and I accordingly ignore it here.

[15] On these points, see the discussion of the relevant literature in Schmalensee (forthcoming).

merging firms" standards in the 1968 Guidelines for highly concentrated industries generally correspond to 30 point to 40 point increases in the HHI. Thus the 50 point standard in the 1984 Guidelines represents only a slight relaxation in most cases. I would be only a bit less comfortable with a standard of 2000 for "high concentration" and a corresponding change standard of 100, though much higher levels would make me nervous.

A major difference between the 1968 and 1984 Guidelines is in the concentration test to be applied to industries that are not highly concentrated. The 1968 Guidelines indicate that mergers that increase HHI by more than 50 points to 90 points were likely to be challenged regardless of the level of concentration. Under the 1984 Guidelines, no mergers that leave HHI below 1000 will be challenged. This important change is clearly warranted; mergers that leave markets atomistic almost never increase the likelihood of collusion noticeably.

The current Guidelines also specify that mergers that leave HHI between 1000 and 1800 will be challenged only if they increase HHI by at least 100 points, thus relaxing the 1968 standards only slightly in this range. Some observers have suggested that in practice this test is currently ignored and mergers are never challenged unless HHI is above 1800. If this is indeed being done (I have not seen conclusive evidence), it is an undesirable departure from the Guidelines. Large concentration increases in moderately concentrated industries at least deserve close scrutiny. I would be more comfortable if the 1000 lower critical level were instead increased a bit, since many markets exceed the 50 percent four-firm concentration ratio to which White informs us this HHI level corresponds. And the 100 point change standard might be increased to 150 or perhaps even 200.

A final issue to consider here is how to treat foreign firms in the measurement of concentration. Landes and Posner (1981) and others have argued that if foreign firms make any sales at all in the United States, and their expansion here is not limited by quotas, their entire worldwide capacity should be included in computations of concentration. They argue that the ability of foreign competitors to *expand* domestic sales constrains the exercise of market power by domestic firms, not the pre-merger level of imports. While the core of this argument is sound, it grossly oversimplifies in treating domestic and foreign capacity as competitively equivalent. In general, I believe that even foreign competition unconstrained by quotas should receive less weight in market definition than domestic capacity.

In many industries, investments in marketing and distribution are necessary to expand sales in any geographic area. Foreign firms may be less eager to make those investments in response to an increase in price than domestic firms, since the real value of United States sales to foreign firms depends on unpredictable fluctuations in exchange rates. Moreover, a close examination of many markets reveals that imports occupy specialized niches, which are glossed over by the approach of the Guidelines to market definition. The French produce a lot of cheese, for instance, but Brie is not a perfect substitute for domestic cheddar. I would thus argue that the obstacles to expanding imports in response to a price increase from domestic producers often extend well beyond quotas and that those obstacles must be explicitly considered in assessing the competitive significance of foreign firms.

Also, I am uncomfortable with the position of the 1984 Guidelines that even quotas will sometimes be disregarded because they do not necessarily last forever. After all, quotas do usually persist well beyond the one-year test period generally used in the process of market definition.

Entry Conditions and Other Factors

Mergers that fail the threshold concentration test are subjected to more detailed analysis by the enforcement agencies. The explicit addition of this second stage is an important advance over the 1968 Guidelines. Among the more important factors considered at this stage are: (1) conditions of entry; (2) the ability of smaller firms to increase output; (3) the nature of the product and terms of sale; and (4) the conduct of firms in the market.[16] Many (or even most) economists would consider these factors, collectively, to be at least as important in determining the likelihood of noncompetitive behavior as the level of concentration.

Unfortunately, those same economists do not agree as to how these factors should be measured or their quantitative importance assessed. Alternative plausible measures of concentration tend to be highly correlated, and analysts can at least use measured concentration in Census-defined manufacturing industries to judge whether any particular level of concentration is unusually high or low. The judgements of economists about the other factors considered here vary much more widely, both in general and in particular cases. No systematic tabulations exist to be used in establishing comparative standards. Without going far—I would argue unacceptably far—beyond the bounds of the professional consensus, it is thus impossible to prescribe detailed quantitative standards or classification systems for the four factors listed above.

I do agree with Fisher that if a proposed merger fails the threshold concentration test, conditions of entry should be investigated next.[17] The position of the Guidelines on the extreme case of contestable markets is theoretically correct: "If entry into a market is so easy that existing competitors could not succeed in raising price for any significant period of time, the Department is unlikely to challenge mergers in that market." However, markets of this sort appear to be very rare indeed. While I can imagine a case in which entry into a concentrated market is so easy that further increases in concentration through merger are plainly not a problem, I cannot imagine encountering more than a handful of such cases in practice.

[16] These four factors are explicitly listed—along with the number and size distribution of sellers and efficiencies—in the administration's proposed amendment to Section 7.

[17] Note that entry that would take place within a year in response to a small price increase is considered in the process of market definition.

Even airline markets, long the favorite example of contestability theorists, do not seem to be contestable in fact. Even though concentration is irrelevant in perfectly contestable markets, several studies have found that prices are higher, all else equal, when fewer airlines fly between two cities.[18] In fact, some knowledgeable observers have argued that the combination of plane size and network economies are in the process of producing a set of regionally dominant airlines relatively immune to entry. At any rate, there is certainly little empirical support for assuming, as the Department of Transportation seems sometimes to have done, that free entry generally makes the exercise of monopoly power impossible in airline markets. (I am thus more nervous about the Northwest-Republic merger than Fisher, though admittedly less well informed.)

More generally, since entry is almost never perfectly free, the enforcement agencies and the courts must frequently ask the question, "How high are the barriers to entry?" The literature provides no generally accepted way of answering this question or even of defining barriers to entry.

Some economists favor Bain's (1965) definition: roughly, "factors that enable established firms to earn supra-competitive profits without threat of entry." Others favor Stigler's (1967) definition: roughly, "costs that must be incurred by an entrant that were not incurred by established firms." Bain's definition seems to me more in line with the relevant theory—both Bain and recent theory find that scale economies and sunk costs can be sources of barriers, while Stigler disagrees—and also more consistent with the notion that effective competition dissipates monopoly rents. Moreover, use of Stigler's definition seems in practice to bias analysis toward findings of low barriers, perhaps because it is easier to argue that both incumbents and potential entrants have to acquire the same assets (plant, equipment, technology, reputation, and so on) than to analyze the possibility that these assets would be acquired on different terms simply because the incumbents can affect the market environment for entrants.

The Guidelines seem closer to Bain than to Stigler, since sunk costs and scale economies are listed as possible sources of barriers. But the basic principles to be applied in assessing entry barriers are not spelled out explicitly. The Guidelines merely state that the "likelihood and probable magnitude of entry in response to a 'small but significant and nontransitory' increase in price" over a two-year period will be considered, and a few potentially relevant factors are listed in a footnote.[19] Since entry conditions are so important, the Guidelines should provide both general principles and complete, annotated lists of factors to be considered. (For example, see Salop, 1986.) Summary formulas or classification schemes should not be used until the state of the

---

[18] See, for instance, Bailey, Graham, and Kaplan (1985, ch. 9). Most studies find the effect of concentration on price in these markets to be relatively small, however.

[19] This footnote states, "Entry is generally facilitated by the growth of the market and hindered by its decline." Since growth affects incumbents and entrants alike, and capital flows to profits, not to growth, growth is irrelevant under either the Bain or Stigler definition. Mechanical application of this "principle" could result in a perfectly competitive and contestable industry being classed as having high barriers to entry because it is declining.

science makes them at least plausible, and that appears unlikely to happen soon. Finally, planning and executing entry in many industries can take well over two years; I agree with Fisher that a longer test period may be appropriate.[20]

The remaining factors listed at the start of this section pose related problems. Assessing the ability of smaller firms to expand production is often relatively easy, for instance, but in a world where imperfect substitutes are the norm and reputations matter, their ability to expand *sales* may be quite another matter.

Similarly, a history of collusive conduct can in principle provide conclusive evidence that, regardless of the level of concentration, noncompetitive behavior is a problem. But real histories are rarely simple to interpret or to weigh. For instance, how should the employment of now legal "facilitating practices" (such as most-favored-nation clauses or advance notification of price changes) be interpreted? How much weight should be assigned to a decade-old conviction for price fixing or predatory pricing?

Finally, recent theory makes it clear that the information available to buyers and sellers about prices, qualities, and competitive moves is a crucial determinant of market conduct and performance. Unfortunately, neither theory nor empirical work has provided any hard and fast rules for evaluating the implications of "the nature of the product and terms of sale." In particular, it is hard to justify the position that the use of long-term contracts by sophisticated industrial buyers should make a merger permissible regardless of other factors, although the clear ability to integrate backward provides powerful evidence of ease of entry.

In the interests of predictability, the Guidelines could say more about how these four factors—particularly ease of entry—and their effects will be assessed. I would also add the principle that the more seriously a merger fails the concentration test, the stronger the burden of proof on those who would use these factors to defend it. But in the interest of accuracy and consistency with established economic doctrine, the Guidelines should not come close to reducing the treatment of these factors to formulas. It is better to recognize that judgement will play an important role in enforcement policy than to pretend to unattainable scientific rigor.

Summary

The problem of devising an optimal merger policy is made complex by the inherent limitations of the courts, the enforcement agencies, and the merger screening process, by the need to provide predictability and to avoid unnecessary costs and delays, and by the evolving and imperfect state of industrial organization economics.

---

[20] The Guidelines state that "the Department will consider the likelihood and probable magnitude of entry in response to a 'small but significant and nontransitory' increase in price" and then note that a two-year time period will be used. This statement seems to say that the response to a price increase lasting two years will be assessed. Since such short-lived price increases are unlikely to justify investment in much longer-lived productive assets, the Guidelines should make clear that what is at issue is the two-year response to a price increase believed to be permanent.

In this light, I find that the current enforcement policy toward horizontal mergers, while certainly capable of substantial improvement, is not fundamentally flawed. But I oppose major legislative changes designed to write that policy into law or to force the courts to consider efficiency arguments they are unlikely to evaluate well or predictably.

■ *I have benefited from helpful comments by Steven Salop and Carl Shapiro and from reading preliminary versions of the other two papers in this symposium.*

References

Bailey, Elizabeth E., Daniel R. Graham, and Daniel P. Kaplan, *Deregulating the Airlines*. Cambridge: MIT Press, 1985.

Bain, Joe S., *Barriers to New Competition*. Cambridge: Harvard University Press, 1956.

Caves, Richard E., and Michael E. Porter, "From Entry Barriers to Mobility Barriers," *Quarterly Journal of Economics*, 1977, *91*, 241–262.

Easterbrook, Frank H., "The Limits of Antitrust," *Texas Law Review*, 1984, *63*, 1–40.

Jensen, Michael, and Richard Ruback, "The Market for Corporate Control," *Journal of Financial Economics*, 1983, *11*, 5–50.

Landes, William M., and Richard A. Posner, "Market Power in Antitrust Cases," *Harvard Law Review*, 1981, *94*, 937–996.

Salop, Steven C., "Measuring Ease of Entry," *Antitrust Bulletin*, Summer 1986, *31*, 551–570.

Scheffman, David T., and Pablo T. Spiller, "Geographic Market Definition under the DOJ Guidelines," Discussion Paper, U.S. Federal Trade Commission, Bureau of Economics, August 1985.

Schmalensee, Richard, "Another Look at Market Power," *Harvard Law Review*, 1982, *95*, 1789–1816.

Schmalensee, Richard, "Inter-Industry Studies of Structure and Performance." In Schmalensee, Richard, and Robert D. Willig, eds., *Handbook of Industrial Organization*. Amsterdam: North-Holland, fortcoming.

Schmalensee, Richard, "Standards for Dominant Firm Conduct: What can Economics Contribute?" In Hay, Donald, and John Vickers, eds., *The Economics of Market Dominance*. Oxford: Basil Blackwell, 1987.

Spiller, Pablo T., and Clifford J. Huang, "On the Extent of the Market: Wholesale Gasoline in the Northeastern United States," *Journal of Industrial Economics*, 1986, *35*, 131–146.

Stigler, George J., "Barriers to Entry, Economies of Scale, and Firm Size." In Stigler, George J., *The Organization of Industry*. Homewood, IL: Irwin, 1967.

Williamson, Oliver E., "Economies as an Antitrust Defense," *American Economic Review*, 1968, *58*, 18–34.

[13]

Journal of Economic Perspectives—Volume 4, Number 3—Summer 1990—Pages 75-96

Innovation and Cooperation: Implications for Competition and Antitrust

Thomas M. Jorde and David J. Teece

Nobel Laureate Robert Solow and his colleagues on MIT's Industrial Productivity Commission recently noted (Dertouzos, Lester, and Solow, 1989, p. 7): "Undeveloped cooperative relationships between individuals and between organizations stand out in our industry studies as obstacles to technological innovation and the improvement of industrial performance" and later (p. 105) that "interfirm cooperation in the U.S. has often, though not always, been inhibited by government antitrust regulation." These striking conclusions warrant further exploration.

Unfortunately, industrial organization textbooks still discuss horizontal cooperation and competition almost exclusively in terms of standard cartel theory. (On the other hand, vertical cooperation/contracting is viewed differently, and some textbooks provide treatments of supplier-buyer relationships in which cooperation is viewed as enhancing efficiency.) Both in the textbooks and in policy discussion among economists, cooperation among competitors is highly suspect, being perhaps the last bastion of what was once referred to as the "inhospitality tradition" in antitrust. As a result, very little literature addresses how cooperation among competitors can promote competition, notwithstanding that cooperation among competitors may sometimes be essential if innovating firms are to compete in today's increasingly global markets (Imai and Baba, 1989). Such cooperation is already important in Japan and in Europe.[1]

---

[1]For instance, cooperative R&D and related activities have been important to the success of the Western German machine tool industry. The industry formed a strong association that has a research and teaching institute at Aachen. The West German industry has been described as

---

■ *Thomas M. Jorde is Professor of Law, University of California, Berkeley, California. David J. Teece is Mitsubishi Bank Professor, Walter A. Haas School of Business, University of California, Berkeley, California.*

This paper begins by describing the nature of the innovation process. We then explore socially beneficial forms of cooperation that can assist the development and commercialization of new technology, and suggest modifications to current U.S. antitrust law that would remove unnecessary impediments to organizational arrangements that support innovation and stimulate competition in the United States. The modifications we propose would create "safe harbors" for various forms of cooperative activities among competitors in unconcentrated markets, and they would permit cooperation in concentrated markets if commercialization and appropriability were thereby facilitated. These modifications would bring U.S. antitrust laws closer to what is already in place in Europe and Japan and would promote competition more assuredly than would existing law.[2]

We have no illusion that our proposed changes, standing alone, would dramatically improve the performance of U.S. industry, though specific industries might be transformed. However, the changes we propose in antitrust have the attraction that they do not require the expenditure of public funds. In short, we see existing law as a self-imposed impediment to U.S. economic performance.[3]

The Nature of Innovation

Innovation is the search for, and the discovery, development, improvement, adoption and commercialization of new processes, new products, and new organizational structures and procedures.[4] It involves uncertainty, risk taking, probing and reprobing, experimenting, and testing. It is an activity in which "dry holes" and "blind alleys" are the rule, not the exception. Many of these aspects are well-known and have been frequently analyzed in the economics literature.

"groups of clubs" (Collis, 1988, p. 95) because of the nature of the cooperation displayed. The Italian machine tool industry around Modena is similarly organized, as is the Italian textile industry and the Danish furniture industry. A review of examples of cooperative activity abroad is part of the authors' ongoing research.

[2] There is no necessary conflict between promoting cooperation and competition, if the cooperation improves efficiency or advances innovation. As Schumpeter (1942, p. 85) pointed out, when compared to competition among firms with similar products and technologies, the competition that counts "comes from the new commodity, the new technology, the new source of supply.... This kind of competition is as much more effective than the other as bombardment is in comparison with forcing a door, and so much more important that it becomes a matter of comparative indifference whether competition in the ordinary sense functions more or less promptly."

[3] As this *Journal of Economic Perspectives* issue goes to press, the House Judiciary Committee approved the "National Cooperative Production Amendments of 1990" (H.R. 4611), a bill that incorporates many of the changes we suggest in this article and which we have been advocating since 1988. We discuss the provisions of H.R. 4611 and additional antitrust changes that we believe would advance innovation and U.S. competitiveness later in this article.

[4] Dosi (1988) provides an excellent review of the innovation literature.

However, other aspects of innovation, particularly its organizational requirements, have not been sufficiently explored. The traditional serial model that has served as the basis for current antitrust policy is described below. Its inadequacies are then addressed in light of the "simultaneous" nature of the process, which is particularly relevant in certain industries, like microelectronics, experiencing high rates of technological change.[5]

The Traditional Serial Model

Traditional descriptions of the innovation process commonly break it down into a number of stages which proceed sequentially and theoretical treatments of R&D in industrial organization reflect this model. According to this view, the innovation process proceeds in a linear and predictable fashion from research to development, design, production, and then finally to marketing, sales, and service (Grossman and Shapiro, 1986, p. 319; Tirole, 1988, p. 389). In simple models, there is not even any feedback or overlap between and among stages.

If the serial model adequately characterizes innovation today, then it is mainly the innovation which occurs in some scale-intensive industries. The initial development of nylon at Dupont perhaps fits this model. The Manhattan Project during World War II is also illustrative. The serial model does not address the many small but cumulatively important incremental innovations that are at the heart of technological change in many industries, especially well-established industries like semiconductors, computers, and automobiles. The serial model of innovation is an analytic convenience which no longer adequately characterizes the innovation process, except in special circumstances.

The serial model has enabled economists to model innovation as a vertical process. Inasmuch as antitrust policy toward vertical restraints is very permissive, many economists and legal scholars do not understand how U.S. antitrust laws could stand in the way of the various kinds of standard and non-standard contracting often needed to support the commercialization of innovation. But as we shall see, matters are not so simple.

The Simultaneous Model

The simultaneous model of innovation recognizes the existence of tight linkages and feedback mechanisms which must operate quickly and efficiently, including links between firms, within firms, and sometimes between firms and other organizations like universities. From this perspective, innovation does not necessarily begin with research; nor is the process serial. But it does require rapid feedback, mid-course corrections to designs, and redesign.[6] This concep-

---

[5]This argument is presented at greater length in D. Teece (1989a).

[6]This process has also been termed "cyclic" (Gomory, 1987, p. 72). The popular press has even begun to recognize and discuss the simultaneous nature of innovation and effective commercialization. See "A Smarter Way to Manufacture," *Business Week*, April 30, 1990, 110–117 (discussing "concurrent engineering").

tualization recognizes aspects of the serial model—such as the flow of activity, in certain cases through design to development, production and marketing—but also recognizes the constant feedback between and among activities, and the involvement of a wide variety of economic actors and organizations that need not have a simple upstream-downstream relationship to each other.[7] It suggests that R&D personnel must be closely connected to the manufacturing and to marketing personnel and to external sources of supply of new components and complementary technologies, so that supplier, manufacturer and customer reactions can be fed back into the design process rapidly. In this way new technology, whether internal or external, becomes embedded into designs which meet customer needs quickly and efficiently.

The simultaneous model visualizes innovation as an incremental and cumulative activity that involves building on what went before, whether it is inside the organization or outside the organization, and whether the knowledge is proprietary or in the public domain. The simultaneous model also stresses the importance of the speed of the design cycle, and flexibility. IBM followed this model in developing its first PC, employing alliances with Microsoft and others to launch a successful personal computer system. Sun Microsystems and NeXT Computer launched themselves in this way and have remained in this mode for subsequent new product development. Microprocessor development at Intel often follows this logic too.

When innovation has this character, the company which is quickest in product design and development will appear to be the pioneer, even if its own contribution to science and technology is minimal, because it can be first to "design in" science and technology already in the public domain. Both small and large organizations operate by this model, reaching out upstream and downstream, horizontally and laterally to develop and assemble leading edge systems.

In short, much innovation today is likely to require lateral and horizontal linkages as well as vertical ones. As we discuss below, and particularly for small firms, innovation may require accessing complementary assets which lie outside the organization. If innovating firms do not have the necessary capabilities in-house, they may need to engage in various forms of restrictive contracts with providers of inputs and complementary assets. The possibility that antitrust laws could be invoked, particularly by excluded competitors, thus arises. Lying in the weeds to create mischief for unsuspecting firms engaged in socially desirable but poorly understood business practices are plaintiffs' attorneys and their expert economists entreating the courts to view reality through the lens of monopoly theory and modern variants such as raising rivals. These theories

---

[7]Moreover, the linkage from science to innovation is not solely or even preponderantly at the beginning of typical innovations, but rather extends all through the process. "Science can be visualized as lying alongside development processes, to be used when needed" (Kline and Rosenberg, 1986). Design is often at the center of the innovation process. Research is often spawned by the problems associated with trying to get the design right. Indeed, important technological breakthroughs can often proceed even when the underlying science is not understood.

have been honed in the context of a hypothetical world of unchanging technology. If new technology does arrive it often falls like manna from heaven; behavior which is anticompetitive in the static context may be procompetitive in a dynamic one. Because the study of innovation is largely outside the mainstream of economic research and antitrust jurisprudence, the possibility of expensive and distracting litigation followed by judicial error is significant.

Paradoxically, the giant integrated enterprises are not most heavily at risk. Instead, most at risk are mid-sized enterprises that have developed and commercialized important innovations, because such firms are likely to have some market power (under orthodox definitions) and have the need to engage in complex forms of interfirm cooperation. Because of these risks, managers may choose to forego socially desirable arrangements and investments, and innovation and the competition it engenders will be attenuated.

Organizational Requirements of Innovation

Whether innovation is serial or simultaneous, it requires the coordination of various activities. The serial model suggests a rather simple organizational problem; the simultaneous model a more complex one, often employing various forms of non-standard contracting. To the extent that economists employ just the serial model, they greatly oversimplify the organizational challenges which innovation provides and underestimate potential antitrust problems. Also, they probably exaggerate the importance of research and downplay the importance of other factors. As discussed below, except in special cases, a firm's R&D capability is for naught if it cannot organize the rest of the innovation process efficiently and effectively, particularly if that innovation is taking place in an already-established industry.

For innovations to be commercialized, the economic system must somehow assemble all the relevant complementary assets and create an interactive and dynamically efficient system of learning and information exchange. The necessary complementary assets can conceivably be assembled by administrative processes, or by market processes, as when the innovator simply licenses the technology to firms that already own the relevant assets, or are willing to create them. These organizational choices have received scant attention in the context of innovation. Indeed, the serial model relies on an implicit belief that arms-length contracts between unaffiliated firms in the vertical chain from research to customer will suffice to commercialize technology. In particular, there has been little consideration of how complex contractual arrangements among firms can assist commercialization—that is, translating R&D capability into profitable new products and processes. The one partial exception is a tiny literature on joint R&D activity (Grossman and Shapiro, 1986; Ordover and Willig, 1985); but this literature addresses the organization of R&D and not the organization of innovation.[8]

[8] For a more complete statement of our own views on this, see Teece (1977, 1989b).

If innovation takes place in a regime of tight appropriability—that is, if the technological leader can secure legal protection, perhaps by obtaining an ironclad patent (Teece, 1986)—and if technology can be transferred at zero cost as is commonly assumed in theoretical models, the organizational challenge that is created by innovation is relatively simple. In these instances, the market for intellectual property is likely to support transactions enabling the developer of the technology to simply sell its intellectual property for cash, or at least license it to downstream firms who can then engage in whatever value-added activities are necessary to extract value from the technology. With a well-functioning market for know-how, markets can provide the structure for the requisite organization to be accomplished.

But in reality, the market for know-how is riddled with imperfections (Arrow, 1962). Simple unilateral contracts, where technology is sold for cash, are unlikely to be efficient (Teece, 1980, 1982). Complex bilateral and multilateral contracts, internal organization, or various hybrid structures are often required to shore up obvious market failures (Williamson, 1985; Teece, 1986). This section will examine various market failures and the institutional arrangements which can ameliorate them.

Technology Transfer Efficiency

The transfer of technology among the various activities that constitute innovation is not costless. This is especially true if the know-how to be transferred cannot be easily bundled and shipped out in one lot—which is clearly the case when the development activity must proceed simultaneously and when the knowledge has a high tacit component.[9] In these instances, the required transfer of technology cannot be separated from the transfer of personnel, which is typically difficult if the contractual relationship is arms-length and non-exclusive.

Besides the problems of getting technology-driven concepts to market, there is the converse problem of getting user-driven innovations to developers. In some industries, users other than the manufacturers conceive of and design innovative prototypes. The manufacturers' role in the innovation process is somehow to become aware of the user innovation and its value, and then to manufacture a commercial version of the device for sale to other users. User-dominated innovation accounts for more than two-thirds of first-to-market innovations in scientific instruments and in process machinery used in semiconductor and electronic subassembly manufacture (von Hippel, 1988). Clearly, user innovation requires two kinds of technology transfer: first from user to manufacturer, and then from the manufacturer to the developer-user and other users.

Mirroring the role that users play in stimulating innovation upstream is the role that suppliers play in stimulating downstream innovation. For example, a good deal of the innovation in the automobile industry, including fuel injection,

---

[9] For a review of the characteristics of know-how, see Winter (1987) and Teece (1989b).

alternators and power steering, has its origins in upstream component suppliers. Bendix and Bosch developed fuel injection and Motorola the alternator. The challenge to the manufacturer then becomes how to "design in" the new components and how to avoid sole source dependency. As discussed below, deep and enduring relationships need to be established between component developer-manufacturers and suppliers to ensure adoption and diffusion of the technology.[10] These relationships, while functionally vertical, could well turn out to be viewed as horizontal by a court. Unless the courts have an adequate model of innovation and competition presented to them, beneficial contractual arrangements with attendant restraints could well be viewed negatively.

Scale, Scope, and Duplication Issues

Successful new product and process development innovation often requires horizontal and lateral as well as vertical cooperation. It is well understood that horizontal linkages can help overcome scale barriers in research; they can also assist in defining technical standards. But it is common to assert that if firms need to engage in joint research to achieve these economies, the maintenance of competition requires that firms participating in joint research work go their own way with respect to related activities such as manufacturing. However, a requirement that firms participating in a joint research arrangement commercialize the technology independently can impose an unnecessary technology transfer burden. As discussed above, the imposition of a market interface between "research" and "commercialization" activities will most assuredly create a technology transfer challenge, a loss of effectiveness and timeliness, and higher costs.

Collaborative research also reduces what William Norris, CEO of Control Data Corporation, refers to as "shameful and needless duplication of effort" (David, 1985). Independent research activities often proceed down identical or near-identical technological paths. This is sometimes wasteful and can be minimized if research plans are coordinated. The danger of horizontal cooperation, on the other hand, is that it may reduce diversity. This concern is legitimate and is commonly stressed by economists.[11] Unquestionably, a system

---

[10] A related set of vertical relationships involving innovation has been remarked upon by Rosenberg (1972, pp. 98–102) in his treatise on technology and American economic growth. The machine tool industry in the 19th century played a unique role both in the initial solution of technical problems in user industries, such as textiles, and as the disseminator of these techniques to other industries, such as railroad locomotive manufacture. Rosenberg's description suggests that the users played a role in the development of new equipment. He notes that before 1820 in the United States, one could not identify a distinct set of firms that were specialists in the design and manufacture of machinery. Machines were either produced by users or by firms engaged in the production of metal or wooden products. Machinery-producing firms were thus first observed as adjuncts to textile factories. However, once established, these firms played an important role as the transmission center in the diffusion of new technology.

[11] Nalebuff and Stiglitz (1983) argue that the gains from competition may more than offset the losses from duplication. Also, Sah and Stiglitz (1989) show that in a model with ex post Bertrand competition where there is knowledge of which research projects others are undertaking, the number and range of research projects undertaken will be a constrained Pareto optimum.

of innovation that converges on just one view of the technological possibilities is likely to close off productive avenues of inquiry.

However, a private enterprise economy without horizontal coordination and communication offers no guarantee that the desired level of diversity is achieved at the lowest cost. In addition, cooperation need not be the enemy of diversity. If firms can coordinate their research programs to some degree, duplication can be minimized without the industry converging on a single technological approach. Indeed, Bell Labs has been noted for the very considerable internal diversity it has been able to achieve, at least in the pre-divestiture period.

Rent Dissipation Issues

Innovation has well-known free rider and public good characteristics. Know-how leakage and other spillovers impair incentives to innovate by redistributing benefits to others, particularly competitors and users. To maintain adequate incentives to invest in innovative activity, without providing government subsidies, free riding must be curtailed. This is how economists justify patents, copyrights, trade secrets, and other aspects of intellectual property law.

The organizational form in which innovation takes place, interacting with the protection provided by intellectual property law (Teece, 1986), will affect the degree of rent dissipation which the innovator experiences. If the innovation has value and intellectual property protection is effective, an innovator specializing just in early stage activity is in a good position to capture a portion of the returns from innovation.

But surveys show that intellectual property law has a limited ability to provide protection from imitation,[12] even though there have been recent efforts by the courts to tighten enforcement. For a sample of 48 patented product innovations in the chemical, drug, electronics and machinery industry, one group of researchers found that within four years of their introduction, 60 percent of the patented successful innovations in the sample were imitated (Mansfield et al, 1982). Not surprisingly, the social returns to innovation are greater than the private returns. Underinvestment in innovative activities is to be expected.

A "research joint venture" may not do enough to overcome appropriability problems, unless many potential competitors are in the joint venture. Thus, a

---

[12]See Levin, Klevorick, Nelson, and Winter (1987). These researchers surveyed R&D managers in various industries. The survey shows that, on a seven-point scale (1 = not at all effective, 7 = very effective) for 18 industry categories with 10 or more respondents, managers in only chemicals (specifically drugs, plastic materials, inorganic chemicals, and organic chemicals) and petroleum refining rated process patents effectiveness higher than 4 on the scale, and only these same chemical industries and steel mills rated product patents higher than 5. These findings make very clear that managers have little confidence that patents suffice as mechanisms to protect intellectual property from free riders. The results also show that other methods of appropriation such as first mover advantages (lead time and learning curve advantages), secrecy, and investment in sales or service support were more effective.

single firm or even a consortium with good intellectual property protection will often need to bolster its market position and its stream of rents by other strategies and mechanisms. These mechanisms include building, acquiring, or renting (on an exclusive basis) complementary assets and exploiting first-mover advantages. We use the term *complementary assets* to refer to those assets and capabilities that need to be employed to package new technology so that it is valuable to the end user.[13] Broad categories of complementary assets include complementary technologies, manufacturing, marketing, distribution, sales, and service.

It is essential to distinguish further between generic and specific complementary assets. Generic assets include general purpose facilities and equipment and nonspecific skills; they tend to be disembodied and codified and hence easy to transfer. Specific assets, on the other hand, include highly differentiated system and firm-specific assets and skills. Specific assets and capabilities are typically embedded in the organization; or even if not embedded in the organization (like a specialized machine) are of reduced value in a different organizational context. In a sense, specific assets represent the firm's particular assemblage of physical assets and prior learning. Accordingly, they are difficult for competitors to replicate.

Thus, when imitation of aspects of a firm's technology is easy, it is essential for firms to be world-class—or to be linked to partners who are world-class—in the less imitable complementary activities. Accordingly, the best defense against product imitators may well be the development of a less easily imitable superior manufacturing process to make the product, or it may be the firm's superior service capability. In short, because a firm's comparative advantage in research does not necessarily coincide with an advantage in the relevant complementary assets, the expert performance of the innovator's contractual partners in certain key activities complementary to the easily imitable activities is often essential if the innovator is to capture a portion of the profits that the innovation generates. The antitrust laws must be shaped so that they do not impair such beneficial linkages.

In this regard, many British and American firms responsible for important product innovations have captured very little value from innovations for which they have been responsible because of their weaknesses in manufacturing. Often competitors can quickly reverse engineer new products. Once the new product design is apparent to competitors, success in the marketplace is determined by manufacturing costs and quality. In these circumstances, firms that are excellent at manufacturing—and this excellence is often harder to replicate than a new product is to reverse engineer—can garner practically all of the profits associated with the new product designs. Hence it is critical that

---

[13]There has been almost no treatment in the economic literature of the concept of complementary assets. It does not map easily into the familiar concept of indivisibilities, which is perhaps the closest analogue. For a more complete treatment, see Teece (1986).

innovating firms protect themselves from such outcomes by developing or somehow uniquely accessing the requisite complementary assets. The next section explains why cooperation may be necessary for firms to perform this function.

Governance Alternatives

The previous section has argued that innovation often requires firms to enter complex contracts and relationships with other firms to bring technology to the market, and to hold imitators at bay. This section considers in more detail the range of organizational alternatives available to the innovator to generate, coordinate and control such complementary assets.

Consider first the price mechanism. Theoretical treatments generally assume that the requisite coordination and control can be achieved by the invisible hand. Efficient levels of investment in complementary assets are brought forward at the right time and place by price signals. Entrepreneurship is automatic and costless. This is the view implicit in textbook presentations; in turn, the textbook view seems implicit in U.S. antitrust law.

However, many economists seem to have what Tjalling Koopmans calls an "overextended belief" regarding the efficiency of competitive markets as a means of allocating resources in a world characterized by ubiquitous uncertainty. Market failures are likely to arise because of the ignorance which firms have with respect to their competitors' future actions, preferences, and states of technological information (Koopmans, 1957, part II). In reality, nothing guarantees that investment programs are made known to all concerned at the time of their inception. This uncertainty is especially high for the development and commercialization of new technology. Accordingly, innovating firms need to achieve greater coordination than the price system alone appears to be able to bring about.

A second mechanism for effectuating coordination is the administrative processes within the firm. A company's internal organization can serve to shore up some market imperfections and provide some of the necessary coordination. As Alfred Chandler (1977) has explained, the modern multidivisional business enterprise "took over from the market the coordination and integration of the flow of goods and services from the production of raw materials through the several processes of production to the sale to the ultimate consumer ... administrative coordination replaced market coordination in an increasingly large portion of the economy." Oliver Williamson (1985) has developed an elegant and powerful framework to explain the relative efficiencies of markets and administrative processes. However, one property of large integrated structures is that they have the potential to become excessively hierarchical and less responsive to market needs (Teece, 1989c). Accordingly, at least for some aspects of innovative activity, smaller organizations are often superior.

In between pure market and full administrative solutions are many intermediate and hybrid possibilities, including interfirm agreements. Interfirm agreements can be classified as unilateral (where *A* sells *X* to *B*) or bilateral (whereby *A* agrees to buy *Y* from *B* as a condition for making the sale of *X*, and both parties understand that the transaction will be continued only if reciprocity is observed). Such arrangements can also be multilateral.

An especially interesting interfirm agreement is the strategic alliance, which can be defined as a bilateral or multilateral relationship characterized by the commitment of two or more partner firms to a common goal. A strategic alliance might include (1) technology swaps, (2) joint R&D or co-development, and/or (3) the sharing of complementary assets, such as where one party does manufacturing and the other distribution for a co-developed product. If the common goal was simply price-fixing or market-sharing, such an agreement might constitute a cartel, especially if the agreement included substantially all members of an industry.

By definition, a strategic alliance can never have one side receiving cash alone; it is not a unilateral exchange transaction. Nor do strategic alliances include mergers, because alliances by definition cannot involve acquisition of another firm's assets or controlling interest in another firm's stock. Alliances need not involve equity swaps or equity investments, though they often do. Strategic alliances without equity typically consist of contracts between or among partner firms that are nonaffiliated. Equity alliances can take many forms, including minority equity holdings, consortia, and joint ventures. Such interfirm agreements are usually temporary, and are assembled and disassembled as circumstances warrant. Typically, only a limited range of the firm's activities are enveloped in such agreements, and many competitors are excluded.

Strategic alliances, including consortia and joint ventures, are often an effective and efficient way to organize for innovation, particularly when an industry is fragmented. Interfirm cooperation preserves market selection and responsiveness; in a sense, it is the pure private enterprise solution. The case for planning and industrial policy recedes if a degree of operational and strategic coordination can be attained through private agreements. The benefits associated with less hierarchical structures can be obtained without incurring the disadvantages of insufficient scale and scope.

Antitrust Treatment of Interfirm Agreements

Current U.S. antitrust law needlessly inhibits interfirm agreements designed to develop and commercialize new technology. The problem is that the legal standards for interfirm agreements are ambiguous. While "rule of reason" analysis will generally be applied to contractual arrangements designed to advance innovation, the elements of rule of reason analysis are quite muddled.

In addition, although current law seems to recognize a "safe harbor" for mergers and acquisitions between firms that will have less than 20 percent market share, it does not recognize a similar safe harbor for horizontal contractual arrangements among firms.

The Clayton Act also permits private parties to sue for treble damages for alleged antitrust injuries, and allows state attorney generals to recover treble damages on behalf of persons residing in the state. Successful plaintiffs can also recover attorneys' fees. These remedies are available only in the United States. They provide a powerful incentive for plaintiffs to litigate, and given the current state of the law, a powerful disincentive for businesses to form cooperative innovation arrangements and strategic alliances. While measuring the missed opportunities for cooperative innovation caused by the threat of treble damage litigation is difficult, we believe the loss is substantial. Moreover, these disincentives work to the particular detriment of small and medium-sized innovative firms in industries where the innovative process is simultaneous.

Congress has recognized that these provisions may inhibit technological innovation, and the National Cooperative Research Act (NCRA) of 1984 took two significant steps to remove legal disincentives to cooperative research. First, the NCRA provides that "joint research and development ventures" must not be held illegal per se, and that such ventures instead should be "judged on the basis of [their] reasonableness, taking into account all relevant factors affecting competition, including, but not limited to, effects on competition in properly defined, relevant research and development markets." Second, the NCRA establishes a registration procedure for joint research and development ventures, limiting antitrust recoveries against registered ventures to single damages, interest, and costs, including attorney's fees. Thus, Congress eliminated the threat of treble damages for litigation challenging cooperative R&D arrangements, provided that the parties to the arrangement first register their venture. But R&D is only a small piece of the innovation puzzle.

In our view, the NCRA is not sufficiently permissive. The substantive protections provided by the NCRA—guaranteed rule of reason treatment and reduction of damages—extend only to research, and downstream commercial activity "reasonably required" for research and narrowly confined to marketing intellectual property developed through a joint R&D program. Treatment of other agreements designed to facilitate innovation is thus left uncertain, to be determined only by interpretation of the "reasonably required" standard. The NCRA unwisely precludes joint manufacturing and production of innovative products and processes, which is often necessary to provide the cooperating ventures with significant feedback information to aid in further innovation and product development, and to make the joint activity profitable. The NCRA implicitly accepts the serial and not the simultaneous model of innovation.

In addition, the NCRA gives little guidance concerning the substantive content of its rule of reason approach. While the Act did require that markets be defined in the context of research and not the products that might result from it, the NCRA fails to specify factors to be considered within rule of reason analysis. It simply requires consideration of "all relevant factors affecting competition," paying no special attention to the special characteristics of the innovation process in a quickly changing industry.

Finally, while the NCRA's elimination of treble damages for registered ventures is an important step forward, cooperating firms are still not protected from antitrust litigation. Even after the NCRA, antitrust law still permits private plaintiffs to engage in treble damage litigation against cooperative arrangements facilitating commercialization. Moreover, single damages are still available even against those registered under NCRA. The cost of defending antitrust suits is not materially reduced by the exceedingly narrow circumstances in which the Act permits an award of attorneys' fees to prevailing defendants. Moreover, the threat of litigation, with attendant managerial distraction, can be extremely damaging to the competitive performance of a fast-paced industry.

Businesses seem to have recognized the limited nature of the steps taken by the NCRA. Not surprisingly, only 111 separate cooperative ventures registered under the NCRA between 1984 and June 1988. Our review of these filings indicates that they are very modest endeavors that are aimed at solving industry problems and are not of great competitive moment. We believe that if an approval procedure existed under which procompetitive arrangements could obtain exemptions from further antitrust exposure to private damage actions, then many more competitively beneficial ventures would utilize the NCRA.

In contrast to this picture of U.S. antitrust law, the antitrust and business environment in Japan and Europe is more hospitable to strategic alliances and cooperative arrangements for innovation. The basic Japanese attitude is that joint R&D activities are procompetitive and thus should not be touched by the Antimonopoly Act. Significantly, the literal Japanese translation of "R&D" —*kenkyu kaihatsu*—implicitly includes commercialization; there is no semantic distinction between the concepts of R&D and commercialization.

In Japan, the Fair Trade Commission is responsible for executing and enforcing the Antimonopoly Act of 1947, which (like the Sherman Act) broadly prohibits unreasonable restraints of trade. While the Act provides no specific legislative exemption for joint innovation arrangements, Japan's FTC has been able to exempt cooperative innovation efforts from the scope of the law by virtue of its power as the primary enforcer of the Act.[14] FTC policy also states

---

[14] The basic administrative policy outlining the standards by which such joint innovation efforts are to be scrutinized is contained in a report of Japan's Fair Trade Commission (1984, 37-39). The report states that the evaluation of the anticompetitive effect of joint R&D at the product market stage will depend significantly "on the competition and market shares among the participants and the market structure of the industry to which the participants belong.... In cases where the market shares of the participants are small ... the effects will be small." Although "small" is not defined in the report, Japan's Merger Guidelines state that the FTC is not likely to closely examine cases in which the combined market share of the merging parties is less than 25 percent. See H. Iyori and A. Yesugi (1983, pp. 86–88). Our discussions with MITI and FTC officials confirm that the horizontal merger safe harbors would be equally applicable to cooperative contractual arrangements.

that if anticompetitive effects are alleged, the procompetitiveness benefits of innovation must be balanced, too. Balancing will take place not only within a particular market but also across markets (FTC, 1984), because "there is a possibility of the emergence of competition at the intersection of industrial sectors as a result of joint R&D between firms in different sectors."

In considering anticompetitive effects of cooperative innovation arrangements, Japan's FTC analyzes market shares and market structure. The FTC specifically recognizes the needs of innovators and articulates procompetitive justifications that include: (1) the difficulty of single-firm innovation; (2) the faster innovation created by cooperation and specialization between joint participants; (3) the pursuit of innovation in new fields by utilizing shared technology and know-how; and (4) enhancement of the technological level of each participant through the interchange of technology.

When MITI seeks to promote cooperative R&D activities (for example, as authorized by the Act for Facilitation of Research in Key Technology, or the Research Association for Mining and Manufacturing Technology Act), the FTC is consulted in advance. Once the FTC clears an activity, it is extraordinarily unlikely to pursue antitrust remedies at a future time. Significantly, treble damages are not available to private parties seeking to enforce Japanese antitrust laws, and private suits for single damages are very rare and usually unsuccessful. Thus, Japanese firms cooperating on innovation and commercialization of innovation have little to fear from Japanese antitrust laws.

Under this type of antitrust environment, it is not surprising that collaboration for innovation is frequent. Although regular statistics are not kept in Japan, because there is no reporting requirement for collaborative research and commercialization activities, a Fair Trade Commission report issued in 1984 contains statistics suggestive of the quantity and variety of joint innovation activities in Japan. The survey results indicate that joint R&D projects among corporations in the same industrial sector, which might be classified as horizontal collaboration, represent 19.1 percent of total projects.[15]

The antitrust environment shaping cooperation in the European Community is also markedly different from the United States. In 1968, the European Commission issued a "Notice of Cooperation between Enterprises" which indicates that horizontal collaboration for purposes of R&D is normally outside the scope of antitrust concerns as defined in Articles 85 and 86 of the EEC Treaty. The Commission has consistently taken a favorable position on R&D

---

[15]Questionnaires were sent to 484 manufacturing corporations in the fields of electronics, telecommunications, automobiles, chemicals, ceramics, steel and nonferrous metals, whose stocks were listed in Tokyo and Osaka Stock Exchanges. Data was provided by 242 corporations, representing 1.9 percent of the total manufacturing industry that engage in R&D activities in terms of the number of corporations and 16.7 percent in terms of sales. As to the nature of the joint R&D projects, 54.3 percent of the total cases were developmental research. Basic and applied research were 13.6 and 32.1 percent respectively. In the case of large corporations with capital of more than 10 billion yen, the total basic and application research amounted to 52.1 percent.

agreements unless the large entities involved imply serious anticompetitive consequences.

In 1984, the European Commission adopted Regulation No. 418/85 (hereafter Reg. 418) expanding the favorable antitrust treatment of R&D. For firms whose total market share does not exceed 20 percent, it provides blanket exceptions for horizontal R&D arrangements, including commercialization—which the Commission views as "the natural consequence of joint R&D"—up to the point of distribution and sales.[16] In addition, under Article 85(3), the Commission is authorized to grant exemptions for cooperative efforts that do not fall within the automatic safe harbor. Such exemptions may be granted when a horizontal agreement contributes to economic or technological progress in the research, production, or distribution of goods, and when procompetitive features outweigh anticompetitive aspects.

Proposed Modifications to U.S. Antitrust Law

To insure that antitrust law is responsive to the needs of innovating firms and does not inhibit U.S. firms from competing effectively in global markets experiencing rapid technological change, we believe the following changes are in order:

First, the rule of reason should be clarified to take specific account of the appropriability regime, the pace of technological change, the diversity of sources of new technology, the need to access complementary assets and technologies, and the need to have cheek-by-jowl cooperation to manage the innovation process simultaneously rather than serially.

Second, a safe harbor defined according to market power should be expressly adopted that would shield from antitrust liability interfirm agreements that involve less than 20 to 25 percent of the relevant market.

Third, market definition should be tailored to the context of innovation and should focus primarily on the market for know-how; specific product markets become relevant only when commercialization is included within the scope of the cooperative agreement. Even then, the extent of appropriability should be factored in when analyzing product market issues. The geographic market should be presumed to be worldwide, with the burden upon the challenger to demonstrate otherwise.

[16]Regulation No. 418/85 of 19 December 1984 on the application of Art. 85(3) of the Treaty to categories of research and development agreements, *O. J. Eur. Comm.* (No. L 53) 5 (1985), entered into force March 1, 1985, and applicable until December 31, 1997. The statutory framework of Reg. 418 is complex. It applies to three categories of agreements involving R&D: (1) joint research and development of products or processes and joint exploitation of the results of the R&D; (2) joint exploitation of the results of R&D product or processes pursuant to a prior agreements between the same parties; and (3) joint research and development of products without joint exploitation should the agreement fall within the purview of Art. 85(1). Under Reg. 418, joint exploitation is interpreted to mean joint manufacturing and licensing to third parties. Joint distribution and sales, however, are not covered and required individual exemptions pursuant to Art. 85(3).

Fourth, antitrust law should not bias the selection of interfirm organizational forms; at a minimum, integration by contract or alliance should be treated no less favorably than full mergers.

Fifth, the NCRA should be amended to include joint commercialization efforts to exploit innovation.

Sixth, an administrative procedure should be created, involving both the Justice and Commerce Departments, to allow evaluation and possible certification of cooperative arrangements among firms with higher market shares, when dynamic efficiency gains are likely and rivalry robust. We favor providing the opportunity for firms to either simply register and receive relief from treble damages as with the NCRA, or to apply for a certificate of exemption from the Justice and Commerce Departments that would provide even more protection. However, the quid pro quo would be greater disclosure and scrutiny of business plans. The firms themselves would choose which path to take.

Seventh, private antitrust suits challenging cooperative innovation arrangements should be limited to equitable relief, and attorneys' fees should be awarded to the prevailing party.

The first four of these proposals could be accomplished by courts interpreting the rule of reason and the National Cooperative Research Act. We hope courts will not hesitate to employ the tools of evolutionary, common law interpretation and development to achieve these changes. However, to achieve the complete package of substantive and procedural changes most quickly, and thus assure certainty and predictability, legislation is the best overall solution. At a U.C. Berkeley Conference on "Antitrust, Innovation and Competitiveness" in October 1988, we distributed a draft of legislation that combined a "registration" and "certification" approach for cooperative commercialization ventures. Shortly thereafter, Congressmen Edwards (H.R. 1025) and Congressman Fish (H.R. 2264) advanced a "registration" approach to cooperative commercialization efforts and Congressmen Boucher and Campbell (H.R. 1024) proposed a "certification" approach. After three hearings on these bills, Chairman Jack Brooks of the House Judiciary Committee introduced and the Judiciary Committee passed the National Cooperative Production Amendments of 1990 (H.R. 4611). H.R. 4611 would amend the National Cooperative Research Act to extend its registration approach to joint production ventures.[17] At the same time, Attorney General Richard Thornburgh and Commerce Secretary Robert

---

[17] Professor Jorde testified on July 26, 1989, in favor of both a registration and certification approach. See "Legislative Proposals to Modify the U.S. Antitrust Laws to Facilitate Cooperative Arrangements to Commercialize Innovation" (with David Teece), in *Hearings Before the Subcommittee on Economics and Commercial Law*, Committee on the Judiciary, U.S. House of Representatives (July 26, 1989). Legislation advancing a registration approach for production joint ventures has also been introduced in the Senate by Senators Patrick Leahy (D-VT) and Strom Thurmond (R-SC) (S.1006). Three aspects of H.R. 4611 bear noting. First, relevant market definition under rule of reason analysis would specifically consider the worldwide capacity of suppliers. Second, foreign participation in a production joint venture would be limited to 30 percent of the voting securities or equity interests, and all production facilities would have to be located in the United States or its

Mosbacher announced the Bush Administration's support of a registration approach for production joint ventures.[18]

As mentioned above, we support *both* a registration and certification approach. We do not see them as alternatives. Rather, we believe they should be combined into a single, two-track approach. Firms could choose the level and then form of protection most appropriate for their joint activity. Greater disclosure could buy greater protection.

The case for these changes rests on three fundamental pillars. The first is that the innovation process is terribly important to economic growth and development, because it yields social returns in excess of private returns, and because innovation is a powerful spur to competition. Hence, if antitrust policy is going to err, it ought to do so by facilitating innovation, rather than inhibiting it. This principle is well-understood in Europe and Japan.

Second, economic theory tells us that if certain organizational arrangements are exposed to governmentally-imposed costs while others are not, firms will substitute away from the burdened forms (in this context, interfirm agreements) and in favor of the unburdened forms (in this context, hierarchy), even when the former are potentially economically superior. According to Aoki (1989), the slowdown in total factor productivity in the United States can be attributed in large part to a mismatch between organizational form and the requirements of new technology; in particular, he is concerned that hierarchical solutions are overused, at least in the United States. As we have explained at some length above, we are concerned that present laws do not give full recognition to the interorganizational requirements of the innovation process; failure to do so is damaging when innovation must proceed according to the simultaneous model.

Third, cartelization of industries experiencing rapid technological change, and which are open to international trade and investment, is very difficult. So long as these industries remain open and innovative, antitrust policy should err on the side of permitting rather than restricting interfirm contracts.

Beneficial cooperation will eventually expand if antitrust laws are revised along the lines we propose. The response may not be immediate, particularly with respect to consortia, because the experience base in U.S. industry in this area is thin, because of our antitrust history, and because U.S. firms, at least in the postwar period, have been large relative to their foreign competitors. Accordingly, the need to cooperate has not been as powerful in the past as it is now. However, once organizational learning accumulates, we expect consortia to begin to flourish even in the absence of government funding. We also expect

---

territories. Third, apparently production joint ventures would not be limited to efforts designed to commercialize joint R&D, nor need they be related to innovation.
[18]See Department of Justice release, "Thornburgh Mosbacher Send Revision Legislation to Congress" (May 7, 1990) (supporting and detailing "legislation designed to facilitate joint production ventures"), reported at *Antitrust and Trade Regulation Report*, p. 701 (Vol. 58, No. 1465) (May 10, 1990).

the reinforcement of bilateral alliances already common in U.S. industry. We briefly discuss the kinds of activities that might take place.

Cooperative Manufacturing and Commercialization

In a number of circumstances, cooperative activity beyond early stages will benefit innovating firms. As discussed, sometimes this is true because of scale, risk, and appropriability considerations. Sometimes it is true because prohibition of cooperative commercialization imposes a significant technology transfer problem, for instance from the research joint venture (if there is one) back to the funding companies. In most cases, firms will not wish to cooperate all the way from research through to commercialization. But in some instances they will, or they will wish to cooperate simply on a downstream production venture. When cartelization of the industry is not a threat, we see no reason for antitrust restraints.

The now defunct U.S. Memories, Inc. consortium wanted to invest $500 million to $1 billion to develop and manufacture for its members and for the market advanced dynamic random access memories (DRAMs). With fabrication facilities costing hundreds of millions, acting alone is beyond the financial resources of many companies in this industry who might otherwise wish to have some control over their DRAM supply. This proposed consortium had to contend with a number of difficulties, including threats of third party litigation (Jorde and Teece, 1989b). While antitrust was not the main reason for the failure of this enterprise, the antitrust environment did nothing to help it succeed. A certification procedure would have provided important certainty to this venture, and others like it. A registration procedure would provide less certainty, but still would be a significant advance over current antitrust law.

Similarly, in the area of superconductors, it is likely that the real challenges will come not in developing superconductors, but in their commercialization. Applying superconductors in systems like railroads, computers, and electricity distribution will require great amounts of time, resources, and capital—probably greater than any single business can muster internally. Accordingly, a public policy stance that treats only early stage activity as potentially requiring cooperation is misguided and will thwart both early and later stage activities. Most firms will not have much incentive to engage in early stage, joint development if later stage, stand-alone commercialization appears too expensive to accomplish profitably.

Cooperative Innovation Designed to Achieve Catch-Up

Cooperative activities in Japan and Europe have frequently been motivated by a desire to catch up with the world's technological frontier, which in the postwar years was usually the technology of U.S. firms. However, U.S. firms are increasingly slipping behind the frontier. For instance, U.S. firms are now behind in areas like ceramics and robotics, and in products like VCRs, facsimiles, and HDTV. Just as foreign firms have found cooperative ventures useful for catch-up in the past, U.S. firms could utilize cooperation for this purpose. For example, U.S.-based firms, acting together and with foreign firms, may still have a slender chance of competing in the market for high definition televisions (HDTV) and related products expected to evolve in the 1990s. In the absence of cooperative interfirm agreements, we doubt that development of HDTV systems is possible in the United States. If America's potential "reentrants" to the consumer electronics business combine to attempt reentry, they cannot be sure of avoiding serious antitrust problems involving treble damages, particularly if they are successful.

At minimum, the legislative changes proposed would facilitate unfettered information exchange and strategic coordination with respect to reentry strategies. If such efforts facilitated profitable reentry into high technology businesses when reentering would otherwise not occur, or would occur in a more limited and unprofitable way, we do not see why antitrust concerns ought to interfere.

Cooperation in Response to Foreign Industrial and Technology Policy
In high technology industries, both European and East Asian nations have active industrial and technology policies that significantly impact market outcomes, both in their own countries and abroad. Airbus is a case in point. The dominant U.S. attitude is one of laissez-faire, and many economists are of the view that the United States should send a letter of thanks to foreign governments who subsidize exports to the United States. Such a view is insensitive to the dynamics of technological change, to the importance of cumulative learning, and to reentry costs.

Some U.S. policy makers, however, favor retaliation against foreign countries which have active industrial policies. We support a modification of U.S. antitrust laws which in some circumstances would permit a competitive response by U.S. industry acting collectively. The proposals we advance to encourage greater cooperation among U.S. firms do not require government expenditures nor do they involve the government "picking winners." But they would soften the tensions emerging in the United States between technology, antitrust and trade policies.

Conclusion

The past two decades have wrought significant changes in the business environment. Markets have become globalized, sources of new technology are increasingly pluralistic, and "simultaneous" systems of innovation have substituted for linear, hierarchical ones. Moreover, the ability of foreign firms to utilize technology developed in the United States has increased markedly. Imitation is easier, not harder, in spite of recent court decisions which have strengthened patents.

Accordingly, innovative firms confront significant challenges in capturing value from new technology. Success in research and development does not automatically translate into a financial success, even if the technology developed meets a significant market need. To succeed financially, innovative firms must quickly position themselves advantageously in the appropriate complementary assets and technologies. If they are not already integrated, the best solution often involves bilateral and multilateral cooperative agreements.[19]

U.S. antitrust policy, like so much of our economic policy, has been preoccupied with static rather than intertemporal concerns. Despite important recent developments, it is informed by naive theories of the innovation process, and in particular is insensitive to the organizational needs of innovation. U.S. antitrust scholars still harbor suspicion of cooperative agreements among competitors, and do not appreciate the benefits. This suspicion fuels uncertainty about how the courts would view interfirm arrangements to promote technological progress and competition.

The policy changes we advance are certainly no panacea for the severe problems U.S. high technology industry is currently experiencing. But in bringing American policy closer to Europe and Japan, we will at least purge dogma that no longer deserves a place in U.S. industrial policy. In time, reduced antitrust exposure will help clear the way for beneficial cooperation, thereby reducing incentives for mergers and acquisitions.

The 1990 centennial of the Sherman Act would be a good occasion to set things right. The economics profession, which in the past has had a significant impact on the law of vertical restraints, can provide the intellectual leadership necessary to propel adjustments in the horizontal area, thereby helping to align U.S. policies with the technological and competitive realities of today's global economy.

■ *This paper is based in part on Jorde and Teece (1989a) and Teece (1986). We are extremely grateful for financial support from the Alfred P. Sloan Foundation, the Smith-Richardson Foundation, The Pew Foundation, and the Sasakawa Peace Foundation. We wish to thank Joseph Stiglitz, Carl Shapiro, and Timothy Taylor for valuable substantive and editorial comments. Bill Baxter, Oliver Williamson, and Dick Nelson made helpful comments on earlier drafts and oral presentations. We implicate none of the above in our conclusions.*

---

[19]As Richard Nelson (1990) notes, a wide variety of new kinds of organizational arrangements is emerging to support innovation. He predicts, and we concur, that some will succeed, and some will not. Our concern is that because the requirements of innovation are not well understood in mainstream economics and in contemporary antitrust analysis, there is significant danger that the performance of U.S. firms will be impaired by outdated antitrust law.

References

Aoki, M., "Global Competition, Firm Organization, and Total Factor Productivity: A Comparative Micro Perspective." Paper presented at the International Seminar on Science, Technology, and Economic Growth, OECD, Paris, June 1989.

Arrow, Kenneth J., "Economic Welfare and the Allocation of Resources for Invention." In National Bureau of Economic Research, ed., *The Rate and Direction of Inventive Activity.* Princeton: Princeton University Press, 1962, pp. 609–625.

Chandler, Alfred D. Jr., *The Visible Hand: The Managerial Revolution in American Business.* Cambridge: Harvard University Press, 1977.

Collis, David, "The Machine Tool Industry and Industrial Policy, 1955–1982." In Spence, A. Michael, and Heather A. Hazard, eds., *International Competitiveness.* Cambridge: Ballinger, 1988, pp.

David, D., "R&D Consortia," *High Technology,* October 1985, p. 42.

Dertouzos, Michael L., Richard K. Lester, and Robert M. Solow, *Made in America: Regaining the Productive Edge.* Cambridge: MIT Press, 1989.

Dosi, Giovanni, "Sources, Procedures, and Microeconomic Effects of Innovation," *Journal of Economic Literature,* September 1988, *26,* 1120–1171.

Fair Trade Commission (Japan), *Research and Development Activities in Private Enterprises and Problems They Pose in the Competition Policy* (*Minkan kigyo ni okeru kenkyu kaihatsu katsudo no jittai to kyoso seidaku jo no kaidai*), 1984.

Gomory, R., "Dominant Science Does Not Mean Dominant Product," *Research and Development,* November 1987, p. 72.

Grossman, Gene M., and Carl Shapiro, "Research Joint Ventures: An Antitrust Analysis," *Journal of Law and Economics,* Fall 1986, *2,* pp. 315–337.

von Hippel, Eric, *The Sources of Innovation.* Cambridge: MIT Press, 1988.

Imai, Ken-ichi, and Yasunori Baba, "Systemic Innovation and Cross Border Networks." Paper presented at Seminar on the Contributions of Science and Technology to Economic Growth, OECD, Paris, June 1989.

Iyori, H., and A. Yesugi, *The Antimonopoly Laws of Japan,* New York: Federal Legal Publications, 2nd edition, 1983.

Jorde, Thomas M., and David J. Teece, "Innovation, Cooperation, and Antitrust: Balancing Competition and Cooperation," *High Technology Law Journal,* Spring 1989a, *4,* pp. 1–113.

Jorde, Thomas M., and David J. Teece, "To Keep U.S. in the Chips, Modify the Antitrust Laws," *Los Angeles Times,* July 24, 1989b, Part II, p. 5.

Kline, S. J., and Nathan Rosenberg, "An Overview of Innovation." In Rosenberg, Nathan, and R. Landau, eds., *The Positive Sum Strategy.* Washington, DC: National Academy Press, 1986, pp. 275–305.

Koopmans, Tjalling, *Three Essays in the State of Economic Science.* New York: McGraw Hill, 1957.

Levin, Richard, A. Klevorick, R. Nelson, and S. Winter, "Appropriating the Returns from Industrial Research and Development," *Brookings Papers on Economic Activity,* Winter 1987, *3,* 783–820.

Mansfield, E., A. Romeo, M. Schwartz, D. Teece, S. Wagner and P. Brach, *Technology Transfer, Productivity, and Economic Policy.* New York: W. W. Norton, 1982.

Nalebuff, Barry, and Joseph Stiglitz, "Information, Competition and Markets." *American Economic Review,* May 1983, *72,* 278–284.

Nelson, Richard, "Capitalism as an Enigma of Progress," *Research Policy,* 1990, *19,* 193–214.

Ordover, Janusz, and Robert Willig, "Antitrust for High Technology Industries: Assessing Research Joint Ventures and Mergers," *Journal of Law and Economics,* May 1985, *28,* 311–33.

Rosenberg, Nathan, *Technology and American Economic Growth.* Armonk: M. E. Sharpe, 1972.

Sah, Raaj, and Joseph Stiglitz, "Technological Learning, Social Learning and Technological Change." In Chakravarty, S., ed., *The Balance between Industry and Agriculture in Economic Development.* New York: St. Martin's/International Economic Association, 1989, pp. 285–298.

Schumpeter, J. A., *Capitalism, Socialism and Democracy.* New York: Harper Brothers, 1942.

Teece, David J., "Technology Transfer by Multinational Firms: The Resource Costs of Transferring Technological Know-how," *The Economic Journal,* June 1977, *87,* 242–261.

Teece, David J., "Economies of Scope and the Scope of the Enterprise," *Journal of Economic Behavior and Organization,* 1980, *1,* 223–247.

Teece, David J., "Towards an Economic Theory of the Multiproduct Firm," *Journal of Economic Behavior and Organization*, 1982, *3*, 39–63.

Teece, David J., "Profiting from Technological Innovation," *Research Policy*, December 1986, 285–305.

Teece, David J., "Inter-organizational Requirements of the Innovation Process," *Managerial and Decision Economics*, 1989a, *10*, 35–42.

Teece, David J., "Innovation and the Organization of Industry." Unpublished working paper, Center for Research in Management, University of California at Berkeley, 1989b.

Teece, David J., "Market Entry Strategies for Innovators: Avoiding Pyrrhic Victories," *Strategic Management Journal*, 1991.

Tirole, Jean, *The Theory of Industrial Organization*. Cambridge: MIT Press, 1988.

Williamson, Oliver E., *The Economic Institutions of Capitalism: Firms, Markets, Relational Contracting*. New York: Free Press, 1985.

Winter, Sidney J., "Knowledge and Competence as Strategic Assets." In Teece, David J., ed., *The Competitive Challenge*. Cambridge: Ballinger, 1987.

Part IV
Antitrust Regulation in Great Britain and Japan

[14]

The Journal of

LAW & ECONOMICS

VOLUME I   OCTOBER 1958

BRITISH MONOPOLY POLICY 1944–56

JOHN JEWKES
Oxford University

I. INTRODUCTION

Now that the Restrictive Trade Practices Act of 1956 has come into force, British policy with respect to monopoly enters a new phase. It is opportune, therefore, to attempt to assess the consequences of the earlier Monopolies and Restrictive Practices (Enquiry and Control) Act of 1948, to survey the information about monopoly in British industry brought to light by the reports of the Monopolies and Restrictive Practices Commission set up under the Act of 1948, to examine the changes in policy and procedure embodied in the new Act of 1956 and to speculate, in turn, about the effects this may have upon the operation of industry.

It may be helpful at the outset to sketch in a little of the earlier history. Between the two world wars belief in Britain in the merits of competition had almost entirely disappeared. This was largely attributable to the prolonged period of depression suffered by a number of the basic British industries, notably coal mining, iron and steel, ship building and textiles. In these industries it came to be generally assumed that long period decline could best be met by organized control over output and prices. This doctrine was accepted by the governments of the day, both Conservative and Labour, and in several industries statutory schemes were introduced whereby a majority of the producers could impose output quotas and minimum prices upon whole industries. The official sanction thus conferred upon restrictive practices bred a feeling that monopoly was desirable in itself and led to the growth in other industries of voluntary schemes for controlling markets. Judicial decisions in restraint of trade cases reflected this popular feeling; the idea that "what was good for producers must be good for the community" remained unchallenged. We shall see later that the almost pathological dread of surplus capacity and ruinous competition, implanted in the minds of British business men in the years between the wars, has left its mark and still colours their thinking about a post-war world where such conditions no longer rule.

Unlikely as it may have appeared in 1939, a change in public thinking was in the offing. This can hardly be said to have been due to the enunciation of any new economic truth or the presentation of any old economic truth in a fresh and exceptionally persuasive form. The post-war disposition in Britain to place greater reliance upon competition must rank among those mysterious and unpredictable switches in broad economic thinking, so numerous in history, in which irrationality has played at least as great a part as rationality.

The first straw in the wind was a somewhat vaguely worded paragraph in the White Paper on Employment Policy of 1944.

> There has in recent years been a growing tendency towards combines and towards agreements. . . . Such agreements or combines do not necessarily operate against the public interest; but the power to do so is there.

The suggestion in the White Paper was that a high and stable level of employment would be difficult, if not impossible, to maintain should monopoly in industry be common. The argument was always dubious. It ran as follows: if there is a depression, or a threat of a depression, then the standard methods of expansion might not produce an increase in the demand for labour but might, instead, be absorbed by the monopolists in the form of higher prices for their goods. In these days it hardly seems worth while to discuss this theory. Post-war experiences makes it clear that, provided the forces of inflation are strong enough, full employment will follow even if monopoly exists on an extensive scale. It is, however, easy to understand why the theory proved so acceptable in 1944. For in all the schemes of post-war reconstruction the abolition of unemployment ranked first and any measure which could be held to contribute to that end was hardly likely to be questioned.

The next important event in this brief history was the passing of the Monopolies and Restrictive Practices Act of 1948. A Labour Government was responsible for it. This may, at first sight, appear surprising. The British Socialist Party had not traditionally been opposed to industrial monopoly; it was more disposed to stress the alleged evils of competition. Monopoly, the socialists often argued, was inevitable, either in the form of restrictive agreements or large scale amalgamations, and this constituted a natural stepping stone to the next stage in industrial evolution—the nationalization of industry. Indeed, while the Labour Government was engaged in 1948 in trying to restore competition to one sector of British industry, it was also busily creating statutory monopolies in coalmining, transport, iron and steel, electricity and civil aviation by its various nationalization schemes. It is interesting to go back to the Parliamentary debates in 1948. The two major political parties welcomed the objects of the Monopolies Bill and by now both were readier to accept the idea that competition could make a contribution to enterprise and efficiency, although the Labour Party was able to convince itself that a case still existed for monopolies in nationalized industries while the Conservatives, perhaps believing that enquiries into industrial monopolies would reveal that these were less serious than generally believed, stressed the urgent need for parallel studies of the consequences of restrictive practices among trade unions.

The Act of 1948 had an eight years run. But, with the return to power in 1950 of the Conservatives, criticism of the procedure and indeed of the findings under the Act became more general and the final outcome was the Act of 1956. This move, once again, was the resultant of a mixed set of forces, some of them political, some economic, some exerted by those who felt that changes were being brought about too precipitately. Perhaps the following four factors were the most important.

First, there was a steadily growing conviction in at least some sections of the Conservative Party that only through competition and free enterprise could British industry maintain itself in the post-war world and raise exports to the level at which the perennial balance of payments strains could be removed. Mr. Thorneycroft, then President of the Board of Trade, in moving the Second Reading of the 1956 Bill, put this matter quite clearly:

> The background of any Bill on this subject was a free enterprise society, and the purpose of any such Bill must be to secure that the virtues of free enterprise, initiative, adaptability and risk taking were not throttled by restrictions which industry imposed on itself. Agreements between traders were tempting ways of avoiding competition; they thrived in the thirties when it was powerfully argued that such devices mitigated unemployment and staved off bankruptcy by avoiding cut-throat competition. Today the problem had undoubtedly changed, but many of the principles continued. . . . It was now claimed that they ensured supplies at stable prices whilst the manufacturers competed in quality and service. If people were free to select where competition operated, it would tend to operate where it had the least marked effect.

The second factor was the dissatisfaction of business men themselves with the working of the Act of 1948. This is a matter which will be discussed in more detail later but the gist of their criticism can be set down here. Many of the reports of the Monopolies Commission proved to be highly critical of the conditions and practices revealed. The Commission was an administrative body and, while it could call for any relevant evidence from an industry under examination, and while it normally discussed the case with that industry, the interpretation of the facts as finally set down in the reports of the Commission could at no point be challenged by the industry. Industrialists, therefore, began to plead for something more closely approximating to a judicial procedure, under which the evidence submitted to the judging body could be made subject to cross examination—a procedure which they held would provide a fairer form of hearing.

The third reason was a burst of public indignation, vigorously fostered by some newspapers, at what were considered to be the sinister activities of certain firms and industrial associations in the enforcement of their restrictive agreements. For the most part these related to the methods pursued to enforce resale price maintenance agreements. In particular, the activities of the British Motor Trade Association in obtaining evidence of, and in preventing, price cutting in motor car tyres came under fire. The Monopolies Commission, in its report on "The Supply and Export of Pneumatic Tyres," produced evidence which naturally enough led to an outcry about "star chamber" methods and invoked spontaneous public sympathy for small retailers who, it was considered, were being unfairly hounded about by the larger corporations.[1] This undoubtedly explains the important place which resale price maintenance occupies in the 1956 legislation.

Fourthly, the Government, as a result of one of the reports of the Monopolies Commission itself, was placed in a position in which it could hardly refrain from new legislation. Under the Act of 1948 it had been assumed that, after the lapse of a few years, in the course of which the Monopolies Commission would have produced reports and recommendations upon a number of industries, thereby accumulating experience and establishing precedents, it would be possible to reach conclusions as to whether certain groups of practices should be declared illegal merely because of their presence and without regard to proof of their undesirable consequences in any specific case. The Board of Trade was, therefore, empowered to request of the Commission from time to time reports upon the general effects on the public interest of specified practices. Under this provision the Commission had been instructed in December 1952 to report upon collective discrimination, i.e. practices of exclusive dealing, collective boycotts, aggregated rebates and other discriminating trade practices. The terms of reference for this report were, indeed, inconveniently narrow, for the Commission was instructed to consider the consequences of collective discrimination without passing judgment on common price agreements, the enforcement of which is usually the principal purpose of collective discrimination. Despite this hampering restriction, the majority of the Commission produced in June 1955 a report in which it was recommended that these practices should be declared illegal, although with provision for excep-

---

[1] Monopolies and Restrictive Practices Commission, "Report on the Supply and Export of Pneumatic Tyres," p. 52.

tions on specified grounds. This forthright declaration involving, as it would have done, legislation which, for the first time, would have turned certain forms of monopolising into a criminal offence, confronted the Government with a choice. Either it must accept the recommendations of the report or it must produce some revised scheme of its own. In framing the Act of 1956 it chose the latter course.

A more detailed examination of the provisions of the Act of 1956 and of some of its earlier consequences will be made in a subsequent article. It is sufficient here to note that the Act involved interesting, and it may prove in time highly significant, departures in policy. First, it made a clear distinction between restrictive practices involving agreements between the parties (price and output association, etc.) and monopolies arising from the domination of one or a few large producers. Second, the two forms of economic monopoly were to be handled in different ways. The single producer monopoly cases would, as heretofore, be reported on by a new Monopolies Commission (smaller than the old Commission) to the Board of Trade. As for monopolies through agreement, a Register of Restrictive Practices was to be kept and a Court was to be set up, the Restrictive Practices Court, as a branch of the High Court, which would try cases submitted to it and would be guided by provisions laid down in the Act of 1956. This was a new constitutional development. All restrictive agreements had to be registered and open to public scrutiny. Third, one form of restrictive agreement, resale price maintenance enforced by collective action of firms, was declared illegal although, at the same time, the legal enforcement by individual firms of their own resale price maintenance schemes was to be made simpler and more effective. In brief, in the Act of 1956 there was something for everybody. The Register of Restrictive Agreements might be expected to go some way towards satisfying those who regarded publicity as an important defence against monopoly. The creation of the Restrictive Practices Court in part met the demand of indignant business men that cases should be examined by judicial procedure. The prohibition of collective resale price maintenance paid heed to the popular public outcry against industrial star chambers. The separation and treatment of single producer monopoly might be expected to reassure those who were anxious that the process of monopoly control should not endanger the full exploitation of the economies of large scale operation in industry. And the Government could claim that so wide reaching a measure as the Act of 1956 was ample evidence of their determination to foster competition and private enterprise.

Attention may now be devoted to a fuller examination of the Act of 1948.

II. The Monopolies and Restrictive Practices (Enquiry and Control) Act, 1948

There was nothing in the Act of 1948 to imply that monopolistic control of the market was necessarily contrary to public interest. The underlying assumption was that monopoly might or might not have socially adverse effects and that each case should therefore be decided strictly on its merits. For that purpose a Monopolies Commission was set up to examine cases submitted to it by the Board of Trade. The Board of Trade might request the Commission simply to report on the facts, or to go beyond that and render a judgment as to whether the conditions found to exist were contrary to the public interest and, if so, to make suggestions as to suitable remedies. It was then for the Board of Trade (or other competent government department) to decide what action should be taken. It seems to have been presumed that discussions between the appropriate government department and the industry would often lead to a voluntary decision by the industry to desist from the practices deemed to be undesirable. If sanctions proved necessary these were to take the form, in each case, of a statutory order approved by Parliament. The whole procedure was, and was intended to be, informal and flexible. The Commission held its proceedings in private although, of course, its reports were published. No cross examination of witnesses was permissible. No penalties for past actions were prescribed. In deciding whether the public interest was adversely affected, the Commission was restricted to a consideration of practices currently being pursued.

No guidance of any consequence was given to the Commission as to the meaning of public interest. Indeed, in the Second Reading of the Bill in Parliament, the responsible Minister had frankly confessed his failure to find a satisfactory definition:

The phrase, the public interest, occurs a number of times in the Bill and some have suggested that we should set out a definition. . . . I can sincerely inform the House that we have tried our best to work out such a definition and have failed. This is a matter that can, and should, be safely left to an impartial tribunal.

It is therefore not surprising to find that the clauses in the final Act referring to public interest proved to be useless generalities. The major condition to which the Act applied was that one producer, or several producers acting jointly, should be responsible for at least one-third of the national supply of a commodity or service—a provision so wide that, interpreted literally, it might well have comprehended practically the whole of British industry. But, beyond that, the Commission was left free to interpret the facts in the light of its own conceptions of what was economically and socially desirable.

To anyone familiar with the extensive code of laws and the elaborate administrative machinery operating in the United States or Canada for the control of monopoly, the British Act of 1948, and what followed from it, may appear very much as a small scale, half-hearted and casually informal approach to a problem of great magnitude. This impression could well be intensified by a recital of a few other simple facts. The total annual cost of the operation of the Monopolies Commission has never exceeded about £100,000.

The Commission consisted of ten (later fifteen) members of whom only the Chairman was full time. Between 1948 and 1956 the Commission produced twenty reports concerning the supply of Dental Goods, Cast-Iron Rainwater Goods, Electric Lamps, Insulated Electric Wires and Cables, Matches and Match-making Machinery, Insulin, Certain Semi-Manufactures of Copper and Copper-based Alloys, Calico Printing, Imported Timber, Pneumatic Tyres, Buildings in the Greater London Area, Hard Fibre Cordage, Sand and Gravel in Central Scotland, Certain Rubber Footwear, Certain Electrical and Allied Machinery and Plant, Linoleum, Certain Industrial and Medical Gases, Standard Metal Windows and Doors, Tea, Electronic Valves and Cathode Ray Tubes. In addition, a Report was published on Collective Discrimination in general. This list is testimony to the heavy labours of a part-time body of Commissioners and a small official staff. Yet many of these references cover small industries or small parts of larger industries and, in total, the work of the Commission can have covered only a tiny fraction of the industrial system. Indeed it is something of a mystery why these particular cases were chosen by the Board of Trade for submission to the Monopolies Commission for there were many other well known and large scale monopolies in operation which were left unchallenged. And the nationalised industries—particularly coal mining, iron and steel, transport—were expressly excluded from investigation by the Commission.

No one, of course, can say whether, in 1956, British industry was more competitive than it would have been if there had been no Monopolies Act of 1948. But it is reasonable to suggest that the work of the Commission was not without result.

In only three of the twenty industries examined did the Monopolies Commission record a clean bill of health or anything approaching it. In one other case, while the Commission found clear evidence of restrictive practices, it was not called upon to give its opinion as to whether the practices were contrary to public interest. In the remaining sixteen cases, at least a majority of the Commission recorded a verdict that practices had been found which were contrary to public interest and recommendations were made for preventive action by the Government. In at least six cases there was a thorough-going criticism of the practices revealed which appears to have had a notable influence on public opinion and to have established beyond doubt that the work of the Commission was of value. It is not easy to assess the consequences of the measures taken by the Government on the basis of these reports. Of the sixteen cases mentioned above where action was recommended by the Commission, four of the later ones were set on one side as more properly the interest of the Restrictive Practices Court established under the 1956 Act. In the remaining cases there appears to have been only one Order submitted by the Government to both Houses of Parliament, restraining an industry from certain prescribed acts. For the rest the Government, while in the main accepting the recommendations of the Commission, sought by discussion with the industry concerned to implement its wishes by voluntary agreement. From any evidence available, it appears that the offending industries have shown themselves willing to comply with the requests and the instructions of the responsible government departments.

These results, therefore, are not very concrete. But observation suggests that the less tangible consequences of the work of the Commission cannot be ignored. In a number of industries, not examined by the Commission, it is known that restrictive practices have been discontinued. Above all, the strong tide which flowed between the wars has been arrested and even reversed: British business men can no longer assume that the Government and the public will remain indifferent to their efforts to create monopolies.

III. THE DEFENCE SET FORTH BY THE BUSINESS COMMUNITY

When the time arrives at which it becomes possible to make a final assessment of what was done under the Monopolies Act of 1948, it may well prove that what was most significant was not the practical steps taken to increase competition but the increased understanding of the whole problem of monopoly arising out of the reports of the Commission and the reactions to those reports by the business community. The Monopolies Commission, indeed, has not always spoken with one voice; the principles which have informed its findings have not remained wholly consistent from one report to another (this is especially true after the Commission was enlarged in order to expedite its work and when different sub-committees became responsible for different reports). But, taken as a whole, the reports have reached a very high standard in the accumulation of relevant facts and in the presentation of the case for and against the restrictive practices found to exist. And, in some of the reports, the analysis constitutes a permanent addition to the best literature on the whole subject of monopoly and competition. In what follows the twenty reports have been drawn upon to indicate some of the more interesting topics to be found there.

British industrialists responded to the work of the Monopolies Commission with a mixture of pained surprise, exasperation and indignation. This was hardly to be wondered at. For the restrictive practices which they now found challenged were precisely those which had been positively encouraged before the war. Their world had suddenly become topsy-turvy.[2] They were being

---

[2] Thus in the Report on the Calico Printing Industry (par. 185), where price fixing and output control was found, the Federation declared "an industry which has been sorely tried and harassed over many years and cannot even now have confident hope in the foreseeable future has achieved a degree of stability it has long sought but never enjoyed until now. Those engaged in it hold a firm and even passionate conviction that to impair the organization built up as a result of patient effort and considered thought to meet unexampled difficulties can only end in a condition of chaos for those who work in it and whose capital

BRITISH MONOPOLY POLICY 1944–56 9

compelled to rethink what they had been allowed to regard as the axioms of sound business judgment and action. They were unpracticed in finding reasons to justify restrictive practices. It is, therefore, of more than ordinary interest to examine the grounds on which they set forth their defence.

In the great majority of the industries which have come before the Commission, business men and their counsel have been concerned not so much to deny the existence of monopoly as to seek to defend and justify it. In the process they have employed a very odd mixture of early socialist doctrine and fashionable economic theory. And intertwined with this are to be found some of the more naive deductions falsely drawn from the theory of perfect competition.

It is particularly intriguing to find business men in these days resurrecting the interpretation of the competitive system as set down by the Fabian socialists in the early part of the century. The Fabian doctrine will be familiar: a competitive system inevitably leads to surplus industrial capacity since there is no central coordination of total supply and demand. This leads to sales below cost of production and to ruinous competition. The decline in profits deprives industry of the resources for re-equipment and thereby inhibits technical advance; falling prices compel manufacturers to debase quality, to multiply uneconomically the varieties of goods being produced and, ultimately, to force down wages. All this, it is suggested, is more likely to happen when overhead costs are a high proportion of total costs. The general result is that the industry becomes unstable; all firms, efficient and inefficient alike, are dragged down to unprofitable trading. Only after a prolonged period of cut-throat competition will firms disappear and then the community will suffer in the opposite sense—there will not be sufficient capacity to meet its needs.

British socialists hardly ever use arguments of this kind now. But apparently they commend themselves to British business men. The following are but a sample of many similar possible quotations drawn from the documents submitted to the Commisison by various industries.[3]

---

is embarked in it, and that it would be nothing short of a calamity in the public interest for the industry to suffer thereby as it would do. Its whole well being is at stake."

And in the Report on the Supply of Semi-Manufactures of Copper (par. 284) where price fixing and supporting restrictive devices were found, the industry urged the Commission to "pay great regard to the fact that it is virtually the unanimous feeling of this industry and of the men who are running this industry, that this type of organization is necessary for their well being, remembering after all that these men are where they are because in their own personal lives they have established that their judgment in this industry is sound. . . . There is an overwhelming feeling of men of great ability in the industry, with very great practical experience, that this type of organization is fundamentally important to them and is necessary for the well being of the industry and those they serve."

[3] See in particular: Electric Lamps Report, par. 238; Calico Printing Report, par. 174; Semi-Manufactures of Copper Report, par. 269; Metal Windows Report, par. 195; Linoleum Report, pars. 154–55.

10   THE JOURNAL OF LAW AND ECONOMICS

To sum up, the Association declare that "so far from stifling competition our system has made competition more effective in its operation and more rapid in producing its results. 'Price leadership' combined with a common price has stimulated competition in quality, maintained a market price below that which would have prevailed under the old price competition and a rate of technical progress that is quickened by the pressures created by the system" [Rubber Footwear Report, par. 246].

Without common price arrangements [the manufacturers contend] "prices would be forced down to a wholly uneconomic level." Although in theory the long-term price in a free market must be high enough to cover the normal costs of the highest cost producer whose output is needed to meet demand, in practice there may be "prolonged periods when prices are barely sufficient to cover the normal costs of the lowest-cost producers, with the result that the financial structure of the producing industry is weakened, and its technical progress retarded, while its weaker members may be driven out of business." Bankruptcy "does not necessarily eliminate excess productive capacity but may merely cause the apparent excess capacity to pass under new ownership, with a lower capitalisation for the same physical assets." If, however, the excess capacity is eliminated for some reason, and if "the period of weak demand is a temporary phenomenon superimposed upon a long period upward trend," the removal of excess capacity may ultimately leave a smaller aggregate capacity than the industry requires. If this happens, either the surviving firms emerge "in an even more dominating position" and will raise prices to a point "at which even the highest-cost producer . . . can earn handsome profits," or new productive capacity will have to be constructed [Electrical Machinery Report, par. 689].

The pleadings of the business men may be examined under two heads, those which relate to monopoly by agreement and those which relate to monopoly through fewness of producers.

PRICE AND OUTPUT AGREEMENTS

Broadly the defence of restrictive agreements has run as follows:

1. There is a condition in an industry (never clearly defined but variously described as unregulated, cut throat, full-blooded, unrestricted, unbridled, all out, open, ruinous, indiscriminate or blind price competition or as the unmodified impact of supply and demand) which is bad in that it brings about instability, slows up technical progress for various reasons, and tends to debase quality.

2. There are various modified forms of competition which are better suited to modern conditions and which do not carry with them the drawbacks of unregulated competition. Thus, in the absence of price competition, firms will compete more vigorously in offering better quality or service. If firms are not compelled to compete in the home market they can engage more effectively in the competition arising in foreign markets. Where firms observe common prices, they can the more vigorously compete in reducing costs, etc.

BRITISH MONOPOLY POLICY 1944–56 11

3. The beneficial results which are normally claimed for unregulated competition can in fact be achieved, and sometimes achieved more quickly or more economically, through regulated competition. Here the defenders of regulated competition exploit to the full the muddle in which economic theory on the subject of monopoly and competition now finds itself. Thus in the Tyres Report the manufacturers argued that the essence of competition is a uniform price; but, in practice, this uniform price under unregulated competition will be brought about only slowly by the higgling of the market; price discussions between manufacturers will speed up the attainment of the uniform price; price discussions are, therefore, a part of the market process. In one case, that of Metal Windows, it is actually argued that when manufacturers quote identical prices this has the effect of granting to the consumer "complete freedom of choice."

4. Unbridled competition tends to destroy competition. The familiar form of this argument is that, in the absence of resale price maintenance, small distributors will be driven out of existence and competition thereby restricted. But it can take other forms. Thus in the Semi-Manufactures of Copper Report it is suggested that unregulated competition would lead firms to specialize and this would, in effect, give to these firms "a real degree of monopoly power."

5. Although, at first sight, the price and output associations may appear monopolistic, yet in practice they are not so—either because the associations are not 100% complete or because there is competition from products which are near substitutes.

6. None of the conditions traditionally associated with monopoly are, in fact, present. Thus prices, although fixed by agreement, are not unreasonable; rates of profit are not above the level found in other industries. Uniform prices are, indeed, to be found but, it is pointed out, uniform prices, as laid down in standard economic theory, constitute evidence of perfect competition.

7. In a few cases, it is claimed, the price agreements are needed for the defence of small firms against monopolistic buyers and therefore are a healthy manifestation of "countervailing power."

In most of the cases which came before it, and in its general Report on Collective Discrimination, the Monopolies Commission (or at least a majority of its members) submitted solid grounds, both in fact and in logic, for rejecting the defence of the industrialists. Many of the arguments and counter-arguments will be familiar to those in any country who have made a study of monopoly. But there are two topics, occupying a peculiar place in the British discussions, which merit comment.

COMPETITION AND THE DEBASEMENT OF QUALITY

If one is to judge from the statements made before the Monopolies Commission, it is widely held among British business men that where price competition rules then there is a strongly established tendency for the quality of goods and services to deteriorate. The argument, in the course of time, has become highly elaborate. Price competition between manufacturers will lead them to lower the quality of their goods (hence the case for common prices ex-factory); price competition between the distributors of those goods will result in inadequate after-service and render the goods less satisfactory in operation (hence the case for resale price maintenance). The argument runs both positively and negatively: if there is price competition, quality will be lowered; if there is no price competition, then competition will be diverted into more useful channels and one of these will be the rivalry between firms to surpass each other in the high quality of the goods offered. At times, it seems almost that the manufacturer conceives it as one of his social functions to provide goods and services of a certain minimum grade even though the consumer himself is satisfied with something inferior. Thus in the Tyres Report (par. 455) Dunlop, defending the practice of resale price maintenance and full after-service by retailers, commented:

> The only way . . . to make buyers use this service is to make them pay for it, in the expectation that having paid for it, they will use it.

And at one stage even a minority of the Monopolies Commission accepted this view (pars. 563–64) arguing that "reputable" dealers in tyres provide a service which "makes some contribution to road safety" and that such a dealer is "entitled to protection from cut-rate competition from persons providing no service."

The argument is puzzling because it raises so many other questions which apparently the business men did not put to themselves but which, fortunately, were very much in the minds of members of the Monopolies Commission. Even if there be price competition, why should not a firm, feeling the effects of it, respond by putting on the market a better article at the same price? If price competition tends to debase quality, why should not quality competition in effect lead to debasement of prices? Why should business men apparently engage in competition in quality with a light heart while showing such morbid fear of price competition?

Again, as to the elementary facts. Is it really the case that, in the intense competition in a number of British industries between the wars, there was a progressive fall in the quality of the goods being produced? The evidence suggests otherwise: in that period, particularly in the export trade, British industries were losing their low grade trade and they maintained to a higher degree their position in the higher quality products. Is it true that, at present, in the export market where price competition is inescapable, British industrialists offer poorer quality goods than in the home market? The industrialist would be the first to deny this. Is it true that those British industries which are known to be competitive are less interested in quality than those known to be monopolistic? There is nothing to support such a view. Is it true that in those countries, such as the United States, where industrial competition is active, the quality of the products is generally lower than in those countries where monopoly is common, such as Britain? The converse is more likely true.

At times, indeed, in reading through the reports of the Monopolies Commission, it almost appears that the British businessman has argued himself into a position in which he doubts whether the consumer can *ever* possess sufficient discretion and knowledge to exercise his choice in a rational fashion (this again is reminiscent of some inter-war socialist argument). Sometimes it seems to be suggested that, even where the consumer is in full possession of the relevant knowledge, he will tend to choose, among all the possible combinations of price and quality, a lower quality than is in his own best interests. It should, therefore, be one of the duties of business men to correct this self-harming bias on the part of the consumer. More frequently, the argument seems to be that the consumer does not and cannot possess sufficient knowledge to make a wise choice. Thus he will not be in a position to judge whether the water pipes being fitted into his new house are made of a durable metal, or whether the electricity cable is safe, or whether the motor car tyres he purchases will in fact give as long a life as is claimed for them.

In countering these arguments the Monopolies Commission has, in the main, shown itself robustly liberal in outlook. Why, it has asked, should the consumer not be allowed to be the judge of his own interests? Where, for technical reasons or through the absence of experience, it is difficult for the consumer to judge, why should he not employ the specialized knowledge of agents, such as architects, or even make use of the experience of other consumers? Where questions of personal or communal safety arise, does not this constitute a case, not for action on the part of self-appointed price associations, but for government intervention in the maintenance of minimum standards? But, despite the cogency of such arguments, some of these doubts as to whether consumers can really look after themselves have passed over into and have influenced the form of the 1956 legislation.

It is purely speculation on my own part but it appears to me that, at the root of this fear on the part of the business man of the danger of debasement, lies his knowledge that his price agreements will always be precarious unless the number of varieties of a product can be cut down to a tolerable minimum. The original fixing of standard minimum prices or of output quotas, and the policing of prices once they have been agreed upon, become progressively more difficult the more numerous are the qualities, with the corresponding different prices, of the product available to the consumer. Or, to put it in other words, having perceived clearly the *conditions* necessary for the maintenance of price associations, the business man seeks to present these conditions as a social *justification* for the price agreements themselves.

The second peculiarity of the defence of monopoly as set forth by British business men is their confident belief that only under conditions of monopoly will research and technical progress be properly encouraged. This topic must be left for treatment in a subsequent article.

MONOPOLY AND OLIGOPOLY

Among the cases studied by the Monopolies Commission there are not many which deal with the single producer or the oligopolistic position. Since 1948 the main emphasis of British monopoly policy has been centred on agreements and not on market control arising through the fewness of producers. Indeed, it is doubtful whether public opinion has yet become aware that size can constitute a problem. One indication of this is that when in 1952 the Nuffield and Austin motor car interests were merged into the British Motor Corporation controlling about one half of the total national output of passenger and commercial vehicles, and when in 1957 Courtaulds and British Celanese amalgamated to give an 85% control of the rayon industry, little or no anxiety was expressed anywhere as to the possible dangers of the market control which would be exercised by such business aggregations.

It is true that the Monopolies Commission, in the course of its work, revealed that two British firms controlled two-thirds of the electric lamp production; four firms nearly one-half of the insulated electric wires and cables; one firm over nine-tenths of the matches; three firms the whole of the insulin; one firm about one-half of the motor car tyres; one firm 44% of the rubber boots; one firm 96% of the oxygen; one firm 40% of the standard metal windows; and one firm 58% of the electronic valves. Even in these cases, however, the Commisison normally concerned itself with the study, along the more traditional lines, of price and output agreements. It was not until the Tyres Report, issued in 1955, that the Commission commented: "We are dealing here with a situation quite different from that which has had to be considered in most of the Commission's enquiries" and then proceeded to expound and accept the familiar theory relating to oligopoly—that price competition in the ordinary sense will be impossible since all the firms recognize that aggressive market policy on the part of one will provoke responses on the part of the others and leave all the firms in a less satisfactory position. And it was not until the publication of the Report on the British Oxygen Company, issued at the end of 1956, that the Commission was confronted with an uncomplicated case of a single large producer.

In dealing with oligopoly (a few large producers) price leadership (one large producer and a number of smaller ones) or monopoly (a single producer), it could hardly be claimed that the Monopolies Commission has made much progress either in the analysis of the problems or in the devising of policy with respect to them. In some ways the Commission has, indeed, added to the existing obscurities. This comes out most obviously in the Tyres Re-

BRITISH MONOPOLY POLICY 1944–56 15

port. Here the Commission began by accepting the standard text book argument regarding oligopoly:

> The industry is dominated by some half a dozen firms . . . they all know that any aggressive market policy on the part of one would provoke a response from the others which might lead to a prolonged period of full-blooded competition . . . with disastrous effects on the profits of all. . . . In these circumstances it seems improbable that price competition of the kind which is normal in industries where there are many independent manufacturers will develop between the manufacturers of tyres, at any rate without radical changes in the structure of industry.[4]

Now if this argument is sound then, in this industry, because of its structure, there is no possibility of price competition and that would seem to be the end of the matter. But at that point the Commission appears suddenly to have become suspicious of its own logic. For in its enquiries it discovered that the manufacturers of tyres, through their association, The Tyre Manufacturers' Conference, did in fact engage in discussions regarding prices and it concluded:

> It may well be that, in present conditions, without these discussions there would be little price competition between tyre manufacturers, but it is certain that with them there will be less. . . . We therefore conclude that the T.M.C.'s price discussions are . . . on balance against the public interest.[5]

In brief, the Commission, as practical men, were prepared to accept the idea that under oligopoly there might be *some* price competition.

It is a pity that, having allowed fact to encroach, even though slightly, upon theory in this way, the Commission did not go further and, with all its knowledge and experience, examine in full the validity of the assumption that in an industry with (say) five or six producers, of something like the same size, price competition is impossible or unlikely. Are the class-room economics good enough in thinking about the real world?

There are two reports of the Commission, those relating to rubber footwear and to insulin, which in themselves throw doubt upon the dogma that fewness of producers excludes the possibility of price competition. In the manufacture of rubber boots there are nine producers, five of which are of considerable size with Dunlop, the largest, accounting for about two-fifths of the total national output. This surely is, or is a close approximation to, what is meant by an oligopolistic situation. In this case the industry sought to justify its practices of price agreement by appealing to the "price leadership" arguments (the whole of the industry's case in this report can be read as a fascinating illustration of how effective a smokescreen can be thrown out in defence of monopoly

---

[4] The Monopolies and Restrictive Practices Commission "Report on the Supply and Export of Pneumatic Tyres," par. 480.

[5] Ibid., par. 489.

by those who have a knowledge of economic jargon and are prepared to make an ingenuous use of what often passes in these days for economic theory). The Commission was able effectively to dispose of the "price leader" arguments. But in so doing, the Commission pointed out that there *was* some price competition in the industry from one large producer, the British Bata Shoe Co. Ltd., and, even more important, that in its opinion, if there had been no discussion of common prices among the producers, price competition might well have occurred more widely. That is to say, if this industry can be held to be oligopolistic in structure, oligopoly is not inconsistent with price competition, provided there is no common action deliberately designed for the fixing of prices.

The rubber footwear case is not altogether a clear cut one—because it can be argued that what appeared to be price competition was in fact only price differentials for differences in quality. But in the second case, that of insulin, this complication does not arise.[6] From 1923 onwards the whole of the insulin in Britain has been produced, at first by five and later by three firms (Burroughs Wellcome & Co.; the A. B. Partnership and Boots Pure Drug Co. Ltd.) which have been manufacturing exactly the same article (since the standardization of insulin is enforced for medical reasons). Between 1923 and 1940 the price of the standard pack of insulin fell continuously from 25/- to 1/-. In 1950 the price was still only 1/5½. How did this happen? Up to 1940 the pace was undoubtedly set by an importer, C. L. Bencard, who purchased insulin from the Nordisk Insulinlaboratorium in Copenhagen and who took the initiative, sometimes along with Boots, in making price reductions. In this period there was no formal price collaboration between the British manufacturers. Subsequently the three manufacturing firms met to discuss prices. But even then Boots, presumably not having been informed of the theory of oligopoly, continued as a restless partner of the trio. In 1944 Boots reduced prices which were "reluctantly followed by other firms." This company later threatened to leave the price association unless they were granted freedom to alter prices as they wished. And they extracted an acknowledgement from the other firms that "a price agreement was not an essential factor in a technical collaboration arrangement."

If there are many cases similar to the two mentioned above then it seems that what is really needed, in the study of the consequences of this particular structure of an industry, is detailed examination, not of what is supposed to happen to price competition under oligopoly, but what actually does happen.

In the one clear cut case of single-producer monopoly to come before the Commission,[7] the essence of the matter was that one firm, the British Oxygen

[6] The details are to be found in The Monopolies and Restrictive Practices Commission "Report on the Supply of Insulin," pp. 10–16.

[7] The Monopolies and Restrictive Practices Commission "Report on the Supply of Certain Industrial and Medical Gases" 1956. In its "Report on the Supply and Export of

Company Ltd., was responsible for virtually the whole of the national supply of oxygen. The grounds upon which the Company sought to defend itself were four:

1. That the monopoly had been achieved purely as a result of efficiency.

2. That monopoly supply in this industry is inherently more efficient than any other arrangement. Capital equipment is extremely costly (for example, in the case of cylinder oxygen, the cylinder is twenty times as expensive as its contents). Transport charges are very high. Any interruption in the supply of industrial or medical oxygen would have serious consequences. In the absence of a national monopoly, either there would be several firms competing over the whole of the national market, in which case there would be duplication of equipment and increased costs; or there would be one firm catering for each local market, in which case there would be a series of local monopolies.

3. The Company's policy as to prices and profits indicated that it had not sought to exploit its monopoly position.

4. That its record in research and technical progress was good.

The Commission apparently accepted the contention that there might be technical advantages in a national monopoly but they argued that the Company had, in fact, employed its market power both to extend the range of its monopoly and to charge unduly high prices.

We recognize . . . that in this industry there may be substantial economies in operating as a monopoly, but, as our own enquiry has shown, there are also serious dangers in the control of virtually all the supplies by a single group which has not been content to rely on its advantages of scale and experience but has continued for many years to pursue a policy of suppressing and restricting competition. Among the things done with this objective have been the control exercised over plant and equipment, the taking over of other producers, the use of fighting companies and the incorporation of exclusivity terms in contracts. It is impossible to say how far competition would have developed if B.O.C. had not taken these steps, but we do not think that there is any doubt that B.O.C.'s policy of deliberately restricting competition has had the effect of depriving the public of the possible advantages of greater competition. We have also found that among the "things done" as a result of the "conditions," B.O.C. has taken advantage of the position which it has built up to charge prices which we regard as unjustifiably high, and has pursued a price policy which is in other respects open to objection.

But what was to be done under such circumstances? Here the Commission split badly. One group suggested that a government department should exercise a loose supervision over prices and profit rates. A second group advocated nationalization. A third group sought to create "a quasi-competitive atmosphere within the British Oxygen Company" by insisting that each region of

Matches and the Supply of Match Making Machinery" 1953, the Commission dealt with a similar type of case, but here there were certain complicating factors.

18   THE JOURNAL OF LAW AND ECONOMICS

the Company should publish a separate price list, with prices based on regional costs, and that these prices should be split between price ex-works and transport costs to the several possible destinations.

These multifold and conflicting recommendations really raised more questions than were answered. Is it really the case that a single producer of oxygen will in the nature of things tend to show lower costs than competing firms? The Commission presented very little evidence for its positive answer to this question. Thus it commented that monopolies of oxygen supply exist in France and Holland but curiously enough it had no comments as to what happens in the United States. Even if competition would make for higher costs in the short period, might it nevertheless justify itself by obviating the continuing monopoly tactics of the kind which it had been shown B.O.C. pursued? Even if it were possible to create two or three companies in this industry instead of one, would this in fact provide a worthwhile degree of competition?

But neither in this case, nor indeed in any other which has come before it, has the Commission yet raised the fundamental question: if the structure of industry is such that price competition, in the nature of things, is unlikely, should changes be enforced in that structure, as for example by the breaking up of existing companies, to restore the possibility of competition? Whether that question will ever be asked time alone will show; it must be confessed that up to the moment the indications are few that it is likely to be asked.

Yet the Commission has in the course of its excellent reports, provided some highly relevant, although up to now strangely ignored, evidence with a direct bearing on this issue. If it can be shown that the economies of large scale operation are so general and so persistent that the bigger firms in an industry are usually more efficient than the smaller, this will, very properly, deter even the staunchest advocate of competition from recommending the dismemberment of monopolistic producers. In fact, in the ten reports in which the Commission has provided evidence of the relative costs and profits of different sized firms, there is only one, that relating to electronic valves and cathode ray tubes, where it was found that the largest producer showed the lowest costs. In other cases, there seems to have been no evidence that size and efficiency moved together.

Thus in the Tyres Report:

It is not always the same manufacturer who shows the lowest profits or the higher costs and vice versa. Nor is it invariably the smaller manufacturers whose costs are higher and profits lower than the larger manufacturers. On the other hand, the company with the highest profit in 1952 made the second highest profit in both 1948 and 1951; a second company's profits was below the average in all these years; while the profit of Dunlop and India together (the largest producer) was close to the weighted average in the same periods [par. 434].

BRITISH MONOPOLY POLICY 1944–56 19

In the Report on Rubber Footwear:

Dunlop's (the largest producer) costs were considerably above those of the lowest producer in four of the five lines costed [par. 219].

In the Report on Metal Windows and Doors:

About three-quarters of the costs submitted by Crittall (the largest producer) and well over half those submitted by another of the three largest members were below the weighted average, while about one-quarter of the costs of each of these two companies were the lowest costs submitted. In the case of the third of the three largest companies, however, over half of the company's costings were the highest submitted and only 1% were below the weighted average [par. 137].

In the Report on Calico Printing, where common prices were being charged, the evidence suggests that the profits on net turnover or on capital of the C.P.A. (the largest producer) had not been higher than those of the smaller firms (Paragraphs 147–49). In the Report on Semi-Manufactures of Copper, the Commission reached the following conclusion:

There is no apparent correlation between the rate of profit achieved and the size of the concern, or the range of products made, or membership or non-membership of the associations. although the larger units with a wide range of production tend to achieve rates of profit at or below the average level and some concerns with a very limited range of products achieved rates of profit well above the average [par. 245].

In the Report on Electric Lamps the Commission came to the conclusion that the two largest firms showed costs which were in the middle of the range for the whole industry (par. 215 and Table 9, Appendix 15). In the Report on Insulated Electric Wires and Cables the conclusion was:

In the samples submitted the costs of the largest cable maker, the B.I.C.C., are not among the five lowest for any one of the six types of mains cable or the seven types of rubber cable; their costs are among the three lowest for a number of types of covered conductor, but in only one of these cases did more than four members submit costs [par. 249].

In the Report on Matches and Match-making Machinery the Commission showed that the largest firm, responsible for more than one-half of the industry's output, was not the lowest cost producer (pars. 166–69).

In a succeeding article an analysis will be made of the purposes of the Restrictive Practices Act 1956 and the early work of the Restrictive Practices Court set up under that Act and an attempt will also be made to assess the value of the evidence so far presented before the Monopolies Commission in favour of the view that monopoly is the most effective driving force behind technical progress.

[15]

ENGLISH LAW AND AMERICAN LAW ON MONOPOLIES AND RESTRAINTS OF TRADE

RICHARD C. BERNHARD
University of California, Riverside, California

THE Restrictive Trade Practices Act of 1956[1] has been on the statute books long enough for the adjudication of a number of significant cases under that act, and the first volume of *Reports* on those cases has now appeared. These proceedings indicate the way in which the law of Great Britain is to be applied, and provide a basis for judging that act as a legal tool of an economic policy. A comparison between the British and the American law dealing with monopolistic conditions and with restraints of trade is, therefore, warranted at this time. The economic postulates underlying the law of each country, the scope of the law, and the particular legal instruments of enforcing the declared policy should all be compared. (What is meant by the law in this connection is, of course, not merely the bare statutes but rather the meaning or interpretation—the specific applications—which courts give to the existing legal doctrines and statutes. The law on this matter we shall define, following Holmes, as the conduct that the courts will probably compel one to follow.)

A comparison of the scope and application of legal rules will be easier if the development of the law in England and in the United States is sketched briefly. The ancient common law doctrines against restraints of trade were largely dormant in Great Britain after the decision of the House of Lords in December 1891 on the famous Mogul Steamship Company case.[2] From that time on, blatantly monopolistic practices by firms in an industry were often sanctioned. Firms had the rights of collusive action that workingmen came to enjoy in their bargaining with employers. Only occasionally was there expression by judges of the earlier opposition to collusive actions. These occasional protests were finally expressly discarded in 1937 by the House of Lords in *Thorton v. Motor Trade Association*.[3] The compulsory price maintenance agreement of the industry, at issue in this case, was held lawful and legally enforceable on the basis that, as Lord Wright said, ". . . the interest of the combination is to promote and protect the legitimate trade interests of the

---

[1] 4 & 5 Eliz. 2, C.68.

[2] Mogul Steamship Co. v. McGregor, Gow & Co., [1892] A.C. 25. This decision affirmed a decision of the Court of Appeal, 23 Q.B.D. 598 (1889).

[3] [1937] A.C. 797.

LAW ON MONOPOLIES AND RESTRAINTS OF TRADE   137

respondent Association and its members and is not a combination wilfully to injure."[4] Thus, the English law had a void on matters of monopolistic practices by members of a trade. It tolerated, or was unconcerned about, practices which would generally have been considered restraints of trade— so long as the actions were intended to advance the economic interests of the group and were not done simply out of malicious spite.[5] Economic mayhem was tolerated if it was motivated by avarice, but not if it was motivated by spite.

The gap in the English law was filled, at least in part, with the passage of legislation in the years 1948 and 1956; the last legislation being the more significant enactment arising out of the earlier act.[6] The 1948 law, the Monopolies and Restrictive Practices (Inquiry and Control) Act[7] is, as its preface says, "An Act to make provision for inquiry into the existence and effects of, and for dealing with mischiefs resulting from . . . any conditions of monopoly or restriction . . ." Its major accomplishment was inquiry and information, as others have pointed out.[8] Its measures "for dealing with mischiefs" were not directly employed and were significantly modified by the Act of 1956.

While English law, for well over half a century, tolerated collusion on the part of firms in an industry, the law in the United States was developing a vast body of rules by court decision and by occasional additions to statute law, most of which followed the line of increasing vigilance over actions that smacked of collusion or monopoly power in the American market. The law dealing with monopolies and restraints of trade in interstate commerce starts with a few general provisions of the Sherman Act of 1890. These are broad statements of policy, like constitutional enactments, as the Supreme Court has itself noted. The Sherman Antitrust Act was not formulated as a set of detailed prescriptions. The drafters believed that they were merely carrying over into national law the existing body of common law doctrines regarding monopoly and restraints of trade found in the law of the various states.[9] The same rules that applied within the individual states should be applicable to interstate commerce.

[4] *Id.* at 814.

[5] For a summary of this doctrine, see the opinion of Lord Cave in Sorrell v. Smith, [1925] A.C. 700, 711–12; and the opinion of Viscount Simon in Crofter Hand Woven Harris Tweed Co. v. Veitch, [1942] A.C. 435.

[6] The 1948 legislation was amended by a minor change enlarging the Commission in 1953, 1 & 2 Eliz. 2, C. 51.

[7] 11 & 12 Geo. 6, C. 66.

[8] See: Jewkes, British Monopoly Policy 1944–56, 1 J. Law & Econ. 1 (1958); Dennison, The British Restrictive Trade Practices Act of 1956, 2 J. Law & Econ. 64 (1959).

[9] See, for examples; Stanton v. Allen, 5 Denio (N.Y.) 434 (1848); Central Ohio Salt Co. v. Guthrie, 35 Ohio St. 666 (1880); Santa Clara Valley Mill & Lumber Co. v. Hayes, 76 Cal. 387, 18 Pac. 391 (1888).

The recent English legislation is, in comparison with American legislation, more specific, or more limited in its provisions. There is, of course, room for judicial interpretation, as in all law; but there is not the same scope for developing rules regarding broad, ill-defined conditions such as "monopoly" or a "lessening of competition." Under the more general phraseology of the Sherman Act, it has been possible to develop the law to a great extent by interpretation. The English statute's first major provision is that all agreements between different parties which in any way limit the freedom of the parties in the terms on which they may sell or buy, their freedom in the amount of sales or purchases they may make or in the amount or kinds of production they may undertake must be registered. Such agreements are declared against the public interest unless, on the basis of certain criteria specified in the act, they can be shown to be, on balance, in the public interest. The *prima facie* presumption against restrictive practices may be removed, and the restraints justified where one or more of the following circumstances are considered by the Restrictive Practices court of preponderant importance:[10] first, if the collusion (the restrictive practice) is necessary to protect the consuming public against some injury, or if the restriction gives the public positive benefits;[11] second, if the collusive dealings of the traders is necessary to counteract monopoly power held by others; third, if the restrictive activity is necessary to prevent serious unemployment in an industry or in an area; fourth, if the elimination of the collusion would cause an appreciable drop in exports.

The English statute imposes on those special courts set up to pass on

---

[10] In section 21 of the Act, these major justifications are given as follows:

   (a) that the restriction is reasonably necessary, having regard to the character of the goods to which it applies, to protect the public against injury . . . in connection with the consumption, installation or use of those goods;

   (b) that the removal of the restriction would deny to the public . . . other specific and substantial benefits or advantages . . .

   (c) that the restriction is reasonably necessary to counteract measures taken by any one person not party to the agreement . . . restricting competition . . .

   (d) that the restriction is reasonably necessary to enable the persons party to the agreement to negotiate fair terms . . . from, any one person not party thereto who controls a preponderant part of the trade . . .

   (e) that, having regard to the conditions actually obtaining or reasonably foreseen at the time of the application, the removal of the restriction would be likely to have a serious and persistent adverse effect on the general level of unemployment in an area, or in areas taken together, in which a substantial proportion of the trade or industry . . . is situated;

   (f) that . . . the removal of the restriction would be likely to cause a reduction in the volume or earnings of the export business which is substantial either in relation to the whole export business of the United Kingdom or in relation to the whole business . . . of the said trade or industry . . .

[11] One might conjecture, after seeing the way the parties defended their restrictive practices, that industry did not view the passage of this legislation with too much misgiving because businessmen thought they could justify their joint policies under this clause.

LAW ON MONOPOLIES AND RESTRAINTS OF TRADE 139

restrictive agreements the responsibility of weighing possible economic benefits from coordinated action of traders in a market over against the detriments to the country. (A judge presides over these special courts and determines matters of law, but lay members of the court outnumber judges co-opted from the regular courts of law.) The responsibility is to determine advantages and disadvantages to the nation, but the disadvantages are presumed and require no specific proof or demonstration. The basis of the decision is public policy, a criterion that English judges have, in the past, often considered dangerously vague and liable to abuse. In judging the public interest, the 1948 legislation stipulates that among the factors to be considered are the best allocation of the country's resources and the economic progress and development of the nation.[12] This is a somewhat novel assignment for courts of law.

The importance given to the various factors that the court must consider, or the way in which the factors are weighed, is of the greatest significance in the effect of the legislation on the economy. In the second major case before the Restrictive Practices Court, *in re Yarn Spinners' Agreement*,[13] this weighing was deftly handled; and it seems clear from this and subsequent cases that the court is going to give a relatively heavy weight to the basic presumption against restrictive practices. In other words, it seems that the court is not going to let anything but fairly important considerations override the *prima facie* objection to such schemes. As the court weighed the factors in the cotton spinning industry, it declared that the industry's scheme of price maintenance had: (1) no great or appreciable effect in raising prices to the public as consumers of cotton goods, (2) a significant effect in helping to maintain employment in that industry, (3) a beneficial effect in allowing some modernization expenditures, although the public derived no benefit from this technical improvement in the form of lower prices, (4) a detrimental effect on exports, and (5) a seriously detrimental effect on the national economy because, under the scheme, an incorrect allocation of productive resources was maintained. Too much labor and capital was kept in an industry that should contract.

These were the findings of the court, findings that may cause some economists to quibble; but here they must be taken as a court's determination of those economic matters that the law says the court must weigh in reaching a decision. They are the court's findings of fact. Taking all the factors together, the court declared the industry's agreement against the public interest and therefore void. The consideration that seems to have been given the greatest weight, if one can judge from the words of the decision, was the misallocation

[12] In Section 14 of the Act of 1948, the public interest was defined in terms of efficiency in production, technical progress and economic development, *and* in terms of the "fullest and best use" of resources.

[13] L.R. 1 R.P. 118 (1958).

of resources which the scheme fostered. This seems to have tipped the scales.

The perspicacity with which the court considered the industry's arguments, its avoidance of intricate, hypothetical economic analysis, and the deftness and subtlety with which it weighed the various factors commands the writer's admiration. The decision is, however, essentially a lawyer's decision. (At one point in the court's proceedings, the presiding judge indulged in one of those casual British understatements when he remarked, "that the evidence of economists and accountants could be rather shorter than it has been."[14] Economists may argue over specific findings, or over the logical consistency of the various facts. The court was not interested in formal economic logic. However, as the Act was applied in this case, it gives promise of being a deft instrument of administering an economic policy; and it makes one more aware than ever of the occasional arbitrariness of the *per se* doctrine which condemns all collusion as such. And, after reading American cases, it seems strange to hear a court judging on the basis of the misallocation of a country's productive resources.

United States courts have also, on a few occasions, sanctioned restrictive agreements in situations where it seemed to the judges economically advisable, namely, in the case involving the technologically obsolete hand blown glass industry,[15] and in the Appalachian Coals case.[16] However, casuistical arguments had to be used in each case to get around the fairly clear doctrine against all collective trade restrictions. (There is also the problem of the demarcation of that vague boundary between legitimate trade association activities and illegal collusion on price and production.) American courts have no explicit authority to weigh the economic benefits and injuries to the general public involved in any concerted control over the market. The law makes the economic presumption that that type of agreement is detrimental and therefore all such agreements are condemned irrespective of the merits that any particular agreement might have. To permit agreements, courts in the United States must, like Tom Sawyer, call the instrument by another name than what it would commonly be designated.

The Yarn Spinners case is all the more significant in indicating the direction of English law in that it concerned one of those industries for which there are extenuating circumstances. It is a contracting industry with excess capacity; but at the same time it needs modernization. Further, the industry has many older workers who, if thrown out of work, will find employment elsewhere only with the greatest difficulty. Nevertheless, the court declared the agreement contrary to the public interest. Subsequent decisions, with one exception, have been similar in tenor to the decision in the Yarn Spin-

---

[14] *Id.* at 117.

[15] National Association of Window Glass Mfgs. v. United States, 263 U.S. 403 (1923).

[16] Appalachian Coals, Inc. v. United States, 288 U.S. 344 (1933).

LAW ON MONOPOLIES AND RESTRAINTS OF TRADE   141

ners case. The case in which collusion of firms in an industry was permitted, *in re Water-Tube Boilermakers' Agreement*,[17] was decided favorable to the industry on the basis that the particular scheme of price quotations followed by the firms aided the export market. This advantage in selling abroad was deemed more important than the detriments which presumably followed from the practice.

Those parts of the English and the American law that have been described so far have, at their basis, the same economic principle or postulate. The postulate is that there is a very high probability that restrictive agreements amongst members of a trade are detrimental to the economic welfare of the country. English law, however, permits more subtlety in appraising the situation in which collusion is practiced by firms. If the precedent of the Yarn Spinners case is followed, the English law will achieve all the benefits of this part of American law without some of the awkwardness of a very rigid rule.

Enforcement of the law on restrictive practices differs somewhat. Up to the present, the Restrictive Practices court has been content to declare agreements against the public interest and therefore non-enforceable. As the court said in *in re Chemists' Federation*, ". . . the effect of the act is to render the restrictive terms void merely and not illegal. The courts will not enforce a void agreement, but normally, if the parties choose to accept it as binding in honour, they are at liberty to act under it."[18] The court supposes that, once agreements are declared against the public interest and non-enforceable, members of an industry will change their practices. Only if the restrictive practice continues will the court consider the issuance of an injunction making the practices not only without legal sanction but illegal with penalties attached. As the court added in the Chemists case, "If Parliament had intended a liability to penalties to arise automatically, we think it would have made the restrictive terms illegal as well as void. We think that Parliament intended a milder approach in accordance with the ordinary rule that an injunction is not granted unless the commission or repetition of an offense can reasonably be apprehended."[19]

In the cases so far, therefore, the industries have been dismissed with the admonition, "Go and sin no more." It will be interesting to see what the court will do if there is evidence that some industries continue in their sins against the public interest. It will also be interesting to see what evidence the court will accept of such sins. Will English courts accept as evidence of collusion all those conditions that have, at one time or another, been accepted by courts in the United States? Market collusion by American firms is not

[17] L.R. 1 R.P. 285 (1959).

[18] L.R. 1 R.P. 75, 113 (1958).

[19] With this point of law determined by the court, part of Prof. Dennison's statement, ". . . that an agreement is against the public interest (and therefore illegal) unless the contrary can be proved," is liable to misinterpretation. See his article, op. cit. supra n. 8 at 66.

merely admonished; it is punished. The persistence of business practices
in restraint of trade in the American economy despite penalties makes the
methods of enforcement in Great Britain seem a little naïve. English businessmen are probably more law abiding than the American business community; but it is still not certain that Adam Smith would want to change
his statement about their inclination to meet and conspire at the expense of
the public.

Resale price maintenance, the authority of a producer to control the price
at which his product is sold by wholesalers and retailers, is another point
on which the law in the two countries should be compared. In the United
States, certain states have laws allowing producers to fix the price at which
buyers can resell their products. American courts, however, have not been
sympathetic in interpreting this legislation, so its force has been weakened.
Under the Restrictive Trade Practices Act, a contract between a buyer and
a seller fixing the resale price is made legally enforceable; but that law is
most careful to stipulate that suppliers may not jointly organize and enforce
a price maintenance scheme. Such collusion is made illegal. Further, no
supplier can refuse to sell to a dealer, or discriminate against a dealer who
has violated a price maintenance agreement. On the part of buyers such as
retailers, it is unlawful to take any joint action in discriminating against,
or refusing to do business with, any supplier who does not follow or enforce
a fixed resale price policy.[20] Popular sympathy for victims of penalties
placed by certain industries on small dealers who violated the industry's
price maintenance scheme was aroused; and, as a result, the law is more
positive in condemning collective resale price maintenance plans than it is
in its proscription of collective price fixing.

Another important difference between the law in Britain and in the United
States arises out of the development in American law—by court interpretation and by legislative enactment—to a point where the law is now concerned
about monopoly as such, not merely concerned about certain practices whereby several parties conspire to influence the market. What is becoming illegal
under federal law in the United States is monopolizing—as the law now
defines monopolizing; and, since this is now considered the crime, it is possible that perfectly legitimate business actions by one firm may, if they
"inadvertently" lead to monopoly power, put a firm in jeopardy of the law.
In the case against the Aluminum Company of America in 1945,[21] in the
1946 case against the manufacturers of cigarettes,[22] in the 1953 United Shoe
Machinery case,[23] in the 1957 DuPont–General Motors case,[24] and in the

---

[20] The price maintenance provisions are in sections 24-26 of the Act of 1956.

[21] 148 F.2d 416 (1945).

[22] American Tobacco Co. v. United States, 328 U.S. 781 (1946).

[23] 110 F. Supp. 295 (1953).   [24] 353 U.S. 586 (1956).

1958 Bethlehem-Youngstown steel case,[25] legitimate business transactions created monopoly power which the courts held illegal. Alcoa's continued plant expansion and aggressive sales policy; the tobacco-buying practices, the sales policy, and the million-dollar-a-year advertising budgets of the major cigarette manufacturers; the United Shoe Machinery Corporation's vigorous sales efforts; and DuPont's profitable investment in General Motors stock were all perfectly legitimate business actions as such; but all contributed to illegal results, monopoly power in a market, and therefore should have been modified in some way or should not have been undertaken. The merger of Bethlehem and Youngstown steel companies would *lessen* competition, and it has been forbidden.

From leading cases such as these, it is easy to see that the scope of the federal law in the United States is vastly greater than the scope of the English law. The U.S. law is concerned with monopoly power and with the preservation of competitive conditions. Under this larger responsibility for competitive and monopolistic conditions in industry, there are two other particular matters that may come under judicial scrutiny. First, the sales policy of an individual firm may be checked to see that the firm does not practice unwarranted discrimination between customers.[26] Second, transactions in which a purchaser is required to take one article as a condition of obtaining another which the seller controls—tying contracts—are considered monopolistic and against the law.[27]

The American law's concern over monopoly as such stems, in part, from an increasingly literal interpretation of Section 2 of the Sherman Act which prohibits monopolization. Earlier interpretations of this provision considered it merely as a condemnation of restraints of trade which could be used as devices to obtain a monopoly. Certain actions were condemned, not monopoly. This was in strict accord with the common law meaning of the words. Now, however, the courts are inclined to interpret the words as a prohibition of monopoly power. In their concern over monopoly, U.S. courts are not at all interested in enforcing, or establishing, anything even vaguely resembling the economists' pure or perfect competition. Competition for lawyers and for courts retains its ordinary day-to-day meaning. This is as true of the American courts as it is of the English courts. In one important antitrust case, the U.S. Supreme Court said: "There is no showing that four major competing units would be preferable to two, or . . . that six would

[25] United States v. Bethlehem Steel Corp. & Youngstown Sheet & Tube Co., 168 F. Supp. 576 (1958).

[26] See: Corn Products Ref. Co. v. FTC, 324 U.S. 726 (1945); FTC v. Morton Salt Co., 334 U.S. 37 (1948); FTC v. Simplicity Pattern, 360 U.S. 55 (1959).

[27] See: Times-Picayune Publishing Co. v. United States, 345 U.S. 594 (1953); Black v. Magnolia Liquor Co., 355 U.S. 24 (1957); Northern Pacific Ry. Co. v. United States, 356 U.S. 1 (1958).

be better than four."[28] English courts take the same attitude. In the Yarn Spinners case, the court said, "Even if the industry were reduced to the five large combines, who now control about 40 per cent. of it, . . . it would not necessarily diminish competition."[29] The growth of oligopoly may, it is true, be considered by U.S. courts when a merger is contemplated, but they can do this only if it can be shown that it would mean a lessening of competition in some market.[30] Oligopoly cannot be attacked as such.

While American courts are gingerly tackling the assignment of preserving competition and checking monopoly power, the specification of these conditions is still, and probably always will be fuzzy. For the law, "monopoly invoves the power to eliminate competition."[31] This has many elements— the power, and the purpose or intent, and the size of the firm.[32] In considering how much control over a market a firm has, it is virtually impossible to establish an unequivocal measure. To devise an unquestionable measure of market control, one must first frame an absolute specification of a completely distinct and separate commodity, or one must designate an industry that is economically and legally distinguishable from all others. Such absolute distinctions cannot be made in practice. Products of many modern industries (like cellophane) have many different uses and in each use there is a considerable range of substitutes with technical characteristics that make each a more or less satisfactory alternative. Therefore, all delineations of product and industry are shadowy in certain areas and tentative. Only in a hypothetical world are there completely distinct and separate products and industries.

How American courts have wrestled with the problem of monopoly, with the effects of certain transactions on the state of competition, and with the element of size is a separate subject. But they have had to wrestle with these issues! One would like to see the ingenuity of the English legal minds dealing with the same problems. They will be spared this arduous labor, because English monopoly legislation provides that when the supply of a third or more of a commodity is in the hands of one party, the monopoly commission may be requested to study the effects of the situation on the economy; and, if the condition appears contrary to the public interest, the

---

[28] United States v. National Lead Co., 332 U.S. 319, 352 (1947).

[29] L.R. 1 R.P. 118 (1958).

[30] On this point, see United States v. Bethlehem Steel Corp. & Youngstown Sheet & Tube Co., 168 F. Supp. 576 (1958).

[31] See: Transamerica Corp. v. Board of Governors of the Fed. Reserve Sys., 206 F.2d 163, 169 (1953); cited in United State v. Dupont, 353 U.S. 586, 592–93 (1956).

[32] For discussions of the legal meaning of monopoly, see: United States v. Griffith, 334 U.S. 100, 105-07 (1948); United States v. Paramount Pictures, 334 U.S. 131 (1948); and especially Judge Wyzanski's summary of the legal views on monopoly in United States v. United Shoe Mach. Corp. 110 F. Supp. 295 (1953).

LAW ON MONOPOLIES AND RESTRAINTS OF TRADE   145

monopolies commission may persuade the large supplier to change his policies, or they may propose an order for Parliament designed to remedy the situation. Ultimately, the matter is thrown back upon the legislature; and, in a sense, it is a legislative matter to determine if large or complete predominance in a market—apart from illegal actions—is to be permitted, or if it is contrary to the public interest and should be forbidden. If preponderant size in a market had been made a matter for legislative action, would congress have rendered the same judgment on the Aluminum Company of America as the federal courts? Would the United Shoe Machinery Corporation have been considered guilty of achieving, by unnecessarily vigorous sales tactics, an unwarranted predominance in its market? An English firm that held 90% of the market for one product, liquid oxygen, had gained its position by research and sharp business practices. The Monopolies Commission recommended that the firm be subject to price supervision. The government decided to do nothing about the monopoly.[33] However, the firm has agreed to change a number of those practices by which it gained and maintained its monopoly—practices such as price cutting to embarrass competitors, exclusive equipment leasing, and control over the building of plant.[34]

One other contrast between the British and the American law should be mentioned. This is the power of federal courts to specify what a firm or an industry must do to restore competitive conditions in the market, that is, what they must do to remove the taint of illegal monopoly power. This authority is necessarily involved when the law deals directly with the condition of monopoly. English courts will escape this burdensome administrative responsibility as long as the statutes under which they operate are expressed in terms of restrictive practices of members of a trade, not in terms of monopoly and competition.

If one reflects on the nature of recent British legislation and on the cases brought to trial under it, one is reminded of the brilliant exposition of the law on monopolies and restraints of trade given by Holmes in his dissent in the Northern Securities case.[35] Holmes's interpretation of the law and current British practice are quite similar. One element of undetermined significance is different. That is the Monopolies Commission's power to investigate, to advise industry about their public responsibilities, and ultimately to recommend legislation to Parliament.

[33] Annual Report for the year 1958, Board of Trade, Monopolies and Restrictive Practices Acts, 1949 and 1953, page 4.

[34] *Id.*, App. 2.

[35] 193 U.S. 197, 400 (1904).

[16]

OXFORD REVIEW OF ECONOMIC POLICY,VOL.1,NO.3

BRITISH COMPETITION POLICY IN PERSPECTIVE

THOMAS SHARPE
Wolfson College, Oxford

I. INTRODUCTION

Competition policy is the subject of a fresh review under almost every British Government. The most comprehensive recent appraisal was undertaken, at high speed, by a Department of Prices and Consumer Affairs working party in 1978-1979.[1] This review, like others before it, was essentially concerned with modifications which might be attempted within the general existing framework of law and institutions. In fact in its discussion of monopolies, mergers and restrictive trade practices the working party appeared to be particularly anxious to foreclose the range of options available to Government and made little effort to assess whether the general framework is appropriate in the light of the experience of the impact of policies. This approach is explicable when it is recalled that during the period of the review, there were doubts that the UK should have *any* competition policy or that whatever policy existed should be subservient to "industrial policy" - a view which was mooted and resisted in wartime discussions of the shape of post-war policy.

The election of the Conservative government in 1979 has elevated private ownership to a central objective of policy, and this is reflected further in policies designed to encourage private tendering by public undertakings. But the conversion of dominant public undertakings, for example, British Telecom or British Gas, into private ownership does not encourage efficiency or competition unless the process is accompanied by appropriate liberalising measures and a machinery for underwriting the competitive process. And even if a market is "liberalised", in the sense that entry is lawful, a combination of natural monopoly or factors serving to increase the irrecoverable costs of entry, may inhibit or totally deter entrants. After the initial structure of the undertaking has been determined politically (which, in the cases of British Telecom and British Gas, meant no divestiture or division), attention focuses on the dominant incumbent's conduct: what is or is not acceptable business behaviour?

---

[1]   Cmnd. 7198, 1978; Cmnd 7152, 1979.

T Sharpe

Similarly, policies designed to encourage rivalry and efficiency in the provision of services, for example, in aviation, bus transport, refuse collection and the like, are contingent on independent, non- collusive decision-making. Once again, the competitive process must be underwritten, as a guarantee to new or prospective entrants, and an efficient system will contain incentives to reveal collusive behaviour and suitable deterrents to such behaviour.

Most economic studies of competition policy in the United Kingdom, with the exception of certain case studies, concentrate upon the quality of analysis displayed by the authorities rather than the effect of the policy on industrial conduct, structure and performance. Equally, most legal analyses of the competition legislation consciously abstract questions of economic policy and where, as in restrictive trade practices, it is impossible to do so, the conclusion is usually drawn that issues are non-justiciable (Stevens and Yamey, 1965). Issues of legal policy, by which I mean the techniques and instruments employed in order to achieve a given end, and the economic consequences of the deployment of certain legal techniques and instruments, as opposed to others, have largely been ignored. One of the purposes of this paper is to highlight certain legal issues in the belief that the choice of technique in competition legislation has an important effect on the efficiency of UK policy.

Competition law in the United Kingdom unlike, for example, factory safety or pollution laws, seldom serves to regulate behaviour: what takes place is more the selective ad hoc application of public powers, exercised in a non doctrinaire, pragmatic spirit, allowing little opportunity for compensation in favour of those affected by the anti-competitive action of others. This flexibility, while accommodating shifts in emphasis flowing from changing economic theories, is achieved at the expense of the blunting of the educative and deterrent edges of policy: it is most unlikely, for example, that *attitudes* in the UK have been affected by the laws in force; indeed, the laws have reinforced the longstanding suspicion of rivalry and competition held by British industrialists. This situation reflects historical attitudes in the UK toward competition which are worth noting and need to be addressed if reform is seriously contemplated. I shall describe below the overlapping, competing and occasionally contradictory accretions to the law since 1948. I shall then attempt to assess if, and to what extent, the existing institutional framework and laws are sufficient to accommodate the description of economic theory and assessments of certain business practices offered by economists. A conclusion and tentative agenda for reform conclude the article.

II. BACKGROUND

When in 1943 two war-time Whitehall irregulars, Hugh Gaitskell and Professor G C Allen prepared their document "The Control of Monopoly" it was with a background of fifty years of investigation, distrust and disquiet of the anti-competitive excesses of large companies, international trusts and of trade associations. Yet, however powerful this undercurrent of distrust and disquiet may have been, it resulted in little action. The desertion of traditional individualistic competition by British manufacturers owed less at this stage to the desire to extract monopoly profit and more to an attempt to regain industrial prosperity by way of national cooperation, in the face of depression and international competition.

This view gave expression to an older tradition unsympathetic to competition. According to Professor Keller (Keller, 1981)

> "The traditional structure of English life seemed to foster cartelisation: combination
> has been accepted without regulation in England because the entire English social
> system is a series of close groups·... English society is stratified and cellular".

Before the first world war public policy toward competition was unsystematic: the general concern of economists, notably Marshall and Pigou, was translated into specific enquires but with little lasting effect. Government action, particularly in armaments, tended to favour cartelisation in order to maintain capacity or to counter existing monopoly. For example, the Admiralty encouraged the Coventry syndicate in order to counter the virtual monopoly of naval gun mountings enjoyed by Vickers and Amstrong-Whitworth. Shipping rings were the subject of a Royal Commission and, more parochially, shop assistants and radius agreements had been investi-

OXFORD REVIEW OF ECONOMIC POLICY,VOL.1,NO.3

gated between 1907 and 1909. Of greater significance, a very detailed official report was published in 1912 devoted to anti-trust legislation in the British self-governing dominions.[2]

It was apparent that the Dominions had been more forthright in their attitude towards monopoly and cartels. The Canadians had enacted the Combines Investigation Act 1910, the Australians had passed the Industrial Preservation Act in 1906 and the Interstate Commission Act in 1912; the Commercial Trusts Act in New Zealand was passed in 1910. Developments in China were also noted: the penalty for artificial pricing was eighty blows and excess profit was regarded as theft.

After the war the "coral reefs" of official controls - which had relied heavily upon trade associations and business cooperation for their effectiveness - were swiftly dismantled to be replaced by private or quasi-private arrangements. The widespread cartelisation in iron and steel, chemicals, electrical engineering, tobacco, wallpaper, salt, cement, textiles and elsewhere, and the stronger post-war position of trade associations led to the establishment by the Ministry of Reconstruction of a Standing Committee on Trusts. This was the first full investigation of competition in the British economy. The fear of trade associations was real enough. The Committee was unanimous that machinery for investigation of trusts and combines should be instituted similar to that which already existed in the United States and in the colonies.

Under the Committee's scheme the Board of Trade would have primary responsibility for the conduct of investigations but if prima facie a practice was contrary to the public interest, the case would be referred to a newly-constituted tribunal for further investigation and eventual report to the President of the Board of Trade. A minority report, signed by Bevan, S Webb and others went further: not only should a tribunal, with a lawyer as chairman, be appointed, but resort should freely be made to nationalisation, to an excess profits tax, to price control and to local authority involvement as a check to capitalist combination.

In 1920, even though the Board of Trade has prepared a Trading and Monopolies Bill, it was not introduced. In the ensuing years resale price maintenance was scrutinised, and Parliament was occasionally asked to approve Private Members' legislation dealing with rings and trusts or to pass bills designed to provide for the collection of information with respect to trusts and combines and to restrain abuses. All these initiatives came to nothing.

It is wrong, therefore, to see the period before 1948 as a time of inactivity or indifference to anti-competitive business behaviour, cartels and trusts. But for the leading industrialists of the time, for the Weirs, the Duncans, for Montague Norman at the Bank of England, and Horace Wilson at the Treasury, leading members of the 'close groups' referred to above, the weight of informed instinct lay in favour of cooperation and rationalisation, preferably effected by private rather than by public initiative. The stress was on efficiency, but through planning. Market forces led to inefficiency and waste. Competition was inherently ruinous. This hardly provided a sympathetic environment for any serious effort to introduce anti-trust laws in the United Kingdom.

It was only in the course of war-time planning for post-war reconstruction that competition policy emerged as a major priority, on a par with general Government support for trade and location of industry. This was largely owing to the clear association, in the minds of the economists involved, of monopoly power and unemployment. If monopolies and cartels could be controlled, output and real income would be higher than otherwise and unemployment lower. This was the leitmotiv of the war-time discussions. Furthermore, Article VII of the Mutual Aid Agreement with the USA committed the parties to discuss trade policy: to the Americans at least this meant control of international cartels.

The method of control suggested in Gaitskell and Allen's document "Control of Monopoly" envisaged the establishment of a statutory commission on restrictive practices with power to investigate and report on industries which applied to operate restrictive practices, practices which but for the grant of a licence would be prohibited. This body was also entrusted with a broader remit - to keep under review and make a recommendations on the state of company law, patents and other laws which directly and indirectly affected competition. In the eyes of the war-time planners, therefore, competition policy had been elevated to a position of importance, an essential

---

[2]   Cmnd. 6439, 1912-1913.

T Sharpe

complement to post-war commercial commodity and employment policy. The proposed planning structure, enforced rationalisation, direction of industry, state ownership of fundamentally un-competitive industry and natural monopolies, compulsory membership of trade associations and other ideas which emerged from the Ministry of Reconstruction and Board of Trade, were all predicated upon a significant role for competition policy. But this enthusiasm was tempered in practice by indecision about the likely economic effects of cartels and by lack of information about the business practices of dominant firms.

III. THE LEGISLATIVE FRAMEWORK

The subsequent legislative history of UK competition law is more familiar and can be summarised briefly. The Monopolies (Inquiry and Control) Act 1948 established a Monopolies Commission under the chairmanship of a lawyer and abstracted from the central government machinery, but answerable to the President of the Board of Trade. As the title implied, the initial task of the Commission was investigatory and the standard by which the conditions "to which the act applies" or "any things done" by the investigated party were to be judged was whether or not they operated against the "public interest". The Act went on to offer some guidance about the public interest: the Commission could have regard to all matters which appeared to them to be relevant and in particular to efficient production and distribution of goods and full employment.

The role given to the Commission and the relationship between the Commission and the President of the Board of Trade indicated that public interest considerations were not amenable to specific definition; they were complex and economic in character and, ultimately, subject to political determination. The decision to refer a company of the Commission was taken by the President of the Board of Trade and any subsequent enforcement was the preserve of the Minister.

The Act may be fairly described as a reconnaissance. The Commission's first set of reports, particularly the one devoted to *Collective Discrimination*[3] isolated a range of undesirable practices and a majority of a Monopolies Commission recommended a general prohibition, reinforced by criminal sanction, subject to specific exceptions. Applications for exceptions would have to be addressed to an independent body and approved ultimately by Parliament. The minority report, distantly echoing the recommendations of the Committee on Commercial and Industrial Policy After the War, of 1918, relied upon registration, publicity and individual, ad hoc examination.

The unpopularity of the Monopolies Commission, the personal conviction of the ministers involved, judicial prestige and the declared preference of industry, led to the passage of the 1956 Restrictive Trade Practices Act, now consolidated into the 1976 Act. Investigations of monopolies was retained by the Monopolies Commission but cartels passed to a court. (Much earlier, Alfred Marshall doubted the wisdom of legal control over business behaviour. According to him, the law was "slow, cumberous and therefore ineffective".)

This extraordinary Act adopted a highly legalistic approach toward restrictive practices. The agnosticism of 1948 gave way to a presumption that such agreements were contrary to the public interest and subject to registration. The difficulty of defining anti-competitive behaviour with respect to a monopolist gave way to narrow, specific definitions of the type of collusive behaviour on the part of two or more parties which was presumed to be contrary to the public interest, and which fell to be justified before the Restrictive Practices Court at the request of a new officer, the Registrar of Restrictive Trade Practices. Once before the Court, the presumption could only be rebutted by reference to specific gateways, all of which required economic analysis, and even if the restriction passed through the gateway it still had to be judged by the Court to be, on balance, not unreasonable. The supervision of cartels under this Act was thought to be abstracted in all important respects from political control.

---

3   Cmnd. 9504. 1955.

OXFORD REVIEW OF ECONOMIC POLICY,VOL.1,NO.3

An important feature of the scheme, which will be discussed further, is that the legality and civil enforceability of agreements is conditional on the legal expression freely given to the economic relationships by the parties, rather than on the economic effects of the relationships themselves.

The 1956 Act also rendered illegal collective resale price maintenance but introduced a statutory device whereby a contract containing a resale price restriction could be enforced by the manufacturer against a third party, thus completing a triangle made up of manufacturer, wholesaler and retailer which would otherwise remain incomplete owing to the doctrine of privity of contract. Individual enforcement of resale price maintenance ended for all but a narrow range of goods following the passage of the Resale Prices Act 1964, now consolidated in an Act of 1976.

In 1968 a further change in the restrictive practices legislation permitted administrative or political exemptions from the legislation in the face of the perceived need for industrial reorganisation. The same Act of 1968 permitted a civil action for damages or injunctive relief to be brought by any party suffering loss against any or all parties to a registrable restrictive agreement which had not been registered.

In 1965 mergers were brought under the jurisdiction of the renamed Monopolies and Mergers Commisssion (MMC) for the first time. As subsequently amended, mergers which create or increase the market share of the parties of 25% or more of the relevant market, or which involve assets of more than £30 million, are subject to referral to the MMC by the Secretary of State, following the advice of the Office of Fair Trading and scrutiny in private, by the non-statutory Mergers Panel. Mergers are not presumed to be contrary to the public interest, even horizontal mergers which may dramatically increase concentration, and the Secretary of State has no power to intervene unless the MMC finds that a merger may be expected to operate against the public interest. The decision to refer is ultimately a political one and the position of a third party, keen to oppose a proposed amalgamation, is that of a lobbyist and provider of evidence to the MMC, (or given that so few mergers are referred, to the OFT and DTI).

The Fair Trading Act 1973 brought together the existing monopolies and mergers legislation and created a new office and officer, the Office of Fair Trading and its Director General, with the general task of supervising, *inter alia,* competition and consumer issues, maintaining the register of restrictive trade practices and of bringing proceedings before the Restrictive Practices Court. The Act also provided for the investigation of situations in which no one party enjoyed a statutory monopoly - 25% of the relevant market - but where several parties so conducted their affairs as to prevent, restrict or distort competition. Such "complex monopolies" - usually, but not inevitably, oligopolies fell under the jurisdiction of the MMC.

Service agreements came under the scrutiny of the Restrictive Practices Court after 1976 but by far the most important changes in the structure of the laws derives from first, the Competition Act 1980 and secondly, the United Kingdom's membership of the EEC.

The Competition Act permits the selective investigation of individual business practices which, in the judgement of the Office of Fair Trading constitute a course of conduct which prevents, restricts or distorts competition. Such practices are defined as anti-competitive business practices. Their existence is determined by the Office of Fair Trading and, if satisfactory undertakings are not forthcoming, the matter may be referred to the MMC, who must confirm the existence of any anti-competitive practice and offer an assessment of whether the anti-competitive practice operates against the public interest.

The attraction of this scheme is that, unlike a Fair Trading Act investigation, a full industrial inquiry is not required and the matter can be despatched in a matter of months. The main drawback is the temptation to regard all business conduct or practices as potentially restrictive - and therefore an anti-competitive practice - and delegate the economic assessment to the MMC as part of its public interest inquiry. This is quite wrong. The burden is on the Office of Fair Trading to determine the existence, if any, of market power enjoyed by the company under investigation, and then to assess whether the practice in question owes its profitability to its capacity to exclude competitors or to increase their irrecoverable costs of doing business. If, to the contrary, the practice owes its profitability to an increase in efficiency, it is not an anti-competitive practice and should not be referred to the MMC. The temptation to conflate public interest and competitive issues has not always been resisted. (Kay and Sharpe 1982; Sharpe 1983).

T Sharpe

Moreover, strangely, the determination of the existence of market power is, formally at least, an unfamiliar task for UK authorities: in cartels - as in US law - it is irrelevant; elsewhere, the relevant market is defined administratively and occasionally very narrowly, such that a monopoly situation is inevitably deemed to exist. The broader question, of the power to control output and prices, is subsumed at the administrative level in order to give the MMC jurisdiction to investigate supply, but it is not necessarily the case that because an undertaking is subject to investigation, it possesses market power.

Once again, individuals affected by an anti-competitive practice must complain to the Office and seek action. No independent private remedy exists and even if a practice is condemned in strong terms no retrospective remedy exists. The incentive to draw the existence of anti-competitive practices to the attention of the Office is therefore weak yet, as the Office lacks a large investigatory staff and wide investigatory powers, it is critically dependent on the lodging of complaints by concerned bodies.

The United Kingdom's entry into the EEC subjected UK based undertakings to the provisions of Articles 85 and 86. The former renders any agreement which prevents, restricts or distorts competition and which affects trade between member states void unless the agreement is notified and can be granted exemption by the EEC Commision. The latter renders any abuse of a dominant position, which affects trade between member states, a violation. It is customary to regard the enforcement of EEC treaty obligations as the preserve of the EEC Commission. But in respect of Articles 85 and 86, in common with other "directly effective" provisions of the Treaty, it is open to an interested party to plead Articles 85 and 86 in a national court and, slowly, litigation is developing in national courts in the pursuit of injunctions and occasionally damages in the face of breaches of Articles 85 and 86.

To summarise, competition policy in the United Kingdom lacks nothing in complexity. The law begins with the old common law rules against restraint of trade which in recent years have been applied most energetically to long term solus agreements between petrol companies and petrol stations. But the core of the law is found in four statutes: The Fair Trading Act 1973 governs the investigation of monopolies, mergers and oligopolies; the Restrictive Trade Practices Act 1976 consolidates the early legislation of 1956 and 1968 and deals with "registrable" agreements; the Resale Prices Act 1976 similarly consolidates the 1964 legislation and causes most resale price maintenance agreements to be void: the Competition Act 1980 permits the Director General of Fair Trading to investigate what are comprehensively defined as anti-competitive practices. Arching over all of these statutes are the relevant provisions of the Rome Treaty, Articles 85 and 86, which only apply if the relevant restrictions or abuses affect trade between Member States. In the light of the *Laker* and *IBM* disputes, it is worth recalling that acts within the United Kingdom which have an effect within the United States are judged actionable within the US jurisdiction, a legal philosophy to which the UK strongly objects, but which nevertheless effectively serves to discipline the behaviour of American and other companies trading internationally. The German courts and authorities subscribe to a similar policy.

IV. SOME CHARACTERISTICS OF THE PRESENT STRUCTURE

Turning first to the treatment of agreements, the first thing to note about the existing structure is that it represents a curious mixture of narrow legalism, broad discretion, certainty and flexibility.

The law contains two sets of distinctions: the first is that between agreements at the horizontal level and vertical agreements; the second distinction lies between price and non-price vertical restraints - contained in vertical agreements.

Unlike the Sherman Act, Section 1 and Article 85 (EEC), UK law has created a distinct category of horizontal agreement, which falls to be considered under the Restrictive Trade Practices Act - any agreement which is not an agreement to which the Restrictive Trade Practices Act applies *may* be a "vertical agreement". Within this latter category, if the agreement contains restrictions directly or indirectly affecting resale prices, it is governed by the Resale Prices Act. If, alternatively, the agreement contains non-price vertical restrictions, involving, for example, territorial exclusivity, exclusive purchasing obligations or customer reservation clauses, it may either be investigated as part of a Fair Trading Act monopoly inquiry - if the market share test is satisfied -

OXFORD REVIEW OF ECONOMIC POLICY,VOL.1,NO.3

or as a Competition Act reference, if the non-price vertical restraint can be characterized as an anti-competitive practice. The implications of this distinction are discussed below.

Horizontal Agreements

Horizontal agreements must be registered with the Office of Fair Trading. It is the registration requirement which in 1956 led to the decision to adopt a legal test to determine which agreements should be registered as opposed to a test based upon economic effect. If an agreement is not registered within a specific time period, it will be unenforceable and moreover may give rise to civil liability as the suit of an aggrieved third party for any loss caused as a result of its operation. Registrability therefore is a matter of some significance and sensitivity, and is more important in practice than satisfying the conditions of a "gateway", although in the economics literature it is the latter which is emphasised.

The Restrictive Trade Practices Act 1978, Section 6 defines registrable agreements as agreements:

> "(whenever made) between two or more parties carrying on business within the United Kingdom in the production or supply of goods (or services) or in the application to goods of any process of manufacture, whether with or without other parties, being agreements under which restrictions are accepted by two or more parties in respect ..."

and the Section then goes on to consider a number of restrictions relating to price, the terms and conditions under which goods are supplied or acquired, the quantities of goods or descriptions of goods to be produced or acquired, the process of manufacture to be applied to any good and the persons or classes of persons to, for or from whom, or the areas or places in or from which, goods are to be supplied or acquired. It would be seen from the above that the registrability of an agreement depends first, on a jurisdictional limitation, that two of the parties must be carrying on business in the United Kingdom and secondly, that two of the parties must accept restrictions in respect of the matters listed. The concept of "restriction" has been subject to detailed judicial examination and, drawing upon common law interpretations in restraint of trade cases, it is defined as an inhibition upon a pre-existing right. So, for example, a restriction as to use contained in a lease granted to a particular party cannot constitute a restriction for the purposes of the Act on the ground that but for the lease itself, the other party would have no right to pursue the prohibited use in the first place.[4]

More fundamentally, however, once an agreement enters the system by way of Section 6, there are in particular two methods by which an agreement ceases to be registrable: they are, first, if the agreement consists of an exclusive dealing arrangement between two parties, in which case it is not registrable.[5] Secondly, the Act demands that no account shall be taken of any term which relates exclusively to the goods supplied in pursuit of the agreement. It can be seen that one or the other of these provisions, in the hands of a skilful draftsman, can transmogrify what would normally be understood as an agreement between competitors into either an ordinary contract of purchase or sale, with terms such as quantity established, or a vertical agreement between parties at different levels of production. A related question is whether it is possible to so draft an agreement such that the restrictions present are judged to be positive restrictions, for example, an obligation to buy a particular quantity, rather than express or implied negative restrictions. If so, the possibility that an agreement is not registrable is enhanced.

In general, limitations on competition are usually phrased in negative terms, prohibiting charging below a particular price, or imposing limits on production and so on. The draftsmen of the 1956 Act saw the need to extend the definition of "restriction" to restrictions which are expressed in a positive form only to those instances where a benefit or penalty was obliged to be conferred if the

---

4   *Ravenseft v DGFT* [1977] ICR 136.

5   Schedule 3(2).

T Sharpe

agreement was breached or observed.[6] Such provisions, for example, would obviously apply to the situation in which payments would be made for exceeding a production quota.

The importance of judicial determination in this area can perhaps be best explained by reference to a familiar example, the litigation involving *Cadbury Schweppes and J Lyons and Co.*[7] It was admitted that the parties had for some years sought to operate a quota system dividing the market in citrus concentrates between them unequally. An earlier agreement was judged to be registrable and was replaced by an agreement under which Cadbury Schweppes was obliged to purchase 43% of its total sales from Lyons or pay a penalty if less were ordered. It was submitted by the Director General of Fair Trading that Cadbury Schweppes was effectively restricted from manufacturing or purchasing from other sources in excess of 57% of its sales without payment of a penalty, which itself constituted a restriction under Section 6(4). The Judge felt unable to interpret the positive obligation to purchase 43% as a negative provision not to produce more than 57% of combined output and held that the only restriction on Cadbury Schweppes was to purchase not less than 43% of its sales. That restriction related exclusively to goods supplied under a contract of sale and thus fell to be disregarded by virtue of Section 9(3). In this way, by adopting a very narrow interpretation of the word "restriction", the court sanctioned a quota agreement. It should be noted that this result followed notwithstanding the obvious detrimental effect of the quota agreement and the clear intention of the parties to attempt to continue an older relationship which the law had in the first instance proscribed. This case exemplifies the stress UK cartel law places upon the appropriate legal *form*, and the apparent indifference to the economic *effect* of a particular agreement.

The choice of "form" or "effect" as a basis of registration or notification was considered at length by the official investigation into restrictive trade practices referred to at the opening of this paper, but any change from a form based system to an effects based system was rejected on the following grounds. First, that such a change would be unfamiliar and disruptive to industry (notwithstanding many years' experience of a comparable EEC approach) and secondly, that in any event, certain agreements structured in a particular form would inevitably be condemned, their effects being predictable.[8] Unfortunately, this is a non sequitur.

The converse does not necessarily hold, that agreements possessing detrimental effect would inevitably be cast in a particular form and caught thereby. The *Cadbury Schweppes* case is but one example where the intention of the parties and the effects of the agreement were obvious but where the stress on narrow legalism excluded the application of the legislation. (Interestingly, by contrast, in a constitutionally more sensitive area of law, tax, the courts have adopted very robust support for intention and effect over form.).[9]

So for many parties registration is an election. The agreement, being voluntary, can be structured in such a way that in many instances it need not be registered. But even if an agreement is registrable there is little incentive to register it. As between the parties it may be unenforceable but typically parties to such an agreement are unlikely to resort to litigation to maintain their bargain. It is true that parties who can prove loss flowing from the operation of a registrable but unregistered agreement may bring a civil action for damages or injunction. But unsurprisingly in view of the difficulties in establishing the existence of an agreement, proof of loss, and the lack of sufficient financial incentive to take the risk of litigation, there is no reported instance of a legal action. although the Post Office and an area health authority managed to recover over-payments caused by the operation of cartels, but only by negotiation and by exploiting their strong market positions as purchasers.

It follows that if the probability of detection is less than certain, and the probability that single damages will have to be paid is very low, (and, unlike the American situation, damages may be

---

6 S. 6(3)(4).

7 [1975] ICR 246.

8 See Cmnd 7511, 1979 at 7.07.

9 e.g. *Furniss v. Dawson* [1984] AC 474.

OXFORD REVIEW OF ECONOMIC POLICY,VOL.1,NO.3

apportioned between the cartel members) only the most risk-averse parties to a cartel would feel obliged to forego the likely benefits that membership of a cartel may offer. Under the circumstances, it is perhaps surprising that there are not more cartels - or perhaps there are, and they remain undetected?[10]

An important subject of cartel policy is or ought to be measures to prevent collusive tendering. We appear to know little about the existence and frequency with which bids are rigged, particularly in construction projects but, speculatively, bid rigging has few of the problems encountered by formal cartels in maintaining stability and detecting cheating between the parties. Collusive tendering was judged sufficiently important to warrant a discussion paper in 1980, on which no action has been taken. The official view is that by deceitfully representing that bids are independent of one another, the winning bidder may be guilty of a criminal offence, of obtaining pecuniary advantage by deception. But there appears never to have been a prosecution and I doubt whether any policeman or local authority solicitor is aware of the criminal aspect of what in certain circles is a perfectly normal commercial relationship. The precedent of specific criminal legislation regarding auction rings is uninspiring.

Parties will collude in tendering for specific contracts, franchises and other work if the likely gains from cooperation outweigh the expected costs in damages, foregone commercial opportunities and general loss of esteem. Discounting the latter two considerations, the maximum that an aggrieved party can recover is a sum equivalent to the loss experienced by it. If the chances of detection are less than certain, it will *always* be rational for parties to collude. If the chances of detection and substantial payments by way of damages or settlement are remote, it is irrational for parties not to collude. One can only assume that some sanction attaches to public association with a cartel but, in truth, it is difficult to determine the detriment that has attached to the cable cartel members, or to Sealink, Valor, Thorn-EMI, Potterton and other well known and promoted names.

The stress on registration and a degree of formality in the structure of an agreement has made it even more difficult in the United Kingdom to develop a body of case law and attitudes towards non-collusive cooperative behaviour. Such behaviour in oligopolistic markets falls outside the 1976 legislation and if it is analysed at all, it falls under the Fair Trading Act's provisions dealing with complex monopoly situations. For the MMC to have jurisdiction over a complex monopoly situation, two or more parties must possess a market of at least a quarter of the goods supplied and conduct their respective affairs to prevent, restrict or distort competition in connection with the supply or production of the goods in question. This curious addendum, found in Section 6(2) of the Fair Trading Act comes near to conferring jurisdiction upon the MMC by reference to what the MMC should actually be seeking *once* it has assumed jurisdiction, namely, conduct which prevents, restricts or distorts competition. Nevertheless, there is the capacity within the complex monopoly provisions for the case by case analysis of certain patterns of behaviour in the conduct of competition among the few. But it must be said, there is little reflection in the United Kingdom of the energy deployed (productively or not) in the pursuit of undesirable strategic behaviour, price signalling or "facilitating" practices, in the United States.

It is well recognised that collusion may take many forms other than an agreement or arrangement. Under EEC law, there is express reference to a "concerted practice" as falling within the proscription of Article 85(1). Such behaviour as prior notification of prospective price increases, thus eliminating uncertainty regarding the likely behaviour of one player in the market, has been regarded as substituting practical cooperation for normal competition. Whether it is sensible to confine the treatment of horizontal relationships to situations in which the test of registrability is satisfied and thus stultifying any judicial innovation regarding tacit collusion is a difficult question to answer, and is perhaps best reserved for consideration in the context of the appropriateness of judicial as opposed to administrative appraisal, and accusatorial as opposed to inquisitorial proceedings.

---

[10] Unregistered but registrable agreements have recently been detected in passenger ferry services between N. Ireland and Scotland (Townsend Thorensen and Sealink (Scotland) Ltd.), in gas fired central heating boilers, liquified petroleum gas heaters and aluminium ingots.

T Sharpe

Vertical Agreements

Turning to vertical restraints, the critical difference is whether such restraints are price or non-price restrictions: the former is a virtual per se violation, judicially enforced; the latter is subject to a case by case analysis, administered by the OFT and MMC. Agreements between parties at the horizontal level to fix resale prices were banned outright by the 1956 legislation. Vertical price restraints were condemned with virtually no exception in 1964. Non price vertical restraints, such as restricting the resale of a particular good to a network of authorised dealers and refusing to supply to others (e.g. the motor distribution agreement) are judged by the flexible standard of the Competition Act. Is a refusal to supply an "anti-competitive practice"?

The familiar arguments for and against vertical restraints are relevant here though what is perhaps more significant in the legal context is the starkness, in legal consequence, between a finding that a restriction is price as opposed to a finding that a particular restriction is non-price related. The typical non-price vertical restraint is a second-best solution to the inability of parties to contract to specify a standard of behaviour, where the behaviour is both complex, difficult and expensive to monitor. But in essence, the conferral of, say, a local monopoly in respect of a particular product in the hope that a dealer will thereby have sufficient incentive to develop pre- and post-sales advice, warranty work and other features, relies upon a combination of increasing the dealers' reward and reducing the possibility or risks of intra-brand competition. As the dealer is largely free from intra-brand price competition, the only price competition he faces is from competing but different products.

There are circumstances in which it can be demonstrated formally that non-price and price restraints will possess exactly the same economic effect, and moreover there are circumstances in which a simple price restraint may be more efficient than a non-price restraint. It seems curious that if the benefits of selective distribution are achieved by the grant of a spatial monopoly they may be judged favourable. But if the benefits are achieved by express resale price maintenance, this will be condemned. (It is of course possible for an application to be made to the Restrictive Practices Court for an exemption to the prohibition on resale price maintenance, but only books and pharmaceuticals have so far availed themselves of this process, and this reluctance is easily explained by the difficulties inherent in making an application).

With the restrictive trade practices legislation, the virtual certainty than an agreement would not be approved, or passed through one of the "gateways" led parties to a strategic response to such certainty, namely evasion or the construction of agreements which did not fall within the system in any event. Similarly, in respect of resale price maintenance, the strategic response has been the creation of selective distribution networks as a substitute for resale price maintenance, but not necessarily an efficient substitute.

This point was exemplified in the first Competition Act reference, *Raleigh*,[11] in which the bicycle manufacturer's policy of selling only to a selected network of bicycle dealers, and not to large multiple stores, was judged to be an anti-competitive practice and contrary to the public interest (although no effective remedy was introduced). It was clear that the OFT and MMC were aware of the new literature concerning vertical restraints but felt, perhaps correctly, that *Raleigh's* policy was nothing other than resale price maintenance in bicycles, by a different name and by different means. It was understood that *Raleigh* was able to dictate the terms under which bicycles could be resold within the specialist dealer network but would, prospectively, have been unable to dictate these terms in the face of significant concentrated purchases by large multiple stores.

Whatever the truth of this surmise, it is possible to say that there is an artificial distinction between resale price maintenance and non-price vertical restraints established firmly in UK law, which may be inefficient and which certainly creates special incentives on the part of manufacturers to so structure their commercial relationships in the manner which avoids the prohibition on resale price maintenance. In other words, it should not be forgotten, as with horizontal agreements, that parties have considerable freedom as to how they construct the relationships they wish to see and, if one avenue is blocked, the same result can be achieved in other ways.

---

[11] Monopolies and Mergers Commission (1981/82).

OXFORD REVIEW OF ECONOMIC POLICY,VOL.1,NO.3

The institutional brittleness of the law encourages this process, while at the same time creating an illusion of certainty and predictability.

Dominant Positions and Mergers

Monopolies and mergers are subject exclusively to a discretionary and effects based system of laws. Since the Fair Trading Act, the Director General has power to initiate monopoly reference on his own motion but in respect of merger references, his task is to recommend a course of action to the ultimate authority, the Secretary of State.

Naturally, as ideas and theories develop, the position of the MMC changes, as would judicial doctrine. But unlike judicial proceedings, where the principle of *stare decisis* applies, it is somewhat less clear what evidential or probative value past reports can offer. This may reflect the nature of the activity itself: only the most exceptional of situations are officially judged worthy of referral, (this is particularly true of mergers), so that it would be unwise, even illegitimate, to generalise from one single instance to another.

What is investigated represents an official view of what ought to be investigated and there is no *necessary* correspondence between such investigations and the private perception of both public and private welfare losses, caused by the conduct of a dominant firm.

The inability to generalise, from past findings, uncertainties regarding referral and the necessity for referral, the absence of restitutionary remedies to those who have suffered loss and the lack of incentive on the part of private parties to generate information on which the Office of Fair Trade must rely, suggest that from the points of view of education and deterrence, UK policy toward monopolies is weak.

But paradoxically a case can be made for the proposition that the UK really does not have an anti-monopoly policy, as the term is recognised in the USA, Germany and the EEC. What the UK possesses is less a legal framework designed to establish standards of acceptable behaviour, to regulate conduct, to provide remedies for those affected and, generally, to provide some guarantees to prospective entrants in any industry that they will be protected effectively from the anti-competitive excesses of a dominant incumbent. What the UK possesses is a mechanism, whereby certain defects or failures in the market mechanism may be investigated and ad hoc remedies applied.

Market power and its abuse is recognised as one example of market failure. A plausible hypothesis, and one which accords with the distinctly British competition policy tradition which emphasises efficiency, described earlier, is that UK policy is to isolate and remedy specific examples of market failure, whether or not abuses of market power are present. As such failures may embrace situations in which no blame need attach to the undertaking in question but may, for example, exist owing to failures in consumer information, no liability need attach to the undertaking.

In this way, references which address issues of high profits, tie-in sales where market power is not present, restrictions on the exploitation of industrial property rights and other matters which to US anti-trust lawyers appear misplaced, may be explained by a direct, official attempt to isolate and rectify failures in the market place. By contrast, in the USA, the anti-trust laws have played since 1890 a central role in the preservation of the competitive process. They draw inspiration not only from the idea of a competitive society as far as economic activity is concerned but also as the basis of the political liberties enshrined in the US Constitution. As John Sherman proposed:

> "If the concentrated power of this combination are entrusted to a single man, it is a
> kingly prerogative, inconsistent with our form of Government, and should be subject
> to the strong resistance of the state and national authorities. If anything is wrong,
> this is wrong. If we will not endure a King as a political power, we should not endure
> a King over the production, transportation, and sale of any of the necessaries of life.

T Sharpe

If we would not submit to an Emperor we should not submit to an autocrat of trade, with power to prevent competition and affix the price of any commodity."[12]

By contrast, fear of monopoly abuse and concentration in the UK never went so far as to over-whelm the warmth felt toward cooperative endeavour. In no sense do UK competition laws occupy the same, almost constitutional position, as such laws enjoy in the United States. The British approach, under the guise of being pragmatic and ad hoc, is essentially to achieve a different objective, that is - direct intervention in specific market situations in which markets do not appear to work efficiently. It is this impatience with the process of competition which grants the British authorities a mandate to intervene in situations in which their counterparts in the United States would fear to tread, particularly under the present dispensation in the Department of Justice.

Before considering why the privatisation of de facto monopolies creates a fundamental challenge to the traditional outlook, the foregoing may be illustrated by brief references to recent experience.

Following upon the ban on the exclusive purchase of car spares from manufacturers by motor dealers, Ford and other motor manufacturers maintained a policy of refusing to license other manufacturers to manufacture spare parts for sale to authorised, and unauthorised, dealers. This policy was considered by the Office of Fair Trading as an anti-competitive practice and was referred to the MMC. The Commission while broadly sympathetic to the OFT's view that this was an anti-competitive practice, was unable to recommend any significant change owing to what it perceived to be its limited powers under the Fair Trading Act, to challenge the exercise of what had been judicially determined to be Ford's industrial property.

US authorities would not typically intervene in such a situation. Motor cars and their spare parts would be judged as essentially part of the same market, and the manufacturer should have the freedom to determine the prices at which both items should be sold, in the knowledge that any attempt to leverage a position in one product would be reflected in a reduction in demand for the other product. In short, the tie-in is benign and the decision of *Ford* to exploit its industrial property rights, and not share them with others is unexceptional. Moreover, taking the argument somewhat further, if Ford were under an obligation to allow others to manufacture the parts under licence, the terms of the licence would have to reflect the income stream which would otherwise accrue to Ford so as not to constitute confiscation of Ford's property. If this is the case, no benefit would necessarily accrue to the consumer, assuming that royalties were calculated efficiently. I hope this summary does justice to the Chicago school.

There is perhaps an alternative view: it is that, in the purchase of a motor car, while the consumer (even the corporate consumer) is appropriately sensitive to the purchase price, the consumer is fundamentally ignorant not only of the costs of spare parts, but of his likely demand for them. He is myopic, possessed of imperfect information and radically, cannot ascertain his probability of being involved in a crash and of that crash causing damage. As a result the close relationship which may be assumed to exist between the price of spare parts and the demand for the motor car is not present, and it follows that the motor manufacturer is possessed of market power in relation to the spare parts required by a particular car, in the event of damage. In summary, the British authorities, although regrettably not articulating it with any precision, were pointing to a situation of market failure, and their concern was essentially to remedy this. It could be remarked that in addition to recommending licences to other manufacturers, which would inevitably lead to difficulties in calculating the appropriate level of such licence fees, an alternative proposal, well within the MMC's remit, would have been to recommend some form of public listing of the prices of spare parts, such that the consumer would be better informed. Short of public intervention, the Consumers Association or other non-profit bodies could be encouraged to provide such advice in a systematic and reputable way. The market failure would thus be remedied, partially at least.

Car spares is, in my view, a particularly good example of the difference in techniques and assumptions between an anti-trust jurisdiction and a regime designed to render markets more efficient. It is so because car spares is not a situation in which, in the long run, market forces would

---

[12] 21 Cong Record 2457.

OXFORD REVIEW OF ECONOMIC POLICY,VOL.1,NO.3

work. It is an example where uncertainty is radical and, absent official intervention, likely to persist. (This is not to underestimate the efforts made by manufacturers to reveal the running costs of a motor car, or of the pressure exerted by insurance companies in containing costs: cars which are expensive to maintain are expensive to insure, but this knowledge is a long way short of the information required by a consumer to effect an efficient purchase).

V. CHOICE OF TECHNIQUE

If the purpose of UK competition policy is to ameliorate specific examples of market failure, this public function need not be combined with the prospect of a private remedy in favour of the individuals affected. Moreover, if the inquiry is a complex and comprehensive examination of the efficiency of markets, an administrative tribunal, consisting of people with specialist skills, is probably preferable to a judicial body, access to which would be open to any party with sufficient interest.

It is possible, however, the UK policy is evolving toward an anti-trust policy, as the term is recognised abroad. As remarked earlier, competition, private ownership and rivalry are being emphasised as virtues, at the same time as privately owned monopolies are being created. A policy which emphasises efficiency as resulting from free and competitive entry or its credible threat appears to have superseded the claim that official, occasional, intervention or regulation can directly bring about efficient outcomes.

This change of emphasis owes something to the obvious potential for anti-competitive conduct possessed by British Telecom, and perhaps also by the experience of US airline deregulation. But over a longer period it has become generally apparent that the absence of effective rivalry in significant sectors of the British economy (which is not necessarily synonymous with the existence of collusion) has left these sectors unskilled in the art of responding to foreign entry. In television sets or white goods, for example, the absence of effective domestic rivalry over many years resulted in rapid industrial eclipse, in the face of competition from abroad. An earlier view, that the suppression of domestic competition would improve international competitiveness may be turned on its head: if domestic manufacturers have little or no experience of responding to domestic entry, and that entry or its threat is rare owing, in part, to the perceived risks of anti-competitive conduct on the part of incumbents, then a determined challenger may carry the field very rapidly. In the absence of empirical study, the above is no more than a conjecture, but an attractive one.

The focus therefore falls upon entry or prospective entry. This is explicit in the case of British Telecom where the degree to which BT's dominance and market share is reduced ought to be an index of the success of public policy, and of OFTEL. But it is clearly impossible to anticipate in advance the full range of techniques and strategies available to a dominant incumbent in order to inhibit entry.

Certain devices are familiar: the offering of price reductions contingent on the purchase of a full range of goods or services - a requirement which mandates any prospective entrant to enter a market not only on a specific scale but also by requiring a broader range of products or services to be offered than would be initially desirable. Alternatively, the creation of exclusive sales outlets, for example, in beer and petrol, serves to decrease the cross elasticity of substitution between different beers or petrol, in proportion to the costs borne by consumers in switching between suppliers. New entrants must therefore enter both at the manufacturing and retailing level, especially if the solus ties are long term.

The strategic competition and predation literature suggests, however, that stress upon isolated individual practices is insufficient: what is significant is the emergence of a pattern of behaviour which owes its profitability exclusively to its capacity to deter competitors. In detecting such behaviour, the incumbent's *intentions* assume importance and data regarding this, and its long term behaviour in the market place, is extremely difficult for any agency to collect or comprehend. There are exceptions: British Telecom's significant anticipatory tariff reductions on routes on which its sole competitor, Mercury, has indicated (several years in advance) it would serve, is clearly designed to indicate to Mercury that post entry profitability on other proposed routes will be low and that British Telecom has little intention of ceding market share, even at the expense

T Sharpe

of short term profitability. Presumably, it is confident that having established a reputation for aggression, a more cooperative game can be played with Mercury. (In the absence, of course, of any formal registerable agreement).

The scope available to a dominant incumbent to indulge in non price entry deterring strategies is great. The literature isolates the deliberate creation of excess capacity as a prime entry deterring strategy: only if there is excess capacity will the incumbent's threat of expanding output in the face of an entrant be credible. Similarly, the design of a product or the issue of compatible or incompatible standards, may serve to increase the costs of entry to others, without necessarily enhancing the efficiency of the incumbent.

Any model of a passive incumbent, neutral to the prospect of entry, would be misleading. Such undertakings disappear. Yet, as is apparent, it is extraordinarily difficult to isolate such entry deterring strategies: at worst, they are opaque, at best, they are ambiguous. But if such behaviour continues to be riskless, no profitable entry by firms of equal or superior efficiency is likely to take place, especially in the presence of imperfect capital markets.

Increasing the costs and risks of anti-competitive behaviour would therefore seem to be essential if entry is to be credible.

The final question which must be addressed, therefore, is whether the traditional structure and techniques of competition enforcement in the UK, which is the product of ideas dating back to the period after 1918, is appropriate, when the imperative is to encourage entry (and thereby efficiency *via* the competitive process).

Administrative, officially-sponsored and centralised enforcement has certain advantages in the dispassionate analysis of the analytics of market failure. A structure placing a premium on entry, is likely to imply an adversarial relationship between incumbent and entrant. The prospective gains and losses are defined and allocatable, and the entrant has explicit incentives to generate the required data. It would seem to follow that the party with most to gain, should itself initiate proceedings rather than rely upon an official agency. Decentralised enforcement will serve to increase the riskiness of anti-competitive conduct, and also reward the initiator of the action by way of damages.

It must be recognised that it is not always efficient to lock penalties for anti-competitive conduct to the rewards received by the party bringing a successful action. This might encourage a plethora of small actions, each of which requires little effort on the part of the initiator of the action, as opposed to the bringing of larger actions involving substantial, anti-trust restrictions but possessing lower probabilities of success.

The major impediments to private actions in the United Kingdom seem to be a lack of confidence in the judiciary in the handling of economic issues, and secondly, difficulty in establishing the appropriate standard by which conduct should be evaluated. These themes require a further paper, but perhaps it should be recalled that other anti-trust jurisdictions have veered toward stark economy in the form of words used to govern conduct. The corollary of this approach is to entrust to the judiciary the task of evolving concepts such as market power, predation, foreclosure and so forth. Lack of faith in the judiciary has lead the British, for example, in the British Telecom licence, to attempt to enumerate, in advance, as many manifestations of anti-competitive conduct as possible, in an effort to be comprehensive. As remarked above, in the context of entry deterring strategies, the full array of techniques open to the determined incumbent is, in essence, indeterminate. What is required, by contrast, is a statement of governing principles, which will have to be worked out over time in a large variety of factual settings.

But the UK is very far from achieving such an objective. Entry problems are likely to remain subsumed under Competition Act references, which will probably diminish in number owing to the dependence of the Office on a dwindling band of complainants. Governing principles are unlikely to emerge from a structure which starts from the premise that each case is one of first impression and, moreover, in sectors which will inevitably spawn entry and anti-trust problems, for example, telecommunications, aviation and financial services, specialist agencies have or will have exclusive or primary responsibility for investigation and enforcement. Curiously, deregulation in the USA has encouraged the opposite development: specialist agencies have given ground, partially

OXFORD REVIEW OF ECONOMIC POLICY,VOL.1,NO.3

or completely, to the general anti-trust jurisdiction, and the exceptions to this jurisdiction are being reduced. In the UK, old traditions die hard.

References

Kay, J A and T Sharpe (1982), "The Anticompetitive Practice", *Fiscal Studies*, 3, 191-8.
Keller, M (1981) in T McCraw (ed.), *Regulation in Perspective*, Cambridge, Harvard University Press.
Monopolies and Mergers Commission (1981), *Bicycles*, HC 67, London : MHSO.
Monopolies and Mergers Commsssion (1983), *Car Spares*, London : HMSO.
Sharpe, T (1983), "Refusal to Supply", *Law Quarterly Review*, 96.
Stevens, R B and B Yamey (1965), *The Restrictive Trace Practices Court*, London : Weidenfeld.

[17]

ECONOMIC CONCENTRATION AND MONOPOLY IN JAPAN[1]

EUGENE ROTWEIN
University of Wisconsin

I. INTRODUCTION

FOR purposes of a study of monopoly and concentration, Japan affords an especially interesting case. The Japanese economy is a "capitalistic" economy, but not a highly developed one. Development has been pushed hard for almost a century; and, for a country emerging late from feudalism—and an oriental country—Japan has made phenomenal gains. Owing mainly to a severe shortage of resources, the struggle for growth has been especially difficult, however; and the level of economic development Japan has attained still falls far short of levels in Western countries.

Japan does not have a long-standing antitrust tradition. Before the last war cartels were permitted, and when the state intervened (in 1931) it did so with a view to encouraging their growth. There likewise were no legal barriers to the concentration of industrial, commercial, and financial assets. For several

decades preceding the war the *"zaibatsu"* —a relatively small number of family-dominated holding company systems with assets fanning out through large segments of the Japanese economy—had been growing. Long before the beginning of World War II these groups had become a major force in Japanese economic—as well as political—life.

Japan, however, is a country in which deliberate attempts were recently made to alter the industrial structure. As part of a more general effort to promote democracy—or "democratic capitalism"— in Japan, the American Occupation launched a program which called for the dissolution of the *zaibatsu* system and the deconcentration of many *zaibatsu* subsidiaries. The latter phase of the program fell far short of its objective. Though 235 firms were originally scheduled for deconcentration, in the end 25 were broken up. While not thorough, the first phase of the program came closer to its objective. The Occupation liquidated the old holding companies, removed the *zaibatsu* families from control and, by loosening intercorporate stockholding, weakened the relations between *zaibatsu* firms.[2] Beyond this the Occupation sought to keep concentration and monopoly under regulation by introducing an anti-monopoly law which in many respects was even more stringent than the American counterpart.

[1] The material for this study was gathered while I was in Japan on a Fulbright grant from 1959 to 1960. I am indebted to many. Here I should like particularly to mention Toru Nishikawa, whose help in Japan was invaluable; Mrs. Michiko Ariga and Hitoshi Misonou, of the Japanese Fair Trade Commission, who provided important data; Kazuo Sato, Seiji Naya, Francis Colaco, and Kunio Yoshihara, who assisted in various aspects of the study; and Katsutake Hattori, managing director of Mitsubishi Economic Research Institute, who generously extended the use of the Institute's facilities to me. Both the University of Wisconsin and the Center for Japanese Studies at the University of California helped make it possible to secure research assistance for the study. The detailed data on which the findings of this study are based will be made available on request.

[2] For a general discussion of the deconcentration program, see T. A. Bisson, *Zaibatsu Dissolution in Japan* (Berkeley: University of California Press, 1954).

ECONOMIC CONCENTRATION AND MONOPOLY IN JAPAN 263

If the Occupation did not persist in implementing all its aims (partly because of the fear that deconcentration might weaken Japan as an ally against communism), the initial deconcentration momentum has further fallen off considerably since the signing of the peace treaty. The *zaibatsu* began to regroup in 1952; and, owing to statutory changes and ineffective enforcement, the antimonopoly law has been losing its force.

What is the pattern of industrial organization in present-day Japan? Studies which, directly or indirectly, bear on this question do not reveal anything like a general consensus. Some observers have regarded the prewar Japanese economy itself as "competitive." Such is the position, for example, of C. C. Allen.[3] Here the *zaibatsu* themselves are regarded as rivals. The contrary view, however, appears to be more pronounced—especially among American observers. The official Occupation position was that "independent enterprises and free competition existed . . . only in minor segments of the prewar Japanese economy," that her industrial structure "was dominated by the *Zaibatsu*" and that Japan was a land of "international and domestic cartel arrangements."[4] In such general statements as these it is difficult to gauge the extent to which the absence of "free competition" is being attributed to the influence of the *zaibatsu* and cartels as against oligopoly in particular markets. In her study of prewar Japan, Eleanor Hadley, however, asserts that "most Japanese markets" themselves were "oligopolistic." Linking this to the influence of the *zaibatsu* in different markets, she argues that a "live and let live

policy" was common in the prewar Japanese economy.[5] In his study of the dissolution of the *zaibatsu*, Bisson adopts Miss Hadley's view. Pointing out that the deconcentration program of the Occupation fell far short of its aims, he argues—on the supposition that the Japanese economy is highly concentrated and Japanese traditions preclude both individualism and competition—that nationalization of Japanese industry is (and should initially have been recognized as) the only effective remedy.[6]

Among Japanese academicians some have adopted the official Occupation position. Avid "trust-busters" and disappointed with the course of the antimonopoly program, they see government policy as a potentially effective means of accomplishing the initial Occupation objectives. As a whole, however, the postwar Japanese literature dealing with the concentration problem reflects little faith in "democratic capitalism." It is predominantly Marxist; and though in no small measure Western economic concepts are used in the analysis, here "capital" is treated largely as "mo-

[3] See his study, "Japanese Industry: Its Organization and Development to 1937," in E. B. Schumpeter, *Industrialization of Japan and Manchukuo, 1930–40* (New York: Macmillan Co., 1940), pp. 682–83.

[4] Economic and Scientific Section, GHQ, SCAP, *Mission and Accomplishments of the Occupation in the Economic and Scientific Fields* (Tokyo, September, 1949), pp. 20–21. *The Report of the Mission on Japanese Combines* (the report of the Edwards Mission prepared in 1946 for the Department of State and the Department of War) states that "the low wages and concentrated profits which are produced by such a structure [that is, "the excessive concentration of economic power in Japan"] have been inconsistent with the development of a domestic market capable of keeping pace with the increased productivity of Japanese industry; and in consequence Japanese business has felt the need to expand its exports not only to pay for necessary imports of food and raw materials but also to make up for the deficiency of domestic consumption" (see Part 1, p. vii).

[5] See Eleanor Martha Hadley, "Concentrated Business Power in Japan" (unpublished doctoral dissertation, Radcliffe College, 1949), pp. 7, 13–14.

[6] Cf. Bisson, *op. cit.*, pp. 12–13, and chap. iii, esp. pp. 47–57.

nopoly capital" exploiting small business and labor with the support of the state.[7]

This study is concerned primarily with industrial organization in postwar Japan and deals with the prewar pattern only to a minor degree or by inference from the postwar findings. It is principally a quantitative study, and it does not deal with the details of individual markets. Such a study always runs the risk of omitting relevant considerations. But I believe it provides general indicators which throw light on industrial organization in Japan—enough light, it is hoped, to help resolve some of the major issues that have been raised on this question in the literature.

II. MARKET CONCENTRATION

The first question of importance concerns the pattern of market concentration in Japan. Speaking most generally, a study of this pattern does not bear out the contention that the Japanese economy is highly concentrated or oligopolistic. More specifically, an analysis of concentration data prepared by the Japanese Fair Trade Commission—the Japanese antitrust enforcement agency—indicates that, in 1956, 16.4 per cent of the Japanese national income was produced in "high-concentration" industries—a "high-concentration" industry being defined as one in which the output of the top four firms in the industry was at least in the close neighborhood of 50 per cent of the industry output.[8] The "high-concentration" proportions by sector of the economy are as follows: manufacturing 34.6 per cent; mining 22 per cent; transportation 47.3 per cent; communications and other public utilities

100 per cent; finance and real estate 1.7 per cent; agriculture, forestry, fishing, construction, trade, and services 0.[9]

Since the data for manufacturing are more detailed than those for other sectors, they throw light on the trends in concentration over time. Going back to

[8] This finding is based on data in *Saikin ni okeru shuyō sangyō no seisanryoku no doko* ("Recent Trends in the Concentration of Production in Major Industries") (2 vols.; Tokyo: Fair Trade Commission, 1956), *Shuyō sangyō ni okeru seisanshuchu* ("Concentration of Production in Major Industries") (Tokyo: Fair Trade Commission, 1958), and, where no published data were available, on appraisals made by the research department of the Fair Trade Commission (F.T.C.) for purposes of this study. National income data were provided by the Economic Planning Agency. For manufacturing, where the income data were available only for broad categories, the data were distributed among the narrower categories on the basis of the value-added distribution as given in the Japanese *Census of Manufactures*. Although the industry categories are often four-digit Census categories, in many cases—owing to a lack of more detailed concentration data—broader groupings were employed. These are believed to be generally representative of the four-digit subcategories, although in instances where there are many such subcategories within the group and the product types vary markedly there may be errors in the estimates.

[9] In making these estimates, government-operated enterprises, such as government communications and the national railroads, were classified among the high-concentration industries and not included in the unclassifiable "government" portion of the national income. It should also be noted that the estimates do not allow for the effect on the market occupancy of any of the top four firms belonging to a *zaibatsu* group which may co-ordinate its operations with affiliates of the same *zaibatsu* in the industry (cf. below, p. 269). A study of the market occupancy among the top ten firms in each of sixty-four industries in the F.T.C. concentration study, however, shows that even on the most liberal construction (that is, when all alleged *zaibatsu* groups are considered, when the broadest construction is placed on membership in each, and affiliation is assumed to mean co-ordinated operation) the average percentage-point rise in concentration ratios would be 3, with over 50 per cent of the industries showing no change and, on the other extreme, thirteen industries showing changes ranging from 7 to 32 percentage points. In all, three industries among the sixty-four would be added to the high-concentration group. The findings, further, do not allow for the effects of international trade. A study of manufacturing (the area of greatest importance here) indi-

[7] See, for example, *Gendai nippon no dokusen shihon* ("Monopoly Capital in Present-Day Japan") by the Monopoly Capital Study Group (Tokyo: Nippon Hyoron Shinsha, 1958).

ECONOMIC CONCENTRATION AND MONOPOLY IN JAPAN   265

the prewar period, concentration ratios for the top three firms are available for thirty-five major manufacturing industries for the year 1937. The ratios for these same industries are also available for 1950; and a comparison reveals a decline in concentration over the indicated period. Of the thirty-five industries twenty-three showed a decrease in concentration, eleven showed an increase, and in one case there was no change. The unweighted average concentration for the top three firms in these thirty-five industries was 67 per cent in 1937 and 59 per cent in 1950. Moreover, the decreases in concentration were most common in the high-concentration industries. More particularly, among the industries in which the top three firms produced at least 50 per cent of the industry output in 1937 (which totaled twenty-four), nineteen showed a decrease in concentration over the period, with the unweighted average concentration ratio for this group declining from 80 to 67 per cent.

A general pattern similar to the change which occurred over the prewar-postwar period is likewise found within the postwar period itself—specifically for 1950–55, a period which covers the Japanese economic recovery and a substantial measure of economic growth. Here for a sample of sixty-four major industries in manufacturing, forty industries show a decline in concentration, twenty show an increase, and four show no change. The unweighted average concentration ratio for the sample was 64 per cent in 1950 and 61 per cent in 1955. In the high-concentration group (that is, where the top four firms had at least 50 per cent of industry output in 1950) there was a decline in average concentration from 77 to 73 per cent, with twenty-nine of forty-four such high-concentration industries showing a decline, eleven showing an increase, and four showing no change.

The decline in manufacturing concentration from the prewar to the postwar period, as indicated in the sample,[10] is most probably attributable to the economic dislocation resulting from Japan's defeat and to a lesser extent to the effects of the deconcentration program of the Occupation in the immediate postwar period. The downward trend from 1950 to 1955 is probably due principally to the impact of the very rapid economic growth which Japan experienced over the period.

III. THE "ZAIBATSU"

The revival of the *zaibatsu* in Japan is not a surprising development. The origi-

---

cates that the effects would be relatively small. In over half of ninety Census manufacturing industries (covering all manufacturing) imports would reduce the concentration ratios by 2 per cent or less, in over two-thirds they would reduce the ratios by 5 per cent or less, and in only seven cases would they reduce the ratios by more than 25 per cent. In only two cases where concentration ratios are available would the adjustment remove an industry from the high-concentration class. The removal of exports would increase the high-concentration component in manufacturing from 34.6 to 36 per cent (assuming that the removal of exports would not alter the domestic concentration ratios in each industry). Data on international transactions were secured from the Ministry of Finance report on *The Annual Returns of the Foreign Trade of Japan*, 1956. It should be noted that these adjustments cover only the directly measurable effects of international trade. The threat of a further expansion of imports (should domestic prices be raised) may also check the exercise of monopoly power; and, where an industry is heavily dependent on export markets, the competition abroad may compel improvements in efficiency, which would yield benefits to domestic consumers.

[10] Since they constitute a majority of the cases, the sample is most representative of the trend in the high-concentration industries. The coverage of these cases is especially good in the sixty-four-industry sample for the 1950–55 period, while the twenty-four high-concentration industries in the prewar-postwar comparison represent a significant proportion of the thirty-nine industries on the 1950 Fair Trade Commission list in which the top three firms produced 50 per cent or more of the industry output.

266   EUGENE ROTWEIN

nal, or prewar, *zaibatsu* flourished on the Japanese scene because Japan was peculiarly congenial to their growth. The Japan "opened" by Perry was a feudal society. Determined to foster economic growth as rapidly as possible, Japan faced a severe obstacle in the form of a shortage of capital and resources. Under conditions of such pronounced scarcity of economic opportunity, individualism could hardly replace the collectivist spirit of feudal Japan. An extremely diligent people accustomed to group discipline, the energies of the Japanese, however, could readily be channeled into industrial and commercial activity through the *zaibatsu* organizations—themselves representing a congeries of "private collectivisms" which were to become the modern industrial counterpart of the feudal clans.[11] Postwar Japan did not see the disappearance of the conditions which originally spawned the *zaibatsu*, and under the circumstances a reversion to older and traditional forms of doing business—with the careful guarding of scarce economic opportunity for the members of the group—was to be expected.

The present-day or "new *zaibatsu*," like their prewar counterparts, cover a wide range of activities which reflect horizontal relations between firms (that is, there may be more than one affiliate in the same industry), vertical integration, and a conglomerate pattern. Firms belonging (or alleged to belong) to the Mitsui group, for example, are strong in shipbuilding, coal mining, copper, rayon yarn, rayon staple fiber, synthetic fibers,

fertilizer, caustic soda, polyvinyl chloride, banking, fire insurance, life insurance, shipping, foreign trade, and real estate; and, though less strongly, are also found in industries producing pig iron, cameras, soy sauce, and aluminum, among a variety of other products.

Owing to the dissolution of control by the old families, the contemporary *zaibatsu* are not organized along the holding-company lines of their predecessors. More loosely knit, the equity interests of the corporate affiliates of each *zaibatsu* are now joined through intercorporate stockholding. With the holding of stock now widely diffused among a large number of shareholders, moreover, there is no evidence of domination by any single stockholder or stockholding group. Available studies indicate, rather, that, by and large (as in the case of many American corporations), the firms affiliated with each *zaibatsu* are "management-directed."[12]

Apart from the development of intercorporate stockholding relations,[13] the regrouping of the *zaibatsu* in the postwar period is perhaps most conspicuously reflected in the role played by the bank affiliated with each *zaibatsu* group, which gives preference to operating af-

---

[11] This is not to belittle the contribution of small-scale industry to Japanese economic growth, which was important. Cf. William W. Lockwood, *The Economic Development of Japan* (Princeton, N.J.: Princeton University Press, 1954), p. 574. Lockwood generally stresses the importance of the small firm in Japan.

[12] See H. Misonou, "Kabushiki shoyu no keitai to kigyo shihai—nihon Big Business ron note" ("Forms of Stockholding and the Control of Firms—a Note on Big Business in Japan"), in *Kosei Torihiki*, April, 1959, pp. 2–11, esp. p. 10.

[13] In September, 1954, 9.8 per cent of the stock of seventeen major Mitsui companies was owned by other Mitsui affiliates. The equivalent figures for Mitsubishi (twenty-two companies) and Sumitomo (thirteen companies) were 20.5 per cent and 19.4 per cent. By September, 1958, such holdings had risen to 12.2 per cent for Mitsui, 23.5 per cent for Mitsubishi, and 24 per cent for Sumitomo. The ranges of holdings are quite large. In September, 1958, for example, for Mitsui they ran from 3 to 30 per cent, for Mitsubishi from 7 to 90 per cent, and for Sumitomo from 11 to 48 per cent (cf. *Oriental Economist*, XXVII [1959], 66–67, 358–59, 413).

ECONOMIC CONCENTRATION AND MONOPOLY IN JAPAN 267

filiates in the granting of loans and which has been increasingly taking over the unifying function performed by the parent holding company of the earlier *zaibatsu* organizations.[14] An independent investigation conducted for purposes of this study, moreover, bears out the allegation that firms affiliated with the top three *zaibatsu*—Mitsui, Mitsubishi, and Sumitomo—tend to make their purchases from other firms affiliated with

groups mentioned above have been selected for special examination. It should be noted at the outset that, however "importance" is conceived, it would be hazardous to give a single measure of this. Intercorporate stockholding alone (information on which is far from complete) does not suffice as a criterion for judgment. The extent to which any firm's stock is held by others alleged to be in the same group varies widely, and

TABLE 1

BUYING AND SELLING ACTIVITIES OF FIRMS AFFILIATED
WITH THE TOP THREE "ZAIBATSU"*

I. "ZAIBATSU" AFFILIATES	II. AFFILIATION OF FIRMS LISTED AS PRINCIPAL BUYERS BY FIRMS IN COLUMN I				III. AFFILIATION OF FIRMS LISTED AS PRINCIPAL SUPPLIERS BY FIRMS IN COLUMN I			
	Mitsui	Mitsu-bishi	Sumi-tomo	Other or None	Mitsui	Mitsu-bishi	Sumi-tomo	Other or None
35 Mitsui firms............	65	16	16	191	76	12	16	196
31 Mitsubishi firms........	9	39	10	145	18	60	9	149
25 Sumitomo firms........	16	12	31	138	25	19	43	130

* *Zaibatsu* affiliates are identified on the basis of Group III, or the broadest category of affiliates. See text below, page 268, for the explanation of the different *zaibatsu* groupings. If Group I or II is used as a basis for identifying *zaibatsu* affiliates, the pattern given in the table above remains essentially unchanged.

Source: Statements of corporations submitted to the Ministry of Finance, which contain a special section dealing with "principal buyers" and "principal sources of supply." These were taken from "Daigaisha Kan no Kinyu Hyo" ("Table of Financial Interrelations of Largest Corporations"), prepared in mimeographed form by Research Section, Nikko Securities Company, Tokyo, 1959.

the group, although at the same time it also makes clear that each *zaibatsu* is still heavily dependent on firms outside its own group (Table 1). If *zaibatsu* affiliates provide for each other's needs, the *zaibatsu* are far from self-sufficient economic empires.

How important are the *zaibatsu* in the Japanese economy? For purposes of appraising this the three major *zaibatsu*

[14] The heavy dependence of *zaibatsu* affiliates on the *zaibatsu* bank is shown in studies by the *Oriental Economist*, ibid., pp. 123, 353, 463. Of the three banks, the influence of the Mitsui Bank is weakest. With smaller resources than the Mitsubishi Bank, it seeks to provide credit to a large number of firms. For this reason and also because the spirit of autonomy is stronger among its affiliates, Mitsui—despite its widespread interests—is not considered to be as well organized as the other top two *zaibatsu*.

any breakoff point would at best be somewhat arbitrary. Moreover, the relations between the firms are affected by a variety of other factors—for example, participation or non-participation in the meetings of the presidents of the firms (which is limited to a relatively small number of major firms in each group), the closeness of the relationship of the firms to the *zaibatsu* bank, the extent to which management, through interlocking directorates, is shared among the firms, the degree to which firms collaborate in launching a new enterprise (such as, most recently, in the fields of atomic energy and petrochemicals), the importance of traditional ties, and the nature of the relations between the products of the firms, that is, whether horizontal or vertical or a looser conglomerate pattern.

Since we have a "spectrum" rather than cases which uniformly provide us with clear demarcations, it seems best—in order to avoid the suggestion of "precision"—to give a threefold classification depending on the degree of closeness of the relations between the firms which have been alleged in various studies to be members of a given *zaibatsu*. The firms which have been included in Group I estimates are those which, by common agreement, appear to be at or very close to the core of each of the *zaibatsu* organizations. They would generally be regarded as the "principal" or "major" firms in the organizations. Group II includes, in addition to Group I, firms about whose membership in the *zaibatsu* there would be only relatively limited disagreement. Group III includes, in addition to I and II, firms about whose affiliation there would be considerable disagreement. Many on the Group III list would be regarded by some as having only a "weak" or "uncertain" relationship to the *zaibatsu* group based, at most, on continuing or regular relations with a given *zaibatsu* bank.[15]

[15] The Group III list of firms in the top three *zaibatsu* was secured from *Monopoly Capital in Present Day Japan*, pp. 132–43. The perspective of the study is clearly Marxist, and the list is the most inclusive that I have been able to find. It is stated in this study that, considering all the minor and more remote affiliates, the total number of *zaibatsu* firms is far larger than the number listed. But the study bases its own estimates of the importance of the *zaibatsu*—in terms of capital controlled and ranking in different markets—only on the list of the firms given. Presumably it is believed that the general impact of the *zaibatsu* is not substantially understated by the use of this list. The Group I firms have been selected from this list on the basis of the data on the *zaibatsu* in the *Nenji Hokoku* ("Annual Report") of the Fair Trade Commission for 1957 (Tokyo, 1958), pp. 142–43. This list is limited to "major" affiliates. The additional firms for Group II

Using this classification, we may consider, first, the general financial importance of the top three *zaibatsu* in the Japanese economy—specifically as reflected in the percentage of total paid-in capital and total profit of all Japanese corporations accounted for by these *zaibatsu* in 1957. For Group I the percentages are, respectively, 7.4 per cent and 7.5 per cent. For Group II they are 11.7 per cent and 11.1 per cent. And if we employ the most inclusive or Group III category as the basis for the estimate, the percentages grow quite considerably to 17.3 per cent and 17.4 per cent, respectively.[16]

Second, what is the position of the

were chosen from the remainder on the basis of evaluations by Japanese who have made studies of the *zaibatsu* organizations, including Mitsubishi Economic Research Institute. For purposes of ascertaining their own perspective, high officials in the *zaibatsu* organizations were also consulted.

[16] The paid-in capital and profit figures were aggregated from data for each of the firms which were secured from the *Kaisha nenkan* ("Company Yearbook") for 1957 (published by *Nihon Keizai Shinbunsha*), and the totals for all Japanese corporations for this year were provided by Mitsubishi Economic Research Institute. Identification of *zaibatsu* affiliates was made in 1960. There are other groups of firms that have been alleged to constitute *zaibatsu* organizations. These are, principally, the Fuji and Daiichi groups, which are themselves made up mainly of subgroups. Fuji's subgroups are Yasuda, Asano, Mori, and Nissan. Daiichi's are Shibusawa, Furukawa, Kawasaki, Fujiyama, Suzuki-Shoten, and Meiji. Considering all their alleged affiliates as actual affiliates, Fuji and Daiichi each accounted for 5.8 per cent of total corporate paid-in capital in 1957. Were they in all major ways similar to Mitsui, Mitsubishi, and Sumitomo, they would likewise have to be considered as important *zaibatsu*. But although most of the subgroups were regarded as *zaibatsu* before the war, the extent of cohesion within and among them is, at least for the postwar period, generally more questionable than in the case of the other organizations. Caution dictates against grouping them with the latter. A list of all alleged affiliates of Fuji and Daiichi is given in *Monopoly Capital in Present Day Japan*, pp. 141–43, where it is recognized that it is doubtful whether these can be called *zaibatsu* (p. 126).

ECONOMIC CONCENTRATION AND MONOPOLY IN JAPAN   269

zaibatsu in the various markets in which they operate? For purposes of gauging this the 1955 findings of the Fair Trade Commission concentration study of sixty-four major manufacturing industries have been used.[17] This, it should be noted, is heavily weighted with high-concentration industries.

Table 2 indicates the number of first-, second-, and third-ranking firms in such industries which were affiliated with the top three *zaibatsu*. The classification of firms according to "group" is again

policies of the different affiliates are coordinated (and the extent to which this is true is not known), the market power of each *zaibatsu* would be indicated by the combined occupancies of its affiliates in each industry. The resulting occupancies, when the affiliates among the top ten firms in each industry are combined, are given in Table 3. Of the three *zaibatsu*, Mitsui is clearly the most important from this point of view (as it is on an individual firm basis—as indicated in Table 2). Using Group II estimates,

TABLE 2

INDUSTRY RANK OF INDIVIDUAL FIRMS AFFILIATED WITH THE TOP THREE "ZAIBATSU"
CLASSIFIED ACCORDING TO GROUP (SAMPLE OF 64 MAJOR INDUSTRIES, 1955)

	GROUP I: No. OF INDUSTRIES WITH A FIRM OF:			GROUP II: No. OF INDUSTRIES WITH A FIRM OF:			GROUP III: No. OF INDUSTRIES WITH A FIRM OF:		
	1st Rank	2d Rank	3d Rank	1st Rank	2d Rank	3d Rank	1st Rank	2d Rank	3d Rank
Mitsui..........	3	1	2	10	7	8	11	9	11
Mitsubishi.......	3	4	2	4	5	3	4	6	4
Sumitomo........	1	4	3	1	4	3	5	10	5
Total..........	7	9	7	15	16	14	20	25	20

Source: Market occupancies secured from data in Fair Trade Commission, *Saikin ni okern shuyō sangyō no seisanryoku no doko* ("Recent Trends in the Concentration of Production of Major Industries") (Tokyo, 1956).

given. If Group II is taken as the "proper" grouping, for example, then among the sixty-four industries the top three *zaibatsu* had first ranking firms in fifteen, or in about 25 per cent of such industries. It may be noted, too, that a relatively large percentage of the *zaibatsu* affiliates is high-ranking firms. On a Group II basis, forty-five of such firms (representing about 30 per cent of all Group II firms) were among the top three firms in the sixty-four-industry sample.

The above measures are based on the rankings of individual firms. In many cases one *zaibatsu* has more than one of its affiliates in the same industry. If the

the combined market occupancies of the Mitsui affiliates place it among the top three in the industry in almost one-third of the cases and among the top ten in more than one-half of the cases. Most of the market occupancies, however, are not overwhelming. As is shown in Table 4, in the bulk of the cases they are under 25 per cent. On a Group II basis, for example, Mitsui had market occupancies over 25 per cent in nine industries, Mitsubishi in three, and Sumitomo in one. Among the market occupancies under 25 per cent the average is 10 per cent with only eight cases in which the occupancy exceeded 20 per cent. Although in 1957 the *zaibatsu* had a relatively large number of high-ranking

[17] *Op. cit.*

TABLE 3

Industry Rank of Each of the Top Three "Zaibatsu," Combining Market Occupancies of Affiliates among the Top Ten in the Industry, Classified According to Group (Sample of 64 Major Industries, 1955)

	Group I: No. of Industries in Which Rank Is among the:			Group II: No. of Industries in Which Rank Is among the:			Group III: No. of Industries in Which Rank Is among the:		
	Top 3	Top 5	Top 10	Top 3	Top 5	Top 10	Top 3	Top 5	Top 10
Mitsui.........	6	9	12	20	28	35	26	30	37
Mitsubishi......	9	17	21	12	22	29	15	24	30
Sumitomo.......	7	9	12	7	9	13	19	26	36

Source: Market occupancies computed from data in Fair Trade Commission, *Saikin ni okern shuyō sangyō no seisanryoku no doko* ("Recent Trends in the Concentration of Production of Major Industries") (Tokyo, 1956).

TABLE 4

Distribution of Market Occupancies of the Top Three "Zaibatsu," Combining Market Occupancies of Affiliates among the Top Ten in the Industry, Classified According to Group (Sample of 64 Major Industries, 1955)

	No. of Industries in Which Market Occupancy Is:			Average Market Occupancy* (Per Cent)
	Under 25 Per Cent	25–50 Per Cent	Over 50 Per Cent	
	Group I			
Mitsui..............	11	1	0	12
Mitsubishi...........	20	1	1	12
Sumitomo...........	11	1	0	14
All 3 combined.......	21	5	2	21
	Group II			
Mitsui..............	26	8	1	18
Mitsubishi...........	26	2	1	12
Sumitomo...........	13	1	0	12
All 3 combined.......	25	14	5	27
	Group III			
Mitsui..............	24	12	1	21
Mitsubishi...........	28	3	1	13
Sumitomo...........	31	4	2	15
All 3 combined.......	24	17	10	34

* The averages are only for those industries in which the *zaibatsu* have affiliates among the top ten in the industry.

Source: Market occupancies computed from data in Fair Trade Commission, *Saikin ni okern shuyō sangyo no seisanryoku no doko* ("Recent Trends in the Concentration of Production of Major Industries") (Tokyo, 1956).

ECONOMIC CONCENTRATION AND MONOPOLY IN JAPAN   271

firms, in most cases the market control of each *zaibatsu* (even when the top-ranking affiliates are combined) fell short of the levels usually considered necessary for the exercise of a substantial degree of monopoly power.[18]

The question arises as to the control exercised by all three *zaibatsu* combined. The market occupancies for all three are of course considerably higher, as is indicated in Table 4. Is there a basis for supposing, however, that the *zaibatsu* act in concert or that their combined market occupancies are in fact significant? A priori, there is some ground for arguing that this may be the case. Insofar as the *zaibatsu* function as co-ordinating organizations for their own affiliates, they may also facilitate communication and negotiation with the affiliates of the other *zaibatsu* in the many markets in which the different *zaibatsu* operate in common. A further basis for the supposition that the *zaibatsu* are likely to engage in some form of collusion has been found in the different positions of *zaibatsu* firms in their common markets. More specifically, it has been argued—in the treatment of the prewar *zaibatsu*—that a *zaibatsu* firm which was in a strong enough position to price independently and in a manner which undercut affiliates of other and weaker *zaibatsu* in the industry would be reluctant to do so because in other industries the affiliates of other *zaibatsu* would be in a strong enough position to undercut them. Owing to this special complex of inter-

relations, a recognition of a general community of interest among the various *zaibatsu* would emerge, and they would act on a reciprocity or "live and let live" basis in their common markets.[19]

In appraising this view for the postwar situation it is well to note that, although the combined market occupancies of the top three *zaibatsu* are frequently high, there are many industries in which they occupy a distinctly subordinate position—so that their contribution to the adoption of some form of collusive action would vary considerably from case to case. For example, as Table 4 shows, there are twenty-four industries (on a Group III basis) in which the top three *zaibatsu* have less than 25 per cent of the market. Among these there are fifteen industries in which the market occupancy is less than 15 per cent.[20] Also the view under consideration presupposes a substantial unification of interest and action within each *zaibatsu*. A *zaibatsu* firm in Industry A will not be concerned with the effects of its price behavior on the position of an affiliate in Industry B unless there is a higher group interest which transcends the interests of the firm itself. The group interest was important in the prewar *zaibatsu*—though even here there is some difference of opinion concerning its significance.[21] It is con-

---

[18] While no single dividing line can be given, a market occupancy somewhere in the neighborhood of 20 per cent would, I believe, generally be regarded as necessary for the exercise of a substantial degree of monopoly power (cf. G. J. Stigler, "Mergers and Preventive Antitrust Policy," *University of Pennsylvania Law Review* [1955], p. 182; and Carl Kaysen and D. F. Turner, *Antitrust Policy* [Cambridge, Mass.: Harvard University Press, 1959], p. 99).

[19] This is Miss Hadley's view (cf. *op. cit.*, pp. 13–14). Though she does not give it primary emphasis in arguing her general position, as additional evidence for her view Miss Hadley cites some cases of intercorporate stockholding among different *zaibatsu* firms in the same industry (cf. pp. 17–20, 22–23).

[20] If the questionable cases of Fuji and Daiichi are included among the *zaibatsu*, in many cases the market occupancies would be significantly raised.

[21] See, for example, Lockwood, *op. cit.*, p. 229. Lockwood states: "Operating within a clanlike hierarchy of loyalties [*zaibatsu* firms] nevertheless had strong personal and professional incentives to carry on their individual responsibilities with a large measure of autonomy."

272   EUGENE ROTWEIN

siderably more doubtful whether, generally speaking, the requisite degree of unification is to be found among their looser knit contemporary counterparts.

It is not uncommon to find the prewar *zaibatsu* treated as rivals.[22] This view may be largely impressionistic. But for the postwar period there is evidence, based on profit data, which does not indicate the implementation of a special community of interest among the *zaibatsu* (emerging either from a reciprocity relationship or from frequent consultation among *zaibatsu* co-ordinating agencies). A study of the rate of return on investment (before taxes) of ninety manufacturing affiliates of the top three *zaibatsu* in industries in which there is more than one *zaibatsu* (among the top ten firms in the industry) shows that, on the average, the rate of return in 1957 was 13 per cent. The average rate of return for 291 manufacturing firms not affiliated with any of these *zaibatsu* was 13.1 per cent.[23]

While the evidence does not afford grounds for identifying "zaibatsuism" in general with monopoly, it would be incorrect to conclude that, dynamically speaking, there is no functional relation between the existence of the *zaibatsu* system and monopoly power. *Zaibatsu* firms have better access to credit than other firms and, insofar as the affiliates of each tend to do business with one another, they have greater market security. Even though the *zaibatsu* do not show conspicuously high profit rates, their special advantages may contribute to their survival power—particularly in periods of depression; and, through special support given affiliates or the discouragement of entry by outsiders, they may contribute to the perpetuation or growth of monopoly over time.

IV. CARTELS

In prewar Japan, as pointed out, cartels were legal, and insofar as the state intervened it did so with a view to encouraging their growth.[24] The antimonopoly law introduced by the American Occupation after the war sought to prohibit cartels. In the early 1950's, however, demands to permit their formation in various industries began to appear and, since then, a variety of exemptions from the law has been permitted. To mention the major exemptions, the Fair Trade Commission is empowered by law to allow the formation of "depression" and "rationalization" cartels.[25] As its designation indicates, the former is

---

[22] See in addition to Allen's view that of Lockwood, *op. cit.*, pp. 229–32. Though she states that *zaibatsu* behavior cannot be regarded as "competitive," Miss Hadley herself asserts: "Rivalry could certainly be said to have existed among Japan's great combines" (*op. cit.*, p. 26).

[23] These averages were computed from data in *Honpō jigyō seiseki bunseki* ("Analysis of Business Performance in Japan") (Tokyo: Mitsubishi Economic Research Institute, 1957). The ninety *zaibatsu* firms are identified on a Group III basis. A breakdown shows that the Group I and II averages are 12.5 per cent and 12 per cent, respectively. Among the 291 firms not affiliated with the *zaibatsu* many are in industries in which there is more than one *zaibatsu* among the top ten in the industry. Although according to the hypothesis under consideration one would expect the profit figures to reflect a special *zaibatsu* community of interest, it may be argued that collusion among them would benefit the entire industry and so raise the profit rate for the non-*zaibatsu* firms in the industry as well. If we remove these latter firms from the list of 291 non-*zaibatsu* firms, the average profit rate for the remainder (eighty firms in twenty-one industries) is only 1 per cent lower than the rate for the Group III firms in the top three *zaibatsu*. The profit rates should not be

compared with those for U.S. corporations, since—unlike the United States—Japan has permitted asset write-ups to allow for the postwar inflation.

[24] See Lockwood, *op. cit.*, pp. 567 ff.

[25] See Restrictive Trade Practices Specialists Study Team, "Control of Restrictive Trade Practices in Japan" (Tokyo: Japan Productivity Center, 1958), p. 10. (Mimeographed.)

avowedly designed to permit industries to control price and output to check depression or recession reverses. In the latter, the avowed objectives take a variety of forms, such as the improvement of technology and the standardization of products, although it may be presumed that in effect this would often provide legal sanction for the control of output and prices. Cartels for various smaller enterprises are also permitted under the Smaller Enterprise Organization Law and, in foreign trade, under the Export-Import Transactions Law. Beyond this, with the downturn of economic activity in the latter part of 1957 the Ministry of International Trade and Industry—in open circumvention of the anti-monopoly law and without special statutory authority—began to sponsor cartels in many major industries on its own.

Among the most general categories of cartels listed in a major cartel survey by the Fair Trade Commission in 1958 and 1959, there appear 5 depression cartels, 4 rationalization cartels, 150 export-import cartels (30 empowered to control production, 51 authorized to control price, and 34 with power to control production and price), 57 national Smaller Enterprise Organization cartels (the bulk of which, with many regional subdivisions, is empowered to control the use of equipment, production, shipments or price), and 34 cartels organized under the direct sponsorship of the Ministry of International Trade and Industry.[26]

In view of the sketchy character of the available data, no precise estimate of the importance of cartels in Japan can be given. On the basis of such data as are available, however, it appears safe to

[26] See *Annual Report* of the Fair Trade Commission (1958), pp. 115–53, and *Shuyo kartel gaikatsuhyo* ("List of Major Cartels") published by the Fair Trade Commission in 1959.

say that, apart from the effects of any special regulations in the foreign trade sector, the areas of private manufacturing industry in which the government itself formally has the power to control or "approve" minimum or maximum prices constituted a small proportion (approximately 3 per cent) of the Japanese national income in the late 1950's.[27] For the remainder of the private sector of the economy (excluding the regulated utilities), the equivalent figure would be in the neighborhood of 5–6 per cent of the national income, with the bulk of this representing price regulation in agriculture.[28] It should be borne in mind that in addition to excluding the foreign trade

[27] This estimate is based on the classification of industries under price regulation (of various types) in "Wagakuni ni okeru kakaku kisei ichiranhyo" ("Table of Price Regulation in Our Country") and Wagakuni ni okeru kakaku kisei no genjo" ("The Present State of Price Regulation in Our Country"), both mimeographed reports prepared by the Research Section of the Enterprise Bureau of the Ministry of International Trade and Industry (October, 1959). Value-added data for each manufacturing cartel, which were converted to national income estimates, were secured from the *Census of Manufactures*. The industries identified as under the type of cartel regulation indicated include salt, sake, camphor, alcohol, sulfuric nitrates, silk yarn, cotton and spun rayon fabrics, woolen fabrics, flax and ramie fabrics, circular knitting, tires and tubes for bicycles, binoculars, plywood, soft drinks, matches, bamboo shades, canned oranges, and leather cases for binoculars. In the latter three cases value-added data were unavailable, but these should not change the estimate significantly.

[28] The agricultural commodities include: leaf tobacco, wheat, barley, potatoes, raw silk, and one-half the rice output. In addition, among major items, roughly 50 per cent of the rents were under control in 1958. Income originating for the latter was estimated on the basis of "private rental income" as given in the *National Income White Paper* of the Economic Planning Agency, and, since it includes imputed rent, 50 per cent of the total overestimates the rental income under control. Income originating in the agricultural areas mentioned was computed from data in *Statistical Yearbook*, published by the Ministry of Agriculture and Forestry. Though rye is listed as under control, it does not appear in the *Yearbook*.

274 EUGENE ROTWEIN

area, this does not include the cartels in which the government has no legal power to control or approve prices.

In the light of the reappearance of cartels in the postwar period, the question of their effectiveness (especially those of a non-compulsory nature) is important in evaluating the prevalence of monopoly power in Japan. Apart from the unavailability of much pertinent data, this, however, poses an intrinsically difficult problem. On the basis of price-output or profit movements only (which is usually all the information that is available to the outside observer as a basis for judgment), cartel effectiveness can only

be judged through a comparison of such movements with those that might be presumed to have materialized in the absence of the cartel; and, with the exception of those cases which are at the polar extremes of the spectrum of "effectiveness," an analysis of this question is likely to prove inconclusive.

Some light can be thrown on the question, however, by a study of seventeen depression cartels—two under the authority of the Fair Trade Commission and the remainder sponsored by the Ministry of International Trade and Industry. For this group there are announced production curtailment "orders"

TABLE 5

"ORDERED" REDUCTIONS IN PRODUCTION AND ACTUAL
PRODUCTION CHANGES—17 JAPANESE CARTELS*

Cartel	Period of Cartel	"Ordered" Reduction in Monthly Output as a Percentage of Monthly Output in Base Period†	Actual Change in Monthly Output during Cartel Period as a Percentage of Monthly Output in Base Period
Celluloid sheets.........	12/58–12/59	20	− 2
Polyvinyl chloride......	10/57– 9/58	20	−28
Calcium superphosphate.	1/58– 7/58‡	15	− 3
Pulp...................	1/58– 9/58	37.5	− 4
Combed wool yarn......	12/57– 3/59	28	−28
Rayon yarn............	4/57– 3/59	43	−35
Cotton yarn...........	4/58– 3/59	20–30§	−25
Carbide...............	4/58– 3/59	Production to be kept at same level	− 3
Calcium cyanamide.....	8/58– 7/59	2	−15
Methanol	9/58–12/58	5	+12
Formaline.............	9/58–12/58	4	+16
Coal..................	6/58–12/58	5	− 2
Steel thick plate........	3/58– 6/59	33	−25
Shaped steel...........	3/58– 6/59	59	−18
Wire material..........	6/58– 6/59	40	+11
Steel thin plate........	10/58– 6/59	3	−20
Lead.................	4/58–12/58	40	+ 3

* The first two cartels listed are Fair Trade Commission "depression cartels." The remainder were sponsored by the Ministry of International Trade and Industry.

† The base periods are several months up to a year in the year preceding the cartel.

‡ The cartel continued until July, 1959, but for this additional period the restriction is stated in terms of the use of machinery. During this period monthly production did not decline, however.

§ The restriction is not stated in a fashion which makes it possible to give a single figure for the ordered cut in production.

Source: production figures: *Tsusan Tokei Geppo* ("Monthly Statistical Report"), published by the Ministry of International Trade and Industry; production orders: *Shuyo Kartel Gaikatsuhyo* ("List of Major Cartels"), published by the Fair Trade Commission.

(although the cartels are non-compulsory); and, assuming that these "orders" or production curtailment targets are meaningful, an indication of the effectiveness of the cartels can be gained by comparing the targets with actual production movements during the cartel period.[29] The findings are given in Table 5.

The pattern, as is apparent, is mixed. In most cases production declined and in several instances the cartels appear to have been strikingly successful. However, in eleven cases the production cuts did not meet the ordered cuts, and in eight of these cases production either fell substantially short of the target curtailment or actually increased.

The legal life of those cartels considered was relatively short; and perhaps with legal sanction over a longer period their effectiveness would have grown. On the other hand, in several instances in which available concentration ratios indicate that the industries are oligopolistic or at least not atomistic—and where one might expect to find comparatively effective cartel restriction—the response to the production curtailment orders was at best poor.[30] In view of the paucity of data, it is difficult to generalize. But, insofar as generalization is warranted, the record would indicate that—notwithstanding the apparent success in particular cases—the growth of cartels in Japan should not be equated with a widespread growth of highly restrictive practices. This conclusion would hold a fortiori with respect to the large number of legally sanctioned cartels in

[29] The selection of the cartels was dictated by the availability of data both on production curtailment orders and actual production.

[30] For example, the 1955 concentration ratios (top four firms) for celluloid sheets, calcium superphosphate and pulp were respectively 75, 53, and 34 per cent (top eight firms for pulp, 54 per cent).

industries which are atomistic, such as those introduced under the Smaller Enterprise Organization Law.

V. CONCLUSION

This study has dealt with three major aspects of industrial organization in Japan. What do the findings suggest? In the main they indicate that, while it is inappropriate to characterize the Japanese economy as "competitive" (and such simple characterizations would generally be suspect), studies which stress the importance of concentration in the prewar Japanese economy do not afford an adequate basis for judgment on the postwar economy, and in some major respects this is attributable to deficiencies in their treatment of the prewar economy.

The evidence, as seen, does not support the view that Japanese markets are generally highly concentrated. These findings cannot be compared directly with those of studies for the United States, owing to various differences in approach.[31] But

[31] The finding that 16.4 per cent of the Japanese national income is produced under "high-concentration" conditions compares most closely with Stigler's and Nutter's findings, respectively, of 24.4 per cent and 22.9 per cent for the proportion of U.S. national income produced under conditions of "monopoly" in 1939 (cf. George J. Stigler, *Five Lectures on Economic Problems* [London: Longmans, Green & Co., 1949], p. 50, and Warren Nutter, *The Extent of Enterprise Monopoly in the United States, 1899–1939* [Chicago: University of Chicago Press, 1951], p. 21). The differences between the latter two and the Japan study involve the definition of the "industry" and the standards used in classifying industries; and as between Japan and the United States there are probably differences in the importance of concentration in regional markets. Adjustments would also have to be made for international trade in the findings for the United States. It may be noted that the greater importance of agriculture in Japan (15 per cent of the national income as against 8 per cent for the United States) would tend to reduce the high concentration component in private industry as compared with that for the United States. In the area of manufacturing in particular, a study I made of forty-six matching (and mainly oligopolistic) industries for the late 1950's indicates a lower average

even with the incomparabilities removed it is unlikely, conservatively speaking, that the results would reveal a substantially higher level of concentration in Japan than in the United States. In Japan the over-all degree of concentration may indeed be lower.

The *zaibatsu*, of course, pose a special problem. Insofar as they preserve economic opportunities for members of the group, they interfere with economic freedom and can insulate themselves from the full impact of competition. Were collusion between them successfully implemented, they would be able to exert a substantial influence in various of the markets in which they operate in common. But if "zaibatsuism" is not market monopoly, there are also obstacles to an effective general inter-*zaibatsu* conspiracy; and market performance—insofar as it is reflected in profit rates—does not indicate such general conspiratorial action.

The evidence on cartels at a minimum serves as a reminder that the sanctioning of a voluntary cartel is a license to engage in restrictive practices which may be used with widely varying effectiveness. The record would appear to have its counterpart in the prewar Japanese experience when the cartels apparently

often encountered difficulties in achieving their objectives.[32] Even bearing in mind the successful cases, the postwar cartel record may in fact be less impressive than that of the prewar period.

Though the amendments to the Japanese anti-monopoly law and the weakening of the enforcement effort facilitate a spread of monopolistic practices, much in the future will depend on the rate of Japanese economic growth. A continued high growth rate is likely to keep individual markets in a relatively fluid state and intensify the rivalry among *zaibatsu* groups in their drive toward modernization of Japanese industry. A high growth rate will also feed the impulse toward independent action that weakens cartels —the demand for which has been largely a function of economic distress. Independence fed from this source may already be reflected in the apparent low levels of compliance in many of the major depression cartels, since Japan's postwar recessions have been relatively mild and short-lived and the cartels have not operated in a climate marked by a long habituation to the urgency of collective action.

During the postwar period the rate of Japanese economic growth has been extraordinary, and the benefits have been widespread. Between 1951 and 1961 (inclusive of both years) gross national product in constant prices rose by 119 per cent, with an average annual increase (over the preceding year) of almost 10 per cent.[33] In the same period per capita real monthly cash earnings of employees in all industry (excluding agriculture) rose

---

concentration in the United States than in Japan (top four firms: United States, 56 per cent; Japan, 63 per cent). Here the probable greater importance of regional concentration in the United States may be especially significant in interpreting the findings, though, notwithstanding this, concentration in Japanese manufacturing may well be higher. See Adelman's finding, based on a Department of Commerce study, that, in 1947, 24 per cent of American manufacturing income was produced in industries in which the top four firms produced 50 per cent or more of the industry output (M. A. Adelman, "The Measurement of Industrial Concentration," *Review of Economics and Statistics*, XXXIII [November, 1951], 291). The finding of the present study for Japan is 34.6 per cent—though again incomparabilities should be borne in mind.

[32] See Lockwood, *op. cit.*, pp. 230–31.

[33] Economic Planning Agency, *National Income Statistics* (Tokyo, 1960), pp. 178–79, and *Report on 1961 National Income* (Tokyo, 1962). (Mimeographed.)

ECONOMIC CONCENTRATION AND MONOPOLY IN JAPAN 277

by 61 per cent.[34] Since Japan lacks an antitrust tradition, prolonged economic reverses would more readily induce attempts at general restrictionism there than, say, in the United States. Moreover, in the foreseeable future it cannot be expected—owing both to Japanese tradition and a continuing scarcity of economic opportunity—that the *zaibatsu* will disappear. But if the partial effectiveness of Occupation policy did not leave Japan a prey to restrictive practices—unable to exploit opportunities for rapid and sustained expansion—further economic growth may prove to be an important route to a fuller realization of that policy.

[34] Bank of Japan, Statistical Department, *Historical Statistics of the Japanese Economy* (Tokyo, 1962), pp. 43–44.

[18]

JOURNAL OF COMPARATIVE ECONOMICS 2, 126–143 (1978)

The Case of Japan: Price Bargaining and Controls on Oil Products[1]

YOSHI TSURUMI

*Pacific Basin Economic Center, Graduate School of Management, University of California,
Los Angeles, California 90024*

Received March 27, 1978

Tsurumi, Yoshi—The Case of Japan: Price Bargaining and Controls on Oil
Products

This paper shows how the Japanese variant of indicative planning has dealt
with the oil crisis. Goals for leading export industries and for income distribution
have been promoted through "administered competition" (a key policy in the
strong economic growth of the 1960s) and pricing policies (including selective
controls). The "price-bargaining" mechanism (aided by sociopolitical forces)
has proved effective in oil products, even under floating exchange rates. One
noteworthy policy alteration is the encouragement of sales in Japan by large
foreign oil companies but under constraints that tie their interests more closely
to those of Japan. *J. Comp. Econ.*, June 1978, 2(2), pp. 126–143. University
of California at Los Angeles.

Journal of Economic Literature Classification Numbers: 051, 053, 723.

1. INTRODUCTION

Japan is among the nonsocialist industrialized nations that have developed some form of "indicative economic planning" (Komiya,
1975). In contrast to central planning, in which the national economy
can be viewed as a giant, all-embracing firm (Arrow and Hurwicz, 1963;
Spulber and Horowitz, 1976), under indicative planning the economy is
managed through a set of complex interactions between the private and
public sectors. Government and business consult with each other to
determine national economic goals. The government then announces the
goals publicly and sets about shaping an economic environment
conducive to their attainment. Firms are encouraged to compete for both
domestic and export markets, but within a government-policy frame-

[1] The author would like to thank an anonymous referee for helpful comments and
criticism.

work such that the competition will fulfill the national goals. For example, the government may provide firms in favored industries with import protection, special foreign exchange allotments, or subsidized investment capital financing.

While Japanese indicative planning conforms to the above general pattern, it differs from other cases in important specifics. In France, for example, the central vehicle for implementing national economic goals has been the government ownership of three large commercial banks and several key manufacturing firms (including Renault) (Lutz, 1969). In Japan, however, the government has relied on competition channeled through interdependent industrial structures to implement national goals (Y. Tsurumi, 1976a). It has not been widely recognized that government-administered market competition has contributed importantly to the rapid industrialization of Japan in the post-World War II era. Of particular interest here is the pivotal role in the growth of heavy industry (especially steel and chemicals) played by price bargaining between suppliers and users of oil products.

This paper examines how the oil-price bargaining process, having fallen into disuse in the early 1970s, has been revived in response to the sharp increase in oil prices since 1973. That process is now being used to pursue three different policy objectives: (1) the maintenance of Japanese exports in selected key industries; (2) the subsidization of lower and middle-income groups; and (3) the tying of Japanese national interests with those of the international oil companies, as a means of increasing the security of oil imports. The analysis of the revival and adaptation of oil-price bargaining in the new environment of higher oil prices yields useful insights into the response of the Japanese economic system to the "energy crisis."

2. THE EMERGENCE OF MONOPSONISTIC PRICE BARGAINING FOR OIL PRODUCTS IN THE 1950s

In the mid-1950s, Japanese policy makers decided to encourage the development of large-scale metallurgical and chemical industries as the foundation for long-term economic growth (Rapp, 1977; Y. Tsurumi, 1976a; Denison and Chung, 1977). While monetary policy was used to moderate short-term cyclical fluctuations, fiscal tools such as tax incentives for investment and the rationing of foreign exchange were used to favor the growth of selected industries. Thus long-term supply management was made an integral part of Japanese indicative economic planning. It would prove to be the key to her rapid industrial expansion.

The Japanese economy was then, as now, heavily reliant on foreign trade. The hope was that the metallurgical and chemical industries would supersede light industrial and consumer goods as the dominant export earners of foreign exchange. For those industries to become internationally competitive, however, high productivity and low raw-material costs were required. Energy-intensive production methods were therefore deemed desirable, but so were low costs of energy for industrial use.

In keeping with these objectives, previous policy was reversed toward the end of the 1950s to give imported oil preference over domestic hydroelectric power and coal (Patrick and Rosovsky, 1976, p. 800). In addition, industrial users were favored over consumers and energy producers. Assuming the downward trend in real crude-oil prices would continue in the long term, policy makers encouraged investment in oil-refining and oil-fired thermal-electric plants over other energy sources (*Sekiyu Gyokai*, 1966). A two-tier electricity-rate system, which charged significantly lower rates to industrial firms than to households, in effect taxed consumers to subsidize industry, while at the same time discouraging nonindustrial uses of electricity.

The prices of oil products were kept under control by structuring the oil-refining and marketing industry so that the spread between imported crude and processed oil prices would be kept at a minimum. A fragmented oil industry—the result of permitting free entry into both the refining and wholesaling of oil but deliberately keeping refining capacity out of balance with wholesaling capacity in order to impede vertical integration (Y. Tsurumi, 1976b)—was expected to compete vigorously and thus to be relatively weak in price bargaining with highly concentrated user industries. Because oil firms were politically too weak to influence planning policy, the deliberate creation of monopsonistic buyers of industrial oil products proved an effective mechanism for guaranteeing strategic growth industries access to cheap energy. A few large industrial buyers, most notably steel and petrochemicals, were able to drive hard bargains by playing one oil firm against the other.

3. "ADMINISTERED COMPETITION" AND INNOVATION DURING THE 1960s

From the 1950s to the early 1970s, technological innovations spurred Japan's industrial growth and the concomitant rise of her export strength in manufactured goods (Sato, 1977; Y. Tsurumi, 1972). Many of the innovations were new products, especially in electronics; however, the bulk of the technological innovations occurred in production processes, enabling metallurgical, chemical, and machinery products to be made faster, better, and more cheaply than before (Y. Tsurumi, 1976a, Chap. 7). One important stimulus to these innovations was the encouragement of firms to exploit economies of scale while at the same time the government was fostering competition in domestic markets through its policies. Even more important was pressure on the large firms to develop exports in direct competition with European and American firms.

The increases in the productivity of labor, raw materials, and energy that accompanied the innovations supported strong price competition not only in such basic industries as steel, nonferrous metals, and chemicals, but also in electrical machinery, shipbuilding, automobiles, and tele-communication equipment. In addition, keeping Japanese firms geared to winning export markets in competition with foreign prices and product quality sustained the pressure for technological innovations and added investments in modern production facilities. The price and quality consciousness of the large exporting firms was in turn transmitted throughout the Japanese industrial structure, in particular to the firms supplying inputs to the exporting industries.

Thus "administered market competition," with a pronounced export orientation, was the means by which Japanese indicative economic planning transmitted the discipline of international price and quality competition to Japanese manufacturing industries. It was government policy to foster concentration in the key metallurgical and chemical industries, in order to permit the realization of economies of scale. But the export orientation—which dates back to the late nineteenth century and is by now a strongly ingrained cultural trait of Japanese corporations (Y. Tsurumi, 1977a)—prevented the growing concentration from stifling technological innovations and price competition.

This model of "administered market competition" nowhere is more clearly seen than in the automobile and computer industries. In the 1960s, the government identified these two industries as the growth leaders of the future. Foreign investors were discouraged from entering the Japanese market in these industries, other than through technical licensing agreements with Japanese firms. The government was not certain, however, about which of the number of hopeful firms then groping their way forward would emerge as the best. It was decided to let market forces decide the issue—that is, to allow the aspirants to bear the full capital risks in their research-and-development and production facilities. Through market competition, the surviving firms learned to orient their efforts to market needs. Thus, while the Japanese government provided assistance and even protection to its computer and auto firms, it also imposed the discipline of market competition to foster habits that would serve the firms well in foreign markets (Kaplan, 1972; Y. Tsurumi, 1976a).[2,3]

[2] In contrast to French planning—widely regarded as the paradigm for indicative planning—under the Japanese variant the government pays serious attention to incorporat-

Throughout the 1960s, the administered market competition of key manufacturing firms was fostered by the low cost of imported oil. So long as both domestic and foreign demands continued to grow, and so long as the technological frontiers (for both new products and improved processes) continued to expand, the "survival of the fittest" policy under administered competition worked well. Japanese manufacturing firms found it more profitable to expand their market shares through price cutting and product innovations than to attempt to increase their prices through the covert or overt collusion that conventional oligopoly theory would suggest.

4. THE OIL CRISIS OF 1973 AND GOVERNMENT REGULATION OF OLIGOPOLY PRICES

The increase in world crude-oil prices that began in 1971 and 1972 came at the time that many formerly competitive large firms in the Japanese metallurgical and chemical industries were also rapidly increasing their prices. The same industrial giants that had competed vigorously through price cutting and product innovations during the 1960s were now abandoning this behavior. One reason was that, beginning in the late 1960s, the rates of technological innovation in the leading export industries slowed substantially: they now found it increasingly difficult to devise

---

ing growth stimuli into the market competition of private firms. See, for example, Y. Tsurumi (1976a, Chap. 1).

[3] The case of the computer industry is especially interesting. The Japanese government extended long-term, low-interest loans to a national leasing corporation, into which each of the aspirant firms paid an equal amount of equity capital. Although this leasing firm was legally owned jointly by the computer producers, in effect they had to compete with one another to sell computers. Naturally, the firms that had best met customers' needs ended up using the capital provided by the less successful firms for financing the leasing corporation. Thus, the weaker firms ended up subsidizing the subsequent growth of the stronger firms.

In course of time, a number of the less competitive computer and automobile manufacturers went out of business. Their production facilities were often acquired by the successful firms at bargain prices. The resulting concentration in these two industries, far from being opposed or discouraged as it might have been by, say, the United States government, was in fact welcomed by the Japanese government (Kaplan, 1972). The government might have liked even greater concentration than apparently occurred. However, in the case of the computer industry, when interfirm rivalry of six surviving firms prevented outright mergers and acquisitions, the government assisted the formation of three pairs of partners out of the six remaining contenders. By 1978, out of these *de facto* mergers, the Fujitsu group has emerged as the leading victor, leaving behind the NEC-Hitachi and Univac-Oki pairs. In the case of the automobile industry, after outright acquisition of the Fuji Auto Co. by Nissan, the remaining two weaker firms, Isuzu and Mitsubishi, were driven into the orbit of General Motors and Chrysler, respectively, thus ending their effective competition in the passenger-car market in Japan and mainly redefining Isuzu and Mitsubishi as American firms' captive sources of exports from Japan.

new products and better processes (H. Tsurumi, 1976; Y. Tsurumi, 1976a).
At the same time, Japan was witnessing the emergence of market structures in which a few large, mature firms raised prices in concert, perhaps with one firm acting as a price leader.[4] Whereas the Japanese
government had previously enforced its "administered price competition," now it permitted the price increases—ostensibly to strengthen
Japanese firms financially in anticipation of direct competition from
foreign multinational corporations.[5] Consequently, the increases in oil
prices, especially the sharp jump that occurred in 1973–1974, helped fuel
what by Japanese standards was hyperinflation of 30 to 40% per year, as
industrial users of oil pyramided their own price increases on top of higher
oil prices.

It is understandable, then, that one major political outcome of the
oil crisis of 1973–1974 was a surge of public sentiment against big
business. The resulting change in the political climate brought with it a
shift in government policy toward the leading growth firms. In particular,
the Japanese government acquired new legal weapons to regulate not only
industrial investment and output but also market structure, prices, and
(by implication) wages.

Popular opposition to rising prices led to the reemergence of an antitrust agency, the Fair Trade Commission (FTC), that had suffered a
political eclipse during the rapid growth of the 1950s and 1960s.[6] The FTC
capitalized on the oil crisis to obtain from the Diet greater power to regulate monopolistic practices and, more importantly, the wherewithal to
exercise the power. The rise of the FTC motivated its rival, the Ministry
of International Trade and Industry (MITI), to exploit the public mood and
secure broader powers to regulate prices, outputs, and investments in
manufacturing. In addition, MITI became more sensitive to popular pressure in its long-term supply management. In early 1974, MITI (sensitive also to criticisms of its probusiness stand) forced the petrochemical
and metals industries to rescind price increases that exceeded increased
oil and electric-power costs. MITI did, though, make certain that it had the
legal power to exempt certain industrial practices from FTC litigation.
It was clearly understood that the FTC's antimonopoly regulations

---

[4] See Caves and Uekusa (1976). On the behavior of mature oligopolies, see Vernon (1974).

[5] See, for example, Y. Tsurumi (1976b). From 1968 to 1970, this argument was
vigorously promoted by the government and the two large steel firms, Yawata and Fuji,
in order to combat public criticism of the contemplated merger between the two firms
(Economic Planning Agency, 1968). This rationale is open to question on both theoretical
and empirical grounds. To pursue the matter further, however, would be to digress too far
from the topic of the present paper.

[6] On the FTC prior to the oil crisis, see Hadley (1970). The reemergence of the FTC
during the crisis is examined in Y. Tsurumi (1976a).

had to avoid damaging either the growth potential or the export competitiveness of the leading industries.

In short, just as leading firms in Japan had begun to break out of the administered competition of the 1960s, both MITI and the FTC acquired new legal powers that enabled them to increase their control over those firms' decisions. Moreover, political rivalry between MITI and the FTC fueled a new commitment on MITI's part to serve "public" as well as corporate interests. Japanese industry was placed on notice that the government intended, whether directly or indirectly, to see that the past pattern of competition on price and new products was maintained.

5. SOCIOCULTURAL STABILIZERS IN THE JAPANESE ECONOMY

Two further elements of the Japanese response to the dislocations of the oil crisis lie in the sociocultural realm. These elements provided the social and political foundations upon which Japan, after the oil crisis, began to rebuild a national consensus on goals. The ability of Japan to find such foundations is in marked contrast to what has happened in some other advanced industrial nations, most notably the United States.

Following the oil crisis, the Japanese "tribal custom" of aligning the interests of private firms and households with the social good appeared in the form of an informal incomes policy. There has always been strong resistance in Japan to an explicit, official incomes policy. Nevertheless, a combination of potential price controls, corporate diplomacy (e.g., reduced dividends and executive salaries), and workers' concern for preserving traditional patterns of job security helped bring down the annual inflation rate from the 30 to 40% range of 1974 to less than 10% in both 1976 and 1977 (Y. Tsurumi, 1977b). Thus the crisis atmosphere and the combined threats of a prolonged recession and higher oil-import costs helped management and labor to close ranks around a realization that what is good for the nation must be good for each individual group.

The Japanese economy was also found to possess an automatic braking mechanism in the face of threatened hyperinflation. Contrary to the conventional wisdom that people save less and spend more in an inflationary economy, Japanese households materially increased their propensities to save following the oil crisis with its attendant uncertainties about the future (Sato, 1976). The increased saving by the public helped damp the inflationary forces then at work in the economy. Thus, sociocultural factors reinforced what Japanese indicative planners sought to do at that particular juncture.[7]

[7] Of course, an increased saving rate was a general phenomenon in the industrial countries during the past recession.

6. PRICE CHANGES FOR OIL PRODUCTS AFTER THE OIL CRISIS

The pattern of oil-product prices in Japan has undergone marked changes since the oil crisis of 1973–1974. Those changes have been complex and are still only imperfectly understood. It is possible, however, to offer at least a preliminary assessment of the causes and implications of the price changes.

MITI instituted price controls on petroleum products in 1973. Officially, those controls ended in June 1975, when MITI publicly relinquished control of kerosene prices. But in fact, there is evidence that government price controls (*de facto* or otherwise) have remained in effect. Moreover, the controls have been used in often intricate ways as instruments

TABLE 1

WHOLESALE AND FINAL USERS' PRICE INCREASES OF OIL PRODUCTS[a]

	Auto-mobile gasoline[b]	Naphtha	Jet fuel	Kerosene	Diesel[b]	Residual fuel oil
1972 Wholesale price per kl (in yen)	41,207	6,076	—	11,982	10,784	10,088
Wholesale price indexes (1972 = 100)						
1973	109	117	105	108	111	111
1974	173	305	172	169	218	219
1975	201	400	207	230	275	276
1976: May	205	458	240	230	298	298
August	225	458	240	270	298	298
December	224	458	240	270	297	296
1977: January	224	458	240	270	297	296
February	224	458	240	270	297	296
March	224	458	240	270	297	296
April	226	458	255	270	305	304
May	226	458	255	270	304	304
June	226	458	255	270	304	304
July	226	458	255	270	304	304
1977 yen price per kl	99,886	28,995	—	34,125	36,817	34,420
Users' price, July 1977 (1973 = 100)	450	391	250	250	294	274

[a] Computed from price indices published by the Bureau of Statistics, Bank of Japan, Tokyo.

[b] Does not include sales taxes.

of Japanese indicative planning under the system of floating exchange rates.

Table 1 summarizes the price movements of major oil products in Japan from 1972 to mid-1977. One can glean a number of observations from the table. *First*, the rate of (users') price increase for kerosene — widely used for household cooking and heating — has lagged behind the rates of increase for other oil products (except for jet fuel).[8] *Second*, the price of naphtha (an important petrochemical feedstock) increased faster than that of any other product between 1973 and 1975. From mid-1976 to July 1977, however, the naphtha price was held constant while the prices of other oil products, except kerosene, increased in step fashion. *Third*, before the oil crisis, the price of kerosene was higher than that of either diesel or residual fuel oil. Between 1973 and 1975, however, the price of kerosene was held below those of diesel and residual fuel oil; the pre-crisis relationship was reestablished only in mid-1976. *Fourth*, both diesel oil (used by trucks and railways) and residual fuel oil (used in steel, electric power and shipping) registered lower rates of price increase than naphtha (used in the petrochemical industry). *Fifth*, between 1972 and 1977, the wholesale prices of naphtha, kerosene, diesel oil, and residual fuel oil increased faster than the wholesale price of automobile gasoline; yet the price to *users* of gasoline increased the fastest of all the major products (see below, Section 7C).

Why did the aforementioned price movements occur? The answer has to do with the way Japanese indicative planning has adapted to the new conditions of the energy market of the 1970s. In particular, the changes in oil-product prices reflect the efforts of the Japanese government to modify market forces so that the increased costs of oil and other forms of energy are shared among three groups of oil users: (1) industry (especially metallurgy, chemicals, transportation, and electric utilities); (2) owners of automobiles; and (3) households generally.

7. OIL PRODUCT PRICES AND THE NEW GOALS OF INDICATIVE ECONOMIC PLANNING

Beginning in 1974, the government sought to redefine its national economic goals. In keeping with earlier practice, the Economic Federation of Japan (*Keidanren*) — the principal interest group of big business — was extensively consulted, and the mass media were regularly briefed. The emerging new goals were announced publicly in a series of carefully orchestrated messages to the public. First, in the future Japan would be able to attain at best about 6 to 7% annual growth in real national income.

[8] Jet fuel is ignored in the present analysis because of the special conditions of sale for use in international commercial aviation.

Second, existing metallurgical, chemical, and automobile firms would be required to reduce pollution from their production processes, and future growth would be oriented towards "knowledge" and "clean-technology" processes (which remained undefined). Third, consumer interests, particularly the "quality of life" (also undefined), would be given a high priority in the planning of national life (MITI, 1975, 1976).

Meanwhile, the economic recession persisted. Although it was not by design, the prolonged recession hit hardest the textile, aluminum, inorganic-chemicals, and light manufacturing industries—industries that had already begun to lose international competitive strength due to rising labor and raw-material costs and to the appreciating yen. The unemployment rate jumped from about 0.5 to 2.0%, bringing back dismal memories of the 1950s, when even university graduates could not find jobs easily.[9] Middle-aged and elderly persons were thrown out of work due to bankruptcies or severe cutbacks by their employers. The prolonged recession of the 1970's considerably moderated the tendency of the general public to question the nation's commitment to sustained economic growth.

Once the slogan of a "low- but steady-growth economy" began to reorient both labor and management to expect lower income growth than they were accustomed to, the government (with the aid of the mass media) undertook intense efforts to impress "energy conservation" upon the general public. Amid slogans about diversifying future sources of energy supplies, the government declared a policy of shifting from the current dependence on imported oil (about 80% of Japanese total energy use) to the expanded use of nuclear, geothermal, and solar energy. It was hoped that, by 1985, the domestic share of Japanese energy use (including coal) would increase to about 18% of total use from about 10% in 1977.[10]

Since 1975, two specific energy policies for the near to midterm future have emerged in the thinking of the Japanese government. First, heavy energy users who are also internationally weak—e.g., copper smelting and primary aluminum reduction—will be checked from further expansion in domestic markets. Other heavy energy users, however, such as ferrous metals and chemicals, will be assisted by the government in maintaining

[9] Taking into account the lifetime employment system in which firms are expected to retain their employees for life, the effective rate of unemployment inclusive of redundant employees retained by firms was estimated at 6–7% (Y. Tsurumi, 1978a), roughly comparable to the record of the United States.

[10] For 1963–1973, the real GNP growth elasticity of energy use was about 1.14 (MITI, 1975, p. 26). The new government goal is to reduce this elasticity to 0.95 between 1973 and 1985. Because of Japan's very high reliance on energy imports, the government hopes to hold the increase in total energy use to an annual rate of about 6.3%. Accordingly, the maximum targeted growth rate of real GNP is about 6.6 percent per annum (6.3/0.95).

their international competitive strength, even in the face of rising energy
and raw-material costs.

Second, recognizing that Japan will continue for some time yet to depend
heavily on imported oil, the government has quietly given up its long-
standing goal of fostering Japanese oil firms at the expense of foreign
companies. In its place, the government (by deed if not by decree)
has adopted the tactic of seeking to merge the interests of the major
international oil companies with those of Japan. In effect, this implicit
strategy of "exchanging hostages" represents the extension of a practice
of Japanese indicative planning to non-Japanese firms. Joint offshore
oil and gas exploration by Japanese oil-trading firms and foreign major
oil companies is now permitted and even encouraged. Even the govern-
ment-owned Oil Development Public Corporation (*SKK*) has, since 1976,
actively participated in joint exploration efforts. At home, the refining and
marketing activities of subsidiaries of the international oil companies have
been encouraged.

The Japanese government's post-oil-crisis energy policies are now
reflected in the price-bargaining taking place in three different administered markets for oil products: "necessities" (kerosene and propane
gas); industrial uses; and automotive gasoline. We take them up in order.

A. Price Regulation of "Necessities"

The Japanese markets for kerosene and propane gas for household use
are very close to the textbook stereotype of perfect competition. Bulk
suppliers tend to be the smaller Japanese oil-refining and -trading firms,
while wholesaling and retailing are conducted by numerous small firms and
local shops. The products traded are widely used throughout Japanese
society and are virtually homogeneous as far as household customers are
concerned. Many retailers use kerosene as a loss leader in order to
attract customers to their main lines of business (e.g., automotive
gasoline, groceries, hardware, dry goods, or even cosmetics and toiletries).
Customer brand loyalty is nil, and the switching of brands and (more
importantly) of retailers is easily triggered by slight differences in price.
Under these circumstances, the retail price of kerosene can only be raised
by a widespread collusion on the part of kerosene retailers and wholesalers. In fact, in the early 1970s a group of kerosene bulk suppliers was
caught attempting to raise prices collusively.

Since the oil crisis, the markets for kerosene and propane have come
under closer antitrust surveillance by the FTC. More important, they
have been placed under "price guidance" by MITI. MITI administers
"standard" kerosene prices and has proved reluctant to raise them, in
the face of vocal voter opposition to price increases, in spite of intense

lobbying by producers and their retail distributors. When the price of imported crude oil increases, MITI generally permits a smaller increase in kerosene prices than in those of other oil products. MITI can also exercise control over the wholesale prices of kerosene and propane gas because it is empowered to issue permits to oil firms for new refining or marketing facilities. Competition in retail markets holds down retailers' markups. MITI's price and other controls on kerosene confirm our earlier conclusion, based on the price data in Table 1, that there is still tight regulation of this market in Japan, whatever the official line to the contrary.

Typically, price controls in a competitive market like that for retail kerosene in Japan create tendencies toward excess demands or shortages. Those tendencies have been mitigated in the Japanese kerosene market through MITI's controls on investment. The small petroleum firms that specialized in kerosene before 1973 have not been permitted to evade the kerosene price controls by diversifying into other petroleum products. Further mitigating the shortage tendencies in kerosene is the appreciation of the yen against the U. S. dollar, which is the currency in which world oil trade is conducted. The resulting effective decline in the price of imported crude oil has tended to increase the supply of kerosene (as well as of other oil products) in Japan.

B. Monopsony Price Bargaining by Leading Growth Firms

The oil crisis of 1973–1974 directly or indirectly changed some of the particulars in the bargaining process between Japanese oil firms and the major buyers of oil products in key industries. The basic mechanism, however, has remained the same—the toleration of monopsony pricing of oil products sold to firms in the metallurgical, chemical and other leading growth industries as one means of maintaining and fostering their international competitive strength.

The general bargaining position of Japanese oil companies has not improved since the oil crisis, and in some respects it has deteriorated. Japanese steel makers are still able to play one oil supplier off against the other, and their own price-bargaining with large steel-using firms in the automobile, shipbuilding and household-appliance industries makes them more than willing to do so. In transportation, a combination of government ceilings on rates (trucking) and excess capacity (tanker and other ocean-going freight) has stiffened buyer resistance to increases in diesel and residual fuel oil prices. Thus competition among oil firms who must sell to a few very large buyers ensures that the benefits from lower crude oil prices due to the appreciating yen are passed through to oil users.

The return to the pre-crisis pattern of oil pricing after the departure of the early 1970s is perhaps most clearly seen in petrochemicals. Recall that in the early 1970s, the petrochemical industry was able to act as a colluding oligopoly. Thus, until 1975, petrochemical firms were not unwilling to accept the sharp increases that occurred in naphtha prices; this was because the increases could be readily passed along to customers in the form of higher petrochemical prices. Once MITI and the FTC put an end to the price collusion, however, petrochemical firms could no longer simply pyramid their profit margins on top of increased naphtha costs. In addition, in 1975 the worldwide recession reduced the demand for petrochemicals and left the industry with excess capacity. Accordingly, Japanese petrochemical manufacturers were forced to return to their previous practice of hard price-bargaining with firms in the fragmented oil industry.

In short, the pressures of export competition to which the leading growth firms as users of oil products are subject continue to be transmitted throughout Japanese industry. As before the oil crisis, the transmission mechanism is the price-bargaining between oil supplying firms and major industrial users of oil products. The Japanese oil firms that supply industrial users find it difficult to pass even higher crude oil prices, *pari passu*, on to the monopsony buyers of their products. And competition, of course, forces them to pass along any cost reductions from the appreciation of the yen against the U. S. dollar.

The medium-to-large-sized oil firms have been able to retain one advantage they enjoyed before the oil crisis: their access to the retail gasoline market. We now examine the operation of that market.

C. Oligopoly Pricing in Gasoline Markets

Retail prices of gasoline in Japan have risen faster than any other oil-product price since the controls on it were lifted in March 1974. Unlike some other markets (e.g., kerosene), in gasoline the Japanese government has allowed markets to clear. In part, the motive has been to use higher prices to curb gasoline consumption and thereby oil imports. But an additional motive appears to have been to shift a sizable amount of the burden of higher oil costs to middle- and upper-income groups, who (in Japan) own and operate the majority of private cars. It is not an increase in gasoline taxes but an increase in the retail price (before tax) that has raised the price of gasoline by over 400% from 1973 to 1977.

A major source of the increases in gasoline prices can be found in the market structure of gasoline suppliers. Nine brand-name marketers, representing the three largest Japanese oil firms and six subsidiaries of foreign oil companies, dominate the Japanese retail gasoline market. These firms systematically raise prices in unison, with one or another of them acting as price leader. What competition there is tends to be waged through nonprice means. The nine brand-name firms, which all have nationwide retail distribution networks, have enjoyed much larger revenue and profit increases since 1973 than the smaller, fragmented oil companies. The six foreign-owned firms are permitted to concentrate on retail gasoline sales and bulk supply of crude oil to Japanese refiners. Even though the three large Japanese-owned brand-name marketers find it difficult to make profits in the administered price-bargaining for industrial oil products, they do well in retail gasoline sales. The smaller Japanese oil firms have only limited retail gasoline operations.[11]

The variants of "administered competition" in different oil-product markets illustrate the way the Japanese government is implementing the new national economic goals articulated since the oil crisis of 1973–1974. Households are to be insulated somewhat from the harsh effects of higher oil costs on kerosene prices. The international competitiveness of the growth leaders in such industries as metallurgy, chemicals, and automobiles is to be maintained and fostered. And the operating efficiencies of the large international oil companies are to be exploited — provided they are willing to accept the incentive structure that aligns their interests with those of the Japanese government. Who will pay for all of this?—the small and medium-sized Japanese oil companies and the higher-income households who own the bulk of the private cars.

8. THE APPRECIATING YEN: A NEW TOOL OF INDICATIVE ECONOMIC PLANNING

As noted earlier, the hyperinflation that threatened in 1973–1974 was contained by sociocultural forces inherent in Japanese society—an informal incomes policy and households' increased propensity to save— and by MITI's renewed enforcement of administered competition among oligopolists within and between industries. Once new price schedules were established under MITI's administrative guidance in 1974 and 1975, exporting industries such as steel, electronics, household appliances, automobiles, and industrial machinery concentrated on maintaining a high level of production by expanding their exports, mainly to the United States. After a decade of concerted cost cutting and product innovation, these industries easily increased their U. S. sales at the expense of their American competitors, who, some observers felt, were lagging behind in introducing technological innovations and modernizing production processes (Merrill Lynch, 1977).

[11] Recall that the Japanese government (through MITI) controls entry into all oil-product markets, and that (since the oil crisis) it has been national policy to encourage foreign firms to expand their operations in Japan.

All told, the trade account, which had registered a substantial deficit for about a year after the oil crisis, began to show a surplus in the fourth quarter of 1974. The Bank of Japan deliberately let the Japanese yen depreciate from 1974 to the beginning of 1976 in order to encourage Japanese exports. As a result, from 1976 to 1977 the trade surplus continued to increase. Together with capital inflows (mainly recycled petrodollars), the mounting trade surplus began to put pressure on the Japanese yen to appreciate relative to the U. S. dollar. In hopes of discouraging further increases in imports from Japan, the United States government encouraged the Japanese government to allow the yen to appreciate.[12] By the end of November 1977, the yen had appreciated to 240 to the U. S. dollar, an increase of more than 20% from the level of 305 yen immediately following the oil crisis.

The appreciating yen helped further damp domestic inflationary pressures. It of course slowed the growth of exports (although in the short run the foreign demand for Japanese exports proved relatively price-inelastic, especially for such consumer products as color television sets, automobiles, and audio equipment). More importantly, it reduced the costs of imported raw materials and energy. It is not accidental that (as shown in Table 1) the prices of naphtha, diesel oil, and residual fuel oil were relatively stable from 1976 through the end of 1977—a period during which the yen steadily appreciated.

9. STOCKPILING OIL PRODUCTS

One aspect of the Japanese government's response to the oil crisis not yet touched upon is policies to reduce vulnerability to short-term import-supply disruptions. Even with complete success in increasing the share of domestic production in total energy consumption, Japan will continue to rely heavily on imported oil for the indefinite future. The Japanese economy is therefore susceptible to sudden disruption of import supplies and the attendant costs in lost output and consumer welfare.

The Japanese government has taken steps to reduce the costs that oil exporters could impose by suddenly cutting off shipments to Japan. We have already mentioned (in Sect. 7) the diversification of energy sources— in effect reducing the exposure of the Japanese economy to any one oil-exporting country's actions. A second step has been to attempt to increase the inventories of refined oil products held by petroleum firms, as a buffer against sudden disruptions. The precise form of the policy and the locus of the cost burden have, however, been points of contention.

---

[12] The appreciation of the yen against the U. S. dollar is tantamount to *de facto* increases of import tariffs selectively levied against Japanese products. It can be argued that it is politically easier for the U. S. government to let the dollar depreciate than to persuade the Congress to raise tariffs.

When the oil crisis hit, Japan had in total less than a 30-day supply
in various stages of oil production (MITI, 1976b). Since then, the
government has provided low-interest loans to oil firms that stockpile
oil products as a defensive measure against a future oil embargo. With
the loans, Japanese oil firms appear willing to hold inventories sufficient
for a 70-day supply. The Japanese government is, however, committed
(through the International Energy Agency) to build a 90-day defensive
stockpile. The issue is who should pay for the incremental 20-day supply.

The oil industry argues that the Japanese government should cover
the full cost. A defensive stockpile of oil (or any other good) is a
form of public good, because the benefits accrue to the nation as a whole
or (what is close to the same thing) the class of all oil users. As with
other public goods like military defense capacity, the public (through
the government) should bear the costs out of general tax revenues. At
the time of writing (early 1978), the Japanese government appears to
have embraced the public-good argument put forth by the oil firms and
is taking steps to build additional inventories of petroleum products at
government expense.[13]

10. CONCLUSIONS

The increases in oil prices since 1973 have posed serious challenges
for Japanese economic-policy makers. Industrially advanced yet lacking
indigenous oil sources, the Japanese economy is heavily dependent on
imported crude oil. The major policy challenge has been to absorb the
impact of the higher prices on long-term growth strategy as well as on
the distribution of income. A lesser but still important challenge has been
to insure against short-term disruptions of oil-import supplies.

The Japanese government has introduced a number of new policies and
altered the economic institutions of Japan in attempting to meet those
challenges. All told, however, the oil crisis has had relatively little
impact on Japanese indicative planning, particularly on the basic process
through which the prices of key industrial and consumer products are
determined. The device of "administered competition," along with a fragmented oil industry, has been used to adapt long-term supply planning
in leading export industries to the higher oil prices. The Japanese government has also been able to use the pricing system to distribute much
of the cost burden of those prices away from the leading growth industries—for example, to the smaller oil-refining and -marketing firms and
to the (largely middle- and upper-class) owners of automobiles.

---

[13] The stockpiling of imported crude oil and oil products is further increasing government
intervention in the oil industry. Government stockpiling is also planned for other imported
commodities.

Three of the modifications in Japanese indicative planning growing out of the oil crisis are noteworthy and may warrant further examination. One modification is relevant specifically to Japan, while two may be of more general interest. First, the increased regulatory powers of MITI and the FTC may have altered the political balance of Japanese indicative planning, with consequences as yet not foreseen for the relative influence of big business and households. Second, the tactical switch to a policy of "enlightened mutual interest" regarding foreign oil companies' operations in Japan may suggest a way of reconciling economic efficiency with nationalistic goals; one thinks, for instance, of the problems Canada faces with respect to large U. S. corporations. Finally, Japanese experience suggests that floating exchange rates can provide an additional tool of indicative planning rather than posing a sometimes difficult added constraint. Japanese planning, with its emphasis on the discipline of (administered) market competition, seems to have been as effective under floating rates as under the earlier fixed-rate system.

REFERENCES

Arrow, Kenneth J., and Hurwicz, Leonid, "Decentralization and Computation in Resource Allocation." In Ralph Pfouts, ed., *Essays in Economics and Econometrics*. Chapel Hill: Univ. of North Carolina Press, 1963.

Caves, Richard E., and Uekusa, Masu, *Industrial Organization in Japan*. Washington, D. C.: Brookings, 1976.

Denison, Edward, and Chung, W., *How Japan's Economy Grew So Fast*. Washington, D. C.: Brookings, 1977.

Economic Planning Agency, *Economic White Papers*, Preface. Tokyo: 1968.

Hadley, E. *Antitrust in Japan*. Princeton, N.J.: Princeton Univ. Press, 1970.

Kaplan, Eugene, *Japan: The Government —Business Relationship; a Guide for American Businessmen*. Washington, D. C.: Bureau of International Commerce, Dept. of Commerce, 1972.

Komiya, Ryutaro, "Planning in Japan." In Morris Bornstein, ed., *Economic Planning: East and West*. Cambridge, Mass.: Ballinger, 1975.

Lutz, Vera, *Central Planning for the Market Economy*. London: Longmans, 1969.

Merrill Lynch, Pierce, Fenner, and Smith, "Japanese Steel Report." New York: 1977.

(MITI) Ministry of International Trade and Industry, *Showa Gojunen dai no Enerug* (Energy Policy, 1975–85). Tokyo: 1975.

MITI, *Sangyo Kozo no Choki Bision* (A Long-term View of Industrial Structure). Tokyo: 1976a.

MITI, *Energy Statistics*. Tokyo: Bureau of Natural Resources and Energy, 1976b.

Patrick, Hugh, and Rosovsky, Henry, eds., *Asia's New Giant: How the Japanese Economy Works*. Washington, D. C.: Brookings, 1976.

Rapp, W., "Japan: Its Industrial Policies and Corporate Behavior." *Columbia J. of World Bus.* pp. 38–48, Spring 1977.

Sato, K., "Saving of Japan's Worker Households". presented at Japan Economic Seminar, Economic Growth Center, Yale University, New Haven, Conn. Mimeo., December 1976.

Sato, K., "Did Technical Progress Accelerate in Japan?" Discussion Paper No. 418, Department of Economics, State Univ. of New York at Buffalo, October 1977.

Sekiyu Gyokai No Suii (Trends in the Oil Industry). Tokyo: Association of the Oil Industry,
    1966, pp. 118–135.

Spulber, Nicolas, and Horowitz, Ira, *Quantitative Economic Policy and Planning: Theory
    and Models of Economic Control*. New York: Norton, 1976.

Tinbergen, Jan, *On the Theory of Economic Policy*. Amsterdam: North–Holland, 1952.

Tsurumi, H. "A Bayesian Test of the Product Cycle Hypothesis Applied to Japanese
    Crude Steel Production." *Journal of Econometrics*, Fall, 1976.

Tsurumi, Yoshi, "R&D Efforts and Exports of Japanese Manufacturers." In Louis T. Wells,
    ed., *The Product Life Cycle and International Trade*. Cambridge, Mass.: Harvard
    Univ. Press, 1972.

Tsurumi, Yoshi, *The Japanese Are Coming: A Multinational Interaction of Firms and
    Politics*. Cambridge: Ballinger, 1976a.

Tsurumi, Yoshi, "Japan." In Raymond Vernon, ed., *The Oil Crisis*. New York: Norton,
    1976b, pp. 113–127. Also in *Daedalus*, Fall 1975.

Tsurumi, Yoshi, "A Critical Choice for Japan." *Columbia J. of World Bus.*: 14–21,
    Spring 1977a.

Tsurumi, Yoshi, *Multinational Management: Business Strategy and Government Policy*.
    Cambridge: Ballinger, 1977b.

Tsurumi, Yoshi, *Japanese Business: Readings and Research Guide With Annotated Bibliog-
    raphy*. New York: Praeger, 1978a.

Tsurumi, Yoshi, "A Bayesian Estimate of Demand Shifts of U. S. Color TV Market:
    Their Implications for U. S.—Japan Trade Issue." Mimeo., Graduate School of
    Business, Columbia Univ., March 1978b.

Vernon, Raymond, "Competition Policy towards Multinational Corporations," *Amer.
    Econ. Rev.*, **64**, 2:276–282, May 1974.

The legal cartels of Japan

BY TOSHIAKI NAKAZAWA* and LEONARD W. WEISS**

Before World War II Japan encouraged cartels. During the occupation the Diet passed an Antimonopoly act which prohibited them and established a Fair Trade Commission (JFTC) to enforce the new law. In 1953, 15 months after the occupation ended, the Diet amended the law to permit certain types of cartels. Most of them were only legal if approved by the new JFTC.

---

   * Professor, Department of Economics, Keio University, Tokyo, Japan.

   ** Professor, Department of Economics, University of Wisconsin, Madison.

AUTHORS' NOTE: *This is a preliminary report on a study of Japanese cartels which is still underway. The project was financed, in part, by a Fulbright grant and by grants from the University of Wisconsin and from Keio University in Tokyo. It is based in part on extensive interviews at JFTC and MITI in February and June 1987 and an infinity of telephone calls to the same agencies.*

   A number of the references cited below are in Japanese and have Japanese names. We use English translations of their names for clarity. These citations are followed by the phrase [in Japanese].

642 : *The antitrust bulletin*

The cartels that require JFTC approval include recession cartels, rationalization cartels, small and medium business cartels, import cartels, and export cartels. In the 1970's the law also permitted cartels in certain industries faced with capacity adjustments due to rising energy prices.

In addition, Japanese industries were often subject to "administrative guidance" by the Ministry of International Trade and Industry (MITI), the other main agency in our story. MITI is a successor of the Ministry of Commerce and Industry of the 1920's and 1930's, which played a major role in cartel policy in those years. In the 1950's and the early 1960's the leaders of MITI were persons who had been there in the 1930's and many of them felt that cartels were in the nation's best interest.[1] MITI seemed to play a major role in the Japanese "miracle" and had a great deal of influence in the 1960's and 1970's.

As described to us, "administrative guidance" involves a study by MITI staff of some problem often in response to industry requests for help. MITI staff presents its results to a meeting of industry leaders. If it concludes that the industry should cut output by X%, say, we were told that the industry does indeed act as advised. Earlier, administrative guidance involved something much closer to explicit cartel agreements, but the Japanese courts ruled that such agreements could be illegal even if MITI had recommended them.[2] It seems probable that since then administrative guidance really has taken the form of study and advice and that it has sometimes been effective.

One reason administrative guidance worked in the early days is that MITI had powerful means of enforcement, especially control of import licenses and access to low-cost credit. A reason why it is a much weaker reed today is that import licenses no

---

[1]   C. Johnson, *MITI and the Japanese Miracle*, Stanford University Press 1982, p. 86.

[2]   Tokyo Court of Appeals, "The Petroleum Production Case," 33 *Journal of Precedents* 983, 1980 [in Japanese]. The Japanese citation I was given (by phone) was Kosai Keisu, Volume 33, Number 5, page 983.

longer exist in Japan, and cheap credit is less crucial because of Japan's increasingly efficient capital markets.

Attitudes have changed greatly since 1960. MITI's leaders today had no experience with prewar cartels. They seem generally to feel that cartels are sometimes useful, but that competition is usually in the nation's best interest. At the same time the JFTC has acquired a fully trained staff and 40 years of experience and carries more weight than it did in the 1950's.

The change in outlook has been reflected in the statistics. In 1963, 28% of manufacturing shipments were covered by formal cartels.[3] By 1973 this was down to 18%.[4] We are convinced this is less than 10% today. The number of small and medium business cartels has fallen from 652 to 226.[5] The main qualifications to this are that tobacco is a government monopoly, oil refining is effectively a regulated industry, and we do not know to what extent legal cartels have been replaced by illegal ones.

I. Recession cartels

The logic of recession cartels was that industries faced with the short-term problems of a recession should not be forced into price cutting and worse if no long-term adjustment is needed. The danger is that such cartels may be permitted in situations where long-run adjustments are required. Then recession cartels are apt to last many years and bail out industries that should make long-term adjustments. After a few decades the nation would find itself with excess, suboptimal and/or obsolete capacity—often industries that once fitted its resources but do not now, such as Japanese textiles and American steel.

---

[3]   JFTC, *Japanese Cartels*, 1964 [in Japanese].

[4]   JFTC, *Annual Report*, 1976 [in Japanese].

[5]   JFTC, *Annual Report*, 1987 [in Japanese].

644 : *The antitrust bulletin*

The Japanese record was better than many would expect, but it did produce problems. The first two recession cartels were extended for several years but, since 1961, none has run more than 19 months. An industry permitted to form a cartel every few years could present similar problems. The JFTC permitted 74 recession cartels from 1953 through 1987. Of these, 40 went to industries so treated only once, and 12 to 6 industries only twice.[6] One of the latter was shipbuilding which was permitted a second recession cartel in March 1987. The JFTC wrestled with its conscience here, but it finally decided that (a) Japan would remain in the industry, (b) it is notoriously unstable, (c) the depressed market would last for at least a year, and (d) a recession cartel of 12 months was therefore appropriate. This is their ideal for recession cartel decisions.

But some industries were awarded three to five recession cartels: liner board (3), corrugating medium (3), light steel bars (3), cement (4), spinning (4), and polyvinyl chloride (5).[7] We will discuss the last two below.

The JFTC does not enforce recession cartels, no firm has to belong, and participants can drop out at any time. With one exception it has not permitted these cartels to agree on price, so they imposed quotas or shut down specified amounts of capacity. The effects of these rules on price is not obvious, but they undoubtedly increased uncertainty about the cartel's effect. Finally, it should be pointed out that no new recession cartels were approved between 1982 and 1987. One reason was that the most seriously depressed industries were covered by special legislation during that period.

Spinning

Japan was the world's low-cost textile producer in the 1930's and by the 1960's it was once more one of the leaders. Since

---

6   JFTC, *Annual Reports*, 1949–1987 [in Japanese].

7   JFTC, *Annual Reports*, 1949–1987 [in Japanese].

then, however, its exports have stagnated and, in the case of every important natural fiber yarn, its imports now exceed its exports. Yarn production of all sorts peaked about 1970. Spinning has declined by about 20% since then.[8] Japan's main foreign suppliers today are China and Korea.[9]

Cotton spinners got a recession cartel in October 1964 that lasted for 17 months. It coincided with 13 other recession cartels that year, but it turned out to be the start of cotton spinners' decline. In 1975 and again in 1977–1978 all types of spinners—cotton, synthetic, and worsted—were permitted to form cartels. The long-term problem was fairly clear by 1981, but a fourth cartel was permitted in 1981–1982.[10] No limit was set on imports, however. Perhaps temporary cartels (only 5 months in 1981–1982) were the lesser of two evils in this case.

Polyvinyl chloride

Polyvinyl chloride (PVC) illustrates two types of cartels: recession cartels before 1982 and special legislation cartels thereafter. We will discuss recession cartels here. PVC is one of the most important plastics (*e.g.*, saran wrap, plastic pipe, plastic film in agriculture). It was first produced in the United States and Germany in the early 1930's. Japan had two small pilot plants during the war. Japan's real commercial output began in 1949.

MITI made plastics and petrochemicals "strategic industries" in June 1955 and in July 1955.[11] Both characterizations applied to PVC. MITI offered special access to foreign cur-

---

8   MITI, *Yearbooks of Textile Statistics* [in Japanese].

9   United Nations, *World Trade Annuals*, passim.

10   JFTC, *Annual Reports*, 1949–1987 [in Japanese].

11   MITI, *History of Commercial and Industrial Policy*, Vol. 21, 1981.

rency, import licenses, low-cost loans, and tax breaks. PVC
grew rapidly, faster even than MITI had planned, because of
large-scale entry. It seemed more dangerous for a chemical firm
to stay out of such industries than to face excess capacity due to
entry. Some believe that the risk seemed low because of the
availability of depression cartels that would allocate demand if
excess capacity appeared.[12]

PVC recession cartels were approved by JFTC in 1958, 1966
and 1972.[13] They met the normal standards: there were temporary drops in demand, but it was hardly a declining industry.
High oil prices in the 1970's changed all this. Japanese petrochemical firms had to pay OPEC's price for oil, while American petrochemists were subsidized by producers of U.S. "old
and middle tier oil." Two more recession cartels were permitted
(in 1977 and 1981) before the Japanese became convinced that a
long-run adjustment was needed.

The first three cartels seemed to pass the normal test, and
Japan had the second largest PVC industry of the world just 20
years after a late start. MITI at its best? But the U.S. industry
grew almost as fast, starting in our worst depression with no
such "guidance." Japan missed out on the first 15 years of the
industry, but it had many firms large and sophisticated enough
to enter the industry. Two had even operated pilot plants. By
1981, 20 firms had entered.[14] And they had lots of excess capacity, the classic effect of cartels with free entry, especially with
such inducements.

II. Rationalization cartels

The meaning of the term "rationalization cartel" was foggy
in Japan. The essential feature is that they could be long term in

---

12   Johnson, *supra* note 1, at 236–37.

13   JFTC, *Annual Reports*, passim [in Japanese].

14   JFTC, *Annual Report*, 1981 [in Japanese].

character. It is a mark in JFTC's favor that they were almost harmless. Half were industry agreements on grading standards with no commitment by firms to any particular grades. In addition, there were quality cartels that did commit participants on quality—in tires, bearings, and textile dyes—and two cartels aimed at stabilizing prices of scrap copper and scrap iron. We will discuss the tires and scrap iron cartels here.

Tires

In addition to a quality standards agreement, the six tire cartel members agreed not to produce white sidewall or deep tread tires.[15] The white sidewall agreement was meant to reduce costs, but why? We and the Japanese spend lots of money on fashions no less "silly" than white sidewalls. If consumers are willing to pay for such things, why not let them. It is difficult to get worked up about white sidewalls, but deep tread is something else. Here the companies were agreeing to limit tire lives. The cartel ended in November 1968. White sidewalls reappeared. But after the oil price shock in 1974 the industry eliminated the white sidewalls once more.

White sidewalls are passe today. Many American and European tires have white stripes, but they are only seen on foreign cars in Japan. The standard depth of tread is 8 millimeters[16] or .315 inches. The standard U.S. tire is 11/32 inches or .344 inches, about 9% deeper. Exported tires were never controlled by the cartel. The Japanese tires for sale in the United States often have white stripes, and they match or beat U.S. tread depths.[17]

---

[15] JFTC, *Annual Reports*, passim [in Japanese].

[16] Based on a phone call to the Japan Automobile Tire Association in 1987.

[17] Based on several phone calls in Madison and Washington to dealers and manufacturers' representatives in October 1987. The standard is

The cartel ended long ago (in 1968) but some echoes still seem audible.

Scrap iron

Cartels were approved by JFTC on April 1, 1955 for copper scrap and on April 11, 1955 for scrap iron. They were Japan's first postwar "rationalization cartels." The scrap copper cartel ended in 1957, but the scrap iron cartel lasted more than 19 years. The cartel was made up of 74 steel producers. Its purpose was to reorganize the Japanese scrap market and stabilize scrap prices.

Scrap had long been scarce in Japan. In the 1950's Japan was the world's leading scrap importer. At its peak, it accounted for 40% of world imports. By 1984 this was down to 11%. Today Italy is the leading importer of scrap iron. The U.S. has been the leading scrap exporter over the entire postwar period. About three-quarters of Japan's imports come from the U.S. At its peak in 1964, Japan bought 73% of U.S. scrap exports, and its imports from the U.S. accounted for 29% of *all* world scrap imports.[18]

But this gives the wrong impression. In 1964 America consumed 66 million tons of scrap while Japan imported 5 million, of which 3.8 million came from the United States.[19] The world scrap market is not perfect, but prices move fairly closely together in the free world. The cartel could hardly have expected to depress world scrap prices much. The most it could hope for was to stabilize them somewhat.

---

not universal. It was not set by government nor by any sort of industry agreement. It probably derives from the specifications for original equipment tires.

[18] United Nations, *World Trade Annual*, 1964.

[19] American Iron and Steel Institute, *Annual Statistical Report 1967*, and United Nations, *World Trade Annual*, 1965.

Scrap prices sagged in the 1960's due to the growth of the new basic oxygen furnace but they rose in 1971–1973. Japanese imports stopped rising, and its steel industry cut inventories in 1973.[20] Then came the Yom Kippur War, the prices of scrap took off, and they had to replace their scrap inventories at very high prices. The cartel was not renewed when it came up for extension in September 1974.

So they made a speculative error! Who else in the world foresaw the Yom Kippur War and the OPEC oil price shock? We feel the cartel was worse than 74 independent buyers on two counts. First, all Japanese steel firms acted as a unit, but 74 buyers would not have all moved in step. Beyond that, they must have felt that they had some short-run power over scrap prices, but 74 speculators would never attempt to force prices down since none of them could have thought he had such power.

Japan probably lost a lot in 1974 from its scrap cartel, but the rest of the world gained. A main gainer was the U.S. steel industry. Japan may have reduced world scrap prices in 1973, and surely raised costs for the Japanese steel industry in 1974. It so happens that 1974 was the one good year the American integrated steel industry had in the two decades ending in 1988.

III. Special legislation cartels—the depressed industry case

Almost every nation has a few industries that by some means or other have attained a cartel status. Japanese barbers have had a cartel for decades as part of their regulation by the Ministry of Health and Welfare. In the mid-1950's MITI pushed through "special measures laws" that exempted textile machinery and "electronics."[21] The electronics cartel lasted from 1957 to 1975.

---

[20]   MITI, *Monthly Statistics of Iron and Steel*, 1972–1975 [in Japanese].

[21]   Johnson, *supra* note 1, at 226.

650 : *The antitrust bulletin*

But the most interesting were three laws passed in 1978, 1983, and 1987 to help industries under special pressure.

Japanese oil and energy prices rose more in the 1970's than those charged American manufacturers. As a result, those industries that depended heavily on energy or oil were suddenly at a serious disadvantage. In 1978 the Diet passed the *Tokuanho*[22] (Temporary Legislation for Cartelization of Specific Depressed Industries) to deal with the special problems of seven obviously energy- or oil-dependent industries. The law was amended within a year to cover seven more industries. Some of the provisions were efforts to reduce pain, but the legislation also provided for government actions to facilitate long-run adjustment.[23] Primary aluminum was an industry where they worked particularly well.

Tokuanho expired in 1983, but by then there had been another oil shock, so the *Sankoho* (Temporary Legislation for Specific Industrial Structure Reform) was passed covering 11 industries covered by the older law plus 15 more. Among the newcomers was PVC.

Sankoho ended on June 30, 1988 but in April 1987 the Diet passed *Enkatsuho* (Temporary Legislation to Facilitate Industry Structure Reorientation) to help firms particularly hurt by the high value of the yen. It provides for tax advantages, low cost loans, credit guarantees, but *not* cartels. JFTC approval is still required for any industry adjustment process adopted. This law also expires after 5 years.

Aluminum

Aluminum is very energy-dependent. In 1978 Japan had five aluminum firms with 1,642,000 tons of capacity. The run up of

---

22   MITI, *Annual Report*, 1979 [in Japanese].

23   J. M. Peck, R. Levin, and A. Goto, "Picking Losers: Government Policy Toward Declining Industries," 13 *Journal of Japanese Studies*, 79–123, 1987.

oil prices hit the industry particularly hard because it depended upon thermal power for 80% of its 1973 capacity and oil for most of that. A MITI study showed that the industry was inevitably high cost given OPEC's high prices.[24]

The five firms sought a fuel subsidy but got none. They were given the right to import 400,000 tons of primary aluminum per year duty-free. This permitted them to continue rolling and drawing aluminum. Subsidies and low-interest loans were paid to promote shifts from oil to coal, and a joint research program was begun seeking a less energy-dependent method of aluminum production. The most important part of the program, however, was the negotiation of capacity reductions by MITI with the five firms individually. MITI staff then presented the tentative reductions of 530,000 tons capacity as a recommendation. No formal cartel was organized.

By 1982 they had actually reduced capacity by 743,000 tons in 5 years. The program continued under Sankoho. By 1987 Japanese primary aluminum capacity was down to 323,000 tons.[25] A capital-intensive industry eliminated 80% of its capacity in one decade in response to a serious cost disadvantage!

Was MITI necessary for this adjustment? Things like the tariff adjustment, subsidies and low-interest loans were obviously dependent on government. The negotiated capacity reductions may have been essential in 1978 to get the adjustment started. The industry was still operating at prices that exceeded average variable costs, but it was probably not yielding much of a return after depreciation.[26]

---

[24]   MITI, Institute of Industrial Technology, *International Comparisons of Japan's Industrial Technology*, 1982 [in Japanese].

[25]   MITI, *Portrayal of Sankoho*, 1983 [in Japanese].

[26]   The value of shipments always considerably exceeded the sum of wages and salaries and materials including purchased electric power over the entire period, 1973–1986, though of course, the plants that had been closed by 1982, say, might well have had variable costs in excess of value

Each of the five firms was a part of a bank-centered conglomerate though one was also a joint venture with Aluminium Limited. The stocks of the aluminum companies was sold to other firms in the five groups. Whatever else they may do, conglomerates can diversify risks.

Polyvinyl chloride, again

PVC is a petrochemical. Its main material inputs are naphtha and chlorine. Naphtha is a petroleum product and chlorine is produced by electrolysis. The industry was included under Sankoho in 1983 and established a goal of reducing capacity by 490,000 tons (24%). It did cut capacity by 450,000 tons, but they also established four joint marketing organizations that sold all the nation's PVC. The result was a more distinct change in price performance than we usually see. Although the law under which they were established has expired, the joint sales agencies still exist and still sell most of Japan's PVC.

Why did it always come out this way for PVC? Perhaps it was a natural result of the "tacit promise" in the cartel laws, but no other statement in this article has been more controversial. Many deny it existed. The growth in petrochemicals was due to entry that occurred in part because MITI at least promised cheap loans, tax breaks, and free importation of equipment and supplies. And the cartel provisions of the antimonopoly law does seem to contain an implied promise of protection against price wars induced by temporary excess capacity, whether or not the promise came directly from MITI. The change in costs when OPEC quadrupled oil prices can hardly be blamed on MITI, but the common selling agencies didn't have to happen. We hope that this "promise" has now run out, after 34 years.

---

of shipments if they had still been operating. Based on Japanese *Censuses of Manufactures*, Vol. 2, *Reports by Industries, 1978, 1982,* and *1986* [in Japanese].

IV. Conclusions

What did Japan get from her cartels? The recession cartels probably prevented a few bankruptcies and lots of price wars, but consumers lost something on the latter. The social gains, if any, were apt to take the form of lower costs of capital to the affected industries due to reduced risk. We are still working on this one. And there can be little doubt that recession cartels helped to preserve excess capacity in spinning and to create it in PVC. We suspect that in a more slowly growing economy there would have been many more such cases. The rationalization cartels probably did at least as much harm as good. They didn't do much of either because the JFTC was so strict in granting them. Policies to help industries make difficult reductions in capacity has strong appeal, but were cartels a necessary part of those policies? We hope not, since it is just such industries that will seek them as remedies less painful than cutting capacity.

The answer may change drastically if you believe the Japanese miracle required MITI and that MITI required the cartels to play its role. It might seem plausible that a "tacit promise" induced firms to make investments in response to MITI's invitation. But we suspect that the access to import licenses and cheap loans were at least as important as the promise.

Even if you conclude that cartels were a crucial part of MITI's industrial policy and that they were worth whatever they cost, it does not follow that we can carry the whole package over to America with no more loss than Japan had. One reason is that we can't hope for the growth rates they attained, and many of the faults of cartels are worse in a more slowly growing economy. A more basic reason is constitutional. Congressmen do not face early new elections if they vote against their party. As a result, they are much less loyal to their parties and much more to their states' or districts' interests than members of a Diet are. The pressure to use cartels to help local industries, especially those in trouble would be far greater here than there. We are convinced that if the U.S. were to adopt a cartel system, we would soon have a badly malfunctioning economy.

Part V
Expansion of Public Utility Regulation in the US

[20]

The Economic Significance of Public Utilities

By FREDERIC C. BENHAM.

(Sir Ernest Cassel Reader in Commerce in the University of London.)

I

ECONOMISTS often find it useful to adopt the hypothesis of free competition. Free competition is a state of affairs in which no seller controls a sufficient proportion of the total supply to enable a variation of his own supply appreciably to affect the price. It is also a state of affairs in which profits in one industry cannot remain permanently higher than in other industries, and in which the price of everything tends to equal its marginal cost of production.

Public utilities do not fall within this hypothesis. "A public utility," says Mr. Hawtrey,[1] "may be defined as a service in which a tendency to a local monopoly necessitates the intervention of a public authority to defend the interests of the consumer." A public utility usually controls either the whole or a significantly large proportion of the supply of its product within its area, while the relative non-transferability of its product protects it from the competition of similar products from other areas. A public utility might permanently make higher profits than other industries. This is usually prevented by State ownership or control. Finally, the prices of public utility services need not equal their marginal costs of production. In the first place, the latter cannot in practice be determined, since "supplementary costs" cannot accurately be allocated among different units of production. In the second place, discriminatory charging is possible.

It follows that the distinguishing features of public utilities are to be found in conditions which exist in the real world and are assumed by the competitive hypothesis, explicitly or im-

[1] *Public Administration*, Vol. IV, p. 352.

plicitly, to be absent. The relevant conditions are those which make some approach to monopoly possible, by rendering it difficult or impossible for newcomers to enter particular fields. They may be grouped, for our purpose, under five heads.

Firstly, knowledge of existing methods of production and of market conditions in general, is imperfect. Processes are sometimes kept secret. It is possible to create a special demand for a branded product through advertising. Consumers may be unaware of the existence of similar products at lower prices or of the fact that such products really are similar. The heavy initial expenditure on advertising required to enable a substitute to compete effectively may act as a deterrent to potential newcomers. This, however, has little application to existing public utilities.

Secondly, certain parts of the earth have peculiar properties. There may be only one or two deposits of a certain mineral, only one or two passes through a range of mountains, only one or two springs of water in an area, and only one or two sites suitable for certain purposes. Private property in such parts of the earth would legalise a monopoly. This partly explains why the State usually owns or controls roads, water supply, and docks and harbours.

Thirdly, there is the existence of the State (including local authorities). The State may grant patents or copyrights and may exclude potential competitors from any field of industry by law. But the State does not *arbitrarily* select certain services to be treated as public utilities and to be subjected to especially close control, which may involve the creation by law of local monopolies operated either by the State or by companies whose charges and profits may be controlled by the State. The distinguishing features of public utilities are to be found in the reasons which lead the State to subject them to special treatment, and not in the fact that it does so.

Fourthly, there is the existence of industries for the economical operation of which a large specialised equipment or " fixed capital " is necessary. Thus concerns exist whose supplementary costs are large both absolutely and relatively to their prime costs.

Fifthly, some products are relatively non-transferable between consumers or places. This tends to prevent competition from other areas. Given monopoly, and the possibility of dividing consumers into classes, it makes discriminatory charging possible.

The last two conditions are especially relevant to public utilities and indicate their significant characteristics. They will now be considered more fully.

II

The hypothesis of free competition usually involves the assumption that all capital is both perfectly mobile and divisible into indefinitely small (homogeneous) units. This, of course, is not true. "Capital" may refer to tangible property or to unspecialised purchasing power seeking investment. The assumptions in question apply fairly well to the latter, which may be termed "free capital," but not to the former, which consists mainly of what may be termed "fixed capital." A million pounds invested in the supply and distribution of electricity, for example, ceases to be a million homogeneous mobile pounds and becomes a specialised aggregate of fixed capital in the form of generating stations, cables, and so on. In the future, the market value of this aggregate may become either much greater or much less than a million pounds; it will depend upon the rate of interest and the prospective earning power of the aggregate, which in turn may depend upon the rates which the State allows to be charged. The fixed capital itself is specialised to the particular function of supplying and distributing electricity in that area; it cannot readily be transferred to another place or adapted to a different purpose; its value as a collection of buildings, machines, and material to be used for some other purpose will usually be much below its value as a "going concern." This fact tends to deter newcomers from such industries and to give them a monopolistic character.

In the first place, future prospects must be tempting to induce newcomers to turn large amounts of free capital into specialised equipment which lasts a long time and the value of which is small except in that particular field. It is not enough that profits are higher this year. What of five years, ten years, hence? Are new inventions or changes of taste or other alterations in general conditions likely to make the equipment less valuable by reducing its earning power?

In the second place, existing concerns may be making greater profits than concerns in other industries, so that new free capital can apparently earn more in that field than elsewhere, and it may appear likely that this will continue. But the entry of a new concern may change the position. The optimum size of the industrial unit in such a field is large. It is not a question of adding a small increment to the capital involved in that field, but of adding a large block. A small village may be large enough to enable one general store to pay well, while two would both make losses. In the same way one public utility undertaking may be making good profits, but the entry of another similar undertaking might cause both to make only low profits, or losses. This is especially likely when, as is often the case, the product can be sold only within a restricted local area.

In the third place, there is the possibility that the existing firm or firms may cut their prices to drive out the new competition or to maintain their own sales. Given heavy supplementary costs which are more or less fixed, it may be profitable to underbid rival concerns by selling at a little above prime cost rather than to lose the business. "Rate wars" between railways are, of course, the outstanding example of this. The less elastic the demand for the product, the more will it be in the interests of all the firms concerned to cease these practices and to combine, at least to the extent of maintaining common prices, if not still more closely.

Thus, in these ways, newcomers tend to be deterred from entering such fields and, if they do enter, they tend to combine with existing concerns. The tendency to monopoly is especially marked when supplementary costs are large relatively to prime costs. This is the case with all public utilities.

Public utilities share this last feature, however, with other industries, such as the heavy iron and steel industries. It is our fifth condition which separates them from these other industries. Their products are relatively non-transferable, since they consist of services supplied by means of fixed rails, pipes, wires and so on. The heavy iron and steel industries, for example, have to meet competition from the products of other areas. Public utilities have not; the only competition they need fear, as a rule, is from substitutes. As we have seen, this tends to make them "local monopolies." Combined with the possibility of dividing consumers into classes, it also opens the way for discriminatory charging. Such discrimination is, in fact, widely practised not only by railways, but by all types of public utilities. It constitutes perhaps the chief of the problems to which their existence gives rise.

The two special features which have been emphasised tend to make public utilities local monopolies charging discriminatory prices. Other features, however, have been selected by various writers as distinguishing public utilities from other industries. Professor Glaeser,[2] for example, says that public utilities satisfy an economic need which is a common necessity. This, however, taken alone, would include bread and boots and might be held to exclude telephones. Again, we are told[3] that the product is highly standardised and the business is a cash one. But many standardised products are manufactured and sold for cash, so that the point does not seem fundamental. Local authorities sometimes engage, for various reasons, in municipal trading, or exercise especially close supervision, from hygienic and other motives, over the supply of certain commodities such as milk and meat, or undertake the provision of houses or other " necessities." A little reflection, however, will show the fundamental differences between the supply of such commodities as milk or houses and that of public utility services. The former can be, and often are, left to comparatively uncontrolled private enterprise. The latter cannot. Gas in Great Britain and railways in America, to name only two examples, were at first left to private enterprise, but the need for closer regulation soon became apparent.

Professor Ely[4] stresses the fact that public utilities are subject to " increasing returns." The same thing can be said of some other industries. If we go further and ask *why* it is true (up to the point at which fixed capital is fully utilised) of public utilities, we find that it is a consequence of the first of our two distinguishing features.

Finally, many writers emphasise the fact that public utilities make use of the right of eminent domain. They may interfere with, and use, streets and highways. They may monopolise specially favoured sites, as in the case of docks and harbours. They may be given the right to compel landowners to sell, or to give them passage, as in the case of railways. All this means that they come into contact with public authorities from the first, and that they may have to submit to control in return for the grant of privileges. Historically, this has been very important. But, as Pigou[5] points out, it is not fundamental from the standpoint of analysis; " it is not, and should not be treated as, a distinction of principle." For why should they need special treatment just because they exercise the right of eminent domain? Why should not competition tend to prevail in the same way as in other fields of industry? The fact is, of course,

---

[2] Quoted in Doran : *Materials for the Study of Public Utility Economics*, p. 189.
[3] By M. L. Cooke. *Ibid.*, p. 187.   [4] *Ibid.*, p. 183.
[5] *Economics of Welfare*, third edition, p. 331.

that the circumstances which lead public utilities to use this right are the circumstances which tend to make them local monopolies : namely, the two features which we have discussed.

Thus these two features are the only ones which need be stressed. Others that have been suggested are either aspects or consequences of these two or are of minor significance.

III

The Theory of Monopoly, including Discriminating Monopoly and Monopolistic Competition, has considerable application to public utilities. Monopoly power is always subject to some limitations. It is often exposed to potential, if not actual, competition. It is always exposed to competition from substitutes,[6] which will become more intense, *ceteris paribus,* as the price of its product rises. Such influences affect the elasticity of the demand for its products, but it is the demand schedule reflecting such influences which is taken as given. Maximum prices may be set by direct State regulation or by the fear of such regulation, or of boycott by consumers, if they are exceeded. This is merely equivalent to cutting off the top of the demand curve with a straight line in graphic representation. The Theory of Monopoly still applies.[7]

The difficulty is that the Theory of Monopoly assumes that the aim of the monopolist is maximum profit. It can tell us what the monopolist will do, on that assumption, after the State has fixed conditions. But it cannot tell us what should be the aim of the State in fixing maximum prices and other conditions, or in itself operating public utilities. It is possible to show by general economic analysis what the probable consequences of different kinds of action will be. This might help statesmen and others to decide what action to take. Similarly, it is possible to take some aim as given, purely for the purpose of analysis, and to inquire how it can best be achieved. The question of what the aim *should* be, however, falls outside the province of economics. It is a question of opinion and not a question of fact. Let us postpone consideration of it for a while and turn to a very relevant point. Public utilities control quite a large proportion of the capital of Great Britain.[8] They present special

---

[6] I am using " substitutes " in its widest sense, to include such cases as the following : " There is no substitute for tin in white-metal bearings; but if tin were unobtainable, machinery could be adapted to use roller or ball bearings " (A. P. L. Gordon, *Rationalisation for Tin,* p. 29).

[7] See F. Zeuthen, *Problems of Monopoly and Economic Warfare,* especially pp. 15 to 23.

[8] See *Britain's Industrial Future,* Ch. vi.

economic problems. The economic *effects* of different kinds of regulation are of great significance, and discussion of them falls within the realm of science, as distinct from opinion. Why then have English economists written so little about this subject? Why are most books and articles upon public utilities written by Americans? And has a coherent body of clear and accepted conclusions emerged from such discussion as has taken place?

IV

The chief reason why so much has been written about public utilities in America is to be found in her constitutional system. The State cannot override the written Constitution, and the fourteenth amendment to the Constitution declares that no individual may be deprived of life, liberty, *or property* without due process of law. Hence, when the States began to make regulations, through Public Utility Commissions, which affected the charges and therefore the earnings of privately-owned companies (by fixing the maximum rates for railways in the 'seventies) the question at once arose of whether they were not acting unconstitutionally in doing anything of the kind. This was answered by the Supreme Court in favour of the States, in the famous case of *Munn* v. *Illinois* (1876). But the regulations made by State Commissions and (since its establishment in 1887) by the Inter-State Commerce Commission, were still subject to review by the Courts. For the question always remains of whether any particular rates or charges are fixed so low as to be " confiscatory " and, therefore, unconstitutional. In this way the economic problems presented by public utilities have been forced on the attention of judges and lawyers and so, indirectly, of academicians.

A further reason is that American public utility undertakings, and especially railways, arose and developed comparatively free from State control. This was partly because nineteenth-century America was individualistic and, in general, was opposed to restrictions on freedom of enterprise. It was also partly due to the relatively small density of population. This made railways, in particular, less profitable ventures than in Europe. The State had to provide subsidies to get the lines constructed and was in no position to insist upon much regulation, even if it had wished to do so.

The consequence of this became apparent when regulation began. The question was whether any given scale of charges provided sufficient revenue to yield a " fair return " upon the company's capital. It was difficult enough to decide what percentage upon the capital constituted a " fair return," but that was as nothing compared with the difficulty of deciding what " capital " was. For the amount shown on the balance-sheets was flatly rejected as quite useless and the whole question had to be approached *ad initio*. This explains why so much American writing on public utilities centres around the determination of the " fair value " of the property.

In England, these reasons have been absent. The State is supreme. Thus, to take an example, the Traffic Act of 1894 " practically debarred a railway company from altering the rates that were in force in 1892, no matter how far those rates might be below the revised maxima awarded to the companies in 1891 and 1892 after a most searching inquiry."[9] From such a Parliamentary decision there is no appeal—and consequently there is little or no discussion of the issues involved.

Again, in England almost every public utility undertaking owed its very existence to an Act of Parliament and came from the first under some measure of State control. This was partly because, owing to her dense population, such undertakings offered good prospects of profit, so that the companies submitted calmly to regulation in exchange for the privilege of being allowed to establish them.[10] In particular, a certain amount of capital was usually " authorised " from the start, and subsequent issues have also had to receive Parliamentary sanction. Thus the problem of " fair value " either has not arisen or has in effect been " solved " by a short cut, as when the 1921 Railways Act fixed a standard revenue in sterling. Possibly, especially in the light of American experience, this was the best practical solution. But the fundamental problems are just as real in England and on the Continent (where they have not become pressing because most public utilities are publicly owned) as in America. On the whole, they have been solved without much public discussion. On the whole, they have been neglected by non-American economists. Can we be sure that our solutions have been the best ones ?

Not very much light is thrown upon the subject by the results of American discussion. Much interesting material has accumu-

[9] Cleveland Stevens, *English Railways*, p. 321.
[10] Thus the earliest railway acts provided maximum tolls which might be charged for the use of the railways. This policy had already been adopted in the case of canal companies, which merely provided the waterways. When it was realised that railway companies would themselves act as carriers, maximum fares and charges were also imposed.

D

lated, especially upon such issues as whether the original cost
of production or the present cost of reproduction should be the
basis of " fair value," the proper treatment of depreciation,
and the " peak-load " problem. Especial mention should be
made of the writings of J. M. Clark. Yet no coherent body of
accepted conclusions has emerged. For example, in the famous
case of *Smyth* v. *Ames* (1898) the Supreme Court said that a
fair return should be earned upon the value of the property,
" and in order to ascertain that value, the original cost of construction, the amount expended in permanent improvements, the
amount and market value of its bonds and stock, the present as
compared with the original cost of construction, the probable
earning capacity of the property under particular rates presented
by statute, and the sum required to meet operating expenses
are all matters for consideration, and are to be given such weight
as may be just and right in each case." Then the Court, perhaps
afraid lest it had been too definite, added " we do not say that
there may not be other matters to be regarded in estimating the
value of the property." Since this decision apparently still
carries great weight, we may return to the main argument.

V

The economist, as such, has no special qualifications for considering what the aim of the State should be, nor would such
a discussion fall within the realm of economics or of any other
science. But the economist can assume a certain aim as given—
whether he personally favours it or not is irrelevant—and pursue
the strictly scientific inquiry as to how that aim can best be
attained. What aim can most fruitfully be assumed as given,
for the purpose of applying economic analysis to the problems of
public utilities?

The answer, I think, is obvious. Most modern States accept
the competitive, or capitalist, system. May we not assume,
therefore, that they accept the broad results towards which this
system tends? May we not, in fact, assume that they accept
the system just *because* it tends to produce these results? It so
happens that within the sphere of public utilities competition
cannot operate as freely and in quite the same way as in most
other industries. But the differences are, so to speak, accidental.
There is, therefore, no reason to suppose that the State wishes
to achieve results in this sphere different in nature from those
achieved in the rest of the economic field by competition. This
provides the assumption which seems most plausible and fruitful.

It is then possible to consider in what ways public utilities should be regulated or operated in order to attain ends similar to, and harmonising with, those attained by competition in other fields.

What *are* the broad results which competition tends to bring about? Briefly, it tends to satisfy demand as well as possible from limited " means " or " factors " of production. Demand is, of course, effective demand. The distribution of wealth and income at any time is a given fact. The State may modify this distribution through the machinery of Public Finance—for example, by a progressive income-tax. It is then the distribution as thus modified which is the *datum*. The satisfaction of demand is a question partly of *how much* is produced and partly of *what* is produced. Thus the system tends simultaneously towards two results. The first is that of producing as much as possible under the limiting conditions, per unit of " means " employed. The second is that of producing that assortment of goods and services, out of all the assortments possible under the limiting conditions, which consumers most prefer.

The two results are variables dependent upon one another, since the proportions of different goods demanded will vary with variations in (physical) productivity, while productivity depends partly on what assortment is produced. Again, the assortment produced affects the distribution of income, which is taken in the first place as given. Nevertheless, the brief statement given above is sufficiently accurate for our present purpose.

It is sufficiently accurate to show, given this aim, what are the dangers of monopoly. It is said that a monopolist aiming at maximum profit may charge " excessive " prices or make " excessive " profits. In so far as this modifies the distribution of income it may do so in the direction of either greater or less inequality.[11] We have no warrant, under our assumption, for assuming any such modification to be either desirable or undesirable. But monopoly profits must imply restriction of output. Their existence shows that new " free " capital could earn more in the monopolistic industry than elsewhere. But outside free capital is kept out and the monopolist will not invest more of his own because the increased production would

[11] Usually greater. But a monopoly owned by comparatively poor shareholders and selling to comparatively rich consumers is conceivable. Monopoly profits made by the State from selling to consumers richer than the average citizen will nevertheless increase inequality if used to relieve still richer classes of some taxation.

compel him to lower his prices in order to sell it all, and would thus lower the return on the capital already invested. His marginal costs equal his marginal receipts, as under competition, but he takes account of the lowered price of his product in reckoning the extra receipts which will accrue to him, and this is not done under competition. Hence the assortment of goods and services produced is not that assortment which consumers most prefer : it contains too little of the monopolised good and too much of other goods. Restriction of output in this sense occurs when monopoly profits exist—whether part of the output is destroyed or not, and whether fixed capital is fully utilised or not. It may occur even when the monopolist is making losses, if the prices of some or all of his products are higher than they would have been under competition. By restriction of output he may keep down his losses, just as a more prosperous monopolist increases his profits. Again, a monopoly may be more efficient (possibly owing to the fact that the advantages of a comparatively large business unit in that industry are greater when there is a monopoly), as well as less efficient, than competing firms would be. In the former case, the prices of his products may be lower than they would be under competition. Nevertheless, if he is making monopoly profits, there is restriction of output. The (assumed) aim of the community is not being achieved as fully as possible.[12]

The State does not permit complete freedom of enterprise. It establishes a framework of regulations within which the system works. Thus hours and other working conditions are often laid down by law, measures are taken designed to promote health and safety, and so on. Sometimes other aims are apparent, as when electricity is conveyed by underground wires instead of more cheaply by overhead wires, since the latter are deemed more unsightly. When water is charged for on some basis other than quantity consumed, the aim may partly be the hygienic one of encouraging its use. Nevertheless, on the whole our assumption seems plausible and justifiable. We thus have a basis for the economic analysis of public utility problems. It is suggested that these problems deserve more attention from trained economists, on account both of their theoretical interest and of their practical importance, than they have hitherto received.

---

[12] This point is sometimes overlooked by those who emphasise the need for protecting the consumer. For example, it is overlooked by R. G. Tugwell in his illuminating monograph *The Economic Basis of Public Interest*.

[21]

The Market for Regulation: The ICC from 1887 to 1920

By THOMAS S. ULEN*

There is a great reassessment under way among economists concerning federal regulation of business. The first series of studies on regulation has almost invariably found that consumer welfare is less than it would be without that regulation. With the usual lag, these results have now begun to effect national policy to the extent that air and surface transportation have been substantially deregulated. A second series of studies is now appearing which goes beyond the measure of static costs and benefits of regulation to ask how we came to have the particular regulations that we do have. In this regard there are at least two contending theories (see George Stigler; Richard Posner). The economic theory of regulation hypothesizes that special interest groups, for whom the benefits of federal regulation are large, persuade Congress and the Executive to enact laws (for example, entry restrictions and minimum price schedules). Politicians are prepared to supply such regulation because its costs can be spread over so many voters as to make it almost unnoticeable while its benefits accrue to small, identifiable groups. Against this hypothesis is the public interest theory of regulation. The suggestion of this second hypothesis is that the government introduces regulation at the behest of consumers in order to maximize consumer welfare in industries where competition cannot be relied upon to do so.

I propose in what follows to study the origins and growth of federal railroad regulation to see to what extent these competing theories of regulation explain the historical record. It is also possible that neither hypothesis above can illuminate the area and that some third hypothesis will have to be proposed.

*University of Illinois.

I. The Demand for Regulation Before 1887

When President Cleveland signed the Interstate Commerce Act in February 1887, the era of *laissez-faire*, which had flourished only intermittently in the nineteenth century, ended. Thereafter, the issue of whether government should regulate independent business was dropped. Instead the question became how to make regulation more effective and, after 1920, how to extend it to other industries. As work by Oscar Handlin, Louis Hartz, Jonathan Hughes, and Morton Horwitz has demonstrated, this more pragmatic approach was indeed the time-honored one: government and the public never doubted its determination to regulate, but did differ at times on who should be regulated and how it should be done.

The rapid extension of the railroad network into new regions where settlement was sparse, and the increasing density of the rail service in older, more heavily populated regions in the decade after the conclusion of the Civil War has been much remarked. These developments in surface transportation in the early 1870's caused unease among three separate groups. These same groups constituted the principal demanders of federal railroad regulation:

1) The farmers in the upper Midwest and on the edges of the Great Plains were persuaded that they faced, in the form of the railroad, a monopoly. In this case farmers felt that through rates on interstate shipment of grain were excessive, thus lowering farm incomes below what they would have been had there been more competition. They demanded legislation from their state governments limiting the rates which could be charged by railroads and by warehouses, which were often owned by railroads. Although upheld in the famous *Munn v. Illinois* decision, this attempt to regulate in-

terstate commerce had already been abandoned in all the Granger states save one by 1877. The reason for this was that railroad investment shunned those states with the most restrictive legislation, and it became clear that monopolistic railroads were better than no railroads at all.

2) A second group which grew restless with the railroads in the 1870's was merchants and farmers in the East. As Lee Benson has noted, merchants in New York City felt that price discrimination by railroads on freight hauled into and out of the nation's largest port harmed their business as transhippers. Their allies in opposing the roads were farmers in upstate New York, who also felt themselves to be victims of discriminatory rate making in that their ton-mile rate was greater than the rate paid by farmers further west. Together these groups persuaded the New York State Assembly to hold the important Hepburn Committee hearings in 1879, whose results influenced Congress' actions in the mid-1880's.

3) The last group which became exercised as the rail network became more dense was the railroads themselves. More railroads in a given area meant more competition and thus lower profits. At first informally, the railroads tried to collude on prices charged, but these loose conspiracies of the early and mid-1870's fell prey to secret rate cutting by the members, particularly so during the depression after the Panic of 1873. From the beginning of the recovery in late 1877 railroads began to develop more sophisticated collusions. This development served, when effective, to increase the anger of the consumers of rail services.

The interests of these three groups were different. Therefore, when they expressed a demand for legislative relief, the sorts of legislation that they favored and that might have resulted ought to have been different. In principle there are three different bills being demanded. This is strictly true if only one of the group is to succeed. To the extent that none succeeds fully but each groups succeeds a little bit, the resulting legislation may well be internally inconsistent. The

farmers in the West would have had as their main goal the lowering of rates on through freight. Eastern merchants and farmers would have been most concerned to have short-haul rates fall through legislation outlawing price discrimination. The railroads would have had two different strategies in this market of regulation: if they felt confident of being able to outbid and exclude the other interest groups, then they would have wanted legislation which reduced the costs to them of earning near-monopoly profits through collusion. They might have desired, for instance, that the government act as a manager for the collusion or that cheating on the cartel contract be punishable as simple breach of contract. If, however, the railroads had strong doubts about their ability to exclude other special interests, they would have chosen a more defensive strategy. In that case, the best that the roads might have been able to achieve would have been a watering down of the restrictions which the other groups might have succeeded in achieving.

The interactions among these three groups in the years just before and after the passage of the Interstate Commerce Act in 1887 reveals much about the origins and growth of federal regulation of independent business. The story of the farmers in the Midwest has been admirably told by George Miller and I. L. Sharfman; that of the Eastern merchants and farmers by Benson. I shall confine my attention in what follows to the activities of the railroads. Additionally, I shall look in some detail at the legislation which Congress supplied in 1887 to see if the provisions of the Act allow one to draw inferences about which interest group or groups succeeded in the bidding before Congress. Lastly, the amendments to the Interstate Commerce Act made in the early years of the twentieth century and in the Transportation Act of 1920 will suggest a third hypothesis about the origins and growth of regulation.

II. The Railroad Interest in Federal Regulation

In the *First Annual Report on the Internal Commerce of the United States 1876*, Joseph

Nimmo remarked that railroad cartels—called "pools"—were operating between all major regions of the country and had been doing so for ten years. Among the cartels upon which Nimmo reported, two stand out. The Southern Railway and Steamship Association had been established in 1876 by railroads and steamers in the South to control rates and market shares for the shipment of cotton from the interior to all ports in the South. An innovative technique adopted by that cartel in order to compel adherence to its rates and market-share allotments was the joint ownership by all members of the rolling stock used in through shipments of freight. The second late-nineteenth century railroad cartel of note is the Joint Executive Committee (*JEC*). That collusion embraced the major trunk lines and their many independent feeders between St. Louis and Chicago in the West and the eastern seaboard ports north of Baltimore. It is this second cartel upon which I wish to concentrate.

The *JEC* was the successor to a series of informal rate-setting agreements among freight agents of the trunk lines. As the received theory of cartels would predict, these informal arrangements were not successful, being repeatedly broken by secret cheating. The organization which appeared in June 1879 was a different matter. The colluders had experience with unsuccessful cartels, knew the shortcomings, and deliberately set out to erect internal enforcement mechanisms which would bring them higher profits with more certainty. The cartel took the following steps: 1) it compiled and published statistics weekly on the amount of flour, grain, and provisions carried by each member; the figures were verified by independent agents of the Chicago Board of Trade and only once did a member complain of their inaccuracy. 2) The *JEC* retained a Board of Arbitrators to hear testimony about and decide internal cartel disputes. The arbitrators were paid a retainer of $10 thousand per year and included such famous men as Thomas Cooley, Charles Francis Adams, and David Wright. 3) From March 1881, the cartel granted the commissioner, Albert Fink, the power to

match immediately any price cut by a member. The effect of this device was to allow the loyal members of the collusion to act as a bloc—thus preserving some structure in the cartel—and to reduce the attractiveness of unilateral cheating. 4) The cartel empowered the commissioner to impose various economic sanctions on a discovered cheater. All or part of good faith deposits were forfeited upon a proven allegation of cheating, and for the smaller roads which cheated, the loyal cartelists refused to transfer freight with them. 5) Lastly, the cartel, at regular intervals, diverted freight among its members such that roads which were above their market-share allotments sent freight to those roads which had carried a share of the cartelized output less than that specified in the agreement.

The effect on cartel stability of these elaborate internal enforcement devices was remarkable. In the seven years before the passage of the Interstate Commerce Act in 1887, the cartel was successful in maintaining near-monopoly rates in more than three-quarters of the 328 weeks surveyed. Cheating and a breakdown of the cartel agreement occurred in fewer than one-quarter of the weeks surveyed (see my dissertation). Moreover, cartel success fluctuated with the demand for the transport services of the cartel. Cheating occurred when business was tapering off, usually because of the entry of new firms or because of a modest harvest in the Midwest and the Plains. Success in jointly monopolizing profits was most likely when demand was expanding.

In light of these findings, it seems less likely that the railroads had an exceptional interest in aggressively securing the government's aid in managing their collusion. Although it is possible that the monopoly profits foregone during the relatively infrequent periods of cheating were substantial, it is more likely that they were not substantial enough to warrant a concerted effort to bid for congressional power. This is especially so when one recognizes that there is little a priori reason to believe that the resulting legislation, even if ideally framed, would have necessarily been more effective than the internal enforcement devices used before 1887 to compel adherence to the cartel contract. The punishment meted out for disobeyance of a statute law would not necessarily have been more of a deterrent to cheating than was the sort of punishment which the cartel was already meting out.

That an Act to Regulate Commerce was not necessary to the relatively stable operation of railroad cartels is borne out further by examining the provisions of the Act. Clauses 2 through 7 of the Act dealt with the sort of cartel agreement that the railroads had worked out formerly among themselves. None of these said anything specific about the legality of collusion, that being thought better handled by the common law, or, later, by the Sherman Act. One device which the *JEC* had relied upon for the smooth functioning of its collusion—the transfer of tonnage to equalize actual and allotted market shares—was specifically out-lawed in section 5. It should not be thought, however, that this illegality of pooling freight or revenue caused more instability in the cartel. Instead, a new means of promoting loyalty was developed. A road which was carrying less than its contractually allotted market share was allowed, by the other members of its rate bureau, to announce a lower rate until the resulting increase in business to that road equalized its actual and allotted shares. None of the cartels' other internal enforcement devices was affected by the Act. Nor can any of the other provisions in sections 2 through 7 be said to have greatly affected the probability of cartel stability.

And yet, in the years just after the passage of the Interstate Commerce Act the success of the cartel increased. Since the above considerations suggest that the presence of the Interstate Commerce Commission was not the factor responsible for this increased success, an alternative explanation must be found. The one which best fits the facts is this: the ICC was, like many first efforts, ineffectual; it neither greatly increased railroad profits nor consumer's surplus. Instead, the same factors which had led to stability in railroad collusion before 1887 accounted for it after 1887. The ship-

ment of grain, flour, and provisions from the Midwest to the East boomed between 1887 and 1893. Just as importantly, entry into railroading, as measured by the volume of investment in the industry, fell continually and rapidly from 1886 to the end of the century. When the demand for transport services was sharply curtailed by the severe downturn of 1893–96, the railroad collusions broke down in much the same fashion as they had when demand fell before 1887.

III. The Growth of Regulation After 1896

During the depression that lasted from 1893 to 1896, approximately one-fifth of all the rail mileage in the country went into receivership. Even among the healthy roads, the pressures of decreasing demand were so severe that the resulting rate wars were said by contemporaries to have been the worst of the late-nineteenth century. This set of circumstances, when combined with an ineffectual federal regulatory agency and a Justice Department which already had filed suit against several railroad cartels for violation of the Sherman Act, led the railroad industry to seek alternatives to collusion. The merger of independent businesses was the means adopted. In the trunk line territory between Chicago and the Atlantic ports, the eight independent roads of the early 1890's combined into three, with strong financial interests overlapping in two of those.

Almost as if to put its seal to the end of an era, the Supreme Court held in *United States v. Trans-Missouri Freight Association* and in *United States v. Joint Traffic Association*, that railroad collusion of the sort practiced since 1887 violated section 1 of the Sherman Act. These decisions meant that there would be no turning back for the railroad industry. They had opted for the "merger to monopoly" route, creating altogether different regulatory problems than those which had agitated the public in the 1880's.

This chain of events must be traced in order to understand the subsequent efforts by the Congress to breathe life into the ICC. In 1903 the Elkins Act strengthened the penalties for discrimination and for non-posting of rates. Three years later the Hepburn Act gave the commission the power to set maximum rates, made thirty-day prior notice of rate changes the law, and imposed treble damages on those found guilty of receiving rebates. The Mann-Elkins Act of 1910 cleared some of the terrible confusion which had attended the 1887 Act's long haul, short haul clause and also empowered the ICC to suspend proposed rate changes. In these acts it is difficult to discover the interests of any single group being represented, other than possibly the ICC itself. As Albro Martin has shown, the more efficient railroads were not served by these provisions. Nor has the case yet been made that the public interest was much served by these extensions of regulation. That something else was precipitating refinements of the regulations dealing with surface transportation must be more closely considered. This seems the more pressing in view of the capstone of this edifice of regulatory legislation, the Transportation Act of 1920. Congress gave the ICC the power to specify minimum rates, to determine entry and exit from the railroad industry, to specify the amount and kind of capital formation which roads might undertake, and to preside over matters of consolidation. In a gesture to the original Act to Regulate Commerce, the ICC was granted the power to approve the pooling of freight and revenues.

IV. Conclusion

The history of federal railroad regulation between 1887 and 1920 cannot be fully comprehended using either the public interest theory or the economic theory of regulation. The Act to Regulate Commerce cannot be said to have resulted in a consistent piece of legislation. Bidding for congressional action is not a zero-sum game in which, in this instance, only one of the three groups identifiable as interested in action will have its desires alone written into law. Each group got something in the Act, which made the result palatable in the short run. But as circumstances in the economy changed over the long run, the inconsistencies of the origi-

nal regulation became evident and adjustments were made. It is not at all clear whether any of the original interest groups continued to express a demand for these alterations. Indeed, there is evidence that none of these had a clear interest in extending and tightening the regulation to the extent that resulted in 1920. The only group which may have had sustained interest in the events from 1903 on was the ICC itself.

REFERENCES

Lee Benson, *Merchants, Farmers, and Railroads*, Cambridge, Mass. 1955.

Oscar Handlin, *Commonwealth: A Study of the Role of Government in the American Economy, Massachusetts, 1774–1861*, New York 1947.

Louis Hartz, *Economic Policy and Democratic Thought: Pennsylvania, 1776–1860*, Cambridge, Mass. 1948.

Morton J. Horwitz, *The Transformation of American Law, 1780–1860*, Cambridge, Mass. 1977.

Jonathan R. T. Hughes, *The Governmental Habit*, New York 1977.

Albro Martin, *Enterprise Denied*, New York 1971.

George Miller, *Railroads and the Granger Laws*, Madison 1971.

R. A. Posner, "Theories of Economic Regulation," *Bell J. Econ.*, Autumn 1974, *5*, 335–58.

I. L. Sharfman, *The Interstate Commerce Commission*, New York 1931.

G. J. Stigler, "The Theory of Economic Regulation," *Bell J. Econ.*, Spring 1971, *2*, 3–21.

T. S. Ulen, "Cartels and Regulation," unpublished doctoral dissertation, Stanford Univ. 1978.

Munn v. Illinois, 94 U.S. 113 (1877).

United States v. Joint Traffic Association, 171 U.S. 505 (1898).

United States v. Trans-Missouri Freight Association, 166 U.S. 290 (1897).

U.S. Bureau of Statistics, *First Annual Report on the Internal Commerce of the United States 1876*, "Part Second...on the Commerce and Navigation...," Washington 1877.

[22]

GOVERNMENT CONTROL OF BUSINESS
BY CLYDE O. RUGGLES

DURING recent decades there has been a marked increase in the scope and character of government control of business. Much of this control has been brought about, and much more has been proposed, on the theory that an increased segment of business ought to be subjected to what in important respects is equivalent to "public utility regulation." This is in striking contrast to the early American conviction that we should depend upon competition to fix fair prices and to bring about low rates and good service, even in the public service industries. It is the purpose of this article: (1) to indicate our early faith in the effectiveness of competition, even among industries "affected with a public interest"; (2) to characterize some of the attempts to extend government regulation to non-utility competitive industries within recent decades; (3) to discuss certain aspects of public utility control; (4) to consider the desirability of extending such control to competitive industries; and finally (5) to look at the requirements for more efficient functioning of public utility industries under regulation and the implications of such requirements for other industries.

Early American Faith in Competition

The early Americans' fear of too much government regulation of their lives, including control over economic activities especially, is reflected in their conviction that *written* constitutions, both state and federal, were necessary safeguards against arbitrary government control of all sorts. In these written constitutions the powers of the legislative, executive, and judicial departments of government were defined in order not only to delegate power but also to limit the exercise of power. Early Americans were determined to prevent any such precise and arbitrary regulation of economic affairs as had been practiced in some of the European countries with which they were only too familiar.

Adam Smith's *Wealth of Nations* was published in 1776, a year marked by early American decisions involving important economic and political issues; and in general early Americans approved the theory of laissez faire which was developed in that important book. It is true that the colonies, and later the states, for a time did attempt to regulate the prices of various commodities, principally because a lack of roads, transportation facilities, and organized markets had created the danger that consumers might be compelled under such conditions to pay monopoly prices. As transportation service improved and more adequate markets came into existence, however, the laws regulating prices were permitted to become a dead letter or were repealed — "partly because there was no machinery adequate to enforce them, partly because of resentment that a few of the states did not take part in the movement," [1] but mainly because of the conviction that such regulation was not in the public interest.

The degree to which our early legis-

[1] See 33 *Harvard Law Review* 838, 839 (April, 1920), which includes a list of these early laws.

lators shared the frequently quoted view of Thomas Jefferson that that government is the best that governs least can be illustrated from the history of the railroad industry. The railroad industry is one in which government interference might have been expected to show itself more readily than in almost any other early industry. But there was virtually no federal regulation of railroads for more than a half century after they began operation. Instead, reliance was placed upon competition to bring about low rates and satisfactory service. Indeed, the government through land grants and other forms of subsidy greatly encouraged the building of competing lines. A Senate report during the deep depression of the middle 1870's proposed that the Federal Government itself should build and operate some double-track, exclusively freight railroads from the agricultural areas of the Mississippi Valley to the grain markets of the Atlantic seaboard. The Senate committee concerned took the position that competition offered by publicly owned and operated railroads charging very low rates would force private railroads to meet such rates.[2] But at that time there was reluctance to have the government engage in business; hence no action was taken on building the proposed yardstick railroads, to bring about indirect control of freight rates through government competition.

The lack of interest in the regulation of railroads may be seen in the action taken on a resolution introduced in the United States House of Representatives in 1868. This resolution raised the question whether Congress had the power to regulate freight rates and pas-

senger fares of interstate railroads. It seems strange now that the answer to that query was not obvious. The resolution was referred to the Committee on Roads and Canals, which presented a divided report. The majority of the committee declared that Congress had been given the power to regulate interstate commerce in the commerce clause of the Constitution, but said that they did not have adequate information upon which to base any recommendations for legislation.[3] The minority pointed out that American railroads "under private enterprise had been developed into an extraordinary network within a brief period of time," and that "if such vast interests and investments were committed to the control of the Federal Government they could not fail to accelerate the growth of corruption in connection with federal legislation and hasten the development of centralism" which was "the greatest danger that now threatens our country."[4]

For some time the states likewise refused to regulate railroads, partly because they doubted whether they had the power and 'partly because they staked their faith on competition as the best way to secure satisfactory service at low rates. In the Iowa legislature, for example, a bill was introduced in 1866 to regulate both freight rates and passenger fares, but because of doubt about the state's power to enact such legislation the matter was referred to the Attorney General. His report was to the effect that the state had "no power to restrict and regulate the tariff of prices for passage and freight over the several railroads of this State."[5] Also, in a decision of the Iowa Supreme

[2] Senate Report No. 307, "Transportation Routes to the Seaboard," 2 parts, 43rd Congress, 1st Session (1874).

[3] House Report No. 57, 40th Congress, 2nd Session, June 9, 1868, pp. 1–7.
[4] Ibid., pp. 7–20.
[5] *Iowa House Journal*, 1866, pp. 124–129.

Court in 1869 concerning local taxation in aid of railroads, the court found occasion to say that railway corporations were not organized for the purpose of developing the material prosperity of the state; that such a result was a mere incident of their business; that railroads were organized solely to make money for their stockholders; and that the legislature had no more power over their property and rights than it had over the like property and rights of natural persons or other private corporations.[6]

When the high Civil War prices for grains decreased strikingly in the late 1860's, there was increased interest in government regulation of railroads. But even in states whose population was almost wholly dependent for income upon the prices of grain crops, legislation regulating railroads failed to pass as late as 1870. A good example is the defeat of such legislation in Iowa at that time; as a matter of fact, the proposed bill passed the House but failed in the Senate.[7] Analysis of the vote on this legislation indicates that, whereas the legislators from the older eastern parts of the state voted for regulation, representatives from newer parts of the state with no railroad or only one railroad voted against regulation because, as they said, they did not want to discourage the building of more railroads.[8]

Reluctant Change of Attitude. But even in the Iowa situation just described, where the result was the defeat of regulatory legislation, there was evident a beginning of loss of faith in competition among railroads as a method of securing low rates and good service; that is why the legislators from

the eastern part of the state voted in favor of regulation. The attitude of the public in the State of Illinois beginning about 1870 is an even clearer example of the change. Illinois adopted an amendment to its constitution in 1870 requiring the legislature to regulate railroad rates and the charges made by grain elevators. It was the legislation of this state which brought before the courts the issue whether the states had the power to regulate such businesses. Nevertheless it is evident from the decisions of the Illinois Supreme Court and of the United States Supreme Court on this point that as late as the decade of the 1870's both the state and federal courts, although their decisions permitted government regulation, were very reluctant to endorse it even for industries "affected with a public interest."

The *Munn* case, which crystallized the issue, was argued twice before the Illinois Supreme Court and was finally decided by a divided court in 1873. "On the first argument at the last term the court after much deliberation was unable to reach a satisfactory conclusion. In the meantime the court had undergone a change by the election of two new members, and it was deemed expedient and proper that they should take a part in the decision." [9] The majority opinion of the court emphasized the fact that the constitution of the state had vested all legislative power in the "General Assembly" and that "that body could not withstand the appeals that went up to them from the producers and shippers of the great and indispensable wants of man . . . to provide some remedy against the oppression and extortions to which they were subjected by this organized combination of monopolists, already such a

[6] *Hanson v. Vernon*, 27 Iowa 28, 53.

[7] *Iowa House Journal*, 1870, pp. 442–443; *Iowa Senate Journal*, 1870, pp. 378, 465, 482, and 615.

[8] See also *Iowa Agricultural Report*, 1869, pp. 183–185 and 187.

[9] *Munn et al. v. The People*, 69 Illinois 80, 88, 91, 93 (1873).

Government Control of Business   35

formidable power, with but one heart, and that palpitating for excessive gains." The minority opinion expressed the belief that the court had rested its conclusion "in part upon the ground that these parties exercised a public employment," which view the minority did not accept.[10]

The United States Supreme Court also divided on whether Illinois had the power to enact such legislation. The majority of the court, emphasizing the significance of a seventeenth-century opinion of Lord Hale, reached the conclusion that the Illinois grain elevators were affected with a public interest. But there was a note of caution in their opinion: "In passing upon this case we have not been unmindful of the vast importance of the questions involved. This and cases of a kindred character were argued before us *more than a year ago* by the most eminent counsel, and in a manner worthy of their well-earned reputations. *We have kept the cases long under advisement in order that their decision might be the result of our mature deliberations.*" [11] One legal authority has pointed out that, while there was a certain plausibility in the application of Lord Hale's principle to the Illinois law, the Court's decision was so broad as to cover any form of private property.[12]

The foregoing events reveal that regulatory legislation, even for industries affected with a public interest, did not have public support until approximately a century after the adoption of our Constitution, and that judicial sanction for such legislation was very reluctantly given. The fear of monopolistic practices detrimental to the public interest, however, finally brought about such regulation. The deep-seated feeling regarding the need of preventing monopolistic practices is seen in the fact that, although pooling by railroads was prohibited by the Act to Regulate Commerce passed in 1887, the Supreme Court in 1897 held that the Sherman Antitrust Act, passed in 1890, also applied to the railroads.[13]

Attempts to Extend Utility Control to Competitive Industries

While there has been much interest in stimulating competition through enforcement of antitrust legislation in the case of certain industries, government regulation has also attempted in the case of other industries to control what has been considered as harmful and destructive competition or to protect the public interest in various other respects. Many of the attempts to extend what is essentially public utility regulation to non-public utility enterprises have reached the United States Supreme Court within the last 25 years. Some of the issues involved in these cases deserve brief consideration.

In 1920 a middle-western state attempted in one bold stroke to extend public utility status to a sizable part of the economy. An act was passed by a special session of the Kansas legislature largely as the result of strikes in the coal mines of the state. Under this act the following business activities were declared to be affected with a public interest: the manufacture and prepara-

---

[10] Ibid., p. 100.

[11] 94 U. S. 77, 88 (1877). Italics supplied.

[12] Breck P. McAllister, "Lord Hale and Business Affected with a Public Interest," 43 *Harvard Law Review* 759 (March, 1930); see also G. H. Robinson, "The Public Utility Concept in American Law," 41 *Harvard Law Review* 277 (January,

1928); Walton Hamilton, "Affectation with a Public Interest," 39 *Yale Law Journal* 1089 (June, 1930).

[13] *United States* v. *Trans-Missouri Freight Association,* 166 U.S. 290 (1897). A similar decision was made in 1898 in the case of *United States* v. *Joint Traffic Association,* 171 U.S. 505.

tion of food for human consumption; the manufacture of clothing for human wear; the production of any substance in common use for fuel; and common carriers and other public utilities. The state public utilities commission was abolished, and regulation of public utilities was transferred to the Kansas Court of Industrial Relations, which was created to regulate all the foregoing industries.[14] The act vested in the industrial court power on its own initiative or on complaint to summon the parties and hear any dispute "over wages or other terms of employment" in the industries mentioned; and, if the court should find the peace and health of the public imperiled by such controversy, it was required to make findings and "fix wages and other terms for the future conduct of the industry."

The constitutionality of this act was tested when a case concerning the regulation of wages in a small packing plant in Kansas reached the United States Supreme Court. The court in a unanimous decision held that "the mere declaration by a legislature that a business is affected with a public interest is not conclusive of the question whether its attempted regulation on that ground is justified"; that "the circumstances of its alleged change from the status of a private business and its freedom from regulation into one in which the public have come to have an interest are always a subject of judicial inquiry"; that the "public may suffer from high prices or strikes in many trades but the expression 'clothed with a public interest' as applied to a business means more than that the public welfare is affected by continuity or by the price at which a commodity is sold or a service rendered"; that "the circumstances which clothe a particular

kind of business with a public interest, in the sense of *Munn* v. *Illinois* and other cases, must be such as to create a peculiarly close relationship between the public and those engaged in it, and raise implications of an affirmative obligation on their part to be reasonable in dealing with the public."

Regarding the business activities specified in the Kansas law "as affected with a public interest," the Court said:

It has never been supposed, since the adoption of the Constitution, that the business of the butcher, or the baker, the tailor, the wood chopper, the mining operator, or the miner was clothed with such a public interest that the price of his product or his wages could be fixed by state regulation. It is true that in the days of the early common law an omnipotent parliament did regulate prices and wages as it chose, and occasionally a colonial legislature sought to exercise the same power; but nowadays one does not devote one's property or business to the public use or clothe it with a public interest merely because one makes commodities for, and sells to, the public in the common callings of which those above mentioned are instances. An ordinary producer, manufacturer, or shopkeeper may sell or not sell as he likes, . . . and while this feature does not necessarily exclude businesses from the class clothed with a public interest, . . . it usually distinguishes private from quasi-public occupations.[15]

The Court pointed out further that there was no monopoly in the preparation of food and that the prices charged by the small packing plant involved were fixed by competition throughout the country at large. Also: "If . . . the common callings are clothed with a public interest by a mere legislative declaration, which necessarily author-

[14] Kansas Special Session Laws, 1920, Chapter 29.

[15] *Charles Wolff Packing Co.* v. *Court of Industrial Relations*, 262 U.S. 522, 537 (1923).

izes full and comprehensive regulation within legislative discretion, there must be a revolution in the relation of government to business." [16] Such regulation of the common callings, the Court said, would "be running the public interest argument in the ground."

Regarding the question whether the Court's sanction of the regulation by Congress of the wages of railroad employees in 1916 was adequate precedent for approval of the Kansas legislation, the Court stated that it was "not too much to say that the ruling in *Wilson* v. *New* [17] went to the border line, although it concerned an interstate common carrier in the presence of a nationwide emergency and the possibility of great disaster"; that there was little danger that there would be shortage of food, clothing, or fuel supply in any state with uninterrupted interstate commerce; that the Kansas law so far as it pertained to the fixing of wages in a packing house, was in conflict with the Fourteenth Amendment.

Within a few years after the foregoing unanimous decision, the Court by a five to four decision refused to uphold a New York law which prohibited the resale of theater tickets by brokers at a price in excess of 50 cents over the price printed on the ticket. The Court repeated its statement in the *Wolff* case, that a business was not affected with a public interest merely because the legislature so declared, and it refused to uphold such regulation of the resale price of theater tickets.[18] In a dissenting opinion Mr. Justice Holmes stated that a state legislature should be permitted to do "whatever it sees fit to do unless it is restrained by some express prohibition in the constitution"; that "the notion that a business is clothed with a public interest and has been devoted to the public use is little more than a fiction intended to beautify what is disagreeable to the sufferers." [19]

In 1928 the Court in a six to three decision found a New Jersey law regulating employment agencies unconstitutional because it provided for control of prices in a business not affected with a public interest. The law required private employment agencies to secure a license from the state and made issuance or revocation of the license contingent upon approval by the state Commissioner of Labor of the proposed schedule of fees to be charged. The majority opinion of the Court conceded that extortion, discrimination, and fraud as practiced by employment agencies might necessitate some regulation, but held nevertheless that these practices did not justify price fixing. The minority opinion challenged the distinction between price control and other regulation, and contended that there was no valid difference "between regulation of price, if appropriate to the evil to be remedied, and other forms of appropriate regulation which curtail liberty of contract or the use and enjoyment of property." [20]

In 1929 the Court, with one dissent, held unconstitutional a Tennessee law which attempted to regulate the retail price of gasoline. The majority opinion said that "gasoline is one of the ordinary commodities of trade differing, so far as the question here is affected, in no essential respect from a great variety of other articles commonly bought and sold by merchants and private dealers in the country"; that the size of a business or the fact that the public has a

---

[16] Ibid., p. 539.
[17] 243 U. S. 332.
[18] *Tyson & Brother* v. *Banton*, 273 U.S. 418 (1927).

[19] Ibid., p. 446.
[20] *Ribnik* v. *McBride*, 277 U.S. 350, 373.

"feeling of concern in respect of its maintenance" did not make the industry one affected with a public interest; and that the state had no power to fix the price of gasoline.[21]

In 1932 the Supreme Court in the case of *New State Ice Company* v. *Liebmann* held that Oklahoma had no power to extend public utility status to the manufacture and distribution of ice for sale. The Oklahoma law made a certificate of public convenience and necessity a requisite for going into the ice business. On the basis of this law the New State Ice Company, the holder of a license to do business in Oklahoma City, sought to prevent Liebmann, who was without such a certificate, from going into the ice business in the same city. Liebmann contended that the ice business was not affected with a public interest and that the state had no right to prevent him from going into that business. The majority opinion of the Court held that the ice business was a private one; that there was no monopoly in the business because of the possibility of shipping ice into markets that might charge high prices; that electrical refrigerators, with electric rates regulated by law, prevented monopoly prices for ice; that no emergency was shown to call for such regulation; and that the protection of natural resources was not involved. The Court expressed the view that the law itself by keeping out new entrants might foster monopoly and thus go counter to the public interest. Mr. Justice Brandeis, together with Mr. Justice Stone, dissented. The former stated that he regarded control of entry into a business through a certificate of public convenience and necessity as a modern device by which the public might create

monopolies to curb unbridled competition and lessen wastes; that granting such certificates in a particular case was primarily a matter for a state to determine; and that the Court should not prevent a state from trying "novel social and economic experiments without risk to the rest of the country." [22]

The foregoing decisions handed down by the Supreme Court in the period from 1920 to 1933 reveal an unwillingness on the part of the Court during most of this period to sanction control, for example, over wages, prices, and entry into business, except for industries "affected with a public interest" in the sense used in *Munn* v. *Illinois*. In 1934, however, the Court by a five to four decision upheld a New York State law regulating the price of milk, and thus reversed its previous position regarding the validity of price regulation and the meaning of the phrase "affected with a public interest."

The New York State law, passed in 1933, declared the production, distribution, and sale of milk to be a business "affecting the public interest and health," on the ground that uneconomic practices in the business constituted an emergency impairing conditions in the industry and even the public health. It established a Milk Control Board with temporary power to fix wholesale and retail prices of milk. Violation of the law by a grocer brought the case to the courts, and the case reached the United States Supreme Court on the complaint that fixing the price of milk resulted in taking property and liberty without due process of law.

Although the dairy business was not considered "in the accepted phrase a public utility," the Court said that no

[21] *Williams* v. *Standard Oil Company of Louisiana*, 278 U.S. 235, 240.

[22] *New State Ice Co.* v. *Liebmann*, 285 U.S. 262, 311.

"constitutional principle bars the state from correcting existing maladjustments by legislation touching prices"; that there is nothing particularly "sacrosanct" about price as an object of regulation. The expression "affected with a public interest" was interpreted to mean "no more than that an industry for adequate reason is subject to control for the public good." And, according to the majority of the Court, an inadequate return to producers and distributors of milk had threatened sanitary standards in the business, which in turn affected the health and "prosperity" of the people of New York State.[23] Thus the Court appears now to be willing to permit the phrase "affected with a public interest" to mean whatever legislative bodies see fit to have it mean, and to consent to price regulation in such industries as the states or Congress may feel necessary.

Characteristics of Utility Regulation

Even though the Supreme Court may now sanction a rather general extension of important aspects of control over public utilities to other industries, there still remains the all-important question whether such control is either wise or workable. Certain economic and regulatory problems are involved in this question, and an examination of some of the outstanding characteristics of public utility regulation will serve to throw light on those problems.

Surely the experience of the United States with the group of industries that it has regulated to the greatest extent and for the longest period of time, the utilities, should be carefully considered in any effort to extend similar controls to non-utility enterprises. The following selected aspects of public utility

regulation suggest themselves as important for this purpose:

Entry into or Exit from Business. It should be emphasized that during the early history of this country, as far as government regulation was concerned, we made little distinction between public utilities and other industries. As already indicated, both groups were comparatively free from government regulation, since we were determined that there should be competition among all industries. Thus, railroad charters were freely granted for the building of parallel lines. The Federal Government did not exercise control over the building or the abandonment of a railroad until almost 100 years after our railroads began to operate. And not until 1920 did we reverse our public policy by giving authority to the Interstate Commerce Commission to grant or refuse certificates of public convenience and necessity for the building or abandonment of lines directly or indirectly serving interstate commerce. Since the Commission has had this power, however, it has authorized abandonment of over 30,000 miles of railroad, much of which never did have economic justification.[24]

Concerning the various types of so-called local utilities, it was our early practice to be liberal in granting franchises and in encouraging duplication of expensive plants and facilities. Even medium-size and small-size communities insisted upon competition between local utilities. Indeed, long-term and even perpetual franchises were granted in order to assure competition in the furnishing of various utility services. But that policy proved unwise and has been virtually abandoned. Entry into the utility business now generally re-

---

[23] *Nebbia v. New York*, 291 U. S. 502 (1934).

[24] 58 ICCR 139.

quires a certificate of public convenience and necessity, and abandonment of utility service now requires the consent of public authority. Despite our early encouragement of the duplication of competing plants, we now generally favor the granting of limited or exclusive certificates or franchises that give the utility a monopoly in the furnishing of a service within a given area.

Obligation to Serve. The early public utilities were not obliged to render service unless their charters and franchises so stipulated. The Interstate Commerce Commission in the first year of its existence refused to require a railroad to furnish freight cars for shipments to destinations on another railroad.[25] From their own point of view, however, most of the railroads soon found the practice of not allowing their cars to be sent to destinations on other roads to be unsound, and in 1910 the failure of one railroad to permit some of its coal cars to be so sent was held by the Interstate Commerce Commission to be illegal. Even so, the Commission gave no order in the case and indicated that it was the duty of the railroads to work out equitable car service rules among themselves.[26] And it was not until 1917 that the Esch-Pomerene Act, which was later incorporated into the Transportation Act of 1920, finally gave the Commission authority to regulate the exchange and interchange of railway equipment.

A good example of the absence in early days of any positive requirement that a municipal utility should render service is seen in an 1858 decision of the New Jersey Supreme Court regarding a gas company in Paterson which refused to serve a prospective customer whose place of business was located on a street in which the company had a gas main. The court pointed out that the franchise was permissive throughout; that the gas company could either serve or refuse to serve customers even on a street already piped for service. Indeed, the court expressed surprise that any gas company would undertake to serve all customers in Paterson, although the city had at that time a population of less than 20,000. The wording of the decision is amusing and instructive:

The Paterson Company is authorized to make and sell gas, which, in the absence of any indication to the contrary, implies that they may fix their own price, and choose their own customers, like any other manufacturer. If the duty of furnishing gas to those requiring it was meant to be imposed, it would doubtless be expressed, and not be left to mere inference. If it is to be inferred, what is to be the limit? Why have not all the inhabitants of the town the same right to demand it as those having buildings on the streets along which the pipes are placed? The charter sets forth the general purpose of lighting all the streets and buildings, and the court below seems to have held that the company has no choice in the matter. But what company in the state, or elsewhere, could have ventured to assume such a responsibility as that?[27]

Quality of Service. The quality of utility service has been subjected to much detailed regulation because price (or rate) regulation means little if the quality of the service or product is not also controlled. Early gas franchises, for example, provided that gas should have a certain candle power—gas at that time being used principally for lighting. After electricity displaced gas for illumination and the latter was used largely for cooking and for various

---

[25] 1 ICCR 688, 693.
[26] 22 ICCR 39, 41.

[27] *Paterson Gas Light Co.* v. *Brady*, 27 N. J. Law 245; 72 Am. Dec. 360 (1858).

industrial purposes, the early standard of candle power became obsolete and was replaced by a standard of heat units. The quality of electric service has likewise been subjected to government control. Indeed, the use of electric power is now so general that adequate quality and continuity of service are necessary both for domestic uses and for industrial processes.

Regulation of Prices. The same sort of "free economy" policy that was followed for some time with regard to entry into business, obligation to serve, and quality of service was also followed with regard to utility prices. Some early railroad charters definitely provided that rate making was a function of the railroads' boards of directors. Even under the Act of 1887, the Interstate Commerce Commission, although it could find railroad rates to be unreasonable, was given no power to determine what the rates should be — and at a time when rail carriers had been operating for more than 50 years. Not until the Act of 1906 [28] was the Commission given power to set maximum rates, and not until 1920 was it given control over minimum rates.[29]

From the time of the early New Jersey Supreme Court decision previously mentioned, holding that the Paterson Gas Light Company had the same right as any other manufacturer to fix its own prices,[30] the attitude toward the regulation of the rates of utilities other than carriers likewise underwent a marked change. Even in the early history of utilities there seems to have been some fear that competition might not be effective; for while franchises were freely granted to competing

companies, rates were sometimes fixed in the franchises for the life of the franchise or at least for very long periods of time. Now, as the result of an evolutionary development similar to that of the regulation of the railroads' rates, the other utilities are subjected to comprehensive control of their prices.

For many years we insisted that utilities should operate under a free economy in spite of the fact that expensive public utility plants should not have been duplicated to render *identical* public utility service within a given community. Most communities went through the same experience: at first wasteful competition and then later consolidation of competing plants into a single unified system — an experience that is reflected in the word "consolidated" found in the title of many present-day utility companies. Obviously, the operation of these early utilities under a free economy meant higher unit costs and service of lower quality than would have been furnished by single, integrated companies.

There can be little doubt about the savings that can be secured through integration. The Consolidated Edison Company has recently become the largest integrated electric utility in the United States with assets of more than $1.2 billion, as the result of approval of its merger with two of its subsidiaries, Brooklyn Edison Company and New York and Queens Electric Light and Power Company. The company is to reduce rates by $6 million annually in the New York City boroughs of Manhattan, Bronx, Brooklyn, and the part of Queens served by the company, and to write off a substantial amount in plant accounts of the three utilities involved.[31] In London, where less large-

[28] 34 Stat. 584.
[29] 41 Stat. 474.
[30] See footnote 27, p. 40.

[31] *Electric World*, Vol. 124, No. 5 (August 5, 1945), p. 118.

scale integration has occurred than in this country, the cost of electricity is higher than in large American cities.

Moreover, because high unit costs of service cut down volume of consumption, a vicious circle is set up: the drop in consumption tends to push up the unit costs even higher. And the most practicable way to break this vicious circle is to cut costs through integration and in other ways, and to adopt such vigorous programs of marketing the service as will bring about enough increased consumption to sustain the low level of rates. But if a monopoly of a certain market is granted through a franchise or a certificate of public convenience and necessity, legalizing complete integration of physical facilities, the utility must not be permitted to operate as though under a free economy. It should then be regulated as a monopoly. Hence, for utility industries government control is necessary over entrance into business or exit from it; over the obligation to serve and the quality of service; and, finally, over prices (rates). But does such a need for regulation apply also to competitive industries, where the circumstances are strikingly different?

Is It Wise to Extend Utility Control to Competitive Industries?

Admittedly the basic issue is whether the public interest will be served by extension to non-utility industries of some such control as we have exercised over public utilities. And a decision on this issue to a large extent would appear to depend on how successful public utility regulation has been, and on whether the control of non-public utility enterprises presents such significantly greater difficulties as to make it not feasible.

But has the regulation of public utilities been successful so far? The writer had occasion to make a study of state public utility commissions in 1937, which led him to the conclusion that state regulation of utilities left much to be desired.[32] While some of the state utility commissions have accomplished worth-while results, altogether too many of them have made very poor records, partly because they have not had adequate financial support to be able to attract competent personnel and partly because political pressure has unfavorably affected not only the selection but also the tenure of commission personnel. The average salary of commissioners as revealed in the foregoing study was only $5,000, and public utility commissions offered too little hope that able men could count on having careers either as commissioners or as expert members of the staffs of the commissions. There was insufficient assurance that governors would not interfere with security of tenure by making room for those whom they wished to appoint in order to pay their political debts or to secure future political favor in seeking higher political office. Furthermore the budgets of the commissions were not adequately sustained by the legislatures during the depression of the 1930's, and hence many commissions lost capable members of their staffs who should have been retained if the public's interest was to be served. Indeed, one of the outstanding reasons urged for publicly owned and operated yardstick power plants has been that government regulation of public utility rates has not been so effective as it should have been in protecting consumers.

[32] *Aspects of the Organization, Functions and Financing of State Public Utility Commissions* (Harvard University, Graduate School of Business Administration, Division of Research, Business Research Studies, No. 18, 1937), p. 90.

But if government control of the utility industries has been ineffective, the question naturally arises whether the attempt similarly to regulate non-public utility enterprises can succeed. In reaching a conclusion on the feasibility of extending public utility control to non-utility enterprises, the problems involved in the application of major aspects of this control to non-utilities need to be appraised.

An attempt to regulate entry into or exit from business for many non-utility enterprises involves complex economic issues. The size of the market which a utility is to serve can be fairly accurately determined, and by means of certificates of public convenience and necessity the *supply of utility service* can be definitely controlled. Such government control of supply is essential to effective regulation of utility prices. If we are unable to exercise similar control over the supply of non-public utility commodities and services, their quality, and their possible substitutes, we cannot hope to control their prices. But determination of the extent of consumer demand and control of the supply in conformity with this demand, not to mention control of the quality of products or services, is very difficult, to say the least, in the case of non-public utility enterprises.

The regulation of prices of agricultural products, for example, shows the need of having direct or indirect control of supply. The importance of this fact was not appreciated when the Federal Farm Board was established in 1929, and the Federal Farm Board itself explained its failure to maintain farm prices in its annual report in 1932 by this statement:

No measure for improving the price of farm products other than increasing the demand of consumers can be effective over a period of years unless it provides a more definite control of production than has been achieved so far. In a few limited and specialized lines, cooperative associations have made progress toward such control. For the great staple products, however, the problem still remains. . . .[33]

The Agricultural Adjustment Acts, beginning in 1933, did involve various plans for disposal of surplus products, for withholding them from the market, and for direct control over production — in other words, sought to raise farm prices by means of various forms of control of the supply of agricultural products to reach the market.

Even so, the attempt to control agricultural prices may well prove to be ineffective in the long run because of the difficulties encountered in such control of supply. One complication is the fact that for many agricultural commodities there are substitutes. Another complication is the fact that such control may fail if it runs counter to worldwide agricultural production and to prices that result from international rather than domestic economic forces. Attempts to fix minimum prices of coal, for example, would call for the fixing of prices not only in accordance with qualities of coal but also in accordance with prices of various substitute fuels such as gas and oil, some of which may be secured from international sources.

Similar complications are not encountered in the regulation of the prices of the products or services of public utilities. There are comparatively few outstanding wholly unpredictable economic factors in the regulation of utility prices and of the quality of service. While some electric power utilities, for example those which serve highly industrialized regions, find the

[33] *Third Annual Report of Federal Farm Board,* 1932, p. 62.

demand for service somewhat affected by substitute services of electric power generated by industry itself or by the swings of the business cycle, the impact of these factors is of minor importance indeed compared with the effect of unknown and unpredictable forces, nation-wide or international in scope.

In the case of regulation of utilities, price control, which is a vital feature of that regulation, has been in the main a fixing of *maximum* prices on the theory that utilities through franchises and certificates of public convenience and necessity have been given such control over their market that they are in a position, if not regulated, to charge unfair prices to *consumers*. On the other hand, in attempts to regulate some non-public utility industries where competition has been considered detrimental, it has been *minimum* prices that have been fixed in the interest of *producers*. Under the regulation of maximum prices, as with utilities, a mangement desiring to increase the rate of return on some legally determined valuation or rate base can only secure it by reducing the costs of products or services through greater volume of sales or through technological advances, in the hope that regulatory agencies will permit a share of the gains from such increased efficiencies to be retained. But fixing *minimum* prices, as with non-utility industries, on the theory that there is too much competition, will encourage capital to continue in such industries when in fact it ought to seek investment where it could be more profitably employed. In other words, fixing minimum prices or providing subsidies encourages the maintenance of the supply, or even an increase in the production, and thus discourages a proper adjustment of the supply to the demand. The result then is a tendency

to perpetuate the very economic unbalance which gave rise to the fixing of minimum prices.

Attempted price control under such conditions may create more problems than it will solve. For one thing, it will create a demand for *substitutes* for the regulated commodity or service. This in turn will make necessary an extension of control over increasing segments of the economy in order to prevent the demand for various substitutes from interfering with the demand for those commodities or services for which prices have been fixed.

Moreover, control of prices in the many non-utility enterprises in a country the size of the United States would call for regulatory agencies on a scale hitherto unknown. It is true that under the exigencies of war that brought shortages in the supply of certain goods and services, we have had to have recourse to price control. But the economic, organizational, and administrative problems involved even under these special circumstances of limited supply have been all too obvious.

Mere mention of control over entrance into business or exit from it for all the various non-utility enterprises and even cursory consideration of factors involved in the regulating of the supply, the quality, and the prices of commodities or services for which there are many substitutes serves to indicate that price control in the non-utility industries will be far less likely to succeed than in the utility industries.

Requirements for More Efficient Functioning under Regulation

In view of the difficulties that will be encountered in any attempt to regulate the *prices* of non-public utility industries, the query may be raised whether more effective competition among such industries rather than government price fixing does not promise more worthwhile results. Obviously, this does not mean an attempt to return to a laissez-faire policy such as existed in our early history, but it does mean much more effective control in the public interest of what is recognized at the present time as "monopolistic competition." There is a vast difference between attempting to apply what is essentially public utility regulation to competitive industries and providing the proper "rules of the game" under which the non-public utility industries are permitted to operate. While this article is confined to a consideration of the extension of public utility regulation to competitive enterprises, it may be pointed out here that, as business becomes more complex, there will be increasing need for positive regulation to prevent unfair competition and various kinds of trade practices and business conduct that would otherwise retard progress by keeping prices higher than they would be without any restraint of trade. We grant patent rights, for example, to stimulate technological advance, not to enable the holders to reap rewards by throttling competition.

Indeed, it may be seriously questioned whether we have not made a mistake in regulating utilities by reducing the competition between the *different types of utilities,* as for example between gas and electric utilities. Although gas and electric utilities are competitive for cooking, refrigeration, and for various industrial uses, census returns reveal that even under government regulation the "composite" company, which combines the two services under a single management, has become the dominant type.[34] While there are certain econo-

mies in combining these two competing utility services within a single company, it is very doubtful whether the *tangible gains* may not be of less importance to the public than the *intangible losses.*

Under a single management, competition between gas and electricity for cooking, refrigeration, and various industrial and other uses is likely to be a sham battle. If the education and experience of the top executive have been in the electrical field, he is not so likely to appreciate the need for appropriating annually large sums for research into possible increased utilization and marketing of gas as would an executive who had devoted all his talents and time to the gas industry. Moreover, those employees of the utility who are responsible for the sale of gas or electric service and appliances are not likely to feel the need of an aggressive sales policy if the company's executives are known to favor "pushing" the use of electricity for certain uses and of gas for certain other uses. In Massachusetts the gas utilities sought regulation by the Commonwealth on the theory that it would protect them from competition both from newer processes in gas making and from electric utilities.[35]

It is highly important to the public that intensive competition rather than "composite company" policy should determine the extent to which each of the utility services is to be used. When company policy rather than keen competition determines the role of gas or electric service, there is likely to be a "birth control" of ideas which in turn may greatly retard both improvement in the quality of service and reduction in its cost. Businessmen are paid to

---

[34] *Census of Electric Light and Power Industry, 1937,* pp. 23–24.

[35] Leonard D. White, "The Origin of Utility Commissions in Massachusetts," *Journal of Political Economy,* Vol. XXIX (March, 1921), pp. 189–191.

worry, and this applies to executives in *different types* of competing utility services as well as to those in non-utility industries. The gains to consumers through technological advances may be intangible, but they are vital — and they are likely to be greater when the competition between different types of service is real rather than apparent.

In contrast to the public policy of permitting gas and electricity to be under the same management, the attitude of the Federal Government toward the desirability of competition between telegraph and telephone service may be cited. Beginning in the decade following 1900, the American Telephone and Telegraph Company attempted to secure control of the Western Union Telegraph Company. In its annual reports, the A.T. & T. pointed out that the most satisfactory and economical communication service by telephone and by telegraph could not "be accomplished by separately controlled or distinct systems"; that there should be no "competition in the accepted sense of competition" between these services; that it was "possible to 'telephone' messages but while the operating cost would be somewhat larger than in the case of 'telegraphing,' the plant cost would make telephoning messages prohibitive over long distances under ordinary conditions." [36] These convictions of executives of the Bell System were translated into policy through the purchase of sufficient Western Union stock to enable the A.T. & T. to exercise a controlling influence in the transmission of intelligence by wire. But a threat of action on the part of the Attorney General brought from the A.T. & T. the explicit statement that it would "dispose promptly of its entire holdings of stock

of the Western Union Telegraph Company in such a way that the control and management of the latter" would "be entirely independent of the former." President Wilson in his correspondence with the Attorney General expressed satisfaction that the A.T. & T. should "thus volunteer to adjust its business to the conditions of competition." [37] Without doubt, competition between long distance service by telegraph and by telephone has greatly stimulated research in communication and has accelerated the progress of long-distance telephone service over what it would have been had the A.T. & T. been permitted to control the telegraph industry.

Another contingency which it is wholesome for either privately or publicly owned utilities to face is that the public might readily change from one type of ownership and operation to the other. There should be no legal obstacles in the way of the public's entering into the utility business if it desires to do so (or, for that matter, in abandoning public ownership and operation and perhaps even leasing publicly owned property for private operation). If the public is able to secure better utility service at lower costs through publicly owned and operated plants, it is certainly foolish not to follow that plan. But there is no merit in public ownership and operation merely because it is public, any more than there is merit in private ownership and operation merely because it is private. And the public should not fool itself regarding the comparability of the results, particularly with regard to inequalities arising from payment of taxes, receipt of subsidies or other economic subventions, and of course from regulation itself.

[36] See Annual Report of the A. T. & T., 1909, pp. 31–34, and 1910, pp. 49–58.

[37] See Annual Report of the A. T. & T., 1913, pp. 24–27.

Government Control of Business   47

Changing the mode of ownership and operation does not set aside economic forces, nor does it change human nature. Managers of publicly owned and operated utilities should not be exempt from effective regulation. Indeed, such regulation is their own protection in the long run. Some state utility commissions that have the power to regulate municipally owned and operated utilities have greatly helped these utilities to make a long-range success by protecting them, for example, against unsound accounting, depreciation, or other policies urged by city councils which might be eager, on the one hand, to secure rate reductions or, on the other hand, to transfer utility revenue into the general municipal funds against the interests of utility consumers.

Furthermore, public management, as well as private, needs the spur to efficiency that comes from reasonable and intelligent regulation. The private utilities have objected strenuously in recent years to regulation which they claim "interferes with management"; and doubtless much regulation has been of that character — not only interference with management but, when not based on thorough and comprehensive data, unintelligent interference. But there is a vast difference between regulation that interferes with management and regulation that holds management responsible for reasonable results. The public interest demands that there should be intelligent regulation based upon reasonable standards of performance and applied to every utility, whether the TVA, a municipal plant, or any other form of utility.

Utility regulation of this type will require much improvement in the character of the administrative agencies that are to do the regulating. Legislative bodies, such as Congress, the state legislatures, and the city councils, are not equipped to cope directly with the issues involved in such regulation. The Supreme Court has recently gone on record to the effect that the courts themselves should leave to public utility commissions much more leeway in the methods of arriving at conclusions regarding business problems arising in public utility regulation provided the "end result" is justified.[38] The Court is to be commended for its recognition that the commissions are in a position to profit by firsthand knowledge on those economic and business problems that must be considered in arriving at fair and reasonable end results.

But there is a danger in giving the public utility commissions more leeway, as has been well recognized in discussions at meetings of the American Bar Association and in legal periodicals — the danger of arbitrary action by those commissions. This is a real danger, and the public should take it seriously and should attempt to avoid it by improving the commissions in such a manner that they are capable of attaining end results that the courts will recognize as equitable. Only in this way will the danger of arbitrary and unintelligent action be reduced to a minimum.

Obviously public utility commissions and their staffs must be of high caliber if they are to take over increased functions of regulation, some of which were formerly exercised by Congress, state legislatures, and the courts. And it seems equally important that they be so financed that they will be able to establish reasonable standards of performance, and thus be in a position to form equitable judgments regarding the results of utility management.

Only under this kind of regulation

[38] *Federal Power Commission v. Hope Natural Gas Company*, 320 U. S. 591 (January, 1944).

are we likely to have the best management which can be rendered. The public interest requires more, not less, regulation of public utilities — but that regulation should be the positive type, based upon "performance yardsticks" or standards that will greatly stimulate efficiency in management. The converse is also true: regulation of public utilities or of competitive industries which does not stimulate efficiency and place the responsibility upon the industry regulated for its inefficiencies is obviously not in the public interest. So far, no close approach to ideal regulation has been attained, even for utilities. It would be far more difficult to accomplish in the case of competitive industries, where price regulation would in turn require a knowledge and control of economic forces that not only are unpredictable but also are beyond the control of a regulatory agency except in a very limited way in dire emergencies.

Summary and Conclusions

Our early determined opposition to regulation even of public utilities was not changed until about a century after the adoption of our Constitution. But, even then, only a very limited regulation of these industries was inaugurated, first by the states and shortly thereafter by the Federal Government. This early regulation was half-hearted and much of it was unsound and unworkable.

Perhaps the best way to summarize the weaknesses inherent in this early regulation is to point to the *statutory* regulation of railroad passenger fares and freight rates. Passenger fares were sometimes fixed by statute in accordance with the earnings from the passenger business per mile of line; those railroads with the highest earnings were to charge lowest fares while those with

the lowest earnings were to charge the highest fares — a policy which obviously was not workable when strong and weak roads were competitors. In some early state laws freight rates were actually fixed for all commodities from A to Z; sometimes they were put on a rigid basis of mileage, and sometimes, with equal rigidity, they were set in relation to a specific date, as in an Illinois law stating that freight rates should not be higher on any day than the rates which existed on the corresponding day of the year 1870.[39] Unfortunately, the legislatures which fixed these fares and freight rates failed to understand the economic issues involved in the laws they passed. Even worse, many of them after fixing the rates adjourned for two years, sometimes for a longer period, leaving rates frozen until changed by later legislatures.

Even when statutory regulation of rates was superseded by that of regulatory commissions, neither the early state nor federal commissions had any power to make rates. It has already been indicated that although the Interstate Commerce Commission was created by the Act of 1887, it had no power to fix maximum rates until 1906, and no power to fix minimum rates until 1920. The various state utility commissions went through similar cycles regarding power over rate making.

Early governmental regulation of prices was limited in the main to the industries "affected with a public interest." As has been indicated, the United States Supreme Court refused until the early 1930's to permit various non-public utility industries to be subjected to control similar to that applied

[39] Laws of Illinois, 1871–1872, 640–1, cited in J. H. Gordon, "Illinois Railway Legislation and Commission Control Since 1870," published in 1904, Vol. I of *University of Illinois Studies*, pp. 28–29. Other types of rate making mentioned are also illustrated by this Illinois legislation.

Government Control of Business 49

to public utilities. In 1934, in upholding the New York law regulating the price of milk, the Court held that no constitutional principle bars the state from correcting existing maladjustments by fixing prices through legislation, and that there is nothing particularly "sacrosanct" about price as an object of regulation. At the same time the Court pointed out that the milk business was not a public utility.[40] Since that decision, further legislation controlling the prices of non-public utility enterprises has been upheld, much of it fixing *minimum* prices in the interest of *producers* on the theory that competition in such cases was detrimental.

But in this connection a further point needs to be emphasized: even though price fixing in non-public utility industries has been declared *legal,* it is confronted with some very formidable economic barriers. The public utilities themselves, although we assume they are monopolies, are not able to ignore competitive forces in rate making. In 1929 the Supreme Court reversed the Interstate Commerce Commission and upheld the contention of the railroads that they were entitled to a much higher valuation than the commission had allowed because the Commission had given less consideration to "reproduction value" than the carriers claimed it should have done. It was a great *legal* victory for the railroads, but it had little economic significance. Although the price of railroad securities advanced immediately after the decision, it was only a flash in the pan; for it soon became clear that the railroads, by advancing their rates on the theory that they could secure a current rate of return on the high value approved by the Court, would have lost an increasing volume of

business to competing forms of transport.[41]

Price control, if it is to be effective, calls for control over both the *supply* and the *quality* of the product or service involved. This is not always simple in the case of utilities, and it is even less simple in the case of non-public utility enterprises. Yet in spite of the relative simplicity of utility regulation compared with that of competitive enterprises, we have not yet made a success of public utility control. Control of competitive industries, even though implemented by very elaborate administrative agencies, would face unpredictable and uncontrollable economic forces. There are relatively few commodities or services furnished by competitive industries for which there are not more or less satisfactory substitutes. Even within the United States the market from which such substitutes might be purchased in lieu of the articles whose prices were fixed is a wide one. Thus, only by extension of price control over ever-increasing segments of the economy could the effectiveness of the competition of unregulated substitutes be lessened. And the extension of price control over competitive industries would involve economic forecasting on a scale too vast to be reliable.

We tend to be critical of the childlike faith in the feasibility of the early regulation of passenger fares, on the basis for example that railroads with high earnings per mile of line should charge low fares while those with low earnings should charge high fares. But are we not likewise entertaining a childlike faith if we assume that the regulation of prices can be successful when the resultant of all the economic forces, of which prices are but symptoms, can

[40] See footnote 23, p. 39.

[41] *St. Louis & O'Fallon Railway Co.* v. *United States,* 279 U. S. 461.

be neither predicted nor controlled?

No economic forces of equal complexity are involved in the regulation of public utilities. Yet even in the comparatively simple market for electric power regulatory commissions are powerless to control the prices at which some of the service is sold. This circumstance holds true for much of the electric power that is sold to certain types of industries.[42] While the rates charged for industrial power service must be filed with utility commissions and must not be discriminatory as between industries with similar economic characteristics of demand and usage of power, the price at which electricity must be sold, if it is to be sold at all, is often beyond the power either of the commission or of the power company to determine. Certain types of industries are free to make their own decision whether they will generate their own power, often as a by-product of the steam they must have for other purposes. Many large industries never buy electric power; some can even sell certain amounts of power to utilities for less than it costs the utilities to generate it.

Certainly, until we can claim greater success in the regulation of industries "affected with a public interest," where in the main the prices of products and services can be controlled because of the extent to which we are able to regulate entrance into or exit from business and to control the quality of product or service sold to consumers, we might be better advised to stimulate competition among the non-utility enterprises instead of attempting to subject them to control similar to that of utilities.

During our early history, the background and convictions of our legislators caused them to oppose government control even of businesses affected with a public interest. The pendulum of laissez faire had swung so far, in the lack of necessary control over carriers and other utilities, that the public could hardly be said to be well served. Now there appears to be danger that the pendulum of regulation will swing too far in the other direction, in the attempt to achieve government control of non-utility industries. Here, in view of the many difficult economic forces involved — forces not only nation-wide but even international in scope, forces so highly dynamic as to defy prediction and control — there would appear to be greater public gain in a type of government control likely to result in *more* effective competition, even to the extent of encouraging capital to move out of those industries that offer the least profitable return. The fixing of *minimum* prices for non-utility industries is liable to encourage complacency and inefficiency in business, resulting in capital's being invested in unprofitable business longer than would be the case without such price fixing by the government.

Even if the Supreme Court has removed the legal obstacles to price regulation in industries that are not public utilities, we should not attempt such regulation where the impact of complex economic forces can neither be anticipated nor controlled and where society's interest in efficiency and in technological advances will be adversely affected.

[42] Concrete cases are given in the author's *Problems in Public Utility Economics and Management* (New York, McGraw-Hill Book Company, 1938), pp. 357–401.

[23]

The theory of economic regulation

George J. Stigler
The University of Chicago

The potential uses of public resources and powers to improve the economic status of economic groups (such as industries and occupations) are analyzed to provide a scheme of the <u>demand</u> for regulation. The characteristics of the political process which allow relatively small groups to obtain such regulation is then sketched to provide elements of a theory of <u>supply</u> of regulation. A variety of empirical evidence and illustration is also presented.

■ The state—the machinery and power of the state—is a potential resource or threat to every industry in the society. With its power to prohibit or compel, to take or give money, the state can and does selectively help or hurt a vast number of industries. That political juggernaut, the petroleum industry, is an immense consumer of political benefits, and simultaneously the underwriters of marine insurance have their more modest repast. The central tasks of the theory of economic regulation are to explain who will receive the benefits or burdens of regulation, what form regulation will take, and the effects of regulation upon the allocation of resources.

Regulation may be actively sought by an industry, or it may be thrust upon it. A central thesis of this paper is that, as a rule, regulation is acquired by the industry and is designed and operated primarily for its benefit. There are regulations whose net effects upon the regulated industry are undeniably onerous; a simple example is the differentially heavy taxation of the industry's product (whiskey, playing cards). These onerous regulations, however, are exceptional and can be explained by the same theory that explains beneficial (we may call it "acquired") regulation.

Two main alternative views of the regulation of industry are widely held. The first is that regulation is instituted primarily for the protection and benefit of the public at large or some large subclass of the public. In this view, the regulations which injure the public—as when the oil import quotas increase the cost of petroleum products to America by $5 billion or more a year—are costs of some social goal (here, national defense) or, occasionally, perversions of the regulatory philosophy. The second view is essentially that the political process defies rational explanation: "politics" is an imponderable, a constantly and unpredictably shifting mixture of forces of the most diverse nature, comprehending acts of great moral virtue (the emancipation of slaves) and of the most vulgar venality (the congressman feathering his own nest).

The author obtained the B.B.A. degree from the University of Washington, the M.B.A. degree from Northwestern, and the Ph.D. degree from the University of Chicago. He is presently Charles R. Walgreen Distinguished Service Professor of American Institutions at the University of Chicago, and has published numerous articles and texts in the field of economics. Dr. Stigler is Vice Chairman of the Securities Investor Protective Commission.

Let us consider a problem posed by the oil import quota system: why does not the powerful industry which obtained this expensive program instead choose direct cash subsidies from the public treasury? The "protection of the public" theory of regulation must say that the choice of import quotas is dictated by the concern of the federal government for an adequate domestic supply of petroleum in the event of war—a remark calculated to elicit uproarious laughter at the Petroleum Club. Such laughter aside, if national defense were the goal of the quotas, a tariff would be a more economical instrument of policy: it would retain the profits of exclusion for the treasury. The non-rationalist view would explain the policy by the inability of consumers to measure the cost to them of the import quotas, and hence their willingness to pay $5 billion in higher prices rather than the $2.5 billion in cash that would be equally attractive to the industry. Our profit-maximizing theory says that the explanation lies in a different direction: the present members of the refining industries would have to share a cash subsidy with all new entrants into the refining industry.[1] Only when the elasticity of supply of an industry is small will the industry prefer cash to controls over entry or output.

This question, why does an industry solicit the coercive powers of the state rather than its cash, is offered only to illustrate the approach of the present paper. We assume that political systems are rationally devised and rationally employed, which is to say that they are appropriate instruments for the fulfillment of desires of members of the society. This is not to say that the state will serve any person's concept of the public interest: indeed the problem of regulation is the problem of discovering when and why an industry (or other group of like-minded people) is able to use the state for its purposes, or is singled out by the state to be used for alien purposes.

1. What benefits can a state provide to an industry?

■ The state has one basic resource which in pure principle is not shared with even the mightiest of its citizens: the power to coerce. The state can seize money by the only method which is permitted by the laws of a civilized society, by taxation. The state can ordain the physical movements of resources and the economic decisions of households and firms without their consent. These powers provide the possibilities for the utilization of the state by an industry to increase its profitability. The main policies which an industry (or occupation) may seek of the state are four.

The most obvious contribution that a group may seek of the government is a direct subsidy of money. The domestic airlines received "air mail" subsidies (even if they did not carry mail) of $1.5 billion through 1968. The merchant marine has received construction and operation subsidies reaching almost S3 billion since World War II. The education industry has long shown a masterful skill in obtaining public funds: for example, universities and colleges have received federal funds exceeding $3 billion annually in recent years, as well as subsidized loans for dormitories and other construction. The veterans of wars have often received direct cash bonuses.

---

[1] The domestic producers of petroleum, who also benefit from the import quota, would find a tariff or cash payment to domestic producers equally attractive. If their interests alone were consulted, import quotas would be auctioned off instead of being given away.

We have already sketched the main explanation for the fact that an industry with power to obtain governmental favors usually does not use this power to get money: unless the list of beneficiaries can be limited by an acceptable device, whatever amount of subsidies the industry can obtain will be dissipated among a growing number of rivals. The airlines quickly moved away from competitive bidding for air mail contracts to avoid this problem.[2] On the other hand, the premier universities have not devised a method of excluding other claimants for research funds, and in the long run they will receive much-reduced shares of federal research monies.

The second major public resource commonly sought by an industry is control over entry by new rivals. There is considerable, not to say excessive, discussion in economic literature of the rise of peculiar price policies (limit prices), vertical integration, and similar devices to retard the rate of entry of new firms into oligopolistic industries. Such devices are vastly less efficacious (economical) than the certificate of convenience and necessity (which includes, of course, the import and production quotas of the oil and tobacco industries).

The diligence with which the power of control over entry will be exercised by a regulatory body is already well known. The Civil Aeronautics Board has not allowed a single new trunk line to be launched since it was created in 1938. The power to insure new banks has been used by the Federal Deposit Insurance Corporation to reduce the rate of entry into commercial banking by 60 percent.[3] The interstate motor carrier history is in some respects even more striking, because no even ostensibly respectable case for restriction on entry can be developed on grounds of scale economies (which are in turn adduced to limit entry for safety or economy of operation). The number of federally licensed common carriers is shown in Figure 1: the immense growth of the freight hauled by trucking common carriers has been associated with a steady secular decline of numbers of such carriers. The number of applications for new certificates has been in excess of 5000 annually in recent years: a rigorous proof that hope springs eternal in an aspiring trucker's breast.

We propose the general hypothesis: every industry or occupation that has enough political power to utilize the state will seek to control entry. In addition, the regulatory policy will often be so fashioned as to retard the rate of growth of new firms. For example, no new savings and loan company may pay a dividend rate higher than that prevailing in the community in its endeavors to attract deposits.[4] The power to limit selling expenses of mutual funds, which is soon to be conferred upon the Securities and Exchange Commission, will serve to limit the growth of small mutual funds and hence reduce the sales costs of large funds.

One variant of the control of entry is the protective tariff (and the corresponding barriers which have been raised to interstate movements of goods and people). The benefits of protection to an industry, one might think, will usually be dissipated by the entry of new domestic producers, and the question naturally arises: Why does the industry not also seek domestic entry controls? In a few industries

---

[2] See [7], pp. 60 ff.
[3] See [10].
[4] The Federal Home Loan Bank Board is the regulatory body. It also controls the amount of advertising and other areas of competition.

FIGURE 1

CERTIFICATES FOR INTERSTATE MOTOR CARRIERS

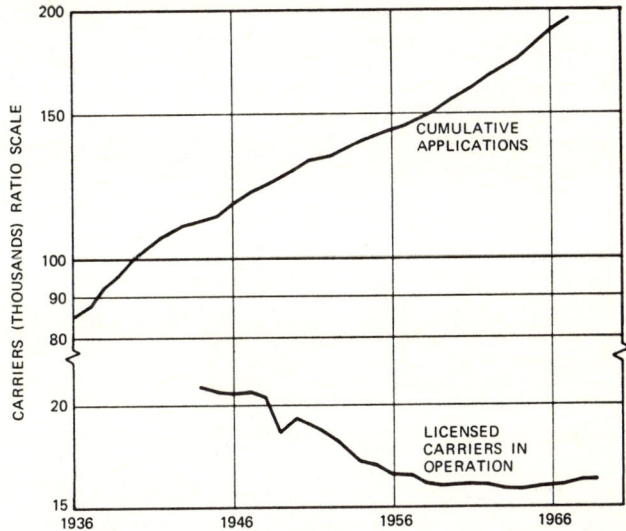

SOURCE: TABLE 5

(petroleum) the domestic controls have been obtained, but not in most. The tariff will be effective if there is a specialized domestic resource necessary to the industry; oil-producing lands is an example. Even if an industry has only durable specialized resources, it will gain if its contraction is slowed by a tariff.

A third general set of powers of the state which will be sought by the industry are those which affect substitutes and complements. Crudely put, the butter producers wish to suppress margarine and encourage the production of bread. The airline industry actively supports the federal subsidies to airports; the building trade unions have opposed labor-saving materials through building codes. We shall examine shortly a specific case of inter-industry competition in transportation.

The fourth class of public policies sought by an industry is directed to price-fixing. Even the industry that has achieved entry control will often want price controls administered by a body with coercive powers. If the number of firms in the regulated industry is even moderately large, price discrimination will be difficult to maintain in the absence of public support. The prohibition of interest on demand deposits, which is probably effective in preventing interest payments to most non-business depositors, is a case in point. Where there are no diseconomies of large scale for the individual firm (e.g., a motor trucking firm can add trucks under a given license as common carrier), price control is essential to achieve more than competitive rates of return.

☐ **Limitations upon political benefits.** These various political boons are not obtained by the industry in a pure profit-maximizing form. The political process erects certain limitations upon the exercise of cartel policies by an industry. These limitations are of three sorts.

TABLE 1

IMPORT QUOTAS OF REFINERIES AS PERCENT
OF DAILY INPUT OF PETROLEUM
(DISTRICTS I — IV, JULY 1, 1959 — DEC. 31, 1959)

SIZE OF REFINERY (THOUSANDS OF BARRELS)	PERCENT QUOTA
0–10	11.4
10–20	10.4
20–30	9.5
30–60	8.5
60–100	7.6
100–150	6.6
150–200	5.7
200–300	4.7
300 AND OVER	3.8

SOURCE: HEARING, SELECT COMMITTEE ON SMALL BUSINESS, U. S. CONGRESS,
88th CONG., 2nd SESS., AUG. 10 AND 11, 1964, [12] P. 121.

First, the distribution of control of the industry among the firms
in the industry is changed. In an unregulated industry each firm's
influence upon price and output is proportional to its share of industry output (at least in a simple arithmetic sense of direct capacity
to change output). The political decisions take account also of the
political strength of the various firms, so small firms have a larger
influence than they would possess in an unregulated industry. Thus,
when quotas are given to firms, the small firms will almost always
receive larger quotas than cost-minimizing practices would allow.
The original quotas under the oil import quota system will illustrate
this practice (Table 1). The smallest refiners were given a quota of
11.4 percent of their daily consumption of oil, and the percentage
dropped as refinery size rose.[5] The pattern of regressive benefits is
characteristic of public controls in industries with numerous firms.

Second, the procedural safeguards required of public processes
are costly. The delays which are dictated by both law and bureaucratic thoughts of self-survival can be large: Robert Gerwig found
the price of gas sold in interstate commerce to be 5 to 6 percent
higher than in intrastate commerce because of the administrative
costs (including delay) of Federal Power Commission reviews [5].

Finally, the political process automatically admits powerful
outsiders to the industry's councils. It is well known that the allocation of television channels among communities does not maximize
industry revenue but reflects pressures to serve many smaller communities. The abandonment of an unprofitable rail line is an even
more notorious area of outsider participation.

These limitations are predictable, and they must all enter into the
calculus of the profitability of regulation of an industry.

☐ **An illustrative analysis.** The recourse to the regulatory process is
of course more specific and more complex than the foregoing sketch

---

[5] The largest refineries were restricted to 75.7 percent of their historical quota
under the earlier voluntary import quota plan.

suggests. The defensive power of various other industries which are affected by the proposed regulation must also be taken into account. An analysis of one aspect of the regulation of motor trucking will illustrate these complications. At this stage we are concerned only with the correspondence between regulations and economic interests; later we shall consider the political process by which regulation is achieved.

The motor trucking industry operated almost exclusively within cities before 1925, in good part because neither powerful trucks nor good roads were available for long-distance freight movements. As these deficiencies were gradually remedied, the share of trucks in intercity freight movements began to rise, and by 1930 it was estimated to be 4 percent of ton-miles of intercity freight. The railroad industry took early cognizance of this emerging competitor, and one of the methods by which trucking was combatted was state regulation.

By the early 1930's all states regulated the dimensions and weight of trucks. The weight limitations were a much more pervasive control over trucking than the licensing of common carriers because even the trucks exempt from entry regulation are subject to the limitations on dimensions and capacity. The weight regulations in the early 1930's are reproduced in the appendix (Table 6). Sometimes the participation of railroads in the regulatory process was incontrovertible: Texas and Louisiana placed a 7000-pound payload limit on trucks serving (and hence competing with) two or more railroad stations, and a 14,000-pound limit on trucks serving only one station (hence, not competing with it).

We seek to determine the pattern of weight limits on trucks that would emerge in response to the economic interests of the concerned parties. The main considerations appear to be the following:

(1) Heavy trucks would be allowed in states with a substantial number of trucks on farms: the powerful agricultural interests would insist upon this. The 1930 Census reports nearly one million trucks on farms. One variable in our study will be, for each state, trucks per 1000 of agricultural population.[6]

(2) Railroads found the truck an effective and rapidly triumphing competitor in the shorter hauls and hauls of less than carload traffic, but much less effective in the carload and longer-haul traffic. Our second variable for each state is, therefore, length of average railroad haul.[7] The longer the average rail haul is, the less the railroads will be opposed to trucks.

(3) The public at large would be concerned by the potential damage done to the highway system by heavy trucks. The better the state highway system, the heavier the trucks that would be permitted. The percentage of each state's highways that had a high type surface is the third variable. Of course good highways are more likely to exist where the potential contribution of trucks to a state's economy is greater, so the causation may be looked at from either direction.

---

[6] The ratio of trucks to total population would measure the product of (1) the importance of trucks to farmers, and (2) the importance of farmers in the state. For reasons given later, we prefer to emphasize (1).

[7] This is known for each railroad, and we assume that (1) the average holds within each state, and (2) two or more railroads in a state may be combined on the basis of mileage. Obviously both assumptions are at best fair approximations.

We have two measures of weight limits on trucks, one for 4-wheel trucks (X_1) and one for 6-wheel trucks (X_2). We may then calculate two equations,

$$X_1 \text{ (or } X_2) = a + bX_3 + cX_4 + dX_5,$$

where

X_3 = trucks per 1000 agricultural labor force, 1930 ,
X_1 = average length of railroad haul of freight traffic, 1930,
X_5 = percentage of state roads with high-quality surface, 1930.

(All variables are fully defined and their state values given in Table 7 on page 20.)

The three explanatory variables are statistically significant, and each works in the expected direction. The regulations on weight were less onerous; the larger the truck population in farming, the less competitive the trucks were to railroads (i.e., the longer the rail hauls), and the better the highway system (see Table 2).

□ The foregoing analysis is concerned with what may be termed the industrial demand for governmental powers. Not every industry will have a significant demand for public assistance (other than money!), meaning the prospect of a substantial increase in the present value of the enterprises even if the governmental services could be obtained gratis (and of course they have costs to which we soon turn). In some economic activities entry of new rivals is extremely difficult to control—consider the enforcement problem in restricting the supply of domestic servants. In some industries the substitute products cannot be efficiently controlled—consider the competition offered to bus lines by private car-pooling. Price fixing is not feasible where every

TABLE 2

REGRESSION ANALYSIS OF STATE WEIGHT LIMITS ON TRUCKS
(T VALUES UNDER REGRESSION COEFFICIENTS)

DEPENDENT VARIABLE	N	CONSTANT	X_3	X_4	X_5	R^2
X_1	48	12.28 (4.87)	0.0336 (3.99)	0.0287 (2.77)	0.2641 (3.04)	0.502
X_2	46	10.34 (1.57)	0.0437 (2.01)	0.0788 (2.97)	0.2528 (1.15)	0.243

X_1 = WEIGHT LIMIT ON 4-WHEEL TRUCKS (THOUSANDS OF POUNDS), 1932-33

X_2 = WEIGHT LIMIT ON 6-WHEEL TRUCKS (THOUSANDS OF POUNDS), 1932-33

X_3 = TRUCKS ON FARMS PER 1,000 AGRICULTURAL LABOR FORCE, 1930

X_4 = AVERAGE LENGTH OF RAILROAD HAUL OF FREIGHT (MILES), 1930

X_5 = PERCENT OF STATE HIGHWAYS WITH HIGH-TYPE SURFACE, DEC. 31, 1930

SOURCES: X_1 AND X_2: THE MOTOR TRUCK RED BOOK AND DIRECTORY [11], 1934 EDITION, P. 85-102, AND U.S. DEPT. OF AGRIC., BUR. OF PUBLIC ROADS, DEC. 1932 [13].

X_3: CENSUS OF AGRICULTURE, 1930, VOL. IV, [14].

X_4: A.A.R.R., BUR. OF RAILWAY ECONOMICS, RAILWAY MILEAGE BY STATES, DEC. 31, 1930 [1] AND U.S.I.C.C., STATISTICS OF RAILWAYS IN THE U.S., 1930 [18].

X_5: STATISTICAL ABSTRACT OF THE U.S., 1932 [16].

unit of the product has a different quality and price, as in the market for used automobiles. In general, however, most industries will have a positive demand price (schedule) for the services of government.

2. The costs of obtaining legislation

■ When an industry receives a grant of power from the state, the benefit to the industry will fall short of the damage to the rest of the community. Even if there were no deadweight losses from acquired regulation, however, one might expect a democratic society to reject such industry requests unless the industry controlled a majority of the votes.[8] A direct and informed vote on oil import quotas would reject the scheme. (If it did not, our theory of rational political processes would be contradicted.) To explain why many industries are able to employ the political machinery to their own ends, we must examine the nature of the political process in a democracy.

A consumer chooses between rail and air travel, for example, by voting with his pocketbook: he patronizes on a given day that mode of transportation he prefers. A similar form of economic voting occurs with decisions on where to work or where to invest one's capital. The market accumulates these economic votes, predicts their future course, and invests accordingly.

Because the political decision is coercive, the decision process is fundamentally different from that of the market. If the public is asked to make a decision between two transportation media comparable to the individual's decision on how to travel—say, whether airlines or railroads should receive a federal subsidy—the decision must be abided by everyone, travellers and non-travellers, travellers this year and travellers next year. This compelled universality of political decisions makes for two differences between democratic political decision processes and market processes.

(1) The decisions must be made simultaneously by a large number of persons (or their representatives): the political process demands simultaneity of decision. If *A* were to vote on the referendum today, *B* tomorrow, *C* the day after, and so on, the accumulation of a majority decision would be both expensive and suspect. (*A* might wish to cast a different vote now than last month.)

The condition of simultaneity imposes a major burden upon the political decision process. It makes voting on specific issues prohibitively expensive: it is a significant cost even to engage in the transaction of buying a plane ticket when I wish to travel; it would be stupendously expensive to me to engage in the physically similar transaction of voting (i.e., patronizing a polling place) whenever a number of my fellow citizens desired to register their views on railroads versus airplanes. To cope with this condition of simultaneity, the voters must employ representatives with wide discretion and must eschew direct expressions of marginal changes in preferences. This characteristic also implies that the political decision does not predict voter desires and make preparations to fulfill them in advance of their realization.

---

[8] If the deadweight loss (of consumer and producer surplus) is taken into account, even if the oil industry were in the majority it would not obtain the legislation if there were available some method of compensation (such as sale of votes) by which the larger damage of the minority could be expressed effectively against the lesser gains of the majority.

(2) The democratic decision process must involve "all" the community, not simply those who are directly concerned with a decision. In a private market, the non-traveller never votes on rail versus plane travel, while the huge shipper casts many votes each day. The political decision process cannot exclude the uninterested voter: the abuses of any exclusion except self-exclusion are obvious. Hence, the political process does not allow participation in proportion to interest and knowledge. In a measure, this difficulty is moderated by other political activities besides voting which do allow a more effective vote to interested parties: persuasion, employment of skilled legislative representatives, etc. Nevertheless, the political system does not offer good incentives like those in private markets to the acquisition of knowledge. If I consume ten times as much of public service A (streets) as of B (schools), I do not have incentives to acquire corresponding amounts of knowledge about the public provision of these services.[9]

These characteristics of the political process can be modified by having numerous levels of government (so I have somewhat more incentive to learn about local schools than about the whole state school system) and by selective use of direct decision (bond referenda). The chief method of coping with the characteristics, however, is to employ more or less full-time representatives organized in (disciplined by) firms which are called political parties or machines.

The representative and his party are rewarded for their discovery and fulfillment of the political desires of their constituency by success in election and the perquisites of office. If the representative could confidently await reelection whenever he voted against an economic policy that injured the society, he would assuredly do so. Unfortunately virtue does not always command so high a price. If the representative denies ten large industries their special subsidies of money or governmental power, they will dedicate themselves to the election of a more complaisant successor: the stakes are that important. This does not mean that every large industry can get what it wants or all that it wants: it does mean that the representative and his party must find a coalition of voter interests more durable than the anti-industry side of every industry policy proposal. A representative cannot win or keep office with the support of the sum of those who are opposed to: oil import quotas, farm subsidies, airport subsidies, hospital subsidies, unnecessary navy shipyards, an inequitable public housing program, and rural electrification subsidies.

The political decison process has as its dominant characteristic infrequent, universal (in principle) participation, as we have noted: political decisions must be infrequent and they must be global. The voter's expenditure to learn the merits of individual policy proposals and to express his preferences (by individual and group representation as well as by voting) are determined by expected costs and returns, just as they are in the private marketplace. The costs of comprehensive information are higher in the political arena because information must be sought on many issues of little or no direct concern to the individual, and accordingly he will know little about most matters before the legislature. The expressions of preferences in voting will be less precise than the expressions of preferences in the

---

[9] See [2].

marketplace because many uninformed people will be voting and affecting the decision.[10]

The channels of political decision-making can thus be described as gross or filtered or noisy. If everyone has a negligible preference for policy A over B, the preference will not be discovered or acted upon. If voter group X wants a policy that injures non-X by a small amount, it will not pay non-X to discover this and act against the policy. The system is calculated to implement all strongly felt preferences of majorities and many strongly felt preferences of minorities but to disregard the lesser preferences of majorities and minorities. The filtering or grossness will be reduced by any reduction in the cost to the citizen of acquiring information and expressing desires and by any increase in the probability that his vote will influence policy.

The industry which seeks political power must go to the appropriate seller, the political party. The political party has costs of operation, costs of maintaining an organization and competing in elections. These costs of the political process are viewed excessively narrowly in the literature on the financing of elections: elections are to the political process what merchandizing is to the process of producing a commodity, only an essential final step. The party maintains its organization and electoral appeal by the performance of costly services to the voter at all times, not just before elections. Part of the costs of services and organization are borne by putting a part of the party's workers on the public payroll. An opposition party, however, is usually essential insurance for the voters to discipline the party in power, and the opposition party's costs are not fully met by public funds.

The industry which seeks regulation must be prepared to pay with the two things a party needs: votes and resources. The resources may be provided by campaign contributions, contributed services (the businessman heads a fund-raising committee), and more indirect methods such as the employment of party workers. The votes in support of the measure are rallied, and the votes in opposition are dispersed, by expensive programs to educate (or uneducate) members of the industry and of other concerned industries.

These costs of legislation probably increase with the size of the industry seeking the legislation. Larger industries seek programs which cost the society more and arouse more opposition from substantially affected groups. The tasks of persuasion, both within and without the industry, also increase with its size. The fixed size of the political "market," however, probably makes the cost of obtaining legislation increase less rapidly than industry size. The smallest industries are therefore effectively precluded from the political process unless they have some special advantage such as geographical concentration in a sparsely settled political subdivision.

If a political party has in effect a monopoly control over the governmental machine, one might expect that it could collect most of the benefits of regulation for itself. Political parties, however, are

---

[10] There is an organizational problem in any decision in which more than one vote is cast. If because of economies of scale it requires a thousand customers to buy a product before it can be produced, this thousand votes has to be assembled by some entrepreneur. Unlike the political scene, however, there is no need to obtain the consent of the remainder of the community, because they will bear no part of the cost.

perhaps an ideal illustration of Demsetz' theory of natural monopoly [4]. If one party becomes extortionate (or badly mistaken in its reading of effective desires), it is possible to elect another party which will provide the governmental services at a price more closely proportioned to costs of the party. If entry into politics is effectively controlled. we should expect one-party dominance to lead that party to solicit requests for protective legislation but to exact a higher price for the legislation.

The internal structure of the political party, and the manner in which the perquisites of office are distributed among its members, offer fascinating areas for study in this context. The elective officials are at the pinnacle of the political system—there is no substitute for the ability to hold the public offices. I conjecture that much of the compensation to the legislative leaders takes the form of extra-political payments. Why are so many politicians lawyers?—because everyone employs lawyers, so the congressman's firm is a suitable avenue of compensation, whereas a physician would have to be given bribes rather than patronage. Most enterprises patronize insurance companies and banks, so we may expect that legislators commonly have financial affiliations with such enterprises.

The financing of industry-wide activities such as the pursuit of legislation raises the usual problem of the free rider.[11] We do not possess a satisfactory theory of group behavior—indeed this theory is the theory of oligopoly with one addition: in the very large number industry (e.g., agriculture) the political party itself will undertake the entrepreneurial role in providing favorable legislation. We can go no further than the infirmities of oligopoly theory allow, which is to say, we can make only plausible conjectures such as that the more concentrated the industry, the more resources it can invest in the campaign for legislation.

☐ **Occupational licensing.** The licensing of occupations is a possible use of the political process to improve the economic circumstances of a group. The license is an effective barrier to entry because occupational practice without the license is a criminal offense. Since much occupational licensing is performed at the state level, the area provides an opportunity to search for the characteristics of an occupation which give it political power.

Although there are serious data limitations, we may investigate several characteristics of an occupation which should influence its ability to secure political power:

(1) *The size of the occupation.* Quite simply, the larger the occupation. the more votes it has. (Under some circumstances, therefore. one would wish to exclude non-citizens from the measure of size.)

(2) *The per capita income of the occupation.* The income of the occupation is the product of its number and average income. so this variable and the preceding will reflect the total income of the occupation. The income of the occupation is presumably an index of the probable rewards of successful political action: in the absence of specific knowledge of supply and demand functions, we expect

---

[11] The theory that the lobbying organization avoids the "free-rider" problem by selling useful services was proposed by Thomas G. Moore [8] and elaborated by Mancur Olson [9]. The theory has not been tested empirically.

licensing to increase each occupation's equilibrium income by roughly the same proportion. In a more sophisticated version, one would predict that the less the elasticity of demand for the occupation's services, the more profitable licensing would be. One could also view the income of the occupation as a source of funds for political action, but if we view political action as an investment this is relevant only with capital-market imperfections.[12]

The average income of occupational members is an appropriate variable in comparisons among occupations, but it is inappropriate to comparisons of one occupation in various states because real income will be approximately equal (in the absence of regulation) in each state.

(3) *The concentration of the occupation in large cities.* When the occupation organizes a campaign to obtain favorable legislation, it incurs expenses in the solicitation of support, and these are higher for a diffused occupation than a concentrated one. The solicitation of support is complicated by the free-rider problem in that individual members cannot be excluded from the benefits of legislation even if they have not shared the costs of receiving it. If most of the occupation is concentrated in a few large centers, these problems (we suspect) are much reduced in intensity: regulation may even begin at the local governmental level. We shall use an orthodox geographical concentration measure: the share of the occupation of the state in cities over 100,000 (or 50,000 in 1900 and earlier).

(4) *The presence of a cohesive opposition to licensing.* If an occupation deals with the public at large, the costs which licensing imposes upon any one customer or industry will be small and it will not be economic for that customer or industry to combat the drive for licensure. If the injured group finds it feasible and profitable to act jointly, however, it will oppose the effort to get licensure, and (by increasing its cost) weaken, delay, or prevent the legislation. The same attributes—numbers of voters, wealth, and ease of organization—which favor an occupation in the political arena, of course, favor also any adversary group. Thus, a small occupation employed by only one industry which has few employers will have difficulty in getting licensure; whereas a large occupation serving everyone will encounter no organized opposition.

An introductory statistical analysis of the licensing of select occupations by states is summarized in Table 3. In each occupation the dependent variable for each state is the year of first regulation of entry into the occupation. The two independent variables are

(1) the ratio of the occupation to the total labor force of the state in the census year nearest to the median year of regulation,

(2) the fraction of the occupation found in cities over 100,000 (over 50,000 in 1890 and 1900) in that same year.

---

[12] Let n = the number of members of the profession and y = average income. We expect political capacity to be in proportion to (ny) so far as benefits go, but to reflect also the direct value of votes, so the capacity becomes proportional to ($n^a y$) with $a > 1$.

TABLE 3

INITIAL YEAR OF REGULATION AS A FUNCTION OF
RELATIVE SIZE OF OCCUPATION AND DEGREE OF URBANIZATION

OCCUPATION	NUMBER OF STATES LICENSING	MEDIAN CENSUS YEAR OF LICENSING	REGRESSION COEFFICIENTS (AND T-VALUES)		R^2
			SIZE OF OCCUPATION (RELATIVE TO LABOR FORCE)	URBANIZATION (SHARE OF OCCUPATION IN CITIES OVER 100,000*)	
BEAUTICIANS	48	1930	−4.03 (2.50)	5.90 (1.24)	0.125
ARCHITECTS	47	1930	−24.06 (2.15)	−6.29 (0.84)	0.184
BARBERS	46	1930	−1.31 (0.51)	−26.10 (2.37)	0.146
LAWYERS	29	1890	−0.26 (0.08)	−65.78 (1.70)	0.102
PHYSICIANS	43	1890	0.64 (0.65)	−23.80 (2.69)	0.165
EMBALMERS	37	1910	3.32 (0.36)	−4.24 (0.44)	0.007
REGISTERED NURSES	48	1910	−2.08 (2.28)	−3.36 (1.06)	0.176
DENTISTS	48	1900	2.51 (0.44)	−22.94 (2.19)	0.103
VETERINARIANS	40	1910	−10.69 (1.94)	−37.16 (4.20)	0.329
CHIROPRACTORS	48	1930	−17.70 (1.54)	11.69 (1.25)	0.079
PHARMACISTS	48	1900	−4.19 (1.50)	−6.84 (0.80)	0.082

SOURCES: THE COUNCIL OF STATE GOVERNMENTS, "OCCUPATIONAL LICENSING LEGISLATION IN THE STATES", 1952 [3], AND U.S. CENSUS OF POPULATION [15], VARIOUS YEARS.

* 50,000 IN 1890 AND 1900.

We expect these variables to be negatively associated with year of licensure, and each of the nine statistically significant regression coefficients is of the expected sign.

The results are not robust, however: the multiple correlation coefficients are small, and over half of the regression coefficients are not significant (and in these cases often of inappropriate sign). Urbanization is more strongly associated than size of occupation with licensure.[13] The crudity of the data may be a large source of these disappointments: we measure, for example, the characteristics of the barbers in each state in 1930, but 14 states were licensing barbers by 1910. If the states which licensed barbering before 1910 had relatively more barbers, or more highly urbanized barbers, the predictions

---

[13] We may pool the occupations and assign dummy variables for each occupation; the regression coefficients then are:

size of occupation relative to labor force: −0.450 (t = 0.59)
urbanization   : −12.133 (t = 4.00).

Thus urbanization is highly significant, while size of occupation is not significant.

would be improved. The absence of data for years between censuses and before 1890 led us to make only the cruder analysis.[14]

In general, the larger occupations were licensed in earlier years.[15] Veterinarians are the only occupation in this sample who have a well-defined set of customers, namely livestock farmers, and licensing was later in those states with large numbers of livestock relative to rural population. The within-occupation analyses offer some support for the economic theory of the supply of legislation.

A comparison of different occupations allows us to examine several other variables. The first is income, already discussed above. The second is the size of the market. Just as it is impossible to organize an effective labor union in only one part of an integrated market, so it is impossible to regulate only one part of the market. Consider an occupation—junior business executives will do—which has a national market with high mobility of labor and significant mobility of employers. If the executives of one state were to organize, their scope for effective influence would be very small. If salaries were raised above the competitive level, employers would often recruit elsewhere so the demand elasticity would be very high.[16] The third variable is stability of occupational membership: the longer the members are in the occupation, the greater their financial gain from control of entry. Our regrettably crude measure of this variable is based upon the number of members aged 35–44 in 1950 and aged 45–54 in 1960: the closer these numbers are, the more stable the membership of the occupation. The data for the various occupations are given in Table 4.

The comparison of licensed and unlicensed occupations is consistently in keeping with our expectations:

(1) the licensed occupations have higher incomes (also before licensing, one may assume),

(2) the membership of the licensed occupations is more stable (but the difference is negligible in our crude measure),

(3) the licensed occupations are less often employed by business enterprises (who have incentives to oppose licensing),

(4) all occupations in national markets (college teachers, engineers, scientists, accountants) are unlicensed or only partially licensed.

---

[14] A more precise analysis might take the form of a regression analysis such as:

Year of licensure = constant

$$+b_1 \text{ (year of critical size of occupation)}$$
$$+b_2 \text{ (year of critical urbanization of occupation)},$$

where the critical size and urbanization were defined as the mean size and mean urbanization in the year of licensure.

[15] Lawyers, physicians, and pharmacists were all relatively large occupations by 1900, and nurses also by 1910. The only large occupation to be licensed later was barbers; the only small occupation to be licensed early was embalmers.

[16] The regulation of business in a partial market will also generally produce very high supply elasticities within a market: if the price of the product (or service) is raised, the pressure of excluded supply is very difficult to resist. Some occupations are forced to reciprocity in licensing, and the geographical dispersion of earnings in licensed occupations, one would predict, is not appreciably different than in unlicensed occupations with equal employer mobility. Many puzzles are posed by the interesting analysis of Arlene S. Holen in [6], pp. 492-98.

TABLE 4

CHARACTERISTICS OF LICENSED AND UNLICENSED
PROFESSIONAL OCCUPATIONS, 1960

OCCUPATION	MEDIAN AGE (YEARS)	MEDIAN EDUCATION (YEARS)	MEDIAN EARNINGS (50-52 WKS.)	INSTABILITY OF MEMBERSHIP*	PERCENT NOT SELF-EMPLOYED	PERCENT IN CITIES OVER 50,000	PERCENT OF LABOR FORCE
LICENSED:							
ARCHITECTS	41.7	16.8	$ 9,090	0.012	57.8%	44.1%	0.045%
CHIROPRACTORS	46.5	16.4	6,360	0.053	5.8	30.8	0.020
DENTISTS	45.9	17.3	12,200	0.016	9.4	34.5	0.128
EMBALMERS	43.5	13.4	5,990	0.130	52.8	30.2	0.055
LAWYERS	45.3	17.4	10,800	0.041	35.8	43.1	0.308
PROF. NURSES	39.1	13.2	3,850	0.291	91.0	40.6	0.868
OPTOMETRISTS	41.6	17.0	8,480	0.249	17.5	34.5	0.024
PHARMACISTS	44.9	16.2	7,230	0.119	62.3	40.0	0.136
PHYSICIANS	42.8	17.5	14,200	0.015	35.0	44.7	0.339
VETERINARIANS	39.2	17.4	9,210	0.169	29.5	14.4	0.023
AVERAGE	43.0	16.3	8,741	0.109	39.7	35.7	0.195
PARTIALLY LICENSED:							
ACCOUNTANTS	40.4	14.9	6,450	0.052	88.1	43.5	0.698
ENGINEERS	38.3	16.2	8,490	0.023	96.8	31.6	1.279
ELEM. SCHOOL TEACHERS	43.1	16.5	4,710	(a)	99.1	18.8	1.482
AVERAGE	40.6	15.9	6,550	0.117(b)	94.7	34.6	1.153
UNLICENSED:							
ARTISTS	38.0	14.2	5,920	0.103	77.3	45.7	0.154
CLERGYMEN	43.3	17.0	4,120	0.039	89.0	27.2	0.295
COLLEGE TEACHERS	40.3	17.4	7,500	0.085	99.2	36.0	0.261
DRAFTSMEN	31.2	12.9	5,990	0.098	98.6	40.8	0.322
REPORTERS & EDITORS	39.4	15.5	6,120	0.138	93.9	43.3	0.151
MUSICIANS	40.2	14.8	3,240	0.081	65.5	37.7	0.289
NATURAL SCIENTISTS	35.9	16.8	7,490	0.264	96.3	32.7	0.221
AVERAGE	38.3	15.5	5,768	0.115	88.5	37.6	0.242

(*) 1-R, WHERE R = RATIO: 1960 AGE 45-54 TO 1950 AGE 35-44.

(a) NOT AVAILABLE SEPARATELY; TEACHERS N.E.C. (INCL. SECONDARY SCHOOL AND OTHER) = 0.276

(b) INCLUDES FIGURE FOR TEACHERS N.E.C. IN NOTE (a)

SOURCE: U.S. CENSUS OF POPULATION, [15], 1960.

The size and urbanization of the three groups, however, are unrelated to licensing. The inter-occupational comparison therefore provides a modicum of additional support for our theory of regulation.

■ The idealistic view of public regulation is deeply imbedded in professional economic thought. So many economists, for example, have denounced the ICC for its pro-railroad policies that this has become a cliché of the literature. This criticism seems to me exactly as appropriate as a criticism of the Great Atlantic and Pacific Tea Company for selling groceries, or as a criticism of a politician for currying popular support. The fundamental vice of such criticism is that it misdirects attention: it suggests that the way to get an ICC which is not subservient to the carriers is to preach to the commissioners or to the people who appoint the commissioners. The only way to get a different commission would be to change the political

3. Conclusion

support for the Commission, and reward commissioners on a basis unrelated to their services to the carriers.

Until the basic logic of political life is developed, reformers will be ill-equipped to use the state for their reforms, and victims of the pervasive use of the state's support of special groups will be helpless to protect themselves. Economists should quickly establish the license to practice on the rational theory of political behavior.

Appendix

TABLE 5

COMMON, CONTRACT AND PASSENGER MOTOR CARRIERS, 1935–1969[1]

YEAR ENDING	CUMULATIVE APPLICATIONS			OPERATING CARRIERS	
	GRAND–FATHER	NEW	TOTAL	APPROVED APPLICATIONS[3]	NUMBER IN OPERATION[2]
OCT. 1936	82,827	1,696	84,523	–	–
1937	83,107	3,921	87.028	1,114	–
1938	85,646	6,694	92,340	20,398	–
1939	86,298	9,636	95,934	23,494	–
1940	87,367	12,965	100,332	25,575	–
1941	88,064	16,325	104,389	26,296	–
1942	88,702	18,977	107,679	26,683	–
1943	89,157	20,007	109,164	27,531	–
1944	89,511	21,324	110,835	27,177	21,044
1945	89,518	22,829	112,347		20,788
1946	89,529	26,392	115,921		20,632
1947	89,552	29,604	119,156		20,665
1948	89,563	32,678	122,241		20,373
1949	89,567	35,635	125,202		18,459
1950	89,573	38,666	128,239		19,200
1951	89,574	41,889	131,463		18,843
1952	(89,574)[4]	44,297	133,870		18,408
1953	"	46,619	136,192		17,869
1954	"	49,146	138,719		17,080
1955	"	51,720	141,293		16,836
JUNE 1956	"	53,640	143,213		16,486
1957	"	56,804	146,377		16,316
1958	"	60,278	149,851		16,065
1959	"	64,171	153,744		15,923
1960	"	69,205	158,778		15,936
1961	"	72,877	162,450		15,967
1962	"	76,986	166,559		15,884
1963	"	81,443	171,016		15,739
1964	"	86,711	176,284		15,732
1965	"	93,064	182,637		15,755
1966	"	101,745	191,318		15,933
1967	"	106,647	196,220		16,003
1968	"	(6)	(6)		16,230[5]
1969	"	(6)	(6)		16,318[5]

SOURCE: U.S. INTERSTATE COMMERCE COMMISSION ANNUAL REPORTS [17].

1 EXCLUDING BROKERS AND WITHIN-STATE CARRIERS.

2 PROPERTY CARRIERS WERE THE FOLLOWING PERCENTAGES OF ALL OPERATING CARRIERS: 1944–93.4%; 1950–92.4%; 1960–93.0%; 1966–93.4%.

3 ESTIMATED.

4 NOT AVAILABLE; ASSUMED TO BE APPROXIMATELY CONSTANT.

5 1968 AND 1969 FIGURES ARE FOR NUMBER OF CARRIERS REQUIRED TO FILE ANNUAL REPORTS.

6 NOT AVAILABLE COMPARABLE TO PREVIOUS YEARS; APPLICATIONS FOR PERMANENT AUTHORITY DISPOSED OF (I.E., FROM NEW AND PENDING FILES) 1967-69 ARE AS FOLLOWS: 1967–7,049; 1968–5,724; 1969–5,186.

TABLE 6

WEIGHT LIMITS ON TRUCKS, 1932-33*, BY STATES (BASIC DATA FOR TABLE 2).

STATE	MAXIMUM WEIGHT (IN LBS.)		STATE	MAXIMUM WEIGHT (IN LBS.)	
	4-WHEEL[1]	6-WHEEL[2]		4-WHEEL[1]	6-WHEEL[2]
ALABAMA	20,000	32,000	NEBRASKA	24,000	40,000
ARIZONA	22,000	34,000	NEVADA	25,000	38,000
ARKANSAS	22,200	37,000	NEW HAMPSHIRE	20,000	20,000
CALIFORNIA	22,000	34,000	NEW JERSEY	30,000	30,000
COLORADO	30,000	40,000	NEW MEXICO	27,000	45,000
CONNECTICUT	32,000	40,000	NEW YORK	33,600	44,000
DELAWARE	26,000	38,000	NO. CAROLINA	20,000	20,000
FLORIDA	20,000	20,000	NO. DAKOTA	24,000	48,000
GEORGIA	22,000	39,600	OHIO	24,000	24,000
IDAHO	24,000	40,000	OKLAHOMA	20,000	20,000
ILLINOIS	24,000	40,000	OREGON	25,500	42,500
INDIANA	24,000	40,000	PENNSYLVANIA	26,000	36,000
IOWA	24,000	40,000	RHODE ISLAND	28,000	40,000
KANSAS	24,000	34,000	SO. CAROLINA	20,000	25,000
KENTUCKY	18,000	18,000	SO. DAKOTA	20,000	20,000
LOUISIANA	13,400	N. A.	TENNESSEE	20,000	20,000
MAINE	18,000	27,000	TEXAS	13,500	N. A.
MARYLAND	25,000	40,000	UTAH	26,000	34,000
MASSACHUSETTS	30,000	30,000	VERMONT	20,000	20,000
MICHIGAN	27,000	45,000	VIRGINIA	24,000	35,000
MINNESOTA	27,000	42,000	WASHINGTON	24,000	34,000
MISSISSIPPI	18,000	22,000	WEST VA.	24,000	40,000
MISSOURI	24,000	24,000	WISCONSIN	24,000	36,000
MONTANA	24,000	34,000	WYOMING	27,000	30,000

* RED BOOK [11] FIGURES ARE REPORTED (P. 89) AS "BASED ON THE STATE'S INTERPRETATIONS OF THEIR LAWS [1933] AND ON PHYSICAL LIMITATIONS OF VEHICLE DESIGN AND TIRE CAPACITY." PUBLIC ROADS [13] FIGURES ARE REPORTED (P. 167) AS "AN ABSTRACT OF STATE LAWS, INCLUDING LEGISLATION PASSED IN 1932."

1. 4-WHEEL: THE SMALLEST OF THE FOLLOWING 3 FIGURES WAS USED:

    (A) MAXIMUM GROSS WEIGHT (AS GIVEN IN RED BOOK, P. 90-91).

    (B) MAXIMUM AXLE WEIGHT (AS GIVEN IN RED BOOK, P. 90-91), MULTIPLIED BY 1.5 (SEE RED BOOK, P. 89).

    (C) MAXIMUM GROSS WEIGHT (AS GIVEN IN RED BOOK, P. 93).

EXCEPTIONS: TEXAS AND LOUISIANA—SEE RED BOOK, P. 91.

2. 6-WHEEL: MAXIMUM GROSS WEIGHT AS GIVEN IN PUBLIC ROADS, P. 167. THESE FIGURES AGREE IN MOST CASES WITH THOSE SHOWN IN RED BOOK, P. 93, AND WITH PUBLIC ROADS MAXIMUM AXLE WEIGHTS MULTIPLIED BY 2.5 (SEE RED BOOK, P. 93). TEXAS AND LOUISIANA ARE EXCLUDED AS DATA ARE NOT AVAILABLE TO CONVERT FROM PAYLOAD TO GROSS WEIGHT LIMITS.

TABLE 7

INDEPENDENT VARIABLES
(BASIC DATA FOR TABLE 2 — CONT'D)

STATE	TRUCKS ON FARMS PER 1,000 AGRICULTURAL LABOR FORCE	AVERAGE LENGTH OF RAILROAD HAUL OF FREIGHT (MILES)	PERCENT OF STATE HIGHWAYS WITH HIGH-TYPE SURFACE
ALABAMA	26.05	189.4	1.57
ARIZONA	79.74	282.2	2.60
ARKANSAS	28.62	233.1	1.72
CALIFORNIA	123.40	264.6	13.10
COLORADO	159.50	244.7	0.58
CONNECTICUT	173.80	132.6	7.98
DELAWARE	173.20	202.7	21.40
FLORIDA	91.41	184.1	8.22
GEORGIA	32.07	165.7	1.60
IDAHO	95.89	243.6	0.73
ILLINOIS	114.70	207.9	9.85
INDIANA	120.20	202.8	6.90
IOWA	98.73	233.3	3.39
KANSAS	146.70	281.5	0.94
KENTUCKY	20.05	227.5	1.81
LOUISIANA	31.27	201.0	1.94
MAINE	209.30	120.4	1.87
MARYLAND	134.20	184.1	12.90
MASSACHUSETTS	172.20	144.7	17.70
MICHIGAN	148.40	168.0	6.68
MINNESOTA	120.40	225.6	1.44
MISSISSIPPI	29.62	164.9	1.14
MISSOURI	54.28	229.7	2.91
MONTANA	183.80	266.5	0.09
NEBRASKA	132.10	266.9	0.41
NEVADA	139.40	273.2	0.39
NEW HAMPSHIRE	205.40	129.0	3.42
NEW JERSEY	230.20	137.6	23.30
NEW MEXICO	90.46	279.0	0.18
NEW YORK	220.50	163.3	21.50
NO. CAROLINA	37.12	171.5	8.61
NO. DAKOTA	126.40	255.1	0.01
OHIO	125.80	194.2	11.20
OKLAHOMA	78.18	223.3	1.42
OREGON	118.90	246.2	3.35
PENNSYLVANIA	187.60	166.5	9.78
RHODE ISLAND	193.30	131.0	20.40
SO. CAROLINA	20.21	169.8	2.82
SO. DAKOTA	113.40	216.6	0.04
TENNESSEE	23.98	191.9	3.97
UTAH	101.70	235.7	1.69
VERMONT	132.20	109.7	2.26
VIRGINIA	71.88	229.8	2.86
WASHINGTON	180.90	254.4	4.21
WEST VIRGINIA	62.88	218.7	8.13
WISCONSIN	178.60	195.7	4.57
WYOMING	133.40	286.7	0.08

(1) AVERAGE LENGTH OF RR HAUL OF (REVENUE) FREIGHT = AVERAGE DISTANCE IN MILES EACH TON IS CARRIED = RATIO OF NUMBER OF TON-MILES TO NUMBER OF TONS CARRIED. FOR EACH STATE, AVERAGE LENGTH OF HAUL WAS OBTAINED BY WEIGHTING AVERAGE LENGTH OF HAUL OF EACH COMPANY BY THE NUMBER OF MILES OF LINE OPERATED BY THAT COMPANY IN THE STATE (ALL FOR CLASS I RR'S).

(2) PERCENTAGE OF STATE ROADS WITH HIGH-QUALITY SURFACE: WHERE HIGH-QUALITY (HIGH-TYPE) SURFACE CONSISTS OF BITUMINOUS MACADAM, BITUMINOUS CONCRETE, SHEET ASPHALT, PORTLAND CEMENT CONCRETE, AND BLOCK PAVEMENTS. ALL STATE RURAL ROADS, BOTH LOCAL AND STATE HIGHWAYS SYSTEMS, ARE INCLUDED.

References

1. ASSOCIATION OF AMERICAN RAILROADS, BUREAU OF RAILWAY ECONOMICS. *Railway Mileage by States.* Washington, D. C.: December 31, 1930.
2. BECKER, G. S. "Competition and Democracy." *Journal of Law and Economics,* October 1958.
3. THE COUNCIL OF STATE GOVERNMENTS. "Occupational Licensing Legislation in the States." 1952.
4. DEMSETZ, H., "Why Regulate Utilities?" *Journal of Law and Economics,* April 1968.
5. GERWIG, R. W. "Natural Gas Production: A Study of Costs of Regulation." *Journal of Law and Economics,* October 1962, pp. 69-92.
6. HOLEN, A. S. "Effects of Professional Licensing Arrangements on Interstate Labor Mobility and Resource Allocation." *Journal of Political Economy,* Vol. 73 (1915), pp. 492-98.
7. KEYES, L. S. *Federal Control of Entry into Air Transportation.* Cambridge, Mass.: Harvard University Press, 1951.
8. MOORE, T. G. "The Purpose of Licensing." *Journal of Law and Economics,* October 1961.
9. OLSON, M. *The Logic of Collective Action.* Cambridge, Mass.: Harvard University Press, 1965.
10. PELTZMAN, S. "Entry in Commercial Banking." *Journal of Law and Economics,* October 1965.
11. *The Motor Truck Red Book and Directory,* 1934 Edition, pp. 85-102.
12. U. S. CONGRESS, SELECT COMMITTEE ON SMALL BUSINESS. *Hearings,* 88th Congress, 2nd Session, August 10 and 11, 1964.
13. U. S. DEPARTMENT OF AGRICULTURE, BUREAU OF PUBLIC ROADS. *Public Roads.* Washington, D. C.: U. S. Government Printing Office, December 1932.
14. U. S. DEPARTMENT OF COMMERCE, BUREAU OF THE CENSUS. *United States Census of Agriculture, 1930,* Vol. 4. Washington, D. C.: U. S. Government Printing Office, 1930.
15. ———. *United States Census of Population.* Washington, D. C.: U. S. Government Printing Office, appropriate years.
16. ———, BUREAU OF FOREIGN AND DOMESTIC COMMERCE. *Statistical Abstract of the U. S., 1932.* Washington, D. C.: U. S. Government Printing Office, 1932.
17. U. S. INTERSTATE COMMERCE COMMISSION. *Annual Report.* Washington, D. C.: U. S. Government Printing Office, appropriate years.
18. ———. *Statistics of Railways in the United States, 1930.* Washington, D. C.: U. S. Government Printing Office, 1930.

[24]

By *Thomas K. McCraw*
ASSOCIATE PROFESSOR OF HISTORY
UNIVERSITY OF TEXAS, AUSTIN

Regulation in America:
A Review Article

❡ *Professor McCraw surveys the state of the art of understanding regulatory commissions in American history, evaluating the relevant literature in history, economics, political science, and law.*

With accelerating momentum over the last quarter-century, the subject of economic regulation by state and federal commissions has undergone rigorous reinterpretation. Although the process of revision is far from mature, studies in each relevant discipline — history, political science, law, and especially economics — have begun to reshape the terms of discussion and to advance alternative models of regulatory behavior. In so doing, they have questioned not only some long-held views of business-government relations, but also associated themes such as the nature and results of Progressive and New Deal reforms, the wisdom and efficacy of planned interference with market forces, and the character of the American polity itself.

Certain difficulties still block the formation of a satisfactory new synthesis. For one thing, the scope of "regulation" defies precise definition, since every economic activity is regulated in some degree.[1] Commissions of various types exist in all fifty states and throughout the federal establishment, but some have little in common with others besides the presence of "board" or "commission" in their titles. Then too, regulation properly conceived includes structurally different (commissionless) but functionally similar roles played by institutions like the Antitrust Division of the Department of Justice and the price support apparatus of the Department of Agriculture. It also includes intra-industry regulatory mechanisms such as trade associations, rate bureaus, and price leadership

Business History Review, Vol. XLIX, No. 2 (Summer, 1975). Copyright © The President and Fellows of Harvard College.

[1] Even public utility regulation raises definitional issues. See James W. McKie, "Regulation and the Free Market: The Problem of Boundaries," *Bell Journal of Economics and Management Science*, I (Spring, 1970), 6–26.

systems. This essay will address only the commission aspects of regulation, beginning with two widely known but troublesome concepts or images: the "public interest" notion, and the recently dominant "capture" thesis. Some of the scholarship of regulation, and practically all the journalism, converges on one or the other, or on some combination of the two.

"Public Interest"

The "public interest" seems an unusually vague construct, indefinable and analytically counterproductive. Part of the problem comes from its multiple meanings and evolving redefinitions over time. In the nineteenth century, "public interest" enterprises had social overhead functions, such as banking, transportation, and several other industries later called "public utilities." Some of these enterprises combined great economic power with a propensity toward corruption, and they required regulation for the protection of potential victims. Others, notably railroads, tended toward "natural monopoly" and needed a surrogate for the lost discipline of the market. More recently, still other industries, such as broadcasting and air transport, appeared to need regulation as an escape from chaotic or destabilizing competition, which injured not only themselves, but the public as well.

American law reflected these economic premises. Beginning in the nineteenth century and culminating in the *Nebbia* decision of 1934, the law marked off certain types of enterprise as "affected with a public interest" and therefore subject to a strong application of the police power. But as society became more and more interdependent, and as consumer markets for standardized products became larger and larger, the number of industries logically "affected with a public interest" grew unmanageably large. As time passed, the "public interest" as an economic and legal notion had less and less utility, and became an unsatisfactory litmus test of why some industries in America are closely regulated, and others are not.[2]

In the political sense, insofar as it can be distinct from the legal or economic one, "public interest" has been roughly analogous to such phrases as "public good," "common good," or "general wel-

---

[2] On the "public interest" in American utility law, see Harry N. Scheiber, "The Road to *Munn*: Eminent Domain and the Concept of Public Purpose in the State Courts," *Perspectives in American History,* V (1971), 327–402. *Nebbia v. New York,* 291 U.S. 502 (1934). Most textbooks of public utility economics provide a summary of the evolution of "public interest" law; an example is Part I of Paul J. Garfield and Wallace F. Lovejoy, *Public Utility Economics* (Englewood Cliffs, N.J., 1964).

fare," expressing in the eighteenth and nineteenth centuries a conviction that the societal whole is greater than the sum of its parts, and by the mid-twentieth an intuition that consumer interests are more vital than they used to be. In political science, the notion is related to the theory of public goods, and also to pluralist thought, for which it serves as a point of departure.[3]

In a confusing amalgam of these usages, "public interest" is a thread of continuity at the heart of regulatory ideology, from its origins down to the present. The phrase "the public good," for example, appeared in the statute that created the first important regulatory tribunal, the Massachusetts Board of Railroad Commissioners, established in 1869 and dominated throughout its first decade by Charles Francis Adams, Jr. In commissions, Adams, like many others, detected "a new phase of representative government," made necessary by the unprecedented complexities of industrial technology. Commissions would take as their guide "the interest of the community," which informed regulators would harmonize with the interests of businesses. Unlike legislatures, the new agencies would sit continuously, investigating and deliberating within a universe of dispassionate expertise. Shunning turmoil, they would deal with industrial problems not as dramatic episodes, but as evolving processes calling for careful, meticulously considered responses. Statistics would replace emotions as the basis for action.[4]

For seven decades afterward, from the 1870s through the New Deal, state and federal commission regulation proliferated over railroads, gas and electric utilities, radio and television broadcasting, truck and air transport, and a few other enterprises. Although the reasons for regulation varied according to the industry involved, the notion of the "public interest" continued to dominate the rhetoric of reformers, the utterances of presidents, and the decisions of commissioners. It served as an ideological glue binding together the quasi-legislative, quasi-executive, quasi-judicial duties of regulators. In the 1930s, the doctrine reached its rhetorical zenith, a paradoxical result in view of the New Deal's frequent recognition of and assistance to private interest groups. Legislative draftsmen inserted the phrase repeatedly into the flood of regulatory law that

---

[3] The concept is examined at length in Glendon Schubert, *The Public Interest* (Glencoe, Ill., 1960); Richard E. Flathman, *The Public Interest: An Essay Concerning the Normative Discourse of Politics* (New York, 1966); Carl J. Friedrich, ed., *The Public Interest* (Nomos V, New York, 1962); and Virginia Held, *The Public Interest and Individual Interests* (New York, 1970).

[4] Massachusetts *Acts and Resolves*, 1869, Chapter 408, Section 4, p. 701; Charles Francis Adams, Jr., "Boston, I," *North American Review*, CVI (January, 1868), 18, 25; Adams, "Railroad Inflation," *North American Review*, CVIII (January, 1869), 158, 163–164.

created the Federal Communications Commission, the Securities and Exchange Commission, and the Civil Aeronautics Authority (now Board). The "public interest" occurs a dozen times in the Communications Act, a dozen and a half in the Securities Exchange Act, and more than two dozen in the Civil Aeronautics Act, as a guide for regulators and as a justification for the immense discretionary powers those statutes bestowed.[5]

The New Deal also produced the outstanding theoretical elaboration of administrative regulation, written by James Macauley Landis, a draftsman of both the Securities Act and the Securities and Exchange Act. Pupil and friend of Felix Frankfurter, commissioner of the FTC and the SEC (and, later, dean of the Harvard Law School and member of the CAB), Landis was one of the brightest men of his time. In his Storrs Lectures at Yale, published in 1938 as *The Administrative Process*, he delivered the most eloquent celebration of commission regulation ever written. Recognizing the ambiguity of the "public interest," Landis nonetheless affirmed the validity and efficacy of broad administrative discretion founded on that doctrine.[6]

THE "CAPTURE" IMAGE

Significantly, Landis devoted much of his analysis to a defense of regulation, for the idea had long since encountered critical attack. Deriving from many different sources and premises, this critique resolved into an alternative image of regulation at once more tough-minded, easily grasped, and above all more descriptive of what seemed to be going on within the regulatory agencies.

Early skeptics had questioned just how independent the regulatory machinery was likely to be, or should be. For one thing, the appointment of expert, nonpartisan regulators (or even bipartisan commissions) and their removal from the normal political process seemed a step toward elitism, away from the nation's democratic traditions. For another, genuine independence might be unsustainable against presidents or governors who wished to interfere with scientific deliberation, or thwart it through the ap-

[5] A typical declaration of the principle came from Commissioner Joseph B. Eastman of the ICC, who wrote to his colleagues in 1931: "For a long time I have quarreled with the idea that in a complaint case involving freight rates this Commission is merely a jury to decide between the parties upon the basis of the particular facts which they happen to bring to our attention in that case. The Commission is much more than that; it is an expert tribunal with a definite responsibility for the railroad rate structure of the country and its proper adjustment in the general public interest." ICC Docket No. 22876, May 4, 1931, Eastman Papers, Robert Frost Library, Amherst College, Amherst, Massachusetts.
[6] Landis, *The Administrative Process* (New Haven, Conn., 1938). On the "public interest," see especially 51–52.

pointment of cronies and hacks. Even more likely, considering what usually went on inside the lobbies of legislatures, regulated corporations could direct their potent economic influence as readily toward regulators as toward other public officials. These arguments, all related to experience as well as to deductive notions of "capture," persisted as a running debate throughout the Progressive Era. In 1925, President Calvin Coolidge symbolically crystallized the "capture" theme by appointing to the Federal Trade Commission a man (William E. Humphrey) who brought a 3–2 majority against what most old progressives conceived as the "public interest." The ensuing despair brought loud protest, together with calls for the FTC's abolition from some of its erstwhile friends.[7]

The New Deal temporarily quieted criticism of this sort. Franklin D. Roosevelt appointed aggressive regulators like Landis and William O. Douglas, and attempted to undo history by firing Humphrey. Thus, during the thirties, intellectually respectable criticism of regulation came from other sources, many of them based on theoretical objections that held it to be "a headless fourth branch of government," unresponsive to executive leadership. It was to this kind of attack, rooted more in political science than in evidence of sellout, that Landis replied when he wrote *The Administrative Process.*[8]

The "capture" idea persisted nevertheless. The New Deal's multiplication of regulatory agencies, together with its programs of assistance to specific interest groups, simply multiplied the fields available for "capture." Over the next two decades, observers noted that the CAB and FCC in particular seemed to follow doctrines that equated the "public interest" with whatever the most powerful elements of the communications and airline industries wanted. By the 1950s, scholars such as Samuel P. Huntington and Louis L. Jaffe had begun to analyze the ties between regulator and regulated, and the inherent flaws in regulatory thought. In 1955, Marver H. Bernstein published a devastating book that synthesized into a coherent whole all the diverse objections that had gathered force since the New Deal. And in 1960, James M. Landis, in a stunning turnaround, catalogued the breakdown of the regulatory system he himself had celebrated twenty-two years before.[9]

[7] G. Cullom Davis, "The Transformation of the Federal Trade Commission, 1914–1929," *Mississippi Valley Historical Review*, XLIX (December, 1962), 452 *ff.*
[8] The Humphrey episode is examined in William E. Leuchtenburg, "The Case of the Contentious Commissioner: Humphrey's Executor v. U.S.," in Harold M. Hyman and Leonard W. Levy, eds., *Freedom and Reform: Essays in Honor of Henry Steele Commager* (New York, 1967), 276–312. The focus of Landis's attention is evident in *The Administrative Process*, 4.
[9] Huntington, "The Marasmus of the ICC: The Commission, the Railroads, and the

By that time, the attack on regulation had become a staple of the broad re-evaluation of American institutions that began in the 1950s and reached maturity in the 1960s. Liberal reform as a whole underwent a searching critique and redefinition, its viability questioned by disillusioned analysts who looked beneath society's veneers and found the results of pluralist democracy ugly and repulsive. In a context of prolonged national crisis and self-examination, the regulatory agencies remained prime targets. By the late 1960s, a common assumption held that the commissions, like so many American institutions, had sold out, that they had suffered "capture" by regulated interests, that the "public interest" had become a tragic joke.

Detailed indictments quickly followed. Portraits of uniformly abysmal performance emerged from a series of immature, predictable, but incisive exposés published by the young associates of Ralph Nader. Less sensational but equally damning studies by other journalists and scholars suggested that however flawed the work of "Nader's Raiders" might be, their conclusions had merit. By the 1970s, the "public interest" as a credible standard for interpreting regulatory behavior had few defenders. In its place reigned the "capture" thesis, which was rapidly nearing the status of a truism, a cliché of both scholarship and popular perceptions. "If nearly a century of regulatory history tells us anything," observed economist Robert Heilbroner, "it is that the rules-making agencies of government are almost invariably captured by the industries which they are established to control." [10]

HISTORIANS AND REGULATION

Over much of the literature of "capture," one historian exerted a uniquely powerful influence. Gabriel Kolko anticipated the crest of the thesis in each of his two books on regulation, *The Triumph of Conservatism* (1963), and *Railroads and Regulation* (1965). In Kolko's models, argued *a priori* and buttressed by impressive new

Public Interest," *Yale Law Journal*, LXI (April, 1952), 467–509; Jaffe, "The Effective Limits of the Administrative Process: A Reevaluation," *Harvard Law Review*, LXVII (May, 1954), 1105–1135; Bernstein, *Regulating Business by Independent Commission* (Princeton, N.J., 1955); Landis, *Report on Regulatory Agencies to the President-Elect* (U.S., Senate, Committee on the Judiciary, 86th Cong., 2d sess., 1960).

[10] Edward F. Cox, *et al.*, *"The Nader Report" on the Federal Trade Commission* (New York, 1969); Robert Fellmeth, *The Interstate Commerce Omission* (New York, 1970); Mark J. Green, *The Closed Enterprise System* (New York, 1972); Green, ed., *The Monopoly Makers* (New York, 1973). Examples of additional critical literature include Louis M. Kohlmeier, Jr., *The Regulators: Watchdog Agencies and the Public Interest* (New York, 1969); and Paul W. MacAvoy, ed., *The Crisis of the Regulatory Commissions* (New York, 1970). The quotation is from Heilbroner, *et al.*, *In the Name of Profit* (Garden City, N.Y., 1972), 239.

evidence of the sort conventionally esteemed by historians, "capture" inhered in the American polity, because of the centrality of capitalist power. Thus, wrote Kolko, railroad men themselves "were the most important single advocates of federal regulation from 1877 to 1916." From the beginning, "the Interstate Commerce Commission entered into a condition of dependency on the railroads, and the railroads quickly began relying on the Commission as a means of attaining their own ends." Even more startling, what was true of the railroads applied to American business in general: "Federal economic regulation was generally designed by the regulated interest to meet its own end, and not those of the public or the commonweal." [11]

Kolko's ideas failed to convince many of his colleagues. Some historians pointed out that he ignored contrary evidence and misunderstood basic economics; others argued that he fallaciously assumed a polarity between the public interest and private interests; still others asserted that even the selective evidence he did present, though useful, did not begin to sustain his thesis, in part because he often failed to distinguish what businessmen received from what they originally wanted.[12] Still, Kolko's books asked new, challenging questions, and neither the questions nor his evidence could be dismissed easily. Consequently, they became staples of graduate seminars and professional convention sessions. Activists enlisting in the causes of the 1960s found Kolko's the most usable of pasts. More important, his work influenced scholars in disciplines other than history. Here the attraction seemed to be neither the strength of evidence nor the conclusiveness of argument, but the distinctly theoretical approach. At bottom, Kolko's analysis was a straightforward deductive system, very like the deductive models of economists and sociologists. The Kolko model argued not only that "capture" inhered in the system from the outset, but also that the American political economy made the design and subsequent behavior of commissions inevitable, and therefore predictable. Such a theory had immense appeal, the more so because it seemed a uniquely clear explanation of contemporary experience. Nor was the appeal confined to Kolko's ideological allies on the Left. His insistence that competition in the American economy was increasing

[11] Kolko, *Railroads and Regulation 1877–1916* (Princeton, N.J., 1965), 3, 233; Kolko, *The Triumph of Conservatism: A Reinterpretation of American History, 1900–1916* (New York, 1963), 59.

[12] A collection of Kolko criticism appears in Otis L. Graham, Jr., ed., *From Roosevelt to Roosevelt: American Politics and Diplomacy, 1901–1941* (New York, 1971), 70–109; see also Robert U. Harbeson, "Railroads and Regulation, 1877–1916, Conspiracy or Public Interest?" *Journal of Economic History*, XXVII (June, 1967), 230–242.

at the turn of the twentieth century, and his implicit ideal of a decentralized society attracted admiration from many quarters, notably the "Chicago school" of free market economists.[13]

As "capture" became first an alternative to "public interest," then a cliché in its own right, questions arose about *its* validity. How could the Interstate Commerce Commission be simultaneously the captive of railroad, truck, and barge transporters, when these industries had overlapping markets and were partial competitors? In what sense was the Federal Power Commission the captive of the natural gas industry, whose field prices it regulated so stringently that production brought inadequate returns, leading to what critics called "regulation-induced shortages"?[14] How well did the "capture" thesis fit those few points of regulatory history where scholars had made detailed investigations?

Most of the existing histories pertain to railroad regulation alone, probably because it offers the richest source materials and the longest perspective for evaluation. In consequence, however, the aggregate portrait of regulation by historians is very narrow. Of eight book-length studies to appear since Lee Benson's pioneering *Merchants, Farmers, and Railroads*, all except three have concerned railroad regulation.

Benson's thesis, that "New York merchants constituted the single most important group behind the passage of the Interstate Commerce Act," seems in retrospect less convincing and less significant than the other points he established in arguing it. His vast body of evidence demonstrated that the movement for national railroad regulation was a many-faceted phenomenon that embraced agricultural, mercantile, and eventually railroad interests themselves. On this last point, a pivotal one for "capture," Benson found the railroad men belated supporters who joined the movement because "it would have been fairly dangerous to attempt to cap it tight." As for the "public interest," Benson portrayed the struggle as hardly "a victory by the 'people' over the 'corporations,'" but instead a fight over who would receive what proportion of the new wealth generated by the economic explosion of the period. Fundamentally,

---

[13] Membership in the "Chicago school" is not a hard and fast category, but one important member is George J. Stigler (see note 33 below). Other Chicago-associated scholars apparently influenced by Kolko include Thomas G. Moore, *Freight Transportation Regulation: Surface Freight and the Interstate Commerce Commission* (Washington, D.C., 1972); and George W. Hilton, "The Consistency of the Interstate Commerce Act," *Journal of Law and Economics*, IX (October, 1966), 87 *ff.*

[14] This point is discussed briefly in James Q. Wilson, "The Dead Hand of Regulation," *The Public Interest*, XXV (Fall, 1971), 46–49; on the FPC, see Paul W. MacAvoy, "The Regulation-Induced Shortage of Natural Gas," *Journal of Law and Economics*, XIV (April, 1971), 167–199.

the origin of the ICC was a story of warring interest groups, no one of which represented the entire public or felt motivated by an ideology of the general welfare. Instead, economic men fought each other over the division of industrial spoils. Without regulation, the railroad magnates had the power to keep a disproportionate share for themselves, even during periods of instability within the industry. Benson's behavioral methodology, informed by pluralist theory from political science, cut through the rhetoric of the period, and in the process demonstrated the inadequacy of both "public interest" and "capture" as models of the origins of national railroad regulation.[15]

Studies by Gerald D. Nash, Edward A. Purcell, Jr., and K. Austin Kerr confirmed the pluralist implications of Benson's book, though Nash differed in his nomination of the leading interest group (Pennsylvania oil men in place of Benson's New York merchants), and Purcell argued that the very process of suggesting one leading proponent disguised the national consensus basic to the ICC's creation. Kerr carried the model of group interaction into the period of World War I, showing how external conditions favored first one interest, then the other, and especially how the growing potency of railway brotherhoods injected a third major force into the old dualism of carriers versus shippers.[16]

These same points emerged in Albro Martin's *Enterprise Denied.* Yet Martin consistently viewed the struggle from the perspective of railroad executives, and took rhetoric and ideology much more seriously. Evaluating congressional and ICC action between 1897 and 1917, Martin contended that railroad entrepreneurship was stunted by "archaic progressivism." He thus portrayed the era as a starving time for railroads, accompanied by a rise in the political fortunes of shippers, with whose cause midwestern legislators identified "reform." Though the book suffered from an untenable conclusion,[17] Martin exhibited an unusually sure sense of the ways in

[15] Benson, *Merchants, Farmers, and Railroads: Railroad Regulation and New York Politics, 1850–1887* (Cambridge, Mass., 1955), 212, 245. An earlier work that included substantial analysis of nineteenth century state commissions in one area was Edward Chase Kirkland, *Men Cities and Transportation: A Study in New England History, 1820–1900* (2 vols., Cambridge, Mass., 1948). Benson's conclusion that railroad men supported regulation somewhat reluctantly was consistent with an earlier report by Thomas C. Cochran, in *Railroad Leaders 1845–1890: The Business Mind in Action* (Cambridge, Mass., 1953), 189–199.

[16] Nash, "Origins of the Interstate Commerce Act of 1887," *Pennsylvania History*, XXIV (July, 1957), 181–190; Purcell, "Ideas and Interests: Businessmen and the Interstate Commerce Act," *Journal of American History*, LIV (December, 1967), 561–578; Kerr, *American Railroad Politics, 1914–1920* (Pittsburgh, 1968).

[17] Martin, *Enterprise Denied: Origins of the Decline of American Railroads, 1897–1917* (New York, 1971). Martin concluded that the ICC's regulatory action in the decade following passage of the Hepburn Act (1906) induced a capital starvation that precipitated the secular decline of American railroads. The fallacy here was Martin's insufficient

which businessmen made decisions. In effect, the book, together with a later article by Martin that clarified the controversy over pooling, totally inverted the thesis of Kolko's *Railroads and Regulation*. Whatever "capture" had occurred was the railroads by the ICC. Wherever Kolko had found "political capitalism" operating to the benefit of the industry, Martin discovered "archaic progressivism" undermining it. Where Kolko's implicit premise appeared to be the illegitimacy of the American polity, Martin's seemed to be the nonsense of regulatory meddling with a market system.[18]

Two state studies provided additional insight into early railroad politics, in its midwestern setting. These were George H. Miller's *Railroads and the Granger Laws* and Stanley P. Caine's *The Myth of a Progressive Reform*.[19] Miller's book, a model of careful scholarship, argued that although the so-called "Granger" legislation of the four upper-midwestern states in the 1870s may have had the support of farmers (some of whom were more or less "radical"), the laws derived more directly from the region's shippers. "When set against the background of previous rate law and policy," observed Miller, "the laws appear far less radical and in no sense agrarian." [20] In the Middle West, the railroad problem meant discriminatory rates, not general rate levels. It meant interstate and intercity rivalry as much as carriers versus shippers. The dilemma pressed hard: if regulation were too stringent, railroads might refuse to extend their services, or stop them altogether, cutting the umbilical lifelines of towns serving as trans-shipment points for agricultural commodities. Within such a context of total dependence, the "public interest" had a sharper, more self-evident substantive meaning than it had for other regions and other industries. As for "capture," it was irrelevant to regulatory experience in the Granger states. The railroads fought commission regulation with every tool they possessed. When this effort failed, they often ignored the new laws, and when that policy proved unsatisfactory they turned to the courts for relief. Thus Miller's book again confirmed the group-struggle pattern of regulation. It also provided a valuable institutional approach to a question too little explored by historians — the transitions and continuities in nineteenth-century

---

emphasis on a much stronger factor in the railroads' eclipse — the onset of severe intermodal competition, both for freight, from trucks, and for passengers, from interurban electrics, automobiles, and airlines.

[18] Martin, *Enterprise Denied, passim*; Martin, "The Troubled Subject of Railroad Regulation in the Gilded Age — A Reappraisal," *Journal of American History*, LXI (September, 1974), 339–371.

[19] Miller, *Railroads and the Granger Laws* (Madison, Wis., 1971); Caine, *The Myth of a Progressive Reform: Railroad Regulation in Wisconsin 1903–1910* (Madison, Wis., 1970).

[20] Miller, *Railroads and the Granger Laws*, ix.

state economic policies from optimistic promotion to disillusioned regulation.[21]

In Stanley P. Caine's monograph on Wisconsin, the principal actor was Robert M. La Follette, who, as the state's governor from 1901 to 1906, attempted to add railroad regulation to his list of essential programs. As La Follette himself told the story in his autobiography, he managed to secure a genuinely progressive commission, which inaugurated an era of regulation in the "public interest." Several historians accepted this version uncritically, but Caine did not. Instead, he argued that the alleged victory over corporate interests was an illusion; that the new law did not give the commission clear power to initiate rates, but made it a judicial institution of appeal from the decisions of railroad corporations. The new tribunal quickly assumed an accommodating posture, and the railroad men who had fought its creation grew to admire it. To Caine, this sequence indicated "a betrayal of reform ideals." The very title of his book, *The Myth of a Progressive Reform*, implied a normative judgement that the "public interest" had not been served.[22]

Although most regulatory histories pertained to railroads, three studies addressed other aspects of the subject. The best known of the three, Kolko's *The Triumph of Conservatism*, argues the same thesis as his *Railroads and Regulation*, substituting business in general for the railroads' role. The other two examine the early careers of the Federal Trade Commission and the Securities and Exchange Commission. The first to appear was G. Cullom Davis's article, "The Transformation of the Federal Trade Commission, 1914–1929." Davis found in the FTC the same sort of inconsistency within one agency that scholars of railroad regulation had collectively discovered among different railroad commissions. As the FTC struggled with its vague mandate during the Progressive Era, World War I, and the prosperity of the twenties, "unfair methods of competition in commerce" successively acquired different mean-

[21] The litigation over the Granger laws produced one of the landmark cases in public utility law, *Munn v. Illinois* [94 U.S. 113 (1877)], in which the opinion of Chief Justice Morrison R. Waite explicitly relied on the "public interest" doctrine in affirming the power of states to regulate enterprises that "stand in the very 'gateway of commerce' and take toll from all who pass." Miller's book provided an insightful new perspective on this decision, tying it to earlier state policies, as did Harry N. Scheiber in the article cited in note 2 above.

[22] Caine, *The Myth of a Progressive Reform*, especially Chapter 10. Caine's analysis was strongest in clarifying the motives of La Follette and other principals, the legislative trade-offs that usually characterize regulatory statute-making, and the policies of the new commission itself. Nowhere, however, did he show that rates in Wisconsin were too high, or that a substantial general decrease would have benefited the shippers or the public without unduly injuring the corporations. Instead he seemed to take this difficult question for granted.

REGULATION IN AMERICA 169

ings for different groups. By the close of the commission's first decade, its early enemies had become champions, its early advocates new opponents. In Davis's scheme, the "public interest" alternated with "capture" depending on the identity of the commissioners, which in turn varied with the incumbent of the White House and ultimately with the mood of the nation. In effect, Davis found the commission, like Mr. Dooley's Supreme Court, following the election returns. The high court itself added to the FTC's woes by confining its discretionary powers to the narrowest of functions.[23]

Michael E. Parrish's fine study, *Securities Regulation and the New Deal*, emphasized the intelligence and professionalism of the architects and early members of the Securities and Exchange Commission, but also noted the effects of concentrated industry pressure, both on the shape of the legislation and on the policies of the SEC. Even during a national economic depression, when businessmen in general and securities dealers in particular were in extremely low repute, industry input could still have powerful impact. The SEC confronted entrenched economic arrangements that antedated the New Deal, and that were likely to be upset by an overturning of the exchange apparatus, with devastating effects not only on the guilty few but also on innocent multitudes of investors. The SEC negotiated a fine line between merely symbolic action on the one hand and overkill on the other, a policy that represented neither a rout of the villains nor a surrender to them, but "half a loaf." Considering the complex situation, this was a substantial achievement. It minimized the effects of private corruption on the national economy, and "held the possibility of more orderly, enduring economic growth in the future." [24] Parrish detailed the financial community's utter hostility toward regulation, its near-willingness to hold national recovery hostage to its determination to avert reform. During the post-enactment period, the mutual reliance between industry and commission for information, the shifts back and forth of important personnel, were characteristics consistent with the possibility of "capture," but not in themselves conclusive evidence.

Taken as a whole, historical writing offers few clear patterns of regulatory behavior, except that it demonstrates the inadequacy of either "capture," the "public interest," or the two in tandem as satisfactory models. Most historians have emphasized the political

---

[23] Davis, "The Transformation of the Federal Trade Commission, 1914–1929," *Mississippi Valley Historical Review*, XLIX (December, 1962), 437–455.

[24] Parrish, *Securities Regulation and the New Deal* (New Haven, Conn., 1970), 219, 232. This book covered much of the same ground as Ralph F. De Bedts, *The New Deal's SEC: The Formative Years* (New York, 1964), but was better researched and more analytical.

aspects of regulation, with the one common conclusion that regulatory politics involved an intricate, complex struggle among intensely competitive interest groups, each using the machinery of the state whenever it could, to serve particularistic goals largely unrelated to "public interest" ideology except in the tactical sense.

ECONOMISTS AND REGULATION

A continuing problem for both scholars and reformers has been the elusiveness of hard evidence concerning regulation's actual effects. Unlike their corporate counterparts, commissions issue no profit and loss statements telling in an instant whether the quarter or year has been good or bad. No regulatory agency lists its common stock on traders' exchanges, where a rise or fall might indicate success or failure. Nor do most commissioners, like elective politicians, face voters at regular intervals for endorsement or rejection. Consequently, the new attention that economists gave to regulation in the 1960s and 1970s had prodigious significance. In these studies, a "bottom line" appeared, purporting to provide quantitative assessments of regulation's impact.

Economists had long been interested in the subject. Institutional economics supplied some of the intellectual foundations of the commission movement, and prominent scholars like John R. Commons, William Z. Ripley, Balthasar H. Meyer, and Rexford G. Tugwell sometimes wrote regulatory laws, served on commissions or commission staffs, and made regulation an academic subdiscipline. By the 1930s, however, institutionalism had begun to wane, and the subsequent triumph of Keynesianism and macroeconomics inevitably made regulation a less exciting topic, prosaic in comparison with the glamour of fiscal policy, growth economics, and "fine tuning."

The studies emerging in the 1960s and 1970s grew less out of the old institutional tradition than from the intellectual revival of price theory, whose methods in themselves raised questions about the pricing functions exercised by state utility commissions and by Federal agencies such as the ICC, CAB, and Federal Power Commission. Adding a measure of ideology to the cold logic of price theory was the related work of scholars associated with the "Chicago school," whose near-worship of the market as allocator of resources led to a distaste for that very interference with market forces that lay at the heart of the commission movement. Irrespective of premises Left or Right, the explicit test for most economists was the performance of an industry under regulation. The collective conclusion, much more decisive than those of the empirically-oriented historians, held that regulation was an expensive failure. In a harsh summary verdict, one influential economist wrote in 1963: "What the regulatory commissions are trying to do is difficult to discover; what effect these commissions actually have is, to a large extent, unknown; when it can be discovered, it is often absurd." [25]

The ICC, the oldest Federal commission, which had weathered innumerable storms and had by the 1930s attained a uniquely high reputation, was now found guilty of enormously costly errors. Its policies of minimum rate regulation, its reluctance to allow market forces to select optimal modes for particular freights, its custodial preservation of obsolete services, were ill serving the industries concerned and making a mockery of the "public interest." By the 1970s, "the immediate cost to the economy of such regulation-induced inefficiencies in surface freight transport is estimated at $4 billion to $10 billion a year." [26]

For airline regulation, the same dismal picture emerged. The Civil Aeronautics Board had prevented since its creation during the New Deal the entry of a single new trunk line carrier into the business. It had facilitated the rise of fares to unnecessarily high levels, preventing normal price competition and indirectly promoting useless and expensive types of competition, such as excessive flights, elaborate decors, massive media advertising, and extravagant inflight services. For the one important city-pair market not subject to CAB regulation, the intrastate Los Angeles-San Francisco route, normal business competition had cut the going rate nearly in half, suggesting what deregulation might accomplish elsewhere. In

[25] Ronald H. Coase, "Comment," *American Economic Review*, LIV (May, 1964), 194. The rapid rise of interest in regulation among economists may be traced through two relatively new journals, both devoted largely to regulatory topics: the *Journal of Law and Economics*, and the *Bell Journal of Economics and Management Science*. A third indication is the large project begun in the late 1960s by the Brookings Institution, which resulted in a number of books on regulation, many of which are cited below.

[26] The quotation is from John R. Meyer and Alexander L. Morton, "A Better Way to Run the Railroads," *Harvard Business Review*, LII (July–August, 1974), 143, citing an unpublished paper by Thomas G. Moore. Moore's views are elaborated also in a book that conveniently surveys the literature of its subject: *Freight Transportation Regulation: Surface Freight and the Interstate Commerce Commission* (Washington, D.C., 1972). Important studies include John R. Meyer, Merton J. Peck, John Stenason, and Charles Zwick, *The Economics of Competition in the Transportation Industries* (Cambridge, Mass., 1959); Ann F. Friedlaender, *The Dilemma of Freight Transport Regulation* (Washington, D.C., 1969); George Wilson, *Essays on Some Unsettled Questions in the Economics of Transportation* (Bloomington, Ind., 1962); Wilson, "The Effect of Rate Regulation on Resource Allocation in Transportation," *American Economic Review*, LIV (May, 1964), 160-171; and Richard N. Farmer, "The Case for Unregulated Truck Transportation," *Journal of Farm Economics*, XLVI (May, 1964), 398–409. An interesting attempt to apply theory to early railroad experience is Paul W. MacAvoy, *The Economic Effects of Regulation: The Trunk-Line Railroad Cartels and the Interstate Commerce Commission Before 1900* (Cambridge, Mass., 1965).

focusing its policies on other priorities, such as the promotion of new, technologically advanced aircraft, the subsidized extension of air service to small towns, and an apparent determination to maximize the size of the industry, the CAB had lost sight of the overall consumer interest.[27]

Price regulation of the natural gas industry by the Federal Power Commission brought similar inefficiencies, according to the leading student of this question.[28] In the first place, gas field production bore little resemblance to "natural monopoly," being instead diversified among numbers of relatively small producers. Regulation therefore lacked the logical foundation that supported early railroad commissions. Then too, the policies of the FPC tended to freeze prices during periods of sustained inflation, discouraging a proper market level of production, retarding the development of the industry, and diverting users to less economical sources of energy. By the 1970s, the policy had injured the entire economy, as the energy problem became acute and one important fuel source lay poorly developed because of regulatory constraint.

Within the states, public utility commissions seemed to pursue unwise policies toward the electric power industry. One influential hypothesis held that regulation had no serious effect at all.[29] In an equally challenging argument, two scholars theorized that utilities tend to overcapitalize, and consequently to operate at outputs other than the optimal. This excessive-capitalization theory encouraged a host of spinoff studies, and gave its originators a type of immortality by incorporating their names into the phenomenon they described: "the Averch-Johnson effect." Still other scholars discovered additional errors common to state utility commissions.[30]

[27] Richard E. Caves, *Air Transport and Its Regulators — An Industry Study* (Cambridge, Mass., 1962); William A. Jordan, *Airline Regulation in America: Effects and Imperfections* (Baltimore, 1970); George C. Eads, *The Local Service Air Line Experiment* (Washington, D.C., 1972); Theodore Keeler, "Airline Regulation and Market Performance," *Bell Journal of Economics and Management Science*, III (Autumn, 1972), 399–424; George W. Douglas and James C. Miller III, *Economic Regulation of Domestic Air Transport: Theory and Policy* (Washington, D.C., 1974).

[28] Paul W. MacAvoy, *Price Formation in Natural Gas Fields* (New Haven, Conn., 1962); MacAvoy, "The Effectiveness of the Federal Power Commission," *Bell Journal of Economics and Management Science*, I (Autumn, 1970), 271–303; MacAvoy, "The Regulation-Induced Shortage of Natural Gas," *Journal of Law and Economics*, XIV (April, 1971), 167–199.

[29] George J. Stigler and Claire Friedland, "What Can Regulators Regulate? The Case of Electricity," *Journal of Law and Economics*, V (October, 1962), 1–16; see also Harold Demsetz, "Why Regulate Utilities?" *Journal of Law and Economics*, XI (April, 1968), 55–65. An enlightening discussion of the evolution of utility pricing theories is R. H. Coase, "The Theory of Public Utility Pricing and Its Application," *Bell Journal of Economics and Management Science*, I (Spring, 1970), 113–128. Elaborations of this theme may be found in any of several standard textbooks on public utility economics, one of the best of which is Alfred E. Kahn, *The Economics of Regulation* (2 vols., New York, 1970, 1971).

[30] Harvey Averch and L. L. Johnson, "Behavior of the Firm Under Regulatory Constraint," *American Economic Review*, LII (December, 1962), 1053–1069; discussions of

Economists tended to be less critical of those commissions with few or no pricing powers, but they hardly ignored them altogether. Scattered throughout the literature were indictments of the Federal Communications Commission, the Securities and Exchange Commission, state insurance commissions, and others. Sometimes regulation itself was held to inhibit technological innovation, a grievous charge to lay at the door of a uniquely American institution.[31]

The distinctive contributions of the economists were their theoretically-based methodology, their quantification of regulatory inefficiencies, and their ability to predict probable effects of hypothetical changes in commission policy. Partly because their inquiries were typically less holistic than those of the historians, they were better able to keep a rigorous focus, and to specify precisely what it was they were trying to show. On the other hand, they paid less attention to historical sequence and factual detail. Seldom did they attempt the kind of combined cultural and economic analysis so fruitful in the work of historians such as Ellis W. Hawley and Richard Hofstadter.[32]

A few economists did theorize about the entire regulatory process. One ambitious statement came from George J. Stigler, a leading member of the "Chicago school," who propounded a rudimentary model of regulation from its origins, through enactment, and into operation. Unhappy with assumptions that the "public interest" emerged automatically from regulation, Stigler showed equal impatience with the "capture" thesis: "This criticism seems to me exactly as appropriate as a criticism of the Great Atlantic and Pacific Tea Company for selling groceries, or as a criticism of a politician for currying popular support." In some respects, Stigler's was the Kolko model updated. Whatever "capture" had occurred was not so much of the commissions as it was of prior political

---

the "A–J effect" are summarized in William J. Baumol and Alvin K. Klevorick, "Input Choices and Rate-of-Return Regulation: An Overview of the Discussion," *Bell Journal of Economics and Management Science*, I (Autumn, 1970), 162–190.

[31] The following are examples of recent scholarship on these topics: on the FCC, Roger G. Noll, Merton J. Peck, and John J. McGowan, *Economic Aspects of Television Regulation* (Washington, D.C., 1973); R. H. Coase, "The Federal Communications Commission," *Journal of Law and Economics*, II (October, 1959), 1–40; on technological aspects, William M. Capron, ed., *Technological Change in Regulated Industries* (Washington, D.C., 1971); on one aspect of SEC regulation, Jeffrey F. Jaffe, "The Effect of Regulation Changes on Insider Trading," *Bell Journal of Economics and Management Science*, V (Spring, 1974), 93–121; on state insurance commissions, Paul L. Joskow, "Cartels, Competition and Regulation in the Property-Liability Insurance Industry," *Bell Journal of Economics and Management Science*, IV (Autumn, 1973), 375–427.

[32] Many of the institutionalists did approach problems in this way, as have a few more recent economists such as J. K. Galbraith. For the historians, see, in particular, Hawley, *The New Deal and the Problem of Monopoly: A Study in Economic Ambivalence* (Princeton, N.J., 1966); and Hofstadter, "What Happened to the Antitrust Movement? Notes on the Evolution of an American Creed," in Earl F. Cheit, ed., *The Business Establishment* (New York, 1964), 113–151.

power, which expressed itself through the creation of a regulatory mechanism. The new apparatus did not necessarily take the form of a commission, but could be an import quota system or tariff schedule. The virtue of Stigler's argument was its recognition that the regulatory process goes beyond purely economic phenomena, that "the problem of regulation is the problem of discovering when and why an industry (or other group of like-minded people) is able to use the state for its purposes, or is singled out by the state to be used for alien purposes." [33]

Regulation in the Literature of Political Science and Law

An appropriate source of answers to Stigler's question would appear to be political science and law. As was the case in economics, the contributions from scholars in each of these two disciplines outnumbered those of historians, a logical circumstance considering that regulation is barely a century old, that it remains controversial, and that the commissions' embrace of legislative, executive, and judicial roles within a single institution raised theoretical and practical issues of keen interest to lawyers and students of government.

Although the characteristic approaches of the two disciplines were not identical, each one emphasized matters of procedure, responsibility, and equity. Where the distinctive method of historians was empirical, and of economists a theory-oriented testing of market efficiency, that of political scientists and lawyers centered on due process, legitimacy, and reform. The resulting scholarship fell into two broad categories. The first included a number of quasi-histories, written within a generation of the establishment of particular commissions and directed toward prescriptions for improvement as well as toward analysis. A second category focused on elaborations or critiques of interest group politics in America, and included books addressing the questions of "public interest" and "capture." This second category fitted into the pluralist versus anti-pluralist debate within both political science and law.

Three books on the Federal Trade Commission typified the first group, the prescriptive quasi-histories. In *The Federal Trade Com-*

---

[33] Stigler, "The Theory of Economic Regulation," *Bell Journal of Economics and Management Science*, II (Spring, 1971), 3–21. See also Stigler, "The Process of Economic Regulation," *The Antitrust Bulletin*, XVII (Spring, 1972), 207–235. A few other economists have attempted interdisciplinary approaches. See, for example, Roger G. Noll, "The Behavior of Regulatory Agencies," *Review of Social Economy*, XXIX (March, 1971), 15–19; and Paul L. Joskow, "Pricing Decisions of Regulated Firms: A Behavioral Approach," *Bell Journal of Economics and Management Science*, IV (Spring, 1973), 118–140.

mission: A Study in Administrative Law and Procedure,[34] Gerard
C. Henderson, a practicing lawyer, found the early FTC insufficiently judicial in its proceedings, sometimes guilty of unfairness,
and ready to dissipate its energies in cases involving no broad public
concern. Some of the same suggestions appeared in another study
of the FTC, published in 1932 by Thomas C. Blaisdell.[35] Antici-
pating much New Deal scholarship, Blaisdell found the commission's
performance during the 1920s clearly unsatisfactory. The vague
FTC Act implicitly identified competition *as* the "public interest,"
on the apparent assumption that competition in all cases promoted
socially desirable results. Such a premise Blaisdell found contro-
verted by American economic history. "Means were confused with
ends," he wrote, in a comment significant not only for the FTC, but
for other aspects of regulatory experience. Blaisdell contrasted the
Federal Trade Commission's woes with the more successful record
of the ICC, whose problems with the courts were resolved only
through repeated action by Congress.[36] In still a third book on the
FTC, former commissioner Nelson B. Gaskill identified some of
the same problems, suggested a few new remedies, and like both
Henderson and Blaisdell advanced the hope that intelligent trade
regulation on a broad scale could be achieved, despite the FTC's
manifest failures. The overriding need, wrote Gaskill, was a clear
enunciation of policy, by both Congress and the commission.[37]

In 1962, Henry J. Friendly updated these views, in a brief but
important book entitled *The Federal Administrative Agencies: The
Need for Better Definition of Standards.* Ending with a prescriptive
chapter typical of regulatory scholarship, Friendly sought salvation
through the creation of "a body of substantive law." Delineating
the ways in which procedural delay denied justice, Friendly showed
how due process carried to extremes could actually thwart the
"public interest." Even so, he rejected the remedy of heavy reliance
on presidential control over commissions recommended in the Landis
report of 1960, and also in the extensive work of Emmette S. Redford, a leading figure among scholars of regulation within political

[34] New Haven, Conn., 1924.
[35] Blaisdell, *The Federal Trade Commission: An Experiment in the Control of Business*
(New York, 1932).
[36] *Ibid.*, 293, 307. The comparison was made central in Carl McFarland, *Judicial
Control of the Federal Trade Commission and the Interstate Commerce Commission 1920–
1930* (Cambridge, Mass., 1933). Also on the important subject of judicial review of
regulation, see Louis L. Jaffe, *Judicial Control of Administrative Action* (Boston, 1965);
and Martin M. Shapiro, *The Supreme Court and Administrative Agencies* (New York,
1968).
[37] Gaskill, *The Regulation of Competition* (New York, 1936). This book examined not
only the FTC, but also the recently expired National Recovery Administration. It was a
broadside more than a scholarly work.

science.[38] Displaying a faith in regulation consistent with the book's dedication to Felix Frankfurter, a pioneer of legal scholarship and teaching in the field, Friendly concluded with an affirmation: "The administrative agencies have become a vital part of the structure of American government. Nothing is accomplished by merely negative criticism or by petulant proposals to abolish them." [39]

Such feelings echoed the tradition of reform-oriented scholarship emblematic of the 1930s. In that decade I. Leo Sharfman completed his huge study, *The Interstate Commerce Commission*,[40] which comprises five thick books and remains the most exhaustive analysis of a commission yet written. Its conclusions tended to confirm the ICC's high reputation of the time. Also in the thirties, E. Pendleton Herring published a thoughtful analysis of several agencies, and a short prosopographical study of the careers of federal commissioners.[41] At the close of this productive decade of scholarship, Robert E. Cushman completed the broadest of the prescriptive quasi-histories, *The Independent Regulatory Commissions*, a massive study that grew out of Cushman's work on Franklin D. Roosevelt's Committee on Administrative Management.[42] Packed with suggestions for improvement, Cushman's book also contained a cross-national analysis of the American and British experiences in regulating business — a useful methodology mostly neglected since.

A landmark of regulation in the scholarship of political science was Marver H. Bernstein's book of 1955, *Regulating Business by Independent Commission*.[43] In a survey of the entire field, Bernstein

[38] Friendly, *The Federal Administrative Agencies: The Need for Better Definition of Standards* (Cambridge, Mass., 1962). Friendly was a Federal judge at the time. His book, heavily footnoted, provided a convenient guide to the legal literature on administrative procedure, a topic I have only touched on in this discussion. Representative of the voluminous publications of Emmette S. Redford are *Administration of National Economic Control* (New York, 1952); *American Government and the Economy* (New York, 1965), and *The Regulatory Process: With Illustrations from Commercial Aviation* (Austin, Texas, 1969).

[39] Friendly, *The Federal Administrative Agencies*, 175; one example of the influence of Friendly's views may be found in William L. Cary (a former chairman of the SEC), *Politics and the Regulatory Agencies* (New York, 1967).

[40] Sharfman, *The Interstate Commerce Commission: A Study in Administrative Law and Procedure* (4 vols. in 5, New York, 1931–1937). Sharfman was an economist, not a lawyer or political scientist. I have included his work in this section because it more closely resembles the work of the 1930s political scientists than that of recent economists.

[41] Herring, *Public Administration and the Public Interest* (New York, 1936); Herring, *Federal Commissioners: A Study of Their Careers and Qualifications* (Cambridge, Mass., 1936).

[42] Cushman, *The Independent Regulatory Commissions* (New York, 1941). The Committee, known popularly as the "Brownlow Committee," after its Chairman, Louis Brownlow, was one of a long series of *ad hoc* groups studying regulation and organization in the Federal establishment. Subsequent studies produced the Hoover Commission Report (numbers 1 and 2), the Landis Report, and the Ash Council Report.

[43] Princeton, N.J., 1955. In the mid-1950s, there was nothing like a consensus on regulation within political science. Bernstein's views may be contrasted with those of Redford, *Administration of National Economic Control* (note 38 above), and of Robert E. Lane, *The Regulation of Businessmen* (New Haven, Conn., 1954). See also the uncritical

weighed arguments for and against regulation and came down
heavily on the negative side. Generalizing freely, the author propounded a "life cycle" theory, which held that commissions typically
pass through successive phases, beginning with exuberant prosecution of mandate but ending with ossification and debility. In the
area of documentation, the book left something to be desired, but
Bernstein's arguments seemed so thoughtful, reasonable, and self-
assured that they practically set the terms for the critical attack that
followed in the 1960s.

This attack, as noted above, came largely from economists and
from reformers like "Nader's Raiders," who made heavy use of the
economic literature and of the theories and arguments summarized
by Bernstein. In political science, the analysis tended to become
much broader, and to address issues of which regulation formed
only a part. Especially noteworthy was the work of the critics of
pluralism. Dismayed by the results of "broker-state" government in
the New Deal pattern, unpersuaded by celebratory assurances from
1950s writers that countervailing pressures from diverse interest
groups yielded a genuine "public interest," these scholars detailed
the distance between the aims of Progressive and New Deal reformers on the one hand, and the contemporary reality of American life
on the other.

Three books both exemplified and influenced the anti-pluralist
persuasion: Henry S. Kariel's *The Decline of American Pluralism*,
Grant McConnell's *Private Power and American Democracy*, and
Theodore J. Lowi's *The End of Liberalism*.[44] The three differed
in many particulars but held unanimously that pluralist theory
disguised the exploitation of public authority by private groups for
private purposes. The "public interest," far from emerging automatically from the inter-group struggle, was simply lost in the
shuffle. Regulated industries were the clients of their commissions.
The American Farm Bureau Federation, in alliance with other
powerful groups, dictated policy to the Department of Agriculture.
Big Labor won big gains for itself, but often ignored the rest of
society. Meanwhile, the "public interest" led nobody's list of
priorities.

"Capture," in other words, applied not just to commissions but
to the entire American polity. The system had degenerated from
an original dream of constitutional democracy and the general

---

quasi-history by James E. Anderson, *The Emergence of the Modern Regulatory State*
(Washington, D.C., 1962).
    [44] In the order listed: Stanford, Cal., 1961; New York, 1966; and New York, 1969.

welfare to a hopelessly fragmented mélange of small, autonomous constituencies sensitive only to self-interest The tragedy was that the government had lent its authority to these constituencies, piece by sovereign piece, and that the pluralist postulate of universal access to power had encountered the incontrovertible fact that such access depended on systematic, articulate, well-funded organization. Some groups could not meet these tests. Unorganized or, as in the case of the poor, unorganizable, they stayed out in the cold, away from the American banquet.[45]

The anti-pluralist indictment inspired a variety of responses, some of them holding that the legal order in the United States had always provided mechanisms to protect the weak and unorganized. As one scholar put it in 1972, "probably never before in our history has legal policy been so supportive of the rights of individuals and groups affected by administrative action to be heard and to influence the action taken." To some writers, the advent of public interest law — an institutional adaptation to some of the problems identified by the anti-pluralists — represented a hopeful sign that the existing system might yet work, given adequate funding for public interest lawyers.[46] Some of the most promising studies by legal scholars, such as those of Richard A. Posner, attempted to combine economic theory with jurisprudence, in order to establish first principles of regulation, whether of the commission variety or of the older market-common-law type.[47]

AN ASSESSMENT

The collective findings in history, economics, political science, and law have been sufficient to establish a few broad conclusions:

1. Neither "public interest" nor "capture," nor the two in combination adequately characterize the American experience with regulation over the last century. Sometimes regulation materialized

[45] The solutions offered by the anti-pluralists varied, and in each book, the diagnosis seemed superior to the prescription. Lowi proposed a return to basic constitutional principles and the promotion of "juridicial democracy." McConnell suggested the strengthening of mechanisms that permitted the entire people to act as one. Invigoration of broad constituencies would limit the scope of "capture," promote citizen participation, and give substantive content to the "public interest."

[46] Carl A. Auerbach, "Pluralism and the Administrative Process," *The Annals*, CD (March, 1972), 1. On public interest lawyers, see Simon Lazarus, *The Genteel Populists* (New York, 1974), Chapter 10; Joseph C. Goulden, *The Superlawyers* (New York, 1972), Chapter 10; and Richard C. Leone, "Public Interest Advocacy and the Regulatory Process," *The Annals*, CD (March, 1972), 46-58.

[47] Posner, "Natural Monopoly and Its Regulation," *Stanford Law Review*, XXI (February, 1969), 548-643; Posner, "Taxation by Regulation," *Bell Journal of Economics and Management Science*, II (Spring, 1971), 22-50; Posner, *Economic Analysis of Law* (New York, 1973); Posner, "Theories of Economic Regulation," *Bell Journal of Economics and Management Science*, V (Autumn, 1974), 335-358.

with the support or even initiative of the industry involved (as with broadcasting), sometimes with the reluctant assent (as with the ICC), and sometimes against the rigid opposition (as with the Granger commissions and the SEC). Commissions often came into existence with broad popular support, sometimes amid obvious public apathy, but never in the face of mass-based, articulate opposition.

2. Once established, commissions did respond readily to pressures from organized interest groups. Such groups included not only the regulated industry, but also that industry's market elements (shippers, for example, in the case of the ICC), and occasionally the industry's labor force. Whenever actual "capture" by one of these elements did occur, it followed patterns not peculiar to commissions but common to a whole range of bureaucratic interdependency between government agencies and organized interest groups, whether in labor, agriculture, defense, or other private interests able to use the power of the state for their own benefit.

3. Regulation in America has been a multi-functional pursuit, a circumstance that has offered scholars a choice, when they generalize about the regulatory process as a whole, between extreme caution on the one hand, and extreme likelihood of error on the other. Regulation is best understood as an institution capable of serving diverse, even contradictory ends, some economic, some political, some cultural. Regulatory experience over the last century suggests several major ends or functions:

    a. the function of disclosure and publicity
    b. the function of cartelization
    c. the function of containing monopoly or oligopoly
    d. the function of economic harmony among industries
    e. the function of promotion or advocacy
    f. the function of legitimizing parts of the capitalist order
    g. the function of consumer protection.

Obviously, such a list could be longer, or differently stated. The functions could overlap, as in early railroad regulation, when efforts to control rates through disclosure and publicity aimed at stabilization and economic harmony. More often than not, regulatory functions among different commissions, and sometimes even within the same agency, could conflict. The Civil Aeronautics Board, to take one example, has not succeeded in its efforts to promote orderly airline development and technologically advanced aircraft, while simultaneously trying to stabilize rates at levels attractive to travellers with modest incomes. In the broader sense, items (b) and (c) above proceed from conflicting premises concerning the efficacy of competition, reflecting not only different market imperatives of different industries, but also ideological splits within American society. The perennial conflict over competition underlies a large proportion of the controversy over regulation, including both the "public interest" and "capture" images of it.

Despite the danger of internal inconsistency, regulators have identified whichever function they wished to emphasize at the moment with the "public interest." They could hardly have done otherwise. Almost nobody ever declares his hostility to the "public interest." Yet such rhetoric could go beyond either symbol or cant. It could often signify an intelligent conviction that a particular policy would yield broad societal benefits. For scholars, the notion has little use as a static entity, but it may offer a helpful signal at those points where it visibly changes. Industries or societies in different stages of development need different things. The same industry or society, moving from one phase to another, fulfills or forgets old needs and acquires new ones. The "public interest," therefore, however defined, cannot remain static, even within the mind of an individual. Time makes it dynamic; and historians specialize in change over time.

They have less experience, however, in other aspects of regulation equally essential to understanding: the structures, markets, and competitive characteristics of the industries involved. As the histories of railroad regulation suggest, a firm grasp of the "railroad problem" and the distinctive features of the industry — its high ratio of fixed to variable costs, its powerful tendency toward huge integrated systems — are indispensable to the study of attempts at its public control. If, as seems likely, the inherent nature of an industry is the most important single context in which regulators must operate, then the range of policies open to them has been narrower than many observers have hitherto believed.[48]

These problems indicate once more that regulation is so broad a

[48] The logical starting place here is the work of Alfred D. Chandler, Jr., though it customarily deals less with regulated enterprises than with manufacturing. See, in particular, *Strategy and Structure: Chapters in the History of the Industrial Enterprise* (Cambridge, Mass., 1962); "The Structure of American Industry in the Twentieth Century: A Historical Overview," *Business History Review*, XLIII (Autumn, 1969), 255–298; and Chandler, ed. and comp., *The Railroads: The Nation's First Big Business* (New York, 1965). See also Alfred S. Eichner, *The Emergence of Oligopoly: Sugar Refining as a Case Study* (Baltimore, Md., 1969). A superior analysis of both the evolution of big business and of its historiography is Glenn Porter, *The Rise of Big Business 1860–1910* (New York, 1973), which emphasizes the capital-intensive nature of modern enterprise. A strong statement of the relationship between production process and industry structure appears in Robert T. Averitt, *The Dual Economy: The Dynamics of American Industry Structure* (New York, 1968), Chapter 3.

topic that its proper study compels the use of methods from many disciplines. Besides those discussed here — history, economics, political science, and law — another promising perspective might come from organizational theory.[49] Despite the vast literature on regulation, scholars still have only a vague idea of what went on inside the commissions, in the interplay of contending sub-groups, the relationships among commissioners and career staff members, and especially the connections between regulatory policy and perceived bureaucratic imperatives. Like other organizations, commissions seldom followed paths that would diminish their own importance, but instead promoted policies that would insure their institutional survival and growth. The inconsistent patterns of regulatory behavior over the last hundred years may mean not only that regulation is a multi-functional undertaking, and that different industry structures governed regulators' options, but also that commissions' highest loyalties sometimes went neither to the "public interest" nor to the regulated industry, but to regulation itself. Regulation was their business, and they did not intend to close up shop.[50] In promoting regulation as a value in itself, they generated an independent social force whose cumulative influence over time may have been substantial, but which remains mostly unexplored by scholars.

Multiple approaches are therefore essential for the realization of the major dividend available from the study of regulation: the illumination of that shadowy zone where public and private endeavors met and merged, where regulator and regulated experienced a confusion of identity and assumed each others' roles. Seldom in American history did the goals of private groups form a perfect identity with those of the rest of society, but seldom a perfect antithesis, either. Instead, sets of goals overlapped, now finely, now amply. Within the zones of overlap, private groups plausibly claimed service to society, and "capture" coexisted in fleeting calm with "public interest." Fleeting, because each zone suffered a double indeterminacy: who made the decisions, the public official or the businessman? And what were the precise

---

[49] Discussions of historians' application of organizational theory include Louis Galambos, "The Emerging Organizational Synthesis in Modern American History," *Business History Review*, XLIV (Autumn, 1970), 279–290; James H. Soltow, "American Institutional Studies: Present Knowledge and Past Trends," *Journal of Economic History*, XXXI (March, 1971), 87–105; and Robert D. Cuff, "American Historians and the 'Organizational Factor,'" *Canadian Review of American Studies*, IV (Spring, 1973), 19–31. Cuff's own *The War Industries Board* (Baltimore, 1973), is in many respects a model organizational study.

[50] An early suggestion of "regulation-mindedness" appears in Louis L. Jaffe, "The Effective Limits of the Administrative Process: A Reevaluation," *Harvard Law Review*, LXVII (May, 1954), 1113.

boundaries of the zone? Constantly shifting from internal and external pressures, the zones formed arenas whose only permanent qualities were confusion, controversy, and uncertainty. Did a given action by a businessman or regulator denote the presence of "public interest," or of "capture"? Did it deserve congratulation, or condemnation? Prize, or prosecution?

The theme is ancient, of course, a continuous thread of American history back at least to the time of Hamilton. Writing twenty years ago, Robert A. Lively described "the incorrigible willingness of American public officials to seek the public good through private negotiations," and offered as a leading exhibit the early corporate enterprises promoted by the states.[51] In this sense, "capture" and "public interest" derived from a single source, and have been intertwined ever since. The gradual obsolescence of the public purpose corporation, and the concurrent rise of modern industrial capitalism, set a context hospitable to the evolution of a regulatory system with as many private purposes as public, as many promotional functions as restrictive, and as much continuity with a recent past as divergence in a new age.

[51] Lively, "The American System: A Review Article," *Business History Review,* XXIX (March, 1955), 93.

Part VI
The Era of Deregulation

[25]

Regulation, Deregulation, and Economic Efficiency: The Case of the CAB

By JOHN C. PANZAR*

The current wave of deregulatory enthusiasm makes it easy to forget that the creation of the CAB and its regulatory authority was itself a result of the political and economic forces which prevailed a relatively short time ago. Since deregulation nowadays is viewed as a move toward economic efficiency, it is tempting to argue that it represents a triumph of the public interest over the special interests which, presumably, were responsible for the formation of the CAB cartel. This would be a serious oversimplification, because 1) it is possible to view the *CAA* of 1938 as a response to a potential market failure *then*; 2) deregulation may give up the possibility of achieving optimal, first best resource allocation *now*; and 3) regulatory machinery which could have been used to pursue either economic efficiency or cartel profit maximization clearly did neither. While the last point requires no elaboration, the first two are somewhat novel, and rather provocative.

The concept upon which most of my arguments are based is that airline markets are, even today, more accurately described as being structurally contestable rather than competitive. Even the strongest proponents of deregulation concede that few air traffic markets can efficiently support more than a small number of firms actually operating *in* the market. (Forty-five years ago this number was almost certainly one.) Efficient market performance is expected to result from the large number of *potential* entrants and the easy entry and exit dictated by the

technology, in other words, because the market is easily *contested.*[1]

I. The Airline Industry of the 1930's and the Civil Aeronautics Act of 1938

Let us attempt to understand and evaluate the *CAA* of 1938 from the perspective of an economic analyst in 1935, when the report of the Federal Aviation Commission (*FAC*) was transmitted to Congress and the drafting of the Act began. Assume that the analyst is familiar with modern regulatory theory and the development of the industry up to that time, but blissfully ignorant of our recent experience of forty years of CAB regulation.[2] Given the premise that, for most routes, it was economic for only one carrier to transport the mail and impossible for an airline to be viable carrying passenger traffic alone, airline markets can be considered to have been joint-product natural monopolies. This posed potential problems for the design of an institutional structure capable of fostering economically efficient development in the industry.

Judging from the legislative history, Congress viewed various manifestations of "excessive competition" as the most serious potential problem. The most striking expressions of this concern are the ringing denouncations of competitive bidding for

*Bell Laboratories. The views expressed are my own and do not necessarily reflect those of Bell Laboratories or the Bell System. I would like to thank Robert D. Willig for helpful comments and suggestions and Elizabeth Bailey and Michael E. Levine for pointing me in the right direction. They are not responsible for where I ended up.

[1] William Baumol, Robert Willig and I study this concept in detail in "The Theory of Value in Contestable Markets," (monograph in preparation).

[2] An invaluable source of quantitative information on the industry *before* regulation is contained in Robert Serling's compendium of airline schedules, 1929–39. An excellent guide to the legislative history of the Act, complete with excerpts from Congressional hearings, is provided in *Civil Aeronautics Board Practices and Procedures* (hereafter, the Subcommittee report).

airmail contracts in the congressional debate. At first, this seems somewhat surprising. While economies of scale might dictate that there be only one firm operating *in* the market, competition *for* the market might have been effective.

Michael Levine (1975) has argued that Congress and the public were overly influenced by the disastrous results of earlier competitive bidding regimes. Prior to 1934, the high-handed behavior of Postmaster General Brown as well as the wide latitude permitted him by the Watres Act, made that period one of *de jure* rather than of *de facto* competitive bidding. After repeated scandals, President Roosevelt cancelled all existing mail contracts and ordered the Army to carry the mail. That disastrous experiment led to the establishment of the *FAC* and to yet another attempt at letting airmail contracts by competitive bidding. That temporary measure was transformed into a curious regulatory regime in which the U.S. Post Office awarded the contract to a low bidder, but the ICC was mandated to adjust rates to fair and reasonable levels. Ludicrously low rates ($.001/ton mile) were bid, since the airlines fully expected that the mail rate would be raised, and made due in the interim by exploiting the (effective) passenger service monopoly conferred by the airmail contract. Thus Levine concluded that "...Congressional attempts to use competitive contracting were doomed to failure by lawlessness and incompetent institutional design..." (1975, p. 323). In other words, the concept had not been given a true trial.

There was, nevertheless, a valid reason why routes could not have been *efficiently* allocated by competitive bidding. Passenger transport, while still not generally viable on a stand-alone basis, was already emerging as the more important of the joint products provided by the industry. A competitive bidding system for letting airmail contracts, even if it worked perfectly, would succeed only in eliciting the mail rate which would yield zero profits in conjunction with *monopoly* pricing of passenger service. This will never lead to socially optimal prices if there is any elasticity of demand for air travel.

This unfortunate situation would persist until either passenger service became viable on its own or it became economic to split the mail among two or more carriers; that is, until markets were no longer natural monopolies. In this environment it was sound economic policy to consolidate the responsibility for determining mail rates and passenger fares in a single entity.

While the above argument, combined with some minimal concern over monopoly exploitation, can be used to explain the rate authority given to the CAB, one must still find a rationale for the certificate of public convenience and necessity which the Act required to enter an airline market. It is clear that the industry wanted this provision to protect their markets from "fly-by-night companies" and "chiselers"; that is, those willing to provide service at a lower rate. (See the testimony of Colonel Edgar S. Gorrell, president of the Air Transport Association, as quoted by the Subcommittee report pp. 210–12.) But what reason did Congress have for incorporating this provision into the statute?

The reasoning of the highly influential *FAC* report is quite clear on this point (see the Subcommittee report, p. 213). Certificates of convenience and necessity were to be required for two equally important reasons: to ensure safety and to prevent excessive competition. The authors' concerns on the latter score seem to spring from the common carrier functions that might be required of certificated carriers. They refer to the possibility of cream skimming by fly-by-*day* and seasonal entrants which would be able to forgo the additional expenditures required to fly at night and/or maintain year-round service.

Recent investigators do not seem to have taken this explanation seriously. The Subcommittee report, for example, points to "...other vaguer concerns such as a presumed similarity between railroads and airlines..." (p. 207) as being the driving forces behind the *CAA*. While this conclusion may be partially due to the contradictory impression created by the *FAC* report's equally clear *pro*competitive language, I believe historical factors also play a role: in this instance the prevailing opinions of regulatory economists at the time the Subcommittee report was written in 1975.

After the Great Depression, the issue of cream skimming was minimized to the point where it became almost "axiomatically" impossible. Alfred Kahn succinctly summed up this conventional wisdom: "If a natural monopolist is producing and pricing as efficiently as possible, there is no need to bar competitive entry: it is economically unnecessary and will not take place anyhow" (p. 223). However, recent research on pricing and entry in regulated markets has made it clear that there may exist situations in which it is *impossible* for a firm (or regulator) to set prices which do *not* provide profitable opportunities for cream skimming by potential entrants, even when the firm is operating under natural monopoly conditions and producing and pricing efficiently. The natural monopoly may be *unsustainable*.

To illustrate, consider a single product market in which the demand curve intersects the average cost curve within the natural monopoly region but beyond its minimum point. Any viable price quoted by a monopolist required to serve all demand can always be undercut by a cream skimmer operating at minimum average cost. (See my paper with Robert Willig for a discussion of this and more complicated, multiproduct examples of unsustainability.) The end result in such markets is problematic; what is clear is that *no free entry noncooperative (Nash) equilibrium exists*. Depending upon the dynamics built into the model, an endless cycle of price cutting, entry, and exit could theoretically result. Such markets readily might be described as disorderly and chaotic. (With a single product one way out of this dilemma is contract bidding. The firm awarded the contract would be *protected* from entry and *required* to serve all demand at the quoted price. However, as argued earlier, this simple approach is incapable of efficiently dealing with the case of multiple products.) Ironically, the contestability of airline markets, which makes monopoly exploitation difficult, makes it

more likely that unsustainability will be a problem.

This argument, in conjunction with equally clear recommendations that desirable entry *not* be impeded, suggest that Congress was merely being prudent by requiring certificates of public convenience and necessity and that it intended to rely upon the judgment of an expert agency to determine a balanced entry policy. Senator Truman's confession (quoted on p. 81 of the Subcommittee report) that it was, unfortunately, necessary to *trust* the Board not to block the entry of new firms into the industry seemed incredibly naive just a few years ago. But that was before Kahn, Bailey, and Levine arrived upon the scene.

II. Regulatory Reform and Deregulation

Recent history would seem to indicate a clear triumph of economic efficiency over the "dead hand" of regulation. While I would be among the last to suggest that deregulation was a mistake, I argue that the issues are more complicated than is commonly thought; since, if anything, recent results in regulatory theory suggest that regulation by enlightened, but not omniscient, regulators could in principle achieve greater efficiency than deregulation. Thus, this solution also involved a tradeoff between pragmatism and theoretical optimality.

Academic criticism of the CAB tended to be of two types, typified by Levine (1965) and by George Douglas and James Miller. The first group questioned the need for *any* governmental *economic* regulation of the airlines, by appealing to the impressive performance of the (relatively) unregulated California intrastate market. In contrast, the Douglas-Miller approach was evolutionary rather than revolutionary. They proceeded by carefully building analytical theoretical models of industry behavior under the CAB's price and entry regulation and deriving recommendations for a more enlightened regulatory policy. A result of this division of labor was that very little attention was given to a *theoretical* analysis of unregulated airline markets.

The problem is interesting and nontrivial because of the monopolistically competitive nature of airline markets. Product differentiation is an unavoidable result of the variation in flight departure times, and the effects of flight frequency and load factor on service quality.[3] The basic results of my analysis are that 1) when the direct benefits (to consumers) of increasing flight frequency are exhausted, socially optimal choices of price and frequency result in zero profits for the industry; but 2) a noncooperative, free entry equilibrium always results in higher prices, lower load factors, and greater frequency than are socially optimal, and the employment of inefficiently small aircraft.

However, much of this inefficiency can be overcome by regulating *maximum* price and allowing free entry. Furthermore, these efficiency gains do not require an omniscient regulator, since in many interesting cases the optimal price is that which, with free entry, results in the maximization of passengers carried. Thus the optimum could, in principle, be achieved iteratively using readily available data.[4]

Why then was deregulation chosen over regulatory reform, and *how* was it achieved? Deferring the first issue to the conclusion, let me briefly summarize the "recipe" for successful deregulation put forward by Elizabeth Bailey. Academic criticisms of CAB regulation were reinforced by the thorough analysis of the Subcommittee report, which marshalled persuasive evidence to counter the objections and dire predictions put forward by the Board and the industry. Some protection for special interests who figured to suffer from deregulation, such as labor and small communities, was incorporated into the legislation. Finally, under Kahn, the board initiated a strongly pro-

competitive policy which served to convince Congress of the feasibility of competition and to prompt some carriers to feel that, shorn of the Board's *protection*, they would be better off without its *restrictions*.

From this argument and the upsurge in air travel and industry profits, it is tempting to conclude that (nearly) everyone has been made better off and to speculate that such a Pareto improvement is almost a necessary condition for changing the status quo. Let me inject a note of caution. *Basic* coach fares have risen steadily under deregulation. The gains in consumer's surplus and profits achieved by the proliferation of (discriminatory) discount fares are partially offset by the costs born by business travelers due to higher load factors. They constitute a large group of travelers harmed by deregulation without compensation. (The extent of their losses due to stochastic delay can in principle be quantified using the methodology developed by Douglas and Miller.)

III. Conclusions

What can be learned from this brief survey of regulatory entry and exit? More specifically, what accounts for the contrast between public policy toward (inherently) imperfect airline markets in the 1930's with that in the 1970's? I submit that the differences resulted from the interplay of three basic forces. 1) A change in public attitude. Competition was viewed with as much suspicion then as regulation is today. This shift is, in part, due to the superior relative performance of competitive airline markets in the interim. 2) The increase, due to market growth, of the efficient number of firms *in* most markets from one to two or more. 3) The basically contestable nature of airline markets, which implies that, if anything, entry will tend to be excessive rather than insufficient. When most markets are natural monopolies, entry *might* lead to *serious* difficulties with regard to nonexistence of equilibrium and subsequent loss of service. When natural monopolies are not present,

---

[3] Douglas and Miller (p. 178) recognized these issues and cited an unpublished paper by Douglas yielding results consistent with those reported here, which are from my 1979a paper.

[4] This simple, myopic regulatory rule also emerged from the analysis of the somewhat different models employed by Arthur DeVany and by me in my book.

entry will tend to cause only the (presumably) minor inefficiencies usually associated with monopolistic competition. Thus not only has the regulatory process failed to live up to its *theoretical* potential, the "downside risks" of the competitive alternative have been sharply reduced.

REFERENCES

E. Bailey, "Deregulation and Regulatory Reform: U.S. Domestic and International Air Transportation Policy During 1977–79," in Paul Kleindorfer and Bridger Mitchell, eds, *Regulated Industries and Public Enterprises: European and United States Perspectives*, Lexington 1980.

A. DeVany, "The Effect of Price and Entry Regulation on Airline Output, Capacity, and Efficiency," *Bell J. Econ.,* Spring 1975, *6*, 327–45.

George Douglas and James Miller, *Economic Regulation of Domestic Airtransport: Theory and Policy*, Washington 1974.

Alfred Kahn, *The Economics of Regulation: Principles and Institutions*, Vol. II, New York 1970.

M. Levine, "Is Regulation Necessary? California Air Transportation and National Regulatory Policy," *Yale Law J.*, July 1965, *74*, 1416–47.

_____, "Regulating Airmail Transportation," *J. Law Econ.*, Oct. 1975, *18*, 317–59.

John Panzar, (1979a) "Equilibrium and Welfare in Unregulated Airline Markets," *Amer. Econ. Rev. Proc.*, May 1979, *69*, 92–95.

_____, (1979b) *Regulation Service Quality and Market Performance: A Model of Airline Rivalry*, New York 1979.

_____ and R. Willig, "Free Entry and the Sustainability of Natural Monopoly," *Bell J. Econ.*, Spring 1977, *8*, 1–22.

Robert Serling, *Birth of an Industry*, Chicago 1969.

U.S. Congress, Senate, Committee on the Judiciary, Subcommittee on Administrative Practice and Procedure, *Civil Aeronautics Board Practices and Procedures*, Washington 1975.

[26]

Deregulation and the Theory of Contestable Markets

Elizabeth E. Bailey†
William J. Baumol††

Until recently, the need to regulate monopoly was considered virtually axiomatic, and the imposition of rules governing entry, exit and pricing was deemed a priority. The deregulation movement has raised pragmatic questions about these orthodoxies, and, more recently, a new body of economic analysis called the theory of contestable markets has provided a conceptual basis for the view that many markets that are subject to economies of scale should not be regulated by the conventional methods.[1]

The new theory has shown that neither large size nor fewness of firms *necessarily* means that markets need function unsatisfactorily. Impediments to entry and exit, not concentration or scale of operations, may be the primary source of interference with the workings of the invisible hand. Indeed, because regulators have been predisposed to interfere with both entry and exit,[2] the new analysis suggests that they have been among the primary causes of unsatisfactory industry performance.

Contestability theory focuses increased attention upon entry barriers and redefines their character. Economies of scale, for example, have frequently been considered an impediment to entry; contestability analysis shows, however, that they need not permit excessive profits or prices or any of the other manifestations usually associated with market power, even when scale economies make an industry a natural monopoly or an

† Dean, Graduate School of Industrial Administration, Carnegie-Mellon University.
†† Professor of Economics, Princeton and New York Universities. The authors are grateful to George Eads, Ann Friedlaender, Judy Gelman, Daniel Kaplan, Steven Salop and David Sibley for their extremely valuable comments on an earlier version of this paper.

1. The tradition which asserts that even in oligopolistic industries barriers to entry are not always sufficiently great to permit monopoly profits traces its roots to Chadwick, *Results of Different Principles of Legislation and Administration in Europe: of Competition for the Field as Compared with Competition Within the Field of Service*, 22 J. ROYAL STATISTICAL SOC'Y 381 (1859). A similar position is taken in Demsetz, *Why Regulate Utilities?*, 11 J. L. & ECON. 55 (1968). These conclusions have recently been extended to the multiproduct case, and derived from a formal theory applicable to the full spectrum of market forms. *See* W. BAUMOL, J. PANZAR & R. WILLIG, CONTESTABLE MARKETS AND THE THEORY OF INDUSTRY STRUCTURE (1982). Much of the material in the first half of this paper draws on this recent work. For a measured appraisal, see Spence, *Contestable Markets and the Theory of Industry Structure*, 21 J. ECON. LITERATURE 981 (1983).

2. There is no shortage of examples. Thus, the ICC has long prevented railroads from abandoning unprofitable routes, while before deregulation, the CAB kept many potential entrants out of the most profitable markets.

oligopoly. It is the presence of sunk costs rather than economies of scale that is of vital significance for both theory and practice.

In sum, the theory of contestability calls for a major reorientation of both the charters and the operating programs of regulatory authorities. Many of its conclusions are consistent with the philosophy of deregulation. But the new analysis does not adopt the Panglossian view that a completely unconstrained free market is necessarily the best of all possible worlds. It claims only that where public measures are called for, the types of market intervention that ought to be undertaken are, in many cases, rather different from those that have traditionally been employed, and that there are *some* cases in which intervention is inappropriate even though it was previously thought to be desirable.

In the following pages, we begin by describing the basic principles of contestability theory. Next, we examine the efficiency attributes of contestable markets, the conditions that contribute to the contestability of a market, and the general implications for regulatory policy that follow from this analysis. Finally, we review some of the major regulatory reform activities that have been undertaken in Congress, the executive branch, and the independent regulatory agencies during the past few years and evaluate these moves in terms of contestability. We shall see that, by and large, the new directions of public policy have been remarkably consistent with what contestability theory would suggest.

I. Contestability Theory as an Alternative Ideal

A. *Perfect Contestability Contrasted With Perfect Competition*

The theoretical foundation of both regulatory and antitrust activity has traditionally relied heavily on the economic concept of perfect competition. Perfect competition has long been used as a standard ideal for the structure and performance of a market, though it is widely recognized to be unattainable in reality. The new analysis proposes the use of a different ideal: what is termed the "perfectly contestable market." Like perfect competition, this exemplary market form is undoubtedly unattainable except as an approximation. But while perfect competition and perfect contestability are both unattainable ideal states, there are many industries whose structure and performance may usefully be measured against the latter but not the former. To see why this is so let us first define the two concepts and indicate the criteria by which they can be taken to constitute the standard of perfection in industrial structure and performance.

An industry is traditionally deemed to be perfectly competitive if it possesses all three of the following attributes: (i) It is made up of a very large

Contestable Markets

number of firms, each of which provides so negligible a proportion of the industry's total output that no one firm's output decisions can have any discernible effect on price; (ii) the industry's products are perfectly homogeneous in the sense that no buyer distinguishes between the products of any two suppliers even in terms of any accompanying services, packaging or marketing procedures;[3] (iii) entry into and exit from the industry is totally unimpeded.

For the purpose of comparison with contestability analysis, the first of these three attributes is particularly noteworthy. It automatically rules out from the competitive category any industry in which, for example, scale economies make small firms relatively inefficient and consequently prevent their long-run survival in a free market. Because so many industries are characterized by technology that makes small enterprise completely impractical, the norm of perfect competition becomes not only unachievable, but, for many sectors of the economy, irrelevant. The concept of a perfectly contestable market is designed to provide a benchmark that applies in markets for which the concept of perfect competition is not very useful. An oligopolistic or even a monpolistic industry can be perfectly contestable if it is characterized by complete freedom of entry and exit—the last of the three attributes of perfect competition.

Formally, a market is defined to be perfectly contestable if no price in that market can be in equilibrium when its magnitude is such as to enable an entrant to undercut it and nevertheless earn a profit. Thus, a market that is protected by substantial entry barriers is clearly not contestable, because the barriers permit an equilibrium involving monopoly prices and monopoly profits. In the absence of barriers, those prices and profits would be undermined by entrants seeking to take advantage of the profit opportunity they provide. Thus, the matter can be looked at in a second and equivalent way. A market is perfectly contestable if firms can enter it and then, if they choose, exit without losing any of their investment. If this condition is satisfied, no prices set by the incumbents that offer profits to entrants can long endure. Thus, freedom of entry and exit are the key requirements of contestability.

The second version of the formal definition of a contestable market is tantamount to a requirement that there be no sunk costs.[4] A sunk cost, by

---

3. The product homogeneity attribute of perfect competition does not play any substantial role in the discussion that follows. It has been argued that heterogeneity of products can introduce a variety of inefficiencies. For example, it has been asserted that it tends to lead to a number of (slightly differing) products which exceeds anything justifiable in terms of costs and consumer benefits (as measured by the consumers' preferences) and that it leads firms to operate wastefully via unused capacity. The classic discussion of this subject is found in E. CHAMBERLIN, THE THEORY OF MONOPOLISTIC COMPETITION (1962).

4. Contestability theory draws heavily upon earlier work relating to barriers to entry originating

definition, is an outlay that cannot be recouped without substantial delay. If entry into a market requires a new enterprise to sink considerable amounts of capital, there must be violation of the requirement of perfect contestability that absolutely costless exit be possible. What is crucial is not the amount of capital that is required for entry, but the amount of this capital that is sunk.

Entry involving highly mobile capital, even if it is very substantial in quantity, may be followed by easy and rapid departure. Even if exit from the industry as a whole is difficult, mobility of capital may permit easy and rapid entry into and exit from particular markets in that industry. Similarly, industries using capital for which a strong second-hand market exists, or using capital that can readily be leased, are likely to exhibit the easy entry and exit characteristics needed for contestability. In light of these considerations, we can define the degree to which an industry is contestable. For we see that the smaller the share of investment that is composed of capital that is sunk, the more contestable that industry will be.[5]

A contestable market works most effectively if, in response to a profit-making opportunity, new firms can enter quickly, earn profits at least temporarily (before incumbents can institute countermeasures) and then leave without any loss of investment in sunk capital. This suggests that where incumbents can counterattack quickly, contestability will prevail only if hit-and-run entry can be carried out even more rapidly. It may appear that in the race between entry and retaliatory measures by incumbents the latter will generally prevail and so will preclude contestability; incumbents may be able to cut price almost instantly—as soon as entry

---

with J. BAIN, BARRIERS TO NEW COMPETITION (1956); it also draws from the literature on limiting pricing growing from the work of P. SYLOS-LABINI, OLIGOPOLY AND TECHNICAL PROGRESS (1962). Perfectly contestable markets contrast with the circumstances considered in the more usual oligopoly models in which both incumbent firms and new entrants must sink some costs. For markets in which sunk capacity is important and leads to strategic behavior when entry threatens or after it occurs, there is a well-developed literature, ably summarized in Dixit, *Recent Developments in Oligopoly Theory*, 72 AM. ECON. REV. 12 (1982).

5. Preliminary empirical evidence confirms that market behavior does indeed follow such a pattern—that is, the smaller the share of sunk outlays, the more closely the behavior of the firms in an industry follows the pattern to be expected in a contestable market. I. Kesides, Toward a Testable Model of Entry: A Study of the U.S. Manufacturing Industries (1982) (unpublished manuscript at Princeton University). Preliminary experimental evidence explores the conjecture that sunk costs weaken the discipline of contested markets, and finds that the disciplining power of market contestability is impressive. *See* Coursey, Isaac, Luke & Smith, *Market Contestability in the Presence of Sunk (Entry) Costs*, 15 BELL. J. ECON. (forthcoming, 1984). Preliminary experimental evidence also indicates that prices appear to be near competitive, rather than monopoly, levels when as few as two identical decreasing cost firms compete for a market large enough for only one of them. *See* Coursey, Isaac & Smith, *Natural Monopoly and Contested Markets: Some Experimental Results*, 27 J. L. & ECON. (forthcoming, 1984). These discussions suggest that the applicability of the standard of contestability is considerably wider than some of the initial discussions imply. *See, e.g.,* Dixit, *supra* note 4.

Contestable Markets

occurs or, for that matter, as soon as it threatens. But if entry into a market entails no sunk costs, a potential entrant has no reason to fear retaliation by incumbents, since it can leave the market without loss if such retaliation materializes. In many markets, rapid retaliation may not be possible; regulation, long-term contracts, or other impediments can slow the response of incumbents to entry. Moreover, a new firm can forestall retaliation by entering into contracts, before it actually opens for business, with customers it lures from incumbents.

B.   *Virtues of Competitive and Contestable Markets*

Analysts have been attracted by the concept of perfect competition, despite its lack of realism and its inflexibility, because it has implications that can readily be used as standards of optimality for industrial performance. These include the preclusion of excess profits, the elimination of inefficient firms, the absence of cross subsidy, and pricing consistent with the allocation of resources available to the economy that is most efficient in serving the preferences of consumers. For purposes of comparison with contestability, it is useful to review each of these four attributes and to indicate why each is a necessary characteristic of a perfectly competitive industry.

Excessive profits are defined by economists as any long-run profits exceeding the cost of capital as determined by the markets for debt and equity. Such excess profits are eliminated in the long run by freedom of entry in a perfectly competitive industry. If the current cost of capital is twelve percent and a particular competitive industry offers a return of eighteen percent, new firms will be attracted into that industry, expanding outputs and driving down prices to the point where all excess profits have been squeezed out. The reason that inefficient enterprises cannot persist in a perfectly competitive industry is similar: cost inefficiencies invite replacement of the incumbents by entrants who can provide the same outputs at lower cost.

Cross subsidy, a problem that has long been of concern to regulators,[6] may be defined, roughly, as the sale by a multiproduct firm of some of its outputs at prices that are indefensibly low relative to their costs, with the resulting revenue shortfalls being offset by the charging of indefensibly high prices for other company outputs. For obvious reasons, cross subsidy is considered unfair both in its disparate treatment of the firm's customers and in its effects upon competing sellers of the products that are under-

---

6.   For example, this issue has been the subject of more than a decade of hearings on telecommunications pricing before the FCC, with AT&T and its large business customers pitted against Western Union, MCI and other entrants. *See, e.g., In re* MCI Telecomm. Corp., 70 F.C.C.2d 666 (1979).

priced (i.e., those products which receive the internal cross subsidy). In perfectly competitive markets, cross subsidy is ruled out by the inability of firms to earn any excess profits. If no product of a firm can contribute more to revenues than its cost of capital, then that enterprise can have no source of funds with which to provide cross subsidies to any of its other outputs.

Of the four beneficial consequences of perfect competition, the most difficult to explain is the relationship between its pricing and efficiency in the allocation of the economy's resources. As already indicated, under perfect competition each firm is so miniscule a part of its industry that its output decision has no effect on price. The market-determined price therefore represents the addition to revenue from the production of another unit. The most profitable output of a good is, then, that output at which the marginal cost, the addition to the firm's total cost caused by the production of an additional unit, equals the given price.[7] Thus, perfect competition drives firms to equate marginal costs and prices—and that, according to economic analysis, is precisely the price behavior required for efficiency in the use of resources to serve consumers.[8]

These are the primary virtues of perfect competition that account for its widespread use as a criterion for industry performance. To what extent does perfect contestability share these attributes?[9] To begin with, perfect contestability precludes both excess profits and inefficient firm operations in the long run, for much the same reasons that perfect competition precludes them. Should either phenomenon arise temporarily, it would make possible profitable operation by firms charging prices below those of the

---

7. Thus, if the market price of X is $10, while its marginal cost (including the cost of the additional capital required) is $9.25, the firm can add to its profit by expanding its output, for it gains $.75 on each additional unit produced. Gradually, however, diminishing returns will increase marginal cost and erode the profitability of further expansion until a marginal cost equal to the $10 price is attained, and it pays the firm to set its output there.

8. The reasoning underlying this standard result is fairly straightforward. If a consumer purchases a unit of good X, the cost his purchase causes, i.e., the value of the resources used up in meeting this demand, is by definition precisely the marginal cost of X. Thus, if the price of each good is equal to the marginal cost of that item, the prices consumers pay are the same as the costs caused by their purchases. Money cost then becomes a perfect proxy for the real social cost incurred in providing a unit of a good to the consumer. Then, if consumers use their *money* resources optimally from their own point of view, i.e., in a way which best serves their preferences, they will automatically be using the economy's *real* resources for the satisfaction of consumer desires as efficiently as is possible. In contrast, if the price of X were low relative to its marginal cost while the reverse were true of good Y, then consumers would be attracted to buy more of X and less of Y than the true economic costs call for. For example, suppose X and Y are perfect substitutes for consumers but the marginal cost of X and Y are $5 and $4, respectively. If, however, the price of X is $5 while that of Y is $5.50 consumers will spend their money efficiently by purchasing X in preference to Y. But that, clearly, is not compatible with efficiency in the use of the economy's resources.

9. For a full examination of the issue with all its technicalities, see W. BAUMOL, J. PANZAR & R. WILLIG, *supra* note 1, at 191-345. A more intuitive discussion is provided in Baumol, *Contestable Markets: An Uprising in the Theory of Industry Structure*, 72 AM. ECON. REV. 1, 4-5 (1982).

Contestable Markets

incumbents. Since entry into a perfectly contestable market is costless, this opportunity for short-term profits would attract entry—and that in turn would soon force down prices and profits. Furthermore, with no possibility of excess profits on any of a firm's products, there can be no source of cross subsidy. Thus the first three virtues of perfect competition are realized in perfectly contestable industries, and these traditional concerns of regulators become groundless.

The possibility of economies of scale in perfectly contestable industries makes the evaluation of the fourth criterion—the equation of price with marginal cost—more complex. The argument for the case of perfect competition is inapplicable in the presence of economies of scale: efficient sized firms are large enough to affect price by their output decisions. However, if scale economies, though significant, do not create a natural monopoly, perfect contestability ensures marginal cost pricing. Moreover, even in the case of natural monopoly, perfect contestability ensures that the lowest price consistent with the continued provision of the good is charged.

Consider the case in which scale economies do not result in natural monopoly. Then maximum efficiency is consistent with two or more firms operating in the industry. A price exceeding marginal cost will create an opportunity for profitable entry. The entrant can (slightly) undercut the incumbents' price, and sell slightly more units than some of the incumbents. The profit on the additional sales must more than cover the reduction in profits resulting from the price reduction on the preceding units. Similarly, if price is below marginal cost, an entrant can offer a slightly lower price than the incumbents, and sell slightly fewer units. The additional profits from the reduction in output must more than cover the decrease in profits resulting from the decrease in price. Thus prices above or below marginal costs invite entry, and therefore price will be in equilibrium only if it equals marginal cost.[10]

In natural monopoly, a single producer can achieve a lower total cost than can any group of firms and total costs are usually large relative to marginal costs.[11] Only one efficient sized firm can remain. Moreover, marginal cost pricing is likely to involve costs that exceed revenues, and so

10. A problem can arise if products in a perfectly contestable industry are heterogeneous, each supplier offering his own special brands with their own special features. However, it can be shown (through an argument similar to that made above) that if each variant is sold by at least two different suppliers, perfect contestability will lead to marginal cost pricing. *See* W. BAUMOL, J. PANZAR & R. WILLIG, *supra* note 1, at 314-21, 329-45.

11. It is tempting to compare marginal costs with *average* costs but in a multiproduct firm (and virtually all firms in reality are multiproduct enterprises) average costs cannot even be defined, because of the outlays which are almost always incurred in common on behalf of several of the firm's products. To give the trivial but standard example, there is no way to determine what part of the salary of the president of the firm is "caused" by the supply of product A rather than product B, and therefore constitutes a legitimate portion of A's average cost.

117

Yale Journal on Regulation   Vol. 1: 111, 1984

no such firm can afford such a pricing policy. However, contestability does ensure that a natural monopolist will be able to prevent entry only if it sets the lowest prices consistent with the financial viability of the firm. Otherwise an entrant could slightly undercut his prices, taking the entire market for himself, and earn a normal profit. Similarly, costless entry precludes inefficient operation. Moreover, with no above normal profits on any goods, there is no opportunity for cross subsidy, even by a contestable monopoly.

This discussion reveals the reason contestability analysis departs from the tradition which classified scale economies as a barrier to entry. Contestability analysis defines an entry barrier as something which provides incumbent firms sufficient protection from entry so that they can obtain above normal profits or exhibit other forms of unacceptable performance. But we have seen that perfect contestability guarantees the absence of excess profits, inefficiencies and cross subsidies even in the presence of scale economies. It can also be shown that even in the presence of a natural monopoly, contestability rewards the firm for selecting the prices that are most efficient given the requirement of solvency of the enterprise. Thus, scale economies are not a source of undesirable performance in a contestable market and cannot be considered a form of entry barrier.

But scale economies do affect the usefulness of contestability relative to perfect competition as guides for policy. We have seen that to be perfectly competitive an industry must be populated by a large number of miniscule firms. But even if each of these dwarf enterprises operates with exemplary efficiency, the overall result may be inefficient. Suppose, for example, that the industry's technology provides substantial economies of scale or what has come to be called *economies of scope*—i.e., economies that derive from the simultaneous production of several goods or services.[12] In these circumstances, large and diversified firms may be able to supply goods far more cheaply, in terms of resources used, than can the many small firms of perfect competition.

---

12. Economies of scope are defined formally as follows: Let $C(x,y)$ be the cost of production by a single firm of quantity x of some good, X, and quantity y of another commodity, Y. Let $C(x)$ be the cost of producing x if it is done by a completely specialized firm and $C(y)$ have an analogous connotation. Then production of X and Y is characterized by economies of scope if $C(x,y)$ is less than the sum of $C(x)$ and $C(y)$. That is, economies of scope are present if the multiproduct firm's production of x and y together incurs a cost lower than the sum of the cost of x alone, when produced by a specialized firm, and the cost of y when produced by another specialized enterprise. For example, a telecommunications network can serve many routes more efficiently than it can only a few. If calls from New York to Los Angeles have just been transmitted via Chicago and the Chicago portion of the route encounters a surge of traffic which strains its capacity, the New York-Los Angeles calls can be (and are) rerouted, say, via New Orleans. Thus, simultaneous provision of service to these four regions makes it possible to operate with lower capacity in both New Orleans and Chicago. For similar reasons shoe factories usually produce footwear of different sizes and styles, automotive firms usually produce both cars and trucks, etc.

Contestable Markets

This type of inefficiency is referred to as *inefficiency in industry structure*, as distinguished from inefficiency in the operations of individual firms. We see now that perfect competition, with its requirement that all firms be small, may be inconsistent with efficiency in industry structure; when that is the case and markets are free, perfect competition will be unable to survive. In an industry characterized by perfect contestability, however, industry structure *must* be efficient. If an industry is perfectly contestable and its outputs can be produced more cheaply by four firms than by three or six or any other particular number of enterprises, then in the long run that industry must indeed be composed of four firms. A two-firm or a nine-firm industry structure cannot survive the market pressures introduced by perfect contestability.

To see why this is so, suppose that by happenstance the hypothetical industry contains nine enterprises even though four-firm production is least costly. Some of those nine firms can be depended upon to seize the cost-reduction opportunity offered by the availability of economies of scale and scope. These economies will permit the more enterprising firms to undercut the prices of rivals who are slower to grasp the expansion opportunity. Costlessness of exit will then make it easy for those laggard rivals to leave the industry. If no incumbent in the industry is sufficiently enterprising to take advantage of the opportunity to undercut prevailing prices, outsiders sufficiently large to benefit from the economies of scale and scope will be happy to do so, since in a contestable industry they bear neither entry cost nor risk. In due course, surplus firms will be driven from the industry, and a four-firm structure that minimizes the total cost of its bundle of outputs will emerge. Such a four-firm industry may be perfectly contestable, but it can hardly qualify as perfectly competitive.

This, then, is the sense in which it can be said that while perfectly competitive and perfectly contestable markets are both ideals, the latter is more ideal than the former. After all, one must be tempered in one's praise of the many-firm structure of perfect competition in those cases in which the availability of economies of scale and scope means that an oligopoly structure can (perhaps) achieve far lower costs and offer far lower prices to consumers.

The perfectly competitive structure is simply not attainable in a broad group of industries. The idea of transforming the automobile, steel, or telecommunications business into an industry composed of a huge number of tiny enterprises is absurd on its face. That is why perfect contestability is a standard of structure and performance that is more pertinent than pure competition given the character of modern technology.

119

Yale Journal on Regulation   Vol. 1: 111, 1984

C. *Some Features of Contestable Markets*

Several attributes of a contestable industry are particularly significant for regulatory policy and therefore merit explicit discussion. We will begin by discussing several of the requirements that must be satisfied in order for a market to be contestable; then we will consider some of the implications of contestability for market behavior.

Freedom of exit is a crucial ingredient of contestability. In a contestable market, freedom of exit is merely the obverse of freedom of entry. Any impediment to exit by definition increases the riskiness, and hence the real cost, of opening for business. A potential entrant will hesitate long before embarking on an enterprise from which it will be difficult to withdraw if his entry proves to have been a mistake. This means that the traditional resistance of regulators to exit—for example, their refusal to permit the abandonment of unprofitable routes by railroads or airlines—is hardly without cost to the economy. However laudable the motivation for opposition to exit—be it the preservation of service to isolated consumers, the safeguarding of jobs, or the maintenance of tax bases in financially troubled communities—the fact is that it has an unintended adverse consequence: preclusion of, or restraints on, exit discourage entry and thereby reduce the competitive threat posed by the availability of potential entrants. The moral is that when subsidies do serve the public interest, regulators should consider ways to provide those subsidies directly rather than attempting to encourage cross subsidy by making exit difficult.

This immediately suggests a second necessary feature of contestable markets: the availability of a pool of potential entrants able to respond quickly to an entry opportunity and to choose the timing, place, and manner of entry that best suits the circumstances. It is their *threat* that disciplines incumbents and forces them to serve consumers efficiently.[13] A regulatory process in which lengthy hearings and evidence of public convenience and necessity are prerequisites to entry is precisely what is not required.[14] Contestability is also subverted by the regulatory custom that requires potential entrants to commit themselves well in advance to the timing and manner of their proposed entry.[15] Contestability requires that firms have what can be described as *standby* authority to enter a

---

13. The role of potential entry and its threat was first emphasized by Bain, and he, too, maintained that it has generally not been given adequate attention. J. BAIN, *supra* note 4.

14. For example, hearing processes at the CAB tended to take from one to four years to complete, and even then almost no new authorizations were granted for routes that already had two or more authorized carriers. Normally, in a route case at most one new carrier was selected for the route. *See* Bailey, *Deregulation and Regulatory Reform of U.S. Air-Transportation Policy*, in REGULATED INDUSTRIES & PUBLIC ENTERPRISE: EUROPEAN & UNITED STATES PERSPECTIVES 29, 29 (1980).

15. For example, CAB rules also required proposed operating schedules to be submitted at the beginning of a route case.

Contestable Markets

market—authority that need not be exercised so long as good performance by incumbents precludes profit opportunities for entrants, but that can be used quickly when unsatisfactory incumbent performance offers entrants the prospect of profit.

In addition to these two crucial elements of contestability, there is a third feature that facilitates, but is not absolutely necessary to, contestability: sluggishness in the responses of incumbents, particularly the pricing responses, to entry. This does not mean that incumbents should be prevented from competing fully and effectively by adjusting prices. The entire purpose of the competitive process from the viewpoint of the general welfare is that it forces firms to offer low prices and to provide service and products of high quality. Contestability theory does suggest, however, that regulation-induced lags in pricing may well be salutory. While slowness in incumbents' pricing responses to entry is conducive to contestability, it is by no means essential. Potential entrants can and do sometimes make binding contracts with their future customers, and if such contracts can be agreed upon quickly, the fact that entry takes a longer time becomes irrelevant. Once the contract is signed, a retaliatory price reduction by incumbents will have lost its sting.

We turn now to some pertinent consequences of contestability for regulation. One key characteristic of contestable industries is the dependence of their structure—including not only number of firms but also the degree of their integration, the number of different items in their product lines, and the dispersion in the sizes of enterprises—upon the forces of the market. This efficiency attribute of long-run equilibrium in a perfectly contestable market means that any structure compatible with equilibrium must offer the lowest cost that is attainable. This implies that regulatory attempts to influence the structure of an industry, perhaps seeking to increase the number of firms it contains, are often doomed to failure. Newly introduced enterprises either will not survive or will replace some incumbents, but in the long run the number of firms will be unaffected. In such circumstances, regulators are all too often tempted to keep firms alive by subverting competitive pressures—specifically, by establishing what amounts to a cartel, in which each enterprise is protected from the competition of the others. But an arrangement of that sort is a monstrosity that keeps up the appearance of competition by assuring the survival of firms as an end in itself, by completely undermining the competitive process and imposing a heavy cost upon the consuming public.

A second implication of contestability for regulation relates to the good behavior that perfect contestability imposes upon business firms. As we have seen, the discipline imposed by the possibility of hit-and-run entry precludes pricing above marginal costs, excess profit, inefficient operation

121

or structure, and cross subsidy, even in an oligopoly. If a perfectly contestable industry is a natural monopoly, the last three conditions are met and the firm must charge as low a set of prices as long-run financial viability permits. Thus, when an industry is contestable, not only is regulatory intervention designed to influence industry structure ineffective, but it is also unnecessary for the protection of the interests of consumers.

Finally, we observe from what has just been said that in a contestable industry the absence of entry should not be taken as a sign of predatory behavior by incumbents, but, on the contrary, as an indication of good behavior on their part. In a perfectly contestable industry, as we have seen, entry can be prevented only by performance that satisfies competitive standards. Thus, if an industry is reasonably contestable a regulator should certainly hesitate before deciding that a history without entry constitutes grounds for intervention.

One other issue should be noted at this point: Since *perfect* contestability is highly improbable in reality, it is necessary to consider the state of affairs that is likely when the requirements of contestability are fulfilled only approximately. Unfortunately, since the entire analysis is so new, the case of imperfect contestability and the attributes of a "workably contestable" market are only now being explored.

In a recent note, Marius Schwartz and Robert J. Reynolds[16] of the Department of Justice argued that slowness of entry can cause serious problems for performance even if the lag is only moderate. They assert that, in such circumstances, rather than acting like perfect competitors and earning zero economic profits, incumbents will find it rewarding to adopt prices that yield them monopoly profits during the period before entry occurs—and then exit gracefully when the entrant opens for business, undercuts the incumbent, and takes the market over. These authors offer several other scenarios designed to show that slight departures from the requirements of contestability can cause large deviations from contestable behavior.

In reply, Baumol, Panzar and Willig[17] undertake to show that Schwartz and Reynolds do not use the right criterion of proximity to contestability. In their view, it is the magnitude of sunk costs, rather than the entry lag, that is the crucial issue. It is clear that as sunk costs approach zero the risks associated with entry also become negligible because an entrant who finds in retrospect that his entry decision was an error can then

---

16. Schwartz & Reynolds, *Contestable Markets: An Uprising in the Theory of Industry Structure: Comment*, 73 AM. ECON. REV. 488 (1983).

17. Baumol, Panzar & Willig, *Contestable Markets: An Uprising in the Theory of Industry Structure: Reply*, 73 AM. ECON. REV. 491 (1983).

Contestable Markets

pick up *almost* all of his marbles and depart with commensurately little loss. Thus, if sunk costs are small but not zero, the discipline exercised by the threat of potential entry remains potent.

The meager empirical evidence also supports this view. But it must be granted that results on this subject are still highly preliminary and do not yet lend themselves to confident generalization. Much of what can be concluded about this issue now derives from particularized observations, such as those in the discussion below of recent regulatory issues. It may be added, however, that we are as unsure about approximations to perfect competition as we are about approximations to perfect contestability. The literature on workable competition is suggestive and illuminating, but it rests neither on rigorous formal analysis nor on a clear-cut body of empirical evidence.

II.   The Implications of Contestability Theory for Regulatory Policy

We have argued that perfect competition is neither an attainable nor a desirable benchmark for industries in which economies of scale or scope are substantial; in such cases, attempts to approximate perfect competition may in fact be highly inefficient. However, the divergence of such industries from the patterns of perfect competition does not justify the sorts of regulation that have traditionally been imposed. Regulators should seek policies that promote contestability. If an industry behaves as if it is contestable, most of the benefits of perfect competition can be obtained without government intervention. In short, our position is that the equilibrium of a contestable market is often a better standard for public policy than the competitive model, particularly in the presence of economies of scale and scope.

Short of doing everything possible to foster contestability, regulators should certainly cease doing those things that work against it. Direct regulatory attempts to impede entry or exit or to interfere with the timing or manner of entry must, at the very least, be questioned severely. Moreover, regulators should keep their eyes open for entry barriers erected by firms and should take steps to discourage the maintenance of those barriers.[18]

In addition to entry barriers introduced artificially by regulators or incumbent firms, there are in many industries what may be described as "natural" barriers, i.e., barriers that arise out of technological circumstances. For example, the technology of an industry may require heavy sunk investments on the part of entrants, as we have seen. An investment

---

18.   We will not pursue this subject here because it has been raised and discussed long before the advent of contestability analysis, and this analysis has, so far, not shed any new light on that part of our subject.

that cannot easily be moved elsewhere is an impediment to exit, which, as has been shown, is in turn a prime obstacle to entry. However, as one critic has noted to us in conversation, "One cannot regulate away the need to sink costs." What, then, can be done to weaken the barrier to entry that is found when entry requires heavy sunk investments?

In these cases, regulators are just beginning to experiment with new methods to ensure that no excessive profits are earned from sunk-cost facilities. Rather than relying exclusively on traditional rate and entry regulation, they have turned to two rather novel approaches. The first of these entails government intervention to ensure equal access to the sunk facility. If the facility is privately owned, the government requires that all firms seeking to use the facility be given access to it, that the access price be reasonable,[19] and that all users be charged the same price. If the sunk facility is in the hands of a local public authority, then that authority is encouraged not to discriminate among private users in its access policies.

The second approach is to isolate the sunk investments, leaving a relatively contestable part of the industry's operations to be controlled by market forces, while the portion with substantial amounts of sunk capital is regulated or even operated by the public sector. Thus, some new legislation and some regulatory decisions are characterized by a flexible case-by-case approach, in which markets subject to strong competitive pressures from substitute services and markets in which technology does not require heavy sunk costs are freed from traditional regulatory constraints and are permitted more open entry and more flexible pricing.[20] Those segments of an industry that have large sunk costs or for which there is a problem of "nonsustainability," that is, absence of an equilibrium,[21] must continue to

---

19. See the discussion of airport access, *infra*, text accompanying notes 44-45, or the discussion of access to local telephone systems, *infra* at Sec. II.D. The lesson that continued regulation to maintain open access may be appropriate holds even more strongly for industries that are characterized by large sunk costs and long lead times, such as the electric power industry. For example, it is important to design and apply criteria for guaranteeing access to transmission systems and power pooling activities. *See* P. JOSKOW & R. SCHMALENSEE, MARKETS FOR POWER: AN ANALYSIS OF ELECTRIC UTILITY DEREGULATION (1983).

20. See the discussion of the Fresh Fruit & Vegetable Decision, *infra*, text accompanying note 28, or the discussion of the AT&T settlement, *infra*, text accompanying note 66. Another example is the 1979 Amendments to the National Health Planning and Resources Development Act of 1974, Pub. L. No. 96-79, 93 Stat. 589 (codified in scattered sections of 42 U.S.C.), which attempts to distinguish between, and treat rather differently, in-patient institutional services and noninstitutional and out-patient services. For in-patient services, continued regulation is called for and the utility of contestability analysis is not great because of both sunk cost problems and third-party reimbursement mechanisms. However, contestability analysis is consistent with freeing from entry regulation those portions of the noninstitutional and out-patient services that are characterized by fixed, but no sunk, costs. *See* J. GELMAN, COMPETITION AND HEALTH PLANNING (F.T.C., 1982).

21. In the single product case, no equilibrium is possible if a natural monopoly firm is producing in a rising portion of its average cost curve. The disequilibrium occurs because any group of customers who together demand an amount of the product equal to the level at the minimum point on the average cost curve can supply themselves at a lower price. Thus, they have an incentive to leave the

Contestable Markets

be regulated.

We now turn to a description of reform measures undertaken in the transportation and communications industries during the late 1970's and early 1980's. We focus in each case upon two or three aspects of reform that reflect the features of contestability that have been emphasized. Our descriptions are brief rather than thorough. They outline a framework for policy which is consistent with contestability theory. The major lesson that emerges from this analysis is that contestability theory provides no mechanistic prescriptions or inviolable rules for regulators or for authors of regulatory reform legislation. However, it does offer substantial insights that can strengthen the effectiveness of their work.

A. *Reform of Railroad Regulation*

The sunk cost and longevity of railroad capital may suggest that the railroad industry is one in which contestability analysis cannot conceivably apply. However, the railroad industry is more contestable than has been traditionally acknowledged, because there is strong competitive pressure from other modes of transportation—such as trucking—on the rates charged for shipment of a wide variety of commodities. Contestability analysis tells us that even in markets in which sunk costs are substantial, pricing power may be held in check by the availability of substitute suppliers whose cost structure is compatible with contestability. In these circumstances, the theory suggests that rate regulation is not required.

The railroad legislation passed in 1976, the Railroad Revitalization and Reform Act (4R Act),[22] is in harmony with this suggestion. From the standpoint of contestability, the most pertinent provision of the legislation is one that offers a railroad freedom in pricing where there is no evidence that it holds a position of "market dominance."[23] The 4R Act provided that market dominance "refers to an absence of effective competition from other carriers or modes of transportation, for through traffic or movement."[24] The Interstate Commerce Commission (ICC) has listed four

---

natural monopoly. The absence of a stable price can occur in the multi-product case as well, and is particularly likely to occur when there is strong demand substitutability and product-specific scale economies. In public policy terms, lack of a stable price equilibrium in the face of open entry and exit may require entry regulation. *See* Faulhaber, *Cross-Subsidization: Pricing in Public Enterprise*, 65 AM. ECON. REV. 966 (1973); *see also* BAUMOL, PANZAR & WILLIG, *supra* note 1.

22. Pub. L. No. 94-210, 90 Stat. 31 (codified as amended in scattered sections of 45, 49, 15 & 31 U.S.C.).

23. The 4R Act prohibited the ICC from deciding that a rate was excessively high without a finding that the carrier filing the rate had market dominance. *Id.* § 202(b), 49 U.S.C. § 10,709. In 1980, Congress limited the ICC's jurisdiction to determine that rates are reasonable to those rates established by rail carriers which the ICC finds have market dominance. Staggers Rail Act of 1980, Pub. L. No. 96-448 § 201(a), 49 U.S.C. § 10,701a (Supp. V 1981).

24. 49 U.S.C. § 10,709(a).

types of competitive checks that are to be considered in determining whether there is market dominance over the transport of a particular product: intramodal competition, intermodal competition, geographic competition (the ability to transport the product to or from a different location) and product competition (the availability of substitutes for the product).[25] In principle such an approach is entirely consistent with the implications of contestability analysis. When an industry can be segmented into independent components, it is desirable to free from regulation those parts of the industry in which competing firms lack market power.

The 4R Act also granted the ICC the authority to exempt the rail carriage of certain goods and passengers if the rail carriage was of "limited scope" and regulation was not otherwise desirable.[26] The Staggers Rail Act of 1980 extended this authority, allowing the ICC to exempt a movement if it finds that rate regulation is not needed to carry out the transportation policy of the Act, and that either the carriage is of "limited scope" or that regulation "is not needed to protect shippers from the abuse of market power."[27] Perhaps the best-known recent example of such an exemption is the ICC's decision to permit railroads total freedom of pricing in the transportation of fresh fruits and vegetables.[28] This action also accords well with the prescriptions of contestability theory as was recognized by economist Darius Gaskins, who was Chairman of the ICC when the exemption was passed.

It is noteworthy that the 4R Act did not automatically extend freedom from regulation to segments of the industry in which a railroad was alleged to dominate the market. Consider, for example, coal transport. Leaps in the price of petroleum, first in the mid-1970's and then again in 1979 and 1980, caused the demand for coal to rise substantially. Railroads are the chief transporters of coal to major coal-using facilities, such as electric power plants. Once these plants have been constructed, their relocation is largely precluded. It is clear that Congress was right in continuing regulation of rates when the ICC finds that a carrier has market dominance.[29]

25. *See* Market Dominance Determinations & Consid. of Product Competition, 365 I.C.C. 1, 118 (1981).

26. 49 U.S.C. § 10,505.

27. *Id.* § 10,505(a).

28. Rail Gen. Exemption Auth., 361 I.C.C. 211 (1979).

29. *See* 49 U.S.C. § 10,701a(b)(1). For a more thorough discussion of ICC activity during this period, see Gaskins & Voytko, *Managing the Transition to Deregulation*, 44 LAW & CONTEMP. PROBS. 9 (1981); *see also* A. FRIEDLAENDER & R. SPADY, FREIGHT TRANSPORT REGULATION (1981); Eads, *The Reform of Economic Regulation*, in AMERICAN ENTERPRISE INSTITUTE, TELECOMMUNICATION AND TRANSPORTATION (1982).

Contestable Markets

The theory of contestability suggests that in such cases policymakers should consider ways to encourage potential competition from other sources. But the case of the railroads illustrates that this must be done with care and that the most obvious paths may be beset by hidden perils. For example, if railroad *A* is required to permit competing railroad *B* to lease space on any of *A*'s tracks—that is, to grant *B* what are known as trackage rights—the arrangement would appear to enhance competition by permitting *B* to bid for shipments along routes that parallel *A*'s but can reach their ultimate destination only by traversing some of *A*'s track. This is indeed so if the price for trackage rights is settled voluntarily in a free competitive market. However, if regulators force the provision of trackage rights at a noncompensatory price, this action will amount to a subsidy to railroad *B* that effectively drives *A* from the field and undermines competition and efficiency rather than enhancing them.

Similarly, some proponents of enhanced competition have proposed that the right of eminent domain be granted to coal slurry pipelines in order to force railroads to permit the pipelines to cross rail property.[30] It is asserted that this will increase greatly the competitiveness of coal transportation. But here, too, there is a pricing complication. Environmental groups claim that the pipelines will make heavy use of scarce water supplies and that disposal of waste products from the pipelines will exact a heavy pollution cost. The pipelines should be forced to bear the full costs of water use and waste disposal through direct charges or other measures. Otherwise, heavily subsidized entities will be pitted against firms that are required to cover their own costs, resulting in inefficiency and environmental degradation rather than real competition.

Whatever the true facts in these matters, the moral is clear. The enforced introduction of competition must not be accompanied by artificial prices for incumbents or entrants; otherwise, more harm than benefit may flow from it, and no contribution to contestability will result.

B.   *Aviation Deregulation*

The Airline Deregulation Act of 1978[31] rested upon such a degree of confidence in the inherent structural competitiveness of the domestic U.S. airline industry that it went further in deregulating than any other piece of recent legislation. Regulatory barriers to entry of the type that had

---

30. *See, e.g.*, Tarlock, *Western Water Law and Coal Development*, 51 U. COLO. L. REV. 511, 538 (1980). One pipeline company has won right of way disputes with railroads in the Eighth and Tenth Circuits. Energy Transp. Sys., Inc. v. Union Pac. R.R. 619 F.2d 696 (8th Cir. 1980); Energy Transp. Sys., Inc. v. Union Pac. R.R., 606 F.2d 934 (10th Cir. 1979).

31. Pub. L. No. 95-504, 92 Stat. 1705 (codified as amended in scattered sections of 49 U.S.C.).

Yale Journal on Regulation Vol. 1: 111, 1984

been favored by the Civil Aeronautics Board (CAB) were removed within three years of its passage.[32] Under the Act, the CAB can no longer block new jet carriers from entering the industry, nor can it conduct lengthy route cases to decide which additional carrier will be permitted to serve a particular pair of cities.[33] The new legislation recognizes the benefits of permitting potential competitors to respond to profit opportunities by entering markets freely. Even though the number of actual competitors in most markets might not change very much as a consequence, the Act gave airline managements complete freedom in the structuring of their route networks,[34] relying on this freedom as an adequate check on market power. The Act also provided for complete freedom of pricing, effective one year after entry became unimpeded.[35] The only exception to the deregulatory tone was for air services involving small communities: to avoid curtailment of these services, the Act provided direct subsidies for a ten-year period.[36]

In some ways the airline industry presents a particularly close approximation to contestability. As discussed above, the more mobile the capital and the smaller the sunk costs involved in an industry, the more that industry approaches perfect contestability. The major component of capital equipment in the airline industry, the airplanes themselves, can readily be moved from market to market. Such items of equipment are, in Alfred Kahn's words, "marginal costs with wings." This is true even though, because of technological economies of scale with respect to aircraft size, the majority of U.S. city-pair markets are natural monopolies (and so are likely to be served by only one carrier even under free entry) and all markets are likely to show high concentration.[37]

The evidence on route networks since deregulation corresponds well to the theory. Because of the economies of aircraft size, the cost of accommodating a passenger in an otherwise empty seat is quite small. Airlines thus have a strong incentive to establish hub-and-spoke operations. Flights from various origins arrive at an intermediate point where passengers change planes to proceed to their ultimate destinations. By combining passengers with different origins and destinations, a carrier can increase the

---

32.   49 U.S.C. § 1551(a).

33.   *Id.* § 1371(d)(7)(A).

34.   *Id.* § 1302(a)(4).

35.   *Id.* § 1551(a)(2)(B).

36.   *Id.* § 1389. For a description of the events leading up to the Airline Deregulation Act and a more complete analysis of its features, see S. BREYER, REGULATION AND ITS REFORM 197-221 (1981).

37.   As described in D. GRAHAM & D. KAPLAN, COMPETITION AND THE AIRLINES: AN EVALUATION OF DEREGULATION 54 (1982) (CAB Staff Report), the average number of large aircraft operators providing nonstop service was less than four carriers even in the densest markets (those having more than 500 passengers per day).

Contestable Markets

average number of passengers per flight and thereby reduce costs. Essentially, the broader scope of operations lets the carrier take advantage of the economies of scale in aircraft size. Because of these advantages of hub-and-spoke operation, both the trunk and local service carriers[38] have increased their use of hubbing in the deregulation period when entry has been free. For example, in 1978, only three of the sixteen regulated airlines had twenty percent or more of their total domestic departures out of their leading city; by 1981, the number had increased to ten airlines. On the other hand, open entry has not led to extreme proliferation of carriers on routes. The average number of carriers per route has increased, but the increase has been moderate. For instance, in the post-deregulation period, approximately two carriers per route serve in the moderate-density, short-haul markets, whereas three to four carriers per route serve in the densest markets.

The condition of contestability theory that incumbents' prices must be relatively "sticky" is not met in aviation. In many cases, incumbent airlines respond immediately to meet a new competitor's lower fares. So it may not be surprising that the evidence on pricing policy since deregulation is more complex. In theory, after a transition period, potential rather than actual competition should serve to police markets. In particular, if all airlines face the same market demands and have access to the same productive techniques as those available to incumbent firms, actual entry should not be needed to limit prices, and price wars and related strategic behavior by incumbents should not be observed. We know that during the first year or two after deregulation, trunk carriers were held to lower price ceilings than local service carriers. Bailey and Panzar[39] showed that despite the presence of economies of density in city-pair airline markets, potential competition by trunk carriers was effectively policing the pricing behavior of local service carriers in their long and medium-haul routes. However, in trunk markets during that period, and in virtually all markets since then, actual (as distinguished from potential) competition has been found to play a significant role.

Graham, Kaplan and Sibley have concluded that the presence of newly

---

38. Sixteen trunk carriers were certificated in 1938; this number had shrunk through mergers to ten carriers by the time of passage of the Airline Deregulation Act. Trunk carriers are large jet aircraft operators serving dense city-pair markets. In contrast, local service carriers are specialty carriers, certificated by the Board in the mid-1950's to provide subsidized feeder service to small communities in nonoverlapping regions. By 1978, these carriers, too, were largely jet operators, but typically used smaller, two-engine jets rather than the three-engine and four-engine jets typical of the trunk carriers. For a history, see E. BAILEY, D. GRAHAM, & D. KAPLAN, DEREGULATING THE AIRLINES (forthcoming, 1984).

39. Bailey & Panzar, *The Contestability of Airline Markets During the Transition to Deregulation*, 44 LAW & CONTEMP. PROBS. 125, 134-44 (1981).

Yale Journal on Regulation   Vol. 1: 111, 1984

certificated carriers has a substantial effect on fares in the markets they serve.[40] They also found that fares are higher in markets served by the four airports[41] in which there is a shortage of landing slots and higher also in markets in which concentration is quite pronounced. Price wars have broken out on the denser routes normally flown by three-engine and four-engine jets. Moreover, incumbent carriers appear to be calculating whether or not they would be better off if they fail to match the lower fares of new entrants and learn to coexist with them rather than matching these fares in order to try to drive out the less-established enterprises. This is, of course, a behavior pattern one would expect from rival oligopolists in the standard analysis, not from players in a perfectly contestable world.

This evidence suggests that the contestability benchmark does not fully hold sway in the first years after deregulation. Why is the industry characterized by fierce rivalry rather than by quiet long-run equilibrium? The pure theory of contestable markets is an analysis of equilibrium conditions, just as the pure theory of perfect competition is. In the current reality in aviation, many of the assumptions underlying stationary equilibrium theory simply are not holding true. For example, the route network was closed to free entry for forty years. It is not reasonable to expect an instant adjustment to a deregulated equilibrium. Instead, market shares of major groups of carriers have been shifting rapidly, with the large trunk carriers losing market share to local service carriers and new entrants.[42] The doubling of fuel prices between 1978 and 1981 has had a profound effect on optimal aircraft deployment, and has meant that two-engine jets have become relatively more efficient than three-engine and four-engine jets. There is thus substantial excess capacity in three-engine and four-engine jets, and undercapacity in two-engine jets. Economic theory suggests that undercapacity will lead to higher prices until more planes can be brought on line. The expected response to overcapacity is price wars. When the excess capacity is substantial, prices will be near variable costs rather than full marginal costs (including the cost of capital). This signals to the investment community that additional capital is not required in the area.

Another standard assumption of equilibrium theory is that all players in the market have the same cost structures. This is not currently true in aviation. Costly labor contracts and associated restrictive work rules nego-

---

40. D. GRAHAM, D. KAPLAN & D. SIBLEY, EFFICIENCY AND COMPETITION IN THE AIRLINE INDUSTRY (1982) (CAB Staff Report).

41. The four are Washington's National Airport, Chicago's O'Hare Airport, and New York's Kennedy and LaGuardia Airports.

42. *See* E. BAILEY, D. GRAHAM & D. KAPLAN, *supra* note 38.

Contestable Markets

tiated during forty years of regulation bind the older trunk carriers; most of the new entrants, however, are not unionized. Thus, new entrants have a cost advantage and can earn profits at prices that are not compensatory to incumbent carriers. A third, and apparently very important, influence impeding contestability is the PATCO job action, which restricted entry into—and has provided an incentive to avoid exit from—major airports. Slots have generally been treated as a vested and non-tradable right of incumbent carriers, with entry by competing carriers largely precluded because of the freeze in capacity.[43]

The factors just discussed have impeded contestability. Given the inherent ability of airlines to move in and out of markets relatively unconstrained by sunk costs, these markets should exhibit more of the character of contestability before a great deal of time has passed. But it is unlikely that perfect contestability will be achieved over the short run since changes in labor contracts and fleet configuration cannot be carried out quickly.

Before leaving this analysis of the aviation industry, two additional implications of contestability analysis should be noted. First, even in aviation, sunk costs are present—particularly at airports. Theoretically, if a particular airline were permitted to own an airport, then it could obtain the monopoly rents associated with that airport, through the prices charged to its passengers or to the other carriers permitted to use the facilities at that airport. Thus, the prevention of control and ownership of airports by particular airlines is important for the contestability of markets in the industry. In general, rules of access to airports should be given careful consideration by policymakers. Accordingly, it is a matter for concern when local airport authorities attempt to deal with slot or noise constraints by banning new entry while permitting incumbent carriers to expand at will.[44] Another matter for concern is the appropriateness of long-term lease arrangements that allocate airport space to particular carriers and that give these carriers the power to determine when, to whom, and at what price to sublease space to their competitors.[45] A similar concern over newcomers' access has arisen with respect to computer reservations. In some regions of the country, travel agents predominantly use a single

---

43. *See* Grether, Isaac & Plott, *The Allocation of Landing Rights by Unanimity Among Competitors*, 71 AM. ECON. REV. PAPERS & PROC. 166, 167 (1981).

44. For example, San Diego sought in 1979 to exclude new airlines but did not plan to restrict new access by existing incumbents. After the FAA and CAB intervened the airport authorities withdrew their proposal. Orange County's John Wayne Airport had a similar plan which is currently under challenge in federal court. Pacific Southwest Airlines v. County of Orange, No. 81-3248 (C.D. Cal. 1983).

45. *See* AIRPORT ACCESS TASK FORCE, REPORT AND RECOMMENDATIONS (1983) (made pursuant to 49 U.S.C. § 2223) (1982).

131

system which is typically supplied by one large carrier. It has been charged that if a carrier denies access to a competitor, uses market information obtained from the reservation system to pressure travel agents to ticket on its own airline, or adopts other anticompetitive practices, the beneficial effects of entry deregulation can be stymied, at least in the short run.[46]

Second, contestability theory has important implications for merger policy. Any merger involving overlapping routes would never have been approved under the 1968 Justice Department guidelines, since, as we have mentioned, four-firm concentration ratios for virtually all city-pair routes are near one hundred percent.[47] Nevertheless, ease of entry and exit ought to be a uniform characteristic of airline markets. Thus, the assessment of mergers for such markets should rely on a functional analysis of the degree of contestability of markets rather than on market share and concentration ratio data. As long as there are comparable airlines with stations at one or both ends of the overlapping markets, the CAB does not consider a competitive problem to be present. Bailey[48] cites the case of the Houston-New Orleans market in the Texas International and National merger case. In spite of the two-firm concentration ratio of seventy-five percent after the proposed merger, the presence of eleven carriers with facilities already functioning at both ends of this market led to approval of the merger. Contestability theory indicates that it is precisely that sort of case-by-case analysis, taking into account ease of entry and exit as well as scale effects within markets, that should be used by policy-makers to evaluate the appropriateness of mergers. Indeed, it appears that the Justice Department has moved in this direction.[49]

46. In December 1982, the Conference Committee on the 1983 appropriations for the Department of Transportation was sufficiently concerned about this issue that it ordered a joint CAB and Department of Justice investigation into computer reservation system practices. *See* 128 CONG. REC. H9510, H9515 (daily ed. Dec. 13, 1982) (conference report on H.R. 7019); CIVIL AERONAUTICS BOARD, REPORT TO CONGRESS ON AIRLINE COMPUTER RESERVATIONS SYSTEMS (1983).

47. *See* Merger Guidelines of Department of Justice, 2 TRADE REG. REP. (CCH) ¶4510, at 6884 (May 30, 1968). However, the 1982 Merger Guidelines, 47 Fed. Reg. 28,493, explicitly consider potential entry both in identifying the firms to be included in the relevant market, 47 Fed. Reg. 28,495, and in assessing the ability of existing firms to raise price, 47 Fed. Reg. 28,498. Consideration of the prospects for entry into airline markets might well lead the Justice Department not to challenge an airline merger. This, of course, is entirely consistent with the implications of contestability analysis.

48. Bailey, *Contestability and the Design of Regulatory and Antitrust Policy*, 71 AM. ECON. REV. 178, 181 (1981). For a fuller description, see CIVIL AERONAUTICS BOARD, ANTITRUST POLICY FOR THE AVIATION INDUSTRY (1982).

49. 1982 Merger Guidelines, *supra* note 47, at 28,495-98.

Contestable Markets

C. *Trucking Regulation and its Partial Reform*

Theory suggests that, with the possible exception of barge transportation, trucking should be perhaps the most contestable of the economy's industries; but it has long been subjected to regulatory entry control. The largest class of ICC-regulated carriers—general freight carriers—specialize in less-than-truckload services, making multiple deliveries and pick-ups along regular routes. Regulatory control has taken the form of certificates describing the commodities permitted to be hauled and the specific cities along which each such commodity may be carried. These interventions have undercut the ability of carriers to serve routes at minimum cost since the restrictions have made it difficult to utilize capacity fully, especially on backhauls. Breyer cites studies indicating that regulated general-freight vans return empty more than one-third of the time, and that a reduction in their regulation could increase load factors by ten percent.[50] Studies also indicate that ICC restrictions on the ability of "exempt" carriers (such as private carriage by firms of their own goods, carriage of goods within states and carriage of agricultural commodities) to haul goods for movements subject to regulation has resulted in an excessive amount of empty backhauling.[51]

The Motor Carrier Act of 1980[52] liberalized entry into the less-than-truckload portion of trucking and exempted additional types of motor carrier transportation from economic regulation.[53] From the perspective of contestability, these route liberalizations offer an important opportunity for enhanced efficiency. In a recent study that attempts to distinguish between economies of scale and economies of scope in the trucking industry, Chiang offers important new evidence about how greater freedom of entry may contribute to market efficiency.[54] She found that there are strong economies of joint production in distribution networks associated with short-haul and intermediate-haul trucking shipments, particularly for small and medium-sized firms. Mergers in trucking are undertaken by firms seeking to obtain the full range of benefits afforded by these economies of scope. These findings illustrate an important feature of contestable markets: if left alone, contestable markets will tend to move toward the

---

50. *See* S. BREYER, *supra* note 36, at 225 nn. 47-48.
51. *See* P. MACAVOY & J. SNOW, REGULATION OF ENTRY AND PRICING IN TRUCK TRANSPORTATION 24-27 (1977).
52. Pub. L. No. 96-296, 94 Stat. 793 (codified as amended in scattered sections of 49 U.S.C.).
53. Additional exemptions are set forth in 49 U.S.C. § 10,526(a). Entry restrictions are eased by *id.* §§ 10,922, 10,762, & 11,145.
54. W. Chiang, Economies of Scale and Scope in Multiproduct Industries: A Case Study of the Regulated U.S. Trucking Industry (1981) (Ph.D. Dissertation, Dep't of Civil Engineering, MIT). For a discussion of other cost studies of multiproduct industries, see Bailey & Friedlaender, *Market Structure and Multiproduct Industries*, 20 J. ECON. LITERATURE 1024 (1982).

most efficient organization of productive forces.

Chiang's study shows also that there is no evidence of global economies of scale in trucking, which suggests that such firms will not attain monopoly size in an unregulated environment. Thus, regulatory inhibition of entry in trucking has been perverse in at least two respects: it has promoted inefficiency in market structure, and it has been unnecessary for the control of monopoly. Moreover, there is no evidence that barriers to entry would have emerged in trucking had regulatory intervention not occurred. Most of the trucking industry's costs are variable, consisting of trucks and drivers. The consolidation of shipments by networking or centralizing repair or administration can produce economies of scale, but these are unlikely to confer monopoly power; firms benefitting from these economies cannot raise prices much above their costs without losing business to enterprises on nearby routes that could readily extend their operations.

The Motor Carrier Act of 1980 introduced zones of price flexibility for general commodity carriage, thereby somewhat increasing the opportunity for competition.[55] Available evidence suggests that decontrol would lead to lower prices. For example, when poultry and frozen foods and vegetables were reclassified in the 1950's to fall under an agricultural exemption, rates declined over a five-year period by thirty-three percent for poultry and nineteen percent for frozen foods.[56] Breyer cites studies that show that rates are lower in intrastate than in interstate markets,[57] and that rate reductions followed the relaxation of regulations in countries such as West Germany and Australia.[58]

D. *Telecommunications Regulation and the Antitrust Case*

Although Congress has now considered legislative reform of telecommunications regulation for several years, the most dramatic regulatory changes have actually emerged from the Federal Communications Commission (FCC), the Department of Justice and the federal courts. The decisions can be characterized as attempts to isolate the segment of the telecommunications market still considered to involve technological natural monopoly, i.e., local telephone service, from segments that can, perhaps, no longer be taken to constitute natural monopolies, such as long distance services and the provision of terminal equipment. The situation has been

---

55. 49 U.S.C. § 10,708.

56. J. SNITZLER & R. BYRNE, INTERSTATE TRUCKING OF FRESH AND FROZEN POULTRY UNDER THE AGRICULTURAL EXEMPTION (1958) (Dep't of Agric. Mktg. Research Div., MRR-244); J. SNITZLER & R. BYRNE, INTERSTATE TRUCKING OF FROZEN FRUITS AND VEGETABLES UNDER THE AGRICULTURAL EXEMPTION (1959) (Dep't of Agric. Mktg. Research Div., MRR-316).

57. *See* S. BREYER, *supra* note 36, at 229 n.52.

58. *Id.* at 229 nn.54-55.

Contestable Markets

complicated primarily by the large costs common to local and long distance services and by the possible economies and externality benefits associated with joint operation of these services within a single firm.

FCC and court decisions that permit subscribers to buy terminal equipment from firms other than AT&T's subsidiary, Western Electric, and to attach the equipment to AT&T's lines raise few problems in terms of contestability analysis.[59] So long as production of this equipment is not a natural monopoly and the equipment manufactured by firms other than Western Electric does not produce noise or other forms of "harm" for the telephone network, contestability analysis suggests that regulatory policy should encourage access to local telephone systems on equal terms because of the large sunk costs associated with the provision of local service. Freedom of entry is preferred, according to the theory, over arrangements that bar local phone companies or other firms from selling telephone equipment.

The issues involving local versus long distance services are more complex, in part because of the common cost problem and in part because of the efficiencies derived from coordinated operation of an integrated network. For example, such an efficiency arises because AT&T commonly routes calls during busy periods through distant switching centers if nearer ones are operating at full capacity.[60] This is only one of a variety of network-wide planning decisions that may make production less costly when local and long distance operations are contained within one firm.[61]

On the other hand, the natural monopoly characteristics of long distance services and the large sunk costs associated with those services are being modified by technological change. Cable technology has at least to some extent been replaced in long distance markets by wireless microwave transmissions systems and, more recently, by satellites. These new techniques have opened new policy options, since, for example, it may be possible for several different firms to use microwave or satellite technology to transmit calls on many routes without significantly increasing unit costs. In a series of decisions beginning in 1959 with *Above 890*, the FCC has given a number of firms the right to use microwave transmissions for private line services, i.e., services not involving any connection with the Bell local exchange network.[62] The D.C. Circuit, in the 1977-78 *Execunet*

---

59. Hush-a-Phone Corp. v. United States, 238 F.2d 266 (D.C. Cir. 1956); Carterphone Device, 13 F.C.C.2d 420, 14 F.C.C.2d 571 (1968); Interstate Foreign Message Toll Tel. Serv. (Registration Program), 56 F.C.C.2d 593 (1975), 58 F.C.C.2d 736 (1976).
60. BELL TELEPHONE LABORATORIES, INC., ENGINEERING AND OPERATIONS IN THE BELL SYSTEM 31, 87-92 (1977).
61. *See* Southern Pac. Com. Co. v. AT&T Co., 556 F. Supp. 825, 868-70 (D.D.C. 1983).
62. Allocation of Frequencies in the Bands Above 890 Mc., 27 F.C.C. 359 (1959), *modified*, 29 F.C.C. 825 (1960). *See, e.g.*, Microwave Com., Inc., 18 F.C.C.2d 953 (1967), *reconsid. denied*, 21

rulings, overturned FCC decisions and extended freedom of entry beyond the provision of private line services, permitting entry in direct competition with Bell long distance service.[63] The *Domestic Satellites* decision permitted firms other than AT&T to use satellites to provide specialized communications services.[64] Similarly, emerging technological developments such as cellular mobile radio are threatening to erode the natural monopoly attribute of local service.[65]

The consent decree involving the Justice Department and AT&T[66] is far more wide-ranging than anything done by the FCC, as it imposed a major change in market structure. It required a complete separation of local and long distance services. Local service is now offered by a series of regulated monopolies, consisting of groupings of former Bell System operating companies. Long distance service is provided in a much more competitive environment. The Bell System is also permitted to enter unregulated markets, such as the computer market, in which the technology is becoming less and less distinguishable from that in communications.

Contestability analysis can provide some framework for discussion of the issues surrounding local and long distance service, but it does not necessarily offer definitive answers. To the extent that the consent decree has succeeded in separating markets characterized by sunk costs and natural monopoly from markets that are reasonably contestable, the decree would seem consistent with contestability analysis. Similarly, contestability analysis favors the realization of economies of scope between telecommunication and computer services which the decree permits. However, to the extent the decree prevents the realization of economies of scope between local and long distance services or results in substantial quality differences across regions with attendant degradation in all service or prevents competition when new technologies, such as cellular mobile radio, reduce sunk costs requirements, questions are raised by the analysis. These uncertainties reflect the critical importance of technological considerations in the application of contestability theory.

F.C.C.2d 190 (1970), *modifs. granted,* 27 F.C.C.2d 380 (1971); Specialized Common Carrier Servs., 29 F.C.C.2d 870 (1971), *aff'd sub nom.* Washington Util. & Transp. Comm'n v. FCC, 513 F.2d 1142 (9th Cir.), *cert. denied,* 423 U.S. 836 (1975).

63.   MCI Telecom. Corp. v. FCC (*Execunet I*), 561 F.2d 365 (D.C. Cir. 1977), *cert. denied,* 434 U.S. 1040 (1978); MCI Telecom. Corp. v. FCC (*Execunet II*), 580 F.2d 590 (D.C. Cir.), *cert. denied,* 439 U.S. 980 (1978).

64.   Domestic Communications-Satellite Facils., 35 F.C.C.2d 844, 38 F.C.C.2d 665 (1972). *See also* United States v. FCC, 652 F.2d 72 (D.C. Cir. 1981).

65.   Allocation of Frequencies in the 150.8-162 Mc/s Band, 12 F.C.C.2d 841, 14 F.C.C.2d 269 (1968), *aff'd sub nom.* Radio Relay Corp. v. FCC, 409 F.2d 322 (2d Cir. 1969); Mobile Radio Communications, Inc., 29 F.C.C.2d 62 (1971); Cellular Communications Sys., 50 RAD. REG. 2D (P & F) 1673, 51 RAD. REG. 2D (P & F) 143 (1982).

66.   United States v. AT&T Co., 552 F. Supp. 131 (D.D.C. 1982), *appeal dismissed,* United States v. Western Elec. Co., 714 F.2d 178 (D.C. Cir. 1983).

Contestable Markets

Conclusion

The new contestability theory clearly makes no pretense of solving all problems, but it does seek to identify the proper questions—how to identify circumstances in which deregulation should occur and, where continuing regulation is appropriate, what forms it should take. By focusing attention on sunk costs as a major reason for regulatory intervention, and by specifying a variety of tools and methods to minimize the market power associated with them, the contestability perspective offers some degree of direction to policymakers. Policy analysts should begin by determining what regulatory or other obstacles stand in the way of contestability and then should consider ways to reduce or eliminate them.

Contestability theory also offers a coherent analysis of market structure issues, and underscores how important investigation of actual conduct and performance is in the presence of concentration attributable to scale economies. Because there may well be sunk costs and entry barriers at an industry level, a market-by-market analysis within the industry may have to be undertaken. The new theory supports policy measures that attempt to separate out those portions of an industry in which market failures attributable to natural monopoly or other elements play an important role from those portions of the industry in which fixed, but not sunk, costs predominate, so that competition and consumer choice can contribute to quality and restrain costs. If particular markets are readily contested, there may be no need for continued intervention in these markets. Similarly, the theory suggests that even in industries where deregulation may be called for in some areas, continued regulation to maintain open access may be appropriate. In this and other ways the new theory sheds light on the appropriateness of traditional patterns of regulation and the avenues available for deregulation.

Our discussion of particular regulated industries confirms once again that reality is more complex than any theoretical model, so that the latter can never be expected to provide standardized procedures that produce cut-and-dried solutions to the problems encountered in practice. We may seek to determine appropriate boundaries between regulated and unregulated portions of an industry, but boundaries based on technological considerations alone may prove misplaced. An analysis such as that provided by contestability theory, while not free of difficulties, can reasonably aspire to offer the practitioner greater confidence and clearer insight into the pertinent issues.

[27]

How Natural Is Monopoly?
The Case of Bypass in Natural Gas
Distribution Markets

Harry G. Broadman†
Joseph P. Kalt††

Public utility markets in the United States are commonly subject to both price and entry regulation. However, as dissatisfaction with much of the nation's regulatory system has mounted within the last decade, the wisdom of protecting utilities from competitors has come increasingly under attack.[1] Numerous court cases and administrative rulings by regulatory agencies,[2] as well as developments in the economics literature,[3] have pointed to the benefits of allowing existing buyers of a utility's services to "bypass" the utility and transact for the services with either incumbent firms or new entrants.[4] The issue of entry deregulation has been at the heart of debates over regulatory reform in such industries as telecommunications,[5] cable and satellite television transmission,[6] the postal service,[7] and electricity generation.[8]

---

† Chief Economist, U.S. Senate Governmental Affairs Committee and Professorial Lecturer at the School of Advanced International Studies, Johns Hopkins University. When the research underlying this article was completed, Dr. Broadman was on the faculty at Harvard University, on leave from Resources for the Future.

†† Professor of Political Economy, John F. Kennedy School of Government, Harvard University.

This research was supported by Harvard University's Energy and Environmental Policy Center and by Resources for the Future. The views expressed herein are the authors' alone and should not be attributed to their respective institutions; nor do these views reflect any exercise of official legislative or regulatory responsibility.

1. For an excellent review of relevant literature, see Bailey & Baumol, Deregulation and the Theory of Contestable Markets, 1 YALE J. ON REG. 111 (1984).

2. See infra Parts I, II.

3. See infra Part III.

4. For a more general and formal definition of bypass, see infra Part III.

5. See, e.g., Copeland & Severn, Price Theory and Telecommunications Regulation: A Dissenting View, 3 YALE J. ON REG. 53, 74 (1985).

6. See, e.g., Owen, The Rise and Fall of Cable Television Regulation, in CASE STUDIES IN REGULATION 86, 91-92 (L. Weiss & M. Klass eds. 1981).

7. See, e.g., Sherman, Pricing Policies of the U.S. Postal Service, in REGULATED INDUSTRIES AND PUBLIC ENTERPRISE: EUROPEAN AND UNITED STATES PERSPECTIVES 95 (B. Mitchell & P. Kleindorfer eds. 1980).

8. See, e.g., P. JOSKOW & R. SCHMALENSEE, MARKETS FOR POWER: AN ANALYSIS OF ELECTRIC UTILITY DEREGULATION 22 (1983).

Yale Journal on Regulation   Vol. 6: 181, 1989

The bypass issue recently has come to the fore in the natural gas industry. Legislative changes mandated by the Natural Gas Policy Act of 1978 (the NGPA)[9] and administrative reforms taken by the Federal Energy Regulatory Commission (FERC)[10] have fundamentally transformed the way in which the wellhead and pipeline segments of the industry are regulated.[11] These actions have created pressure to change the industry downstream at the level of the local distribution company (LDC). Large industrial customers served by LDCs are increasingly seeking ways, previously forbidden or drastically constrained, to buy cheaper gas either directly from trunk system supplies of nearby interstate pipelines or directly from producers. In the latter case, the gas is transported to the end-user via pipeline "contract carriage."[12]

---

9. Pub. L. No. 95-621, 92 Stat. 3352 (codified at 15 U.S.C. §§ 3301-3342 (1982)).

10. See, e.g., Regulation of Natural Gas Pipelines after Partial Wellhead Decontrol, FERC Order No. 436, 50 Fed. Reg. 42,408 (1985) (to be codified at 18 C.F.R. §§ 2, 157, 250, 284, 375, 381) [hereinafter FERC Order No. 436]; Regulation of Natural Gas Pipelines after Partial Wellhead Decontrol, FERC Order No. 500, 52 Fed. Reg. 30,334 (1987) (to be codified at 18 C.F.R. §§ 2, 284) [hereinafter FERC Order No. 500].

11. The natural gas industry comprises three major segments: (1) the wellhead or production segment, in which natural gas is extracted from the ground (often as a joint-product with petroleum) and then sold by producers to pipeline companies; (2) the pipeline segment, dominated by interstate pipeline companies that transport the gas over long distance "trunk" pipelines to the "city gate" and then re-sell it to local distribution companies and large industrial direct end-users; and (3) the local distribution segment, in which utility companies distribute the gas locally and resell it to industrial, smaller commercial, and residential customers. The rates charged by both interstate pipeline companies and LDCs for the gas supplies and transportation services that they sell are regulated. In general, both types of firm are also subject to entry and exit regulation. Firms seeking entry must obtain a "certificate of convenience and necessity." Those seeking exit must be granted permission for "abandonment." Finally, both are typically awarded exclusive territorial franchises that carry with them various types of "service obligations" that must be fulfilled. For an overview of these issues and the recent policy changes that have taken place in the gas industry, see Broadman, Natural Gas Deregulation: The Need for Further Reform, 5 J. Pol'y Analysis & Mgmt. 496, 496-99 (1986).

12. Historically, interstate pipeline companies have mainly operated as "private carriers," taking title to and reselling the gas that they transport. Recently, pipeline companies have increasingly operated as "contract carriers," serving not as merchants of gas supplies, but rather selling transport services to parties who have arranged to purchase gas directly from producers. Under the Natural Gas Act of 1938, ch. 556, § 7, 52 Stat. 821, 824-25 (codified as amended at 15 U.S.C. § 717 (1982)) (the NGA), pipelines that operate as private carriers generally have the discretion to decide to whom they will provide service. Also, the NGA authorizes the pipelines to decide the relative extent to which they will engage in private carriage or contract carriage. Thus, unlike most other transportation industries, natural gas pipeline companies are not statutorily subject to the rules of "common carriage" that would obligate them to serve all customers who request service. LDCs also have operated mainly in the private carriage mode, and they, too, are increasingly offering contract carriage service. For more discussion, see Broadman, Montgomery & Russell, Field Price Deregulation and the Carrier Status of Natural Gas

How Natural Is Monopoly?

Interstate pipeline companies burdened by excess "deliverability" of gas supplies are seeking new downstream customers, especially large industrial end-users.[13] These pressures challenge the traditional control of downstream gas markets by LDCs.

The argument over bypass of LDCs has been spirited, pitting bypassing industrial end-users against "captive" residential customers.[14] The debate has also raised the difficult issue of the appropriate boundary between federal and state regulatory authority. Perhaps most important, it has prompted a fundamental reassessment of the role of LDC service obligations and other elements of the traditional arrangement between LDCs and public utilities commissions (PUCs). Natural gas bypass policy is now being determined through high-stakes court cases,[15] state legislation,[16] politicized PUC decisions,[17] and heated arguments before FERC commissioners and administrative law judges.[18]

This Article provides an analysis of the issues surrounding bypass in local natural gas distribution markets. Its ultimate objective is to develop a conceptual framework for analyzing both the extent of natural monopoly in these markets and the desirability of institutionally protecting LDCs from competitive entry. Part I describes relevant institutional developments in the gas industry. These include regulatory and legislative changes that have increased the incidence of proposals for and, in some cases, the consummation of bypass. Part II reviews the involvement of state legislatures, state and federal regulatory bodies, and the courts in the development of natural gas bypass policy. Part III develops a conceptual framework for analyzing whether natural monopolies exist in these markets and whether protecting LDCs from competitive entry is worthwhile. Part IV provides a taxonomy of the costs and benefits of permitting bypass. This Article concludes with a discussion of the principal lessons for policy-making. Our conclusions mirror the recent developments in the

Pipelines, 6 ENERGY J. 127 (1985).

13. See Kalt & Schuller, Introduction: Natural Gas Policy in Turmoil, in DRAWING THE LINE ON NATURAL GAS REGULATION: THE HARVARD STUDY ON THE FUTURE OF NATURAL GAS 1 (J. Kalt & F. Schuller eds. 1987) [hereinafter DRAWING THE LINE].

14. For a sample of the controversy, see Blaydon, State Policies Under Pressure, in DRAWING THE LINE, supra note 13, at 157; Johnston & Sullins, Comments on Blaydon, in DRAWING THE LINE, supra note 13, at 170; Stewart, Natural Gas on a Frontier of New Challenges, PUB. UTIL. FORT., May 14, 1987, at 9, 13.

15. See infra notes 35-39, 58-60 and accompanying text.

16. See infra notes 50-57 and accompanying text.

17. See infra notes 45-49 and accompanying text.

18. See infra notes 61-86 and accompanying text.

economics literature concerning the wisdom of regulation.[19] While
there are theoretical circumstances under which bypass in certain
types of naturally monopolistic industries can be inefficient, there
is less need for the current scope of entry restrictions in local
natural gas distribution markets than is commonly practiced.

I. The Incentives and Constraints That Shape Bypass

Modern regulatory reform of natural gas markets began in
1978 with gradual wellhead price deregulation under the NGPA.
Since then, reform has been working its way steadily downstream.
The phenomenon of LDC bypass stems most directly from major
modifications in federal interstate pipeline regulation introduced
in October 1985 under FERC Order 436.[20] FERC Order 500,
which was issued in August 1987, also directly affects the
prospects for LDC bypass.[21]

Order 436 gives pipeline customers potentially greater access
to contract carriage service on the interstate trunk system.[22]
Customers served by a pipeline that receives blanket authorization
to become a "nondiscriminatory contract carrier" or an "open
access carrier" under Order 436 also receive a greater opportunity to purchase gas in the open, spot market or directly from
gas producers.[23] To the extent that these direct transactions
provide end-users with lower costs or delivery under more
reliable terms, they create incentives for customers to bypass the
merchant function of the LDC.

In general, three factors create the incentive for bypass of
LDCs. First, an LDC may be saddled with relatively expensive
contracts with its pipeline-suppliers, resulting in an overall level
of rates that is not competitive with either other gas sources or

---

19. See Bailey & Baumol, supra note 1.

20. FERC Order No. 436, supra note 10. For a detailed description and critique, see
Broadman, Deregulating Entry and Access to Pipelines, in DRAWING THE LINE, supra note 13,
at 125.

21. FERC Order No. 500, supra note 10. See generally WASH. LETTER, Aug. 14, 1987
(newsletter of the Am. Gas Ass'n, Arlington, Va).

22. FERC Order No. 436, supra note 10, at 42,409-10, 42,424-26.

23. Rather than requiring a pipeline to obtain permission from FERC for contract
carriage on a case-by-case basis—the traditional route followed to engage in such
service—Order 436 allows a pipeline company to get blanket, or pre-approved, authorization
to operate as a contract carrier. One stipulation of receiving this blanket authority is that
if the pipeline company offers contract carriage service to one party, it must offer such
service to all parties; that is, it must operate as a "nondiscriminatory contract carrier" or
"open access carrier." Id. at 42,424-25.

How Natural Is Monopoly?

alternative fuels.[24] Second, an LDC's rate design or structure may be economically inefficient. Relatively high rates may be charged to large industrial customers, which often have elastic, "interruptible" demand, while relatively low rates are charged to residential and small commercial customers, which typically have inelastic, "firm" demand.[25] Finally, an LDC may not offer the type of service that its end-users desire. For example, some large industrial customers require firm private carriage distribution service, but their LDC suppliers do not offer it to them.[26] More often, unmet demands for LDC contract carriage service provoke bypass.[27] If an LDC is unwilling to provide its own "unbundled" contract carriage service to match the service provided by the interstate pipeline, or if such service is not competitively priced, end-users will have incentives to bypass both the merchant and transport functions of the LDC. The distinction between complete and partial bypass is important. As this Article argues more fully below,[28] the situations in which the social interest lies in constraining entry arise primarily in connection with attempts to bypass the transport function in ways that lead to wastefully duplicative physical investments.

Order 436 eases restrictions on a pipeline company's ability to enter downstream end-use markets by building new facilities and selling either pipeline-owned gas or pipeline contract carriage transportation services directly to end-users.[29] It eliminates the need to gain approval for entry through the traditional and lengthy process of applying for a certificate of convenience and necessity under Section 7 of the Natural Gas Act of 1938 (the

24. See, e.g., Blaydon, supra note 14, at 167.

25. See, e.g., J. KALT, THE REDESIGN OF RATE STRUCTURES AND CAPACITY AUCTIONING IN THE NATURAL GAS PIPELINE INDUSTRY 12-19 (Energy and Environmental Policy Center, Harvard University, Discussion Paper Series No. E-88-04, 1988).

26. See Mojave Pipeline Co., 35 Fed. Energy Reg. Comm'n Rep. (CCH) ¶ 61,199, at 61,459, 61,466 (May 19, 1986) (Docket Nos. CP85-437 et al.) (order consolidating proceedings for comparative hearing) [hereinafter Mojave Pipeline].

27. See INTERSTATE NATURAL GAS ASS'N OF AM., THE INTERPLAY OF FEDERAL AND CONSUMING STATE REGULATIONS (Research Report 86-3, 1986) [hereinafter INGAA]. Of course, the relevant decisions regarding rates and other terms of LDC service do not rest solely with the utilities. Such matters are also under the purview of the PUCs. These state agencies have their own agendas and objectives that may or may not accord with the LDC's. For a general discussion of the role of PUCs, see 2 A. KAHN, THE ECONOMICS OF REGULATION 10-11 (1971). See also Lambert, Bypass in the Natural Gas Industry, PUB. UTIL. FORT., Apr. 3, 1986, at 11.

28. See infra Part III.

29. FERC Order No. 436, supra note 10, at 42,467-76.

NGA).[30] A company that agrees to operate as a nondiscriminatory contract carrier can now receive expedited and pre-approved authorization of entry. In return, it must bear all the risk of cost recovery from the new investments.[31] This expedited entry permits pipeline companies to seize rapidly and aggressively market opportunities as they arise.

Notwithstanding the incentives toward bypass that Order 436 generates, some of its provisions act as disincentives to bypass. Under Order 436, an LDC may reduce its firm contract demand for pipelines' gas or firm transport demand for pipelines' capacity to zero over a period of five years.[32] Alternatively, the LDC can convert its firm contract demand to firm transport demand, also over a five-year period.[33] In either case, these provisions give LDCs the ability to reduce their gas costs, thereby discouraging bypass investment.[34]

In June of 1987, in *Associated Gas Distributors v. Federal Energy Regulatory Commission*,[35] the Court of Appeals for the District of Columbia remanded portions of Order 436 to FERC. However, the court approved the central goal of the Order: to open natural gas markets to greater competition by changing the nature of pipeline regulation. As a result, the court affirmed both the open access carriage and expedited entry provisions of Order 436.[36]

Order 500 is FERC's response to the court's remand.[37] Although Order 500 leaves the basic thrust of Order 436 intact, it affects the terms under which LDCs can alter their contractual relationships with pipelines.[38] In *Associated Gas*, the court had ruled that there was no legal basis for allowing LDCs to reduce

---

30. Natural Gas Act of 1938, ch. 556, § 7, 52 Stat. 821, 824-25 (codified at 15 U.S.C. § 717 (1982)).

31. FERC Order No. 436, supra note 10, at 42,467.

32. Id. at 42,425-26, 42,438-47.

33. Id. Contract demand is the maximum amount of gas supplies (as opposed to transport capacity) that a pipeline is obligated to provide to a customer.

34. This ability is contingent upon the LDC's pipeline volunteering to be nondiscriminatory contract carriers. Because these reductions and conversions of contract demand and transport capacity amount to a form of pipeline bypass, pipeline companies have a disincentive to apply for nondiscriminatory contract carrier status. Indeed, they may prefer to attempt to bypass the LDC in concert with end-users.

35. 824 F.2d 981 (D.C. Cir. 1987), cert. denied, 108 S.Ct. 1468 (1988).

36. 824 F.2d at 1044. See also Regulation of Natural Gas Pipelines after Partial Wellhead Decontrol, FERC Order No. 436-A, 50 Fed. Reg. 52,217 (1985) (to be codified at 18 C.F.R. §§ 2, 157, 284, 375).

37. FERC Order No. 500, supra note 10.

38. Id. at 30,347-48.

How Natural Is Monopoly?

their firm contract demand or firm transport demand unless pipelines were relieved of their corresponding city gate service obligations and their wellhead take-or-pay liabilities.[39] Thus, Order 500 retains the Order 436 conversion provision and eliminates the reduction provision.[40] Inasmuch as this modification limits LDCs' abilities to bargain with relatively costly pipeline-suppliers, the prospects for bypass are increased.[41] Moreover, Order 500 authorizes pipelines to devise inventory charges for customers to provide for a type of cost-sharing scheme that mitigates pipelines' exposure to take-or-pay liabilities.[42] Again, all other things equal, this creates greater pressure for end-users to bypass their LDCs.

There is little doubt that FERC wants the market, rather than regulation, to govern gas sales and investments. As FERC promotes this objective in downstream markets, however, conflicts between federal and state regulators arise. When interstate pipelines can bypass LDCs and deal directly with gas customers, they challenge the scope of state PUC regulation. FERC has articulated its views on the impact of bypass on state-federal relations in Order 436 and Order 500. For example, Order 436 states that unless "pipelines engage in unfair competitive practices or other circumstances are present that would make it unfair for a pipeline to bypass the distributor," "[t]he Commission will not insulate the LDC markets from the competitive incentives that are the foundation of the final rule."[43] This implies that if there are effects at the local level from FERC actions that create pressures on state policies, it is the PUCs' responsibility to devise policies that minimize or eliminate them. In the case of bypass, this can mean adjustments such as improved LDC rate design or the unbundling of LDC transportation.

The direct competition between pipelines and LDCs that bypass causes raises complicated questions of state and federal rights. From the states' perspective, bypass threatens the presumed

---

39. 824 F.2d at 1021-30. A "take-or-pay" provision is a typical component of a wellhead contract between natural gas producers and a pipeline. Together with the contract's price provisions, it specifies the minimum payment that must be made to the producer by requiring that the pipeline pay for a certain quantity of gas, regardless of whether delivery is actually taken.

40. FERC Order No. 500, supra note 10, at 30,347-48.

41. An LDC could still combat bypass by making transportation services available and by securing cheaper gas supplies. Alternatively, an LDC can now also unbundle and offer contract carriage service and face a bypass threat only if pipelines not serving the LDC can build spurs to its customers and offer gas that is sufficiently less expensive to compensate for the new investment costs.

42. FERC Order No. 500, supra note 10, at 30,355.

43. FERC Order No. 436, supra note 10, at 42,468.

exclusivity of LDC service franchises. Even more fundamental, states may see bypass as a threat to their abilities to implement economic and social policy through gas utility rates and policies.[44] The argument supporting federal jurisdiction over bypass stresses that neither the shareholders of affected industrial gas users nor the ultimate buyers of such users' products reside entirely, or even predominantly, within the state where the gas is used. Accordingly, only federal authorities can take account of an appropriately broad range of interests when formulating policy.

II.   Recent Actions Affecting Bypass Policy

The tensions over appropriate bypass policy have been highlighted recently by specific activities of various PUCs and state legislatures, as well as by suits filed in the federal courts and before FERC. Although systematic data on these activities are not available from one central source or collected in a uniform manner, enough information can be obtained to put together a rough profile of recent legislative, judicial, and administrative actions. This Part outlines that profile.

A.   Bypass Policy-Making by PUCs

According to a recent survey by the Interstate Natural Gas Association of America (INGAA) of twenty-two PUCs that regulate firms comprising 84% of the national gas market, ten had addressed proposals for bypass between 1981 and 1985.[45] The INGAA survey indicated the degree to which PUCs believe that they have the legal authority to approve or to reject bypass proposals. Whereas two of the PUCs surveyed, regulating 11% of the market, asserted that they had such authority, eighteen, or 62% of the market, claimed their authority on bypass is legally untested and hence uncertain. Only two PUCs, or 11% of the market, stated that they do not possess the authority to rule on bypass.[46]

Different PUCs have adopted different roles in court and FERC cases dealing with bypass. Some have taken an activist posture,

---

44. See, e.g., Mojave Pipeline, *supra* note 26, at 61,460 (discussing motion of California PUC to dismiss Mojave application).

45. INGAA, *supra* note 27, at 10.

46. *Id.* at 11.

How Natural Is Monopoly?

usually in opposition to bypass;[47] others have been passive, letting the LDC and aligned parties sue the prospective bypassing customer and supplier on their own.[48] With respect to their own regulatory policies, certain PUCs have responded to prospective bypass by encouraging LDCs to offer contract carriage service as a method of preempting new competition.[49]

B. The Role of State Legislatures

State legislatures also have begun to play significant roles in determining the environment in which bypass incentives operate. For example, Indiana recently passed legislation that grants its PUC the authority to approve or to deny bypass investment.[50] Other legislatures passed similar statutes many years ago.[51]

Another way in which legislatures have affected bypass policy is by enacting statutes that subject direct transactions between interstate pipelines and industrial customers to the certification process and rate regulation administered by the PUC. This legislation transforms federally-regulated direct connection interstate pipelines into state-regulated public utilities. By the beginning of 1986, only ten states had passed this type of legislation.[52] Thus, in most states, bypass facilities are not consid-

---

47. See, e.g., Mojave Pipeline, supra note 26, at 61,460.

48. See ANR Pipeline Co., 34 Fed. Energy Reg. Comm'n Rep. (CCH) ¶ 61,238 (Feb. 20, 1986) (Docket Nos. CP84-386 et al.) (order setting case for hearing) [hereinafter ANR Pipeline I]. See also infra notes 62-68 and accompanying text.

49. A survey of 44 PUCs by the Missouri Public Service Commission indicates that LDCs in nine states do not transport gas on a contract carriage basis. For the 35 PUCs indicating that contract carriage does take place in their states, the survey results suggest that the conditions under which such service is offered vary considerably from state to state. For example, only ten of the surveyed PUCs have instituted a program of mandatory LDC contract carriage, California's unfolding program being the most far-reaching. In the 25 other states, LDCs have discretion whether to offer access to LDC contract carriage. See Pub. Serv. Comm'n of Missouri, The Instigation of Developments in the Transportation of Natural Gas and Their Relevance to the Regulation of Natural Gas Corporations in Missouri Section VI (1986). Independent of whether or not access to LDC contract carriage is mandatory or voluntary, however, LDCs may or may not be required to post tariffs for contract carriage service with their PUCs. Of the 35 states in the Missouri Public Service Commission survey that have LDC contract carriage, only 24 mandate that associated tariffs be filed. Id.

50. Ind. Code Ann. § 8-1-2-87.5 (Burns 1988). Indiana's law was passed in 1985.

51. See, e.g., Mich. Comp. Laws Ann. § 483.103 (West 1987). The Michigan statute dates back to 1929. See INGAA, supra note 27, at 10.

52. See INGAA Poll Finds Widespread Implementation of State Carriage Program, Inside F.E.R.C., Dec. 23, 1985, at 9. New York, Pennsylvania, Iowa, and Florida have mandatory transportation. Illinois, Michigan, New Jersey, Colorado, Indiana, and Ohio have active voluntary transportation programs.

ered to be public utilities in statutory terms.[53] Moreover, as is true in Mississippi,[54] some states exempt utilities that serve very small numbers of customers from PUC regulation.[55]

State legislatures have also been active in developing statutes to regulate LDC contract carriage. West Virginia, for example, recently has enacted enabling legislation that instructs its PUC to design rules for mandatory contract carriage by LDCs that operate within the state.[56] Under their legislative mandates, PUCs in states such as New York, Pennsylvania, and California have already moved to allow their respective LDCs to establish contract carriage service.[57]

C. Actions by the Judicial System Affecting Bypass Policy

Because of the conflict over jurisdiction and resource allocation that bypass engenders, it is not surprising that litigation also is shaping bypass policy. Aside from Associated Gas,[58] the most significant case on the bypass issue is the May 1987 settlement of District of Columbia Hospital Energy Cooperative Inc. v. Washington Gas Light Co.[59] The plaintiffs were a group of seven Washington, D.C. hospitals that had arranged for direct discounted spot purchases of gas from Yankee Resources, an independent supplier based in Ohio. The hospitals sought to have the local transportation of that gas performed by their LDC, Washington Gas Light Co. (WGL). When WGL refused to provide the contract carriage service requested, the hospitals sued WGL. The essence of the hospitals' allegations was that it was anti-competitive for WGL to attempt to extend a franchise monopoly in the transmission and distribution of gas into an unsanctioned monopoly in the purchase and sale of gas to end-users. Whether the hospitals ultimately would have sought complete bypass of

53. PUCs can assert that their jurisdiction covers direct sales made locally by an interstate pipeline, but these assertions inevitably must meet with the approval of the legislature and the courts. For a sampling of PUC decisions in this regard, see Burkhart, Gas System Bypass: Can States Regulate Direct Sales by Interstate Pipelines?, Pub. Util. Fort., July 9, 1987, at 45.

54. Miss. Code Ann. § 77-11-307 (1988 Supp.).

55. See INGAA, supra note 27, at 10.

56. W. Va. Code § 24-1-2 (1986); see also United Fuel Gas Co. v. Battle, 153 W.Va. 222, 167 S.E. 2d 890 (W.Va. 1969), cert. denied, 396 U.S. 116 (1969).

57. Lambert, supra note 27, at 16.

58. Associated Gas Distribs. v. Federal Energy Regulatory Comm'n, 824 F.2d 981 (D.C. Cir. 1987), cert. denied, 108 S. Ct. 1468 (1988).

59. No. 85-3720 (D.D.C., filed Nov. 20, 1985).

How Natural Is Monopoly?

WGL's system is not known. In any event, under the terms of the settlement, WGL agreed to seek regulatory approval from the District of Columbia Public Service Commission to carry out contract carriage service for gas customers within the District of Columbia. WGL filed its contract carriage tariff in June 1987.[60]

The Role of FERC in Shaping Bypass Policy

Several bypass cases before FERC are having a profound effect on the nature of bypass policy. Two of the more important cases were settled before FERC reached a final decision. One such case involved a Columbia Nitrogen fertilizer plant in Georgia that sought to bypass its LDC, Atlanta Gas Light Company (Atlanta Gas).[61] The proposed bypass would have entailed building a spur line of less than one mile in length to connect the Southern Natural Gas Pipeline Company (Southern Natural) to the fertilizer plant. Columbia Nitrogen estimated that at the rates that Atlanta Gas was charging, it would have been able to save approximately $3 million annually through the bypass investment. Atlanta Gas argued that because it was Southern Natural's largest customer and Columbia Nitrogen was in turn Atlanta Gas' largest customer, the "loss of load" engendered by the bypass (approximately 70,000 million BTU per day of interruptible sales) would have increased its overall average gas costs and imposed a larger portion of its fixed costs upon residential and small commercial customers. Atlanta Gas was joined in opposing Southern Natural's application before FERC by other customers of Southern Natural, the Consumers' Utility Counsel of Georgia, and most important, the Georgia Public Service Commission (the GPSC). Before FERC was able to reach a decision, the GPSC instituted rules allowing Atlanta Gas to offer both contract carriage service and market sensitive rates to industrial end-users. Upon the appearance of the improved service offering and lower tariffs, Columbia Nitrogen withdrew its bypass proposal.

---

60. While the case focused on the hospitals' desire for contract carriage access to WGL's system, the hospitals recently appealed the rates that WGL filed for such service, alleging that they are set too high. See Chandler, Bargain-Price Natural Gas Flowing to Area Hospitals, Wash. Post, Aug. 29, 1987, at D9, col. 5.

61. Southern Natural Gas Co., FERC Docket No. CP85-529 (1985) (application withdrawn prior to official action) [hereinafter Southern Natural]. See Fertilizer Plant Would Bypass Distributor Under Southern Natural Deal, INSIDE F.E.R.C., May 27, 1985, at 1; Southern Natural Customers, State Regulators Fight Bypass, INSIDE F.E.R.C., July 15, 1985, at 6.

A similar FERC case involved Bethlehem Steel Corporation's (Bethlehem) plant in Burns Harbor, Indiana and the LDC serving that plant, the Northern Indiana Public Service Company (NIPSCO).[62] Bethlehem had proposed to build a short pipeline to connect its Burns Harbor plant directly to the ANR Pipeline Company (ANR), one of the trunk lines from which NIPSCO purchases its gas.[63] Bethlehem alleged that access to alternative supplies for its interruptible demand would allow it to lower its costs.[64] While Bethlehem would have used the bypass spur with ANR to fulfill its interruptible requirements, Bethlehem still would have relied on NIPSCO for its firm demands.[65] Thus, Bethlehem was proposing only a partial bypass of NIPSCO's system. NIPSCO alleged that the Bethlehem-ANR bypass would shift significant costs to NIPSCO's residential and small commercial customers.[66] Bethlehem argued before FERC that NIPSCO's rates were inappropriately "inverted," with interruptible rates exceeding those for higher quality firm service.[67] Ultimately, Bethlehem and ANR withdrew their proposal in return for a significant adjustment of NIPSCO's rates for interruptible sales to Bethlehem.[68]

The most important FERC adjudication on bypass to date is FERC's recent decision on a case involving Panhandle Eastern Pipeline Company (Panhandle), National Steel Corporation (National Steel), and Michigan Consolidated Gas Company (MichCon).[69] National Steel arranged for direct purchases of gas supplies in Oklahoma from Union Texas Corporation at facilities that are connected to Panhandle's system.[70] National Steel argued that at MichCon's current rates, it could realize significant cost savings if it bypassed MichCon.[71] National Steel, however, stated that if MichCon lowered its rates it would regain the opportunity

---

62. ANR Pipeline I, supra note 48. Both authors served as consultants to Bethlehem Steel Corporation for this case.

63. Id. at 61,409-10.

64. Id. at 61,411.

65. Id. at 61,409, 61,411.

66. Id. at 61,410.

67. Id. at 61,411.

68. ANR Pipeline Co., 39 Fed. Energy Reg. Comm'n Rep. (CCH) ¶ 65,031 (Apr. 15, 1987) (Docket Nos. CP84-386 et al.) (initial decision dismissing proceeding without prejudice), aff'd, 39 Fed. Energy Reg. Comm'n Rep. (CCH) ¶ 61,205 (May 26, 1987).

69. Panhandle Eastern Pipeline Co., 38 Fed. Energy Reg. Comm'n Rep. (CCH) ¶ 63,009 (Jan. 22, 1987) (Docket Nos. CP86-232 et al.) (initial decision) [hereinafter Panhandle I].

70. Id. at 65,034.

71. Id. at 65,034.

How Natural Is Monopoly?

to supply National Steel.[72] Moreover, National Steel asserted that the plant would further diversify its supply options with other fuels even if the proposed bypass was approved.[73] MichCon argued that Panhandle was proposing to charge discriminatory rates for its transportation service that made competition with the bypass virtually impossible.[74] MichCon further contended that the loss of National Steel as its customer would lead to a reduction of about $10 million in annual revenues.[75] The costs covered by these revenues necessarily would have to be spread among MichCon's remaining customers.[76]

Despite MichCon's arguments, FERC decided against MichCon and affirmed the administrative law judge's decision to grant Panhandle and National Steel their application for the bypass.[77] The first decision had noted, in part, that "the potential detriments to MichCon and its customers will occur regardless of whether the application . . . is granted because National Steel has a viable other supply option,"[78] and that "any potential detriment to MichCon's other customers from granting the application . . . is speculative since MichCon would not file for a rate increase with the Michigan Public Service Commission solely because of the loss of National Steel's load."[79] Thus, it was FERC's judgement that because National Steel had alternate supply arrangements available, it already had effectively bypassed MichCon.[80] In addition, because MichCon did not intend to seek an increase in its rates if the National Steel bypass were approved, FERC concluded that any resulting losses would not have to be made up through higher rates for the remaining customers.[81]

The most hotly contested bypass case to date is currently before FERC.[82] The Mojave case involves the applications of two

72. Id. at 65,036.
73. Id. at 65,035.
74. Id. at 65,038, 65,039.
75. Id. at 65,038.
76. Id. at 65,038.
77. Panhandle Eastern Pipeline Co., 40 Fed. Energy Reg. Comm'n Rep. (CCH) ¶ 61,220 (Sept. 10, 1987) (Opinion No. 275-A, Docket Nos. CP86-232 et al.) [hereinafter Panhandle II].
78. Panhandle I, supra note 69, at 65,076.
79. Id.
80. Panhandle II, supra note 77, at 61,752.
81. Id. at 61,752, affirming Panhandle I, supra note 69, at 65,076.
82. Mojave Pipeline, supra note 26. See also Mojave Application is 'Subterfuge' to Evade Jurisdiction, CPUC Charges, Inside F.E.R.C., July 1, 1985, at 10; CPUC Can't Meet Hinshaw Test in Jurisdictional Dispute, Mojave Says, Inside F.E.R.C., July 15, 1985, at 8. Dr. Kalt is serving as a consultant in the Mojave case.

interstate pipeline companies, Mojave and Kern River, to serve directly enhanced oil recovery (EOR)[83] gas customers in central California. The proposed systems would allow EOR customers to bypass the intrastate distribution facilities of Pacific Gas and Electric (PG&E) and Southern California Gas (SoCal).[84] The bypass applications are a response to EOR producers' complaints that they have been disfavored customers in California, receiving low-quality yet expensive service from PG&E and SoCal.[85] The California Public Utility Commission (the CPUC)—a party to the case in opposition to the bypass—has responded by implementing new rules designed to improve opportunities for service and to rationalize rates for the EOR gas market. The CPUC, PG&E, and SoCal argue that approval of the bypass will in turn impose a greater share of the utilities' fixed costs upon the remaining customers and result in duplication of facilities.[86] The EOR producers contend that if the threat of bypass were removed, they would again be subject to the market power of the LDC and the political objectives of the CPUC. The producers also argue that competition will block the actual construction of new facilities if they are wastefully duplicative.

The Mojave case will have a major effect on the future of bypass policy if for no other reason than the size of the market at issue and the number of parties involved. One of the case's more interesting characteristics is the fact that the EOR producers' position suggests that they find the political risks of conducting business with competing pipelines regulated by competing levels of government more palatable than the political risks of conducting business with LDCs regulated by the California state government alone. That may well be a harbinger of future bypass proposals.

E. Bypass Policy Lessons Learned from the Legal Battles

The recent litigation over bypass illustrates the major themes around which cogent assessments of relevant public policy should be structured. The public clearly has an interest in avoiding

---

83. "Enhanced oil recovery" refers to a process in which steam or other agents are applied to the drilling procedure to increase the amount of petroleum obtained from a given deposit. Mojave Pipeline, supra note 26, at 61,458.
    84. Id. at 61,459, 61,460.
    85. Id. at 61,466.
    86. Id. at 61,459-61.

How Natural Is Monopoly?

wasteful use of scarce resources, and if bypass facilities merely duplicate services already available from state-regulated LDCs, they are wasteful. Yet, public policy with respect to bypass does not determine whether bypass facilities are built or not; it only determines whether market entrants are able to compete for the chance to provide their services. As the cases mentioned above show, the mere prospect of new entry can engender improvements in LDC rates and services that out-compete a proposed bypass and therefore eliminate the need for building bypass facilities.

The foregoing cases highlight the equity issues that bypass policy raises. Industrial gas users stand to benefit the most from allowing the possibility of bypass while LDCs and their non-bypassing customers find the competition introduced when bypass is permitted threatening. This split is mirrored in the federal-state tensions over bypass policy, with state regulators particularly sensitive to in-state, residential consumers' interests and the federal authorities seeing a broader, national set of gas users. Assertions in the political arena, or even in the courts, rarely provide guidance for policymakers to use in the face of such conflicts. Accordingly, a systematic framework for analyzing the costs, benefits, and probability of consummated bypass should be developed.

III. Bypass and the Theory of Entry Regulation

Up to this point it has been necessary to define only loosely what is meant by bypass. However, a more formal definition is needed to develop an analytical framework of the economic determinants and the costs and benefits of bypass. A customer bypasses a regulated utility when it discontinues the purchase of a service or product from the utility and instead: (1) buys the service or product from a utility in another service area (horizontal competition); (2) buys the service or product from a party upstream from the utility (vertical competition); (3) produces the service or product itself through, for example, internal production of synthetic natural gas or electrical cogeneration (vertical integration); or (4) buys a service or product that is a close substitute for that provided by the utility. An example of this final form of bypass is the use of dual-fired boilers or other means of fuel switching.

The central economic implications of bypass can be segregated along familiar efficiency and equity lines. Within the context of regulatory practices that traditionally have protected exclusive territorial franchises from the threat of entry, a crucial question of regulatory efficiency is presented: when is an incumbent utility susceptible to inefficient entry? Inefficient bypass may be defined as entry that engenders social costs in excess of social benefits. Addressing the efficiency of bypass raises other questions as well. How can competition exist in a market presumed to be a natural monopoly? If a regulated utility and competitors can co-exist, is the granting of an exclusive franchise to the utility warranted? Should the utility continue to be subject to a legal obligation to serve all customers in its service area if it is open to the threat of entry by new competition? And, on what basis should entry be regulated?

From an equity standpoint, if PUCs follow a de facto policy of guaranteeing gas utilities' fixed cost recovery, bypass can engender redistributions of the burden of fixed costs. In these circumstances, it is unlikely that bypass will ever be unanimously welcomed. This most certainly does not mean that bypass is necessarily a zero-sum or negative-sum event, but it does underscore the political tensions that have been mentioned previously. The purpose of this and the following Part is to examine the susceptibility of gas distribution markets to entry and to analyze the types of costs and benefits that come with bypass.

A. The Economics of Entry Regulation

Against a backdrop of perceived sizeable reductions in economic welfare and growing administrative burdens resulting from the regulation of a variety of industries, economists have been turning their attention toward re-examining the conditions under which government involvement in the marketplace is socially beneficial. This process has reaffirmed the importance of the conditions of entry in affecting the ability of a market to perform efficiently. This principal has been formalized in the theory of contestability.[87]

A monopolistic or oligopolistic market is contestable when the threat of entry is sufficient to maintain the price and output levels that would occur if the market were competitively struc-

---

87. See W. BAUMOL, J. PANZAR & R. WILLIG, CONTESTABLE MARKETS AND THE THEORY OF INDUSTRY STRUCTURE (1982); Shepherd, Contestability Versus Competition, 74 AM. ECON. REV. 572 (1984).

How Natural Is Monopoly?

tured. In general, three conditions must prevail for a market to be contestable. First, entry into and exit from the market must require the expenditure of few or no sunk costs. Second, all potential entrants must have access to the technology employed by the incumbent firms. Finally, the incumbent firm must not be able to adjust prices instantaneously when faced with the threat of entry. When these conditions exist, hit and run entry and exit are possible. This threat will cause even a firm in a monopolistic market to set its price and output at the competitive equilibrium because the ability of entrants to attack targets of profitability quickly provides discipline on incumbents' pricing and service offerings.[88]

The efficacy of contestability as a threat hinges centrally on the mobility of capital. Clearly, the natural gas distribution industry is not characterized by highly mobile, quickly deployed and redeployed capital. This characteristic of the industry belies the possibility of hit and run entry and renders reliance on contestability to control monopolistic pricing futile.[89] As a result, under conditions in which distribution markets are not (or cannot be made) structurally competitive, there is a rationale for public utility-style price regulation. The question then arises whether entry into such markets should also be regulated.

Notwithstanding a general recognition of the benefits of easy entry, the answer to the foregoing question must be informed by the possibility that an industry that is most efficiently structured as a monopoly or oligopoly might not be able to sustain that structure if entry is unregulated. For example, if one large LDC or pipeline can serve a given market more cheaply than some multiple number of firms, entry by multiple firms would constitute a wasteful duplication of facilities. Whether a policy of unregulated entry would lead to such a result depends upon the rates that the incumbent can charge and the services that it can provide. In particular, if potential entrants anticipate that rates after entry will be insufficient to allow them to cover their costs, entry will be deterred and the incumbent's natural monopoly will be sustainable.[90]

---

88. See Bailey & Baumol, supra note 1, at 120.

89. Similar conditions prevail in the pipeline segment of the industry. See Broadman & Toman, Non-Price Provisions in Long-Term Natural Gas Contracts, 62 LAND ECON. 111, 112 (1986).

90. The genesis of the "sustainability" literature is Panzar & Willig, Free Entry and the Sustainability of Natural Monopoly, 8 BELL J. ECON. 1 (1977).

Yale Journal on Regulation   Vol. 6: 181, 1989

A central determinant of the sustainability of a market that is naturally and efficiently structured as a monopoly is the market's contestability. In fact, while contestability provides a justification for laissez faire in markets that are not naturally monopolistic, the tables are turned in markets where efficiency requires a single firm.[91] If an entrant's capital is highly mobile and not sunk upon entry, new competitors can engage in hit and run entry into the incumbent's market (or some of its submarkets) whenever the incumbent loads fixed costs into rates such that those rates exceed an entrant's costs. This could leave the incumbent with no set of rates that allows it to recover its costs and deter entry. When hit and run entry is possible, there can be an efficiency justification for restricting freedom of entry into otherwise naturally monopolistic or oligopolistic markets.

Notwithstanding their theoretical appeal, arguments for restrictions on entry into contestable natural monopoly markets have no obvious applicability to questions of bypass in natural gas distribution markets. Hit and run entry is wholly unrealistic in such markets because entrants must sink fixed costs to operate in the market. Because of the need to make distribution investments that cannot be pulled up freely and redeployed elsewhere, a new entrant can anticipate finding itself stuck in an industry already populated by an established competitor. As a result, the entrant's post-entry rates may yield losses. Losses are even more likely to occur if the established incumbent is a natural monopolist and therefore more efficient by definition. The sunk costs of distribution act as a barrier to entry and enhance the sustainability of incumbent companies' market positions.

A new entrant might be willing to get stuck in head-to-head competition with an incumbent utility if the utility has little or no ability to respond with better service offerings or rates of its own. In fact, natural gas utilities typically have the ability to respond to the prospect of entry with so-called "Mickey Mouse," multi-part rates.[92] Rates charged by distribution companies and

---

91. "Where markets are perfectly contestable and monopoly is natural but unsustainable, limitations upon entry may be needed to ensure that the socially optimal set of products can be produced in the most efficient manner." W. BAUMOL, J. PANZAR & R. WILLIG, supra note 87, at 222-23. In short, while contestability is a necessary condition for the deregulation of entry to maximize economic efficiency, it is not sufficient. Sufficiency requires that the market in question be not only contestable, but also sustainable.

92. See Oi, A Disneyland Dilemma: Two-Part Tariffs for a Mickey Mouse Monopoly, 85 Q.J. ECON. 77 (1971).

How Natural Is Monopoly?

pipeline companies commonly can be stated in two parts: a commodity charge and a demand charge. The commodity charge varies with the volume of gas actually provided and generally covers at least variable costs. The demand charge bills customers for access to service without regard to the volume of gas purchased. Thus, this charge provides for recovery of some of the fixed costs. Such rate designs can enable even a natural monopolist facing contestability to sustain itself and deter entry.[93] This conclusion is most true in industrial gas markets, where small numbers of sophisticated parties can meet to negotiate and tailor rates to specific contexts. Higher transactions costs and less sophisticated buyers make this outcome less feasible in residential and small-scale commercial markets. However, these latter markets have not been the targets of bypass.

In sum, the sunk costs of incumbent LDCs deter, rather than encourage, bypass entry. Moreover, the ability of LDCs to respond to the threat of bypass by improving rates and services permits them to sustain themselves in the face of otherwise wasteful entry. Clearly, the long-standing tradition of granting LDCs an exclusive franchise, which obligates them to serve all customers in a market but also protects them from competitive entry, can be interpreted as being based on the notion that LDC markets are not sustainable. Nevertheless, it is reasonable to conclude that sustaining otherwise naturally monopolistic structures in local gas distribution markets does not require draconian prohibitions on entry.

B.   Linkages Between Entry Regulation and Rate Regulation

The feasibility of bypass and the sustainability of LDCs' monopolies are tied directly to the rate structures in the gas industry.[94] The current demand charge-commodity charge rate structure should be taken to its logical limits to permit an improved rate design.[95] A rate design that allows for more efficient signalling of costs and demands will eliminate the consideration of fixed costs from LDCs' charges for marginal gas and transportation service. Moreover, the allocation of the various

93. See, e.g., Perry, Sustainable Positive Profit, Multiple Price Strategies in Contestable Markets, 32 J. ECON. THEORY 246 (1984).

94. See, e.g., OFFICE OF PIPELINE AND PRODUCER REGULATION AND OFFICE OF ECONOMIC POLICY, FEDERAL ENERGY REGULATORY COMM'N, GAS TRANSPORTATION RATE DESIGN AND THE USE OF AUCTIONS TO ALLOCATE CAPACITY 30-31 (1987) (on file with authors) [hereinafter RATE DESIGN].

95. See J. KALT, supra note 25, at 30.

classes and priorities of service, such as firm and interruptible demand, on the basis of price rather than politically-determined criteria of preference would permit improved distributions of these services.[96] Movement in this direction will require new approaches and contractual institutions. These include inventory fees, which charge for customers' use of LDC storage facilities and gas inventories; exit fees, which charge for leaving LDC systems; and reservation fees, which charge for the right to call on LDC services. Other needed reforms include the increased availability of fully unbundled transportation and sales services and the introduction of more market-based allocations of access to LDC facilities of the kind contemplated at the federal level in FERC's recent auction proposal for reservation rights on interstate pipelines.[97]

The observation that a naturally monopolistic LDC can effectively deter entry with appropriate rate designs provides, by reverse implication, insight into the origins of customers' interests in bypass. Specifically, inappropriate LDC rate designs or the inability to provide customers with the services that they demand are the underlying roots of bypass. As commonly phrased by LDCs and their respective PUCs, the difficulty of rate design lies in allocating fixed costs from jointly used facilities across customer classes and types of service.[98] Local gas distribution markets are not made up of a single, homogeneous class of customers. They include residential, commercial, and industrial gas users, each of whom commonly has different demand characteristics and desires different types or qualities of service. In addition, customers commonly differ in their needs for such attributes of LDC operations as gas brokerage services, storage services, and price and contract term reliability.[99] LDCs with economies of scope can attempt to serve these various needs from a single physical plant, allowing customers to share the use of at least some LDC facilities.[100]

---

96. Id. at 31.

97. RATE DESIGN, supra note 94.

98. See supra notes 45-49 and accompanying text (discussion of LDC and PUC responses to bypass).

99. These demands underlie the bypass cases reviewed supra notes 58-86 and accompanying text.

100. Economies of scope arise when the total cost of producing (or delivering) two or more products (or services) jointly is less than the sum of producing (or delivering) each separately. For more discussion, see Bailey & Baumol, supra note 1, at 118.

How Natural Is Monopoly?

The allocation of the costs of jointly used facilities across LDCs' rates presents both economic and political problems. To be sure, it is relatively easy for economists to describe and advocate first-best multi-part rate structures[101] or second-best "Ramsey" prices,[102] which load fixed costs into prices in inverse proportion to the elasticity of customer demand. Nevertheless, it must be stressed that LDCs and PUCs do not make rates in an environment where economic efficiency is the sole objective of the parties involved. Most often, the parties to the ratemaking process—including LDC management, PUC commissioners and staff, involved politicians, and the various classes of customers—have conflicting private and social concerns over the burden of cost recovery.

As the discussion of recent cases suggests,[103] the LDC rate-making process easily can result in rate designs and corresponding allocations of types of service that lead to proposals for LDC bypass. To the extent that an LDC's service offerings leave certain customers' demands unmet, affected customers will have incentives to pursue bypass. Similarly, to the extent that the politics of ratemaking impose burdens that exceed the costs of bypass on particular customer classes, those classes have an incentive to pursue bypass. Even second-best Ramsey pricing may not be sustainable in the face of entry.[104] However, Ramsey pricing generally is not practiced by PUCs, and its sustainability is largely irrelevant in debates over bypass. The ultimate lesson is that the prospect of bypass pressures PUCs to institute more rational first-best pricing policies.[105]

The fact that some bypass proposals can arise because of untoward aspects of state regulatory processes does not mean that such proposals are somehow economically unjustified. Improved costs or quality of service for customers of a bypass constitute real economic benefits. However, the fact that a prospective or actual instance of bypass can impinge on state regulatory processes and lead PUCs to design different rate or service offerings does

---

101. See supra notes 92-93 and accompanying text.

102. Ramsey pricing refers to the scheme developed in Ramsey, A Contribution to the Theory of Taxation, 37 Econ. J. 47 (1927). The most comprehensive restatement is in Baumol & Bradford, Optimal Departures from Marginal Cost Pricing, 60 Am. Econ. Rev. 265 (1970). Advocacy for defense of such second-best rate designs against bypass is contained in MacAvoy, Spulber & Stangle, Is Competitive Entry Free? Bypass and Partial Deregulation in Natural Gas Markets, 6 Yale J. on Reg. 209, 237-40 (1989).

103. See supra notes 58-86 and accompanying text.

104. See MacAvoy, Spulber & Stangle, supra note 102, at 239-40.

105. See, e.g., Bailey & Baumol, supra note 1, at 121-22; Perry, supra note 93.

Yale Journal on Regulation   Vol. 6: 181, 1989

suggest that there can be both winners and losers, benefits and costs from bypass competition.

IV. The Benefits and Costs of LDC Bypass

As a general rule, public policy choices involve some implicit or explicit comparisons of winners and losers, gains and losses. Economically efficient policies seek to promote activities in which the former exceed the latter. The possibility that bypass can produce both winners and losers means that it is useful to contrast socially economic bypass with socially uneconomic bypass.[106] In the common case in which the bypasser is an industrial end-user, the beneficiaries generally include stockholders, final consumers of the affected industrial products and, in some instances, labor.[107] The parties presumed to be harmed include LDC stockholders and customers remaining after bypass. A socially efficient bypass is one in which the gains to the bypassers exceed the losses to LDC stockholders and remaining customers. In such a case, regulation of entry is unwarranted and the prospect of bypass should be allowed. When losses to the remaining customers exceed the gains to the bypassers, economic standards of efficiency indicate that the bypass should not occur.

These policy conclusions risk being mischaracterized as policy choices. Policymakers encounter bypass as a request by a new competitor for the right to try to enter a market. The policymakers' decision does not cause bypass facilities to be built or force customers to switch suppliers. There is simply a choice whether to allow the competition to take place. The competition, in turn, will determine whether entry is successful. In fact, the policymaker can seldom be expected to have ex ante knowledge of the full costs and benefits of a particular bypass proposal. Thus, the policymaker must determine whether competition between incumbent utilities and potential entrants can be relied upon to weed out socially uneconomic bypass proposals if a proposed bypass is allowed to compete to enter the market. This is the implied policy problem of deregulating entry into gas distribution markets.

---

106. For the sake of simplicity let us refer to the presumed beneficiaries of bypass as the "bypassers".

107. A socially economic bypass can then be said to be one in which the gains to the bypassers exceed the losses to the remaining customers. The parties presumed to be harmed directly by bypass can be designated the "remaining customers."

How Natural Is Monopoly?

The question posed by this policy problem involves the sustainability of the LDC's traditional monopoly (or oligopoly) position. As was stressed above, the sunk costs of established utilities act as a barrier to entry; indeed, they act as a barrier to entry by even efficient bypass.[108] When coupled with the PUC-conferred ability to respond to the threat of competition by means of rate and service redesigns, efficient utility service can be expected to be sustainable against the threat of entry.

One implication of allowing the market to decide the fate of bypass proposals is that even if inefficient entry is weeded out, the competition leading to such a result may alter utilities' pre-existing rate structures and service offerings.[109] To the extent that this process rationalizes rate structures in accordance with marginal cost pricing principles, or the process results in improved service offerings to potential bypassers, it is not a zero-sum process. In this instance, competition yields improved efficiency. In fact, the competition that weeds out uneconomic bypass need be no worse than zero-sum as long as PUCs and their utilities do not worsen rate designs by shifting forgone fixed cost recovery from prospective bypassers into other customers' rates for incremental service. Stated differently, if the only benefit to prospective bypassers from bypass competition is a reduction in contributions to their utility's overhead, the implied burden on other ratepayers need not exceed an equivalent amount.

A. A Framework for Analyzing the Benefits and Costs of Bypass

From a welfare perspective, the benefits of bypass are the consumer surplus gains realized by bypassers, while the cost of bypass and the process of allowing competition over bypass are the burdens. In this framework, the efficiency test for bypass amounts to assessing whether the winners' gains from bypass outweigh the losers' losses.

The losses attributable to bypass can take the form of a cost-shift from bypassers to remaining ratepayers, but a dollar-for-dollar cost-shift is not a necessary result of bypass competition. Any contribution to LDC overhead that is lost from bypassers can be borne by other ratepayers, utility stockholders, and the utility itself. In other words, the costs of bypass may take the form of a cost-shift, a profit-squeeze, or a cost-squeeze. The textbook

---

108. See supra notes 87-93 and accompanying text.
109. See supra notes 58-86 and accompanying text.

result of a dollar-for-dollar cost-shift to other ratepayers represents a limiting, extreme case.[110] The experience of public utility
regulation suggests that LDCs seldom operate on the knife-edges
of both technical efficiency and zero economic profits.[111] That is,
there is "fat" that gets squeezed when a political equilibrium is
upset by an event such as bypass. Of course, to the extent that
the result is improved LDC cost efficiency, there are no losers
from the process; there are only pure efficiency gains. When the
burden of bypass falls on other ratepayers and on stockholders,
however, an economic welfare analysis must compare these
parties' losses to the benefits that bypassers realize.

B. The Benefits of Bypass

There are four generic classes of socially productive benefits
that may be attributable to subjecting LDCs to competition from
potential entrants: (1) rate effects,[112] (2) service effects,[113] (3) risk
effects,[114] and (4) competitive effects.[115] Beneficial rate effects result
from the ability of actual or prospective bypass to lower the
marginal expense of delivered gas to bypassing end-users. Any
induced reduction in the expenses that affected end-users pay at
the margin to acquire delivered gas could result in increased gas
use. As long as expenses at the margin are not below the
marginal resource costs of service, this increased use yields net
social benefits. Of course, an LDC could choose to offset such
benefits by responding perversely with higher incremental rates
for remaining customers.

Dissatisfaction with the quality of LDC service can also be an
important impetus to bypass.[116] Two attributes of service are

110. See supra Part III.

111. See Joskow, Inflation and Environmental Concern: Structural Change in the
Process of Public Utility Price Regulation, 17 J.L. & ECON. 291 (1974).

112. These are illustrated by ANR Pipeline I, supra note 48, discussed supra notes
62-68 and accompanying text; and Southern Natural, supra note 61.

113. These are illustrated by the moves toward LDC contract carriage in states such
as California, New York, Pennsylvania, and West Virginia. See Lambert, supra note 27, at
16. See also supra notes 50-57 and accompanying text.

114. These are illustrated by Mojave Pipeline, supra note 26, discussed supra notes
82-86 and accompanying text.

115. These are illustrated by Panhandle I, supra note 69 and Panhandle II, supra
note 77, discussed supra notes 69-81 and accompanying text; and District of Columbia
Hosp. Energy Coop. Inc. v. Washington Gas Light Co., No. 85-3720 (D.D.C., filed Nov. 20,
1985), discussed supra notes 59-60 and accompanying text.

116. See supra Part II.

How Natural Is Monopoly?

frequently at issue. The first is delivery reliability. Low priority service is a de jure or de facto reality for many industrial customers of LDCs. The political, if not economic, need to grant higher priority to other users is frequently manifested, for example, in the inability of industrial end-users to purchase firm service from LDCs. This does not mean that LDCs can or should ignore political necessities in establishing priorities of service. Rather, it suggests that, in the process of establishing de jure or de facto priorities, certain customers demands may go unmet. In such circumstances, bypass may be the only mechanism by which industrial end-users are able to buy service of the quality that they desire. The second aspect of service at issue is access to unbundled LDC transportation service. As federal policy has moved interstate pipelines into an era of increasingly unbundled, open-access transportation, many end-users that are sophisticated enough to take advantage of the implied opportunities have been blocked from doing by lack of access to unbundled LDC transportation.[117] The prospect of bypass can induce LDCs and their PUCs to respond to these customers' demands, and consummated bypass directly can link them to the nation's emerging open access transportation grid.

Closely related to the service effects of bypass are the risk effects. Industrial end-users can not only demand the reliability of physical deliveries that gives rise to service benefits of bypass; they can also require reliability in the contractual terms and conditions of gas delivery service. If de jure or de facto low priority before PUCs manifests itself in relatively high risks of changes in the terms and conditions under which LDC service is available, industrial end-users' costs can be raised (as they self-insure),[118] long-term planning can be inhibited, and investment can be discouraged. State PUCs have a difficult time binding themselves to credible bargains of the type that some industrial gas users demand. This problem appears to have been magnified in recent years.[119] Bypass or the threat of bypass can provide an answer. Prospective bypass may induce LDCs, and especially their respective PUCs, to improve the reliability of the terms and conditions under which local distribution services are provided. When bypass actually takes place, it commonly involves

---

117. See supra Part II.
118. For example, firms can self-insure through fuel switching installations.
119. See Kalt, Lee & Leonard, Reestablishing the Regulatory Bargain in the Electric Power Industry, in FINAL REPORT OF THE BOSTON EDITION REVIEW PANEL Appendix V (W. Hogan ed. 1987).

turning from state-regulated distribution entities to FERC-regulated pipeline facilities. Although there is no theoretical necessity that federal jurisdiction provide more reliable terms and conditions of service, permitting bypass to occur allows end-users to vote with their feet. At the very least, access to both state and federally-regulated facilities sets up inter-jurisdiction competition and establishes a method by which bypassing end-users can hedge the risks that they face. This form of competition is not inherently wasteful;[120] it allows users to reduce risks while encouraging investment and lowering the costs of self-insurance.

Apart from allowing improvements in rates, service, and reliability, bypass can produce generalized competitive benefits. For example, insofar as prospective bypass induces LDCs to offer unbundled transportation, or consummated bypass links large end-users directly to open access interstate systems, additional competitors are introduced into the market. This not only tends to dampen any latent upstream monopoly power, but also effectively offsets structural monopolies in local gas brokerage that LDCs enjoy. Finally, competition from bypass coupled with remaining customers' and LDC stockholders' resistance to the burden of a cost-shift may induce efficient cost reductions for all LDC operations.[121]

C. The Costs of Bypass

Bypass is not free. The most significant costs are those associated with building and operating the bypass facilities themselves. Whether or not new physical facilities are economically duplicative, their use of labor and capital represents a real resource cost. From a policy perspective, these costs reduce any benefits bypassers realize. New facilities can be considered economically duplicative only to the extent that their costs are not offset by benefits of the kinds that we have described. When the benefits of a bypass extend beyond simple delivery of gas to include improved service quality or risk reduction, the observation of an apparent physical duplication of facilities provides little insight into the outcome of a social cost-benefit test.

---

120. A classic discussion of inter-jurisdictional competition is provided by Tiebout, A Pure Theory of Local Expenditure, 64 J. Pol. Econ. 416 (1956).

121. See supra notes 110-11 and accompanying text.

How Natural Is Monopoly?

It is important to note that some degree of physical duplication of facilities may well be optimal. For example, many gas and electric utilities maintain capacity reserve margins to insure against the risk of short-run increases in demand or to provide needed capacity during maintenance periods. End-users' bypass investments can function in much the same way. Similarly, end-users may have dual-fired boilers or other types of fuel-switching capabilities; to the extent that these facilities are tantamount to bypass investments, they also can be viewed as constituting duplications of physical facilities. Nevertheless, such investments are usually considered socially beneficial insofar as they result in a more flexible energy-using capital stock.

If the construction of bypass facilities permits an affected LDC to avoid building, repairing, or maintaining facilities of its own, the resulting avoided costs appropriately can be thought of as a benefit of bypass. Equivalently, the net cost of bypass facilities can be thought of as being less than the gross cost when bypass displaces investments that an LDC would otherwise have to make. A consummated bypass displaces the variable costs that an affected LDC would otherwise incur. This also is a benefit of bypass. Of course, the savings in LDCs' variable costs are offset by the variable expenses of operating the bypass facilities. A priori, it is not possible to say which supply system, LDC or bypass, has the lowest operating costs. The comparison depends upon such factors as the relative distances over which the alternative systems travel and the extent of any technological improvements embodied in the bypass' newer facilities.

Conclusion

The most critical lesson of this analysis of bypass is that, given the complexities and uncertainties associated with assessing whether a particular bypass proposal produces positive net social benefits, public policy towards bypass should carry a presumption in favor of competition. Thus, if there is to be a bias in bypass policy, it should be towards rather than away from bypass. The question should not be "when is competition excessive?" but rather "when is regulation necessary?"

The core of the argument for bypass rests upon two themes. First, entry and the threat of entry have the capacity to discipline regulated gas distribution markets in socially productive ways. Bypass and its threat can increase the pressure on local utilities to hold down their costs, rationalize their rate structures, and

Yale Journal on Regulation   Vol. 6: 181, 1989

improve the range and quality of their service offerings. Second, entry by socially inefficient bypass proposals is unlikely to be successful. Because LDCs and PUCs can respond to the prospect of entry with improved rate designs and because LDCs' fixed costs are largely sunk, significant deterrents to inefficient entry exist. Particularly in the context where bypass commonly a-rises—industrial markets populated by relatively small numbers of sophisticated participants—efficient natural monopoly in local gas distribution can be expected to be sustainable. Accordingly, restrictions on entry can be relaxed.

Effective threats of bypass clearly impinge on the rate-making process for local gas distribution utilities. This has both economic and political implications. Reforming LDC rate structures so that they are more in line with basic principles of economic efficiency not only would be an important step in improving LDC market performance overall, but it also would reduce artificial incentives for bypass. Indeed, it is arguable that one of the reasons why bypass has become such a major policy issue is that PUCs have not encouraged LDCs to offer flexible and fuel-sensitive rates and services to industrial end-users. In fact, many PUCs have followed a regulatory policy of excessively tilting rates, not to mention service priorities and quality, in favor of residential and small commercial customers. In part, these policies have grown out of the politics of LDC regulation. These policies have generated a belief among PUCs and LDCs that competition in gas markets stops at the city gate. Yet, if there is one conclusion to be drawn from recent FERC actions, it is that wellhead competition in the gas industry reverberates directly downstream from the wellhead to the city gate and to the burner-tip. As a result, any attempt to devise an effective bypass policy in downstream markets necessarily must entail significant reform of LDC rate structures.

The analysis presented in this Article should make it clear that a blanket ban on bypass would be unsound public policy. On the one hand, with the introduction of more efficient pricing schemes, the incidence of bypass proposals and the amount of bypass actually consummated surely will diminish. On the other hand, opportunities for credible threats of bypass must be preserved, for the mere threat of bypass enhances the performance of both LDCs and PUCs. The argument in favor of allowing bypass is not that bypass itself is desirable. Rather, permitting bypass engenders positive effects by enhancing competition throughout the natural gas market.

[28]

Deregulation: Looking Backward and Looking Forward

Alfred E. Kahn†

We have a surfeit of deregulatory anniversaries to celebrate or deplore: it is now more than thirty years since the Federal Communications Commission (FCC) authorized substantial competition in long-distance communications,[1] more than eleven since we deregulated the airlines, and almost ten years since we did substantially the same to the railroad and trucking industries.[2] Can we, by examining this long and varied experience with deregulation, draw any conclusions about the likelihood and desirability of its continuation in the decade ahead?

In this attempt to place deregulation in historical perspective, I feel compelled to emphasize, in contradiction of the widespread

---

† Robert Julius Thorne Professor of Political Economy, Emeritus, Cornell University; Special Consultant, National Economic Research Associates, Inc.; Chairman, New York Public Service Commission, 1974-77, and Civil Aeronautics Board, 1977-78. This is a revised and expanded version of a paper presented at the fiftieth anniversary session of the American Economic Association, Transportation and Public Utilities Group on December 28, 1989. I acknowledge with gratitude the criticisms of Richard Rapp, Douglas Jones, Irwin Stelzer, William Shepherd, Judith Greenman and Robert Crandall, and the assistance of Tina Fine.

1. Allocation of Frequencies in the Bands Above 890 Mc, 27 F.C.C. 359 (1959), *modified on reconsideration* 29 F.C.C. 825 (1960) (authorizing large users to provide their own communications services via microwave).

2. Other major milestones were the deregulation of stock exchange brokerage commissions in 1975-76, see Roberts, Phillips & Zecher, *Deregulation of Fixed Commission Rates in the Securities Industry*, in THE DEREGULATION OF THE BANKING AND SECURITIES INDUSTRIES 151 (1979); the progressive relaxation of FCC restrictions on cable television competition with over-the-air broadcasters during the 1970s, see S. BESEN, T. KRATTENMAKER, A. METZGER JR., & J. WOODBURY, MISREGULATING TELEVISION 4-20 (1984); *see also* Besen & Crandall, *The Deregulation of Cable Television*, 44 LAW & CONTEMP. PROBS. 77 (1981); the FCC's reluctant allowance of direct competition in the offer of interexchange telecommunications service on a common carrier basis. MCI Telecommunications Corp. v. FCC, 561 F.2d 365 (D.C. Cir 1977); In re Establishment of Policies and Procedures for Consideration of Application to Provide Specialized Common Carrier Services in the Domestic Point-to-Point Microwave Radio Service, 29 F.C.C. 2d 870 (1971); In re Applications of Microwave Communications, Inc., 18 F.C.C. 2d 979 (1967). *See generally* 2 A. KAHN, THE ECONOMICS OF REGULATION: PRINCIPLES AND INSTITUTIONS 129-52 (1988); G. FAULHABER, TELECOMMUNICATIONS IN TURMOIL: TECHNOLOGY AND PUBLIC POLICY (1987). *See also* text accompanying *infra* note 20.

Yale Journal on Regulation   Vol. 7: 325, 1990

popular impression that President Reagan deserves most of the credit—or blame—how much of it occurred between 1978 and 1980.[3]

While deregulation has dramatically transformed the transportation industries, its effect on the traditional public utilities, while substantial, can easily be exaggerated. Two years ago, in a symposium on "The Surprises of Deregulation," Robert Crandall shrewdly observed that the greatest surprise in the case of telecommunications was how little had actually occurred.[4]   Customer premises equipment aside, the overwhelming majority of transactions continue to be thoroughly regulated. And AT&T, which had agreed to divest its putatively naturally monopolistic services and confine itself to competitive operations, continues nonetheless to be heavily regulated.[5]

I have been guilty of some such exaggeration myself, in speculating several years ago that we might at last be witnessing the fulfillment of Horace Gray's ancient celebration of "the passing of the public utility concept:"[6]

> Gray intended his title to be historically descriptive, and not merely hortatory. The celebration was premature. . . .

> In contrast, the last decade has witnessed such dramatic modifications and abandonments of the traditional institution that I suggest it is now possible to talk realistically about the passing of the public utility concept. . . .

> The institution of closely regulated, confined, franchised monopoly, which produced reasonably satisfactory results for all parties, including the public, until around 1970, has proved progressively unsuited to the drastically altered condition of the American economy since that time. I think history is on the way to proving that Horace Gray was something of a

---

3.   Even so knowledgeable a student as Roger Noll has credited President Reagan with dismantling the Civil Aeronautics Board (CAB), merely because it happened during his term. Noll, *Regulation After Reagan*, REGULATION, Number 3, 1988, at 13. Also, most people credit Reagan with deregulating crude oil, even though it was President Carter who set the process on a definite two and a half year time schedule; his successor's contribution was to compress the remaining nine months into one immediately on taking office.

4.   Crandall, *Surprises from Telephone Deregulation and the AT&T Divestiture*, 78 AM. ECON. REV., PAPERS & PROCEEDINGS 323 (1988). The same is true of electric power and local distribution of gas.

5.   *See* G. FAULHABER, *supra* note 2, at 85-87.

6.   Gray, *The Passing of the Public Utility Concept*, 16 J. LAND & PUB. UTIL. ECON. 8 (1940).

Regulation in the 1990s

prophet—a premature one (if it is not excessively redundant of me to say so), and a simplistic one, but something of a prophet nonetheless.[7]

More cautious than Gray, I hedged my predictions and prescriptions. Where deregulation had been incomplete, I observed, the reciprocal interpenetration of markets by regulated and unregulated companies required regulatory prevention of cross-subsidization and abuse of monopoly power. I also professed agnosticism about the feasibility of competition across the board in electric generation, dithered on the desirability of deregulating basic cable television service and petroleum pipelines, described my own efforts to ensure effective protection of shippers captive to the otherwise deregulated railroads, and recognized that similar exploitation was almost certainly happening in some thin airline markets. Still, considering the continuing pervasive regulation of the public utilities, I, like Gray, could justly be described as a "premature prophet" of their passing.

There is, however, also a great deal going on, almost all of it in the direction I predicted. Of especial significance, the major issues of regulatory policy these days in the public utility arena are not whether or how to return to the closed world of franchised, thoroughly regulated monopolies, but how to accommodate traditional regulation to the increasing intrusion of competition. Among the leading examples of that intrusion are:

> the growth of electric generation by non-utility enterprises—both "qualifying facilities" under the Public Utility Regulatory Policies Act (PURPA)[8] and so-called independent power producers;[9]

---

7. Kahn, *The Passing of the Public Utility Concept: A Reprise*, in TELECOMMUNICATIONS TODAY AND TOMORROW 3, 4, 5, 27 (E. Noam ed. 1983) (footnotes omitted) [hereinafter Kahn, *A Reprise*].

8. Pub. L. No. 95-617, 92 Stat. 3117 (1978) (codified at 16 U.S.C. § 2601 (1988)). *See generally* Joskow, *Regulatory Failure, Regulatory Reform, and Structural Change in the Electric Power Industry*, 1989 BROOKINGS PAPERS ON ECONOMIC ACTIVITY: MICROECONOMICS 124, 153-74, 184-85.

9. Non-utility generation accounts for only about four percent of total national capacity. *See* EDISON ELECTRIC INSTITUTE, 1989 CAPACITY AND GENERATION OF NON-UTILITY SOURCES OF ENERGY (1989). But it accounts for one third or more of planned additions. J. WILE, THE DEMAND FOR NEW GENERATING CAPACITY (Nat'l. Econ. Res. Assoc. 1989), provides an estimate of 30 percent of planned additions. Mason Willrich quotes a figure of 44 percent of "capacity under construction or advanced development." *The Competitive Wholesale Electric Generation Act, 1989: Hearings on Amend. 267 to S. 406 Before the*

Yale Journal on Regulation   Vol. 7: 325, 1990

- the deregulation of certain wholesale bulk power sales, where the Federal Energy Regulatory Commission (FERC) has satisfied itself that the transactions were at arms' length and untainted by monopoly or monopsony power;[10]

- the requirement by an increasing number of state utility commissions that local electric companies obtain their additional power requirements via competitive bids;[11]

- the decision by many states to permit electric companies to exercise discretion in pricing, within a stipulated range, in order to meet competition, forestall cogeneration, and retain or attract industry;[12]

- the proposal by FERC to permit local gas distribution companies to replace long-term commitments to buy gas from open access pipelines with arrangements to purchase transportation alone;[13]

- the total deregulation of telephone equipment, which is now highly competitive;[14] and

- the burgeoning of private communications networks, to such a point that more business phones are now linked in the

---

Senate Comm. on Energy and Natural Resources, 101st Cong., 2d Sess. 5-6 (1989) (statement of Mason Willrich, Pres. and CEO, PG&E Enterprises).

10.   R. FITZGIBBONS, BEYOND THE FERC NOPRS: TRENDS IN ELECTRIC UTILITY REGULATION (Nat'l. Econ. Res. Assoc. 1989).

11.   Fourteen commissions have done so, twelve others are considering it. Willrich, supra note 9, at 5.

12.   R. FRAME, COMPETITIVE INDUSTRIAL RATES (Nat'l. Econ. Res. Assoc. 1987).

13.   Batla, Order 500 Joins Order 451 on the Critical List, NATURAL GAS, Dec. 1989, at 1. In 1982, interstate pipelines owned 78 percent of the natural gas they carried; by 1987 that share had fallen to less than one-third. For the remainder, the pipelines provided the transportation as a separate service. ENERGY INFORMATION ADMIN., OFFICE OF OIL & GAS, U.S. DEP'T OF ENERGY, GROWTH IN UNBUNDLED NATURAL GAS TRANSPORTATION SERVICES: 1982-87, at ix-x (1988).

14.   See Crandall, After the Breakup: U.S. Telecommunications in a More Competitive Era (Nov. 1989) (unpublished manuscript on file with author). See also Noll & Owen, United States v. AT&T: An Interim Assessment, in FUTURE COMPETITION IN TELECOMMUNICATIONS 172-86 (S. Bradley & J. Hausman ed. 1989).

Regulation in the 1990s

first instance to their own switches than to those of the local telephone company.[15]

Among such quasi-public utilities as financial service institutions and transportation, the processes of market interpenetration and unregulated pricing are even further advanced.

Despite these developments, most transactions at the core of the traditional public utilities, such as the local provision of telephone, electric and gas service, continue to be tightly regulated, and there seems little prospect or desirability of that situation changing fundamentally in the next decade. In these circumstances, my predictions and prescriptions about the future course of deregulation in the structurally competitive industries, on the one side, and the structurally monopolistic markets, on the other, will necessarily differ from one another.

There will, however, be a common theme and a consistent set of conclusions:

> The case for deregulation has been that direct regulation typically suppressed competition, or at least severely distorted it, and that competition, freed of such direct restraints, is a far preferable system of economic control. I read the recent experience as having essentially vindicated that proposition, making substantial reversal of the deregulatory trend unlikely.

> Where competition is not feasible throughout an industry or market, as in the traditional public utilities, entry of unregulated competition can introduce distortions so severe as to make the mixed system the worst of both possible worlds. The preferable remedy is not to suppress the competition, but to make the residual regulation as consistent as possible with it. That seems to be the direction in which regulators are moving.

> The abolition of direct economic regulation is by no means synonymous with *laissez faire*. On the contrary, it may call for government interventions no less vigorous than direct regulation itself, but fundamentally different in character and intent. The progressive realization of this fact in recent years makes

---

15. P. W. Huber, The Geodesic Network: 1987 Report on Competition in the Telephone Industry 2.5-2.7 (Antitrust Division, U.S. Dep't of Justice 1987).

for a bifurcated prognosis for the 1990s: the historic trend of
direct economic deregulation is unlikely to be reversed, but
government will play an increasingly active role in attempting
to preserve competition and remedy its imperfections. And that
is what it should do.

I. The Prospects for Reregulation

One way of trying to judge whether the recent deregulatory
trends are likely to continue or be reversed is to consider the root
causes of these remarkable historical changes[16] and appraise the
likelihood of their persistence.

Perhaps the most fundamental of these has been the rediscovery
all over the world of the virtues of the free market. It was obviously
no accident that many of the comprehensive governmentally-administered cartelizations overturned during the late 1970s and early
1980s were established during the Great Depression, when confidence in the market economy was at its nadir. While the present enthusiasm for market capitalism will doubtless be subject to ebbs and
flows in the years ahead, it is difficult to envision an early return to
centralized governmental command and control systems, of which
our regimes of economic regulation were an exemplar in microcosm.

There is no sign of let up, either, in the technological explosion
that made inevitable the collapse of almost all the historic regulatory
barriers against competitive interpenetrations in telecommunications,
and bids fair to do the same among financial institutions. It was the
development of microwave that presented large users with the
irresistible opportunity to escape the regulatorily-dictated over-
charging of interexchange services. Similarly, the geometrically
declining cost and increased versatility of switching has made
possible the proliferation of privately-owned networks and privately-
provided sophisticated telecommunications services; and fiber optics
will probably doom the present artificial separation of cable television
and information services from telephony.

A. *Vested Interests in Deregulation*

The deregulations of the last fifteen years were powerfully
motivated also by changes in the configuration of the private

---

16.   *See generally* Kahn, *The Political Feasibility of Regulatory Reform: How Did We Do It?*,
in REFORMING SOCIAL REGULATION: ALTERNATIVE PUBLIC POLICY STRATEGIES 247 (1982).

Regulation in the 1990s

interests most directly affected. The Staggers Act[17] was passed in large measure because of the growing disenchantment of the railroads with their historic regulatory bargain with government that protected them from competition but also systematically impeded them from competing effectively, forced them to maintain thousands of miles of track on which they were losing money, and limited their ability to raise their charges to customers with relatively inelastic demands. Similarly, airline deregulation owed a great deal to the unhappiness of United Airlines with the CAB's systematic denial to it of the ability to enter new markets or desert old ones. The insistence of large customers that they be released from the burdens of cross-subsidization to which they had been subjected by the FCC and state commissions was an important part of the reason for the breakup of AT&T's monopoly; in the same way, the competitive encroachments on the formerly protected markets of the electric and gas utilities came about because of the desire of large industrial customers to take advantage of emerging opportunities to make bulk purchases at bargain rates in the field and from outside suppliers with excess capacity. And one reason for the receptivity of the electric industry to competitive generation was the reluctance of many of its members to undertake construction of new baseload generating stations, because of the stunning regulatory disallowances of previously incurred construction costs to which they had been subjected in the early and mid-1980s.[18]

It is the converse of the foregoing proposition that is the more relevant for the future. There are now vested interests in deregulation itself—politically or economically powerful entities that, having now achieved freedom from regulation, will not readily surrender it. That is part of what I intended when I said that my colleagues and I at the CAB were going to get the airline eggs so scrambled that no one was ever going to be able to unscramble them. Although many of the thousands of new truckers and small bus companies

17. Staggers Rail Act of 1980, Pub. L. No. 96-448, 94 Stat. 1895 (1980) (codified as amended in scattered sections of 11, 45, and 49 U.S.C.).

18. As the foregoing account already suggests, while the deregulation movement was powerfully motivated by historical factors affecting the economy at large and economic policy generally, its explanation must be sought also in circumstances peculiar to the individual industries affected. For example, it is highly unlikely that our regulatory policies affecting the electric utilities would have been so substantially changed had that industry continued to perform as it had during the decades of the 1950s and 1960s. In contrast with telecommunications, where the most powerful motivating force was technological progress, in the energy sector the motivating force was, in important measure, technological and institutional failure. *See, e.g.,* Joskow, *supra* note 8, at 149-63; R. F. HIRSH, TECHNOLOGY AND TRANSFORMATION IN THE AMERICAN ELECTRIC UTILITY INDUSTRY (1989).

and many of the hundreds of railroad ventures that have taken over the trackage and thin routes that larger companies were unable to operate profitably, and many of the cogenerators and small-scale generators of hydro- and wind power that have eagerly entered the doors opened by deregulation have already gone bankrupt, and many more will, the survivors are not going to permit the government to retract the invitation to compete. Moreover, the previous incumbents now have a freedom to manage their own operations, configure their own service offerings and set their own prices that will be very hard to take away. Where the deregulatory process has been only partial, the companies that remain thoroughly regulated devote most of their energies to demanding "symmetry," by which they mean not a restoration of restraints on their newer competitors, but corresponding freedom for themselves. The principle applies symmetrically to deregulation and regulation: once instituted, they tend to be progressive and cumulative.[19]

These forces explain why the process can be essentially inadvertent, as it was in the case of telecommunications. No planner laid out in advance the path of decisions from Hush-a-Phone and Above 890 through Carterphone, MCI, Specialized Common Carriers, Execunet, AT&T's stonewalling response, the Modified Final Judgment concluding the ensuing antitrust litigation, and the FCC's MTS/WATS Market Structure and three Computer Inquiries. Yet each step led logically to the next, and they were all in the same direction.[20]

The same process is underway in the financial services field. Once we permitted brokerage houses to offer the equivalent of demand deposits and retail chains to provide home mortgages and credit card services, once we removed ceilings on interest rates payable by savings institutions, it was inevitable that we would loosen the previous restraints on the permissible lending and investment activities of the savings institutions and permit commercial banks to underwrite commercial paper.

19. On the tendency of regulation to spread, see, e.g., A. KAHN, *supra* note 2, at 28-32. For a study of the effects of deregulation, see Kahn, *Applications of Economics to an Imperfect World*, 69 AM. ECON. REV., PAPERS & PROCEEDINGS 1 (1979).

20. *See* text accompanying *supra* notes 1-2. *See also* Kahn, *The Future of Local Telephone Service: Technology and Public Policy*, in TOWARD THE YEAR 2000 88-90 (1987); Crandall, *supra* note 14.

Regulation in the 1990s

B. *Distortions and Tensions of Partial Deregulation*

In the electric and gas utilities, similarly, partial deregulation has introduced a host of asymmetries and distortions, which have been and are still being resolved primarily by further liberalizations. The basic problem is that the rates charged by the utility companies, which inevitably play a central role in deciding which competitive transactions take place and which do not, contain a very large component of capital carrying charges on investments valued at embedded (i.e., at depreciated original) cost, not marginal cost. Under partial deregulation, therefore, many competitive purchase and production decisions are made on the basis of comparisons between those economically meaningless, traditionally regulated rates, on the one side, and competitive costs or prices on the other. Businesses will decide whether to generate their own electric power or construct their own communications systems by comparing the current, true economic cost to them of doing so with the regulated rates they would otherwise have to pay. Where those rates are higher than the marginal or avoided costs of the electric or telephone company itself—as they have been by wide margins in recent years, because of the presence in rate base of high-cost, excess generating capacity, or inadequately depreciated telephone plant[21]—the decisions by customers to provide the service themselves can produce inefficient results.

For the same reason, when differences in regulated rates cause large-volume buyers to shift their patronage from one electric company to another, or from a gas pipeline or distribution company to producers in the field, it need not be that the marginal costs of the new supplier are lower than the avoided costs of the former one. Often, in fact, their short-run marginal costs are identical—for example, when both suppliers are part of the same power pool. The most powerful inducement for high-volume gas customers to desert their historic pipeline and distribution company suppliers has been the billions of dollars of sunk costs embodied in the rates of their former suppliers because of commitments they had made to take or pay for very high-cost gas at a time when supplies were critically short. As a result, a large number of transactions have been entered into because of decisions distorted by regulation itself, and there is

21. *See* Rohlfs, *'Miles to Go': The Need for Additional Reforms in Capital Recovery Methods,* TELECOMMUNICATIONS IN A COMPETITIVE ENVIRONMENT 63 (Nat'l Econ. Res. Assoc. 1989). *See also* A. KAHN, *supra* note 2, at 146-50; Kahn, *The Uneasy Marriage of Regulation and Competition,* TELEMATICS, Sept. 1984, at 1, 2, 8-17.

Yale Journal on Regulation   Vol. 7: 325, 1990

no assurance that the supply function is distributed among competitors on the basis of their comparative efficiency.

The legal obligation of utility companies to serve on demand, which requires them to incur the costs of installing the capacity necessary to fulfill that obligation, creates a similar distortion. So long as they were monopolies, their customers had, in effect, a corresponding obligation to pay rates reflecting those sunk costs if prudently incurred. In contrast, the customers who are now free to shop around or to supply their own needs can escape that obligation. If their shift is feasible only because, while evading the costs of keeping the option available to them, they nevertheless retain the right to return to their local utilities and demand service without penalty when their economical supplies elsewhere dry up, or their own generators fail, or their own telephone circuits are busy, the shift may involve not an improvement, but a loss in economic efficiency.[22]

C. *Regulatory Adaptations*

The still emerging resolution of these distortions has had several components.

Legislatures and regulatory commissions have been giving the utility companies increased freedom to reduce prices as low as their incremental costs to meet competition. Occasionally, this freedom has extended to the point of total deregulation of some services or transactions, such as Centrex, telephone equipment on the customer's premises, and some electric bulk power sales.

Also, both regulators and the passage of time have presided over a partial writing off, settling out, accelerated recovery, and disallowance of the heavy sunk costs—the multi-billion dollar take-or-pay obligations of the gas pipelines, the long-term contractual purchase obligations of the local gas distribution companies, the

---

22. On the separate problem of option demand and the possibility of market failure in satisfying it, see Weisbrod, *Collective-Consumption Services of Individual-Consumption Goods*, 78 Q. J. OF ECON. 471 (1964); Kahn, *The Tyranny of Small Decisions: Market Failures, Imperfections, and the Limits of Economics*, 19 KYKLOS 23 (1966). On the possible distortion of competition consequent on the failure to impose such a charge in the telephone industry, see A. KAHN, *supra* note 2, at 238-39. For the most thorough exposition of the case for such charges, see Weisman, *Default Capacity Tariffs: Smoothing the Transitional Regulatory Asymmetries in the Telecommunications Market*, 5 YALE J. ON REG. 149 (1988). *See also* Weisman, *Competitive Markets and Carriers of Last Resort*, PUB. UTIL. FORT., July 6, 1989, at 17; Weisman, *Optimal Re-contracting, Market Risk and the Regulated Firm in Competitive Transition*, 12 RES. IN L. & ECON. 153 (1989).

Regulation in the 1990s

inflated costs of recently constructed or abandoned electric generating plants, and inadequately depreciated telephone company plant—that have constituted the major source of discrepancy between the companies' average revenue requirements for regulatory purposes and their own incremental costs.[23]

In a few cases, regulators have partially relaxed the utility's obligation to serve customers who choose to escape their *de facto* obligation to help carry fixed costs. Regulators have also considered permitting the utility companies to impose a capacity reservation charge—the leading example of which is the gas inventory holding charge contemplated by FERC—on customers who wish to retain the option of service on demand.[24] In a few recent cases, where buyers have had access to alternative suppliers, FERC has permitted the utility's obligation to be limited explicitly to the volumes and circumstances stipulated in long-term contracts.[25]

The importance and promise of individually negotiated long-term contracts can hardly be exaggerated, both as a newly permissible form of competition and as a device for reestablishing and redefining the relationship between utility companies and individual customers in a manner compatible with competition. In the electric power industry, for example, the increasing tendency of the utility companies to acquire their supplies by long-term contract has helped to introduce competition into generation. Before the Staggers Act, such contracts for rail transport were legally unenforceable: all rail and truck carriage had to be at openly posted, uniform spot rates. As a result, electric companies that had built generating plants in the Southwest designed to burn coal from Wyoming and Montana found themselves subjected to very sharp increases in the rail rates charged them by the single railroad or pair of end-to-end carriers to which they were captive. Since 1980, in contrast, most of the coal shipped by rail has been covered by long-term contracts.

The ability, newly available under deregulation, to enter into such arrangements, adapted to the particular needs of the individual shipper and providing for rewards and penalties based on performance of the transportation function, is said to have been an essential

---

23. In the case of the electric companies, the discrepancy has been reduced in many areas by marginal costs moving up toward average charges as growth in demand has outpaced additions to capacity.

24. *See* Kahn, *A Reprise*, *supra* note 7, at 18-21 (tracing dissolution of this obligation in the case of the airlines and motor carriers, and even incipient efforts in the electric utilities).

25. R. FITZGIBBONS, *supra* note 10, at 11.

Yale Journal on Regulation   Vol. 7: 325, 1990

factor in the rapid spread of just-in-time inventory and logistical control systems, which have produced cost savings estimated in the scores of billions of dollars a year.[26]

There has been no abatement in the zeal of regulatory commissions to protect residential and small commercial customers, almost all of whom remain captive to the local utility companies, from being forced to assume the sunk costs that the competitive markets can no longer be forced to bear. To some extent, they have continued to do so by discouraging "cream-skimming" competition—for example, by competitive providers of long-distance telephone service intrastate, or by proprietors of "smart buildings," providing telecommunications services for their tenants.[27] Increasingly, however, regulators have been developing methods consistent with, rather than obstructive of, the new competition—a tendency most fully developed in the field of telecommunications.

The simplest of these new methods has been a rate freeze for basic telephone service, accompanied by stipulations that service quality not deteriorate. The freeze may consist in a simple directive or undertaking to maintain existing rates for a number of years. Alternatively, it may provide for automatic adjustment to reflect inflation or changes in taxes or interstate separations. The indexations typically incorporate an automatic downward adjustment predicated on a targeted improvement in productivity, thereby ensuring a continuation of the long-term decline of these rates in real terms.

Such freezes or "social compacts" have some obvious virtues, both political and economic. They provide direct, straightforward protection for consumers of the services that are the subject of most

---

26.   R. DELANEY, FREIGHT TRANSPORTATION DEREGULATION, SEMINAR T9 ON ROAD TRANSPORT DEREGULATION: EXPERIENCE, EVALUATION, AND RESEARCH 6 (Arthur D. Little, Inc.).

27.   At times regulatory commissions have simply prohibited the utility companies under their jurisdiction from offering special competitive rates to attract customers, particularly where (1) the competitor's marginal or avoidable costs were no lower than those of the customer's traditional supplier, and (2) the consequence of the transaction would have been merely to shift the sunk costs inflating the rates of the latter from the departing customer to the remaining ones. *See, e.g.,* In re Lukens Steel Co., No. P-810310 (Pa. Pub. Util. Comm'n, Jan. 13, 1984) (petition denied). In this case, the Pennsylvania Power and Light Co. sought to attract a large industrial customer from the Philadelphia Electric Co. with a favorable rate, even though both companies were generating their electricity from a common pool dispatching power from the lowest marginal-cost supply source. Similarly, the New York Public Service Commission dismissed the petition by some towns in Westchester County to be served by New York State Electric and Gas rather than Consolidated Edison. Interoffice Memorandum from Jean Cleary, Staff Counsel, to State of New York Public Service Commission (July 12, 1974).

Regulation in the 1990s

intense regulatory concern. More important in the present context, they sever the link between those rates and the revenues from the more competitive services, and in this way, in principle, prevent cross-subsidization of the latter offerings by the former. By so doing, once again in principle, they make it possible to give the utility companies greater freedom to compete for the business on which they are challenged. Finally, by focusing regulation on prices rather than rates of return, and fixing the course of those prices over a period of time, these freezes or indexations mitigate the cost-plus character of traditional regulation, and therefore enhance the incentives of the companies to improve their efficiency.

These beneficent tendencies are sometimes reinforced by an explicit or implicit acceptance of a wider than usual range within which achieved rates of return are permitted to vary. Sometimes there is an accompanying provision for companies and ratepayers to share surplus profits, up to limits (before sharing) that would have seemed unacceptably high by historical standards. The consequently wider range of possible earnings, for longer periods of time, presumably provides carriers with enhanced incentives not only to minimize costs, but also to undertake risky investments and innovations that would be discouraged if the returns from successful ventures were limited to levels traditionally regarded as reasonable.[28]

Finally, the FCC now subjects AT&T's basic and non-basic interstate services to separate rate caps—ceilings on average prices (rather than on each individual one) indexed to inflation minus a productivity target. It has decided to do the same with the services

---

28. The accompanying divorce of basic service rates from the companies' overall costs and revenues relieves regulators to some extent of responsibility for scrutinizing the heavy expenditures the companies are making in fiberoptic transmission and digital switching, with a view to their possible disallowance. Since these outlays are typically justified only partly in terms of minimizing the costs of basic service, and in part in order to be able to offer new services the market for which is highly uncertain, regulators have naturally been concerned that subscribers interested only in the former not be burdened by the costs and greater risks properly attributable to the latter. Threatened with disallowance of some portion of these outlays from rate base, while lacking the prospect of being permitted to retain supernormal profits if the ventures prove successful, the companies may refrain from undertaking relatively risky innovations that may nevertheless be socially desirable. Freezes and indexations of basic service rates and variable rates of return tend to remove those obstacles. *See* Kahn & Shew, *Current Issues in Telecommunications Regulation: Pricing*, 4 YALE J. ON REG. 191 (1987).

Yale Journal on Regulation   Vol. 7: 325, 1990

of the local companies under its jurisdiction, and some states as well are now actively considering rate caps for intrastate services.[29]

These various regulatory devices tend to permit the utility companies to compete effectively for business by offering rates as low as their incremental costs, if necessary. In this way, they correct the worst competitive distortion introduced by partial deregulation, while limiting the ability of a company to recoup net revenue losses from basic service customers. They also limit the extent to which the company may compensate for reductions in competitive rates by raising rates for non-basic services.

Of course, such arrangements openly invite the companies—and, insofar as the adoption of rate caps is coupled with the opportunity for a wider range of achieved rates of return, encourage them—to introduce a finer discrimination in the prices they charge for their several services. This is only a more polite way of saying that deregulation permits a fuller exploitation of monopoly power.[30]

The counter-considerations—in my judgment compelling—are the necessity of giving the utility companies freedom to meet the

---

29. In re Policy and Rules Concerning Rates for Dominant Carriers, No. 87-313 (F.C.C. Supplemental Notice of Proposed Rulemaking, adopted March 8, 1990); In re Policy and Rules Concerning Rates for Dominant Carriers, No. 87-313 (F.C.C. Report and Order and Second Further Notice of Proposed Rulemaking, adopted March 16, 1989). For a description of the FCC's plan and of a similar one adopted by the California Public Utilities Commission, see Norris, *Price Caps: An Alternative Regulatory Framework for Telecommunications Carriers*, PUB. UTIL. FORT., Jan. 18, 1990, at 44. On the pioneering British "RPI minus 3" scheme, see Stelzer, *Regulating Telecommunications in Britain: A New Alternative to the U.S. Approach*, TELEMATICS, Sept., 1986, at 7.

The Florida Commission has in effect grafted a kind of rate cap on the formal scheme of variable rates of return that it accepted for Bell South, by explicitly excluding the Company from the right to share in any surplus earnings that are the consequence of increases in its average rates: "Southern Bell will not be permitted to enhance its profits through rate increases. . . . We will allow any rate increases to be netted against rate decreases." In re Petitions of Southern Bell Telephone and Telegraph Company for Rate Stabilization etc., No. 880069-TL and 870832-TL, Order No. 20162, slip. op., at 7-8 (Fla. Pub. Serv. Comm'n, Oct. 13, 1988).

These direct restraints on prices—whether in the form of freezes, indexation provisions, "social compacts," or rate caps—do not represent an abandonment of traditional rate of return regulation. They typically contemplate periodic reexamination of the results and readjustment of the formulas when and as rates of return range outside of acceptable limits. In the last analysis, therefore, they are all forms of rate of return regulation. *See, e.g.*, Noll, *Telecommunications Regulation in the 1990s*, in 1 NEW DIRECTIONS IN TELECOMMUNICATIONS POLICY 11 (P. Newburg ed. 1989). The potentially significant difference, in principle, is that these various formulas may contemplate substantially longer regulatory lags, and therefore imply a willingness on the part of both the commission and the company to accept returns fluctuating and persisting within some range wider than would be permitted under traditional regulation.

30. This is Joseph P. Gillan's objection to rate caps. Gillan, *Reforming State Regulation of Exchange Carriers*, TELEMATICS, May, 1989, at 17.

Regulation in the 1990s

increasing competition they encounter in the provision of "non-basic" services, and their entitlement to recover prudently incurred costs. The former is grounded in considerations of both economic efficiency and of retaining whatever contribution the competitive markets may continue to make to holding down the rates for basic service. The latter requires that the companies be allowed an opportunity to recover the consequent net revenue losses elsewhere, as the market will allow. The resulting discriminations are therefore in the interest of subscribers to basic service, and they tend also to minimize the aggregate distortions in customer choices created by the need to price above marginal cost in order to recover total costs.[31]

D. *Possible Reversions to Regulation*

Each of these adaptations of regulatory policy to competition represents a further loosening of restraints, rather than a reversal of the deregulation process. Each therefore seems to support the general expectation that the trend of the last ten to fifteen years will persist. There are, however, two opposing possibilities.

The first is the far-from-negligible danger of a misguided intensification of protectionism, in the event that we either fail to cure the fundamental macroeconomic causes of our national balance of trade deficit or we "solve" the problem by falling into a recession. The public's enthusiasm for free competition varies inversely with the unemployment rate.

The second possibility lies in the microeconomy of the electric utility industry. Major sections of the country are likely to need substantial additions to generating capacity within the next several years. At present, a large portion of the increase is expected to be supplied by non-utility generators using natural gas as their fuel. It seems likely, however, that the present large natural gas supply bubble will be exhausted during the 1990s, resulting in a sharp increase in the field price. In that event, a large portion of those expected additions to non-utility generating capacity may well not materialize, and we may see the commissions and the public alike turning back toward total reliance on their local utility companies. In these circumstances, the recent vogue of regulatorily-required

---

31. *See* Baumol & Bradford, *Optimal Departures From Marginal Cost Pricing*, 60 AM. ECON. REV. 265 (1970).

Yale Journal on Regulation   Vol. 7: 325, 1990

least-cost planning[32] could well result in restoration of the traditional "regulatory compact"—the mutual commitment on the part of the companies to ensure the required expansions of capacity and of the commissions, having lent their approval, to provide reasonable assurances to the companies of recovering prudently incurred costs.[33]

II. The Merits of Continued Non-Regulation

The future course of regulation and deregulation will be determined not only by the changing configurations of private interests, prevailing political and economic philosophies and macroeconomic conditions, but also by how we collectively appraise the record so far. The difficulty is that the performance of even a single industry is multi-faceted and never susceptible to a definitive evaluation; even less is it possible to reach a simple, unequivocal verdict about the effects of deregulation on the diverse collection of industries that have been affected by it in varying ways and degrees over the last fifteen years.

Nevertheless, I believe most economists would agree on the following two broad propositions:

> *First*, wherever even quite imperfect competition is feasible, it is superior to command-and-control regulation. This proposition has a corollary: where such regulation continues to be necessary, as in major sectors of the traditional public utilities, it should, to the greatest extent possible, be designed in such a way as to be compatible with competition rather than obstructive of it; and

> *Second*, if competition is to work well, it requires a great variety of governmental interventions to remedy imperfections and market failures—interventions that, however validly they may be characterized as regulatory, differ fundamentally from the kind of direct economic regulation previously administered by such agencies as the CAB and ICC, and still practiced by most of the state public utility commissions.

---

32. Burkhart, *Least-Cost Planning: A State Survey*, PUB. UTIL. FORT., May 14, 1987, at 38.

33. On the previous dissolution of this implied "regulatory compact," see Kahn, *Competition: Past, Present, and Future--Perception versus Reality*, in UTILITIES STRATEGIC ISSUES FORUM 2, 3, 9-10 (Elec. Power Res. Inst. 1988), and Kahn, *Who Should Pay for Power Plant Duds?* Wall St. J. Aug. 15, 1985, at 26, col. 3.

Regulation in the 1990s

To these propositions I would attach a third, somewhat less obvious one. A central part of the case for deregulation is the severe deficiencies of regulation—deficiencies of information, wisdom, and incentives, along with a strong inherent tendency to suppress competition.[34] If, however—as I will argue presently—the response to the imperfections we have observed in the performance of the deregulated industries is that a large share of the fault lies in the failure of government to perform its essential competition-supplementing functions, such as antitrust enforcement, then the case for deregulation may rest upon assumptions about the ability of the government to fulfill those supplementary responsibilities just as unrealistic as the assumptions behind the case for direct economic regulation. This last consideration could, in some situations, take us full circle, back to an acceptance of full-scale regulation as the less imperfect of the two alternatives. In most instances, I believe, it does not.

A. *Reading the Record: The Superiority of Competition*[35]

The deregulated industries are unquestionably more competitive today than they were previously. This is not to deny the significance of the increased concentration at the national level in less-than-truckload (LTL) carriage or, marginally, in airlines,[36] or to claim that the competition is sufficiently effective in all markets to have fully taken over the role previously played by governmentally-enforced price ceilings. It is to say that market concentration route-by-route has definitely declined, on average, in markets of all sizes and dimensions,[37] and that the several indicia of competitive behavior

___

34. *See* A. KAHN, *supra* note 2, at 1-46.

35. Not surprisingly, the record of the effects of deregulation on performance is much fuller and more susceptible to the drawing of conclusions—favorable or unfavorable—in the case of industries and markets that have been thoroughly deregulated than for the core public utilities; for this reason, the following account has relatively little to say about the latter.

36. For a discussion of the anticompetitive consequences of the same air carriers meeting one another in market after market, see Shepherd, *The Airline Industry*, in THE STRUCTURE OF AMERICAN INDUSTRY 217, 225 (W. Adams ed. 1990), echoing my own almost identical observation with respect to the chemical industry many years earlier. Kahn, *The Chemicals Industry*, in THE STRUCTURE OF AMERICAN INDUSTRY 197, 208-09 (W. Adams, ed. 1950).

37. For the changes in airlines between 1983 and 1987, see CONGRESSIONAL BUDGET OFFICE, POLICIES FOR THE DEREGULATED AIRLINE INDUSTRY 17 (1988) [hereinafter CBO REPORT] and, for 1978-83, see CIVIL AERONAUTICS BOARD, IMPLEMENTATION OF THE PROVISIONS OF THE AIRLINE DEREGULATION ACT OF 1978 14 (1984). *See also* SECRETARY'S

Yale Journal on Regulation   Vol. 7: 325, 1990

support the same conclusion.[38] The same is true of telecommunications, particularly in customer and central office equipment, long-distance telephony, and the provision of high-speed, high-volume transmission of data. Because of the competition unleashed by deregulation, average prices of air travel, trucking, and long-distance telephoning are down substantially, producing not only

TASK FORCE ON COMPETITION IN THE U.S. DOMESTIC AIRLINE INDUSTRY, U.S. DEP'T OF TRANSP., 1 INDUSTRY AND ROUTE STRUCTURE 3, 11-12 (1990) [hereinafter SECRETARY'S TASK FORCE REPORT]. The mutual interpenetration by the dominant carriers of their respective regional markets, which has produced that result, has occurred also in LTL trucking. *See* U.S. GENERAL ACCOUNTING OFFICE, TRUCKING REGULATION: PRICE COMPETITION AND MARKET STRUCTURE IN THE TRUCKING INDUSTRY 18 (1987).

38.   On the case of the railroads, see MacDonald, *Railroad Deregulation, Innovation, and Competition: Effects of the Staggers Act on Grain Transportation*, 32 J. L. & ECON. 63, 64-65 (1989); *Hearings Before the Joint Economic Committee*, 101st Cong., 2d Sess. (Oct. 19, 1989) (testimony of Darius W. Gaskins, Jr., former chairman of the Interstate Commerce Commission) [hereinafter Gaskins Statement]. With respect to the increased inter-railroad competition in the Powder River Basin, see BUREAU OF LAND MANAGEMENT, CASE STUDY: IMPACT OF COAL TRANSPORTATION ON WESTERN COAL DEVELOPMENT AND THE FEDERAL COAL PROGRAM (1987).

Critics have laid heavy emphasis on the substantial air fare increases in late 1988 and early 1989, which have reflected the industry's increased facility in playing oligopolistic follow-the-leader. But those criticisms have clearly minimized the underlying competitive tensions—which showed up, for example, in a sharp decline in average yields in the ensuing months, practically all the way back to 1988 levels. This experience elicited universal moaning in the investment community about the consequent erosion of yields and profits. For example:

> [t]he airline industry remains a very competitive business. If Congress thinks this is not a competitive business, perhaps a brief review of some of the promotional fare activity spreading—as competitive battles heat up—in a number of regions will convince them. American, Pan Am and Eastern are battling it out in Miami; America West is entering the Hawaii free-for-all; Eastern will take on Delta in the Northeast-Florida markets and Atlanta in hopes of regaining lost market share. USAir is attempting to slow Midway's expansion plans in Philadelphia. And, it seems everyone wants a bigger piece of the West Coast Corridor market, from American (San Jose) to United (San Francisco-SFO) to Delta (Los Angeles-LAX) to USAir (LAX & SFO) to Southwest (Oakland) to Alaska Airlines (Seattle).

Derchin & Tortora, *The Airline Industry: What Happen [sic] to the Oligopoly?*, in DREXEL BURNHAM LAMBERT, Research 4 (Dec. 8, 1989).

Shortly thereafter, First Boston estimated the industry's operating profits in 1989 at $1.95 billion, or 33 percent below the $2.95 billion reported in 1988—with the entire decline occurring in the second half of the year. PAUL P. KAROS, FIRST BOSTON, EQUITY RESEARCH, INDUSTRY: AIRLINES, FLIGHTLINES: EXPECT BRUTAL FOURTH QUARTER COMPARISONS 1 (Nov. 30, 1989).

Regulation in the 1990s

consumer savings but net welfare improvements in the billions of dollars each year.[39]

The effect of deregulation on the relationship between the structure of prices and costs has been more complicated. In general, regulators tend to equalize rates to different customers despite differences in the costs of serving them; correspondingly, competition since deregulation has apparently—despite some increases in price discrimination, to which I will return—forced prices for the several categories of service into closer conformity with their respective costs.[40] Prominent examples of this economically beneficial change have been the increased sensitivity of air fares to the effects on cost of length of trip and traffic density, and of transportation rates generally to the differences between peak and off-peak and front- and back-haul. In telephony, the prices of long-distance calling and basic residential service have likewise come into closer conformity with their respective costs.[41]

---

39. S. MORRISON & C. WINSTON, THE ECONOMIC EFFECTS OF AIRLINE DEREGULATION (1986); Rose, *The Incidence of Regulatory Rents in the Motor Carrier Industry*, 16 RAND J. ECON. 299 (1985). In the telephone case, see reference to the L. Perl study in Kahn & Shew, *supra* note 28, at 209. It is of course impossible to say with certainty how much of the observed decline in price can be attributed to deregulation—a consideration especially pertinent in the case of the airlines, whose average fares declined secularly under regulation as well. *See* Brenner, *Airline Deregulation—A Case Study in Public Policy Failure*, 16 TRANSP. L.J., 179, 198-99 (1988); Kahn, *Airline Deregulation—A Mixed Bag, But a Clear Success Nevertheless*, 16 TRANSP. L.J., 229, 235-36 (1988). Morrison and Winston have come closest to resolving the question by reconstructing for the post-deregulation period the Standard Industry Fare Level (SIFL) index, according to which the CAB used to set fares, and demonstrating in this way that actual fares have indeed been consistently lower, by many billions of dollars a year, than they would have been had those CAB policies continued in effect. Morrison & Winston, *The Dynamics of Airline Pricing and Competition*, 80 AM. ECON. REV., PAPERS & PROC. 189 (1990).

40. MacDonald observes that the widespread use of long-term contracts for rail carriage has been especially beneficial to large shippers; it could therefore have made possible price discriminations that were previously impermissible. His major finding, however, is that the Staggers Act deserves substantial credit for the accelerated replacement of single-car with much lower-cost multiple-car and unit-train shipments, which have required the predictability and larger volumes that large shippers have been best able to provide. The resulting breakdown of the ICC's historic policy of equalizing rates to large and small shippers and the abandonment of unprofitable routes—the previous mandatory service of which had likewise been beneficial mainly to small shippers—have therefore evidently involved a closer alignment of rates with costs and so resulted, on balance, in a diminution of discrimination. *See* MacDonald, *supra* note 38.

41. Between December 1983 and December 1989, the local telephone charges component of the Consumer Price Index increased 19.3 percent in real terms, while the average price of long-distance calling declined 44.5 percent interstate and 24.1 percent intrastate. FEDERAL-STATE JOINT BOARD, U.S. BUREAU OF LABOR STATISTICS, MONITORING REPORT CC DOCKET NO. 87-339, at 246 (1990). This has been more the indirect than the direct consequence of intensified competition: the FCC initially required local exchange companies to charge long-distance companies rates far above marginal costs for access to

Yale Journal on Regulation   Vol. 7: 325, 1990

Purchasers are being offered a greatly expanded range of price/service options, most strikingly in financial services, telecommunications and transportation.[42]

The removal of regulatory restrictions and the pressures of competition have yielded marked increases in productivity.[43] The failure of the airline industry to realize the huge potential economies of hub and spoke operations under regulation testifies eloquently to the inefficiency of centralized government planning and the superiority of unconstrained profit-seeking in free markets. Similarly, the freedom of both airlines and truckers to vary their effective charges from one moment and one route to another, depending on the relationship between demand and capacity, has contributed powerfully to improved use of equipment and consequent reductions in cost.

All of this has occurred with no evident sacrifice of safety.[44] And, with the glaring exception of the general decline in the quality of the air travel experience, it has on the whole resulted in improved quality as well as variety of service, just as any student of competition would have predicted.[45]

B. *Imperfections of Competition and Derelictions of Government*

There remain three glaring apparent exceptions to the beneficent consequences of deregulation—the deterioration in the quality of air travel, a sharp increase in certain kinds of price discrimination,

---

interstate callers. When institutional customers and interexchange carriers began to bypass the local phone companies in order to evade these inflated charges, the FCC gradually reduced them and substituted a direct charge on ultimate subscribers. *See* Kahn & Shew, *supra* note 28, at 196-97.

42. Prominent among the expanded range of service offerings in transportation have been long-term contract as well as spot rates, sharply increased intermodal carriage, and—thanks to the spread of airline hub and spoke operations—an increased variety of available destinations. SECRETARY'S TASK FORCE REPORT, *supra* note 37, at 3, 149-289 (especially the discussion at 160).

43. For the case of the railroads, see Gaskins Statement, *supra* note 38.

44. *See generally* Rose, Profitability and Product Quality: Economic Determinants of Airline Safety Performance (1989) (unpublished manuscript on file with author, publication forthcoming in J. POL. ECON.); TRANSPORTATION SAFETY IN AN AGE OF DEREGULATION (L. Moses & I. Savage ed. 1989). Statistics compiled by the Federal Highway Administration show a decline in fatal trucking accidents of about 20 percent in 1981-85, as compared with 1976-79, on a per mile basis. Letter from Edward H. Rastatter of the Regulatory Review and Planning Division to Alfred E. Kahn (Sept. 16, 1987). *See also* CAL. PUB. UTIL. COMM'N & HIGHWAY PATROL, REPORT ON TRUCK SAFETY, JOINT LEGISLATIVE REPORT AB 2678 (1987).

45. The one qualification of that prediction would have been a recognition of the strong tendency of the previous regulatory regimes to encourage an inefficient inflation of service quality. *See* text accompanying *infra* note 46.

344

Regulation in the 1990s

and—reflecting a loss of the safety or stability that the previous pervasive restrictions on competition were supposed to preserve—the savings and loan fiasco.

1. *Discomfort and Congestion in Air Travel*

The first thing to observe about the increase in congestion, crowding and delay in aviation is that they reflect success, not failure. A major criticism of regulation had been that, by discouraging price competition, it had on the one side encouraged inefficient competition of a cost-inflating, quality-enhancing character,[46] and, on the other, failed to probe the price elasticity of potential demand. Deregulation has eliminated the distortion and made good the failure. The result has been deeply discounted fares—necessarily for service in fuller planes, with tighter seating and a lower ratio of ticket agents and flight attendants to passengers. It has been the enthusiastic response of travelers to this new option that has taxed the capacity of our airports and air traffic control systems, and the patience of travelers.

Neither an economist nor a government official is competent to decide whether the lower-quality service provided at a lower price is superior to the higher price/quality option exclusively available before. It is the task of an efficiently-functioning market to offer customers the choice, to the extent it is feasible to do so. The inefficiency of regulatory cartelization, corrected by deregulation, was that it suppressed the former option.

To some extent, unregulated competition has had the equally deplorable opposite effect: travelers who pay full fare suffer along with the ones who buy the discount tickets from long lines, uncomfortable seating and delays. This spillover effect might suggest there is no basis for concluding that there has been a net welfare improvement.

There are several reasons for rejecting that implication. First, the superior service option has not disappeared: the airlines compete strenuously for the patronage of the regular full-fare-paying customers, with frequent flyer credits, upgrades, separate lines, and, where feasible, separate business class service.

Second, to the extent that it is not feasible to provide full-fare-paying passengers a fully differentiated service—wider seating than

---

46. For a broad exposition of this proposition across various industries, see A. KAHN, *supra* note 2, at 10, 189 (trucking), 206-20 (securities brokerage and airlines).

their discount-fare-paying fellow travelers, for example—it is a general principle, and on balance a beneficent one, that in a market economy the majority of dollar votes rules, at the necessary expense of minority preferences, when the two cannot be reconciled.[47]

Finally, the general increase in congestion and the failure of the market to offer delay-free travel to customers willing to pay for it are, above all, a consequence of severe derelictions on the part of government. During my tenure as Chairman of the Civil Aeronautics Board, I pointed out that it was the responsibility of government to respond to the increased demands generated by the competitive forces we were unleashing, by expanding airport and air traffic control capacity, and by pricing access to those scarce facilities rationally.[48]

2. *Intensification of Price Discrimination*

Most of the history of economic regulation can be written around the phenomenon of price discrimination. Discriminations by the railroads inspired our first major venture in regulation. Regulators, hostile to even cost-justified price differentiations, have frequently required discrimination, in the interest of "equity." On the other hand, regulators have long recognized the possible economic benefits of discrimination in the presence of economies of scale and scope, and of overall revenue constraints defined in terms of historic or embedded costs.[49]

---

47. *See* Kahn & Shew, *supra* note 28, at 229-32 (discussing "collective consumption decisions").

48. *See, e.g.*, Address by Alfred E. Kahn, Federal Aviation Administration Consultative Planning Conference (Mar. 22, 1978). *See also* Levine, *Landing Fees and the Airport Congestion Problem*, 12 J. L. & Econ. 63, 79-108 (1969).

The Massachusetts Port Authority (Massport) in 1988 shifted the basis for landing fees at Boston's Logan Airport from weight of aircraft to the number of operations. The Department of Transportation (DOT) ordered Massport to withdraw those altered charges on the ground that they were discriminatory, because, among other reasons, they entailed higher charges per passenger on smaller than on larger planes. What DOT failed abysmally to understand was that it was the previous charges that were discriminatory: the change to which it objected was fully justified by differences in the respective marginal costs of serving the two classes of customers. On the other hand, the new fee schedules' failure to differentiate peak and off-peak landings was admittedly an imperfection, which Massport had promised to remedy.

49. Observe, for example, the unrestricted pricing freedom conferred on the railroads by the Staggers Act, within the limits of 180 percent of average variable costs and overall revenue adequacy. 49 U.S.C. § 1701a (d)(2). *See also* T. KEELER, RAILROADS, FREIGHT AND PUBLIC POLICY 98-101 (1983).

346

Regulation in the 1990s

Even ardent deregulators have understood that unregulated price competition in the public utility industries would probably be highly selective and localized, with its benefits available only to some well-situated customers, because of the ubiquity of the monopoly power that counselled regulation in the first place. Many of us have been surprised, however, to find discrimination increasing also with the deregulation of industries that we thought were potentially structurally competitive. Borenstein and Rose have demonstrated unequivocally that price discrimination in the airline industry has in some respects increased, substantially and significantly, as markets have become less concentrated.[50]

Manifestly, the instances of sharply increased price discrimination that deregulation has made possible in airlines and railroads are both a competitive and a monopolistic phenomenon. They reflect intense competition for the traffic most likely to be attracted by price differences among competitors. They have also promoted economic efficiency in very important ways. The ability of the railroads to price down toward incremental cost has improved the distribution of the transportation function among the competing modes; their ability to charge rates for demand-inelastic traffic incorporating wider margins above variable costs has contributed to an improvement in their financial condition, which has helped them to finance major improvements in trackage, equipment and service, without yielding excessive returns in the aggregate. The deeply discounted fares to discretionary air travelers fill seats that would otherwise remain empty and help make possible more frequent scheduling, which is particularly valuable to the full-fare travelers.

Manifestly, however, the discriminations also reflect the exercise of monopoly power no longer curbed by direct price regulation. The reasons for the return of monopoly power to the airline industry, following upon the intensified competition of the early 1980s, and the way in which it has been exercised to produce sharp increases in the unrestricted fares paid by about 10 percent of the

---

50. Borenstein & Rose, Competitive Price Discrimination in the U.S. Airline Industry (1989) (unpublished manuscript available at University of Michigan Institute of Public Policy Studies). Their results do not necessarily conflict with my previous observation that in other respects price discrimination has been reduced significantly. Borenstein and Rose's findings relate to an increased dispersion of the fares charged different passengers on individual routes; my observation related to the structure of fares for different routes, times of day and modes of travel. On the other hand, a marked increase has occurred in discrimination in the fares carriers charge on different routes depending on the extent to which they encounter competition on them. *See* text accompanying *infra* note 51.

travelers, is by now a familiar story.[51] The increasing sophistication with which the leading carriers—particularly the ones with the most fully developed computerized reservations systems—have learned to practice what the industry euphemistically calls "yield management" has enabled them to take full advantage of that monopoly power, while also erecting possibly insurmountable barriers to entry by truly new competitors.[52]

There are three possible ways in which government might respond to this equivocal situation.

It could do nothing. We put up with a great deal of competitive imperfection in industries that we would not think of regulating. It is by no means clear that unrestricted fares exceed the stand-alone costs of serving the minority of passengers who pay them, or that the discrimination to which those travelers are subject is not compensated for by frequent flyer credits[53] and the improved convenience of scheduling that the high fares help make possible. The airline industry is far more competitive than it was; the benefits of that competition have been widely distributed; and the industry is evidently not earning monopoly profits. In these circumstances, it would not be ridiculous to conclude that no remedy was required.

Second, however, the government clearly has neglected responsibilities of which it was never the intention of deregulation to relieve it. These include vigilant policing of safety practices, the provision of the requisite airport and air traffic control capacity[54] and pricing access to them rationally, and vigorous enforcement of the antitrust laws, along with other policies designed to remove

---

51. *See, e.g., Hearings Before the Subcommittee on Aviation of the Senate Committee on Commerce, Science, and Transportation,* 101st Cong., 1st Sess. 6-61, 131-41 (1989) (statement of Kenneth M. Mead, Director, Transportation Issues, Resources, Community and Economic Development Division, U.S. General Accounting Office) [hereinafter Mead Statement]; CBO REPORT, *supra* note 37, at 23-36; SECRETARY'S TASK FORCE ON COMPETITION IN THE U.S. DOMESTIC AIRLINE INDUSTRY, U.S. DEP'T OF TRANSP., 1 PRICING 3-4 (1990); Borenstein, *Hubs and High Fares: Airport Dominance and Market Power in the U.S. Airline Industry,* 20 RAND J. ECON. 344 (1989); Levine, *Airline Competition in Deregulated Markets: Theory, Firm Strategy, and Public Policy,* 4 YALE J. ON REG. 393 (1987).

52. For these complicated reasons, Shepherd is both correct and at best telling only part of the story when, under the heading of "price discrimination," he concludes that "airline pricing behavior has virtually ceased to be a competitive weapon and has become instead a complex process by which an airline tries to maximize the revenue it extracts from its customers." Shepherd, *supra* note 36, at 232.

53. On the especial attractiveness of these credits as a device for retaining the patronage of the full-fare-paying passenger, see Levine, *supra* note 51, at 452-54.

54. An alternative clearly worth considering would be to permit private entrepreneurs to fulfill this function in whole or in part. A leading proponent of privatization is Robert W. Poole, Jr., of the Reason Foundation. *See* Poole, *Toward Safer Skies,* in INSTEAD OF REGULATION (R. Poole ed. 1982).

Regulation in the 1990s

barriers to competition. Prominent among such supplementary policies would be expansion of airport capacity sufficient to keep open opportunities for competitive challenges to hub-dominating carriers and dissolution of preferential arrangements between those carriers and their hub airports.[55] The bill recently introduced by Senators Danforth and McCain is a long overdue initiative along the latter lines.[56]

Finally, however, it is not possible in principle to reject the reimposition of price ceilings to protect travelers subject to monopolistic exploitation, where restoration of more effective competition proves to be infeasible.

My own endorsement of the second approach and reluctance to embark upon the third—a position with which most economists would probably agree—is heavily influenced by the lesson of history that, once introduced, direct (as contrasted with competition-supplementing) regulation has both a logical and almost irresistible tendency to spread. Price ceilings would be of little value if they were not accompanied by the introduction of floors under quality of service. It takes little imagination to see where that logic might lead—to prohibitions of reductions in the frequency of scheduling and in the frequency with which full-fare paying customers are upgraded to first class; stipulations about the minimum quality of meals; maximum charges for head sets; and maximum length of lines at the ticket counter. These examples are not fanciful: all but one of them were adopted under regulation, in mirror image, to prevent competitive evasions of governmentally-set price floors.

3. *The Savings and Loan Fiasco*

The flood of savings and loan bank failures and the consequent multi-hundred-billion-dollar cost to the Federal Government dramatically underscores the second of the three propositions with which I introduced this appraisal of the record—namely, that economic deregulation cannot mean firing the police force. It also, however, inescapably raises the question implicit in the third one: may not

---

55. *See* Mead Statement, *supra* note 51, at 4-5; SECRETARY'S TASK FORCE ON COMPETITION IN THE U.S. DOMESTIC AIRLINE INDUSTRY, U.S. DEP'T OF TRANSP., AIRPORTS, AIR TRAFFIC CONTROL AND RELATED CONCERNS (IMPACT ON ENTRY), ch. 3 (1990).

56. S. 1741, 101st Cong., 1st Sess. (1989). The bill, entitled "A Bill to Amend the Federal Aviation Act of 1958 to Increase Competition Among Commercial Air Carriers at the Nation's Major Airports and for Other Purposes," was introduced by Senators McCain, Danforth and Bradley on October 6, 1989.

Yale Journal on Regulation   Vol. 7: 325, 1990

deregulation in some circumstances put on police forces burdens heavier than they can realistically be expected to bear?

In retrospect, the causes of the massive failures are clear. They were the consequence of our having removed the regulatory ceilings on interest rates payable to depositors, which in turn necessitated a relaxation of the restrictions on the kinds of lending and investment activities in which those institutions were permitted to engage. What we evidently failed to recognize was that removal of these restrictions, while retaining Federal deposit insurance, openly invited the more speculative if not reckless lending and outright fraud that, along with a good deal of bad luck, produced the present debacle. So long as the government guaranteed their deposits, institutions whose assets may have been worth far less than their liabilities could nevertheless continue to attract deposits by offering higher interest rates, and could engage in additional risky investments—as well as continued peculation. If those ventures proved successful, the owners could not only remain in business but could make large profits; if they failed, it would be the Federal Savings and Loan Deposit Insurance Corporation that would be left holding the bag—as indeed it was.[57]

In short, deregulation, particularly in the presence of Federal deposit insurance, enormously increased the necessity for vigilant bank examination, enforcement of capital requirements sufficient to provide a cushion against losses, varying deposit insurance premiums with the riskiness of the lending and investing activities of the insured institutions, and a readiness to close down S&Ls that were effectively insolvent.

C. *The Future Direction: Coming Full Circle?*

This kind of defense of the deregulation record—"It wasn't my fault, the trouble is you other people didn't do your job"—is a trifle glib. It contains more than a trace of justifying the abandonment of direct regulation, because of its severe imperfections, in terms that implicitly demand perfection of performance by such agencies as the Department of Transportation, the Savings and Loan Bank Board

---

57. *See* Andrews, *Is There Any Way Out of the Deposit Insurance Crisis?*, INSTITUTIONAL INVESTOR, Sept. 1988, at 86; Bush, *Former FHLBB Regulators Offer Solutions to the Current FSLIC Crisis*, SAVINGS INSTITUTIONS, Oct. 1988, at 81; O'Driscoll, *Bank Failures: The Deposit Insurance Connection*, CONTEMP. POL'Y ISSUES, Apr. 1988, at 1. O'Driscoll would disagree with this diagnosis only to the extent it assigns blame to the removal of restrictions on the asset side; he contends that diversification alone would have reduced risk.

Regulation in the 1990s

and Congress—higher levels of prescience, conscientiousness, information, incorruptibility or simple effectiveness than can reasonably be expected.

To some extent, similarly, thrusting upon the antitrust authorities both blame for some of the monopolistic consequences of airline deregulation and responsibility for their future remedy implicitly expects more of competition-preserving policies than they can deliver. It is possible to identify fewer than a handful of mergers and code-sharing (i.e., traffic-interchange) agreements that probably should not have been permitted on antitrust grounds; most of the mergers that have reconcentrated the industry were more a reflection of the economies of networking and the inability of smaller competitors to survive in open competition than they were an independent cause of its attenuation. Again, the greatest disadvantage borne today by airlines dependent on the computerized reservations systems of their major rivals is apparently the high booking fees they have to pay; but these raise the inescapable consideration that the high profits of the system owners may be a reasonable reward for an important innovation; and the possible divestiture cure has never, to my knowledge, confronted the possible sacrifice of economies of integration. Yet again, frequent flyer credits augment the monopoly power of the larger carriers, and particularly the ones dominating the hubs used by business travelers; but it would be difficult to attack them directly, because they are a form of price competition. Moreover, the logical remedy of subjecting them to income tax when the purchases that generated them were treated as deductible business expenses would apparently be an administrative nightmare. Finally, an attack on predatory pricing would involve all-too-familiar difficulties of distinguishing unacceptable price discriminations from legitimate competitive responses and welfare-enhancing exploitations of the economies of scale and scope.[58]

---

58. These reservations about the likely efficacy of antitrust should not be construed as in any way diluting my firm advocacy of vigorous competition-preserving and enhancing policies, in preference to reregulation.

On the desirability of a forthright attack on practices that might be regarded as predatory, for example, I am among the minority of American economists who feel that our profession and the courts have gone much too far in the direction of minimizing the likelihood of predation and the threat to competition it may pose. See, for example, the decision by the CAB, under my Chairmanship, to limit the permissible competitive response of the International Air Transport Association carriers to the intensified competition on trans-Atlantic routes of the charters and Freddie Laker—an effort ultimately overturned by President Carter; my warning of the dangers (which have in fact materialized) of a successful price response of the incumbent carriers to the prospective entry of World and Capitol into the transcontinental market, in Kahn, *Deregulatory Schizophrenia*, 75 CALIF. L.

Yale Journal on Regulation   Vol. 7: 325, 1990

Competition can in some circumstances make unrealistic demands on consumers as well—assuming a greater ability on their part to make complex choices, on pain of suffering penalties to which they had not previously been subjected, than they either have or are willing to take the trouble to acquire. A poignant illustration of the resulting dilemma has been provided in recent years by providers of alternate telephone operator services, which have entered into arrangements with non-telephone-company owners of public telephones, hotels, and other such institutions serving transient customers, under which, in exchange for commissions to the owners, they receive the right to provide operator services and charge what they please. The problems arise because the transient caller is an often unwitting captive to such arrangements between the other two parties. The competitive solution would be to permit this kind of free entry, while requiring comprehensive disclosure of the system of charges and, probably also, that callers be offered the opportunity to be transferred without charge to the long distance carrier of their own choice. Conceivably, however, the burden on consumers of digesting such information and choosing may outweigh the benefits of competition; one is reminded of Oscar Wilde's analogous observation: "The trouble with Socialism is that it uses up too many evenings."

Conclusion

I can take solace from the equivocal nature of these observations in the fact that I have been consistent in my equivocation. The beginning of wisdom in the devising of regulatory and deregulatory policies must be, as I put it in celebrating the "passing of the public utility concept,"

> a skepticism of the universal efficiency of both the unregulated market, on the one side, and of government enterprise on the other, sufficient to make it impossible for me simply to abandon the regulatory tool. Competition and regulation are both highly imperfect institutions. So is antitrust. It should not

REV., 1059, 1060-68 (1987); *see also* Kahn, The Macroeconomic Consequences of Sensible Microeconomic Policies, The First Distinguished Lecture on Economics in Government, Annual Meeting of the American Economic Association and Society of Government Economists 11-15 (Nat. Econ. Res. Assoc. 1985).

be surprising, therefore, that there is no single choice between them equally valid for all times and places. . . .[59]

The experience of the last decade or so justifies a somewhat less fatuous conclusion. I believe it has confirmed our historic presumption in favor of competitive markets: against the deregulatory fiasco of the S&Ls must be weighed the regulatory fiascos of nuclear power plant construction and the shortages and extreme distortions of natural gas markets during this same decade. Our recent experience demonstrates also that free markets may demand governmental interventions just as pervasive and quite possibly more imaginative than direct regulation; but its lesson is that those interventions should to the greatest extent possible preserve, supplement, and enhance competition, rather than suppress it. Finally, to the extent direct economic regulation continues to be required, it is preferable that it be of a kind compatible with competition, rather than obstructive of it.

In short, the lesson I take from recent history is that the evolution of regulatory policy will never come to an end. The path it takes—and we should make every effort to see that it takes—however, is the path not of a full circle or pendulum, which would take us back to where we started, but of a spiral, which has

---

59. Kahn, *A Reprise*, *supra* note 7, at 26. For a recent, persuasive exposition of the ubiquity of market failure—as well as regulatory failure—in transportation, see Kay & Thompson, Regulatory Reform in Transport in the UK: Principles and Application (Oct. 1989) (unpublished manuscript on file with Center for Business Strategy, London Business School).

It is important for me to make clear what it is that I have been consistently equivocal about. It has to do with selecting the set of institutional arrangements best suited to achieving economically optimal results, not with the propriety of economic efficiency as the primary goal of regulatory (or deregulatory) policy.

In contrast, the debate between advocates of regulation and deregulation is in very large measure about the latter, not the former issue. Opponents of deregulation will often protest—sometimes truculently, I can attest—that efficiency is not and should not be the sole or even the primary end of economic regulation. While I endorse the proposition that fairness and a more equitable distribution of income should be central goals of public policy, I also insist that proponents of such goals have every obligation to be just as rigorous in thinking about how they may best be served as the advocates of pure economic efficiency. And "best," in a world of scarcity, must mean "at minimum social cost." Restrictions on entry and price competition and distortions of the relationship between prices and marginal cost are usually irrational ways of achieving those ends, and to the extent regulation has served them in these ways, it has typically done so at excessive social cost. From this standpoint, one of the major accomplishments of deregulation has been to force us to seek more rational ways of achieving those goals. Neither privately nor governmentally-administered syndicalism or cartelization is a sensible way either to remedy the failures of unregulated market capitalism or to achieve a more humane distribution of income.

Yale Journal on Regulation   Vol. 7: 325, 1990

a direction. This is in a sense only an expression of a preference for seeking consistently to move in the direction of the first-best functioning of a market economy, rather than the second- or third-best world of centralized command and control.

Name Index